Published by:
A.R.E. Publishing, Inc.
Denver, Colorado

Library of Congress Control Number: 2002101245
ISBN 0-86705-053-5

© A.R.E. Publishing, Inc. 2002

Printed in the United States of America
10   9   8   7   6   5   4   3   2   1

DEDICATION

To Shoshana, Evan, and Bob
To Josh and David
May God be a source of joy and comfort to you all the days of your lives.
With gratefulness for the blessings of your love and you.

In memory of Faye Tillis Lewy, whose spiritual quest inspired many, and who is
now resting in the wings of the *Shechinah*.

ACKNOWLEDGMENTS

THIS BOOK IS THE RESULT OF MANY YEARS OF WORK. It presents many of the theories and theologies with which we have grappled and which we have shared with others along the way through discussions, speeches, classes, workshops, and writings. We thank all who have inspired, encouraged, and supported our efforts. Many of them are contributors to the book, others are found in our address books, and still others are those whose paths we have crossed as we traveled on our individual journeys. In particular, we would like to acknowledge Jim Fowler, John Snarey, Romney Moseley (*z"l*), Sharon Parks, Ken Stokes (*z"l*), Joel Lurie Grishaver, Jeffrey Schein, Michael Shire, Eugene Borowitz, Leonard Kravitz, Bill Cutter, Gabriel Moran, Maria Harris, Gloria Durka, as well as all the angels with whom we wrestled for their inspiration, insights, and encouragement.

We are grateful to all the talented individuals who contributed to this book. We appreciate the sharing of wisdom and insights about God and spirituality with us in order that so many others may benefit. We all hope to draw God near to us, to help others as well as ourselves walk in the light of the Eternal.

We offer special thanks also to Daniel S. Schechter for adding his wisdom on how to be an editor to that of our publishers. The Schechter/Goodman family relationship has spanned six generations, three continents, and many meals, cups of tea, and hours of discussion.

We are grateful to all of you who responded to the editors' comments so supportively, allowing us to learn and grow in this new role.

Thanks also to our publishers, Audrey Friedman Marcus and Raymond A. Zwerin, who, for our good fortune, emulate the attributes ascribed to God: compassionate, gracious, slow to anger, abounding in loving-kindness and truth. In addition, they are endlessly patient. We have tested and relied upon all of these attributes in putting this book together. We are eternally grateful to them for all the advice, support, and expertise they have provided.

Finally, we feel blessed by God to have reached this day, overcoming both moments of great sorrow and joy, pain and illness, to be able to share the wisdom collected in this volume. We are in awe of the mysteries of life, the abilities of scientists, and the healing power of the *neshamah* and the prayers of friends and family. May we all find our way to and with God. May we all continue to be a blessing to God and others. *Ken yehi ratzon*, may it be God's will.

CONTENTS

FOREWORD

Richard N. Levy

HOW CAN WE ENCOUNTER GOD? WHY IS IT THAT people today do not hear the voice of God as our ancestors in the Bible did?

Many of us think that the women and men who were so intimate with God in the Bible could merely go out into the field, or stand at the entrance to their tent and be immediately swept up into the embracing presence of God. We like to believe that they knew instinctively when God was speaking to them, and that they must have been infinitely superior creatures to us, who most commonly feel that God does not speak to us at all.

But when we look more deeply into the text we see that biblical individuals seldom encounter God spontaneously, without assistance, without preparation. Abraham began by leaving Babylonia for Canaan. He settled at Elon Moreh, near an oak tree called the Teacher, and from then on each generation taught the next how God might be encountered. Our biblical forebears did not spontaneously discover God; they had to learn how to access the Divine. Those of us who grew up on a book called *Picture Stories from the Bible*, which told biblical stories in cartoon form, thought we knew how God spoke to biblical figures: in jagged letters, so it was always clear that God was speaking. But, as we grew up, we realized that biblical figures did not hear God's words as jagged letters. They had to be taught to recognize when they were hearing the voice of God, and when they were hearing another person's voice or their own. As a small boy, Samuel needs to be instructed by the priest Eli that the sound he hears is the voice of God. It is only through teaching that we come to understand when God is making Godself known to us, and what God is saying.

This book takes the teacher's role in spiritual education very seriously. It asks us to consider the different stages through which we develop faith and become aware of God's presence in our lives, the different ways in which women and men can live in the presence of God, the ways in which we can help people of all ages rise above the material concerns and the self-involvement that blind us to the deep, pulsing spring of God's presence that flows beneath our feet. This book urges the teachers of our children and their parents to open their eyes to the Godliness around them, to become nothing less than the spiritual guides who point the way for this generation of Jews to surmount the obstacles to faith to encounter the holy world beyond.

What is the "spiritual"? What is "spirituality"? It is an English translation of a word whose root is *ruach*, from the wind of God that hovers over the waters as Creation is about to begin. When God speaks through that wind, *"Yehi Or"* (Let there be light), the wind becomes the breath of God which forms the words of Creation. God infuses that breath into the lump of clay God calls Adam, and that creature — our ancestor — becomes a living being. *Ruach* is sometimes translated as "spirit" instead of "wind" or "breath." This is one of the theories of the origins of the word "spirituality." It suggests that God is manifest in the world through the wind which animates it, and when we breathe in, that wind becomes our breath, animating us; when we breathe out, our breath becomes the wind infusing the breath of our neighbor. Each of us is a membrane through which God moves through the world.

As pointed out in this book, Jews have understood God in many ways throughout the ages, and one person's pathway to God is another person's obstacle. But as the Jewish people in more and more parts of the world have stepped away from concerns over our own survival, we have become more intent on learning how we connect with a reality beyond ourselves, how we can sense the presence of our Creator. As a result, teachers are no longer satisfied to teach facts or ideas to children or adolescents, and we are no longer just teaching children — or adults — who are committed to being Jewish. If parents come from different religions, or if the parents are indifferent to Judaism, we now have to persuade them and their children, in the few hours they spend with us, that being Jewish is worthwhile — that being Jewish can change their lives. Facts, we know, seldom change lives; profound insights and experiences may. Part of why teaching about God is more important than ever is that if we can help give our students an experience of God, we can help that change take place.

First, though, we need to talk about what the word God means — and whether we ourselves believe in God. As Rabbis and educators, most of us don't talk about our beliefs enough — perhaps because we're embarrassed to admit our doubts, to admit that we don't believe at all — or even to admit that we *do* believe. But as this book suggests, there are many beliefs we share that are affirmations of God, and there are enough diverse understandings of how God moves through the world that most of us can testify that God's existence is a part of the world we inhabit.

Most of us — even the most confirmed secularists — believe that there are connections in the world. All of us feel connected to something, whether to friends or relatives, to our students, to an ocean or a sunset, and we know that all of us are made up of atoms and molecules that are connected to each other. Not to feel connected to other parts of the universe is to fly in the face of what we know about science. Once we acknowledge that, it is not a big step to believe that there is a sum of all the connections in the world, that they all fit together — and then to suggest that the sum of all the connections, even the source of all the connections, could be called God. The challenge of the spiritual life is to find all the connections we can — to find the link between a tragic illness and a text's great insight,

between a song that brings tears to our eyes and a stunning sunset, between a hurtful act and the sudden smell of spring. If we want to teach about God, we cannot merely affirm the old saw that God is everywhere — we have to ask, "Why is this event happening now? What is the connection between these events?" — and show that we believe, or are struggling to believe, that there is a connection between seemingly random acts. If we train our students to ask these questions, if we utilize some of the myriad lessons suggested in this book, our students will be able to see God's presence too.

Happily, our tradition has ways to capture that presence and to make ourselves conscious of it. We read a different portion in the Torah every week, suggesting that we ask, "Why is this event happening in the week of *this parashah*?" In the back of most *Siddurim* is a list of blessings, *Birchot Nehenin*, blessings for things enjoyed, through which we experience sunsets, oceans, remarkable human beings, flowering trees, as gifts of God. Our tradition informs that God is present in each beautiful unfolding of nature and in every sad event — each of these, too, is a membrane through which God "moves" through the world. If we are to show our students that being Jewish matters, we must begin to look for — and increasingly find — the presence of God, the presence of meaningful connections in our lives. When a thunderstorm crackles outside our classroom window, let's say the appropriate *berachah* — "Praised are You . . . whose might and power fill the world." When a little miracle happens in our lives, let's not be embarrassed by it. Let's share it with our students, encouraging them to share their miracles, too. When we're struggling with seeing how God is present at a hard time in our lives, let's share that struggle as well.

Even if we teach Hebrew or Jewish history, we need to remember that as teachers in Religious Schools and Day Schools, everything we teach must ultimately help our students see the connection between themselves and the Torah (which God gave to Israel), with the God who gave it, and the people God created. When children learn Hebrew, they are learning the language in which our people has heard the voice of God. We therefore need to teach a religious vocabulary and a grammar that will help them become fluent in prayer, in the saying of the *Birchot Nehenin*, and in other expressions that will strengthen their ability to communicate with God. When we teach Hebrew, we are teaching nothing less than the love language between God and the Jewish people.

And Jewish history? Are we teaching only about Jewish figures in the past, about wars we've lost and won, pogroms and Crusades and oppressive kings and popes and despots? I hope not. I hope we see ourselves as teaching what God meant in telling Abraham that we would be as uncountable as the stars in heaven and that the land of Israel would belong to us. In our schools, we need to open our students to the possibility that Jewish history is the working out of God's providential design for the Jewish people.

It is unlikely that our students will walk into our classroom on the first day of school and be immediately swept up into the embracing presence of God. But if we are earnest teachers of the ways in which the holy can enter our lives, we can be the staunch oaks in the lives of those who learn with us, swaying with the wind of God moving through us, guiding these young descendants of Abraham and Sarah into a receptive space where one day they, too, will meet with God.

INTRODUCTION

God is central to the existence of the Jewish people. The relationship of the Jewish people to God is the focal point of the Torah and the entire Tanach. *Halachah*, prayer and blessings, Torah study, Shabbat and holiday celebrations, *tzedakah*, and even the land of Israel, all connect us implicitly to God. Yet, our understanding of and relationship to God is often assumed, rather than examined, enriched, or expanded. God's omnipresence is no guarantee that we make God fully present in our lives.

In recent years, more Jews have begun to search for God and to seek the light of God's presence in their lives. This quest has led to a greater openness to discuss, explore, and experience God in multifaceted ways. People are seeking a greater sense of spirituality, of transcendence and immanence, awe and wonder, comfort and support, and wholeness and completeness.

This book is addressed to all who are involved in the transmission of Jewish life. Included are chapters for Jewish educators in all settings who work with learners of all ages and types, including the training of other educators, Rabbis and Cantors, parents, and lay leaders. As Jewish educators and guides to Jewish life, we have a responsibility to help nurture and guide people's quests for God and spirituality. We need to let people know of the richness that Judaism provides in knowing, relating, and experiencing God. Essential to our role as educators, parents, Rabbis, Cantors, youth workers, lay leaders, social service workers, is connecting what Judaism has to offer in terms of texts, rituals, prayer, and ideas to people's lives, their practices in the home, and their ways of seeing and acting in the world.

While God is One, views of God are not monolithic in Judaism. Multiple paths exist to understanding and approaching God. In this volume, we have sought the wisdom of a wide range of scholars, educators, and lay leaders to provide insights into these multiple paths, these manifold ways of reaching God and the sacred in our lives. The chapters bear their names and reflect the depth and richness of their understandings and of Jewish life itself.

ORGANIZATION OF THE BOOK

Teaching about God and Spirituality is intended to help all Jews concerned with transmitting Jewish life in their efforts to connect people to God and guide them in their spiritual quests. To do this, it is essential to help those who transmit the knowledge and guide the experiences to further their own knowledge about God and to deepen their spirituality. The book presents ideas, identifies issues, and raises questions for the reader to reflect upon. Our relationship to God and our own spiritual quest is something that the individual needs to examine, though not necessarily resolve, before he or she can offer assistance in guiding others comfortably. This book also contributes in another way to nurturing spiritual growth — by presenting actual teacher training workshops and lesson plans for learners of all ages, including families. These can be used in a wide range of settings and can be adapted for use in classrooms. In order to fulfill these purposes, the book is divided into three parts:

Part I: Professional Development

Part II: Teacher Training

Part III: Lessons, Curricula, Programs

Each of these sections is described briefly below, and also in greater depth in an introduction to each of the parts.

Part I: Professional Development

The Professional Development section presents chapters on Jewish theology — views of God to further the knowledge and understanding of the teacher — and educational theories related to teaching about God and spirituality. The material is presented in traditional ways, from a feminist perspective, and modern perspectives. Key theologians and theological ideas over the ages are presented and critiqued. This section also contains ways of understanding spirituality and Jewish life that come from the social sciences, and also from theology or philosophy. Other chapters in this section draw on educational, psychological, and developmental theories as they relate to teaching about God and spirituality. In a few cases, Jewish educators and professionals present their empirical research. Many of the theories and authors reviewed in these chapters come from secular realms or religions other than Judaism. The relevance of these theories and authors to Jewish education is considered and implications identified.

Two special features distinguish this section. First, the editors have identified implications and questions for critical inquiry for each of these chapters. Therefore, all the chapters on theological background can easily be used for adult group study with lay people and/or professionals, and all the chapters on educational theory can be readily used for professional development workshops. These chapters can be used for individual inquiry, too. The second feature that distinguishes the section is the provision by the editors of activities based on the ideas presented in the chapter, which can be used for professional development workshops or in classrooms with learners. For example, Chapter 1, "The Changing Perceptions of God in Judaism" by Rifat Sonsino, includes activities that teach about the views of God throughout Jewish history that are featured in the chapter. These activities help the reader imagine the link between theory and application, in other words, how theory gets translated into curriculum.

Part II: Teacher Training

Even though all the chapters in the first two sections of the book are readily usable for teacher training, this section offers several different teacher training programs that have been field-tested in various settings. Both one-time programs and ongoing programs are presented. The format of the programs in this section is the same as that used for the lesson plans for the different age levels. That format is described in the following section.

Part III: Lesson Plans, Curricula, Programs

All the programs described in this part of the book have actually been used. Each of them is written up in a particular format, which provides some consistency. The elements of each lesson plan are:

Topic: God or spirituality thematic focus

Target Audience: Population or group for which the program is intended

Time Frame: Program frequency, schedule, and length

Staffing: Listing of professionals and volunteers and their role in the program

Overview: Succinct description of the entire program or curriculum

Purpose: What the program, curriculum, or lesson is trying to accomplish

Objectives: What the participants will do and learn

Content: Major concepts covered

Learning Materials: All books, supplies, and other materials needed to execute the program.

Learning Activities: Step-by-step description of how to implement the program

Evaluation: Presents ways of evaluating the program

Watch Out For: Concerns to consider in implementing the program

Please note that in the case of multi-session lessons, all the titles or topics of all the sessions are mentioned, but only one session is presented in detail.

Many of the lessons were selected for inclusion because they reflect the approaches presented in Part I of the book, Professional Development. Each focuses on theories and approaches for teaching about God and spirituality. In a few cases, authors of the theoretical chapters actually wrote lesson plans for this section.

Reference

The book concludes with a Reference section that features an Appendix; a Glossary; Resources for Learners, Teachers, and Parents; and an Index.

The appendix contains a reprint of the mini-course *God: The Eternal Challenge* by Sherry Bissell [Blumberg], with Audrey Friedman Marcus and Raymond A. Zwerin (A.R.E. Publishing, Inc.) This course for students in Grades 7 up presents source material and activities related to questions about God that encourage students to share their thoughts, feelings, questions, and experiences in seeking God.

The glossary by Sherry H. Blumberg contains a vocabulary for theology and defines prevalent terms used by Jewish and non-Jewish theologians. These terms reveal how great thinkers have spoken and thought about God and spirituality over the ages.

Finally, the bibliography of materials and resources compiled by Roberta Louis Goodman lists books, textbooks, web sites, and films/videos that can be used in teaching about God and spirituality for the different age groups: early childhood, elementary school, middle school/high school, and adults. Listed also are books that educators and parents can use as resources in guiding them on how to teach about God and spirituality. Both Jewish and non-Jewish sources are included. For additional suggestions of books and materials, see the annotated bibliographies at the end of the chapters in Part I.

HOW TO USE THIS BOOK

Teaching about God and Spirituality is designed to be a source and a resource rather than read from cover to cover. It may be read by an individual, studied in *chevruta*, or used by groups of adults, such as parents and professionals, or it may be used for self-growth. The chapters are ready for use as the professional development component of a faculty meeting, a special workshop, an adult education class, a parenting or family education program, etc. The book can be used to do research on the topic of God and spirituality for a sermon, *D'var Torah*, academic paper, or curriculum. Some may prefer to learn by doing, by trying out different programs and curriculum. Lessons are provided for professional development workshops or working with learners of all ages. Some lessons are geared to parents and children at home. All can be used as is, or modified to fit a particular setting. *Teaching about God and Spirituality* is intended to be read and reread and used in a variety of ways as one continues to learn and grow in comfort, skills, and confidence as a teacher of God and spirituality. Whatever gate one uses to enter and explore the wisdom contained in this book, it will promote thinking and doing that enhance learning and teaching about God and spirituality.

The book combines both theory and practice. Just as other subjects in Jewish and general education have a theoretical basis, so, too, does the teaching about God and spirituality. While there is definitely something unique and sacred about teaching about God and spirituality, there is a knowledge base that can be drawn upon. Many of the chapters will help the educator, the spiritual guide, in the formulation of an approach to teaching about God and spirituality.

The theory, both the theological and the educational, is intended to inform practice. While all the lessons for teachers and learners are readily adaptable for instant use in a variety of settings, the lessons chosen for use should reflect the teacher's or transmitter's approach and goals for teaching about God and spirituality. The lessons are creative, outstanding examples of ways of presenting God, but they are intended to stimulate rather than stifle the creation of new and exciting ideas regarding how to encounter God.

GUIDELINES FOR TEACHING ABOUT GOD AND SPIRITUALITY

Throughout our lifetime, we continue to grow in our spirituality and understanding of and relationship to God. Each person is unique in his/her understanding at any given stage of life. However, while this is true, it is important for the teacher or transmitter about God and spirituality to state and reflect upon his or her views before teaching others. Part of seeking involves raising questions, often difficult or challenging ones. This means that we are not always totally comfortable with our relationship to God. Anger and doubt are all part of relating to God. Very likely, your learners will not be in the same place as you are from a spiritual standpoint. Thus, it will be helpful for you to be aware of what is involved in the seeking process by doing your own reflection first.

When teaching others about God and spirituality it is important to consider the following:

- Listen to what the learner has to say.

- Capitalize on the situations that emerge in the classroom that lend themselves to talking about God and spirituality.

- See how you can integrate God into whatever curriculum you are teaching, and not just those entitled specifically "God," "Prayer," and "Spirituality."

- Create a safe, nonjudgmental environment in which learners can explore God and spirituality.

- Affirm that doubting and questioning are part of seeking God and spirituality.

- Affirm that there are many paths to God.

- Use different modalities, intelligences, or ways of helping the learner explore, experience, and express his/her views of God and spirituality.

- Help the learners ascribe their own meaning to the teachings about God and spirituality that are found within Judaism — its texts, liturgy, stories, rituals, and symbols.

CONCLUSION

The more you teach about God and spirituality, the more skillful and comfortable you should become in being a guide.

We hope that this book will inspire both learners and teachers. May it be a resource for many years to come in the quest for the Source of life and blessing. *Baruch Shem Kavod Malchuto L'olam Va'ed.*

INTRODUCTION TO PART I
Professional Development

Roberta Louis Goodman

MORE AND MORE PEOPLE ARE BECOMING SPIRITUAL seekers, searching for purpose and direction in their lives. They want answers to ultimate questions about the meaning of life and their place in the universe. They are looking for values to guide their actions and interactions with children, adults, and society as a whole. They desire connections and relationships to other people and to God — that which is ultimate and eternal, truthful and righteous, that which not just today, but over the generations, provides a framework within which they can live their lives. The role of Jewish educators, clergy, parents, and others therefore becomes one of helping people find their spiritual routes and roots.

Aiding these spiritual seekers requires preparation for those who will nurture, mentor, and guide them. As with any other topic, subject, or challenge, the professional engaged in nurturing people's spirituality and relationship to God benefits from knowledge and skills that can augment experiences and intuition and create a feeling of competency and comfort. Part I of *Teaching about God and Spirituality*, entitled "Professional Development," is designed to achieve these goals.

This section of the book is the longest. It consists of chapters aimed at preparing educators, teachers, administrators, parents, clergy, and others to nurture a relationship to God and uncover a sense of spirituality. These chapters provide background information and educational theories and approaches to teaching about God and spirituality. Each of the chapters in Part I was designed to challenge and enhance the knowledge and skills of Jewish educators, clergy, and parents. Each chapter concludes with implications and questions for critical inquiry that

can be used as a professional development session, a conversation between colleagues, or stimulate thought for the person reading it on his/her own. The suggested activities that follow these chapters may be used with teachers and/or with students.

This first part of the book models the trend found in teacher training and professional education in general — to create professionals who are reflective practitioners. Any profession is a combination of science and art. It requires skills and knowledge that people are able to apply to messy, unclear, different situations to develop competency. To gain this competency, the emphasis in professional preparation is on reflecting on learning and experiences with the aid of a mentor. The implications and questions for critical inquiry included herein reflect the best of the editors' thinking and questioning, and address many issues and situations that each Jewish educator, clergy, or parent confronts. We hope these will further critical thinking about the ideas expressed in the chapters. The entire Part I, "Professional Development," is designed to help you think and reflect. It exposes you to important ideas drawn from the perspectives and experiences of experts, and offers an opportunity to respond to these ideas either on your own or with your peers.

The chapters in Part I present a range of disciplines that contribute to our understanding of how to teach about God and spirituality. These disciplines include theology, practical theology, sociology, history, psychology, Jewish education, religious education, and general education. Some of the leading thinkers in Jewish education and Jewish communal life, the innovators in teaching about God and spirituality, contributed chapters to this book. They come from different movements (Reform, Reconstructionist, Conservative, and Orthodox) and different settings (Jewish colleges, secular universities, synagogues, Day Schools, supplementary schools, adult education programs, North American Jewish educational organizations, among others). The authors are teachers, clergy, executive directors, education directors, academics, and therapists. They bring a variety of perspectives and insights to nurturing spirituality and a relationship to God. Following is an explanation of what each author contributes to our understanding of nurturing spirituality.

DESCRIPTION OF CHAPTERS I TO 26

Views of God

Judaism throughout the ages has produced different views of God. In Chapter 1, "The Changing Perceptions of God in Judaism," Rabbi Rifat Sonsino traces the main views of God from biblical through modern times.

In Chapter 2, "What Is Jewish Feminist Theology?" Dr. Dawn Robinson Rose fills in the "conventional" picture, adding concepts and images of God from feminist theology.

Rabbi Bruce Kadden, in Chapter 3, "What Can We Learn from Christian Theology?" provides another understanding of the main views of God in Judaism by comparing and contrasting major images of God from Jewish and Christian sources.

Issues in Jewish Spirituality

Using an approach characteristic of sociology, Dr. David Ariel describes in Chapter 4, "The Spiritual Condition of American Jews," the phenomenon of seeking and seekers in today's world. Ariel explains the popularity of the emergence of spiritual seeking. He outlines six types of seekers and briefly discusses the implications of the orientation to spiritual seeking for Jewish educational institutions.

Acknowledging the desire of many to find

their spiritual path, Dr. Sherry H. Blumberg outlines a variety of paths that spiritual seekers can take in Chapter 5, "Paths To Jewish Spirituality." Some are based on traditional paths of finding God; others boldly trace new steps, new ways of connecting with God. Blumberg emphasizes that Judaism has many paths to God, enough to embrace most, if not all, Jewish seekers.

The healing movement has awakened spirituality and connections to Judaism for many individuals. Dr. Kerry M. Olitzky, in Chapter 6, "Healing As a Spiritual Search," shares insights into how healing and spirituality are intertwined. He speaks of people's interest in healing, provides a Jewish framework for understanding healing by looking at ancient and contemporary sources, and addresses how educators can be involved in the process.

Theories of Human Development and Learning

Theories of human development and learning provide insights into how people learn and grow in terms of their spirituality and relationship to God. Many theories in general education, religious education, and psychology offer wisdom and guidance into how to nurture spiritual growth and development. Dr. Roberta Louis Goodman, in Chapter 7, "Nurturing a Relationship To God and Spiritual Growth: Developmental Approaches," comments on the adaptations and implications of theories from general education, religious education, and psychology for nurturing the spirituality of Jews. Her chapter focuses particularly on Fowler's faith development theory and Oser's theory of religious reasoning.

In Chapter 8, "Psychological Resources for a Spiritual Judaism," Dr. Barbara R. Grossman points out some important personal or psychological challenges that can be directed religiously or spiritually to help people seek meaning and the sacred in their lives. She offers insights into how to address these concerns. Grossman draws on the Theories of Erikson's psycho-social development, Fowler's faith development, Jung's work on typology, Myers-Briggs on temperament, and others.

Rabbi Craig Marantz, in Chapter 9, "Archetypal Pathways To God: The Subconscious in the Development of Faith," demonstrates how archetypes from Jung's theory can help us understand the narratives and ancestors presented in Jewish texts and nurture our relationship to God.

In Chapter 10, "Educating the Spirit," Dr. Michael J. Shire presents his original research regarding what young people say about their own spirituality and how it is influenced by their Jewish educational programs. Based on this investigation, he suggests a curricular approach to enhancing religiosity in Jewish education.

Dr. Betsy Dolgin Katz focuses in Chapter 11, "Teaching and Learning about God: Considerations and Concerns for Adults," on what the field of adult education has to say that will assist us in nurturing spirituality in a Jewish context.

Curricular Approaches and Strategies

Several of the authors in this book address the organization, design, and implementation of curriculum and curricular approaches and strategies in teaching about God and spirituality. Curriculum is the core of teaching. It is the design and plan to transmit content and material to the learner. The curriculum integrates approaches and articulates strategies for capturing the learner's attention, imagination, and intellect.

In Chapter 12, "Curricular Approaches for Teaching about God," Dr. Sherry H. Blumberg describes special considerations that need to be attended to when designing curriculum on teaching about God and spirituality. She stresses the necessity for spirituality and God to be a planned, explicit part of the curriculum with fully articulated goals, objectives, activities, and outcomes, just like other topics we teach our students. It is not sufficient, she asserts, to deal with issues related to spirituality as they emerge.

Dr. Jeffrey Schein, in Chapter 13, "Text, Teacher, and Student: Enhancing Spiritual

Development," shares his approach to developing curriculum, which combines the triangle of text, teacher, and learner in fostering a relationship to and understanding of God. Schein emphasizes the importance of having learners engage directly with texts, unmediated by the teacher or secondary sources as of way of relating to God.

In Chapter 14, "Educating for Self-Transcendence," Dr. Sherry H. Blumberg offers insight into her view of this important concept that needs to be taught and integrated into the curriculum. Transcendence is an important theological idea, as it comes from seeing God as above and beyond, connecting us to tradition and moving us beyond our selves. Blumberg offers some practical suggestions on how to educate for self-transcendence.

Dr. Neil Gillman, in Chapter 15, "Writing a Personal Theology," presents a strategy that encourages people to write down their own theologies. Ironically, many of Gillman's examples pertain to the Rabbinic students he teaches in a seminary setting where one would expect God to be omnipresent in the institutional culture. Even in this setting, Gillman asserts, it is necessary to devote time to reflection and learning about God to further spiritual growth. Gillman has used this writing strategy extensively with adult learners. The technique, which makes explicit one's relationship to God, is also appropriate with teens, and can aid them in their spiritual journeys.

In Chapter 16, "Tell Me a Story about God," Rabbi Sandy Eisenberg Sasso writes about using stories to foster spiritual growth. She provides advice for parents, as well as educators and clergy, on how to use stories as a spiritual activity. Spiritual learning requires space for the learner to struggle, question, explain, and explore. Sasso shows how the writing, telling, listening to, and interpreting stories is a spiritual activity that parents, educators, and clergy can use to engage children and deepen their spiritual quests.

In Chapter 17, "Parents As Spiritual Guides for Children," Rabbi Julie Greenberg encourages parents to take on the role of spiritual guide for their children. She attempts to help make parents more comfortable with their own spirituality so that they can nurture that of their children. Greenberg presents some practical, easy to do activities for the home that foster a sense of *keshushah* (holiness) and a relationship to God.

Dr. Roberta Louis Goodman, in Chapter 18, "God and Spirituality in Prayer and Praying," addresses how to approach the teaching of God and spirituality in four ways: (1) she describes the three elements that should be part of every curriculum that teaches about God and spirituality, (2) she presents major problems in the teaching of prayer from a developmental perspective, and offers responses and solutions, (3) she discusses the tension between personal and communal aspects of finding God through prayer and praying, and (4) she offers some thoughts on the importance of addressing the question "why pray."

The Arts

The arts provide additional curricular approaches and strategies. The chapters in this sub-section are devoted to addressing how the arts — storytelling, visual arts, dance and movement, drama, and music can be used to foster spiritual growth.

The arts are well suited for fostering spiritual seeking. They are expressive and interpretive, reflective of the artists' struggle to understand and relate to God. The arts often convey content that is spiritual. The elements of creativity, imagination, interpretation, and inspiration come through as we use the arts to explore our spirituality and relationship to God. The arts represent different types of intelligences, tap the different modalities — visual, auditory, and kinesthetic — reach the conscious and unconscious realms, and utilize communicative media other than discussion. Therefore, they are able to reach many people and reach them in different ways. Chapters on the Arts are as follows:

In Chapter 19, "God Dwells in the Story," Dr. Steven M. Rosman describes the sacred power of stories and recommends telling stories about God, about the search for God by others, and

about the "hand of God" that leaves clues for us in nature, in relationships, and in moments of awe and wonder.

In Chapter 20, "Art Therapy and the Spiritual Encounter," Nadine Cohen draws upon the world of art therapy and shares her approach to deepening spiritual exploration. In her chapter she provides an example of a lesson that utilizes the arts to heighten spiritual awareness.

Lynn Lutz Friend is an artist and a teacher. In Chapter 21, "Awakening Spirituality through Art Experiences," she shows how the visual arts can be used to illuminate one's spirituality. She describes a number of examples of art activities based on her work in Jewish schools.

In Chapter 22, "Encountering God in Dance," Dr. JoAnne Tucker describes two specific areas of dance activities that are avenues to finding God: (1) teaching Torah through the process of Dance *Midrash*, and (2) experiencing liturgy in a physical manner.

Drama and music are tools for connecting people to God and *kedushah*. Rabbi Shawn Israel Zevit in Chapter 23, "Using Drama and Music to Enrich Spiritual Seeking," advocates for a "playfully serious" approach to music and drama, and suggests ways to integrate the two as we seek God with our students.

Leaders in Fostering Spiritual Growth

Both professionals and lay leaders have important roles to play in fostering spiritual growth. While it is often assumed that clergy, with their worship and life cycle responsibilities, serve as religious and spiritual figures in the Jewish community, educators and lay leaders contribute to the community's and individual's spiritual development in significant ways. In fact, all three parties need to work together in reaching the seekers of today.

Dr. Hanan A. Alexander in Chapter 24, "God As Teacher: Jewish Reflections on a Theology of Pedagogy," and Rabbi Jeffrey Salkin in Chapter 25, "A Spirituality for Jewish Teachers: Working with God, for God, and through God," present inspiring pieces about the role of teachers and educators as doing God's work. For Alexander, both teaching and study are holy acts. He presents a list of principles of educational practice which God models. These principles include learning through both words and actions; facilitating learning through using dialogue and inquiry; grounding teaching in caring, covenant, obligation, and authority; distinguishing between teaching and training and using them appropriately; using reward and punishment; and being willing to make mistakes and asking for forgiveness. Salkin suggests the need to recognize the sanctity of our work, the acts of creation, revelation, and redemption we each perform as Jewish educators. He also suggests that we remember that God is our master, our true "boss," as, ultimately, we do our work for the sake of God. Adapting these perspectives can help to elevate what we do.

Chapter 26, "Spiritual Mentoring" by Dr. Carol Ochs, presents suggestions for being or becoming a spiritual guide or mentor. Ochs urges educators, clergy, and parents to take on the role and responsibility of nurturing our students and children in their spiritual quests, and provides strategies and supports for engaging in this task.

The special role that clergy can play in fostering spiritual seeking is presented in Chapter 27, "From the Pulpit To the Classroom" by Rabbi Morley T. Feinstein. He provides strategies for nurturing spirituality from the *bimah* through interpreting prayers and weekly Torah readings. Most of all, he emphasizes the need for clergy to share their own views and struggles publicly with congregants as a way of sending a message about putting God in the center of their lives.

Board members as lay leaders of Jewish educational institutions, including synagogues, have their own role to play in nurturing spirituality, according to Dr. Roberta Louis Goodman and Daniel S. Schechter in Chapter 28, "The Role of Volunteer Leaders in Educating about God and Spirituality." These authors advocate for engaging lay leaders in the process of bringing God and the sacred into all aspects of institutional life including, but not limited to, the boardroom. The role and deliberations of board members are sacred and based on sacred principles. An awareness of this is central and fundamental in understanding the work of the communal leader. Professionals have an important role in teaching and guiding board members so that they are able to lead and inspire others in terms of God, spirituality, and *kedushah*.

CHAPTER 1

THE CHANGING PERCEPTIONS OF GOD IN JUDAISM

Rifat Sonsino

INTRODUCTION

IN THE PAST, ONE OF THE MAJOR RELIGIOUS CONCERNS was to determine "who" was God. People lived in a social environment that could take for granted the presence of the Divine. There was no such a thing as a secular life. All life was religious. Social groups identified their own god(s) from among the various divinities known during their time, and swore allegiance to whichever one(s) matched most closely with their ideas, needs, and values. There was *Baal* in Canaan, *Amon* in Egypt, *Marduk* in Babylonia, *Melcart* in Lebanon, *El* in Ugarit, *Zeus* in Greece, *YHVH* in Israel, among others.

In surveying the Jewish sacred literature on this subject, it becomes apparent that almost all Jewish thinkers based their belief on "the unity principle." In other words, except for the early periods in our people's history when our ancestors may have worshiped more than one god at the same time, Jewish teachers and sages promoted the idea that God is one, not two or three or more. In fact, even the number "one" would imply that God could be counted among many. And this was indeed the case during the monolatrous times, when Israel's God was considered the special God of Israel, without denying the fact that other divinities served the neighboring peoples. Once monotheism was firmly established in Israel, God became not only One, but unique, alone. There is no other God besides YHVH, they affirmed.

Traditional sources do not always agree on the specific attributes of God. In other words, Jewish sources maintain the uniqueness of God, but have not turned one particular concept into a dogma. Our ancient Jewish sages taught that human beings, though often achieving greatness, can never transcend their humanity. They cannot become God. The prophet Hosea stated this belief clearly when he asserted in the name of God that "I am God and not man" (11:9). Furthermore, the biblical message is that God cannot be represented by an image (Exodus 20:3-5; Deuteronomy 5:8-9; 34:18) or compared to anything physical in the universe:

"'To whom can you liken Me? To whom can I be compared?' — says the Holy One" (Isaiah 40:25).

Most Jewish thinkers have also argued that God makes ethical demands of us. Morality is connected with the idea of God. Unlike other people who believed that there is one god for good and one for evil, biblical authors maintained that God is the source of everything there is, both good and evil. "I form light and darkness; I make weal and create woe; I the Lord do all these things" (Isaiah 45:7, NJPS).

While it is not possible to review all Jewish perceptions of God throughout history in this one short chapter, we can, however, identify some of the basic assumptions that have been part of the Jewish views regarding the Divine.

IN THE BIBLE

The belief in the existence of God is fundamental in biblical Judaism. However, a survey of the Hebrew Scriptures clearly shows that it is rather difficult to give a precise definition of what the biblical Israelites and later on Jews in historical times meant by the term "God," simply because the perception of the Divine changed through the centuries. Furthermore, the Bible, though a highly theological document, does not provide us with a single and integrated definition of God. Throughout its pages, one can find vestiges of primitive beliefs as well as remarkable expressions of ethical monotheism. Consequently, instead of presenting a unified view of God, it is more appropriate to speak of some of the dominant themes about the Divine that can be culled from its writings.

God Is Unique

The idea of the unity, the singleness if you wish, of God represents a long development in biblical thought, going from polytheism (Genesis 20:13; 35:7) where the term *"Elohim"* (literally, gods) is accompanied by a verb in the plural, to monolatry (e.g., Exodus 15:11) where God appears as *primus inter pares* (first among equals). Within its context, the statement in Deuteronomy 6:4: "Hear, O Israel, YHVH is our God, YHVH is *ehad* (one)," does not mean that God is the only one to the exclusion of others, but that YHVH is the sole deity whom the Israelites were permitted to worship. During exilic times (sixth century B.C.E.), we find clear expressions of spiritual monotheism:

> The Creator of heaven who alone is God,
> Who formed the earth and made it,
> Who alone established it;
> He did not create it a waste,
> But formed it for habitation:
> I am the Lord, and there is none else
> (Isaiah 45:18, NJPS).

God Has a Name

In ancient Canaan, the generic term for god was *El*, just as it was in Ugarit. In Babylonian it was *Ilu*. Later on, among the Arabs, it became *Allah*. That word probably means "(the) strong (one)." In the Bible, we find the term *El* either alone or in combination with other terms, such as *El-Elyon* (Genesis 14:20), *El-Roi* (Genesis 16:13), and *El-Shaddai* (Genesis 17:1). We also find other terms about God, for example, *Eloha/Elohim*, *Adon* (master), *Av* (father), *Melech* (king), *Tzur Yisrael* (Rock of Israel). Yet, the most recognizable name for the Israelite god is the tertragrammaton, the four Hebrew letters YHVH, whose

root meaning is "existence/being." The exact pronunciation of this word is now unknown because, as it was charged with metaphysical potency, the name ceased to be uttered. It was replaced by *Adonai* (Lord). Often in documents the vowels of the word *Adonai* were imposed upon the letters YHVH. This gave rise to a reading of those letters with those vowels to form the mistaken pronunciation *Yehovah* and later Jehovah.

The Gender of God

Hebrew does not have a neutral gender. Everything is either masculine or feminine. Biblical Israel lived in a predominantly patriarchal society where power resided in men. Consequently, God was often viewed as a vigorous and combative male warrior, as reflected in Exodus 15:3, "YHVH is a man of war, YHVH is His name." Yet, there are a number of passages in which this image is softened: God is compassionate (Deuteronomy 4:31), a caring father (Psalms 103:13), even a comforting mother (Isaiah 66:13).

God Cannot Be Represented by a Physical Object

In the Decalogue, God instructs the Israelites not to make for themselves a sculptured image for purposes of worship (Exodus 20:4; Deuteronomy 20:8). Even though some people in the biblical period claimed to have "seen" God (Exodus 24:11; Deuteronomy 34:10; I Kings 22:19), there are no descriptions of what God looks like. In fact, we are clearly told that humans "cannot see Me and live" (Exodus 33:8). At the time of the giving of the Torah, the Israelites "heard the sound of words, but perceived no shape" (Deuterono-my 4:12).

God Acts in the World

In the Bible, God is often defined by actions. God is involved in the lives of people and particularly in the peregrinations of the Israelites and other nations. Not only does God create the universe (Genesis 1-3), but is also behind every historical act: God destroyed Sodom and Gomorrah (Genesis 19), brought the Philistines from Caphtor, the Arameans from Kir, and the Israelites from Egypt (Amos 9:7). As in many other ancient Near Eastern countries, battle victories are attributed to God. Thus, Moses tells his people:

> The Lord your God Himself will cross over [the Jordan] before you; and He Himself will wipe out those nations from your path, and you shall dispossess them (Deuteronomy 31:3, NJPS).

God Has a Covenant with Israel

Even though God is the God of all humanity, biblical Israelites saw themselves bound to YHVH by an enduring Covenant (Deuteronomy 29:13-14). As the text reads: "Of all the peoples of earth the Lord your God chose you to be His treasured possession" (Deuteronomy 7:6). However, this bond does not give the Israelites special privileges. In fact, it imposes upon them greater responsibilities. As the prophet Amos makes it clear: "You alone have I singled out of all the families of the earth, that is why I will call you to account for all your iniquities" (3:2, NJPS). Israel is to be judged by higher standards. It is expected to become "a light to/of the nations" (Isaiah 42:6).

God Is the Law Giver

In the ancient Near East, gods were the source of law, but redaction of the legislation was left to the kings. Furthermore, collections of laws were meant to impress the gods that kings were carrying out justice as expected of them. In ancient Israel, however, YHVH is both the source of Torah and the sole redactor of specific instructions directed not only to priests or other officials, but also to the people at large.

In addition to ritual observance, the Israelite God requires ethical behavior. True, priests are told how to offer sacrifices and Israelites are enjoined to carry out certain practices, but the overwhelming direction in the Bible is that this is not enough. Ritual never replaces ethics. "I desire goodness," writes Hosea, "not sacrifice" (6:6).

Biblical Spirituality

In the biblical period, spirituality was expressed primarily by sacrificial offerings, by pilgrimages to Jerusalem, and by acts that clearly demonstrate the "fear" (*yirah*) or "love" (*ahavah*) of God. These represent two sides of the same coin — loyalty and reverence. Above all, the biblical God requires of the Israelites total covenantal faithfulness (*chesed*). The greatest offense against God is idolatry. The prophets constantly accuse the people of backsliding, and many legal texts in the Pentateuch end with short blessings to encourage steadfastness, and longer curses to frighten men and women lest they succumb to the allures of paganism.

IN TALMUDIC LITERATURE

Like the Bible, Rabbinic literature also embodies a religious doctrine about God without representing a self-contained and logically thought-out system. God is again viewed through various prisms, and there is no apparent attempt to integrate all perceptions into a coherent whole. The following points are worth highlighting.

God Is One

The idea of God's absolute unity is emphasized throughout the Rabbinic texts. True, God is known by different names, but this simply means that the only one God is experienced by human beings in a variety of ways. Thus we read,

> When I judge my creatures, I am called *Elohim*; when I wage war against the wicked, I am called *Tzevaot*; when I suspend judgment for a person's sins, I am called *El Shaddai*; but when I have compassion upon my world, I am called *YHVH* (Exodus Rabbah, Shemot 3:6).

God Inheres in All of Nature

We read:

> A heathen once asked Rabbi Joshua b. Korha, "Why did God speak to the Israelites from the thorn bush?" Rabbi Korha replied: "To teach you that there is no place where the *Shechinah* (the Divine Presence) is not present, even in a thorn bush." (*Exodus Rabbah, Shemot* 2:5)

God Is a Personal God

Though an angelic court surrounds God, the Holy One personally cares for individuals and relates to them directly.

> If a person is in distress, let him not call on [the angels] Michael or Gabriel, but let him call directly on Me, and I will hearken to him straightway. (*Jerusalem Talmud, Brachot* 9)

God rules the universe with two different attributes — *Middat HaDin* (justice) and *Middat HaRahamim* (mercy). Above all, God is compassionate:

> Before God brought on the flood [in the days of Noah], God observed seven days of mourning, for God grieved at heart. (*Tanhumah, Shemini* 11a)

The Nature of Human Beings

God has created human beings with two inclinations: the desire to do good (*yetzer tov*) and the desire to carry out evil acts (*yetzer ra*). Even though God is all-knowing, human beings still have free will to choose between these two. "Everything is foreseen, yet freedom of choice is given" (*Pirke Avot* 3:19). Here this dichotomy is noted, but not resolved.

Two Aspects of Torah

God revealed two Torahs simultaneously — the *Torah Sheh-Bichtav* (Written Torah) and the *Torah Sheh-B'al Peh* (Oral Torah). The first refers to the sacred texts, the second to the authoritative interpretations of these documents. Some say

the first expression refers to the Torah itself, whereas the second refers to the Talmud. The line of authority proceeds from one generation to another, as we read:

> Moses received the Torah from Sinai and gave it to Joshua; Joshua to the elders, the elders to the prophets, the prophets to the men of the great assembly. (*Pirke Avot* 1:1)

The Mitzvot

God's requirements are embodied in a collection of 613 *mitzvot* (commandments), which can be either positive ("do this") or negative ("don't do this"). Some of them are of biblical origin (*d'Oraita*), others come by the authority of the Rabbis (*d'Rabbanan*). The study and performance of these *mitzvot* represent for the Rabbis the way to serve God, namely spiritually. Ultimately, what God wants is for human beings to emulate divine deeds:

> As God clothed the naked . . . visited the sick . . . comforted the mourners . . . buried the dead . . . so should you. (*Sotah* 14a)

Human Suffering and Final Judgment

These early Rabbis took note of human suffering, and taught, "It is not in our power to [understand] the prosperity of the wicked or the suffering of the righteous" (*Pirke Avot* 4:19). However, they added that ultimate justice would be meted out, not in this world, but after death in "the world to come." For the Rabbis, the world in which we live is "like a corridor to the world to come" (*Pirke Avot* 4:21), where "the righteous sit enthroned, their crowns on their heads, and enjoy the brightness of the *Shechinah*" (*Brachot* 17a).

Though the Bible does not speak of hell or paradise or about the resurrection of the dead (except in the last stages of the biblical period, see Ezekiel 12:2), our Rabbinic sages sought to find biblical anchors in the Torah for this belief (e.g., *Sanhedrin* 91b). The Rabbinic Sages popularized this concept in the liturgy.

IN MEDIEVAL TIMES

Under the influence of Muslim thinkers, a number of outstanding Spanish Jews have created a body of philosophical literature wherein God's nature is discussed *in extenso*. Most of these Jewish scholars followed the thinking of ancient Greek philosophers, as mediated through Arabic writings of the time, and adapted them, to the extent possible, to their understanding of Judaism. Almost all of them stressed God's existence, unity, and incorporeality.

Creation of the Universe

One of the basic discussions centered on the issue of "creation *ex nihilo*" (creation out of nothing). Aristotle (384-322 B.C.E.) had argued that matter was eternal — it had always been in existence. Levi ben Gerson (1288-1344) supported this assertion and argued that no thing comes out of anything.[1] Most Jewish philosophers, however, believed in the biblical teaching of creation. So, as early as the tenth century, Saadia ben Joseph al-Fayyumi (892-942), the Gaon or head of the Sura academy in Babylonia, opposed the belief of eternality on the basis that a finite body, such as the world, cannot be infinite. This proves, he said, that the world came to be in time.[2]

The Existence of God

God's existence was mostly defended by using the Aristotelian idea of God as a "prime mover," and the need to make a distinction between "possible" and "necessary" existents, as well as between "potential" and "actual" beings. Thus, Moses Maimonides (1135-1204) wrote:

It is as if you say: this stone, which was in motion, was moved by a staff: the staff was moved by a hand; the hand by tendons; the tendons by muscles; the muscles by nerves; the nerves by natural heat; and the natural heat by the form that subsists therein, this form being undoubtedly the first mover.[3]

God's Knowledge

Another issue of considerable dispute was the notion of God's foreknowledge vs. individual freedom. Some, like Maimonides, argued that in God, human freedom and divine omniscience can be reconciled, because God's knowledge is not like ours (i.e., ours is limited, God's is not).[4] Others, like Levi ben Gerson, taught that God knows the universal order of nature, and is aware of particulars only in so far as it is united with this universal order. Therefore, free will exists.[5]

The Human Being

Most Jewish thinkers held firmly to the belief that the body (the source of evil in life) and the soul (the divine component) are separable, and that we can only connect to God through the development of our minds. Yet, there are some who, like Saadia, argued that both body and soul were created at the same time and constitute a complete whole.[6]

Mysticism

In addition to this intellectual tradition of the medieval Jewish philosophers who followed the neo-Platonic and Aristotelian Greek thought, Judaism developed its own type of mysticism called *Kabbalah* (meaning "reception" [of special traditions]). Its adherents believe that one can achieve knowledge of God through direct awareness or intuition, rather than from logic and rea-

---

[1]See Isaac Husic, *A History of Mediaeval Jewish Philosophy* (Philadelphia, PA: Jewish Publication Society, 1958), 352-358.

[2]Ibid., 29-32.

[3]Moses Maimonides, *The Guide To the Perplexed*, trans. Shlomo Pines (Chicago, IL: University of Chicago Press, 1963), 2:1.

[4]Husic, *History*, 287-288.

[5]Ibid., 345-349. For an intermediate position, see Hasdai ben Abraham Crescas (1340-1410), Ibid., 396-399.

[6]Ibid., 37.

soning. Kabbalists, among others, maintain that God is unknowable (*Ein Sof*, without end), that the Divine relates to the world through the mediation of ten *sephirot* (emanations) emerging from the godhead, and that the human body is a microcosm of the universe in which we live.

In Medieval times, especially during the classical period, the most influential work was the *Zohar*, written around 1289 and attributed to Moses ben Shem Tov de Leon of Guadalajara and Avila in Spain. The main purpose of his *chef d'oeuvre* was to explain the *mitzvot* from a mystical perspective. It deals with topics such as the hidden meanings of the biblical texts, the mysteries of the soul, and the special powers of the Hebrew alphabet. In the post-classical period, the teachings of Rabbi Isaac Luria (the Ari, 1534-1572) of Safed dominated the sixteenth century and beyond. According to the Ari, at the beginning of time, God contracted (*tzimtzum*) and into the emptiness that ensued, divine lights were thrust, shattering the emptiness (*Shevirat HaKelim*). The result is that the world is now broken, chaotic, corrupted. It is our duty to redeem the divine sparks hidden everywhere and to engage in the process of repairing the world (*Tikkun Olam*). This can be achieved through prayer, ritual observance, and doing good deeds.

IN MODERN TIMES

The question of the definition of God continues to exercise many modern Jewish philosophers. Today, no one takes for granted the existence of God. Many, in fact, deny that such a being rules the universe. On the other hand, there are many approaches to the Divine, some of them even mutually incompatible. (See Chart in Appendix A of this chapter, p. 14, also Chapter 2, "What Is Jewish Feminist Theology?" by Dawn Robinson Rose.)

Classical theists consider God as all-powerful, all-knowing, and all-good, a personal God who knows the individual and responds to prayer. Others, such as Milton Steinberg and Harold Kushner, have advanced a position called limited theism that stresses God's goodness, but denies God's omnipotence, thus allowing for free will and the possibility of evil in the universe. Abraham J. Heschel follows the mystical tradition and speaks of experiencing the Ineffable.

A number of Jewish thinkers, among them Mordecai Kaplan, Levi Olan, and Roland Gittelsohn, promoted a religious naturalistic point of view in which God is viewed as energy or force acting within the world through the laws of nature. In this view, God is neither omnipotent nor omniscient, but is the creative principle within the cosmos. Richard L. Rubinstein argued that though the paternalistic God is dead, the God who is the ground of being and the focus of ultimate concern exists. Alvin Reines advances a similar position by defining God as "the enduring possibility of being."

There are existentialist Jewish philosophers, such as Martin Buber and Franz Rozensweig, who seek the Divine through relationship. For religious humanists, like Eric Fromm, God is not a reality but an idea that stands for our highest human powers. Harold M. Schulweis, favoring a predicate theology, prefers to speak of "godliness" rather than of "God." There are also a few, especially after the Holocaust, among them Elie Wiesel, who stress the idea of "the Hidden God." Our job, they say, is to bring God out of hiding by reshaping and mending the world.

A number of women thinkers within the Jewish community have also expanded our understanding of our sacred texts and contributed to our present liturgical creativity.[7] Marcia Falk has written a remarkable prayer book, entitled *The Book of Blessings*,[8] in which, within a humanistic religious framework, she rephrases many of the traditional prayers, often referring to God in the feminine.[9]

[7]For a current theological article on this subject, see "The New Jewish Feminism" by Arnold Jacob Wolf, *Judaism*, Summer, 1998, 351-357.

[8]New York: Summit, 1989.

[9]For a critique of this book, see Simone Lotven Sofian, "Pushing the Envelope: Reflections on *The Book of Blessings*," *CCAR Journal*, Spring, 1999, 84-95.

CONCLUSION

The search for the Divine basically reflects our deep-seated need and desire to find a reasonable explanation for the mysteries of the universe. At some point in our lives, we all want to know the whys and the hows of our existence. The quest for spirituality that now prevails in our society should be an impetus for many committed Jews to engage seriously in theological studies, to identify their religious options, and ultimately to subscribe to that approach that best reflects their personal needs.

However, for dedicated and inquisitive Jews, the study of God cannot remain merely an intellectual exercise. Ultimately, God's essence and presence must have a personal impact. Study should change perspective. It ought to open new vistas. God must become a "living God" through chosen paths of study, social action, and personal devotion.

IMPLICATIONS

1. Judaism is monotheistic. The unity, uniqueness, oneness of God, is not necessarily equated with one concept of or relationship to God. Therefore, concepts, images, and metaphors of God change over time, with experience, and in conjunction with our growing understanding of the past.

2. As time moves on, so, too, do some of our central questions and concerns about God. Although, despite all the changes throughout Jewish history, certain threads and key concepts or views about our understanding of and relationship to God remain unchanged.

3. Every person must establish his/her own personal relationship to God. Every generation must establish its own communal searches for and responses to God.

4. There can be many ways of apprehending God, all within the context of Jewish tradition.

5. Understanding and relating to God is both a personal and a communal journey.

QUESTIONS FOR CRITICAL INQUIRY

1. Does God exist? How does focusing on who God is help us address the question of God's existence?

2. What does it mean that God is ethical, a moral agent?

3. How has the concept, for example, of God as one or unique, changed or stayed the same from biblical through modern times? How have other concepts changed or stayed the same?

4. Why do you think new ideas of God emerged over time? Do you think a person's ideas about God develop and change for similar reasons?

5. Why do you think there are so many names given to God in biblical times and throughout the ages?

6. How can Jews have so many different views about God and still remain one people?

7. What are the main questions and concerns Jews have about God today?

8. Which of the ideas in this chapter about God come closest to your own idea of God?

ACTIVITIES

1. Make a chart of the different names for God used in the time periods that Sonsino identifies. What are the major changes from period to period? How do you explain these changes?

2. Using Sonsino's division of historical periods, make a chart of the major events and ideas in each historical period that affected people's views of and names for God. How have these major events and ideas changed the way we have prayed to God over the ages — in terms of rituals, liturgy, buildings, and prayer garb? (See *The Art of Public Prayer* by Lawrence Hoffman.)

3. Form groups of students according to the different periods. Each group will be attending the God Conference (something like the Zionist Conference). Have each group present the main views about God from their period, and explain why these views are important to the Jewish people. Then debate: What views are most important about God today? Why should all Jews learn about these different views of God from throughout the ages? What, if anything, do the Jewish people lose if the views of God of one period are not accepted? What do they gain by being able to have views of God grow and change?

4. Using a piece of clay that can be easily molded, make one shape. Look at the shape. Then change it into another shape. Do this several times. Then answer the following questions: What was the same about the sculptures you made? What was different? Since the substance of the sculptures stays the same, how does this relate to the idea expressed in the chapter that one tradition can spawn variety and richness in the ways people apprehend its views of God while still remaining true to its essence?

APPENDIX A

	In the Bible	Philo: Spiritual Monotheism	Maimonides: Neo-Arisototelianism	Luria: Mysticism
God's Nature	Different notions, some derived from other Near Eastern religions.	God is the "Soul" of the universe, the universal "Mind," pure spirit or intelligence.	God is pure intellect, the Unmoved Mover of the universe.	God is *Ein Sof*, infinite, revealed to us through the ten *sephirot*. At the same time God is self-limited. Therefore, God needs us to "mend" the world.
Basic Questions	God exists. But is God among us? What is God's name? What does God want of us?	Does God exist? Does God have two parts, body and soul?	Does God exist? How should we interpret the attributes of God?	How can we ascend the ladder of creation and return to God?
God's Unity	An early notion that there may be gods for other nations gave way to a firm belief that there is only one God for all humanity. Angels exist, but only as God's messengers.	God is one. We can prove that God exists.	God is one. We can prove that God exists.	God is one.
God's Name	Proper name of *YHVH*, not to be pronounced. Other names used to describe powers of God or ways in which God relates to the world (*El, Elohim, El Shaddai, Adon, Tzur, Av, Melech*). New names introduced: *HaG'vurah, HaRachaman, HaMakom, Ribono shel olam, Avinu she-bashamayim*, and others.	God can only be called *Ontos*, a Greek term for "That which exists."	Whatever we call God is inadequate, for our language is limited.	*Ein Sof* (The Endless One).
Knowing God	Some texts assert that a few people "saw" God or "met" God, but these texts provide no specific description. We cannot know God.	We cannot describe God. God is unknowable.	God is incorporeal. We cannot say what God "is," only what God "is not."	God is totally unknow-able by the human mind.
God's Relationship To the World	God alone created the world, established a pre-dictable order for it, and continually renews it. God's might and concern for humanity are revealed through histori-cal and natural events. God judges the world. God rewards the good and punishes the wicked.	The "logos" is the means through which God operates in the world.	God created the world out of God's will, *ex nihilo* (out of nothing). God rules the world through "angels," divine intellects. God put in them the forces that gov-ern and shape the physi-cal world.	In observing the physical world, we derive the existence of *Ein Sof* as its cause.

APPENDIX A

	In the Bible	In Rabbinic Literature	Philo: Spiritual Monotheism	Maimonides: Neo-Aristotelianism	Luria: Mysticism
God and the People Israel	God revealed the Torah at Sinai. God brought Israel into the Promised Land. God and Israel are in a covenantal relationship. Israel is to obey God's laws. God is to protect Israel as God's chosen people for all generations.	God gave Israel both a Written and an Oral Torah at Sinai. God "loves" the people Israel. Israel loves God. The relationship is an unbreakable one. God protects us and cares for us. God will resurrect the dead in the world-to-come.	Revelation is God's special gift to Israel. Israel receives the highest form of prophecy.	Israel is the chosen people. The Torah and the mitzvot help us realize our divine potential.	God and Israel are co-partners. Through the performance of mitzvot, we free the imprisoned divine sparks and help to restore the world. Through prayer, our soul ascends to God.
What God "Wants"	God requires observance of mitzvot and ethical behavior.	God requires observance of mitzvot and ethical behavior.	Observing the biblical prescriptions is not enough. We must attempt to understand their spiritual essence.	God is distant from the world. We have free will to shape our world. But God "knows" the choices we will make in a manner that is beyond our comprehension.	God "wants" and "needs" us to better ourselves and restore the world.
God and the Individual	God is a personal God, who hears and answers prayer. God is compared to a parent who cares and watches lovingly over us. God is seen as having human qualities, such as anger, compassion, and a capacity for love.	God is a personal God, who hears and answers prayer. God has the capacity for compassion and anger, but God "prefers" mercy.	We can direct prayer to God, but that is merely our way of talking "about" God. Only through development of our reason can we approach God.	We can pray directly to God and draw nearer to God as our intellectual level increases. The highest goal in life is intellectual and spiritual perfection.	Meditation, prayer, and contemplation give us knowledge about God's relation to our world. People represent the Divine Presence on earth. We can commune with God.
The Problem of Evil	God is loving and just, yet there is evil in the world. Different notions: evil is punishment for sin, is a test, is beyond our comprehension. No single idea.	God is loving and just. Suffering may be a punishment for sin, but why the righteous suffer is beyond our comprehension. This world is not the only one. There is another world, *haolam haba* (the world-to-come) when the righteous will be rewarded and the wicked punished.	Evil is a consequence of the imperfection of the physical world and, therefore, was not caused and cannot be remedied by God. Humanity is endowed with free will and, thus, must choose virtue. But humanity must choose virtue for its own sake, as virtue leads to happiness.	Evil is the denial of good and has nothing to do with God. It is the result of the perishability of matter and the misuse of freedom by human beings.	Evil exists in the world as a result of *sh'virat hakeilim* (the breaking of the vessels). God needs us to eliminate evil.

APPENDIX A

	Spinoza: Pantheism	Buber: Dialogue	Steinberg: Limited Theism	Kaplan: Naturalism	Fromm: Humanism
God's Nature	God and the universe are one. God is nature. The laws of nature were set by God, and everything follows their structure.	God is the "Eternal Thou," always awaiting for us to relate to God. God is an eternal presence that cannot be defined, described, or proven.	God is a Power and a Mind, the Being of all beings, purposive and ethical. But God is not all-powerful. God is like a parent who loves us but cannot save us from pain.	God is the totality of those forces in the world that render human life worthwhile. God is Power or "Process."	God is a symbol, an idea, of our highest potential, the most desirable good.
Basic Questions	What is God? How can we know God?	How can we open ourselves to genuine "I-Thou" encounter?	How do we reconcile the notion of God with the problem of evil and free will?	How can we attain self-realization?	How can the idea of God lead us to better ourselves?
God's Unity	God is one. There is no dualism of mind and matter.	God cannot be defined in any way. God can only be "met."	God is one.	God is one, in the sense of being a totality of forces leading to human self-realization.	God is a unique idea, a symbol in our minds, but not a reality in itself. God represents the supreme goal for humanity.
God's Name	No unique name.	The "Eternal Thou."	No unique name.	"The power that makes for salvation."	No unique name. Any name for God makes God an idol.
Knowing God	God is the totality of the universe. The more we know about the structure of the world, the more we know about God.	One can meet God through a genuine dialogue with others.	We cannot know God completely. Our human knowledge is inadequate. We must accept the existence of God on faith. Logic alone cannot bring us to belief.	The human mind cannot know the totality of God. God is a power and thus has no appearance.	Imitating God means knowing God.
God's Relationship To the World	The laws of nature are manifestations of God. God does not act independently of the world. God is the world.	God waits everywhere in the world for us to let God in through a genuine dialogue.	God has a relationship with the world and needs humankind's help to improve it.	The world has not reached its finality, but is continually being renewed by God.	God has no relationship to the world as such. Our idea of God places God in the world.
God and the People Israel	God has no special relationship to Israel or to any other people. The laws of nature, God, operate equally for all.	Sinai was not a one-time revelation of laws for all time. Revelation is possible at any time.	No particular notion.	Tradition has permanent values that we cannot afford to ignore.	God has no special relationship to any people. But the idea of God should inspire all people.

APPENDIX A

	Spinoza: Pantheism	Buber: Dialogue	Steinberg: Limited Theism	Kaplan: Naturalism	Fromm: Humanism
What God "Wants"	God "wants" nothing. God as nature simply "is."	God "wants" genuine encounter with mankind.	God needs and wants us to work for a more decent world.	Our prayers are for ourselves, not directed to some supernatural being. God is not supernatural, and thus does not "want" anything.	Our idea of God should move us to self-betterment, greater justice, and love. We thus should strive to "imitate" God.
God and the Individual	God is not a personal God. God is the laws of nature. The world is determined. Our only freedom comes through knowledge.	Whenever we have an "I-Thou" relationship with another person, we also encounter God, the "Eternal Thou." We receive a revelation of God's presence.	God allows us free will so that we can work together with God.	A God who makes a difference in one's personal life should be designated as a personal God.	God has no "relationship" with people outside of our idea of God. God is an inner human experience. We cannot know God.
The Problem of Evil	Good and evil are relative to human experience and have nothing to do with God.	Evil is the predominance of relating to others in an "I-It" fashion. Evil can be transcended through an "I-Thou" encounter. God's face is hidden before "radical evil."	Evil is part of the lower levels of evolutionary development. God cannot be blamed for evil and tragedy. Evil is part of the makeup of the universe and part of nature that has not yet been conquered.	Evil is that part of universe that God has not yet subdued. The world has not reached its finality, and our responsibility as co-partners with God is to eliminate all evil from the universe.	Whatever hinders good is evil. Since God is an image of our higher selves, God has nothing to do with evil in the world. It is therefore the task of people to eliminate evil through greater truth, goodness, and kindness.

APPENDIX A

	Heschel: Depth Theology	Reines: Polydoxy & Hylotheism
God's Nature	God is the source of insight and intuition and is "in search of" humanity.	God is the enduring possibility of being.
Basic Questions	How and where do we meet God? How do we apprehend God as God "looks" for us?	What is the source of a religion's authority? Each person has "radical freedom" to choose beliefs and practices, so long as they do not impinge on the freedom of others.
God's Unity	God is one.	There is one God only insofar as "being" is unique and singular.
God's Name	We call God by the many names found in Jewish tradition.	God has many names, from which every individual may choose.
Knowing God	God is beyond the scope of our minds. The world gives us a glimpse of God.	We cannot "know" God any more than we can "know" being.
God's Relationship To the World	God created the world and remains the object of "radical amazement."	God is the past, present, and future possibility of being in the world.
God and the People Israel	God and Israel are bound together by the Covenant of Torah.	God has no special relationship with Israel or any group of people.
What God "Wants"	Divine revelation is the basis of what God "wants." We are to sanctify time.	There is no supernatural entity that "wants" anything from us.

APPENDIX A

	Heschel: Depth Theology	Reines: Polydoxy & Hylotheism
God and the Individual	We humans can know God's "feelings." God loves humankind. We accept God's existence through our intuition.	God has no relationship to humanity as we understand it. If we act to improve the world, however, we better the enduring possibility of being.
The Problem of Evil	We do not know how to solve the problem of evil, but its source is humanity, not God.	What we call "evil" is the imperfection inherent in all existence.

BIBLIOGRAPHY

Falk, Marcia. *The Book of Blessings*. New York: Summit, 1989.

> Falk uses different language and alternative metaphors, drawing primarily upon feminist theology in her rendering of many traditional blessings. She also includes some new blessings for special occasions that are not found in traditional sources.

Husic, Isaac. *A History of Mediaeval Jewish Philosophy*. Philadelphia, PA: Jewish Publication Society, 1958.

> While written many years ago, this work remains an important exploration of Jewish philosophy in Medieval times.

Maimonides, Moses. *Guide To the Perplexed*, translated by Shlomo Pines. Chicago, IL: University of Chicago Press, 1963.

> This translation enables English readers to access the seminal work by Maimonides on Jewish law and practice.

Sofian, Simone Lotven. "Pushing the Envelope: Reflections on *The Book of Blessings*." *CCAR Journal*, Spring, 1999.

> This review comments upon the work of Marcia Falk.

Wolf, Arnold Jacob. "The New Feminism." *Judaism*, Summer, 1998, 351-357.

> A noted scholar, Rabbi Wolf reviews some of the main contributions and issues that feminists have brought to the discussion of theology.

CHAPTER 2

WHAT IS JEWISH FEMINIST THEOLOGY?

Dawn Robinson Rose

RELIGIOUS TRUTHS

JEWISH FEMINIST THEOLOGY, LIKE FEMINIST OR liberation theologies in the Christian milieu, is based on the very modern revelation that dearly held religious "truths" — however divinely inspired — have been received and interpreted by human beings. Being human, and therefore limited, these receivers were shaped/ influenced by a myriad of factors and preoccupations, such as material and historical circumstance; community, national, and international politics; and, in ways we are just beginning to understand, gender.

Prior to the modern era, religious truths and the laws, liturgy, ritual, and societal norms derived from them were treated as divine in their entirety, universal (meaning binding upon everyone), and thereby unassailable. From the seventeenth through the nineteenth centuries, however, thinkers such as Spinoza (a Jew), Marx (also a Jew), and Feuerbach critiqued religious truth and the institutions they upheld as originating from and supportive of social and material hierarchies. After all, who had access to the centers of learning, the leisure of study and writing, the power of publication? Who supported theologically the divine right of kings to rule and of Inquisitions to torture? Institutionalized religion in the hands of the ruling class was thereby revealed as conservative, even reactionary, created by those in power for the maintenance of the status quo. In America, one of the earliest examples of this dynamic was the theological arguments for the institution of slavery: Southern white churches focused on the god-like responsibility of white folk to care for and chasten "inferior blacks." At the same time, Black slave churches, preoccupied with bondage and suffering, focused on God as liberator and Jesus as comforter.

Radical priests in South America would construct (out of the philosophical critique and examples such as the above) liberation theologies fueling revolutions in support of the poor against wealthy dictatorships. Here, the very criticism against theology or religious truth — its human component — became its greatest strength; for if religious truth is dependent upon the social positioning of the knower and is still in any way valid, then the "truths" known by the poor and disenfranchised are also valid. In other words, the poor did not have to believe what the establishment taught (e.g., that their poverty was part of a divine plan and so forth), but rather could trust their gut, so to speak, and follow their hearts to a belief in a loving God who supported their liberation and the amelioration of their wretched condition.

Alongside liberation theologians who challenged the political and material hierarchies supported by religious knowledge, early feminists, too, began to challenge religious dicta concerning the "natural" or "divinely ordained" subordination of women to men. An early product of this fledgling movement was *The Womens Bible* written by Elizabeth Cady Stanton, in which Stanton explains and reinterprets selective passages to prove that women were indeed intended to be the equal of men.

FINDING A VOICE

The same intellectual, political, and spiritual foment which gave rise to rebellion in the Christian sphere was also felt in the Jewish community. A minority group in a Christian culture, however, and in some ways more overtly oppressive of women, the processes of revolt were often quite different, although an essential part of the complaint — the biblical interpretation of woman as subordinate — remained the same.

For Jewish women of the nineteenth and early twentieth centuries, religiously sanctioned oppression was felt most strongly in traditionally Jewish households and in ritual observance. In traditional households, women were often expected to forgo the sparkling New World promises of education and career, instead prioritizing their husbands' Talmud study and remaining for countless lifetimes in the sweatshop labor force, meanwhile bearing numerous children and keeping house. Relegated to the balcony of the synagogue, shut away from public performance and ritual status, Jewish women's spiritual expressions remained privatized and unpublished (except for a tiny canon of personal prayer books), and thus lost to the generations.

An early and most obvious response in the context of a wider, more secular society which offered so many options socially and spiritually was simply to escape, to assimilate. Some carried their reforming spirit into the public arena, joining the fray against poverty, capitalism, and sexism. Others sought religious expression through forms of spiritualism, transcendentalism, and, of course, Christianity.

The women of less traditional households, such as German Reform, were more financially and socially integrated in the New World. Although less constrained by poverty, they were also barred from synagogal ritual. There is much evidence to suggest, however, that they redirected their religious and spiritual impulses toward highly organized philanthropic work both inside and outside of the Jewish community.

It was not until after the World Wars and the Holocaust that Jewish women would begin to question more pointedly their roles in community and synagogue. Just as women all over America were chafing against the newly set, postwar boundaries in the labor force and at home, Jewish women had gained new insight and had developed new needs. One of the first signposts of this sea change came in the form of a single issue of a relatively obscure journal called *Davka* [literally, "really" or "truly" in Hebrew]. It contained a number of articles questioning the place of Jewish women in Judaism. On the cover was a famous picture from the Holocaust of two women, dressed like men, who had served as spies and had been active in the Resistance. It was clear from the photo that they were now in Nazi hands and about to be executed. The unwritten caption might as well have been: "We earned our equality then — why do we not have it now?"

As the Women's Movement in America proclaimed more and more loudly the equality of women, and steps forward continued to be made in all areas of American life, many Jewish women continued to face a contradiction: in the wider society they were [becoming] equal in [secular] education, in various careers, and experimenting with equality in personal relations. Yet the jarring reality upon entering synagogue was the centuries-old subordination and with it, feelings of alienation, disempowerment, distance — certainly little or nothing supportive of a spirituality to address contemporary needs and experiences.

Christian women from various denominations had long been experiencing much the same. Such groups, although diverse, found in common their womanhood, their religious oppression, their needs for spiritual expression and meaning, and for many, a conviction that, however oppressive, some things were worth salvaging of their various religious traditions and communities. An aid in understanding these groups and their progress might be following the schema. Described as a three-step process, one must remember that these steps fluidly overlap and circle around, each informing and catalyzing the next. These steps are: (1) contradiction, in which women perceive that what is upheld as religious truth contradicts their own knowledge and experience; (2) critique, in which those women examine their religious tradition in order to discern from whence comes the contradiction; and (3) construction, in which women, naming and embracing their own experience, religious knowledge, and spirituality, construct new theology to express and support their own needs and experience.

SETTING A NEW AGENDA

The earliest publications, *Womanspirit Rising* (Christ & Plaskow, 1979), *On Being a Jewish Feminist* (Heschel, 1983), and *The Jewish Woman* (Koltun, 1983), speak most strongly to the first two steps, contradiction and critique. In these controversial volumes, women raised, as one book put it, "The Essential Challenge: Does Theology Speak To Women's Experience?" (Christ & Plaskow, 1979). If by "theology" one meant the intellectual deliberations in seminary, formal doctrines and laws produced, the images of God in liturgy, Torah, and storybooks, the weekly, monthly, and yearly ritual reenactments, even the forms of spiritual expression developed over the centuries — if all this was theology, the world it represented and reinforced, then, no. Christian or Jew, mainstream or normative theology was found to have come from men's lives, and therefore spoke to men's lives. And, extending to the social critique, those theologies, just like the theologies supporting monarch over peasant, white over Black, supported a divine worldview in which women were relegated to a very particular sphere and counseled, in the name of God, to remain there.

In the Jewish community, this dynamic found particularly forceful expression in that Judaism is traditionally a religion of laws more than doctrine. This system of laws, otherwise known as *Halachah*, has been variously understood as divine in origin. The laws are interpreted and adjudicated according to esoteric and complicated systems accessible only to the highly educated elite [male] Rabbinate. It was the *Halachah*, then, that forbade women to engage in rituals such as reading the Torah and being counted in a *minyan*, or having a Bat Mitzvah ceremony. Likewise it was the *Halachah* that forbade liturgical changes, women Rabbis, and even women's study of the Talmud, through which they themselves might learn how to adjudicate the law.

As Rachel Adler poignantly described in her essay, "The Jew Who Wasn't There: Halakhah and the Jewish Woman" (Heschel, 1983),

Halachah not only excluded women from what was commonly held to be the meaningful ritual or spiritual expressions in Judaism, but for those committed to the traditional community, it held the door closed fast against change as well. *Halachah* being "what a Jew is supposed to do, not what a Jew is supposed to think" proclaimed itself outside of the critique of theology, and independent of doctrine. Jewish women, then, found themselves on the horns of a dilemma. For many, such as Blu Greenberg, traditional observance and community was of primary importance (Greenberg, 1981). Certain *halachic* forms such as Shabbat and *kashrut* (kosher observance) were still meaningful religiously, spiritually, and communally, as were notions of historic and universal continuity as a people. For these women, the road to enfranchisement could only be within the *Halachah* — their very spirituality, it might be said, was predicated on the Rabbinic process making the necessary legal changes. But in the meantime, they were not dozing in the balconies. A movement sprang up of traditional (neo-Orthodox, Conservative) women determined to become educated in Talmud by any means possible. Such education in the Jewish community meant status and power. But it is also of itself a traditional form of seeking and worshiping God. And so a form of Jewish feminism (or women's spirituality, as some call it, because so many of these women would hesitate to call themselves feminist) became, just as it was for the men, study.

Not every Jewish woman was willing to wait for the passage of Rabbinic time, however. In a famous essay entitled "The Right Question Is Theological," feminist theologian Judith Plaskow assailed the traditionalist notion that Jewish law existed outside of theology and, therefore, was beyond critique. On the contrary, said Plaskow, Jewish law is a product of the male experience and projection — and the exclusion of the female experience. It reflects the intrinsic, societal othering of women: it makes of women the object of action and discussion, never the subject actor or discussant. Plaskow quotes:

Our legal disabilities [in Judaism] are a *symptom* of a pattern of projection that lies deep in Jewish thinking. They express and reflect a fundamental stance toward women that must be confronted, addressed, and rooted out at its core. (Heschel, 1983, p. 226)

It would not be enough to "fix" the *halachic* strictures on women. Jewish law as a system is predicated on othering and prejudice. Perhaps even the notion of law itself is incompatible with divine revelation accepted and interpreted by both female and male. More to Plaskow's point, however, is that "it is folly to think that justice for women can be achieved simply through *halachic* mechanisms when women's plight is not primarily a product of *Halachah*" (p. 227). Jewish law is but a product of a mind set, a *Weltanshauung*, a stance in the world, which is male and sees woman as Other, a theology in which God is male, men are therefore made *b'tzalmo* — "in the image of God," and women — those Others, over there, are untranscendant.

FINDING NEW FORMS

Having discovered, or begun to discover, the male bias behind and perhaps permeating all of Jewish law, the rest of Judaism then became subject to examination and critique — though some aspects much earlier than others. Of course, the legal strictures in traditional synagogues were an affront and insult to many. Leaving those synagogues for more liberal Reform, Reconstructionist, and Conservative congregations, however, with *mechitzah* removed and given access to the *bimah*, women were still assaulted and disaffected by the inescapable male God language, pronouns, and imagery. Out of pain and protest, movements began to rewrite prayer books, experimenting with everything from merely changing all the pronouns (but leaving everything else more or less intact), to researching and incorporating female-god[dess] imagery whether or not it came from Jewish sources.

It is important to note that with the "mere" act of changing pronouns and other God lan-

guage, the process of new theological construction, overt and intentional, had begun. This is not to say that Jewish women stopped feeling contradiction between their life experiences and Judaism — we did and will for some time to come. Nor is it to suggest that critique was now ended, for behind the language and imagery more would be discovered. Rather, it must be understood that changing a divine He to a She is more than a trivial grammatical act. And, even though its psychological benefit may have been to counter feelings of women's alienation in the synagogue, that was not its only purpose or significance. To the contrary, the change of He to She challenged Jewish concepts of God — Jewish theology — to the core, right back to the first appearance of God in the Torah.

GOD AS SHE

Of course, the change was and is extremely controversial. Typically, arguments range between the grammatical — in Hebrew the masculine is inclusive of both male and female; and the theological — God, in truth is neither gender, or outside of gender (and the male pronouns somehow convey that more effectively). But in truth it seemed that the cause of what Rita M. Gross described as a "knee jerk refusal to speak to God-She" (Heschel, 1983, p. 236) was far more profound. As she explains:

[The use of He] expresses a profound and long-standing alienation between woman and femaleness and the central values of the Jewish tradition . . . That usage and the alienation it reflects is also the basic explanation for the traditional exclusion of women from almost all the most meaningful and most normative dimensions of Judaism — its covenanted, "religious," and "spiritual" aspects (p. 237).

A step forward in constructive theology, a "simple" pronominal shift, leads again to the profound critique of Judaism as a religion created by men, predicated upon the male experience, to the express exclusion of women.

The "knee jerk refusal" might well come from a place of, shall we call it, intuitive knowledge that the change of pronouns begins a domino-like process that would ripple throughout Jewish history and civilization. For example: If God is not He but She, not father but mother, how might our creation myths be different? Who would She have spoken to in the desert, and how would we have become a people? What if God were not angry/warrior/king/judge? What would She be like and which of Her attributes would we, Her faithful, be commanded to imitate? Would She even relate to us by command, or though other venues? What sort of families, communities, and societies would have grown (and still could grow) out of these conceptions of God?

Early research reveals that there already existed in Judaism a tradition of a female aspect or part of God called the *Shechinah*. In the Torah, this was the name for the presence of God that dwelt with Israel within the Ark of the Covenant. Mystics picked up on this theme and developed an entire lovely and complex mythology in which the *Shechinah* was, like Israel, in *galut*, diaspora, or separation — Israel from the Land and the non-transcendent *Shechinah* from the male, transcendent aspect of God. The disunity of the gendered deity was the source of all the discord and trouble on earth, especially for Israel. Israel's task then, was one of *tikkun*, fixing or healing. By engaging in the *mitzvot* and other mystical activities, the Godhead would be reunited, and Israel's way on earth would be safe and bountiful.

Just as the *Shechinah* poignantly expressed the feelings of loss and exile for diaspora Israel, so, too, She became a near perfect metaphor for the alienation of women from Judaism. Moreover, She gave us a place to start, a name, a history to research and build upon, a set of characteristics which, if God were female, She might have, such as presence, compassion, and understanding. Sometimes She is depicted as a dove protecting the helpless beneath Her wings — and so She could be called Mother, and we could derive strength and warmth from Her invocation. Other myths, however, described Her in ways as vulnerable as human women — a sorrowful widow, or a bride kidnapped and raped. (One shudders to think of the historical circumstance which prompted these insights and depictions!)

A HERMENEUTICS OF SUSPICION

The usefulness of the *Shechinah* in Jewish feminist theology is multifaceted, but not without its limitations. She may well be a ready-made female counterpart to the otherwise all-male God; however, She is still but a *counterpart* (e.g., She is ever *missing* something, her homeland, her husband. Her weakness requires a savior). She was conceived by men to embody femaleness as they understood it and, moreover, in those myths She does not stand alone, but is part of a duo (or, more precisely, a constellation of God-attributes called the *Kabbalah*). Therefore, She must be critiqued and reinterpreted — like all the rest of Judaism.

It took theologian Judith Plaskow to introduce Jewish feminists to what, in methodological terms, is the process required of a feminist in conversation with Judaism, traditional or liberal. That is, we must approach with a "hermeneutics of suspicion." Hermeneutics means a mode of interpretation or our overall stance toward texts and tradition. Plaskow explains by quoting her Christian colleague, Elizabeth Schussler-Fiorenza:

> A hermeneutics of suspicion "takes as its starting point the assumption that biblical texts and their interpretations are androcentric [taking maleness as the norm for humanity] and serve patriarchal functions." (Plaskow, 1989, p. 14)

Given this, the question naturally arises, if these texts indeed reflect only the male experience and not Jewish women's, if they indeed "serve patriarchal functions" — including those functions of keeping women in their place — why do we continue to deal with these texts at all? Plaskow answers with theological pragmatism — they are the only texts we have. "Jewish sources," she says, "have formed us for good and for ill, and they remain our strongest link with the Jewish historical experience" (1989, p. 14). Therefore, alongside the hermeneutics of suspicion, we must also read with a hermeneutics of remembrance:

> A "hermeneutics of remembrance" insists that the same sources that are regarded with suspicion can also be used to reconstruct Jewish women's history . . . even the most androcentric text can provide valuable information about Jewish women's past. (1989, p. 15)

RECOVERING THE MISSING TEXT

The first major (and still most comprehensive) text of Jewish feminist theology, Plaskow's *Standing Again at Sinai: Judaism from a Feminist Perspective*, opens with a biblical passage that functions as an example of an androcentric text, which is foundational, and as a central metaphor for the status of women in Judaism. The scene is set in Exodus 19. Moses is instructing the "people of Israel" on how to ready themselves to receive the very covenant, the Ten Commandments, which will enter them into particular relationship with this One God. "Be ready for the third day," Moses says. "Do not go near a woman." Nowhere in the text does Moses address women.

> At the central moment of Jewish history, women are invisible. Whether they too stood there trembling in fear and expectation, what they heard when the men heard these words from Moses, we do not know. It was not their experience that interested the chronicler or that informed or shaped the Torah. (1989, p. 25)

For Plaskow, the task begins here — to recover out of the silence of the text women's voices, stories, and experiences with an eye toward a "reshaping of Jewish memory" (p. 52). But that remembering is only a beginning. If Torah grew out of a patriarchal world view and sustained that view, then so did Rabbinic interpretation. In fact, the very society that sustained and was sustained by those interpretations needs

critical scrutiny. If, at the center of the Covenant, men are othering women, stepping up and away from them to reach for a God who is yet more transcendent, then a central problem in Judaism is that separation, the creation of hierarchy, and Judaism's overall dependence upon separation and hierarchy in order to create holiness and describe the path toward God.

The dynamics of separation and hierarchy in ancient (and modern) Judaism support a theme which signifies that a central characteristic of the Jewish God and God's relationship to His people is dominance. Moreover, this God is dominant in ways that are both like and unlike human dominance: He, like human beings, knows — but unlike human beings, knows everything. He is powerful, but all-powerful. Present, in fact all-present. Anthropomorphically conceived and described, He is the ultimate. As Plaskow explains:

> God represents the superior side of a range of hierarchical differentiation. The image of God as exalted one, compared to whom everything else is of lesser reality and value, both fosters and mirrors the tendency to conceptualize all difference in terms of graded separations. (1989, p. 133)

The dynamic is redundant in itself. Israel sees graded separation between God and man, men and women, *Kohane* and Israelite, and Israel and the nations.

After critiquing the concept of the dominant God, escape from that paradigm (and its ancillary dynamic of hierarchy/separation) requires both a reimaging of God and a new understanding of a relationship to God, which would be non-hierarchical and non-dominant.

One path explored by Plaskow and other theologians, Jewish and Christian, is that of reconceptualizing human relations and community. For example, building from Martin Buber's work *I and Thou*, theologies of relation in which mutuality not dominance is the overriding characteristic are being developed. Simply put, according to these theologies, it is in the context of open, mutual, and reciprocal relations that each person is allowed, even drawn into the fullest disclosure and actualization of one's true being. Because God is "the ground of all being" or, put more crudely, the Being-est, God's self is revealed in that process of coming-into-being. Just as a society divided by hierarchy and otherness previously informed the fledgling concepts of relationship to God as dominant, here relationship to God is informed by personal experiences of mutuality, and the warmth, intimacy, and personal growth it brings. Questions arise from this, such as: Who/what is God now? What is or can be our relation to this Being?

Importantly, this re-conceptualization of relation to God, allows us also to rethink and enact whole new ethics or patterns of relations, personal, communal, and political. A transformative circle, or *praxis* has begun — a theological critique and insight (that God is not about dominance) is put into practice (relationships between individuals are about mutuality and not dominance). From this we learn more about God (God is about mutuality, thus intimacy, warmth, personal growth) which informs us further about how to act, and so on. Moreover, because the original critique (God is not about dominance) has been the foundation of Judaism, the Jewish community, and in fact most of Western society, the transformative circle of *praxis* ultimately targets nothing less than the transformation of all of Judaism, the Jewish community, and Western society (repairing the havoc wrecked upon the rest of the world as well). Up to the present time, however, transformative visioning and enacting has occurred primarily in the context of personal/sexual relations, in the formation of women's *havurot* dedicated to the exploration of non-hierarchical modes of community, and (to the extent the wider world has been addressed) some historical/multicultural exploration for alternative god[dess] imagery, and, finally, certain ecological themes.

RIGHTS AND RITUALS

Probably because many Jewish women experienced discrimination most acutely in the context of liturgy and ritual, the majority of religious Jewish feminist energy and creativity has been spent on issues more closely related to the synagogue. These have included (1) gaining "rights" of access to the *bimah*, the Torah, even the Rabbinate; (2) learning the requisite skills (and providing others with opportunities and supportive atmospheres in which to do so); and (3) creating new liturgy and ritual which is expressive, in some way, of women's lives and experience.

In the area of ritual expression, once again two primary avenues have been explored: rituals already existing in Judaism which were more specifically for women and perhaps lost or downplayed through the ages, and new rituals for female-specific life passages, such as the onset of menses or menopause.

The foremost example of merging existing ritual with new forms is that of New Moon celebrations. The tie between the cyclical moon and woman appears to be profoundly ancient and transcultural. In Judaism, the New Moon, signifying the new month, was a special holiday for women, marked by special feasts, the lighting of candles, and abstinence from work. In modern synagogues, the only vestige of that holiday has been prayers for the new month performed by the entire congregation [once again, often male]. Building on evidence from Rabbinic texts, however, women have come together to form New Moon *havurot*, creating rituals around the moon, around events in their lives such as birth and death, and around relevant themes from the Jewish calendar.

The importance of these groups in the development of Jewish women's spirituality and theology cannot be overstated. Here are Jewish women making space and time just for Jewish women; forming bonds independent of [male dominated] synagogues and even independent of heterosexual relationships; supporting each other in exploration and learning; and creating liturgy, ritual, songs, *niggunim*, and *midrashim* expressive of their lives. As Penina Adelman describes in her landmark book, *Miriam's Well: Rituals for Jewish Women around the Year*, the silence of the Torah and of the Jewish past regarding the experience of women has become "a *tabula rasa* on which to write the stories, past, present, and future of Jewish women" (Adelman, 1986, p. 9). For her, a central focus of this new writing must be our relationship with our own bodies:

> In the context of Rosh Chodesh, Jewish women have begun to foster positive images of the female body by celebrating a young girl's first menstrual period in addition to her Bat Mitzvah, by creating rituals for pregnancy and pregnancy loss, by marking menopause in a way that is appropriate to each individual. In addition, Jewish women are cultivating positive self-images which will enable them to transcend that which differentiates them from Jewish men and to explore the ultimate goal of the spiritual exercise of Rosh Chodesh and Judaism: to explore what it means to be fully *human*. (pp. 9-10)

The power of separate space and energy solely for women and women's relationships with each other has perhaps been most forcibly, and understandably, realized in the context of the Jewish lesbian feminist movement. It is this standpoint that the epistemological/theological bias that Rebecca Alpert calls "male-female complementarity" in Judaism becomes most apparent. By this phrase she means the various (and insidious) ways in which the "truth" that women belong with and are only completed by men is self-evident. Jewish lesbians in lifestyle and community effectively critique and explode this myth, offering newfound insight and energy to the Jewish feminist movement as a whole.

Although the primary foci of Jewish feminist theology over these few decades have been ritual oriented, concurrent efforts have been made to raise the consciousness of the Jewish community concerning previously silenced social issues such as domestic abuse, rape, divorce, "alternative" family structures, and Jewish female body images. More recently, the movement has been criticized by Plaskow and Rose for its parochial stance — or lack of a stance — toward broader

social issues concerning, for example, race and class. Without attention to these fundamental issues, both theologians insist that Jewish feminist theology not only circumscribes its own transformative potential in the world, but fails adequately to understand and embrace the truly multicultural nature of its own current and possible constituency.

NOTES ON TEACHING JEWISH FEMINIST THEOLOGY

The preceding portion of this chapter is presented more or less in the order in which I teach the subject.

Whether at seminary to Rabbinic students or to adults and young adults at synagogues, *havurot*, *Shabbatonim*, or at JCCs, the best first step is to present Jewish Feminist Theology as a natural part of the cultural, intellectual, and theological milieu of the nineteenth and twentieth centuries. Too often Jewish women and men are made to feel as though Jewish Feminist Theology is weird, foreign, dangerous, and, most of all, lacking in rational grounding. As the chapter demonstrates, Christian and Jewish feminist thought grew out of what were already modern theological and philosophical trends. Feminists applied critical approaches common to modern theological and philosophical problems to the question of gender.

However, even though their method came more or less from the mainstream, many feminists were, and are still, branded radical. It is not hard to see why this could occur. Any questioning of time-honored tradition, especially in Judaism, can be viewed as potentially threatening to community and authority. On the other hand, without such questioning, many people, women in particular, are apt to drift away from a religion which appears disjunctive to the times and disenfranchising of the female sex.

Thus, at the beginning of each class on Jewish Feminist Theology, I offer some overview whether large or small of the historical critique of religious truth and where Jewish Feminist

Theology fits into it. Two good and accessible illustrations, I think, can be offered easily: (1) involving the Southern White churches and the Black slave churches; and (2) the construction of new theology to fit the purpose of liberation in South America. This discussion really serves the double purpose of *contextualizing* Jewish Feminist Theology historically in a way that is easy to demonstrate; and, most importantly, it *normalizes* Jewish Feminist Theology as a movement among movements. Jewish theology, philosophy and mysticism have always interacted with its host cultures in this fashion.

From here I move to a discussion of the notion of *praxis*, or the system of theological development which I describe earlier in this chapter as: (1) contradiction, in which women, Blacks, or the poor, perceive that what is upheld as religious truth contradicts their own knowledge and experience; (2) critique, in which those people examine their religious tradition in order to discern from whence comes the contradiction; and (3) construction, in which people, naming and embracing their own experience, religious knowledge, and spirituality, construct new theology to express and support their own needs and experience.

Many of the people taking the class or seminar will be there because they are already experiencing the discomfort of step 1, or already actively pursuing steps 2 and 3. They may even recognize themselves as you introduce the model. I find it a wonderful time to stop and talk about personal experiences — why people have come, what they feel during certain portions of the liturgy, etc. After making the "system" personal — a foundational element in the class or seminar — I walk through various other examples: such as the White church/Black church model, or Luther's revolt against the Catholic Church because of its many corrupt practices during that age, etc. It is important to demonstrate that not only has critique and construction "been done," so to speak, but also that the resulting theologies have been "legitimate" — not just "made up."

The first question is of religious knowledge:

who has it, or, better yet, who gets to claim they have the genuine article? We need to disabuse our students of the notion that theology belongs solely to the past, to the Rabbis, or to the academics. The second and somewhat more sticky question is that of the purposefulness of theologizing. For theology does have its goals: i.e., the preservation of community or tradition, adherence to a code of laws, elevation of the human spirit, creation of a particular kind of individual (e.g., the *mensch*) — and all of this wrapped up with the search for God. The better we can demonstrate to our students that theologies have *always been* a product of human beings theologizing according to their place and time, out of their own experience, toward the fulfillment of their chosen ends, the better chance they have to understand the gender critique and to grasp their own potential for theologizing as women and as Jews. This is a lot to swallow, but it is a message that is reiterated and/or demonstrated again and again throughout the course.

If this is a semester-long class, I spend a week or two on background feminist theory, especially Jean Paul Sartre and Simone de Beauvoir on the concept of *the Other* and the early works of Mary Daly. Both provide excellent and fairly accessible methodological tools and a common vocabulary through which to approach both the traditions and the literature by Jewish feminists. Best, they provide a perfect introduction to Judith Plaskow's *Standing Again at Sinai*, which can serve as a basic background textbook for any Jewish Feminist Theology class.

From here I move to various forms of the written word by Jewish women. I want to give my class a sense of Jewish women's theological heritage. And I do believe a repository of Jewish women's theology already exists, albeit as yet fairly unrecognized and awaiting exegesis. It exists in letters, stories, autobiographies, novels, poems, *midrashim*, even in the bylaws of synagogue women's auxiliaries. I am speaking of Jewish women's wisdom, of good and evil, our notions of causality, our visions of hope, our own messianic visions, understandings of community, friendship, family, God, sin, and redemption. Jewish women were not invited to the *Bayt Midrash* to write commentary on the Talmud or Torah, but that does not mean that we existed all these centuries without a single thought or feeling about good and evil. Our first job is to uncover our lost heritage. *Four Centuries of Jewish Women's Spirituality* (Umansky and Ashton, 1992) is a fine aid in this endeavor. These writings require the development of a special sensitivity and skill, as the "theology" therein is written closely between the lines.

Many theological views from what we may call patriarchal Judaism or the existing "mainstream tradition" are no longer acceptable to many people (such as, if you follow Gods commandments you will have many children and your vineyards will grow many grapes); not everything our foremothers believed will be altogether relevant for today either. It needs to be acceptable in class for students to be disappointed in or to disagree with some of the readings. We are all wrestling with our heritages. Some readings will be profoundly inspiring and enlighten-ing. As for those which are not, well, I try to guide toward archiving rather than throwing out.

Learning the skill to read for theology in Jewish women's literature opens whole new worlds. The classes can be extremely fun and rewarding. In the process, students begin culling out key elements toward their own theology, as well as growing more and more accustomed to the idea of *having* their own theology . . . as Jewish women. For surely they are no different from any woman who wrote *this* poem or lived *that* life.

We move then from the theologies that have been our heritage to the theologies that Jewish women are now creating. We survey the literature of contemporary feminist *midrashim* and explore the meaning of new liturgy and ritual. The final project will be the creation of a constructive theology of their own, however it is expressed: artistically, theoretically, ritually, even autobiographically. That is, for me, the ultimate purpose of teaching Jewish Feminist Theology: empowerment and ownership.

———◆◦◆◦◆———

IMPLICATIONS

1. Contradiction, critique, and construction are three steps that Rose suggests are the process through which women create their own theology.

2. Feminist theology is a movement that crosses religious traditions and binds them together.

3. Judaism has always allowed for critique and reinterpretation, including that coming from the variety of feminist expressions throughout the ages.

4. Feminists can reclaim Jewish sources while preserving the authenticity of those sources.

QUESTIONS FOR CRITICAL INQUIRY

1. How do the three steps of contradiction, cri-tique, and construction apply in how we teach about God?

2. Rose states that through the mere act of changing language, the process of constructing a feminist theology had begun. Why are language and images central to the feminist discussion? What makes language and images so powerful?

3. Rose raises questions about why Jewish sources that serve "patriarchal" functions should be reclaimed for women. Plaskow provides two answers: (1) they are the only texts we have, and (2) they remain our strongest link to Jewish historical experience. What other answers could you give as to why we should continue to deal with these "patriarchal texts"?

4. Recall the moment when students first con-

fronted Jewish texts as being exclusive of
women and women's experiences, or recall a
time when students struggled with the exclu-
sivity of Jewish texts. What do these experiences have in common?

5. Rose presents her experiences of taking her
understanding of feminist theology and
developing her own educational approach.
How would you structure a course in Jewish
feminist theology for your setting?

ACTIVITIES

(Note: For a lesson on this topic, see Chapter 45,
"Your Link in the Chain of Tradition" by Nadine
Cohen, a description of an arts based program
for adults which explores women's spirituality.)

1. Make a list of the names for God that Rose
presents in the chapter. Compare and contrast this list of names to those in Chapter 1,
"The Changing Perceptions of God in
Judaism" by Rifat Sonsino. Pick a prayer and
insert the different God names that Rose
presents. How does each name change the
prayer? How does each name change the way
you think or feel about God? Why do you
think women might feel isolated by masculine terms of God? What do you think is
attractive to women in having these feminine and alternative images of God?

2. Design a class for your setting on Jewish
Feminist Theology. Why would such a class
be important to have? What would be the
goals? What would you cover in the curriculum? What learning experiences and sources
would you include?

3. Rose identifies three important steps in
teaching about God: contradiction, critique,
and construction. Find a way to illustrate
these three steps using a medium with which
you are comfortable, such as a dance, play, or
art piece that interprets a biblical text, or a
midrash about Miriam.

4. Read some of the blessings in *The Book of*

*Blessings: New Daily Prayers for Daily Life, the
Sabbath, and the New Moon Festival* by Marcia
Falk, or listen to the recording *Selections from
Marcia Falk's Blessings* by Fran Avni and Linda
Hirschhorn. Use some of these blessings in a
prayer service. Talk about how the words or
music affected the worship experience.

BIBLIOGRAPHY

Adelman, Penina V. *Miriam's Well: Rituals for
Jewish Women around the Year*. Fresh Meadows,
NY: Biblio Press, 1986.

Gleaned from recent years of development in
a Rosh Chodesh *havurah*, this book describes
13 New Moon rituals for women to corre-
spond to the 13 months of the Jewish calendar. In addition to liturgy, stories, and personal accounts, Adelman also includes
practical advice for groups that are just
beginning.

Adler, Rachel. *Engendering Judaism: An Inclusive
Theology and Ethics*. Philadelphia, PA: Jewish
Publication Society, 1997.

This work of theology and ethics attempts to
cull its primary resources from traditional
Jewish texts and legal frameworks. Of special
interest is Adler's concept of *Brit Ahuvim*:
Marriage between Subjects.

Alpert, Rebecca. "Challenging Male/Female
Complementarity: Jewish Lesbians and the
Jewish Tradition." In *People of the Body: Jews and
Judaism from an Embodied Perspective*, ed. by
Howard Eilberg-Schwartz. Albany, NY: University
of New York, 1992.

An important yet accessible essay investigates
the various ways traditional Judaism and
Jewish society creates and reenforces the
myth that men and women not only belong
together, but are in fact incomplete without
each other.

———. *Like Bread on a Seder Plate: Jewish Lesbians
and the Transformation of Tradition*. New York:
Columbia University Press, 1997.

In this book, Alpert describes various aspects of the lived experiences of Jewish lesbians and offers prophetic rereadings of the Torah toward creating a polemic of social/religious justice and acceptance.

Biale, Rachel. *Women and Jewish Law: An Exploration of Women's Issues in Halakhic Sources*. New York: Schocken Press, 1984.

This book is a (nearly) complete and entirely intelligent explanation of Jewish women's status, problems, and restrictions according to *halachic* Judaism. Although ostensibly only about Jewish law and, by extension, Orthodoxy, it is yet important to women outside of strictly traditional settings insofar as it provides necessary background to Jewish perspectives on such issues as marriage, sexuality, and reproduction.

Christ, Carol P., and Judith Plaskow, eds. *Womanspirit Rising: A Feminist Reader in Religion*. San Francisco, CA: Harper Forum Books, 1979.

A wide-ranging anthology that includes women from Christian, Jewish, and less mainstream feminist religious traditions. The volume is extremely useful both for historical reconstruction of the early debate and the cross-cultural view it affords in contextualizing Jewish issues and concerns.

Falk, Marcia. *The Book of Blessings: New Daily Prayers for Daily Life, the Sabbath, and the New Moon Festival*. San Francisco, CA: Harper Forum Books, 1996.

This compendium of prayers, blessings, and poetry is partly derived from traditional worship services and partly conceived in more original form. Falk concentrates in particular on non-hierarchical names for God and on the incorporation of earth imagery.

Greenberg, Blu. *On Women and Judaism: A View from Tradition*. Philadelphia, PA: Jewish Publication Society, 1981.

A voice from Jewish Orthodoxy, Greenberg assesses feminism's impact on the Jewish community, and argues for a *halachic* solution to women's position in Judaism.

Heschel, Susannah, ed. *On Being a Jewish Feminist: A Reader*. New York: Schocken Books, 1983.

This landmark book, edited by the daughter of the famed theologian and social activist Abraham Joshua Heschel, contains many important early essays, most notably the "debate" between Cynthia Ozick and Judith Plaskow on whether the "right question" is theological, *halachic*, or other.

Kantrowitz, Melanie Kaye, and Irena Klepfisz, eds. *The Tribe of Dina: A Jewish Women's Anthology*. Montpelier, VT: Sinister Wisdom 29/30, 1986.

This work is a collection of more radical or overtly political writings in Jewish feminism. This anthology is especially important not only because of its inclusion of more marginalized voices, but because of its connection of traditions of dedicated Jewish political action/ethics/values to Jewish feminist identity.

Koltun, Elizabeth, ed. *The Jewish Woman: New Perspectives*. New York: Schocken Books, 1983.

One of the earliest books on the subject, this volume includes essays which explore critically the status of women in Jewish law, Jewish women's identity, and their relationship to the feminist movement. Several essays seek reinterpretations of women in the Torah, as well as search for role models in recent Jewish history.

Plaskow, Judith. *Standing Again at Sinai: Judaism from a Feminist Perspective*. San Francisco, CA: Harper & Row, 1989.

To date, this stands as the most comprehensive text in Jewish feminist theology. Written by a theologian, the book attends to scholarly issues such as methodology, while at the same time offers highly accessible discussions around issues of memory, community, identity, God, sexuality, and *Tikkun Olam*.

Plaskow, Judith, and Carol P. Christ, eds. *Weaving the Visions: New Patterns in Feminist Spirituality*. San Francisco, CA: Harper Forum Books, 1989.

Like a grown-up *Womenspirit Rising*, this volume combines essays from Jewish, Christian, post-Christian, and other non-mainstream feminist religious traditions, but this time the voices are stronger and more sure of their methods and their purpose. Target themes include power, naming the sacred, self in relation, and transforming the world.

Rose, Dawn Robinson. "Class As Problematic in Jewish Feminist Theology." In *Democratic Theorizing from the Margins,* Marla Brettschneider, ed. Philadelphia, PA: Temple University Press, forthcoming.

In this article, I critique the Jewish feminist theological effort to date as representative of and sustaining a myth that Jewish feminists are homogeneously middle or upper middle class. I point out the detrimental effects this myth has for Jewish feminist movements both in terms of representing their own constituency and understanding their possible roles in coalition.

Schneider, Susan Weidman. *Jewish and Female: A Guide and Sourcebook for Today's Jewish Woman.* New York: Simon & Schuster, 1984.

A meld of *Jewish Literacy* and *Our Bodies Ourselves*, this volume attempts to cover every possible topic from law to money to alcoholism in the double framework of Jewish and feminist education.

Stanton, Elizabeth Cady, and the Revising Committee. *The Women's Bible.* Seattle, WA: Coalition Task Force on Women and Religion, 1974.

This work is a version of the Bible sensitive to feminist theology.

Umansky, Ellen M., and Dianne Ashton. *Four Centuries of Jewish Women's Spirituality: A Sourcebook.* Boston, MA: Beacon Press, 1992.

An excellent collection of Jewish women's writings in a wide variety of forms: stories, speeches, poetry, etc., which provides evidence of and access to at least some of Jewish women's spiritual heritage.

CHAPTER 3

WHAT CAN WE LEARN FROM CHRISTIAN THEOLOGY?

Bruce Kadden

WITH INCREASED DIALOGUE BETWEEN JEWS AND Christians in recent years, community leaders have recognized that each group can learn much about the other and better understand one's own religion based upon that learning. This insight is obvious for Christians who see the first 2,000 years of Jewish history as part of their history and who see Christianity as emerging from first century Judaism. But Jews also can learn much from Christianity, especially in the realm of theology and spirituality. While it is an oversimplification to say that Judaism is a religion of action, whereas Christianity is a religion of belief, historically Jews have placed much less emphasis on theology than have Christians. In recent years, however, Jews have had a greater interest in spirituality. Some have explored eastern religions, particularly Buddhism. Others have been attracted to a variety of "New Age" practices and beliefs. Some have looked to Jewish sources, particularly the *Kabbalah*, to enhance their spirituality.

While this increased interest in spirituality by Jews has been embraced and encouraged by many, it has also been questioned by others who are concerned that such influences will negatively impact Judaism. Nevertheless, the quest for greater spirituality continues, reflected in part in more classes on meditation and a greater interest in healing rituals. Within Christianity, too, the recent flourishing of interest in spirituality is reflected in such practices as ecumenical Taize services (based on chants and reflective meditation from the services at Taize, France) and other spiritual endeavors. One author has observed "that alongside a decline in traditional religious practice there exists an ever-increasing hunger for spirituality" (Sheldrake, 1991, p. 1).

In order to reflect upon our own beliefs and practices, it is often useful to compare them to others. How does Christianity view spirituality? What can we, as Jews, learn from Christian beliefs and practices? In what ways are we different? What lessons can we learn about the quest for spirituality from contemporary Christianity and how might we apply these lessons to Judaism? We begin our search for the answer to these questions by exploring the history of first century Judaism and the birth of Christianity.

AN HISTORICAL OVERVIEW OF CHRISTIANITY AS IT RELATES TO JUDAISM

Contemporary Judaism and Christianity both derive from first century Judaism. Both were greatly influenced by significant events in the first century: for Christianity, the birth and death of the Jew, Jesus of Nazareth, and for Judaism, the destruction of the Second Temple in 70 C.E. While Judaism and Christianity, therefore, share some history, they have been distinct religions since the early second century and have developed distinct beliefs and theologies.

Like Judaism, Christianity is not monolithic. The Roman Catholic Church and the Eastern Orthodox Churches (Greek Orthodox, Russian Orthodox, Armenian Orthodox, etc.) split from each other in part over the issue of the primacy of the Pope among the bishops. The Protestant Reformation led to the creation of a variety of denominations under the umbrella of Protestantism. Today Protestantism continues to flourish in a wide variety of denominations including Lutheran, Methodist, Episcopalian, and Baptist. Evangelical Christianity has been especially successful in appealing to those Christians who want to deepen their faith. Despite these many denominations, most Christian communities share basic beliefs and practices.

These beliefs and practices are derived both from Judaism and from the interpretation of the life and death of Jesus of Nazareth. Christians believe that Jesus is the Messiah promised to the Jews in the Hebrew scriptures. The title "Christ" is the Greek word for messiah. Christians believe that not only is Jesus the Messiah, but he is also the son of God.

Jesus

Based on the accounts in the gospels and in other ancient sources, most contemporary scholars agree about the basic facts concerning the life of Jesus. He was born about the year 4 B.C.E. (the calendrical calculation which placed the birth of Jesus in year one is in error) to a Galilean Jewish couple, Joseph and Mary. The stories linking his birth to Bethlehem are of questionable historical accuracy, and were likely written to fulfill the messianic prophecies in the Hebrew Scriptures.

Very little is known about Jesus' childhood, but he clearly had a Jewish education and may have studied with Gamliel the Elder. He was baptized by John, a first century Jew, who may have been a member of the Essene community. Jesus' public ministry was comprised of a series of teachings, many in the form of parables, and the performing of miracles. Many of Jesus' teachings are similar to contemporaneous Jewish teachings, which have been recorded in the Talmud. Where Jesus appears to challenge Jewish teachings, it should be understood in the context of first century Judaism when teachers often argued with each other about Jewish teachings and practice. Indeed, since the Mishnah was not composed until the end of the second century, there was no written compilation of Jewish teachings at Jesus' time (other than the Tanach). Jesus criticized certain practices just as the prophets had condemned various practices in earlier generations.

As for Jesus' miracles, it is, of course, impossible to verify their historicity. Some miracles seem to be based on similar stories in the Hebrew Scriptures, while others are similar to those of other first century Jews such as Honi the Circle-maker.

Jesus gained a following of fellow Jews who resonated to his message, though it is difficult to determine the number of his followers. It is clear, though, that many of his followers viewed him not only as a charismatic leader, but also as the Messiah.

Jewish expectations of the Messiah were quite high in the first century. Apocalyptic writings, such as the book of Daniel, were gaining influence. Roman oppression led many Jews to embrace teachings that looked forward to an era when Jews would be free from foreign rule. For the Jews, the Messiah would be a human being, chosen by God, who would be anointed as the leader of the people. The Hebrew world *mashiach*, from which the word messiah is derived, means "anointed one," and originally referred to the kings of Judah and Israel who were anointed with oil in recognition of their status. The Messiah was to be both a physical and spiritual descendant of King David; he would lead a successful revolt against Rome, restore Jewish sovereignty to the land of Israel, and inaugurate an era of peace and justice.

The early Christian Church, cognizant of these beliefs, traced the lineage of Jesus to David. In writing the story of Jesus, the authors of the gospels attempted to demonstrate that he fulfilled teachings about the Messiah contained in Hebrew Scriptures. It is questionable, however, whether Jesus viewed himself as the Messiah. Some scholars have concluded that the sayings of Jesus regarding the Messiah reflect the teachings of the early Christians, rather than the authentic words of Jesus. Certainly, though, Jesus did not view himself as the Messiah in political terms, but rather focused on his belief of the immediacy of the Kingdom of God.

The greatest challenge to the followers of Jesus occurred when he was crucified by the Romans. This act should have ended all messianic speculation, since he failed to fulfill messianic expectations. No doubt many of his followers recognized this failure and abandoned the group of his followers. However, a significant number of Jews continued to believe that he was the Messiah, despite his death, and that he would return imminently to fulfill his mission. They were encouraged by the reports that his body had risen from the grave after three days and that some of his followers had experienced his presence. When Jesus failed to return, his followers continued to practice Judaism while affirming the belief that Jesus was the Messiah.

Proselytism

Like other first century Jewish communities, the followers of Jesus attempted to gain adherents through active proselytism, both among Jews and pagans. Among those Jews to join this fledgling community was Saul of Tarsus, who became known as Paul after his "conversion." Originally an outspoken opponent of the followers of Jesus, Paul is considered by many as the founder of Christianity. He actively brought the teachings of Jesus and his followers to communities throughout the Mediterranean. In order to make Judaism more palatable to the pagans, he relaxed the requirements of Jewish practice for those newcomers. No longer would they have to observe the dietary laws; no longer would males have to be circumcised in order to join the community.

In time, therefore, the communities that followed Jesus included those who were born Jewish and continued to observe traditional Jewish practices and those born as gentiles, who did not observe these practices. Eventually, the latter group greatly outnumbered the former, leading the entire community to abandon Jewish practice and become a distinct religious community. It is not clear exactly when this occurred, but most scholars point to the end of the first century or early second century.

Core Christian Theological Ideas

Over the next two centuries, Christianity would develop its theology, practices, and teachings, which would guide its development. Among the most important theological ideas that Christianity embraced were these:

1. The concept of the trinity, i.e., that God is manifest in three distinct ways: as God (the Father), as the Son (i.e., Jesus), and as the Holy Spirit (or Holy Ghost). Trude Weiss-Rosmarin points out that "the chief and fundamental difference between Judaism and Christianity is that the former is committed to pure and uncompromising monotheism and the latter subscribes to the belief in the Trinitarian nature of the Divine Being" (Weiss-Rosmarin, 1981, p. 15).

2. Christians believe that Jesus was both fully human and fully divine; this paradox is fundamental to most forms of Christianity. Although Jews believe that human beings were created in God's image, Judaism rejects the idea that any human being is divine. Furthermore, the concept of the trinity raises the question of whether Christianity is monotheistic. Many Jewish scholars concluded that Christianity was monotheistic because the idea of the trinity can be understood as expressing three manifestations of one God. The idea of God as Holy Spirit is similar to references in Judaism to God as the Divine Presence. Nevertheless, the belief that Jesus was fully divine sets Christian theology sharply apart from Jewish theology.

3. There will be a second coming of the Messiah. Jesus' crucifixion caused a crisis among those who believed that he was the Messiah, since according to Jewish belief, the Messiah was supposed to live to see his accomplishments. After his death, many of his followers anticipated his imminent return. When this did not occur, the Christian community developed the concept of his second coming. In brief, this doctrine says that Jesus came the first time to show human beings, by the example of his life and by his teachings, how to live their lives. He will return when human beings have taken these teachings to heart and have brought about the transformation of our world.

Christianity Borrows from Jewish Theology

Since Christianity grew out of first century Judaism, it is only natural that it would borrow and adapt various Jewish beliefs and practices. Christianity, for example, adopted into its theology the Pharisaic ideas of life after death and resurrection of the dead. Christianity also reinterpreted various Jewish symbols, such as the bread and wine of Passover, to reflect its theological message. Bread and wine are the main symbols of the central rite of Christian worship that is called the Eucharist or Communion, or the Lord's Supper. This ritual derives from Jesus' Last Supper, during which he identified the bread as being his body and the wine as being his blood. For some Christians, the bread and wine are symbolic of Jesus' body and blood (consubstantiation). According to Catholic theology, however, the bread and wine actually become Jesus' body and blood, a process known as transubstantiation. Whichever interpretation one holds, the importance of this ritual is that it manifests the presence of Christ for the Christian worshiper. Christianity thus took Jewish symbols and ascribed new meaning to them to reflect Christian theology.

As Christianity developed, the question of its relationship to Judaism emerged. While some early Christians despised Judaism and suggested that Jewish scriptures be eliminated from Christian worship, the Church understood that it must be preserved both for its historic and theological significance.

The Hebrew Bible, therefore, forms the beginning of the Christian Bible. Usually referred to as the Old Testament (although some contemporary Christians recognize the pejorative nature of that term), it is usually the source for one of three scripture readings at Christian services. A second reading normally comes from the latter part of the "New Testament," such as the Book of Acts or the Letters of Paul, and the third (and the most important) reading is from one of the four gospel accounts of the life and death of Jesus. These readings parallel the Jewish tradition of reading from the Torah and Haftarah, and usually form the basis of a minister's sermon.

Christian Influences on Judaism

Christian theology and practice also had an influence on the development of Judaism, as each community attempted to define itself. Judaism, in more recent centuries, has not been averse to borrowing from Christian practices. For example, in nineteenth century Germany, the nascent Reform Movement brought the organ into the synagogue and adopted the ceremony of Confirmation. These changes were among many implemented by the Reform Movement in its response to the Enlightenment and its attempt to combat assimilation. By offering a worship experience that was more similar to Christian worship than traditional Jewish worship, Reform Jewish leaders hoped to meet the needs of German Jews who wanted to be more like their fellow German Christians.

Christian Emphasis on Belief

Christianity's emphasis on belief, as opposed to action, can be traced to its origins, particularly its decision to abandon Jewish practice in favor of belief that Jesus was the Messiah. Whereas Jesus made it clear that he did not wish to abolish all of Jewish law, his followers, in their efforts to proselytize among the pagans, did not insist that new members of their community follow Jewish practice. Eventually, when the number of gentiles greatly outnumbered the number of Jews, the community abandoned Jewish rituals. They stopped requiring circumcision of males and did not observe the dietary laws. They stopped observing Shabbat (Saturday) and replaced it with "The Lord's Day" (Sunday — the day of the week on which Christians believe Jesus rose from the grave). They also stopped observing Jewish holidays and began observing Christmas as the day of Jesus' birth and Easter as the day of Jesus' believed resurrection.

In comparing Judaism and Christianity, it has often been noted that Jesus plays the same role in Christianity as Torah does in Judaism. For Jews, the path to salvation is through living a life of Torah, whereas for Christians it is following Jesus. This parallel is also reflected in the area of spirituality. Whereas Jewish spirituality, in whatever form it takes, is based upon the teachings and ideas of the Torah, Christian spirituality is based on the teachings and ideas of Jesus. For Christians, studying and emulating the life of Jesus allows one to live a spiritual life, just as for Jews studying Torah allows us to live a spiritual life. For some Christians and Jews, this might mean a mystic or contemplative life; for others it will mean a life devoted to social activism and serving others.

Alternative Forms of Christian Spirituality

Christian spirituality has taken many forms during its long history. From monks and nuns who spent many hours a day praying to Catholic workers who focused their efforts on serving the poor, Christians have found many ways to serve God.

Contemporary Christian worship ranges from services that are contemplative and sedate to those that are charismatic. Some Christians prefer emotional fervor in their worship services, while others prefer intellectual stimulation.

SOME THOUGHTS ON EDUCATION

In an educational setting, teaching Jewish children and adults to understand the basic beliefs and practices of Christianity will enable us to relate better to our Christian friends and neighbors. We can acknowledge that belief is at the core of Christian faith and provides the foundation of Christian life. We can better appreciate the similarities and differences among Christians of different denominations.

As teachers of Judaism, we might begin by asking our students what they know about Christianity and utilize the material in this chapter and from other resources to expand or correct their knowledge.

Then we might ask the students to compare specific Christian ideas or practices to Jewish ideas and practices in order to recognize the similarities and differences between the two religions. Finally, we can explore with our students the implications of these similarities and differences on both a personal level (how it affects the students' lives) and in a communal level (how it affects the Jewish and Christian communities).

An alternative approach would be to begin with a specific issue of historical import or contemporary significance and try to understand how each tradition has arrived at its position or viewpoint. Then one can explore the implications of each tradition as above.

CONCLUSION

Like Judaism, Christianity continues to evolve to meet the needs of twenty-first century human beings. As Jews, we can admire and learn from Christianity's willingness to speak about belief, even when we disagree with its theological conclusions. We can also admire the ability with which such Christians as Dr. Martin Luther King, Jr. and Mother Theresa put their beliefs into action. We can work side by side in our communities with Christians who are committed to housing the homeless, feeding the hungry, and working for social justice for all. We can pray together with our Christian neighbors at Thanksgiving services, Israel Independence Day and Holocaust Remembrance Day observances. We can study scripture together, learning how each religion has interpreted the stories and teachings that are at the core of our religions. We can dialogue with each other about the beliefs and practices which unite and divide us.

IMPLICATIONS

1. Both Judaism and Christianity have borrowed important ideas, concepts and rituals from one another.

2. Jews and Christians can learn from each other through reading, dialogue, and experience.

3. Christianity like Judaism is not monolithic in its belief systems.

4. Both Jews and Christians are experimenting with ways of enhancing spirituality in people's lives today. This necessitates changes in institutions in terms of prayer, ritual, and education.

QUESTIONS FOR CRITICAL INQUIRY

1. Kadden states, "In order to reflect upon our own beliefs and practices, it is often useful to compare them to others." Based on this statement, what is it that you think we can learn from each other? What is the implication of this for the curriculum of Jewish schools?

2. What are the ways that your institution already interacts with people of other religions? What are the benefits of this sharing? For what reasons do you do this? What are other things that you could do to maximize the learning that comes from sharing one's religion with people from other religions?

3. How has what Christians have done in understanding and relating to the life of Jesus similar or different from the ways in which we understand and relate to the lives of the Patriarchs (Abraham, Isaac, and Jacob), Matriarchs (Sarah, Rebecca, Leah, and Rachel), Moses, Miriam, and others?

4. Kadden provides an analogy in understanding Christian and Jewish spirituality: Jesus is to Christianity what the Torah is Judaism. Do you agree or disagree with this statement?

5. In what ways does the Torah provide a path to Jewish spirituality?

6. Kadden lists three core theological ideas in Christianity: trinity, humanity and divinity of the Messiah, and the second coming of the Messiah? What are the parallel or similar theological ideas in Judaism? What are some other key theological ideas in Judaism of which you think everyone should have some knowledge?

7. In what ways are spirituality, belief, and practice connected in Judaism?

8. What are the implications of this sensitivity and ability to learn from another religion in helping educate mixed marrieds (including their children) who are committed to having a Jewish household? For example, how might you tap into the familiarity and comfort that many Christians have with belief and God talk in Jewishly enriching the spirituality of the household members?

ACTIVITIES

1. Make a list of the main images and names of God that Kadden presents for Christianity. Using this list and the one from Chapter 1, "The Changing Perceptions of God in Judaism," create a collage in which the names and images of God that are the same or similar are in the middle, and those exclusive to either religion are to one side or the other. Compare and contrast the names and images for God. Consider: Do Jews and Christians pray to the same God?

2. Find a way of talking with Christians about their views of God. Have the group develop a series of questions about God and their God beliefs and how it influences their worldview. You can do this by visiting a church and arranging for a special discussion or by inviting some Christians to the class to talk about their views of God.

3. All religions have master stories that identify what is most important to them. Read excerpts from the Exodus/Revelation and the

Passion/Resurrection, called the master stories of Judaism and Christianity by Michael Goldberg, a Rabbi and theologian. You might also watch the Exodus/Revelation section in the film *The Prince of Egypt* (1998, rated PG, 93 min.) or *The Ten Commandments* (1956, rated G, 219 min.) and the Passion/Resurrection scene in the film version of *Jesus Christ Superstar* (1973, rated G, 108 min.). In each of these master stories, identify the key views of God, including God's relationship to the people. Then consider how these master stories helped frame the spiritual paths of each religion.

4. Find and/or take pictures of sanctuaries in various synagogues and churches. Compare and contrast the sanctuary in a synagogue to one a church. In what ways does the architecture, art, ritual objects, symbols, and décor reflect the image of God for each religion? How does each sanctuary capture a sense of the sacred? How does each suggest that worshipers are to relate to God?

BIBLIOGRAPHY

Bamberger, David. *Judaism and the World's Religions.* Watchung, NJ: Behrman House, 1987.

The beliefs, practices, and teachings of each major religion (Hinduism, Buddhism, Islam, and Christianity) as seen through Jewish eyes. Geared to Grades 7-10. Teacher's Guide available.

Holt, Bradley P. *Thirsty for God: A Brief History of Christian Spirituality.* Minneapolis, MN: Augsburg Press, 1993.

This work is a general introduction to Christian spirituality.

Sheldrake, Philip. *Spirituality and History: Questions of Interpretation and Method.* Maryknoll, NY: Orbis Books, 1995.

Sheldrake offers a comprehensive introduction to spirituality from a historical perspective.

Weiss-Rosmarin, Trude. *Judaism and Christianity: The Differences.* New York: Jonathan David, 1981.

A noted Jewish scholar, Weiss-Rosmarin offers a systematic comparison of Judaism and Christianity covering such topics as sin and atonement, faith vs. law, and Jesus.

CHAPTER 4

THE SPIRITUAL CONDITION OF AMERICAN JEWS

David S. Ariel

By ALL INDICATIONS, AMERICAN JEWRY IS STANDING on the brink of a spiritual revival. The evidence for this can be found in the increasing attention to personal Jewish growth, the emergence of serious adult Jewish learning, the resurgence of counter-cultural alternatives, the interest in the mystical dimensions of Judaism, the expansion of the market for Jewish books, the rise of the Internet, and the strength of the *Ba'al Teshuvah* movement. The growing interest in the exploration of one's own personal Jewishness can be seen among those who are engaged in one or another Jewish journey or who identify themselves as Jewish seekers. The rise in the number of people involved in adult Jewish learning and the proliferation of national, regional, and local programs that promote Jewish spiritual growth are sure signs of this phenomenon. (For an overview of such programs, see Chapter 11, "Teaching and Learning about God: Considerations and Concerns for Adults" by Betsy Dolgin Katz, p. 131.) The Jewish counter-culture that began with the Havurah movement in the late 1960s has developed into a syncretistic, spiritual movement — Jewish Renewal — that integrates elements of traditional Judaism, ecstatic Hasidism, and Buddhist meditation.[1] Jewish meditation groups and courses on *Kabbalah* are now offered in synagogues and also for home study. Major trade publishers and Jewish niche publishers are experiencing strong sales of books on Jewish spirituality that are supported by national author tours. Numerous Internet web sites offer "Jewish spiritual resources" from varying religious perspectives. Finally, some Jewish adults — the *Ba'alei Teshuvah* — continue to embrace Orthodox Judaism and its rigorous lifestyle without any ambivalence or ambiguity.[2]

A growing number of younger Jews, primarily between the ages of 25 and 50, increasingly identify themselves as spiritual seekers in pursuit of deeper personal meaning and connectedness.[3] They see spirituality as the deeply held core of values by which they lead their lives. They search for truths that serve as the unassailable anchor of their personal experience. They want to find corroboration in Judaism for what they know in their hearts to be true. They seek wisdom that can guide their public behavior and their relationships with others. Inwardness becomes the measure of whether their public activities have meaning. They are engaged in a lifelong journey in which various forms of Jewish expression are synthesized into an evolving system of personal identity.

The emergence of personal Jewish expression in all its varieties constitutes a spiritual revival, although this revival is not necessarily unified or coherent. What makes this phenomenon unique is that it is taking place largely outside the purview of institutionalized Jewish life, the major Jewish denominations, and most congregations. It is one of the few truly indigenous developments in American Jewish life. It is a genuinely grassroots movement that started on the periphery of Jewish life, but which has recently begun to move into the center.

---

[1] Rodger Kamenetz, *Stalking Elijah* (Harper: San Francisco, 1997). This book and his earlier book, *The Jew in the Lotus*, offer an important window into the Jewish Renewal movement.

[2] Janet Aviad, *Return To Judaism: Religious Renewal in Israel* (Chicago, IL: University of Chicago Press, 1983). Although her analysis is based on observations of *Ba'alei Teshuvah* in Israel, the same can be said about *Ba'alei Teshuvah* in America. Many *Ba'alei Teshuvah*, however, end up in Israel.

[3] Wade Clark Roof, *A Generation of Seekers: The Spiritual Journeys of the Baby Boom Generation* (San Francisco: Harper, 1993). This is the definitive work on the spiritual quest of the baby boomer generation in America.

For the first time in three generations, a growing number of younger Jews are not content with accepting conventional Judaism. They want to know about Judaism for themselves and reject the passivity of vicarious Jewishness, of letting others define Judaism for them. They seek empowerment as Jews to counter the meagerness of the Judaism they were taught in Religious School. It is not sufficient for the Rabbi to lecture, define, and lead. They want to learn, experience, and understand for themselves. But they do not want to learn *about* Judaism, they want to learn Judaism. They seek immediacy, authenticity, and truth. This puts increasing pressure on the Jewish community to respond to this development positively, seriously, and with additional resources.

Many seekers today view Jewish institutions as more concerned with sustaining membership and preserving the institution for its own sake than with the heart and soul of the individual. Abraham Joshua Heschel's critique of the organized Jewish community has turned prophetic. Heschel expressed his criticism of the vacuousness in the American Jewish community and a Jewishness that did not deepen the spiritual and religious life of the individual. He criticized the excessive preoccupation with the communal aspects of Jewish life at the expense of our spiritual lives.

> The concern for the welfare of the community and its institutions that has dominated Jewish life in America has also diverted our attention from the individual. Jews attend Jewish meetings, belong to Jewish organizations, and contribute to communal and national funds: In seeing the forest, we could not see the trees. In building a strong communal life, we have forgotten the spiritual condition of the individual Jew. The private life of the Jew has become impoverished and is reflected in the spiritual vacuousness of many Jewish homes and synagogues. The concern

of the Jewish community should be reversed: Unless the religious spirit of the Jew as an individual is enriched, the life of the community will be a wilderness. If the individual is lost to Judaism in his privacy, the people are in danger of becoming a phantom.[4]

Today's spiritual revival may be a reaction to the situation that Heschel described. This change may reflect the growing assertion of the spiritual — the personal, the private, the inward — into the public arena. When institutions such as the family, voluntary, social, and civic organizations, the workplace, religious organizations, and political institutions no longer meet our deeply personal criteria of meaning, we turn to alternative forms of expression that have greater personal meaning. We ask not what we can do for institutions, but what institutions can do for us. Therefore, many of the spiritual expressions of personal Jewish meaning today take place beyond the traditional institutions of Jewish life. Because these are positive expressions of Jewish meaning in the eyes of the seekers themselves, they represent a deepening of personal Jewishness among individuals who were previously less engaged with Judaism.

This revival reflects the maturation of the growth of Jewish identity that followed the Israeli victory in the Six Day War in June 1967. What began as growing comfort with the public expression of Jewish identity has matured into a growing concern with the personal meaning of Jewish identity — the Jew within. It is no longer sufficient to base Jewish identity on the social, public, communal, or organizational forms of Judaism — or on the imperatives of fighting anti-Semitism and defending Jews in Israel and around the world — unless we also understand what this means to us personally.

The recent spiritual awakening is also an inevitable reaction against the trend of assimilation that has resulted in a weak congregational Jewish educational system. Many congregational

---

[4]Abraham Joshua Heschel, *The Insecurity of Freedom: Essays on Human Existence* (New York: Farrar, Giroux, and Straus, 1966), p. 215. Heschel is often the inspiration for seekers who pursue the Jewish spiritual path.

schools encouraged Jewish identity, but not Jewish knowledge, validated a minimalist form of Judaism, and expected little of either the student, their parents, or their teachers. With the growth of more intensive Jewish education — Day Schools, summer camps, youth groups, and Israel programs — the pendulum has swung the other way toward taking Judaism more seriously. And those Jewish adults whose own Jewish education was inadequate, but whose children are involved in more intensive Jewish education, often want and expect to explore and live Judaism on a more intense level.

The Jewish spiritual revival also reflects the growing acceptance of public religious expression in the United States. It mirrors the penetration of religion into public discourse and political life among many sectors within American society. Spirituality in America is often accompanied by a commitment to societal change rather than a retreat from society.[5] Likewise, many Jewish adults seek ways to express their spirituality in the world rather than withdraw into a private cocoon. At the same time, the spiritual developments within contemporary Judaism echo many forms of expression in contemporary American culture — lifelong and adult learning, increased focus on expanding leisure time activities, creating intentional communities, exploration of new age and healing traditions, openness and eclecticism that blends elements of various traditions, alternative lifestyles, and other non-traditional forms of personal expression.

Although we lack basic statistical and analytical data on the attitudes, aspirations, and journeys of today's Jewish seekers, it is possible to identify today's Jewish seekers as fitting in one or another of six broad categories: Authenticity Seekers, Institutional Revitalists, Adult Learners, Activists, Jewish Renewal, and New Age Spiritualists. These definitions, however, are neither exhaustive nor static. Many people incorporate elements from different spiritual persuasions and

many people move in and out of various groups over the course of a lifetime. The Jewish spiritual revival defies easy categorization because the various forms of expression are fungible. In addition, since the Jewish journey is an adult journey, there is tremendous flux and unpredictability among each individual on the journey. For these seekers, the Jewish journey is a lifelong journey the stages of which evolve and change over a lifetime. Most seekers are not today who they were ten years ago, and will not be the same ten years from now.

Authenticity Seekers

All seekers see themselves in pursuit of genuine spirituality. They crave, above all, authenticity, which to them means a faith and a way of life that are unambiguous, based on certain authority, and which is not self-conscious or temporizing. They want guides who are authentic and who do not just "talk the talk, but also walk the walk." They look for a Judaism that speaks to their hearts and that provides a clear answer to those questions that matter most — how to validate one's own feelings, how to be a good person and lead a moral life, how to relate to other people, how to find balance and perspective between and among the many competing claims on our time, how to create a Jewish home life, and what to believe about God and the presence of God in our lives. They often reject Conservative and Reform Judaism — the denominations in which they were raised — because their Rabbis seem to be uncomfortable with such questions and prefer to advocate rather than to serve as role models. They see Conservative and Reform congregations as too concerned with institutional self-preservation and their Rabbis as lacking spiritual authenticity. They may draw comfortably on those elements of traditional belief and practice that they can integrate into their lives. They want Judaism to provide an

[5]The Great Awakenings of 1730-1750 and 1815-1850 led to the creation of many American colleges, frontier missions, and

fed the abolitionist and women's rights movements.

internal compass that guides them across the terrain of life, the basis for religious practice in their home and daily lives, and the foundation of friendships and relationships with other like-minded individuals. They want "intimacy," the clear comfort of a certain identity that is deeply personal, but also connects them to others.

The search for authenticity finds many forms of expression. Seekers are not necessarily loyal to institutions; they view them instrumentally as vehicles that warrant their affiliation only as long as they serve their needs. Some seekers create or join communities of connectedness outside of institutional Jewish life, such as alternative or intentional congregations (havurot), alternative prayer groups (minyanim), or create their own circle of friends that get together for Jewish holidays. Some seekers idealize the more open-minded and accepting Orthodox Rabbis and teachers as being authentic role models. They seek genuine Jewish experience even if they are not willing to embrace the lifestyle of their idealized Orthodoxy. Thus, they are drawn to Orthodox teachers, but not to Orthodoxy as a way of life. In some ways, they are tourists within an Orthodox theme park who are comfortable making a weekly foray into studying with an Orthodox teacher as long as they can go home afterward.

Authenticity seekers do not necessarily embrace Orthodoxy. Authenticity seekers might pursue a gradual, incremental embrace of Jewish life or they might follow a patchwork of observances that are not necessarily internally consistent. Sometimes seekers adopt particular observances without regard for how a particular ritual fits into a larger context. For example, a woman might study the laws of family purity, be inspired by its notion of holy sexuality, and decide to attend a mikvah, the ritual bath, after her monthly menstruation. This same woman may be just as likely to drive to synagogue on the Sabbath. While the practice of mikvah has traditionally been limited to Orthodox observance, Sabbath observance is more fundamental to Judaism than mikvah and more widely practiced. Within the context of traditional Judaism and its hierarchy of practice, one is more likely to observe Sabbath than attend the mikvah. When mikvah is taken out of its context, all things are possible. There is often such a contradiction between a seeker's idealization of Orthodoxy and an unwillingness to accept the whole package.

Some authenticity seekers embrace Orthodoxy. These born-again Jews are called Ba'alei Teshuvah ("Returnees") to indicate that they have returned to the correct path. Many Returnees were raised in assimilated Jewish homes and have often pursued extended spiritual odysseys before returning home to Judaism. Returnees are critical of non-Orthodox Judaism, which they often see as hypocritical, superficial, lacking conviction, relativistic, and spiritually vacuous. Like other authenticity seekers, Returnees seek genuine Jewish experience. Unlike other seekers, they are not satisfied by anything less than total immersion in Judaism. They are drawn to the various forms of Orthodoxy — modern, Hasidic, and fundamentalist — in which they find the overpowering appeal of unambiguous commitment of both heart and body.

Institutional Revitalists

Despite the generally anti-institutional nature of the present revival, there has been a growing interest in spirituality within mainstream institutions, especially within some Conservative, Reconstructionist, and Reform congregations. Meditation groups, spirituality discussion groups, and healing groups have recently appeared in a surprisingly large number of congregations. Most of these initiatives come from the members, not the Rabbi or educator.

Seekers are sometimes attracted to Conservative congregations that do away with the notion that only clergy can have Jewish expertise. The chasm between the knowledgeable Rabbi and the Jewishly uneducated congregant has been closed due to the success of the Ramah summer camps and the Day School movement. There are now highly educated congregants in many Conservative congregations who, nonetheless, feel disempowered by the hierarchical style of their synagogues. Many of these congregants find authenticity in their own Jewish knowledge, abilities, and skills. Conservative congregations could better hold on to such seekers if they were to eliminate the raised pulpit, promote the participation of members in leading services, and encourage members to learn and employ Jewish liturgical skills. This can be done by creating smaller groups within cathedral congregations that are customized to the needs of various kinds of seekers, by devoting resources to support the educational needs of seekers, and by fostering less formal frontal services within congregations in favor of more participatory services led by the seekers themselves.

Reconstructionist Judaism, founded by Mordecai Kaplan in the 1920s, has evolved from a highly intellectual approach to Judaism to a movement that actively promotes spirituality among its followers. Most Reconstructionist congregations are intentionally small in order to create intimate communities of connectedness. They often share a bias against cathedral congregations in favor of small, informal prayer quorums that foster innovation and personal reflection. Reconstructionists seek to incorporate elements of traditional Judaism with new rituals, unfettered by tradition. The criteria for Reconstructionist Judaism is that the individual, not the past, determines what has meaning today. For example, Jewish rituals are often appropriated out of their traditional context and transformed into new rituals that serve the present moment. There is a comfort with transforming traditions, blending the traditional with the personal, and preserving intimacy within their congregations. There is often the presumption of respect for tradition, but not for the authority of the past.

As the Reform Movement has embraced greater tradition, it has also preserved the freedom to alter or create new traditions. The impact of a robust summer camping and youth group movement, together with a growing number of charismatic young Rabbis, has resulted in the growth of a romantic and revivalist trend within Reform congregations. Reform spirituality is often evident in the inclusion of music and song within the formal religious services. Several influential denominational singers and composers have created a set of popular melodies that have become part of many Reform services. The atmosphere created in many of these congregations and associated movement activities is sometimes revivalist. People are no longer tethered passively to their seats; hand clapping and ecstatic singing are common.

New Adult Learners

For many seekers, the primary mode of spiritual exploration is learning. Adult Jewish learning is one of the most significant, yet least understood, trends within American Judaism today. While there is no quantitative or qualitative data available on adult Jewish learners, the phenomenon is evident within every community and through a variety of national and local programs. The Wexner Heritage Foundation has graduated 1,000 adults in 31 communities from its two-year program of Jewish studies for high potential Jewish leaders. The Florence Melton Adult Mini-School of the Hebrew University in Jerusalem has 4,900 adults enrolled in 44 communities across North America and has graduated 6,000 adults. More than 1,000 adults are enrolled in "Me'ah: One Hundred Hours of Jewish Learning," a two-year curriculum created by Boston's Hebrew College and based on the latest scholarship. Other such programs include those of CLAL — the National Jewish Center for Learning and Leadership, the Jewish Community Center Association's Derech Torah, the Dawn Schuman Institute in Chicago, Washington's Foundation for Jewish Studies, Berkeley's Lehrhaus, New Jersey's Midrasha, the Reform Kolel, the Drisha Institute, and "Eilu ve-Eilu" in Detroit. Orthodox outreach groups, such as Aish Hatorah and Chabad-Lubavitch, reach a large yet unspecified numbers in its various learning programs for non-Orthodox adults. Several colleges of Jewish studies (Boston Hebrew College, Siegal College of Judaic Studies, and Gratz College) reach more than 1,000 adults within their communities and regions.[6]

These new programs are both a response and a stimulus to the growing interest in adult Jewish learning. While adult Jewish learning has long been a part of the fabric of traditional life within the Orthodox community, it has increasingly reached non-Orthodox Jews. Some adult learners take advantage of organized learning opportunities as a form of leisure or recreational activity. Other adult learners are clearly dissatisfied with the pediatric level of their own Jewish education and seek a more adult understanding of Judaism. Others have reached the stage in their own development in which family and professional goals have been achieved and issues of personal identity and meaning come to the fore. Still others are engaged in a lifelong journey of enlightenment that leads them to explore Judaism among other religious and spiritual traditions.

There are two distinct types of adult learners — those who are spiritually oriented and those who are intellectually oriented. The spiritually oriented adult learners are interested in the subjective experience of learning what Judaism has to say to them directly about their own lives. They have great reverence for the sacred texts of Judaism, but are more interested in the guidance of a living teacher. Judaism is dialogical, that is, truth can be found in the spoken word between teacher and student that engages the heart. They seek to recapture Jewish experience through immersion in Jewish text study. They study Torah, Talmud, *Kabbalah*, and Jewish ethics. They believe that through study, a deeper approach to practice and understanding might emerge.

The intellectually oriented adult learners are generally interested in a more cerebral understanding of Judaism. They want to understand the historical origins and dynamics of Judaism. They want to understand Judaism on its own terms and want to apply literary, historical, and philosophical categories of knowledge to Jewish experience. They want to be challenged intellectually, to acquire Jewish knowledge, and to master Jewish skills such as reading Bible, Talmud, Hebrew, or other Jewish texts. They may take a class, read Jewish books, or form a study group with a teacher.

Communal and Organizational Activists

Another group of seekers is not anti-institutional. They are identified by their voluntarism, activism, and participation in the organized institutions of Jewish life including Federations, congregations, and membership organizations. A generation ago, this group was characterized as having a shared outlook known as "civil Judaism."[7] According to Jonathan Woocher, many Jewish activists saw themselves as motivated by a secular version of Jewish values that saw the preservation of the Jewish people, not Judaism itself, as the greatest goal. Civil Judaism drew on Jewish religious values to inform support for social justice, the fight against anti-Semitism, the defense of Jewish rights, and respect for the welfare of Jews and non-Jews. Such actions often took the place of traditional religious behaviors.

As the next generation of Jewish activists entered Jewish life, it was not sufficient for them to rely on a residue of Jewish values as their inspiration. They needed to go back to the source in order to discover why generations of Jews have cared for the poor, the needy, the oppressed, and the displaced within their community, Israel, and around the world, without

---

[6]While these programs represent the more intensive and challenging Jewish learning programs that attract younger seekers, there are many Jewish learning programs that attract a more mature audience. Elder adults may not be looking for authenticity, but for intellectual stimulation, confirmation of their identity, reinforcement of their sense of Jewish identity, and the opportunity to interact with their peers. Many congregations, Federations, community centers, and other organizations offer short-term adult education and enrichment programs to an undetermined number of adults. Elderhostel, a major not-for-profit educational venture, offers popular Jewish content courses and attracts significant numbers of Jewish seniors.

[7]Jonathan Woocher, *Sacred Survival: The Civil Religion of American Jews* (Bloomington, IN: Indiana University Press, 1986). This important work focuses on the Jewish Federation movement in the 1980s, just when Federations were beginning to grapple with issues of Jewishness.

regard to whether the beneficiaries of their concern are Jewish or not. They often indicate that they "know in their hearts" that to be a Jew is to see the world not as it is, but as it can be.

These activists seek the spiritual basis of communal, congregational, and organizational involvement and activism. They want to know the spiritual teachings that serve as the inspiration for the enduring Jewish commitment to *tzedakah*, *tikkun olam*, and *k'lal yisrael*. They believe that all people are created in the image of God, that all Jews share a mutual and reciprocal responsibility to one another, and that helping other people is a Jewish religious duty. They believe that the organized Jewish community is the most effective vehicle for transmitting these values, and that these values have little endurance unless they are validated by the Jewish community at large. While this group is more interested in activism than in learning for its own sake, they often participate in study groups within congregations and organizations, and value inspirational and motivational speeches about Jewish values.

Many of these activists have become staunch supporters of Day Schools. Others have succeeded in business and the professions, have established philanthropic foundations, and are active in Jewish life. They support the organized community's efforts to promote Jewish continuity or the Jewish renaissance. They are committed to a Jewish revival not only for their children, but also for themselves. Many of them have, in fact, experienced a deepened Jewish spirituality themselves.

Jewish Renewal

The Jewish Renewal movement is the only organized contemporary Jewish spiritual movement. It is an outgrowth of the Havurah movement that began in the 1960s, combining elements of Hasidic ecstasy and communal intimacy in a non-institutional and egalitarian culture. As the Havurah movement matured, the influence of two master teachers — Rabbi Zalman Schachter-Shalomi and Rabbi Shlomo Carlebach — became dominant. Schachter-Shalomi's immersion in traditional Hasidism and his openness to Buddhist meditation, Sufi chants, and other mystical traditions coalesced into a teaching of inwardness, mindfulness, and soulfulness. Carlebach's neo-Hasidic melodies gave this movement a liturgy, a tradition of teaching stories and *niggunim* — Jewish melodies that induce ecstasy and self-transcendence. In recent years, this movement has taken shape as Jewish Renewal, a loose confederation of groups across the country. A spiritual retreat center in upstate New York, *Elat Chayyim*, serves to energize the adherents. A recent decision to ordain Jewish Renewal Rabbis is evidence of the movement's aspirations to create a new denomination.

Jewish Renewal promotes authentic Jewish spiritual experience by embracing the mystical traditions of Hasidism. Unlike some New Age groups that dabble in *Kabbalah*, the center of gravity of this group is rooted within traditional Judaism even as they emphasize the mystical tradition to the exclusion of other Jewish traditions. They are also eclectic and incorporate elements from Buddhism and other Eastern traditions. Their greatest accomplishment so far is that they have created small communities across the country and have reintroduced elements of ecstasy, sensuality, music, and dance into the Jewish experience of communal prayer. To Jewish Renewal adherents, Judaism without ecstasy is empty, and the support of a community of people connected together by a common spiritual outlook is indispensable.

New Age Spiritualists

There is substantial evidence that many Jews have turned away from Jewish life, but still seek a spiritual anchor within Judaism. However, for some, Judaism itself carries no greater authority than any other spiritual tradition. These seekers may have been born Jewish, but they have no real familiarity with it. Precisely because Judaism is so foreign to them as individuals, Judaism possesses an exotic attraction. They see Judaism as an occult tradition of ancient wisdom and a guide to esoteric practices such as mystical union, soul travel, reincarnation, healing, and achieving gnosis. These spiritualists are eclectic and draw on a wide range of New Age and other spiritual paths — especially Native American and Buddhist practices — as effortlessly as they draw on Judaism. They seek to find a spiritual path by combining whatever spiritual elements appeal to them from the traditions available to them. They are drawn, in particular, to *Kabbalah*, the Jewish mystical tradition. However, they rely on New Age interpretations of *Kabbalah*, most of which bear little or no relation to actual *Kabbalah*. This group is largely peripheral to Jewish life — even if the significance of this phenomenon is greater than meets the eye.

CONCLUSION

This brief, non-scientific survey of contemporary forms of Jewish spirituality points to both the diversity and momentum of the present Jewish spiritual revival. We cannot predict where this spiritual revival will lead and whether or not it will ultimately have a lasting impact on Jewish life. It is clear, however, that for many seekers, the stakes are exceptionally high. If many seekers embrace Judaism and acknowledge that nothing Jewish is alien to them, the Jewish community must provide validation and support to these seekers. This requires a concerted effort on the part of denominations, congregations, organizations Rabbis, Cantors, and educators to restore heart and soul to the institutions of Jewish life, to make these institutions more responsive to adult seekers, and to support the journey with resources. If the community does not address this need, we face the danger of permanently alienating some of the best and brightest Jews today.

The present revival may reflect the spark of Jewishness that resides in every Jewish soul waiting to be ignited. In every generation, there is a yearning to discover the mystery of Jewish existence that inspired and nourished our ancestors. It is not a legacy that one would want to relinquish easily. The yearning today, however, manifests itself not as a simple return to the innocence of traditional Jewish life that defines and directs all aspects of life. Rather, it can be described as a "second innocence," a yearning to return to the innocence and faith of our ancestors while preserving our autonomy, freedom, and modernity — not by returning to the lifestyle of the past, but rather by integrating the Jewish legacy with who we are today. We should not discount the many miraculous and inexplicable ways in which Judaism retreats from the precipice of near extinction and gains power, endurance, and vitality.

IMPLICATIONS

1. We are all seekers, but of different varieties.

2. Institutions need to address the different ways in which people are seeking spirituality in their lives.

3. For many Jews, inwardness and spiritual seeking are prime factors of what they expect out of Jewish activities, both communal and individual.

QUESTIONS FOR CRITICAL INQUIRY

1. What reasons does Ariel give for this spiritual awakening occurring at this time? How does what he describes resonate with your own experience? What other explanations do you give for the rise in spirituality?

2. What kind of spiritual seeker are you? In other words, where would you place yourself in terms of the categories that Ariel outlines?

3. What is your reaction to Jewish seekers who are introducing New Age spiritual approaches, such as eco-vegetarianism, aroma therapy, meditation, and mantra into living as a Jew? What makes you respond in that way? With what are you comfortable/ uncomfortable? What makes New Age spiritual approaches appealing to many Jews?

4. Ariel argues that most of the efforts focusing on spirituality, e.g., Rosh Chodesh groups, healing services, meditation groups, were instituted by lay people and not clergy or professionals. In your own synagogue, is this the case? Why or why not? For what reasons do you think that this pattern of innovation and change focusing on spirituality has occurred?

5. What are the implications of what Ariel has said for Jewish communal institutions, including synagogues, Jewish institutions of higher learning, and secular colleges that offer Jewish Studies programs, Federations and agencies (e.g., Jewish Community Centers, Jewish Family Services, Jewish camps, youth groups, Hillel organizations on campus, and other nonprofit organizations such as Hadassah and B'nai B'rith)?

6. What type of educational activities would you design for each category of seekers?

ACTIVITIES

1. Ariel identifies many different paths for spiritual seekers. Write about which one fits best for you. What is it that you are seeking? How do you seek it? Does this way satisfy your spiritual questing? Have you ever walked a path different from the one you are on now? What precipitated the change?

2. Experience the *"Shema"* through the lens of three different spiritual paths. Study the text using commentaries. Sing or chant it as it is sung or chanted in your synagogue. Use the *"Shema"* in both Hebrew and English as a mantra for meditation. Reflect on all three of these spiritual paths. How did each of these experiences connect you to God? What was your response to each? Why might someone choose or prefer one over the other? In what ways does your congregation support these spiritual paths?

3. For a month, collect newspapers and magazines, including your synagogue bulletin, local Jewish paper, and other Jewish publications. Analyze each to see which spiritual themes appear and reappear. How do the different institutions or organizations within the Jewish community address these different themes? Of the paths described by Ariel, is there one that is discussed more than others? Are there any other paths besides those he mentions? What was absent, or what didn't you find that you expected to find?

4. Interview a few 20 to 30-year-olds to learn about and understand their spiritual longings, how they find God in their lives, and the ways in which they perceive synagogues and Jewish communal institutions as responsive or non-responsive to their spiritual questing.

5. Locate several different musical versions of some prayers (e.g., *"Shema," "Kedushah," "Adon Olam"*). What type of spiritual experience does each create? What relationship between God and human beings does the music suggest?

BIBLIOGRAPHY

Aviad, Janet. *Return To Judaism: Religious Renewal in Israel*. Chicago, IL: University of Chicago Press, 1983.

> Although her analysis is based on observations of *Ba'alei Teshuvah* in Israel, the same can be said about *Ba'alei Teshuvah* in America. Many *Ba'alei Teshuvah*, however, end up in Israel.

Heschel, Abraham Joshua. *The Insecurity of Freedom: Essays on Human Existence*. New York: Farrar, Straus and Giroux, 1966, p. 215.

Heschel is often the inspiration for seekers who pursue the Jewish spiritual path.

Kamenetz, Rodger. *Stalking Elijah*. San Francisco, CA: Harper & Row Publishers, 1997.

This book (and Kamenetz's earlier book, *The Jew in the Lotus)*, offers an important window into the Jewish Renewal Movement.

Roof, Wade Clark. *A Generation of Seekers: The Spiritual Journeys of the Baby Boom Generation*. San Francisco, CA: Harper & Row Publishers, 1993.

This is the definitive work on the spiritual quest of the baby boomer generation in America.

Woocher, Jonathan. *Sacred Survival: The Civil Religion of American Jews*. Bloomington, IN: Indiana University Press, 1986.

This important work focuses on the Jewish Federation movement 20 years ago, when Federations were beginning to grapple with issues of Jewishness.

PATHS TO JEWISH SPIRITUALITY

Sherry H. Blumberg

THE TORAH'S REFLECTION OF THE DESERT EXPERIENCE stands as both a compelling and a lasting image of our first encounter as a people with God. During those 40 years of physical struggle, strife, and privation, we came to appreciate the immediacy of a God who is involved in our lives — feeding, giving law, working wonders, encouraging us on our way.

Even in the prosperity and comfort of our own time, that earliest encounter still serves as a vivid metaphor for our spiritual connections. Some of us are in exodus from traditional forms of Judaism; others are trying to find meaning in becoming ever more connected to our traditions. Whatever our stage of life or the extent of our observances, each of us is on a spiritual journey — trying to make sense of life, seeking our path to God, searching, questioning, and questing.

This chapter explores a few of the many Jewish spiritual paths. Some are old, others are new. Each has the potential of enabling a person, as an individual or as part of a community, to search for God. Each path brings with it the potential for struggle and tears, doubt and questioning, wonder and joy, challenge and fulfillment.

As Jewish educators, we have the opportunity to suggest spiritual acts and to delineate potential paths that people might explore. People constantly seek to make meaning out of life — seeking answers to ultimate questions, hoping that life cycle occasions will be celebratory events, looking for *kedushah* opportunities for themselves and for their loved ones. All this searching and hoping goes on whether or not we engage them in dialogue. Despite the abundance of answers and spiritual practices available within our rich tradition, our persistent silences about God and spirituality (in the context of the synagogue or Jewish schools, our most significant religious institutions) are usually taken to mean that God does not matter. Faced with that strong implicit message, our congregants often begin to look outside the synagogue and the school for answers. The ashrams, the liberal churches, and the cults are eager to provide their own answers and to embrace those we fail to nurture.

The following, then, are a few of those spiritual paths, along with an explication of how an educator might lead a learner or seeker along the way. Some of these paths are normative for Jews to explore; others are less common.

WHAT IS A SPIRITUAL PATH?

What is a spiritual path and how does it differ from other paths we might take in our life? Although not exclusively religious, a spiritual life includes an appreciation of our natural, physical world, as well as an experience of transcendence and of the immanence of God's presence in this world.

Transcendence is about reaching out and up to God — about rising above the material world so as to be able to see life as part of a greater whole, in the context of a grand design. Immanence is about looking inward to God. Immanence is a sense of closeness and an immediate trust or faith that the inner spark, our soul (if you will) connects the divine in each of us to the God of the universe. Immanence involves finding God in our day-to-day relationships with family members, friends, and others as we experience them as part of God's creation.

Immanence and transcendence are two intimately connected ways of experiencing God and bringing the sacred into our lives. For Jews, and for all spiritual persons, these are called experiences of the holy.

Mainstream Jewish thought has usually shied away from investigating experiences of the holy. Rather, emphasis has typically been placed on the doing of deeds of loving-kindness and on the performance of *mitzvot* — the following of God's commandments. As we are taught in Mishnah *Pirke Avot*: "On three things the world depends — *al haTorah* (on study), *v'al haAvodah* (on prayer), *v'al Gemilut Chasadim* (on deeds of loving-kindness)." Accentuated here is the living by these principles. What is often lost or passed over is the connection between doing for God and experiences of the Holy — experiencing God.

Of course, the mystical path has been a part of Jewish life for centuries. The mystics, by exploring arcane texts and through fasting and meditative disciplines, seek an immediate relationship with or knowledge of God. They posit hidden meanings and secrets (*sod*) imbedded in Torah, and through such techniques as *gematria* (numerology) and *remez* (connecting passages from one part of Torah to another), they build a framework for understanding *sephirot* (God's presence in the world), *Shechinah* (the indwelling aspect of God), and angels. Mystical writings often focus not only on the black letters of the text, but also on the blank spaces in between the words of Torah. Because every aspect of Torah has the potential for meaning, the spirituality of Jewish mysticism might also entail the detailed observance of Jewish traditions and practices. However, it was the mystics' desire for a direct encounter of God that led traditionalists to mistrust the mystics and to regard their path as somewhat suspect, esoteric, and too unconventional.

To trust in the experience of the holy was risky; better to do what was normative and hope for an experience of the sacred to evolve — to happen in time. Therefore, our traditional approach has been more apt to affirm holiness with our words. But, as Eugene Borowitz suggests in *The Masks Jews Wear*, we sometimes still hold back from acknowledging the experience of God in our own lives because as "modern Jews" we may mistakenly believe that the traditional

Jewish paths do not lead to a spiritual life. Because Judaism has too often downplayed the importance of relating to God, many Jews struggle to find their path within Judaism.

There are many possible moments of apprehending the holy and the holiness that fills the earth, the moments in which we can sense God's presence. Jews would do well to work at reclaiming the spiritual aspect of our heritage, and at incorporating it into the more conventional side of being Jewish through *mitzvot*, prayer, and study. Not only do old spiritual paths need to be rediscovered and reclaimed, but new ones also need to be explored.

For example, each of the many names of God can represent an experience of the holy, a way of comprehending and relating to God. God is experienced as *Adonai, Elohim, El Shaddai, Avinu Malkaynu*, the Eternal, the Judge, the Mighty, the Awesome One, the Compassionate, the Parent, the Creator, and the Redeemer. To understand God as being mighty and awesome, working miracles as in the Exodus of the Jews from Egypt, or as the One who gives Torah at Sinai amidst thunder and lightning can be spiritually uplifting. In contrast, Elijah experienced God not in the thunder or the wind, but in the still, small voice of God. For the Psalmists, God was the protecting Shield, who reveled in words of praise and glory. For others, God is experienced as *shlaymut* — a feeling of wholeness or completeness that leads to a quiet gentle feeling that all life has purpose, that one's actions are in harmony with God's design, and that prayer brings comfort to one's soul.

The next section of this chapter describes several paths to God, verbal and nonverbal, traditional and alternative, that affirm the experience of the holy and sacred in our lives and in this world. Most of these paths are informed by Jewish texts that try to give an understanding, meaning, and direction to the spiritual journeys of people today. Therefore, these paths represent a reclaiming or reordering of some of the most beautiful and spiritual understandings from our tradition. They just do so in new forms.

NEW PATHS TO JEWISH SPIRITUALITY

Loyalty and Relationships

The first path is that of Loyalty and Relation-ships. This path includes loyalty to the Jewish people, loyalty to Israel, and loyalty to family and friends.

Loyalty to the Jewish people is experienced as and associated with feelings of pride, belong-ing, connectedness, and duty. It can stem from the concept of chosenness; it can also be con-nected to a defensiveness for the Jewish people in the face of anti-Semitism. Feelings of loyalty often give rise to such acts as joining a congrega-tion, supporting Jewish organizations, giving *tzedakah* to Jewish causes, attending Jewish cul-tural events, supporting Jewish artists, and *kvel-ling* over the accomplishments of a Jew of renown (e.g., a Nobel prize winner, Senator Joseph Lieberman's nomination for Vice-President of the U.S.).

Loyalty to Israel is expressed by support at all times and under all circumstances for Israel. It is an unconditional love for the *Eretz Yisrael*, *Medinat Yisrael*, and *Am Yisrael*. This uncondi-tional love does not mean uncritical love, but it does mean unwavering love. Loyalty to Israel can be expressed through such actions as visiting Israel; buying Israeli products; giving money to Israeli causes, including investing in Israeli busi-nesses; speaking out for Israel in the United States; belonging to political organizations that support Israel; following anything in the media about Israel; and participating in Israeli cultural events. The sacred dimensions of God's covenan-tal promise of the Land to the Jewish people, starting with Abraham, underlies our sense of loyalty to Israel.

Loyalty in marriage, family, and friendship are excellent ways of understanding the metaphor for our own relationship to God. Tanach includes many stories about a person's loyalty to family or friends. One such well-known story is Ruth's loyalty to Naomi. Ruth foregoes the security of staying in her own land and with her own people. She demonstrates her love for her mother-in-law despite the limited support that Naomi is able to offer her. In our relationships with our family and friends, we defend, argue, support, and challenge. We also intensify our relations with each other through our ongoing engagement with one another. The qualities of love, concern, care, commitment, and obligation are needed to remain in relation-ship to another. Buber would have us under-stand that it is through our I-Thou relations, our turning toward another individual and fully lis-tening and appreciating who that individual is, that we meet God.

Curiosity and Dialogue

A second path might be called Curiosity and Dialogue. The joy of discovery and discussion exemplifies this path. For many, the encounter with God comes through the study of sacred texts. The experience of studying text in *chevruta* or larger groupings and of reading commentaries on the text by scholars of today or long ago, pro-vides intellectual, sometimes emotional, connec-tions to God and deepens one's spirituality. Traditionally, the study of Jewish texts is viewed as a spiritual experience as signified by the use of a *brachah* — *La'asok B'divray Torah* — at the start of this activity. What might appear to be a very rational, cognitive, and intellectual activity is actually very personal and spiritual for many. Many adults regularly attend a Shabbat morning Torah study group, but do not stay for the wor-ship service. For them, this behavior presents neither contradiction nor dilemma, since Torah study — not the worship experience — is their spiritual path.

Another example of this path is the tradition of *machloket* (debate, disagreements) found throughout the Talmud and Rabbinic literature. Perhaps the most famous Talmudic arguments are those of Hillel and Shammai, who were in conflict about all aspects of Jewish life from ritual observance through the treatment of the poor. Their debates were a sacred activity as they tried to understand what God wanted and to make that understanding a living, vibrant part of their own lives and the lives of others. *Machloket* continues today as people study, inquire, and debate how to apply Jewish law for today's world.

Equally expressive of this spiritual path can be those engaged in intensive study and inquiry in the sciences, humanities, arts, and other fields. On their paths, they, too, are sharpening their intellect, ideas, and even wit, in pursuit of truth and, in most cases, the creation of a better world. Examples of such a spiritual path are Jonas Salk's pursuit of a polio vaccine to improve the human condition, Albert Einstein's desire to understand and explain the laws that govern the universe, and Leonard Bernstein's pursuit of beauty in both traditional and new forms of music so as to enrich our souls. Those engaged in this kind of study and inquiry do not always regard their work as a spiritual endeavor; they do not always perceive how what they do is connected to God. But in a basic Jewish sense, it is connected, for those people are using God's gifts of the mind to benefit the world.

Passion

The path of Passion involves the ability to transcend oneself and throw oneself wholeheartedly into something. This path refers not only to the passion of love, or the sensual nature of touch, but also the passion for an activity or cause. This is the path of the *Mitzvot Ha-layv* (*mitzvot* of the heart), as contrasted to either the *mitzvot* of the mind or *mitzvot* of the hands, which Abraham ibn Ezra describes in *Yesod Morah* (Foundation of the Teaching). *Mitzvot Ha-layv* is found in unsung heroes like the enduring piano teacher, the devoted Religious School teacher, the caring coach, and the reliable *shammes* at the *shul*. All of these individuals are able to dedicate their lives to helping others succeed and grow, because of their passion for their work and not for reward or recognition. This is also the path of the martyrs of Israel, like Rabbi Akiva, who gave their lives in affirming God, Torah, or *Eretz Yisrael*.

The path of Passion is fraught with danger. Passion can become so self-absorbing that one loses touch with reality in the process. God,

truth, and humility must be maintained as the focus of our passion. Moses Ibn Ezra in *Arugat HaBosem* (literally, the "fragrant flower bed,") delineates this caution: "You must first know your own soul and then you can know the realities of things — self-knowledge is necessary to comprehend the signs of the artisan whence the soul was hewn." When one becomes excessively absorbed in a cause and loses perspective with regard to what is really important, and God's way, passion can go awry and lead to zealotry. Zealotry can lead to false messiahs (e.g., Shabbetai Zvi) and to the committing of misguided acts of violence in the name of God (e.g., assassinations of national leaders).

Justice and Compassion

The path of Justice and Compassion is the path to social action, in which *tzedek, tzedek tirdof* (pursuing righteousness or justice) is a guiding principle, a sacred act. While seeking justice leads to righteousness, justice can be harsh. The person who follows this path must also be aware of the need for compassion as a balance. Compassion requires us to look at each human being individually, in context, while fulfilling the desire for justice. It is the understanding that restitution (making an injured person whole), making peace (mediating the grievances that may have been at the initial root of a conflict), rehabilitation, and not just punishment, are important in the pursuit of justice.

This path of Justice and Compassion appears throughout our sacred texts. Abraham argues on behalf of the people of Sodom and Gomorrah (Genesis 18). The image of justice as being blind comes from the warning to judges and officials not to favor the poor or the wealthy in their decisions (Leviticus 16:18-20). The need for righteous actions can be seen in both the biblical concept of "*peot*," of leaving the corners of the field for the poor and the stranger (Leviticus 23:22) and in the similar injunction against gleaning a vine or tree after first harvesting its fruit, so as to leave those gleanings for the poor, the widow, and the orphan (Deuteronomy 24:19-21).

While pursuing justice is a *mitzvah*, those on this spiritual path see justice and compassion as more than merely fulfilling a commandment or doing good deeds. Rather, the pursuit of justice and compassion must become a driving force, a focal point of their way of being in the world. Those who participated in the American civil rights movement, daring to walk arm-in-arm with Dr. Martin Luther King, Jr. in acts of civil disobedience, followed this path. Others pursue this path by providing sanctuary for refugees, visiting AIDS patients, or building houses for the poor through Habitat for Humanity. Such people are the little known heroes who take a risk, who extend themselves beyond the norm, to do something for those in need who are limited in their ability to help themselves.

People on this path find a way to make a difference in bringing righteous to the world. One example of such a person was Miriam Mendilow, who founded *Yad L'Kashish*, Lifeline for the Elderly. She saw elderly Jews in Jerusalem lose their sense of dignity because they were inactive and ignored, unable to contribute to society. Through a series of workshops, she gave them creative, important tasks, such as mending books for school children, and in so doing restored their self-respect and sense of value in society. Her compassionate pursuit of *mitzvot* was her spiritual path to God.

SELF-TRANSCENDENCE, SELF-CONSCIOUSNESS, SELF-CONTROL

Akin to some of the mystical paths is the modern Jewish path of Self-transcendence, Self-consciousness, and Self-control. Self-transcendence involves moving beyond one's self, connecting to a larger and greater whole. Self-consciousness is the awareness of one's place in the world. It comes with an understanding of the connection between nature and human beings and their interdependent existence. Self-control is the conscious use of will to shape the self and one's actions in the world. At the core of this path, are will, discipline, and choice.

Ecstasy and joy are the primary means of experiencing God along the path of self-transcendence. *Kavanah* (experiencing) takes precedence over *keva* (fixed ritual acts). But moderation is critical to this path. The Musar Movement — founded by Rabbi Israel Salanter (the Rosh) in the late 1800s — recognizing the dangers of an unmoderated pursuit of religious ecstasy and joy, encouraged a highly structured and contemplative form of daily study of ethical literature and ethical practices, so as to strengthen one's inner life. One must always be conscious of the "yoke of heaven" — that we are always in the presence of God.

Wholeness (*shlaymut*) and balance (*shalom*) are both operative principles and goals of self-control. Maimonides, in his introduction to *Pirke Avot*, refers to the appetites of the soul, saying that the soul must be in balance — each of our appetites may be fulfilled, but within reason. Trying to live in harmony with nature, other people, and God has been discussed as a spiritual path since medieval times in such texts as *Sefer HaYirah* and *Orchot Chayyim*. All these texts teach that wisdom emerges not from extremes, the broad swings in emotion, knowledge, or action, but from the resolution, the synthesis of these aspects of life.

Traveling along this path includes meditation, prayer, and reflection — the tools of the pious person who aims to have direct contact, firsthand experience of God. These disciplines are becoming more prevalent in Jewish life today as attested to by the numerous retreats and workshops, the plethora of books being published, and the sermons preached by Rabbis from all four movements — Reform, Reconstructionist, Conservative, and Orthodox. Jewish Renewal has had perhaps the most profound influence in terms of the widespread use of meditation, prayer, and reflection in Jewish worship settings.

Creativity

Another of the paths to God is that of Creativity. Creativity can be found in both the arts and sciences. Through expression using the plastic arts, drama, dance, music, and other creative endeavors, we become partners with God in the creation of beauty. Being on the cutting edge in research or the use of research in the sciences or medicine or engineering is a way of being involved in the ongoing process of revelation. Putting our thoughts and insights, our courage and passion to work in attacking and solving today's social issues (e.g., education, poverty, the environment) are no less than acts of redemption.

"Creative knowing" that combines the human with the sacred is a link to "spiritual knowing." This spiritual path combines several other paths, as it is filled with passion, curiosity, and often self-reflection. Artists, thinkers, or researchers who open themselves up to their positive, creative energy may allow God to flow through them to their work. Creating beauty and participating in acts of redemption together form a spiritual path.

IMPLICATIONS OF THE DIFFERENT PATHS FOR JEWISH EDUCATION

Why the many paths? Just as each human being is unique, each person's vision of God and relationship to God will be unique. As educators, we are entrusted with the special task of helping each individual find his/her own way to God. Just as educators are comfortable with the notion of different learning styles, so, too, do educators need to acknowledge that different ways of understanding and relating to God exist. Judaism is monotheistic, promoting a belief in

one God, but multi-pathed in terms of reaching and encountering God. This is as it has always been. Our biblical ancestors had different names for God and, therefore, different ways of conceiving and relating to God.

With regard to the classroom, how can Jewish educators help our learners see their world, their religion, their friends and family as reflections of *kedushah,* the holiness of God?

To help learners find their paths, the teacher must first find his/her path. As a teacher, you can begin by answering these two personal questions: What seems to be your path? What is the holy potential to be found in the faces of others, in the wonder of nature, and/or in the traditions/texts of our people? Grappling with these questions may not only help you recognize your personal spiritual path, but it may also sensitize you to how challenging and daunting a process this is, and to the many different ways that people shape their spiritual quests.

It is clear, then, that the task for the teacher is to guide the learner, so as to enrich and encourage his/her spiritual style or path. Sometimes, merely showing the learner alternative ways of journeying can be enlightening if not formative. The teacher might convey to the learner that God is found in the creative works of people as well as in aspects of nature. God is seen in the painting, heard in the song, felt in the touch of a hand, experienced in the fragrance of flowers, sensed in the sweetness of Shabbat *challah.* God is present wherever we find holiness, love, and peace. God is present whenever and wherever we let God into our lives.

* ◆ *

IMPLICATIONS

1. There are many "Jewish" paths to God. Having many paths to God is not contrary to monotheism.

2. Judaism is a dynamic religion, as exemplified by the emergent spiritual paths of people today which are described in this chapter.

3. Understanding a variety of spiritual paths can help individual Jews further their own spiritual quests within a Jewish context.

4. We need to match our teaching about God and spirituality to our learners' spiritual paths, just as we would match our teaching of any subject to our learners' learning styles.

QUESTIONS FOR CRITICAL INQUIRY

1. Which of the spiritual paths that Blumberg describes is most like your spiritual path? What makes it similar?

2. What are the stumbling blocks to finding a spiritual path in Judaism that Blumberg identifies? What are the stumbling blocks from your experience? What helps facilitate a rich and deep spiritual life?

3. What have you learned from others as they journeyed on their spiritual path that has affected the way that you help bring others along on their spiritual paths?

4. Brainstorm an educational activity that links your learners to any of the spiritual paths that Blumberg describes — loyalty and relationships, curiosity and dialogue, etc.

5. What are the techniques that you have used that help a learner — child or adult — discover his/her own spiritual path?

ACTIVITIES

1. Make a time line of your life. Include in your time line: joyous times, sad times, major events or milestones in your life or the world around you, major achievements, times that God was present, times that God was absent, times of certainty about your beliefs and values and times of struggle, any questions about God or images of God that you remember. Represent these pictorially. Then share with someone else, and discuss your path.

2. Make three lists about the things you most like to do. Write down: ten things you liked to do as a child or when you were younger, ten things you enjoy doing now, ten things you think you would enjoy doing ten years from now. What things are common in all three lists? What are you most passionate about? What are the special gifts that God has given you (e.g., scientific ability, creativity, ability to argue, caring about others, loy-

alty)? In what ways do your passions and gifts lead you on a spiritual path?

3. Invite to class people whose passions and gifts have lead them on spiritual paths toward a relationship with God. In particular, invite people who are well regarded in the community and not necessarily in professional Jewish roles.

4. Examine the biographies of people who had special passions and gifts in the areas that they were most interested in. Read these biographies to see how these people's passions and gifts lead them on a spiritual path. Some examples are: Yitzchak Perlman, Albert Einstein, Jonas Salk, Martin Luther King, Jr., Debbie Friedman, Elie Wiesel, Marcia Falk, Justice Louis Brandeis, Rachel Cowan, Steven Spielberg, Rabbi Sandy Eisenberg Sasso.

5. Create a videotape of the stories and spiritual paths of the famous people listed above.

SUGGESTED ADDITIONAL RESOURCES

(Note: The description of paths to Jewish spirituality laid out in this chapter comes from the author's own observations and experiences, although it might be likened to a *midrash* built on some of the traditional Jewish paths to God. Below are some resources that are evocative of one or another of the paths described in this chapter.)

Blumberg, Sherry H. "Jewish Spirituality: Toward My Own Definition." In *Paths of Faithfulness: Personal Essays on Jewish Spirituality.* Carol Ochs, Kerry M. Olitzky, and Joshua Saltzman, eds. Hoboken, NJ: KTAV Publishing House, 1997.

This chapter is part of a book that features many definitions of Jewish spirituality.

———. "Forms of Jewish Spirituality." In *Keeping PACE: 25 Years of Theology, Education and Ministry from PACE.* Padraic O'Hare, ed. Dubuque, IA: Brown-Roa, 1996.

Concentrating on the most common paths

(Torah, Worship, and Deeds of loving-kindness), this article also explores mystical, secular, and non-traditional paths to God. (Originally published in the December, 1992 issue of PACE.)

Julia Cameron. *The Artist Way: The Spiritual Path To Higher Creativity*. New York: Putnam, 1992.

This book contains exercises connected with opening up creativity.

Exodus 31 and 35.

The description of Bezalel, the son of Uri, of whom God said, "I have filled him with the spirit of God, in wisdom, and in understanding, and in knowledge, and in all manner of workmanship; and to contrive works of art, to work in gold, and in silver, and in brass . . . , and in all manner of artistic work. And [God] has put in his heart that he may teach . . . . "

Pirke Avot 5:20.

The injunction that "every argument conducted *l'shem shamayim* — for God's sake, will in the end prove fruitful . . . . "

Pirke Avot 6:1.

Rabbi Meir's description of Torah study as leading one to becoming like a "gushing fountain, like a never failing river . . . modest, slow to anger, forgiving of insults," and that ultimately, "it magnifies and exalts you above all things."

Herbert Kohl. *The Discipline of Hope: Learning from a Lifetime of Teaching*. New York: Simon & Schuster, 1998.

In this autobiographical book, in which the author reflects on his life as a teacher, teaching can be seen as a spiritual path that demands the discipline of hopefulness and optimism.

Parker J. Palmer. *The Courage to Teach: Exploring the Inner Landscape of a Teacher's Life*. San Francisco, CA: Jossey-Bass, 1998.

Speaks of teaching as a spiritual enterprise.

William Zinsser, ed. *Spiritual Quests: The Art and Craft of Religious Writing*. Boston, MA: Houghton Mifflin, 1988.

Based on lectures given in 1987 at the New York Public Library by Mary Gordon, David Bradley, Jaroslav Pelikan, Frederick Buechner, Hugh Nissenson, and Allen Ginsberg, the book presents these writers' perspectives on the art and craft of religious writing.

CHAPTER 6

HEALING AS A SPIRITUAL SEARCH

Kerry M. Olitzky

AFTER MY WIFE SHERYL'S FIRST SUCCESSFUL CANCER surgery, during a routine follow-up visit, the surgeon discovered another lump in her neck — a walnut-size growth that he had not previously detected, or one that had perhaps developed in the intervening period between checkups. Without additional testing, he decided to go ahead and schedule her for surgery. Two weeks later, in the midst of that scheduled surgery, while probing with his surgical instruments, he had difficulty finding the growth. Without the assistance of any chemotherapy or radiation, the tumor was reduced to about the size of a grain of rice. Had he waited a little longer, he suspected that it might have disappeared completely. The doctor was puzzled; Sheryl was not. When he explained to her that the tumor was reduced in size, she replied, "I know. I diminished it myself."

WHY THE SUDDEN INTEREST IN HEALING?

Perhaps with some measure of regret, highly educated, rational people living in this post-modern age, have begun to admit to the short-comings or even misjudgments of building a life (and society) based on a firm conviction in the "messianic potential" of human beings. And we have demonstrated particularly in recent history the shortcomings of our humanity — even in the most deceptively cultured of societies. According to one recent study, the large majority of Americans believe in God's power to heal. This overwhelming interest in God as Healer is clear from the list of new books on the subject. Consider the amount of research that is taking place in laboratories, the dollars spent on alternative therapies, and the establishment of mind-body clinics in major hospitals (many funded by

the National Institute for Health). By adding those who offer alternative therapies to their list of accepted providers, even HMOs are admitting that healing is possible through means other than the standard protocols of medical science. As part of this interest in a healing that transcends modern medicine, a growing number of people have decided to do what many of our ancestors tried to teach us to do — to build a life of relationship (what we call covenant) with God. And it is only in the context of such a relationship with the Divine that a discussion of healing can take place.

This role of building a lifelong relationship with God, learning to live in covenant, is a role for educators as well as clergy. It is a relationship that can be fostered by stimulating a sense of awe and wonder in the young. It should continue all the way through the final stages of life, when we review our lives and come to see them as having served a greater good or ultimate purpose. The lessons in the classroom and the lessons in life need to be directed toward nurturing the soul — fostering knowledge of and a relationship with the Divine. Educators are in a crucial position to serve as spiritual mentors. They can help individuals, families, health professionals, and others better understand how Jewish sacred texts, rituals, and prayer can aid in healing. They can also help people probe their own view of God — and understand the views of others — as they guide them toward a relationship with God.

HEALING AND SPIRITUALITY

Who among us in the all too familiar position of confronting the serious illness of a student or loved one has not been moved to utter a prayer of healing? How often have I found myself — as I am sure you have as well — sobbing uncontrollably in the solitary quiet of a hospital chapel, praying for the health of someone who is struggling for his or her life. Not fully understanding the impact of our prayers, wanting to do whatever we can to help, we reach into the very depths of our being and ask God to exercise healing powers, to reach out, so to say, and heal our loved one. In this selfless act, we put all theology and rational reflection to the side and simply ask God in our own words for healing. And somehow, somewhere, we know that such healing is possible. In our own words, we recast Moses' simple entreaty to restore Miriam's health, *"El na, refa na la*; God, please, heal her please" (Numbers 12:13). In this short phrase, barely containing five complete words, we acknowledge that the power to heal rests within the capacity of the individual to be in touch with the divine spirit. We may not — we may never — fully understand this powerful connection of human and divine relationship, but on a personal level, we certainly resonate with Moses' prayer. It may have been Moses' plea for his sister, but it is a journey of the spirit that we, too, have undertaken.

The world of medical science is well-known for its strictly rational approach to wellness. Yet, it is beginning to open up to the possibilities inherent in alternative or complementary medicine, as this field is also called. The Rabbis have known about these possibilities for a long time. Jewish sacred literature is full of examples from the Rabbis' own lives and the lives of the people they served. Although Rabbis may have a greater familiarity with the prayers of our people, their pain and suffering is no less real — and their desire to bring healing no less urgent. According to Rabbi Eliezer, the short, sweet prayer of Moses on behalf of Miriam should be a model for all our prayers of petition (*Berachot* 34a). In times of real prayer, there is no need for verbosity or patronizing, no need for the fixed prayers which mark our tradition — though they have their place, and indeed have sustained our people through its many years of wandering. The utter-

ance of our prayers, however framed, constitutes a statement of faith, a belief in our ability to call on God's power to heal.

A HEALING GOD

Like most teachers, I have many doubts and plenty of questions regarding God, particularly at times of illness and misfortune. (As part of an exploration of God as Healer, we also have to consider the question of why the righteous suffer.) But belief in God informs what I can affirm about God's role in healing. It is this struggle that has guided my exploration as a teacher and as a student of what may be called a theology of healing. Ultimately, regardless of the specified dimensions of one's belief, faith in God is indispensable to healing.

Reward and Punishment

I was raised with a rather traditional concept of reward and punishment. I suspect that most people were, particularly if they attended a synagogue school in North America. This idea was constantly emphasized by my own parents and teachers. It is cited in one form or another throughout biblical literature by a variety of personalities. Isaiah said it most effectively when he wrote: "Tell the righteous it shall be well with them, for they shall eat the fruit of their deeds. Woe to the wicked, it shall be ill with them, for what their hands have done shall be done to them" (Isaiah 3:10-11). There is no doubt that Isaiah believed that all Israel would be rewarded for their righteous behavior and punished for their wicked deeds. As a result, this became an essential ingredient of his message to the people.

I'm convinced that most of us would be satisfied were the wicked punished and the righteous rewarded in this straightforward way, because most of us presumably believe that we would be counted among the so-called righteous. Indeed, even those of us who have doubts about this worldview still try to apply it to the world we see. How often do we hear about some student or colleague who seems undeservedly to be punished continually? Too many of us are aware of people in our school community who have been through a period of bad times (loss of job, a divorce, the tragic death of someone they love) only to find themselves struggling at a later point with a serious illness. Some will call it bad luck, others will try to rationalize the reasons behind it, but some will ask the profound question, "What did he or she do to deserve all this?" The Rabbis of the Talmud considered the same question and advised: "When a person sees suffering come upon him [or her], he [or she] should examine his [or her] ways (*Berachot* 5a). We may never discover a reason for a person's suffering, but we have to be unafraid to search for it, even outside traditional parameters. Illness can teach profound lessons about life and our relationships with others if we are willing to "listen to the disease."

This approach will not satisfy everyone. Perhaps that is why the Rabbis came along and modified the equation of reward and punishment somewhat from what the Bible specifically taught. They sought an explanation for what they experienced in their own lives. By introducing the notion of the "next world" (an afterlife), they suggested that reward and punishment are not restricted to this world. Instead, when considering the balance of good and evil in the world, we must look at this world *and* the next. As a result, some contemporary Rabbis have sought to address the issues that they deemed unsatisfactorily answered by their predecessors while still pursuing the role of the God as Healer.

When I was a child, I like others thought that God was capable of doing anything. It is what my parents taught me, and this idea was reinforced by my own teachers who tried to direct my early religious education. After all, they taught that God created the world and all that is in it. Each year, we relearned the story of Noah in Religious School. As we read the book of Genesis, I was instructed that the world moves from paradise to corruption, all as a result of the actions of humans. It seems as though God had no choice but to destroy the world and every-

thing and everyone in it. As a Religious School student, I reasoned: If God could destroy the entire world, God could easily get rid of me. While this notion was easy to accept when I was young, it became increasingly difficult to affirm as I grew into a rebellious adolescence and beyond.

I began to reexamine this story, together with others that I had learned. I thought, if my parents and teachers had taught me this particular idea that appeared untrue, then the many other things that they taught me must also be false. So along with other members of my peer group, I rejected most of the traditional values of my childhood, and did not revisit them until adulthood. Yet the idea that God would punish me for what I was doing continued to unnerve me, because I realized that some of those teenage pranks might actually have been deserving of punishment. And I knew in the depth of my being that there was more to this question of reward and punishment.

A Limited God

Rabbi Harold Kushner answered some of these concerns in his bestseller, *When Bad Things Happen To Good People.* Kushner's personal experience helped him understand what God may and may not be capable of doing, regardless of what we may ask of the Divine. In his read of Jewish history, divine intervention is not the paradigm that has been suggested by the experience of our ancestors. Instead, he suggests that God is only able to suffer along with us (which God has done with the Jewish people throughout history), and he concludes that God cannot do anything to change natural events in the everyday world. He gives us license to believe in a compassionate and benevolent God who may not be able to cure the sick directly, but who "heals" us nonetheless.

God As Separate from Nature

Rabbi Harold Schulweis addresses the same question, but reaches a different conclusion. Schulweis believes that God and nature are not the same. Instead, he maintains that our only option is to classify nature and its implications as secular (*chol*) and morally neutral, separate from God. This approach frees us from the inclination to defend God for each natural disaster or personal illness. This approach does not place limits on God. It posits that nature is neither hostile nor unfriendly to the moral universe, but rather, is totally irrelevant to it. Schulweis echoes these words of the Rabbis, "The world pursues its natural course and stolen seed sprouts as luxuriantly as seed honestly acquired" (*Avodah Zarah* 54b).

A Golden Mean

In her own attempt to come to grips with a theology of healing, Rabbi Nancy Flam applied the notion of a golden mean — the midpoint between two extremes, as a way of establishing balance in life. Out of her years of experience working within the healing community, she has frequently seen the direct manifestation of Schulweis's theology. Acknowledging the two opposing attributes of God, typically labeled as *din* (usually translated as "justice") and *rachamim* (usually translated as "mercy" or "compassion"), she suggests that the idea of *din* as the meting out of divine judgment is misunderstood. Rather than seeing *din* as the harsh imposition of justice — which the Rabbis say reflects the nature of reward and punishment — Flam understands *din* to refer to an imposition of limits that know no moral boundaries. Like nature, limits have no relationship to morality. Illness and disease emerge within the limits of the physical world. Since the physical world (and its natural limits) was created by God, illness and disease are indeed linked to God as their source, but they are not the result of punishment for a person's deeds.

While illness is an expression of *middat hadin*, according to Flam, healing is its opposite and keeps it in balance. Healing is an expression of *middat harachamim*, also God's creation. (Note that *rachamim* derives from *rechem*, womb, in order to emphasize its relationship to a Creator God, as well.) This *rachamim* makes it possible for us to live within the reality of *din*. It is the Jewish impulse to add *rachamim* so that it overcomes *din*, whether by personal prayer or by those who are charged with the physical care of the body. By seeing the potential balance of *din* and *rachamim* in our lives, we may be better able to recognize God at all times, especially in the context of our illness.

A God beyond Our Comprehension

There is much that we cannot comprehend about God or the plan that God has for all of us. Some scholars believe that God is beyond human understanding so that any attempt to try to understand God or even reach God is presumptuous.

God was as inscrutable for the characters who struggled with the Divine in the Bible as God remains for us. The classic tale of suffering in the story of Job illustrates the theological paradox of unexplained suffering with one addition: we learn at the outset that Job is a good person, undeserving of punishment. We know that Job's friends are wrong when they suggest that Job must really deserve his punishment. If they took an alternative position, they would have to argue that God is malevolent, as the Book of Job presupposes God as all-powerful. Job simply resigns himself to living in an unfair world since there is no mediation with regard to God. He believes that rather than being malevolent, God is simply beyond comprehension. Many of us have chosen to resign ourselves to that position as well. Yet, the idea of prayer or contrition as a mechanism that can influence divine decision suggests that mitigation with regard to God is indeed possible. Nevertheless, the message that emerges from the classic story of Job is confirmed in our everyday life. God is unknowable and beyond our human ability to understand.

FINDING A THEOLOGY OF HEALING

Trying to find a theology of healing that makes sense in the post-modern world presents us with a paradox. While science informs much of how we navigate the world, we have come to understand its shortcomings. Today, we learn that religion is more helpful in unraveling the mysteries of the world. Among other things, we have learned that the existential questions we ask are often more important than are the answers that science provides. It seems to be part of the human condition to be simultaneously rational and meta-rational. Thus, our beliefs about God and healing should be constructed along a progressive continuum that reflects the various stages of our suffering and our faith. We experience different facets of God as we move throughout our lives, and our belief in God changes as we progress through these experiences. Similarly, we confront different aspects of God as Healer as we move forward on our path toward healing. Thus, our theology of healing changes, as well. Our journey is dynamic. As a result, so is our theology. There are times when we keenly feel the power of God's healing presence. It may overwhelm us, filling us with awe and dread. At other times, God seems distant and remote. It appears as though God is disinterested in the world and disconnected from our individual human lives. In part, this sense of alienation and estrangement is the price for living at this juncture in history.

The philosopher/theologian Martin Buber argued that evil may be defined as the absence of relationship and direction in our lives. Since the model for all relationships should reflect the one we establish with God, we can potentially combat the evil of suffering by developing relations with each other and with God. Such a process will help us recognize that we are never alone: God is always there alongside us wherever we go, whatever we are forced to confront in our lives. This will bring the healing presence of God to our midst, bringing healing to the body through the soul.

The Meaning of Illness and Healing in Jewish Tradition

Since Judaism is more of a religion of this world than it is a religion of the next, Jewish spirituality is a spirituality of the mundane as much as it is of the transcendent. Thus, it is not surprising to find that Jews look to illness as a spiritual teacher rather than relegating it exclusively to a challenge of the body that needs to be defeated and vanquished. Judaism teaches that we should embrace illness as a part of who we are, since it is an integral part of the world in which we live. As a result, I believe that Judaism teaches us that one suffers spiritually through illness only when we cannot find meaning in it. When we can find meaning in our illness, suffering is overshadowed, and we are in a better position to find spiritual healing at the same time.

The Human Dimension

For me, the actual experience of illness is more important than any theoretical construct in Judaism. It is the human experience that matters, not the theological constructs that may be found in the classrooms of Jewish theology. However, as a teacher I feel compelled to confront God as the source of suffering in a theoretical framework of a sound theological system. If I acknowledge God as the source of all life as I do, I am more inclined to engage God as a healer. But what is most important is how Judaism considers the individual who is ill — and then helps him or her to galvanize personal resources in order to ameliorate the suffering.

Spirit is the bridge between mind and body that makes us human. As a result of our illness, we may not be able to stand upright in order to praise God — or do anything else. Because of the heavy burden which a serious illness lays on us, we may not even have the desire to stand upright, and may resist praising God even when we are able to. However, the daily recitation of these prayers helps pave a path toward healing. It offers a prism through which to view our entire day and forces us to assume a posture that might otherwise be overlooked in our quest for healing, the alliance between the body and the soul. I find these moments in the morning when I stand alone with God to say my morning prayers to be among the most powerful in the day, much more significant than the afternoon or evening service, or even the proclamation of the "*Shema*" before lying down to go to sleep.

Spiritual Sickness

Illness represents a state in which a lack of spirituality negatively impacts on the physical well-being of the individual. Sickness can ensue when the non-sacred side of one's life dominates and smothers the other side, potentially severing one's connection with God. The writer of Proverbs asks, "One's spirit strengthens oneself in one's illness, but who will lift up a broken spirit?" (Proverbs 18:4). The Malbim (Rabbi Meir Leibush ben Yechiel Michel) offers an answer: "It is the spirit that sustains the body. And even if there is sickness in the body, the spirit has great enough strength to support the illness, giving them strength to bear [the illness] and renew their courage. But if the spirit is broken [referring to spiritual sickness] who will lift it up? For then the sickness will affect the body, too, as it is written, 'A depressed spirit dries the bones'" (Proverbs 17:22). *Metsudat David* adds this explanation: "But when the spirit is broken by sadness and depression, who will lift it up? For the body does not lift it up to strengthen it; rather, it is the spirit that supports the body."

Remembering God

In the midst of illness, it may be hard to remember how you felt before getting sick. Dr. Herbert Benson, a well-known leader in alternative or complementary medicine, suggests that the key to healing is to get the body and spirit to "remember (its) wellness." He works with his patients to achieve this. Dr. Benson argues that if we can get ourselves to remember what it was like to feel healthy before becoming ill, we will then be able to move ourselves in the direction where healing takes place. At the same time, we have to block out everything that might prevent us from doing so. No negativity, no pessimism are allowed; only positive thinking. While this

idea is still controversial in the medical community, it remains as a leading idea in the area of medical healing. But what of the spiritual side of this "remembered wellness"?

I believe that the key to remembering wellness, as per Dr. Benson, is to recall this original relationship with God. Here's how it works. I believe that all Jews possess "historical memory," the collective experience of the Jewish people that dates back to the Covenant at Sinai. If so, regardless of whether or not they have ever accessed it, even if it has receded deep into the unconscious, then it may be possible to reach back into that memory and "remember" it. Pregnant women understand this idea rather well. One friend told me that when she was pregnant, she kept misjudging how much room she would need to pass between two people or objects. She would constantly bump her belly into things, because she "remembered" her size before she was pregnant.

This is what the Passover *Seder* attempts to accomplish in the family context. The *Haggadah* for the *Seder* contains a step-by-step guide to help those sitting around the Passover table to reach back and participate in the Exodus again. It offers a model for the entire week of Passover and beyond. The Torah extends this idea, "If you listen to the voice of *Adonai* your God, and do what is right in God's eyes, and listen to God's *mitzvot*, and observe all of God's laws, all the diseases that I put upon Egypt, I shall not put upon you, for I, God am your healer" (Exodus 15:26). For me, this "historical memory" is crucial to healing in Judaism. When we bring the relationship with God to the forefront of our consciousness by remembering it, we bring healing along with it.

Drawing Close To God

Rabbi David Wolpe, spiritual leader of Sinai Temple in Los Angeles and the author of several bestsellers on spirituality and suffering, once wrote, "Suddenly God seems closer to us because we are awake" (sensitive to God's presence and to our illness). Regardless of our mental or physical state, we are all in need of healing. And in order to achieve healing, we have to draw closer to God.

A CURRICULUM FOR HEALING

Drawing close to God involves four elements that are particularly important, especially for those who did not take the opportunity to foster such a relationship prior to illness. Admittedly, these elements are difficult to establish when ill, but they are key to spiritual wholeness and thereby lead to healing.

The first element is study. Divine light is reflected in the study of Torah; it illumines the dark corners of our souls and casts no shadows. If we believe that "Torah is healing to all flesh" (Proverbs 4:22), then we have to provide our students with the tools to explore it, to probe its depth for meaning, to find in it a rhythm for their own lives. As educators, we do not teach Torah in order for our students simply to learn more text; we teach Torah in order to help our students learn more about themselves.

The second is ritual. Ritual brings order into our lives, anchoring us as we travel through the up and down journey of life. According to Rabbi Nina Beth Cardin, Judaism creates spiritual strength through the performance of *mitzvot*. Rituals are the avenue through which we come into close contact with the Divine. With the observance of Shabbat rituals, for example, divine light is brought from the spiritual realm into the physical realm. Shabbat comes weekly, and its observance is considered equal to all other *mitzvot*. Out of Shabbat come special ideas, such as *Oneg Shabbat* (joy of the Sabbath), for with joy comes healing.

Third is the element of prayer. It is our way of communicating with God, of asking God for healing. The establishment of a regular prayer life helps to nurture the relationship with God. But we first have to help people to pray, to learn to pray before we can explore the liturgy. After the habit of prayer is established, then we may teach the words of prayer and explore their meaning. It is at that point that these words can be applied to real life situations, whether it be "*Mi Shebayrach*" during a Torah service or the daily recitation of a healing prayer in the "*Amidah.*" As educators, we have a responsibility to mine the resources of tradition with our students so that they may navigate their way through life toward healing.

Last is the element that combines the others: presence — of God and of others — in the form of community. The presence of persons and God is what the Jewish tradition describes as *bikkur cholim*, visiting the sick. It is this visitation which makes an appreciable difference in the healing of a person. This idea of a social network sounds simple, rather obvious, but too many people are left to endure their illnesses alone. As educators, we can model community in our classroom and teach our students the responsibility to maintain it. These four elements then — study, ritual, prayer, and presence — are the crucial components to awakening the spirit and drawing close to God.

Sometimes, the straightest route to healing takes us the long way around. Healing does not happen overnight, even when our disease is under control and no longer life threatening. The desert journey of our people taught us how to endure the desert in life for an extended period of time. It is like spiritual DNA. Like the tablets of the Covenant which were said to be written with black fire on white fire, the journey of our people is written with spiritual fire on our genes. It is part of the Jewish religious psyche. It helps fuel the historical memory of the Jewish people. Now we add our personal journey to the collective one of our people. In doing so, our experience helps others to face theirs. As fellow travelers — student and teacher — we make the spiritual trek together.

IMPLICATIONS

1. Times of illness and sorrow may open people to spiritual questions, a search for God.

2. In nurturing a person's spirituality, starting with the needs, questions, and concerns of the seeker is critical in the delivery of learning experiences.

3. Education can play an important role in fostering community, teaching texts that help the individual to experience the Divine and confront life's significant questions, searching for the meaning in prayers, and sharing their experiences with God.

QUESTIONS FOR CRITICAL INQUIRY

1. Olitzky writes: "Judaism teaches that we should embrace illness as part of who we are, since it is an integral part of the world in which we live. As a result, I believe that Judaism teaches us that one's spiritually suffers through illness only when we cannot find meaning in the illness." How is illness part of God's creation? What wisdom do you find in Olitzky's statement? Think about situations in which people you know or you yourself were suffering. What meaning could you find in that situation? What makes it difficult to find meaning in suffering?

2. The author begins the chapter by telling a story about the efficacy of prayer with regard to his wife's illness. From your view, in what ways do you think the soul, heart, mind, and will are stronger than the body/physical being? What do you think prayer can do for those who suffer? for those who care about someone suffering?

3. Olitzky presents many views of the role of God in healing. Which view(s) do you find most compelling? How does this view help answer what is God's role in people's suffering? What answer does this view provide in terms of God's role in comforting and healing people?

ACTIVITIES

1. Participate in a healing service by attending one in your community or by obtaining some liturgy from local or national resources. What are the main images of God used in this service? In what ways, if any, was the prayer service unusual? In what ways did the service connect you to other Jews? How did you feel after the service? Talk to others who went to the service. Find out why they went. What did they perceive as helpful?

2. Create inspirational posters that you think will bring comfort to people in need of healing. Use photos/pictures and sayings from prayers, poems, or other sources.

3. Bring in a grief counselor to talk about loss and about supporting others in times of illness or tragedy. As part of this session, role-play situations, such as talking to a friend about the death of a grandparent or the illness of a parent. Use the views about life after death as vehicles of comfort for those who are bereaved.

4. Read a few selections of texts — poems, Psalms, or other writings — or listen to some songs or prayers that our tradition and/or modern experts have identified. Some good sources for this material are *Sacred Intentions, Restful Reflections,* and *Jewish Paths toward Healing and Wholeness,* the first two by Kerry M. Olitzky and Lori Forman, and the latter by Kerry M. Olitzky (see the bibliography below for complete citations). What does the writing have to say about suffering, healing, wellness, wholeness? What role of God is portrayed in the writing? Why do you think the writing is effective at helping a person heal?

BIBLIOGRAPHY

Bleich, J. David. *Judaism and Healing: A Halakhic Perspective.* New York: KTAV Publishing House, 1981.

This volume provides a straightforward legal treatment of sacred texts related to health and healing, written from the perspective of traditional Judaism.

Brenner, Daniel. *R'fuah: A Guide To Jewish Healing*. New York: CLAL The National Jewish Center for Learning and Leadership, 1999.

This is an attractive, small volume that is very useful. It contains short prayers, texts, and source materials that are designed to be used for situations that require healing.

Flam, Nancy. *When the Body Hurts, the Soul Still Longs to Sing*. New York: National Center for Jewish Healing, 1992.

In the tradition of women's prayers, known as *tekhines*, this is a collection of prayers written by a group of women who long to offer others spiritual uplift based on their experiences.

Freeman, David L., and Judith Z. Abrams, eds. *Illness and Health in the Jewish Tradition*. Philadelphia, PA: Jewish Publication Society, 1999.

Edited by a physician and a Rabbi, this book is a treasury of Jewish source materials on the subject. It provides the reader with texts for any occasion or situation, as well as some guidance on the use of these resources.

Friedman, Dayle A., ed. *Jewish Pastoral Care: A Practical Handbook from Traditional and Contemporary Sources*. Woodstock, VT: Jewish Lights Publishing, 2001.

Jewish pastoral care — an essential activity of Rabbis, Cantors, and many lay professionals — is spiritual accompaniment for people in need. A distinguished group of contributors draws upon the healing resources inherent in Judaism, and presents guidance from the Jewish tradition on responding to people in a variety of situations.

Goldhamer, Douglas, and Melinda Stengel. *This Is for Everyone: Universal Principles of Healing Prayer and the Jewish Mystics*. Burdett, NY: Larson Publications, 1999.

Following a step-by-step method, the authors introduce readers to the universal principles of healing embedded in Jewish mysticism. The book contains both a theoretical approach and practical exercises.

Greenbaum, Avraham. *Wings of the Sun: Traditional Jewish Healing in Theory and Practice*. Jerusalem: Breslov Research Institute, 1995.

Expanding on the teachings of Rabbi Nachman of Bratslav, this book is rich in resources, insights, and inspiration. The author takes the reader through Rabbi Nachman's teachings as they relate to traditional perspectives on healing in the Jewish tradition.

———. *A Call to Live: Jewish Guidance on Healing*. Jerusalem: Azamra Institute, 1999.

This is an insightful online book full of profound resources for those who are facing serious illness. Along with other resources for the journey of healing through Judaism, it is available at http://www.azamra.org.

Jaffe, Hirschel, and H. Leonard Poller, eds. *Gates of Healing: A Message of Comfort and Hope*. New York: Central Conference of American Rabbis, 1991.

This small, pamphlet-sized collection of prayers, meditations, and readings is designed to bring comfort, hope, and consolation to those who are ill, as well as to those who care about them.

Olitzky, Kerry M. *Jewish Paths toward Healing and Wholeness: A Personal Guide to Dealing with Suffering*. Woodstock, VT: Jewish Lights Publishing, 2000.

This book helps readers initiate a new kind of healing dialogue with God and shows them the way to restore their faith and enrich their spirit. By sharing with readers prayers, Psalms, meditations, and rituals — as well as insights from his personal experience — the author helps readers to understand how, when confronted with suffering, they can take steps to heal the soul, a vital counterpart to healing the body.

Olitzky, Kerry M., and Lori Forman. *Restful Reflections: Nighttime Inspiration to Calm the Soul Based on Jewish Wisdom*. Woodstock, VT: Jewish Lights Publishing, 2001.

A collection of short essays, anchored in the secular calendar, fleshed out with Jewish ideas that emerge from the Hebrew calendar, this book is meant to be read at the end of the day to bring peace and relaxation, to calm the spirit and the soul.

————. *Sacred Intentions: Daily Inspiration from Jewish Wisdom*. Woodstock, VT: Jewish Lights Publishing, 1999.

Like its companion volume, this collection of short essays is also based on the calendar. It is designed to give direction and meaningful purpose to the individual as he or she begins the day — and can be considered a companion of sorts to morning prayers.

Wittenberg, Jonathan. *With Healing on Its Wings: Contemplations in Time of Illness*. London: Masorti Publications, n.d.

Featured here are text selections from a variety of traditional and contemporary sources that have been integrated into standard liturgies. In addition, the editor has included select prayers for particular situations, such as before an operation and on recovering from illness.

(Portions of this chapter are adapted from *Jewish Paths toward Healing and Wholeness: A Personal Guide to Dealing with Suffering* by Kerry M. Olitzky (Woodstock, VT: Jewish Lights Publishing, 2000). $15.95 + $3.75 sh/h. Order by mail or call 800-962-4544, or order online at http://www.jewishlights.com. Permission granted by Jewish Lights Publishing, P.O. Box 237, Woodstock, VT 05091.)

CHAPTER 7

NURTURING A RELATIONSHIP TO GOD AND SPIRITUAL GROWTH: DEVELOPMENTAL APPROACHES

Roberta Louis Goodman

INTRODUCTION

A FAMILY DECIDES TO BRING JEWISH RITUAL INTO their daily lives by beginning each meal with "*HaMotzi*." A beautiful sunset inspires a musician to compose a melodic tune. A child is angry at God for her father's illness. A worker driven by a sense of fairness and righteousness blows the whistle on a big business. A parent decides to change jobs and lifestyle in order to spend more time with his family. A college student away from home for the first year finds a mentor in a college professor. A chronically ill senior citizen turns to Tai Chi, Buddhism, and meditation for relieving pain and for spiritual guidance. People of all ages are continuously deriving meaning out of their lives. They are determining how they want to live their lives, cultivating relationships with people, creating their own views of — or dialogue with — God, answering questions about life and death, devising their own value system, forming their views about what is sacred and central to their lives. They are doing this on their own, whether or not we as Jewish educators choose to intervene in their meaning making processes and conceptualization of God. What theories and approaches are available to help us as Jewish educators guide religious growth, nurture each person's relationship with God, and augment their spirituality?

The concept of development has long been affirmed in Jewish tradition. The stories of Joseph reflect how a spoiled, favored child comes to love and provide for his brothers who once sold him into slavery. *Pirke Avot* describes different qualities associated with different ages. The Rabbis recognized that people change over

time. One is instructed not to read the *Zohar* until the age of 40, as a certain amount of preparedness, maturity, and life experience is necessary in dealing with that spiritually challenging text. In biblical, Rabbinic, and Medieval texts, as well as modern texts, the evidence of significant change over one's life is both recognized and affirmed as desirable.

Development is a concept of interest to theoreticians in education, psychology, philosophy, and theology, as well as to practitioners in education and religion. Development implies that noticeable changes occur in a person over the life span. While our society has come to assume that people change in regard to intellectual abilities, physical acumen, social interactions, and emotional capacity, less prevalent is the view that our spirituality and conception of and relationship to God change. A few people interested in human development have developed theories that help explain development in areas of religious life. James Fowler, a Protestant minister and theologian, devised a theory called "faith development"; Fritz Oser, a European philosopher, delineated a theory of religious reasoning. Both theories were influenced by the work of Piaget and Kohlberg.

The purpose of this chapter is to describe the key points of the religious developmental theories of Fowler and Oser and their practical application to Jewish educational settings. Actual activities that can be used to nurture faith development and religious reasoning are included. The chapter is divided into three sections: (1) overview of the work of Piaget and Kohlberg as it applies to developmental theories of religious life, (2) presentation of Fowler's faith development theory and its practical application to the Jewish educational setting, and (3) presentation of Oser's theory of religious reasoning and its practical application to the Jewish educational setting.

PIAGET AND KOHLBERG

The work of both Jean Piaget and Lawrence Kohlberg greatly influenced the work of Fowler and Oser, who adapted some critical concepts from them. These concepts distinguish their work from other popular approaches to human development, such as those of Freud, Erikson, and Maslow. The key concepts that James Fowler and Fritz Oser incorporated into their own theories were: (1) the belief that development is a fundamental, natural process that distinguishes human life, (2) certain types of human development can be described in stages, (3) development is a process that can be discerned and described.

Piaget's Theory of Cognitive Development

Piaget was a Swiss-born biologist who became interested in psychology. Born in 1896, he worked in the Binet laboratory in Paris named for the originator of the early intelligence quotient (IQ) examinations. He became curious as to why children of certain ages tended to make the same mistakes on the IQ tests while older children were consistently able to get the answers correct. Piaget began to inquire into children's intellectual capacities. Through his experiments and observations, he found that children grow in the capacity to understand relationships between objects (Riemer, 1983). At different points in their lives, children develop systems or approaches that have an internal logic to them. At a particular stage in life, their answers to problems and how they come to understand the world is consistent, even though from the perspective of an adult, these might not fully explain the situation. The classic Piagetian experiment is to take two beakers, one that is tall and thin and the other that is short and stout. Fill the tall beaker half way with water. Pour the water from the tall beaker into the short and stout one. Children at the pre-operational stage will consistently say that the tall and thin beaker contains more water than the short and stout beaker.

Through his experiments and observations, Piaget concluded that children's thinking goes through four distinct stages. In general, developmental theories explain the ways in which people of the same stage are similar to one another and the ways in which they are different from people of other stages. In particular for Piaget, each stage is more adequate than the previous stage to describe the relationship between objects. The change from one stage to another is precipitated by the acquisition of an intellectual skill. For example, the toddler's ability to look for objects not in view pushes toddlers from a stage that is based on sensing objects that are present to one in which they can internally represent an object, as through language. This process, called accommodation, means that an element from the environment is incorporated into the system of knowing by forming a new structure, thus altering the previous way of organizing experiences. Assimilation refers to an experience or stimulus being absorbed into existing ways of knowing.

Piaget's stages were sequential and hierarchical, meaning that one moves through them in order. A person does not skip stages or move backwards. A higher stage is considered more adequate to explain phenomenon than a previous stage. Therefore, the previous understanding disappears or is diminished and no longer functions as the way that the person structures his/her cognitive abilities. The stages describe how a person's mind organizes itself. The stages provide insight into the structures of the mind rather than regarding what the person thinks about any particular topic. This structural characteristic gives the stages a universal quality as they encompass people of all cultures, religions, and races.

In Piaget's theory, age is not the same as stage. A person does not automatically grow into a particular stage by virtue of one's age or phase in life. Rather, a person moves to the next stage through interactions with the environment that affect the person's brain and thinking capacity. Most, but not all, children reach Piaget's fourth stage of formal operations. Piaget described no stages beyond this that were generally reached in adolescence. Some of the people who work on cognitive development have since examined the ways in which cognitive development goes beyond formal operational thinking in adulthood.

Piaget was interested in moral judgment. Durkheim was influential in raising questions about moral behavior in the French society in which Piaget lived. Piaget began his studies of moral judgment by observing boys at play. Since the girls often stopped playing when a dispute over the rules arose, Piaget chose to focus only on how the boys resolved their conflicts. Piaget discerned a cognitive progression in regard to how children understand law, responsibility, and justice. Unlike Freud who thought that morality was in the realm of unconscious and irrational forces, Piaget was rationally and intellectually oriented. Piaget saw cognition and affect as developing on parallel tracks in regard to moral judgment (Riemer, p. 43). Piaget's view that moral judgment was a discernible, cognitive process distinguished him from other theoreticians of the time.

Kohlberg's Theory of Moral Development

Kohlberg, who studied at the University of Chicago, was interested in Piaget's work. Although Piaget wrote about moral judgment, it was Kohlberg who furthered the application of the concept of stage development that Piaget worked out — the relation of cognitive development to moral reasoning (Riemer, 1983, p. 45). In the epistemologist's tradition of understanding that the nature of human beings is that they are thinking, intellectual creatures, Kohlberg viewed all human beings, including children, as philosophers. Kohlberg was concerned that theories of the time that explained moral judgment led to moral relativism. He found problematic

theories that attributed moral judgment to a product of early social learning or unconscious processes, as did Freud. He felt that moral reasoning must be connected to action, thereby connecting thought with feeling. Furthermore, these other theories were unable to explain how people resolved value conflicts, which is a central concept in moral reasoning (Riemer, 1983).

Kohlberg, who spent his career as a professor of education at Harvard, wanted to understand how one can educate people toward creating and sustaining a just society. He was fascinated with the *kibbutz* as a social collective that supported a community predicated on justice and equality. His concept of the just community and the just school was influenced by the life story and work of Janusz Korczak. Korczak, who died in a concentration camp with "his children," was the director of an orphanage during the Holocaust. He was an educator and popular Polish radio personality whose work in the orphanage modeled a way of teaching children to act with righteousness and kindness toward one another in the formal classroom and in their day-to-day living situations. Kohlberg's efforts were focused on applying his theory of moral judgment to educational settings and schools in particular, as well as on refining his theory. Kohlberg recognized that the hypothetical dilemmas he created and the dilemmas that emerge in the day-to-day interactions at a school were the material for creating a learning environment in which moral judgment could be nourished and flourish.

Kohlberg conducted his early experiments with boys and Harvard students (all males at the time); that led to the formation of his theory on moral development. Kohlberg presented the students with hypothetical situations that described moral dilemmas. The respondents had to indicate what they would do in the situation. Perhaps his best known dilemma is the Heinz Dilemma. This dilemma presents a situation in which Heinz's wife is going to die unless she receives some medication. The drug is so expensive that the only way Heinz can obtain the drug is to steal it. The question posed is: if you were Heinz, would you steal the drug? Why or why not? The responses are analyzed not so much for the content of what the respondents have to say, but rather for how they go about presenting their argument justifying their choice.

Kohlberg's conclusions are similar to Piaget's theory of cognitive development. Kohlberg found that moral judgment, a person's sense of what is right, changes over time. He identified six stages of development. Each stage was qualitatively different in terms of how people structured moral judgment. As with Piaget, the stages are hierarchical and sequential. Unlike Piaget's theory of cognitive development in which most people attain the final stage, most people never reach Kohlberg's highest stage. Kohlberg's stages reach well past adolescence into adulthood, and his last stage presents an image of a moral individual of the highest regard.

Kohlberg spent a great deal of time doing cross-cultural studies of his theory to prove its universal applicability to people of all countries, races, and religions. In some ways, proving the universality of the theory would have shown that moral judgment was a cognitive capacity and process achievable by all human beings. One implication of this finding was that a just world could be formed and that education could play a critical role in forming it. Tragically, it was on one of his cross-cultural study trips that he contracted a disease that eventually led to his death in 1986.

Application of Piaget and Kohlberg's Developmental Theories To Religious Education

Piaget and Kohlberg have contributed to establishing the notion of making curriculum in a school developmentally appropriate. While Piaget's work is widely influential in helping educators understand the cognitive capabilities of students, Kohlberg's work has important lessons to teach of a religious nature, and his theory is readily adaptable to an educational setting. Kohlberg proposes a theory of moral development and theories of how to adapt moral development to an educational setting. He recognizes

the centrality of hypothetical and actual situations in which values are in conflict as a key to nurturing and shaping moral development. Furthermore, he postulates a vision of justice in living models of a just school and just community toward which one can aspire.

Kohlberg's theory, based on a conception of justice, is useful in a Jewish context, since Judaism is a religion in which ethical behavior, following *mitzvot*, and believing in God are inextricably linked. Piety and righteousness are connected in Judaism as part of living in covenant with God. Even God is viewed as essentially just, in contradistinction to the Greek gods, who were well-known for their capricious, amoral behavior.

Kohlberg's work has been adapted for use in Religious Schools, including Jewish schools. Earl Schwartz wrote a curriculum and book (*Moral Development: A Practical Guide for Jewish Teachers*, A.R.E. Publishing, Inc., 1983, o.p.) on adapting Kohlberg's work to Jewish texts for use in a Day School. Schwartz has created a network of schools — Jewish and Christian Day Schools and public schools in the Twin Cities — that strive to create a just community within a school. He also created a *Va'ad Din*, a court, at the Talmud Torah of St. Paul Day School, to which the students can bring cases involving conflicts between students or even between a student and a teacher. Fifth graders spend a year studying Rabbinic texts related to common types of situations in which students in a school might find themselves: lying and cheating, relationships with peers and teachers, and so forth. In the sixth grade, a selected group of students serves on the *Va'ad Din* to make binding decisions resolving the conflicts presented. In addition, the *Va'ad Din* oversees what happens to lost and found items, applying Rabbinic categories and concepts. (See "Three Stages in a School's Moral Development" by Earl Schwartz in *Religious Education*, Winter 2001.)

Despite the seeming compatibility with Judaism, Kohlberg's theory provides insight into only part of what it means to live as a religious person, Jew or otherwise. Piaget's theory is even more limited in its applicability to understanding the fullness of religious life. In many ways, both Piaget and Kohlberg are part of enlightenment philosophy that upholds rationality. In Enlightenment philosophy, reason and rationality are a unifying force in creating a just civilization through righteous laws. Religion is perceived as irrational and a divider of humanity rather than a unifier. The rise of Fowler and Oser's explicitly religious developmental theories in a postmodern society that appreciates the arational, emotive, social, and religious aspects of life is not a mere coincidence. A tenet of Postmodernism is that the Enlightenment, which emphasized rationality, produced the Holocaust. Post-modernism seeks to give credence to other forms of knowing and being while acknowledging and incorporating rationalism as but one factor among many.

Piaget and Kohlberg contributed several things to the formation of Fowler's and Oser's theories: an understanding of the importance of development as an aim of life and education, the connection between development and stages, and the ability to discern and describe development. In the next two sections, Fowler's faith development theory and Oser's religious reasoning will be presented, along with their implications for Jewish education and recommendations of actual activities for each stage.

In the next several sections of this chapter, I will (1) present faith development theory as it helps us understand the process of meaning making, (2) describe a rubric of activities for nurturing faith, and (3) offer suggestions of actual activities for nurturing faith.

FOWLER'S THEORY OF FAITH DEVELOPMENT

About the Theory

Faith development theory was devised by Dr. James Fowler, a minister, teacher, and thinker. He formed his theory from interviews with people of both genders and different ages, from different religious groups, as well as unaffiliated individuals, and from different socioeconomic backgrounds. All of his subjects lived in North America.

Faith development is about meaning making. "Faith or 'faithing' is the process by which a person finds and makes meaning of life's significant questions and issues, adheres to this meaning, and acts it out in his or her life" (*A Test of Faith* by Goodman, p. 1). Faith is common to all people. Yet, we each choose a particular path in pursuing this universal phenomenon.

Faith has a narrative quality. We are continuously creating and recreating a story or stories about who we are. These stories embody our meaning making systems. They reveal to others, and to ourselves, our values, struggles, conflicts, and hopes. These stories guide our daily decisions, life choices, and actions.

Faith formation occurs in relation to others. These others can be individuals, such as family members, friends, classmates, work place associates, youth group workers, Rabbis, and/or educators. Or, these others can be groups, such as a synagogue, team, youth group, school, and/or *havurah*. What Fowler calls "shared centers of value and power" mediate the relationship between the individual and others. These centers of value and power include: trust, fairness, financial gain, possessions, recognition, strength, beauty, integrity, humanism, holiness, and/or God. Fowler identifies God as one possible center of value and power. By doing so, his theory overcomes the split between rationality and passion, religion and secularism, that has characterized the modern era since the Enlightenment. According to Fowler, all people, whether they are atheists or religious zealots, have faith. How we organize these centers of value and power, whether we assign more importance to financial gain than to fairness, or to beauty than to integrity, or to humanism than to holiness, reflects who we are and how we conduct our lives.

Faith encompasses the whole human being, binding together the rational, affective, kinesthetic, cognitive, conscious, and unconscious. Just as faith binds together these components, so, too, these components can be conduits through which faith is nurtured.

Faith changes over time, both in its content and structure. Faith development theory examines the structural changes in one's faith. Fowler outlines six "stages of faith" which describe people's faith (see below). Although our formal schooling may end, faith, or meaning making, is a lifelong process. The choice, perhaps the obligation, is for us as educators to intervene in people's meaning making processes. We have an important role to play in nurturing faith. By understanding how people construct their faith, we can better address their needs in this area.

The Stages of Faith

Faith development is similar to other theories, such as those of Piaget and Kohlberg, in that there are stages to the process. Fowler outlines one pre-stage and six "stages of faith." These stages are sequential and hierarchical, meaning that one goes through them in order. People do not skip around from one stage to another. A higher stage is considered more adequate than a lower.

The faith stages are structural. The stages tell how people structure their meaning making system. The stages reveal little if anything about the content of each stage. Their structural orientation gives them their universal quality as they encompass people of all religious groupings. We do not go through faith stages in the abstract. We each pursue a path filled with particular ideas, beliefs, experiences, practices, symbols, rituals, and customs. Stage 3 Catholics and Stage 3 Jews share a way of organizing, presenting, discussing, and thinking about their lives, irrespective of the content. In the same way, a concrete operational thinker who is Mexican-American and a concrete operational thinker who is Anglo-American think about the math concepts of sets or addition similarly.

Age is not equated with stage. A person *develops* stage structures, rather than *grows* into a particular stage automatically upon reaching a certain age or phase in his/her life. Therefore, not everyone goes through all six of Fowler's stages. Most people get through at least Stages 1 and 2. Few reach Stages 5 and 6.

The stages of faith are outlined in this chapter accompanied by Jewish educational implications for each stage. Fowler claims that the role of education or of any intervention is not to move a person from one stage to the next. Rather, the task is to fill out each stage. For example, imagine the person who in Stage 1 is not introduced to any Jewish rituals or symbols until she or he is in a higher stage, thus obviously older. This person who lacks an early introduction to Jewish symbols and rituals is likely to feel a void in his or her Jewish upbringing. The introduction of ritual and symbols into a Stage 3 person's life must be done differently from doing so with a Stage 1 person. A Jewish education needs to address a person at every stage of his or her faith development to bring out the richness of our heritage. Different faith issues, transitions, crises, and dangers can arise at each stage. The stages of faith help us appreciate the importance of lifelong Jewish education.

Pre-Stage: Undifferentiated Faith or Primal Faith

Fowler calls this a pre-stage because it is essentially kinesthetic, and non-verbal or "pre-talking." This pre-stage focuses on trust and mistrust. The infant develops a sense of routine, ritual, and mutuality through feeding, dressing, bathing, and sleeping. The interaction between caretaker and child establishes a foundation for images of God.

Stage 1: Intuitive Projective Faith

The use of language and symbols to communicate about objects and experiences signals the onset of Stage 1. A Stage 1 person is self-centered: the world revolves around him or her. Individuals view their perspective and that of others as the same.

At this stage, emotions are central and intense. Individuals have a great sense of mystery, awe, and fear. These underlie their views of God. The ability to think logically is not present. They often do not distinguish between reality and fantasy. This gives free reign to the imagination. Life has an episodic and mysterious quality to it. Rituals create an alliance between the moral and the sacred. One obeys out of a desire to avoid punishment.

Jewish Educational Implications for Stage 1

As Stage 1 individuals are just learning the names of things. Their new verbal capabilities provide an opportunity for introducing Judaism's culture code. They will as easily learn a Hebrew word or expression as an English one. Stage 1 individuals are open to the mysteries of rituals, symbols, stories, and prayers. When talking about symbols, remember to have concrete examples present. Stage 1 individuals flourish on repetition and routine. Their views of God can be quite anthropomorphic. God is a wonderful topic for discussion with those who are at this stage. Their desire for playing and pretending makes them receptive to a variety of experiences through role-playing and imitating others. They enjoy fairy tales. As their comprehension of stories is episodic, do not overemphasize the importance of sequencing of events. Although you as teacher may distinguish between Bible stories and *midrash*, between what is in the biblical text and what is not, making such a distinction is superfluous to this stage.

Stage 2: Mythic Literal Faith

The emergence of concrete operational thinking that includes the ability to distinguish between reality and fantasy generally stimulates the transition to Stage 2. Stage 2 individuals are able to differentiate their perspective from that of others. Life is linear and predictable. Narrative or stories which have a beginning, middle, and end, as opposed to the episodic quality of the previous stage, become a favored way of grasping meaning. Stories of "my" people give an individual a sense of identity. Stories are understood literally. Meaning is both carried and trapped in the narrative. This stage can be self-righteous. Prejudice emerges at this stage.

Symbols are one-dimensional. Stage 2 individuals take pride in participating and helping in the celebration of holidays and life cycle events, or in performing acts, as with the *mitzvot* (com-

mandments). Events have a cause and effect relationship. Good is rewarded and bad is punished. A reciprocal fairness emerges. God appears to be like a consistent, fair, and caring ruler or parent.

Jewish Educational Implications for Stage 2

The sequencing of stories is important to this age group. They can tell the difference between fairy tales and true to life stories and between the biblical text and *midrash*. The stories of their people, especially their heroes and heroines, provide a source of pride and connection for this stage. Their interpretations of texts are still very literal. They can grasp a tremendous number of details and concepts. They can understand a concept like *Hachnasat Orchim* (welcoming strangers) in a literal way through concrete examples.

Although some of the mystery and awe of symbols is lost in this stage, individuals at Stage 2 do enjoy participating and assisting in rituals or celebrations. This comes in part from their desire to please authority figures, such as parents or teachers. They respond to the images of the good emulated by adults. *Mitzvot* provide a tangible and concrete way of enacting behaviors that authority figures and the community value.

Stage 3: Synthetic-Conventional Faith

The emergence of interpersonal perspective taking, the ability to see another person's perception of oneself — the preoccupation with looking at oneself in the mirror, often signifies the beginnings of this stage. How the person appears to others is all absorbing. At this stage, an individual can construct the interiority of oneself and of others. Identity and meaning are functions of roles and relations, yet not held in critically reflective ways. Approval and acceptance from others is sought and valued. Authority is external, coming from the group or selected authority figures, rather than from within oneself. This stage often involves the formation of a personal relationship to an authority figure other than parents — youth group leader, Director of Education, Rabbi, coach, teacher, gang leader, or cult leader. Those at this stage are susceptible to the loss of self to the group, as with gangs, and to total commitment to an authority figures, as with cult leaders.

Formal operational thinking, the ability to think abstractly, emerges at this stage. With that capability comes a sense of the future and an awakening to death. Values and beliefs are tacit and unexamined. These values and beliefs are often fleeting and piecemeal, unsystematic. Sometimes individuals at this stage get stuck in seeing the world and themselves in one way; they fail to imagine alternatives. Symbols are evocative and reflect one's identity. Wearing a *chai* or *Magen David* is one example. God is perceived in mainly interpersonal terms: God as friend, the One who knows and understands me.

Jewish Educational Implications for Stage 3

Stage 3 individuals have the ability to think abstractly, which leads to contemplating their futures, and brings out fears and concerns about: death, messiah, the afterlife, their contribution to society, taking responsibility for their lives and destinies, suicide, making life meaningful, the sacred and the profane, and God. Although capable of thinking abstractly, Stage 3 individuals are neither systematic nor systematized thinkers, nor are they particularly critically reflective. When presenting or discussing these topics, getting the Stage 3 individual to raise questions, see options, and think through statements is essential. In terms of options, the Stage 3 individual who rejects God as an old man with a white beard needs to be shown that our views change and that other views of God exist.

Getting Stage 3 individuals to think critically is tricky because they are sensitive to how others perceive them. They have a tendency (1) not to express any opinion, or (2) to get stuck making some outrageous pronouncement that they feel compelled to defend. As a preferable alternative to "attacking" one of their viewpoints, take a text or statement of an unknown party, and critique it. Until they become comfortable or trusting of the instructor and their classmates/study-mates, they may be slow to open up to criticism of their views. It is crucial to provide opportuni-

ties for creative writing, expository writing, journal writing, or art, with the assurance of acceptance rather than critique.

At this stage, individuals search for a personal God. God has an immanent quality of knowing one and caring for one. Hasidic tales are a favorite of this stage, as they present a close and caring personal relationship to God. This stage is often marked by an acknowledgment of the unfairness of a God who allows children to die of cancer or hunger. Stage 3 individuals struggle with ideals and realities, and can be opened to the complexities of life and God.

Stage 4: Individuative — Reflective Faith

Clashes with and exposure to other value systems lead to the formation of Stage 4. The individual becomes critically reflective of his/her own ideas and views, and those of others. The meanings behind (the why of) symbols and rituals become important while, at the same time, these symbols and rituals lose their evocative power and their mystery. Stage 4 individuals construct systems or theories of belief and meaning which must be internally consistent and defensible. Views become explicit. This stage tends toward rationality and individuality, and may result in a display of overconfidence in critical thought and in the rational, conscious mind.

Membership in a group or organization results from an individual's choosing. The individual takes responsibility for and control over his/her commitments, lifestyle, beliefs, and attitudes.

Jewish Educational Implications for Stage 4

Stage 4 individuals look for systems of thought. So they are receptive to reading or learning about the works of a Buber, Heschel, Maimonides, and so forth, on far ranging topics, such as forgiveness, *tzedakah*, and God. They construct their own theology or philosophy of Judaism and life. Introduction of texts on issues relevant and useful to their lives, such as biomedical ethics, business ethics, caring for the elderly, and the like, can influence their actions as they carry out their daily responsibilities.

Stage 4 individuals hold up the standards of scholarship or scientific works, whether of electrical engineers or philosophers, commonly found in the university. They judge these religious or theological systems on the basis of internal consistency, truth, insightfulness, and presentation. They freely critique and reflect on the meanings expressed by others and themselves.

They develop explanations for their actions, for their adherence to ritual and traditions. Their search for answers and understanding motivates them to learn. "Why" needs to be explicitly answered for them — why do we light two candles on Shabbat? Why do we recite blessings over four cups of wine? etc.

Stage 5: Conjunctive Faith

Dissatisfaction with the flatness and sterility of the orderly meanings and systems that one serves and a recognition of the complexity of life can lead to transition into Stage 5. This stage brings a second naivete, a receptivity to symbolic power reunited with conceptual meanings. This provides an opportunity for introducing and experimenting with new rituals. Multiple names and metaphors for the holy emerge. Experiencing God goes beyond the rational.

An awakening to life's paradoxes and an openness to discovering new meanings from strangers or those unlike oneself occurs. Life is dialectical. The language is of "both" rather than "either/or." Stage 5 individuals show an uncertainty, a doubting. This stage is multi-systemed. Stage 5 individuals tolerate differences and inconsistencies which have implications for realizing *K'lal Yisrael*. The tolerance of Stage 5 can lead to passivity, inaction, cynicism, and complacency.

Jewish Educational Implications for Stage 5

Stage 5 presents the possibility for awakening to and active experimentation with new rituals and traditions in the home and synagogue. Exploring and uncovering deep and rich meanings of symbols and observances can enrich the lives of Stage 5 individuals. God, holiness, the mystery of life, spirituality, and mysticism are topics of interest to this stage. The receptivity of Stage 5 individuals allows the educator to introduce far-reaching views and writings. This stage presents the opportunity for sharing the worship experiences, customs, and valued writings of Judaism's various branches.

Stage 6: Universalizing Faith

A search for a transforming world vision and the willingness to live that vision leads to this stage. Jewish concept terms for people who are at Stage 6 are *lamed vavnik* (one of the hidden 36 righteous who sustain the world) or *tzaddik*. Few people reach this stage. Stage 6 is characterized by an at-oneness with God, a uniting of self and God. Transcendence and immanence of God are experienced as intertwined. These individuals share their unconditional love and commitment to absolute justice. Particularism, in the sense of feeling distinct or different from another human being, is lost. The experience is of one human family. A social consciousness leads to the loss or detachment of self, as seen with Gandhi, King, and Heschel. God's presence is felt in the presence of these individuals.

Jewish Educational Implications for Stage 6

How do you educate for or continue to stimulate the development of a Stage 6 individual? The entire world, both in terms of interactions with people of all religions and beliefs and all texts Jewish and non-Jewish, is the material upon which a Stage 6 individual draws. In reality, there is no way of preparing one to be a Stage 6 individual. If you think you are a *lamed vavnik*, you probably are not one. Similarly, if you are self-conscious that you are a Stage 6 individual, then you probably are not.

A Critique of the Stages of Faith

Perhaps the most common critique of the stages is the feminist critique of Stages 3 and 4. Fowler presents Stage 3 as a more communal and relationship-oriented stage, whereas Stage 4 is much more individually and independently oriented. Carol Gilligan's feminist critique of Kohlberg (Gilligan, 1982) applies here, too. Gilligan claims that women tend to be relationship and group-oriented, whereas men are more independent and individually-oriented. To claim that one orientation is a lesser stage than another is to make women look morally inferior in the case of Kohlberg's moral development, and, extrapolating, is to relegate women's faith to a lesser form of development.

THE TEACHER/FACILITATOR AND PARENT

Teacher/facilitator and parent are roles which involve transmitting the content of Judaism and nurturing faith, meaning making. Stages of faith can be helpful in under standing how our students/learners and children structure meaning. Often, we structure meaning in ways different from our students. Stages of faith help make us aware of these developmental differences, and can guide our expectations, preparation, and presentation as we teach and preach.

Good teachers overlap strategies for auditory, visual, and kinesthetic learners. In the same way, we need to overlap strategies for people at different faith stages.

In the main, the task is to enrich a person's meaning making processes at a particular stage, rather than moving people from one stage to the next. No educational or spiritual advantage is derived from having people in one stage versus another. The richer and deeper the Jewish experience at each stage, the more our lives are filled with meaning. This approach deepens, strengthens, and renews our commitment to living a Jewish life as evidenced by our actions, values, and beliefs.

A RUBRIC OF ACTIVITIES FOR NURTURING FAITH

The key to nurturing faith is helping the individual make connection between himself/ herself and the array of experiences, symbols, rituals, and texts that Jewish life has to offer. This represents an entire approach to Jewish education. Nurturing faith has a cognitive, concrete, and conscious side, even though it involves the whole person (including the affective and the unconscious). This tangible side of faith makes nurturing faith look similar to teaching other Judaic subjects. Certain activities better fit a faith nurturing approach to Jewish education. Outlined below is a rubric of activities for nurturing faith.

- The Arts: Music, creative writing, dance, sculpture, painting, and all other art forms are implicitly expressive and interpretive.

- Nature: Appreciating nature gives us a sense of rhythm, movement, mystery, power, growth, renewal, and origins. By sensing the mystery and wonder in the world, we discover that the world is more than people. Nature presents a physical reality that parallels a psychic understanding.

- Narratives or Stories, Including Those That Contain Metaphor: Stories model the relationship between God and the Jewish people and the relationships among individuals. Stories show us how we got and get from the past to the present. Stories provide a way of knowing about a whole. Embedded within stories are a microcosm of the Jewish worldview and values. Stories teach without being didactic. They are entertaining. Metaphor allows us to make explicit our perceptions and explore new meanings. With stories and metaphor, we are both limited and freed by language. Metaphor and stories are expressive.

- Symbols, Rituals, and Prayer: Symbols hold past meaning and offer the possibility for new meanings. Through ritual and blessing, we act out the symbolic meaning. For example, sounding the *shofar* on Rosh HaShanah: "The symbol makes a connection between what God commands us or expects, what we as Jews do, and how in the doing, we make our lives special."[1] Prayer is a spiritual, meaning making activity; it too can be taught and processed.

- Experience and the Experiential: Experience draws upon the life one has lived. Experience is important because we are all meaning makers. Sharing something explicitly adds a different quality, and often adds understanding to the experience. The experiential occurs when we try to create or simulate an experience, i.e., crossing the Sea of Reeds. The experiential puts one in another person's perspective, another time or space. The experiential extends one's imagination. It has an affective component. Both experience and the experiential are emotive and whole person oriented; they get on the inside, the interiority of one's inner life.

- Definitions, Descriptions, and Categories: Creation, loving, caring, thanksgiving, and *gemilut chasadim* are examples of categories. Deriving definitions, descriptions, and categories is the work of theologians. This approach closely examines a phenomenon, trying to figure out what something is, striving for common understanding.

- Dialogue, Discussion, and Questioning: Dialogue, discussion, and questioning are the most common techniques used (and often overused) in a meaning making approach. They make the issue public and conscious. They help form understanding and insight. They are essentially inquiry oriented, inquisitive.

MEANING MAKING ACTIVITIES BY STAGE

Following are activities by stage that promote meaning making.

Stage 1: Intuitive Projective Faith

(Note: All activities for Stage 1 are reprinted with permission from "God and Prayer and Faith Development" by Roberta Louis Goodman, in *The Jewish Preschool Teachers Handbook*, rev. ed., by Sandy Furfine Wolf and Nancy Cohen Nowak, Denver, CO; A.R.E. Publishing, Inc., 1991, pp. 139-148. Many activities other than those reproduced here can be found in that chapter. While this book is out of print, it can be found in libraries and resource centers.)

B'tzelem Elohim (In the Image of God) — A Visual Art Activity

Objective: The students will associate the creation of human beings *B'tzelem Elohim* with the responsibility for showing caring behavior.

Activity: An important concept in Jewish theology is that human beings are made in the image of God. This concept is introduced in the creation story. God cares for human beings and, like God, we care for each other. Collect and show photographs of people. Have the preschoolers identify pictures that show caring behavior.

Hospitality — A Story Activity

Objective: The students will practice being hospitable to strangers and friends, imitating Sarah and Abraham.

Activity: Have a "Be Kind To Strangers Day" at school. Invite "strangers" — the elderly, another class, grandparents — to visit on that day. Send invitations. Prepare a program. Act out the story of Abraham and Sarah and the three visitors. Share a snack. Come dressed in biblical costumes.

Performing Ritual Acts

Objective: The students will practice doing ritual acts.

Activity: Play *Follow the Leader* using motions

---

[1] Roberta Louis Goodman, "God and Prayer and Faith Development," in *The Jewish Preschool Teachers Handbook* by

Sandy Furfine Wolf and Nancy Cohen Nowak. rev. ed. (Denver, CO: A.R.E. Publishing, Inc., 1991), 141, o.p.

that pertain to rituals: washing hands, affixing a *mezuzah* to a doorpost, lighting Shabbat candles, drinking *Kiddush* wine, walking to synagogue for services, climbing steps to the *bimah*. Go over what the motions represent.

Music Videos

Objective: The students will interpret key concepts in prayers or songs in expressive and creative ways.

Activity: Learn a song, such as *"Oseh Shalom,"* *"Prayer Is Reaching,"* or *"Hineh Mah Tov."* Sing the song. Go over the words. Discuss how students can act these out. Focus on the main concepts. With *"Oseh Shalom,"* for example, concentrate on how we show that things are peaceful: hug, kiss, shake hands, hold hands in a circle. Sing the song and do the motions. As an option, videotape the production for a real music video.

*Praising God[2]

Objective: The students will discuss reasons to praise God and create a way of praising God through music.

Activity: Introduce the word *"halleluyah."* Go over the parts of the word: *hallelu* (praise) and *yah* (God). Altogether it means praise God. Have the students repeat the word several times, with different emotions and intensity: loudly, softly, lovingly, enthusiastically. Ask students to give reasons that we would want to praise God. Sing a song or two that has *halleluyah* in it. Obtain an audiotape of Psalm 150, which is a *halleluyah* prayer. Using hand instruments mentioned in that psalm — harp, tambourine, etc., play along and dance with the tape. You may want to read the psalm in English and identify the instruments as they are mentioned. Call out reasons for praising God as you interpret the psalm while playing and dancing. Create your own interpretation of the psalm.

Stage 2: Mythic Literal Faith

Miracle of the Week Bulletin Board — Stories and Visual Arts

Objective: Students will find evidence of the mystery of creation and life by sharing pictures and stories of miracles in their lives and surroundings.

Activity: Assign a student a week to come up with a picture or story that illustrates a miracle in their lives or surroundings. These pictures or stories can be photographs, drawings, newspaper stories, a story that happened to them, and the like.

Brachah Busters Scavenger Hunt — Nature

Objective: The students will link the *"Birkot HaNehenim"* with items found in nature.

Activity: The students are given a list of the *"Birkot HaNehenim,"* such as the blessing on smelling fragrant woods or barks, on smelling fragrant plants, on seeing the rainbow, at the sight of sea, on hearing thunder, on seeing a sage distinguished for knowledge of Torah, on affixing a *mezuzah*. Ask students to find evidence of these *brachot*. Be creative, not just literal!

Hiddur Mitzvah Corps — Symbols and Rituals

Objective: The students help maintain and prepare ritual objects for use in prayer services.

Activity: *Hiddur Mitzvah* refers to paying attention to the aesthetic beauty involved in performing *mitzvot*. This activity actually has the students beautify and prepare ritual objects and settings for use. Have the students polish silver Torah ornaments. Dust prayer books, *Chumashim*, and non-silver ritual objects. Set the Torah to its place for the next reading. Straighten up the sanctuary. If ritual objects are on display elsewhere in the synagogue, those, too, can be cleaned.

---

[2]This section of the chapter was originally published in a chapter entitled "Faith Development: A Jewish View" by Roberta Louis Goodman, in *The New Jewish Teachers Handbook.* Audrey

Friedman Marcus and Raymond A. Zwerin, eds. (Denver, CO: A.R.E. Publishing, Inc., 1994). All newly added activities have an asterisk (*) in front of the program name.

God's Top Ten — Stories

Objective: The students will associate a story with each of the Ten Commandments.

Activity: *God's Top Ten* by Goodman (Torah Aura Productions, 1992) exemplifies each commandment by using a biblical or *midrashic* story or a folktale. Throughout each story are questions that help students to analyze the story as they grapple with meaning making issues and try to understand each commandment better.

*Living Our Lives B'tzelem Elohim (In the Image of God)

Objective: The students will examine how famous Jews, heroes and heroines, have lived their lives *B'tzelem Elohim*, in the image of God.

Activity: Create or collect biographies of famous Jews. Discuss how their lives were/are lived *B'tzelem Elohim*, in the image of God. Discuss what makes their lives holy. Develop a list of criteria that describe these Jewish heroes and heroines. Compare and contrast this list with the characteristics of a Prophet (See *Bible People, Book 3* by Joel Lurie Grishaver (A.R.E. Publishing, Inc.). Discuss how the lives of a group of biblical figures who were role models (e.g., Abraham, Moses, King Solomon, Esther, Ruth) were lived *B'tzelem Elohim*. Discuss their relationship to God and what made their lives holy. Create a list of criteria that describe these figures. Compare and contrast that list to the one you made of more modern Jewish heroes and heroines and the one for Prophets. What can we learn from these people about how to live our lives? In what ways do they inspire us and provide models for living our lives? What is most important in life? How can we relate to God? In what ways are you like the modern Jewish hero and heroines, Prophets, or biblical figures? How do you live your life *B'tzelem Elohim*, in the image of God?

Stage 3: Synthetic Conventional Faith

A Metaphor Activity: God Is Like . . .

Objective: The students will increase their under-standing of God's character and being through a metaphor activity.

Activity: Have the students make a list of famous people. Then have them write or answer aloud: God is like [insert name of a famous person] because . . . . Keep doing this with several different examples. Then try: God is not like [insert name of a famous person] because . . . . Compare the two lists.

A Spiritual Interview

Objective: The students will critique an individual's understanding of his/her spirituality and views on spiritual issues, such as: prayer and praying, life after death, God, Israel, finding meaning in life, relationships, marriage.

Activity: One week, the students make up questions on these different topics, then interview a person. Or, before the next week, the teacher interviews the person and provides a transcript. Have two or three students take an excerpt from the transcript on a particular topic (e.g., prayer, God, life after death). The group must be prepared to explain and defend the person's views. Once they are ready, go around the room having one group at a time read their section of the transcript. The other students ask them questions and challenge their views.

An alternative way of doing this exercise is to take excerpts from famous Jewish philosophers/ theologians and do the same thing.

On a third week (if the students are ready), have students interview one another in pairs, using the questions they devised.

Create a Prayer

Objective: The students will write prayers about personal events or experiences that happen in their lives.

Activity: Look at a variety of different prayers: blessings, prayers of thanksgiving, petitions. Make a list of events and occurrences that happen in people's lives for which no particular prayer exists: getting your driver's license, a friend moves away, finishing school, passing an examination, a birthday, travel to a special place, and so forth. Write a prayer or two for these occasions.

Panel on God: Discussion

Objective: The students will hear and respond to a panel presentation on some meaning making issues.

Activity: Invite some important or prominent members to speak on this panel. (No Rabbis, Jewish educators, Cantors, Judaic studies professors, or other Jewish professionals should be on the panel.) Ask panelists to prepare a few minute presentation on their relationship to God, spiritual experiences, earliest memories of God, etc. After the presentations, open up the panel for questions. Encourage dialogue as much as possible.

*Awesome Experiences

Objective: The students will examine the quality of "awe" by identifying awesome experiences in their lives.

Activity: Students write about an experience they had that was "awesome." In the description they include: what happened, who was involved, who was present, where were you, how old were you, and what made the experience "awesome."

Have a few willing parties share these experiences which may or may not be obviously religious in nature. Read an "awesome" experience from Jewish texts, such as receiving the Torah at Mount Sinai, crossing the Sea of Reeds (including Miriam's celebration), and so forth. Compare and contrast the students' experiences with these texts. Develop a list of criteria of what makes an experience "awesome" and "awe-inspiring."

Stage 4: Individuative-Reflective Faith

Tray of Symbols

Objective: The participants will describe their connections to various symbols.

Activity: On a tray or table, place a number of symbols associated with prayers and blessings: *kipah*, *tallit*, Shabbat candlesticks, *challah* cover, *Kiddush* cup, *tefillin*, *shofar*, *Seder* plate, prayer book, Torah, or *Chumash*. In pairs, ask people to give their responses in 90 seconds or less, explaining to their partners why they selected a particular symbol in response to each of the following sentences: Choose a symbol that you are comfortable using. Choose a symbol that you are uncomfortable, or less comfortable, using. Choose a symbol that connects you to other Jews. Choose a symbol that brings you close to God. As a total group, process the responses.

My Own Jewish Book of Why

Objective: The participants will make explicit why they observe certain rituals and customs.

Activity: Around a room, place sheets of poster board or butcher paper with a ritual or custom written on each. (Examples are: lighting Shabbat candles, not eating *chametz* on Passover, affixing a *mezuzah*, etc.) Have people circulate, writing on each sheet, why they do or do not observe each ritual. Give people the opportunity to move around and read the responses. Have a discussion of the whys and why nots of ritual observances. Allow for stories to emerge. Focus on the meaning that people derive from these observances and what barriers may be standing in the way for others.

Using *The Jewish Book of Why* by Kolatch (Jonathan David), introduce a more "traditional" Jewish view as opposed to a personal view of the whys of these same rituals and customs. Discuss the reasons that these practices emerge from the view of Jewish tradition.

Discuss how people's explanations and the traditional explanations of why intersect and diverge.

Pirke Avot: A New Anthology for Future Generations — Creative Writing

Objective: The participants will articulate their views on a number of meaning making topics.

Activity: Read a few excerpts from *Pirke Avot* on

topics that relate to how people live their lives. Create a list of topics with which theologians commonly deal, and add some of the group's concerns: justice, truth, meaning of life, righteousness, *tzedakah*, work, family, education, blessing, and joy. Then have participants write their own "*Pirke Avot*: Sayings of Our Ancestors." Share the writings.

Modern Midrashim

Objective: The participants will create their own *midrashim*, tying today's problems to biblical themes.

Activity: In one paper bag, written on separate sheets of paper, place slips of paper with movie titles with which people are likely to be familiar. In another bag, written on separate sheets of paper, place slips with quotable verses or commandments from the Torah.

In small groups, have each group pull out a movie title and a biblical verse. Give them time to create a modern *midrash*. Have each group act out their *midrash*, connecting the movie's plot or characters to the biblical verse. The movie title and the verse must be recited at some point during the play.

*Favorite Names for God

Objective: The participants will identify their favorite names for God.

Activity: Have enough prayer books and *Machzorim* (High Holy Day prayer books) so that each participant can have at least one. Use a variety of prayer books, both familiar and unfamiliar to the group. Having available some feminist prayer books or books of blessings enriches the experience, too. Give people time to look for their favorite names (*Avinu* — our Father) or phrases (*Ribbono Shel Olam* —Master of the Universe) for God. Have them write about: what the name means to them and why they connect to this name. You can do the same thing for the least favorite names or phrases for God. Discuss people's responses and reactions. Consider how names can influence one's perception, relation-

ship, and connection to God. If possible, prepare a list of names for God with their meanings and history as a handout to take home.

Stage 5: Conjunctive Faith

An Illuminated Prayer Book — Visual Arts

Objective: The participants will each interpret a prayer or prayers from the *Siddur* through the visual arts.

Activity: For ideas, look at some illuminated or illustrated *Haggadot*. Give each person a prayer in Hebrew or Aramaic and English on a sheet of paper that can be cut out. Using various art materials, have the participants create an illuminated prayer page. You may want to arrange the prayers so that you cover an entire service or section of a service, e.g., the "*Amidah.*"

A Spiritual Will — Creative Writing

Objective: The participants will each write their own spiritual will.

Activity: We have living wills and ethical wills, as well as inheritance wills. Ask participants to write their spiritual wills.

Experiment with a Ritual or Custom

Objective: The participants will try out a ritual or custom that is new for them and will report on the experience.

Activity: This activity takes two sessions. During the first session, introduce participants to the idea of trying out a ritual or custom that is new to them. The ritual or custom may be something they want to continue doing, such as Havdalah, or it may be something that they anticipate trying only once, e.g., wearing a *kipah* for an entire day, laying *tefillin*, going to a weekday service, washing their hands before they eat. Have each participate report on his/her experience.

Interpreting Prayers through Modern Dance

Objective: The participants will explore the

meanings and interpretations of prayers through modern dance. (See Chapter 37, "Moving Metaphors for God: Enriching Spirituality Through Movement," for ideas on this topic.)

Activity: Have live or taped music available of five or six different melodies to the same prayer or song (e.g., "Shema" or "Adon Olam"). Sing the prayer or song a few times using a familiar melody. Go over the words. Then sing the song using different melodies. In small groups, play one melody and interpret the music through modern dance. You can use a combination of stretching, motion, drama, and dance. Have the dancers and then the audience comment on what they experienced, saw, felt, and learned.

The Mystery and Majesty of Creation

Objective: The participants will explore the wonder, majesty, and mystery of creation.

Activity: Read the first story of creation in Genesis. Identify the wonders of creation that emerge from this story. Send the participants outside with a Polaroid or digital camera to capture some inspiring shots of creation. Do this even if they are living in urban areas. Come back to the classroom and do some creative writing, including prayers, poems, or acrostics. Post the pictures and writings on the wall. Have people circulate around the displays.

Stage 6: Universalizing Faith

Suggesting specific activities for Stage 6 is complex. As stated earlier, few people are or ever will be at Stage 6, and one cannot be intentionally prepared to be a Stage 6 individual. The deliberate effort of becoming Stage 6 contradicts the loss of self, the at-oneness with the world and God, that characterize the Stage 6 individual. Yet, Stage 6 people continue to grow and learn from others. In this sense, they have become "students." All meetings or encounters with people, and all texts, regardless of their origin, provide sources of stimulation for Stage 6 individuals. To label these experiences and textual

readings as facilitated educational "activities" is too limiting.

SUMMARY OF FAITH DEVELOPMENT

Faith development theory is a tool. It offers us a way of understanding human meaning making. People are constantly in motion, constantly making meaning out of their lives. We as Jewish educators can enter this ongoing internal dialogue, nurturing people's meaning making processes. A meaning making approach to Jewish education will help create responsive and committed Jews.

OSER'S THEORY OF RELIGIOUS REASONING

Fritz Oser is a significant figure for those interested in religious development. He heads a Piagetian research institute at Frieburg University in Switzerland. While Oser received much of his education in Europe, he has done work in the United States, spending time at Harvard, as did Kohlberg and Fowler, and at UCLA. Oser and Fowler are contemporaries in the sense that they both conducted much of their research and initially formulated their theories in the 1970s. Most of Oser's work is in German. Several papers of his have been translated and/or written in English in an attempt to widen knowledge of his work among English speakers. Oser has an interest in religious behavior. He attempts to see if there is a way of apprehending and describing aspects of religious development not captured in other theories of human development.

Oser focuses on the religious judgment of individuals. He contends that a cognitive capacity and scheme exist for religious judgment just as cognitive capacities and schemes exist for logic, moral reasoning, mathematics, and so forth. Religious judgment has to do with "how a person copes with contingencies, gives religious meaning to situations, interprets religious messages, and engages in prayer" (Oser, 1991, p. 37). He is concerned with understanding how people come to know the ultimate environment. Furthermore, he is interested in what religious judgment has to do with religious education. Oser is interested in answering questions such as: How do people perceive God during life situations? What is the relationship between our actions and God's actions? How do people make religious judgments when addressing real-life or hypothetical problems? What are the implications for religious education of focusing on religious judgment?

Oser developed an interview and a series of religious dilemmas to discover if patterns existed in terms of how people structure and present their perceptions. Three major dilemmas were based on core religious issues. In some ways, these major dilemmas draw upon archetypal stories and figures found in religious traditions. The narrative construction of these dilemmas as story mirrors how religions present their traditions and people encounter problems and situations in their lives. All the dilemmas contain explicit religious references and follow-up questions, not to any particular religion, but rather to God's relationship to human beings and the world including issues of theodicy, covenant, free will, and so forth. The three dilemmas are:

1. Paul Dilemma – Paul makes a promise to God in a perilous situation. The question becomes whether or not Paul should keep his promise.

2. Theodicy Dilemma – A "Job-like" situation occurs in which bad things happen to a person. The tension focuses on whether or not this person should continue to believe in God.

3. Chance Dilemma – Is luck a gift of God, a sign of God's loving-kindness? (Oser 3, p. 42).

In developing his stage theory, Oser initially interviewed men and women of all ages in a small Swiss town who had different religious denominations and different social status. Later, he did cross-cultural studies of people from around the world, including many Eastern religions that have no understanding of a God, but

do have a sense of an ultimate reality and environment.

The results of his research led Oser to find that people's religious judgment falls into a pattern characterized by five stages. As with other stage theories, Oser found that these stages are sequential, hierarchical, acquired (not automatic), and universal. People go through the stages in order. A higher stage is more adequate as it is more flexible and complex in its construction of the relationship between God and human beings. Movement from one stage to another is not automatic. The cognitive structures that constitute religious judgment are stimulated through a process of growth, of the life situations that come from leaving home, marrying, going to work, parenting, aging, and so forth. Oser found that these cognitive structures are common to all people, even those of different religions. While the content of people's religious traditions and the ways that people view the Ultimate differ, the ways that they structure their reasoning about religious matters are similar.

Oser's stage theory includes five stages. Each of the stages and their implications for Jewish education are described below:

Stage I

Stage 1 individuals can distinguish between reality and fantasy. Reasons for things happening are explainable by the individual. The individual can attribute what happens either to a person or to God. God's interventions in the world are one-dimensional, usually having to do with reward and punishment. The relationship between God and the individual is uni-directional, with the Ultimate Being acting upon the world and/or you.

Stage I Implications for Jewish Education

God can be quite powerful to the individual at this stage. God is the cause of great, mighty, magnificent, miraculous things, many of which are wonderful and others are tragic. Sharing and discussing stories of the miracles or miraculous in our lives in which God acts alone or in partnership with human beings is one way of nurturing individuals at this stage. Examples of stories could include: Jews leaving Egypt to dwell in the Promised Land, founding of the modern State of Israel, discovery of vaccines. Look for and discuss the great, mighty, magnificent events in your surroundings, e.g., change of seasons, sick child receiving a transplant.

Stage 2

Stage 2 emerges when reasons are found in a means-end scheme. In other words, the individual perceives that another reason beyond the obvious, a hidden deeper meaning, explains why the event occurred. The relationship between humans and God becomes two-directional. Human beings take an active interest in God and try to influence God's actions toward them. Prayers, offerings, following religious rules are ways of influencing the Ultimate Being. God can be pleased by the individual's actions and deeds, thereby assuring and protecting the individual's well-being. Punishment can be avoided. Fundamentally, God wants the best for humanity. God's actions are more predictable and limited under this scheme. The actions and well-being of both God and human beings is connected.

Stage 2 Implications for Jewish Education

Use dilemmas to introduce and teach individuals at this stage the different *mitzvot* (commandments) that one can follow as a Jew. Tell them what the *mitzvah* is, give them examples of how they can fulfill the *mitzvah*, and, if possible, create opportunities for doing the *mitzvah*. Try to find *mitzvot* that have them interact with others and help others. Explore ways in which these actions make the world a better place to live and bring a sense of the holy, of God into our lives. Be certain to examine news about both good and bad things that happen in the world and in their lives. Explore both explanations that are reasonable and unreasonable. This activity is important, as individuals in this stage are susceptible to taking blame for bad things that happen in their lives that are not their fault, such as a child

who thinks that her actions were responsible for her parents getting a divorce, or making connections between two things that are totally unrelated, a child who needs glasses thinks God is punishing him because he punched a friend in the eye.

Stage 3

The idea of a hidden cause and the direct connection between our actions and God's actions disappear. As critical thought and abstract thinking emerge, causality of events in life are seen as the responsibility of human beings and not of divine origination. Human beings have their sphere of influence and God has God's own sphere of influence. The individual takes responsibility for his or her own life and the world, justifying the importance of actions and views on the basis of their significance to the individual. Even with the evident trend toward individual autonomy, some ambivalence remains about God's role in the world. A tension exists between the individual's sense of free will and conformity with God. God is able to help only if the human being allows this to happen. Events that are clearly beyond human control, fate, are labeled as "coincidence," "synchronic" (Jung's term) or "*bashert*" (Jewish term). Other types of behavior, such as promise keeping, are important for the individual and not for God. God's sphere and human being's sphere intersect in the areas of spiritual growth, secrets of nature, and hidden forces in life. The challenge is to allow for growth in individual autonomy while still remaining connected to an Ultimate Being, rather than full rejection of the Ultimate.

Stage 3 Implications for Jewish Education

Use dilemmas with Stage 3 individuals as a way of encouraging them and supporting their efforts to take responsibility for their actions. Open them up to a sense of social responsibility, of the possibility for their actions making a difference in the world. Share the lives of others throughout Jewish history and human history who have followed their convictions, making the world a better place for others. Share with them the concepts and values found in Jewish tradition that relate to their interaction with the world. Study what Jewish sources say about what constitutes appropriate and inappropriate behavior in a variety of situations that parallel their own lives: ethics in the work place, relationships with other people, how we treat our bodies, and so forth. Be certain to discuss how these concepts, values, and behaviors are connected to God and our sense of being commanded. Have the individuals apply these concepts, values, and sources to their own lives and situations in the world today. Affirm their individuality, while showing that God can be a source of inspiration and hope in moments of darkness. Show how their accomplishments and moments of joy are a blessing for us all and for God.

Stage 4

This stage continues the theme of life being based on human decisions. The individual is responsible for his/her actions and his/her character is judged by others and by him/herself based on these actions. What changes is the recognition that human beings are not their own creators and originators. What emerges is a sense that God and human beings must relate to one another for the sake of the good and right in a plan or system for humanity. Furthermore, the individual must reach out to others to make the world a better place, to implement this larger plan. God enters our lives through signs that cause us to reflect. Free will is acknowledged as part of God's plan. Our actions are richer, more meaningful because they are connected to this larger sense of purpose.

Stage 4 Implications for Jewish Education

Work with individuals at this stage at identifying "signs," things that happen to others close to us and in our own lives, that are cause for reflection about what is really important — how we spend our time and what we value. For most

individuals at this stage, there is all too much that brings cause for this reflection, e.g., a business associate is killed by drunk driver, a peer has cancer, or a teen joins a gang. Discuss the ways in which these signs point to an ultimate reality and/or Being beyond ourselves. Examine texts from Jewish sources that show how we are partners with God in creation and in redemption of the world. Raise questions about what is the purpose of our lives. What do we want from life? Explore ways that the individual can immediately make the lives of those surrounding him/her, members of one's family, community, and society better, richer, more whole (*shalaym,* complete).[3]

Stage 5

The divine plan falls away and is replaced by a sense that every person is a unique contributor to the ultimate environment. God appears in every human commitment, yet reaches beyond these commitments, too. One way in which the Ultimate Being becomes part of reality is through the connection among human beings. Meaning is found in the world, in encounters with other human beings, as part of a social reality. God and human beings are in solidarity with one another. God's presence in history and revelation are apparent, too. Contradictions exist in a comfortable dialectic: God is both simultaneously immanent and transcendent — where there is holiness there is the profane; hope cannot exist without absurdity and absurdity without hope.

Stage 5 Implications for Jewish Education

Stage 5 individuals are very open to experiencing God and finding God in their lives and in the world around them. The Stage 5 individual is open to discussing good and the evil, right and wrong, and does not find a need for reconciling these contradictions. These individuals are ripe for discussing religious dilemmas that oc-

---

[3]Related to the word *shalom,* peace.

curred throughout Jewish and human history, as well as more current ones that come from their lives or those of others. At this stage, they are likely to be interested in the societal impact of religious dilemmas as well as the impact on the individuals directly involved.

WAYS OF NURTURING RELIGIOUS JUDGMENT

Oser sees nurturing religious judgment as a critical part of religious education. For Oser, the mere dissemination of information about religion is not a compelling way of conveying ideas about the Ultimate that will affect people's actions, beliefs, values, or views. A passive approach to religious education will not work. Oser uses the three dilemmas mentioned earlier (Paul, Job, and Chance Dilemmas) along with the provocative questions developed for each dilemma as a way of stimulating the cognitive religious structures of the individual. Oser further suggests that new dilemmas be introduced and discussed as a way of advancing the individual's religious judgment. In effect, Oser borrows from Kohlberg the emphasis on using dilemmas, both real and hypothetical, as the way to enrich judgment. Kohlberg used moral dilemmas to assess people's level of moral reasoning, but he also recommended using dilemmas as an educational tool for strengthening moral development.

In describing the implications for Jewish education, I offer suggestions about how to nurture Religious Reasoning for each of Oser's five stages. All of the suggestions in some way involve presenting dilemmas. These dilemmas come from three sources: (1) hypothetical, (2) people's own experiences, and (3) the experiences of others, both current and historical, as found in documents and texts, often presented in story form. In the next sections, I describe these three types of dilemmas, give examples of topics that raise religious or theological issues, provide a rationale of why dilemmas are useful, and suggest ways of presenting these dilemmas in a Jewish educational setting.

Three Types of Dilemmas

Dilemmas are very much a part of life. They involve some type of tension and choice. Often they involve choosing between conflicting responsibilities or commitments. Choices have consequences. More than one "good" response is possible. Religious reasoning encourages transcending one's own experiences and considering ultimate questions about life, God, and the universe. Examining religious dilemmas is important, as doing so can hopefully influence people's ways of acting, valuing, thinking, and believing.

Hypothetical dilemmas are ones that in some way seem true to life, appear plausible, but they are fabricated, never actually happened. Oser uses hypothetical dilemmas to determine a person's stage in his theory of religious judgment. Oser's hypothetical dilemmas help the teacher as well as the learner identify what types of questions or concerns are religious in nature. The advantage of a hypothetical dilemma is that it can engage all people equally in a discussion; all have the same knowledge about the situation. A dilemma can help people think through conflicts that they are likely to confront in their lives. Hypothetical dilemmas can also expand a person's religious judgment overall, even on issues that they are unlikely to confront in their lives. The main limitations of using hypothetical dilemmas is that sometimes they can seem contrived, and one does not have the benefit of understanding how a person's response actually affected their life in the short and long term.

As stated earlier, Oser drew upon Kohlberg's work with dilemmas in forming his theory of religious judgment. Interestingly, Kohlberg's moral dilemmas could be turned into religious dilemmas even though Kohlberg himself never asked the religious questions. For example, the famous Heinz dilemma, in which Heinz cannot afford to pay for an expensive drug that will help his sick wife, the question is asked if Heinz should steal the drug. Justice is the focus, but concepts that are related to the dilemmas that are deeply religious, such as the relationship between God and human beings, the relationship among human beings, caring for others, reward and punishment, conviction, commitment, and the like, are ignored. From a Jewish perspective, concepts such as *Brit* (Covenant), *mitzvah* (commandment), *tzedek* (righteousness), or *hesed* (mercy) that mediate the relationship and responsibility between human beings and God are not asked by Kohlberg either in a specifically Jewish or generally religious way. Kohlberg makes the moral secular in trying to make it universal, thereby leaving out religiously-oriented questions that are equally universal. All moral questions are religious in nature.

The second type of dilemma comes from the person's experiences. These are real situations that a person has lived through. Generally, people have some opinion or feelings about their experiences. They are likely to care in some way about how the situation affected their lives, whereas with something that has not happened to them, they may be removed from or not interested in the incident. The consequences of the choices that people make are also known. With other types of dilemmas, especially hypothetical ones, one can only conjecture about the consequences. The limitation of dilemmas from people's experiences is that they can be very personal and even painful to relate. In addition, examining experiences of others is often easier and therefore better suited to expanding one's judgment than having to reflect critically on one's own behaviors.

The third type of dilemma draws upon the experiences of others, both current and historical, as found in documents and texts or passed on orally. These experiences are often presented in story form, as with biblical narratives and Rabbinic literature (especially *midrashim)*, oral history, biographies, short stories, and books. Primary source material, such as diaries, letters, and newspapers contain useful dilemmas. Dilemmas that emerge from present-day situations create a sense of communal or societal awareness. They can be used to pose a dilemma that a person might confront in life as a way of helping them think through how they will

respond if and when the situation becomes part of their lives. For example, a teen swears to God that she will not reveal her friend's secret. Then her friend relates that she is contemplating suicide. Should the teen tell an adult or keep her promise? When no living will is provided by a relative in a persistent vegetative state, should you discontinue life support?

Dilemmas also can be helpful in furthering identity and connection to one's people. Dilemmas can bring to life the types of questions and issues that one's forebears — family, culture, nation, people, or religion — had to confront. Is Abraham deceiving Sarah by not telling her that he is planning to sacrifice Isaac? Is he being more or less caring and compassionate by not doing so? Is suicide ever acceptable? Should the Jews have elected to kill themselves on Masada? By examining the issues involved in these dilemmas, they convey values and perspectives of those involved. This examination can help connect a person to a tradition, group, or history.

Topics that Raise Religious or Theological Issues

Some topics are better suited to raising religious or theological issues than others. While all events probably could be construed to present some religious dilemma, some subjects are more conducive to doing so than others. Presented below are topics with examples of dilemmas from Jewish history, Jewish texts, and present day life that are well suited to enhancing religious judgment:

- Vows – In the Book of Esther, Mordecai makes Esther promise that she will never forget her origins and her people when she becomes Queen and moves into the Shushan palace as wife of King Ahasureus. Shortly thereafter, the King endorses an edict sponsored by Haman to wipe out the Jews in the kingdom. Mordecai tells Esther that she must act or all the Jews will die. After a period of fasting, a traditional way of showing mourning and supplication, Esther approaches the

King and tells him that he inadvertently is destroying her people. The King changes the edict and punishes Haman. Why doesn't Esther tell the King about her ancestors and people from the beginning? Is it because she hides her identity at first and later reveals it that the people are saved — fate or lots? What does this story have to say about God even though God's name is never mentioned? Is it right to celebrate joyfully as the sons of Haman are killed and their family cursed? Is it ever right to wish for the annihilation of a people (no matter how evil they may be), as with Haman and the Amalakites?

- Forgiveness and *Teshuvah* (Repentance) – In the book *The Sunflower* by Simon Wiesenthal, he describes an encounter that he had toward the end of the Holocaust. A seriously wounded Nazi covered in bandages asks Wiesenthal to forgive him for having killed and tormented Jews. Can you grant him forgiveness? Is God the only one who can grant forgiveness? Should you be concerned about comforting his soul? What about your soul?

- Gossip, Lying, and Deceit – You are on a train from the countryside going into New York City on a Saturday night. An acquaintance of yours from a famous, wealthy family is on the same train. You find out that he is returning home in order to teach Sunday School at church the next morning. He inquires as to the institutions you support. You indicate that you support a Jewish seminary when in fact you have not made a contribution of note. You know that he will check up on your donation. You are concerned about your reputation. On Monday, you call the chancellor of the seminary and offer to make a significant donation to the library. Were you just misleading this noted philanthropist or in fact lying to him? Does the fact that you did a *mitzvah* justify stretching the truth? Is pride, one's reputation, a good reason for giving *tzedakah*, making a donation?

- *Tzedek* (Righteousness) – A very wealthy millionaire makes a donation to your institution that provides services to the homeless. In fact, as part of the agreement for receiving the gift, the building is named for her deceased parents. Shortly thereafter, she is convicted of a federal crime that has to do with how she obtained her wealth. Without that money, your institution will not be able to provide the service. Some of your board members are suggesting that you remove the name from your building, as they do not want to be associated with the person, but that you should keep the funds. Is it right to take her parents' name off the building, but keep the money? Do you return the money to the philanthropist and no longer serve this group of homeless individuals? Does the means justify the end?

- *Sh'lom Bayit* (Peace in the House) – Your mother-in-law insists that you open a gift in front of her. She gives you a gift of something that she obviously likes and would wear herself, but is definitely not your style. As this is a repeating scenario, your husband instructs you to tell her that you like it. Telling her that you don't like it will obviously anger him. Your two young children are present when this happens. You want to be honest with her, yet you are concerned about teaching your children to follow the commandment of respecting their elders. What can you say? How can you preserve her respectability, your husband's love for your mother and you, and your integrity?

- *B'tzelem Elohim* – Each human being is created *B'tzelem Elohim*, in the image of God. No life is greater than another, or is it? The Talmud presents the dilemma of two people stranded in the desert. Person A has a flask of water which has only enough water for one person to survive. What should they do? Should the two people share the water? Can B convince A to pass the water on to him? Should the more important or prominent person get the flask of water? Should the person with the larger family and more responsibilities get the water? Should they even argue, or is it God's choice as to what happens? Is there anything else that they should do to try to survive? Why do the Rabbis prescribe a response rather than allow for A and B to choose who should live and who should survive?

- Observance – You are in graduate school majoring in religion at a secular university with a major seminary on its campus. Your professor is a minister who is also your department head. He teaches both at the university and in the seminary. On the first day of class, he tells you that since your seminar meets only once week, there will be no excused absences. You look at the syllabus immediately and see that class is scheduled for Yom Kippur. Ironically, the class is on Freud, an assimilated Jew, who barely left Nazi occupied Austria in time, even though his friends and colleagues warned him to do so. You have to take the class as it is required for graduation. The program is small and the professor is well aware that you are Jewish. After class, you tell him that you are not going to be there on Yom Kippur. He makes no comment, but he is obviously disturbed with your statement. You are disappointed and angered by his insensitivity to your religion. You wonder how a religious person, a minister, could be so uncaring for your religious practices. Do you drop the course and register another semester? Do you report him to the dean? How do you show respect for his religion even though he has exhibited none for yours? How do you show respect for him even though he shows little for you?

These are just a few topics around which religious dilemmas can be devised.

Rationale of Why Dilemmas Are Useful

Dilemmas are a useful educational tool in expanding and strengthening a person's religious judgment. Examining dilemmas can lead to seeing alternative ways of thinking, feeling, and acting. Often we are trapped in our own ways of responding or in the situation itself. Conversations about dilemmas can help us imagine how life could be different or discover other ways of responding.

The characters or people presented in dilemmas can be role models for how to respond in a difficult situation and how to bring God into our lives. They can model the values that are important in Jewish life. They can be a source of inspiration as we tackle the difficulties that life presents. They can provide a sense of hope and encourage us to be courageous as they show us reasons and ways to praise God even when diversity strikes.

The values embedded in each dilemma, especially those from texts or history, can provide a Jewish framework to guide our behaviors. By identifying and naming these values, they give us a world view, a framework for approaching life. These stories involving religious judgment present the collective wisdom of our people about how to act in this world.

Discussing religious dilemmas can connect us to our history, our tradition, and to God. These discussions give us glimpses into our past, a way of comprehending the significance of the struggles and accomplishments of our ancestors, while at the same time helping us to make sense out of their experiences for us today. The dilemmas can help us discern our purpose in life both temporally and eternally. They can provide glimpses into different ways of knowing and experiencing God.

Ways of Presenting Dilemmas

Dilemmas can be presented in many ways. The most common way is to discuss them using a combination of prepared and emerging questions. Learners are asked to explain the choices that they make, to examine alternative responses, and to engage in dialogue with others about the issues.

The presentation of dilemmas can be enriched by examining texts that present Jewish views on the topic under discussion. Non-narrative texts such as *halachic,* legal Rabbinic texts or *Responsa*, and the wisdom literature, can reinforce Jewish perspectives on a text. For example, the dilemma described above on gossip, lying, and deceit by the Jewish philanthropist who stretches the truth would be enriched by looking at Jewish texts related to the topic. While the questions are provocative, challenging the learners to substantiate their views with values and views from Jewish sources, connects them to their tradition and makes that tradition come alive. Questions also serve to enrich and deepen the discussion.

Helping the learners fully examine the issues presented in the dilemma enriches the experience. Certain techniques can be used to help identify the issues and conflicts, the range of responses, the consequences of the actions, and the values at stake, as well as to motivate the learners. These techniques include: role-playing, sociodrama, mock trial, interviews with celebrities, videotaping, debate, and the like. These techniques are particularly helpful when the dilemma is not one directly related to their experiences.

People's experiences can provide an ample source of dilemmas. One way of helping people identify dilemmas in their lives is through developing critical incidents. Writing or talking about a critical incident is a technique for obtaining data about people's perceptions usually used in qualitative research. In a critical incident, a person is asked to describe a situation from his/her own experience. In terms of a religious dilemma, a person might be asked to describe a dilemma in terms of: who was involved, when did it happen, where did it happen, what happened, what religious questions or issues were involved, how did you respond, and what were the consequences of how you responded? Devising a critical incident enables the person to share his/her experience with others. Then both they and the person can reflect on the dilemma.

These are just some ways in which dilemmas can be used in a learning situation to facilitate the development of religious judgment. The centrality of dilemmas as the means for nurturing

religious reasoning is clear from Oser's theory. More research and work by religious educators is needed on how dilemmas are used actively in an educational setting to augment a person's religious judgment. In any event, Oser has provided a way of thinking about religious development that has compelling implications and potential outcomes for Jewish education.

CONCLUSION

The first verse of *Pirke Avot* describes the lineage of the passing of the Torah and authority from one group to the next. That historical connection is critical to understanding how one approaches the Torah today. Much in the same way, the delineation of the lineage from Piaget to Kohlberg to Fowler to Oser in this chapter is critical in understanding how religion and religious views and concerns have come to be part of the conversation regarding human development today.

Piaget introduces the concept that human beings are able to acquire and learn moral practices as they do other cognitive abilities, such as math, language, and so forth. Kohlberg refocuses the importance of nurturing moral judgment within the individual on fostering justice within society. While justice is a very Jewish concept and Kohlberg is very Jewish in his own right, Kohlberg (as does Piaget), leaves out of the equation God and a covenantal relationship to the people. Fowler is able to restore a place for God and Covenant in the conversation about human development, as well as moral development. Oser provides a way of thinking about issues in religious rather than solely moral terms. Both Fowler and Oser present their theories in ways that transcend the differences among those of different religious traditions. While one may follow a particular religious tradition, the way in which human beings develop, make meaning out of their lives, or form religious judgments is universal.

What the lineage here leaves out are some serious critiques from those who are less certain about the validity and helpfulness of hierarchical, linear, universal, sequential stage theories in describing spiritual development. The feminists, particularly represented by Carol Gilligan, challenge some of the core notions that lead to the order of the stages that favor individualism over collectivism. Some thinkers, such as Gabriel Moran, view religious development as drawing on images other than those that are linear. None of the four stage theorists presented in this chapter addresses the danger and power that comes from marginalizing those who do not fit into what are presented as normative patterns of development. Furthermore, stages tell only about structure; they describe little about that which is perhaps the most important, the actual content and substance of people's religious development — their knowledge, attitudes, skills, and commitments. These concerns need to be kept in mind when applying the work of Fowler and Oser, as well as that of Piaget and Kohlberg.

Fowler and Oser do offer important ways of thinking about how Jewish educators can approach nurturing a relationship to God. I have presented my understanding of how these approaches can be implemented in an educational setting. Many active ways and practical suggestions have been provided.

Three main implications emerge from the theories of Fowler and Oser for us as Jewish educators.

1. It is incumbent upon us to facilitate intentionally the learner's relationship to God. The learners in our educational settings are making meaning out of their lives and arriving at views of God on their own, sometimes with, and sometimes without, any connection to Jewish tradition or texts in the broadest sense. Therefore, educational curricula need to incorporate God explicitly into the curriculum.

2. Just as people can grow through educational experiences in their knowledge and appreciation of art, literature, physics, and the like, so, too, can they grow through education in spirituality. Education can have an impact on the ways in which learners understand and relate to God. We can provide learners with content, experiences, and moments of reflection that will expand their knowledge, and, hopefully, enrich their relationship to God.

3. Filling out each stage matters. The content of what constitutes one's ways of knowing and experiencing God is as important as the structure. Education needs to reach the learner at all stages throughout his/her lifetime in order to help fill out each stage. Our task is to help inform the process of learning about and relating to God, always maintaining humility and respect for each other and God.

IMPLICATIONS

1. We as Jewish educators must in some way help inform people's meaning making processes. It is our responsibility to bring tradition, texts, and learning into the process.

2. Faith and religious reasoning can be nurtured, informed, and strengthened.

3. Development is prized and valued in Judaism. These different theories of development outlined in this chapter fit well with this fundamental value.

4. Development occurs in relation to others. Therefore, community plays an important part in one's development.

5. We as Jewish educators have multiple opportunities for nurturing people's faith and religious reasoning. Care needs to be given as to how programs, sermons, and the like are designed to fill out the developmental stages of the participants.

QUESTIONS FOR CRITICAL INQUIRY

1. If you are a teacher or parent, think of the age and development of your learners/children. How do they fit into the theories of Fowler and Oser? How do the theories of Fowler and Oser help explain the behavior of your learners?

2. Do you agree with Fowler's claim that the role of religious education should be to fill out the stage rather than to move a person along? Explain your view.

3. What do you see as the major differences between Oser and Fowler?

4. Over the past few years, in what settings has your own faith and religious reasoning been nurtured? When and how has your own growth been addressed (formally and intentionally — within an institution or organized program, informally and incidentally (among friends or on your own)? What factors contributed to making them powerful experiences?

5. How many of the types of nurturing activities that Goodman identifies in her rubric do you use in your setting? Which are the most powerful for you? What would you most like to try out next or become accomplished at?

ACTIVITIES

1. Read and discuss a dilemma from pp. 89-91.

2. A woman has two sons. The older one is impulsive and physical, but knows how to impress people when necessary, and the younger one is thoughtful and reliable, but doesn't mind taking advantage of situations. The husband has worked hard all his life taking care of the family business. Both sons have worked in the business. The husband knows that he must designate one of his sons to be responsible for caring for the business. His own father picked him to carry on the tradition. He, too, must pick his successor, as the family is dependent upon this business for their livelihood and survival. He favors the elder one because the elder one has catered to him and sought his approval. His wife knows his wishes, but she believes that God has given her the necessary gifts to run the business and take care of the family. Her husband does not consult her on matters related to the family business. Should she intervene, and how might she do it?

   Now, read Genesis 25:19-34, and Genesis 27:1-40. The dilemma above is actually a modern day of version of the dilemma that Rebecca faced. What is the role that God played in helping Rebecca decide what to do? What difficulties did Rebecca's choice present for all the family members? In what ways did Rebecca's choice benefit the family and the Jewish people?

3. See *Test of Faith* by Roberta Louis Goodman (Torah Aura Productions), an Instant Lesson that presents the students with the opportunity to do an abbreviated faith development interview, analyze the responses, and learn more about faith development theory.

4. Prayers enact stories of our people and our lives. In small groups, deconstruct a prayer or sections of prayers (e.g., the *"Shema"* and its blessings, the *"Amidah"*). Analyze each prayer by identifying the following aspects: narratives (stories) and history, key words or messages, concepts, symbols, rituals, theology (names of God, relationship to God, etc.), and values. Then, using poster board or construction paper, markers, magazines, scraps of materials, etc., create a picture of the prayer based on your responses. Set up all the pictures for people to review like a museum. Give each group time to explain their prayer and how it leads them on a spiritual path to God.

BIBLIOGRAPHY

Bellah, Robert N., et al. *Habits of the Heart.* Berkeley, CA: University of California Press, 1985.

Following in the footsteps of De Toqueville, Bellah and his associates undertook this sociological study of American individuals and their attitudes and beliefs about organized religion and religious issues.

Dykstra, Craig, and Sharon Parks, eds. *Faith Development and Fowler.* Birmingham, AL: Religious Education Press, 1984.

This collection of essays is perhaps the most comprehensive critique of Fowler's theory of faith development. The two editors are both prominent theologians.

Fowler, James W. *Stages of Faith: The Psychology of Human Development and the Quest for Meaning.* San Francisco: Harper & Row Publishers, 1981.

Stages of Faith is Fowler's seminal work in which he describes faith development theory and the stages in detail.

Fowler, James W., et al. *Stages of Faith and Religious Development.* New York: Crossroad/ Herder & Herder, 1991.

This volume consists of a collection of articles about faith and religious development by some of the most prominent theologians and thinkers of the time. A variety of theories, both stage theories and other approaches, are included in this volume.

Gilligan, Carol. *In a Different Voice.* Cambridge, MA: Harvard Press, 1982.

In this work Gilligan critiques Kohlberg's moral development theory. Besides questioning a theory devised originally solely on interviews of just men, Gilligan contends that woman's moral development is based more on relationship. Therefore, she contends that Kohlberg's theory is flawed, particularly in terms of his sequencing of Stages 3 and 4. In fact, Gilligan claims that the two stages should have their orders reversed.

Goodman, Roberta Louis. "Nurturing Students' Spirituality and Prayerfulness." In *Connecting Prayer and Spirituality: Kol HaNeshamah as a Creative Teaching and Learning Text,* Jeffrey L. Schein, ed. Wyncote, PA: The Reconstructionist Press, 1996.

The focus of this piece is on what faith development has to say about nurturing prayer, prayerfulness, and spirituality.

———. "Faith Development." In *What We Know about Jewish Education,* Stuart Kelman, ed. Los Angeles: Torah Aura Productions, 1992, pp. 129-135.

This chapter reviews the major work and research in faith development and identifies the implications of this theory for Jewish education.

———. "God and Prayer and Faith Development." In *The Jewish Preschool Teachers Handbook,* rev. ed., by Sandy Furfine Wolf and Nancy Cohen Nowak. Denver: A.R.E. Publishing, Inc., 1991.

The focus of this chapter is on faith development in the earliest stages, for early childhood learners. Examples of activities for nurturing a sense of God and prayer are included.

———. "Test of Faith: An Instant Lesson on Faith Development." Los Angeles: Torah Aura Productions, 1985.

Perhaps the first piece published that uses faith development theory in a Jewish setting, this Instant Lesson is directed at teens and adults. Through its use, students are challenged to think about how they make meaning out of their lives. Activities include: trying to figure out what stage the learner is at and interpreting a story by answering significant meaning making questions.

Grossman, Barbara. "Faith and Personal Development: A Renewed Link for Judaism." In *Journal of Psychology and Judaism,* vol. 16, No. 1, Spring 1992.

Grossman, a therapist, links faith development theory, to other developmental and psychological theories. She analyzes the types of issues and concerns that emerge at Fowler's Stages 3, 4, and 5. (See also Chapter 8 in this volume, "Psychosocial Resources for a Spiritual Judaism" by Grossman.)

Kohlberg, Lawrence. *The Psychology of Moral Development: Volumes I and II*. San Francisco: Harper & Row, Publishers, 1984.

These two volumes contain some of Kohlberg's most important thinking about moral development. Kohlberg dedicates an epilogue to Janusz Korczak, whom he saw as a model of his postulated seventh stage of moral development, a stage beyond justice. This epilogue lays the foundation for seeing the multitude of ways in which Kohlberg's work was inspired by Korczak's actions.

Oser, Fritz K. "Toward a Logic of Religious Development: A Reply To My Critics." In *Stages of Faith and Religious Development*, edited by James W. Fowler, Karl Ernst Nipkow, and Friedrich Schweitzer. New York: Crossroad/Herder & Herder, 1991.

This chapter provides the English speaking reader with an opportunity to access Oser's theory of religious reasoning. Most of Oser's important works are written in German and have not been translated.

Osmer, Richard Robert. *Teaching for Faith: A Guide for Teachers of Adult Classes*. Louisville, KY: Westminster/John Knox Press, 1992.

One of the few disciples of Fowler who actually trained with him, Osmer also is a religious educator, as opposed to being primarily a theologian. His writing is instructive for those who want to apply faith development theory to an adult religious educational setting.

Reimer, Joseph; Diana Pritchard Paolitto; and Richard H. Hersh. *Promoting Moral Growth: From Piaget To Kohlberg*. 2d ed. New York: Longman, 1983.

The lead author, Joseph Reimer, was a student of Kohlberg's at Harvard and today teaches at Brandeis University in the Jewish communal service program. Written as a textbook for college courses, this book provides a good overview of Kohlberg's work in moral development and its connection to Piaget's work.

Shire, Michael. "Faith Development and Jewish Education." *Compass*, vol. 10, no. 1, Fall 1987, 17-18, 24-25.

Shire is one of a few Jewish educators who have written about Fowler's theory of faith development. Shire provides a concise and informative overview of the theory and its stages.

Barbara R. Grossman

CHAPTER 8
PSYCHOLOGICAL RESOURCES FOR A SPIRITUAL JUDAISM

IT IS COMMON TO EXPECT THAT PEOPLE TURN TO GOD in times of suffering, trauma, and loss. However, ordinary life experiences also present many openings for developing and nurturing our relationship to God. The purpose of this chapter is to identify those opportunities, which are implicit in everyday life.

Once we identify and understand the religious value implicit in life's passages, we can use this understanding to enhance spiritual opportunities as they occur. We can also build a language with which to reflect on these experiences. This reflection, in turn, can deepen the meaning of those life experiences and put them into the context of our ever maturing understanding of Judaism.

We do not need to turn to secular psychology to know about human suffering. Our sacred texts describe ancestors who struggle with guilt, who feel emotional pain because they cannot conceive children, or who suffer from jealousy or family dysfunction. Our sacred stories teach us that suffering is universal and that we often turn to God for solace and for answers.

Yet, psychology can be helpful in conceptualizing the ways individuals are stretched and challenged by life's tensions. It can tell us how a community of faith might support and contribute to an individual's development, thus creating and enhancing bonds that build community and mature faith. Also, since many individuals today experience themselves as psychological beings more than as religious beings, the use of psychological language in addition to religious language can become a bridge to conversations about spirituality.

Historically, psychology was part of the religious domain. Interpreting dreams, catharsis, and wisdom are all biblical genres. Less norma-

tive forms of Judaism, such as *Kabbalah* and the traditions of the Hasidic teachers, are even more connected to the psychological. For contemporary, non-Orthodox Judaism to reclaim psychological knowledge for the purpose of understanding religious development is uncommon. Yet, through understanding individual and personal religious experience, we might balance the social action orientation of liberal Judaism with a personalized and reflective approach to religion. Together, these two emphases can offer a comprehensive religious education that deepens our understanding of our religion.

ERIKSON'S EIGHT LIFE CYCLE PHASES AND SPIRITUAL DEVELOPMENT

Resolution of Developmental Issues: Crises of Faith and Ethical Responsibility

Erik Erikson describes eight life cycle phases. These are inevitable maturational constructs that come about due to normal biological and social changes during one's lifetime. That means everyone goes through these phases because everyone ages. Each phase is generally understood as presenting a developmental issue that is resolved either negatively or positively. The subsequent phase is then encountered with more or less preparation, depending on the outcome of the previous phase. Thus, psychology offers a functional map of psychological and developmental lags in an individual's life.

The failure to resolve any one or a number of these phases positively results in some amount of suffering that is cumulative. It is the problem that does not go away; in fact, the magnitude of poorly resolved phases grows with time. Eventually, the individual seeks help in some form, and the project of remediating development commences. Predictably, seeking help does not occur until the individual is capable of reflecting on him/herself and on his/her suffering. The potential for this cognitive achievement of self-reflection starts no earlier than age 12, and considerably later for many persons.

What is less well-known about Erikson's conception of psychosocial phases is that he understood the challenge of each phase as a crisis of faith and ethical responsibility (Erikson, 1964, pp. 111-157). Thus, the crisis of infancy is between trust and mistrust, and the ethical value that can emerge is hope. On this foundation, the second great crisis of emotional and ethical development occurs — the tension between autonomy and doubt or shame. Resolving the conflict in favor of autonomy develops the individual's will, which provides for the exercise of choice and restraint, in common language, willpower.

Developing Character

The third phase offers the opportunity to learn initiative through the quality of play. Unsuccessful progress through this phase results in inhibition, fear of punishment, and guilt. The ethical value of initiative is better captured in the word "purpose." School age children face the challenge of developing a pattern of industry and interpersonal cooperation or impairment due to feelings of inferiority. In the language of religion, this can be understood as strength of character and social relatedness.

The review of this psychological information provides an opportunity to consider the applications of psychological maturity to religious experience. Erikson's work shows that psychosocial development relates directly to the development of faith. Not only does each crisis have the potential to enhance character, but the process of going through the crisis, the experience of disequilibrium or personal chaos, is a test of faith that is rewarded upon resolution with maturity and enhanced spiritual resources. In this view, psychosocial development is, in itself, faith

development; the motivation for development is an act of faith. This insight has important implications for religious education.

One application of this information relates to the quality of parenting and early childhood education. To facilitate a child's successful accomplishment of these maturational hurdles in the context of religious life will bind a child to the trustworthiness of that religion. For a religious community to appreciate the opportunity of educating its parents about the principles of Judaism and how principles relate to a child's success in ethical and religious terms, as well as success in secular terms, is to enrich the parents' understanding of religion and to enable them to bond their children to positive religious values. The alternative is that children are bonded to some other value, such as financial success, artistic creativity, science, athletic prowess, or social action. These are, of course, legitimate values; however, a religious point of view would maintain that religion can offer more ultimate value.

While parent education may not be a huge demand in Jewish circles, there is a market for it in the secular world. Perhaps Jews are confident that they know how to parent successfully, or possibly they are unwilling to admit their inadequacies to their peers within the Jewish community. This may then be an agenda that is applied indirectly. Parents can be guided to assist their children in faith development through curricula developed for them in parent meetings.

The fact is, the resolution of trust versus mistrust, initiative versus guilt, and so forth, powerfully impacts an individual's life in the form of character. As a religious community, we are not just casually interested in the outcome of this development. While religious education promotes good values, the most powerful influence is clearly in parenting. This can be an unexpected source of meaningful religious education and service to Jewish family life for both adults and children. Since parenting is also a chance to rework the adult's own upbringing, improving the adult's parenting can have far-reaching impact on adult development.

Spiritual Quest for a Personal Relationship To God

Another application of this model of psychosocial phase development is for the young adult or the older adult who is searching to define his/her personal relationship to God. This kind of quest requires the experience of the succeeding psychosocial phases because it is during these years that the individual defines a self and becomes interested in intimate relationships. Succeeding phases, then, describe the issues of the teenage years in terms of defining one's identity as a leader, as a sexual being, and as a believer in an ideology versus having identity confusion. Clearly this phase reflects the cumulative effect of previous phases and can be considered, in itself, a "battleground of character." This phase offers the successful adolescent the internalized virtue of fidelity, the capacity to commit and sustain a relationship with a significant other, and a value system or community. This is a key time for spiritual questing because it is the first opportunity to engage in abstract thinking. The successful culmination of this thinking is a deeper attachment to the religion of one's upbringing. Sometimes an alternative community forms the basis of identity.

Building on the virtues of fidelity and competence, the next developmental crisis presents itself in young adulthood with the issue of intimacy versus isolation. Here the opportunity is available to resolve the conflict of individuality versus togetherness and to develop mature love. The alternative outcome, failed relationship or hyper-individualism, is a form of suffering that generates the motivation for many adult spiritual quests.

While this discussion casually itemizes the psychosocial issues as they occur through the life span, each phase is more accurately a very dynamic, indeed an intense struggle to satisfy a mature need or value. The success of the struggle offers the person true joy and a deeper, more trusting bond to the universe. Maturity, in itself, enhances spiritual life. Conversely, the lack of success in resolving these normal crises of devel-opment creates prolonged suffering and often precipitates a spiritual quest. If we are aware and prepared in our religious leadership, both roads can provide a path to Jewish learning.

Through the lens of psychosocial maturity, we see how individualized a personal quest really is. There is no simple recipe to connecting personally with God. The process is influenced constantly by the individual's growth experiences and his or her unique development. For some, trust is the issue, nuanced by particular crises in personal life, such as abandonment, which are the result of parental divorce or neglect. For another, the search for God is driven by the challenge of personal mastery and concerns about whether there is adequate evidence in the universe for personal success. Perhaps the struggle to accomplish in school or work without the appropriate help from a parent or an undiagnosed learning disability evokes such pressure. For still others, the religious quest is influenced by early learning experiences, by feelings of not belonging, or by social awkwardness that comes from a lack of those interpersonal skills necessary for acceptance in a group experience. Such isolation or distrust or insecurity, etc., needs to be solved psychologically as well as theologically when it is the focus of an adult quest.

Psychological models such as Erikson's can assist our community in understanding the personal struggles at stake in adult religious education. The process for adults to mature in their religion is both psychological and intellectual. Sensitivity to the psychosocial challenges that individuals face adds crucial dimensions to religious reflection.

Erikson's model of psychosocial maturation continues with a seventh phase that describes the resolution of caring for others versus self-absorption, and an eighth phase in which the focus is the virtue of wisdom and integrity versus despair. The religious relevance here is unmistakable, and we need to give these phases and age groups due attention by providing opportunities in congregational life for seniors to enhance caring and wisdom.

Carl Jung is famous for saying that the issues

of the second half of life are all spiritual issues thinly disguised (Jung, 1933, p. 229). The purpose of our discussion so far is to investigate how all of life cycle development is spiritual and relevant to religion. Psychosocial maturity becomes explicitly spiritual when we attain the self-reflection and willingness that are necessary to resolve the suffering of our lives.

As a community, therefore, we need to be equipped to respond to personal quest, however it comes. Not appreciating the dynamics of individual development and not knowing how to validate and provide needed learning to remediate individual spiritual needs has cost us a generation of seekers who have sought in Buddhism, Vedanta Hinduism, eclectic mysticisms, and metaphysics what has not been made readily accessible in Judaism. For better or worse, since World War II, Judaism has been engaged exclusively in the communal quest, mostly for survival. As a result, a focus on individual spirituality has been generally overlooked.

The question may arise: Why has there been such a need for support and nurture for personal spiritual quest in the latter part of the twentieth century and the first years of this century? Certainly our great grandparents did not clamor for spiritual direction like this, nor did they threaten to find their spirituality elsewhere if this need was not satisfied. For a perspective on this, we can turn to the faith development work of James Fowler.

FOWLER'S STAGES OF FAITH: INSIGHTS ON ADULT SPIRITUAL DEVELOPMENT

James Fowler offers another life span development model with similarities to, but also significant differences from Erikson's psycho-social model. With Erikson's model, biology and time lead everyone through every phase one after the other. Fowler's work, building on the structural developmental theories and research of Jean Piaget, Lawrence Kohlberg, and others, provides a qualitative model that requires not only psy-

chosocial accomplishment, but cognitive development as well. Both the psychosocial and cognitive aspects of development affect whether the individual retains a faith more typical of that which emerges in childhood and adolescence, or whether one seeks deeper truths. (For more on Fowler's faith development theory, see Chapter 7, "Nurturing a Relationship To God and Spiritual Growth: Developmental Approaches.")

This more advanced developmental stage is characterized by the need for personalized meaning and internalized, rather than externalized, authority. Such individuative and reflective faith takes us beyond traditional culture and traditional religion. Factors that stimulate this stage include college level education that promotes critical thinking and scientific method, as well as competing claims for truth in the non-academic arena such as our communities of diversity provide.

The majority of the North American Jewish population accomplishes a social conformity to a non-Orthodox religious community by late adolescence. Unaffiliated Jews conform to the secular culture. The result in either case is a non-reflective lifestyle. The difference is simply that one is secular and the other is religious. Individuals in both of these groups are not just conforming; the experience of identity comes from the group. In time, it is probable that many individuals become ripe for more development. The "ripeness" will occur as individual adults transition to an individuative and reflective faith, which is highly probable considering the commitment of large numbers of North American Jews to college education. For these Jews, our congregations must generate engaging experiences and learning around God, Torah, and Israel, as well as self.

"Individuative-reflective faith" does not guarantee a religious renaissance. In fact, it can become a cul-de-sac of individualism. For many Jews, traditional religion has been demythologized into an ideology of liberal democratic politics. While the liberal agenda has its value, the idea that this translation of Judaism is adequate has barely begun to be challenged. Indeed, the conversation among Jews about religion at the level of individuative-reflective faith has been sparse and unsophisticated. For the most part, it is not a conversation inside the congregation, but has been occurring at a grass roots level for over a decade through a phenomena called the spiritual renewal movement.

Individuative faith is focused on rational principles. It demythologizes the Bible in a search for values that are worthy of personal commitment. For some individuals, social justice and scientific progress have been popular agendas in the search for meaning. Individuative quests can take the form of a search for self through psychology and/or philosophy. Frequently, this extends to an interest in meditation and mysticism.

TEMPERAMENT, PERSONAL EXPRESSION OF RELIGIOUS MEANING, AND SPIRITUAL RENEWAL

Probably the best predictor for how an individual will express his or her personalized meaning of religion comes from research in temperament theory. Tools such as the Myers-Briggs Temperament Inventory (Kiersey and Bates, 1984), based on Carl Jung's work on typology, suggests a finite number of styles, each of which organizes its values and skills into a coherent logic. The 16 styles can be reduced for the purpose of painting broad strokes for understanding community into two intuitive styles and two sensory styles. The sensory styles have a social action orientation and they outnumber intuitives three to one. They are also the organizational backbone of the synagogue. The intuitive styles are intellectually abstract and more likely interested in meditation and mysticism.

This assessment of differing approaches to religion in a congregation matches the estimate offered by Avram Davis, founder and co-director of Chochmat HaLev in Berkeley, California. In the discussion provided in Judith Linzer's book, *Torah and Dharma: Jewish Seekers and Eastern Religions* (1996), Dr. Davis suggests that the audience for sustained spiritual practice is 25-30%.

For him, this is a tremendous number of people who need to be taken seriously and taken care of, and he makes the observation that organizational-type individuals who typically are in charge of congregational life are not likely to appreciate this interest.

This is the kind of information that temperament research makes available. There is a national organization of teachers who apply the understanding of different temperaments to a format of "teaching to type." Christian religious educators have published applications of temperament to prayer, suggesting that there may be different forms of prayer for differing temperaments (Michael and Norrisey, 1984). Additional applications might include exploring different biblical personalities and their probable styles and role in Israel's history. It would also be beneficial to analyze the holidays for their style characteristics so that over the course of the calendar year, persons of each style might experience religion in a way that is congruent with their primary values.

The awareness that adults who are becoming more individuated will have differing religious needs promises to increase our ability to reach out and connect with more adults in terms of their own needs, not just the needs of family and raising children. This means we can address adults directly with a diverse program and can continue to offer religious value after their children have grown, even if they joined the synagogue originally "for the children."

It is important, however, that we do not confuse style with substance in this discussion. While there are multiple styles of spiritual expression that appeal to individuated religious seekers, the distinction of this level is in the quality of more rigorous thinking. Stories, symbols, assumptions about interpretations are all deconstructed and disembedded from meanings received from authority figures. Implicit understandings are analyzed for rational meaning. This is a dynamic and disorienting experience, and many individuals leave their congregations because they find this process to be alienating. Since this phenomenon is not limited to Jewish experience (it is paralleled in North American Christianity), it is important to recognize what is happening and how it is related to mass higher education in America. With critical thinking and cultural sophistication a more common achievement, religion must respond to the college educated by inviting its participants into an engagement in religion at this level without defensiveness.

A LATER ADULT PHENOMENON: A RENEWED OPENNESS TO DIALOGUE, MYSTERY, CONNECTEDNESS, AND RELIGIOUS EXPERIENCE

Since the boomer generation of the 1960s was the first to enter college in huge numbers, these now middle-agers are arriving developmentally at the opportunity for a rapprochement with tradition. The rational explanations of reality can give way to a more dialogical and dialectical approach. For this advanced group, there is a reverence and a wisdom that sees beyond the ideological system and self-definition of the early and middle adult years. The quality of this level of thinking retains the capacity for critical thinking, yet embraces the symbolic, the myth, and liturgy without reducing it.

I am fond of writing and thinking about this stage that Dr. Fowler calls "conjunctive faith" because its potential for dialogue, relationship, and ambiguity offers to break through the stubborn individualism, the either/or dichotomies within and between communities, ethnicities, and ideologies that have limited the conversation and the problem solving in our society. This is probably the first time in recorded history when this level of wisdom and maturity is possible for so many, which is not to say it is guaranteed to happen. Within the Jewish community, this accomplishment by enough people can create a milieu that makes it possible to nurture individuals in all the other levels of religious development. What is required is an accepting, mentoring, "holding environment" that allows for maturity to grow maximally through study in community of texts, history, self, and God.

Fowler's model shows how the breakdown of traditional religion is inevitable and important developmentally. The individuative stage, therefore, is important but not sufficient. Developmentally, individuals sort through their personal stories and intellectual frameworks and resolve issues of emotional and intellectual meaning. Eventually, individualism runs into deficiencies. Perhaps that is why there appears to be a return to faith communities amongst the middle-aged generation in Judaism, as well as other religions.

Another way of saying this is to describe the North American middle-aged, middle class individual as stuck in a self-imposed isolation of self-reliance and autonomy. This is the summary from research conducted by Robert Bellah, et al (1985) and summarized in his book *Habits of the Heart*. The religious community or congregation provides the opportunity for connectedness. Looked at developmentally, this connection needs to provide more than just belonging. It needs to be intelligent. It needs to allow for differences in opinion and style. It needs to be a community of continuous learning and discovery about what is sacred and holy and what it means to be human. It needs to forge connections between private and public life, material and spiritual life, personal history and communal history.

CONCLUSION

In short, the leadership of our religious community needs to draw on developmental resources to generate a context in which numerous learning communities are ongoing and enriching for those who engage in this partnership of learning. The curricula for each generation will probably be different, but age is not the only determinant of qualitative development. The middle-agers who are now exploring religion are bringing their individuated development, along with the pressure and challenges of intimacy (versus isolation) and generativity (versus self-absorption). They are looking to learn and grow to resolve those issues and enhance their well-being and care for those who depend upon them in their families and work situations. What they need is not ready-made answers, but empathic listening, a process for exploring texts with rich conversation, and prayer, and meditation with learning partners, all of which will enhance maturity.

———— •◆• ————

IMPLICATIONS

1. Life experience provides openings for developing a relationship to God.

2. Teachers should be aware of Erikson's phase theory of human development in order for them to identify teachable moments — ways of connecting the curriculum with the lives of students so as to enhance bonds to their religious values.

3. Parent education needs to focus on assisting parents in connecting psychosocial hurdles with Jewish values, traditions, and texts. One advantage of this approach is that parent education is immediately applicable and relevant to the issues that parents are confronting.

4. Because of the variety of temperaments that could be in one class, adult education courses should combine some personal reflection with content and action.

5. We all need to be patient with people's life struggles and stages. The diversity of life stages that people are in makes for a rich, vibrant, healthy community.

6. Life presents many openings for spiritual growth. Many of these openings emerge from joyful transitions and experiences, as well as from suffering.

QUESTIONS FOR CRITICAL INQUIRY

1. What does Dr. Grossman mean by maturity? How do we define maturity in the Jewish tradition?

2. What is the role of the synagogue in nurturing the individual's spiritual Judaism, as well as in aiding one to find a place in the synagogue community?

3. Dr. Grossman writes about creating "an accepting, mentoring, 'holding environment' that allows maturity to grow maximally through study in community of text, history, self, and God." How does this compare to Eugene Borowitz's statement in his covenant theology that a Jew should develop a relationship to God through Torah within the Jewish community?

4. Recall moments in your life that enhanced your spiritual awareness. What other life events, transitions, experiences might precipitate openings for enhancing spiritual awareness? What could you do in the classroom that would connect your classroom content to these moments of openness?

ACTIVITIES

1. Think about an experience that changed your view about God. Take five minutes to answer in writing the following questions. What was the experience? How old were you? Who else, if anyone, was involved? What view did you hold about God and what was the new understanding? How did this new understanding make you feel about God? How does thinking about this experience make you feel now?

2. Form a circle. Pair off with partners facing each other. Identify one person as "alef" and

the other as "bet." The alefs will rotate clockwise after responding to one of the following questions using the body. Without speaking, partners need to share their feelings and responses. How do I feel when I pray to God? How do I feel when I feel grateful to God? How do I feel when I am angry with God? How do I feel when I can't sense God's presence? How do I feel when I really need God's help? How do I feel when I dance with God? How do I feel when I struggle with God?

3. Grossman talks about how progressing through life phases affects our religious and spiritual development. Looking at Erikson's phases of human development, where are you on the chart? What are the spiritual and God challenges for you at this phase?

4. Design an obstacle course inside or outside — it can have things you need to climb over or crawl under, you can have people carry an egg on the spoon around the course, you could blindfold people, whatever. Have people go through the obstacle course. In what ways is this obstacle course like your life? Thinking about your life, in what ways were Jewish values, texts, and traditions helpful to you in overcoming these obstacles? What obstacles still remain for you? In what ways does having a belief in God help support your journey through this obstacle course of life?

5. Ask people to get physically comfortable in order to go through a guided fantasy. Suggest that they close their eyes to help them concentrate. Then say the following: Imagine that you are a seed. You are getting planted by loving hands. Those same loving hands water you, weed around you, and care for you. You begin to grow. You push your way through the ground and your root has to begin to grow down further into the group. Those loving hands continue to take care of you and you continue to grow. Now it is obvious what kind of plant you are. What is it that you have become? See yourself in full color. Are you a flower? a tree? a vegetable?

The sun is shining on you. Sometimes there is gentle rainfall. Glory in what you have become. At this point, ask people to open their eyes and join the group as a whole. Discuss: What plant were you? How is that plant a metaphor for who you are now? As a plant, what contributed to making you strong and healthy? What contributes to making you strong and healthy in your life? What would have happened if instead of a gentle rain, you had experienced a windstorm? How have you been able to withstand the windstorms in your life?

BIBLIOGRAPHY

Bellah, Robert, et al. *Habits of the Heart: Individualism and Commitment in American Life.* San Francisco, CA: Harper & Row, 1985.

This study presents an examination of contemporary American life modeled on de Toqueville's comprehensive analysis of America in the 1830s. In this updated version, the character of American individualism is explored, along with cultural traditions and practices, including those of religion, that restrain the destructive side of individualism.

Erikson, Erik. *Insight and Responsibility.* New York: W.W. Norton, 1964.

This volume consists of a collection of Erikson's lectures delivered during the years 1956-1963 on various ethical themes viewed from a clinical perspective. The lecture cited in this chapter is entitled, "Human Strength and the Cycle of Generations."

Fowler, James. *Stages of Faith: The Psychology of Human Development and the Quest for Meaning.* San Francisco, CA: Harper & Row, 1981.

This is James Fowler's comprehensive presentation of his theoretical model of six faith stages and semi-clinical interviewing data to support his theory. He includes a discussion of Erik Erikson, Jean Piaget, Lawrence Kohlberg, and theorists in psychosocial and structural development who contributed to his faith development theory.

Jung, C. J. *Modern Man in Search of a Soul*. New York: Harcourt, Brace & World, 1933.

This collection of essays on dream analysis, the primitive unconscious, the relationship between psychology and religion, the spiritual problem of modern individuals, highlights the differences between the theories of Jung and Freud.

Kiersey, David, and Marilyn Bates. *Please Understand Me: Character and Temperament Types*. Del Mar, CA: Prometheus Nemesis Book Company, 1984.

The authors outline a history of the theory of types and provide descriptions of all 16 temperament styles based on Carl Jung's theory of typology with some variations from the original theory. Additional discussions focus on temperament styles in children, in leadership, and in mating.

Linzer, Judith. *Torah and Dharma: Jewish Seekers in Eastern Religions*. Northvale, NJ: Jason Aronson Inc., 1996.

This book explores the contemporary phenomenon of Jews seeking spiritual experience in Eastern religious practices. Included is the author's journey through Zen and yoga and back to Judaism. The author presents a Jewish-Buddhist dialogue that is rich with theological insights for postmodern Judaism.

Michael, Chester, and Marie Norrisey. *Prayer and Temperament: Different Prayer Forms for Different Personality Types*. Charlottesville, VA: The Open Door, Inc., 1984.

The book provides an overview of the four basic temperament styles and associates, each with a major historical form of Christian prayer. Included are specific suggestions for how to apply prayer techniques.

CHAPTER 9

ARCHETYPAL PATHWAYS TO GOD: THE SUBCONSCIOUS IN THE DEVELOPMENT OF FAITH

Craig Marantz

INTRODUCTION

FOR SOME, TEACHING ABOUT GOD AND THE SPIRITUAL life is difficult because they see these concepts as being individual and personal. Views of God and our sense of spirituality are often difficult to explain, and they are perceived as defying the common rigors of rational discourse, of proof. Spirituality involves delving into one's inner life, one's *neshamah* (soul), and the inner life is filled with images, stories, fears, and hopes that are often concealed in our unconscious or revealed in fragments to our conscious self. God and spirituality are difficult to teach because they cannot be reduced to information, to fact and figures, or to simple concepts. Educators cannot easily adapt methods for teaching other subjects to an involving lesson about God and spirituality.

This chapter presents a way of approaching the inner life of individuals, through the use of archetypes — fundamental images. Archetypes inhabit our inner life, our subconscious, our dreams, our values, feelings, and thoughts. Jewish texts are filled with archetypes embodied in symbols, narratives, and dreams. Whether in our inner lives or in our texts, archetypes are powerful sources of spiritual understanding. While a text may tell us something in a straightforward way, it often has deeper symbolic lessons to teach also. By examining the symbols, myths, and dreams in our inner lives and in Jewish texts, our spirituality can be enriched and deepened.

This chapter presents one way in which archetypes can be used in a Jewish educational setting to nurture spirituality. I will show how archetypes help address the problem of overemphasizing the rational. Then I will present the connection among Torah, an archetype, and our inner life. As this chapter unfolds, I will define archetypes in general and show how a particular mythological archetype, the Seeker, is characterized. Working with this characterization of the Seeker as a frame, I will then look at three examples from *midrash* that illustrate the Seeker through the life of Abraham. In studying these texts, we will come to understand how archetypal relationships, namely the connection between Abraham and God, can inform our understanding of the *midrashim*. Following these analyses, the chapter addresses specific ways in which Abraham as Seeker can help us understand our own spiritual development. The last part of the chapter focuses on Peter Pitzele's work on bibliodrama as a technique to train our imagination to summon forth archetypal thoughts and feelings from our subconscious mind.

DEFINING AND DESCRIBING ARCHETYPES

According to Carl Gustav Jung, the archetype originates as an inborn form of intuition, which shapes and forms our most native instincts for understanding the world. Whenever we become aware of a consistently recurring mode of perception, Jung maintains that we are dealing with an archetype, "no matter whether its mythological character is recognized or not."[1]

---

[1]C. G. Jung. "The Concept of the Collective Unconscious," *The Portable Jung,* ed. Joseph Campbell, trans. R.F.C. Hull, (New York: Penguin, 1971), 57.

A variety of archetypes exist, expressing the fundamental ways of being that we have come to know as characterizing humanity throughout history. Patriarch and Matriarch, King and Queen, Prophet, Healer, Warrior, and Trickster are common examples of archetypes (descriptions of these archetypes are found in Appendix A, p. 114). Often, these archetypes are characters that we find in stories portrayed in literature, movies, advertisements, and the like.

In *Star Wars,* for example, the hero, Luke Skywalker, becomes a Jedi knight, a classic expression of the Warrior archetype. Skywalker's awareness of the great universal Force and his ability to utilize this sacred connection to fight evil makes him virtuous. His rival, Darth Vader, also embodies the Warrior. However, Vader uses the Force for evil, giving in to the Dark Side that all Warriors possess.

Archetypes symbolize important roles which people assume along with their ways of acting and being. Think about who in your own family serves as the matriarch or patriarch, keeping the family members connected, offering wisdom, serving as the focus of celebrations. Warriors exist on the "battlefields" of professional and recreational sporting events, in the courtroom fighting for justice or defending innocence, or in the boardroom strategizing over corporate mergers and acquisitions. Whatever the nature of these archetypal roles, it is possible to discuss spirituality as it relates to or shapes the archetypal behavior of these different people. So, for example, we often witness an accomplished sports figure, a triumphant Warrior, thank God for his or her strength and victory.

Archetypes affect not only perceptions, but actions, too. Any regularly repeating actions or reactions are defined as instinctual behavior, no matter if linked with conscious motivation or not.[2] When someone tells us something we don't want to hear about ourselves or our society, we tend to shut them out, ignore their insights, and discount their words and wisdom. As the Bible attests, prophets elicited such responses from the people when they brought a message of rebuke from God.

Jewish texts and history are filled with figures who embody archetypes. Much can be gained from looking deeply into the lives of ancient or modern figures for what they reveal about God and the spiritual.

The biblical and Rabbinic writings about Abraham, a key figure in Jewish tradition, clue us into what we can learn from him about relating to God and spirituality. Abraham embodies two masculine archetypes: Patriarch and Seeker. In particular, I will focus on some *midrashic* examples that show how Abraham embodies the archetype of Seeker. But first, let's examine the characterization of the Seeker. (A brief description of other masculine archetypes may be found in Appendix A, p. 114.)

THE SEEKER

The Seeker is a male archetype of change. He emerges in the human psyche when it is time for a person to modify the paradigms through which he understands the world. The Seeker is able to transform the negative experience of loss into a positive opportunity for change. He is humble and driven by hope. Courage, trust, and risk-taking constitute his hope, which, in turn, creates its own promising new future in self-fulfilling prophecy.[3]

Searching and inquiry mark the Seeker's journey. In his self-discovery, he finds his individuality. His sojourn is deliberate in nature and takes him to holy places in quest of special blessings. His journey may involve physical, geographical movement. It may include symbolic, metaphoric movement. We can better understand the Seeker by analyzing the circularity that marks his movement throughout his life. We can gain insight into the Seeker's life by exploring the nature of his resistance to the status quo, his movement

---

[2]Ibid., 54.

[3]P. M. Arnold, *Wildmen, Warriors and Kings* (New York: Crossroads/Herder & Herder, 1992), 88.

against rules, traditions, and commitments that threaten his freedom and integrity as a Seeker.[4]

The Seeker's wanderings are made more meaningful by the important relationships he has. The Seeker needs the mirror of relationships to discover himself. He tends to ask many questions of those with whom he allows himself to grow close.[5]

Just as a Seeker has many virtues, he also possesses shadow characteristics, traits that stand in opposition to his "brighter" attributes. For instance, the Seeker can be completely irresponsible. Although he may be willing to work for someone, he finds his avocational passions far more compelling and will spend more time on those. As a result, he can be undependable in business and a poor provider. He tends to blame others rather than accept responsibility for his actions. He has few enduring relationships, often resulting in profound loneliness. Sometimes, the Seeker would rather walk away from a difficult problem than deal with it thoroughly.[6]

Simply put, the Seeker's identity forms as he seeks out meaning in life. He finds definitive roles and obligations confining. His own activities are far more fluid than a Patriarch (his alter ego) would ever allow. Access to his identity can be a challenge because he is not always clear about who he is or what he values. However, he lives to explore the possibilities and loves, even demands, the freedom to do so. Consequently, the Seeker's identity typically remains in flux. This leaves him vulnerable, even fragile. If he does ultimately learn self-discipline, the Seeker will never find for himself the personal identity for which he searches.[7]

Abraham and God

Midrash examined collectively comes to portray Abraham as an exemplification of the Seeker archetype. These accounts provide insights into

how we can relate to God and foster our spiritual growth.

Example One

From the precocious age of three, according to R. Ammi b. Abba, Abraham comes to identify with God.[8] So moved is God by Abraham's early faithfulness to the *mitzvot* that the Holy One later blesses Abraham's son, Isaac. In the midst of a famine like the one in the days of Abraham, Isaac and God meet. Much as God once communicated with Abraham, God appears to Isaac and tells him not to go down to Egypt, but to dwell in a land of which God will tell him. God tells Isaac to sojourn throughout Canaan, and the Holy One will accompany him, bless him, and give him an abundance of land and children. Not only that, but God will also keep the oath established with Abraham.

What prompted Abraham to relate to God at such a young age? Given his cultural milieu, it seems unlikely that anyone would have forsaken idolatry enough to train him. Perhaps something instinctive in his nature leaves him open to identification with God. The *Midrash* corroborates this possibility:

> R. Abba b. Kahana explained: The one whose heart is full of sin will ultimately *have his fill from his own ways. And a good man will be satisfied from himself* (Proverbs 14:14). This applies to Abraham who himself recognized the existence of the Holy One, blessed be God. There was no person who taught him how to obtain knowledge of the Holy One, blessed be God. He did it without help.[9]

Here we learn that Abraham possesses a native intelligence that enables him to come to know God. It is not a matter of training or study. Rather, it is his intuition that leads him to understand that God is present in his life.

The context in the Book of Proverbs gives us

---

[4]T. Guzie and N. M. Guzie, *About Men and Women: How Your Great Story Shapes Your Destiny* (New York: Paulist Press, 1986), 34-6.

[5]Ibid., 34.

[6]Ibid., 36-7.

[7]Guzie and Guzie, 37.

[8]*Nedarim* 32a-b.

[9]*Bamidbar Rabbah* 14:2. See also *Bamidbar Rabbah* 18:21.

insight into Abraham's perceptive awareness of God. Proverbs 14 draws a distinction between various acts of wisdom and acts of folly. Verse 6 helps illustrate the difference: "A scorner seeks wisdom, but does not find it; but knowledge is easy to him who understands." Thus, for instance, in his spiritual resistance, Abraham seeks a more sanctified religious existence and, in the process, disparages the idolatrous world in which he and his family live. However, he does not scorn simply for the sake of insulting his father's ways. Rather, Abraham intuits that he must change his lifestyle in order to create a greater connection with God.

It follows, then, that through Abraham's understanding, his knowledge of God's presence becomes more immediate. The more he links his life with the one God, the more he resists his father. The more he bonds with the unity of the Holy One, the more he reflects on the nature of a new spiritual path that he must take to get away from the evil of his father's world. Abraham's rage for his father's world is not anger for its own sake. On the contrary, Abraham's upset forces him to confront the deceit of idol worship and ultimately motivates him to break away from it. This chapter in the Book of Proverbs implicitly captures the wisdom of Abraham's actions in an environment of folly.[10]

Here the Seeker in Abraham is active. He does not possess all the requisite knowledge to relate to the one God. Yet, he transforms his anger and disappointment into meaning amidst the arrogant, dishonest world in which he remains. Just because there is no one to teach him the ways of monotheism, he proceeds with no less hope that he can discover what the concept of one God really means to his spiritual existence.

Example Two

The communication between God and Abraham is not one way. Abraham engages God in debate, and the Holy One shows a willingness to respond to Abraham and does so with compassion:

R. Yitzhak said: At the time of the destruction of the Temple the Holy One, blessed be God, found Abraham standing in the Temple. Said God: *What has My beloved to do in My house?* Abraham replied: I have come concerning the fate of my children. Said God: Your children sinned and have gone into exile. Perhaps, said Abraham, they only sinned in error? And God answered: *She has wrought lewdness.* Perhaps only a few sinned? *With many,* came the reply. Still, he pleaded, You should have recalled on their behalf the covenant of circumcision. And God replied: *The hallowed flesh is passed from you.* Perhaps had You waited for them they would have repented, he pleaded. And God replied: *When you do evil, then you rejoice!?* Thereupon he put his hands on his head and wept bitterly and cried: Perhaps, Heaven forbid, there is no hope for them. Then came forth a Heavenly Voice and said: *God called your name a leafy olive tree, fair with goodly fruit:* as the olive tree produces its best only at the very end, so Israel will flourish at the end of time.[11]

Here Abraham defends the honor of his children before God, Who is profoundly upset with the waywardness of his children. Abraham stands up for them even to the point of tears. God hears him and responds empathetically, giving Abraham hope, even when it seems he has none, that God will ultimately redeem his children even though they have transgressed.

Example Three

There are various examples in the *Midrash* in which God infuses Abraham's life with promise, blessing, and reassurance. In turn, Abraham's faith in God deepens.

The proximity of Deuteronomy 6:11 to the *"Shema"* (v. 4ff) indicates how important it is to God that Abraham believes in the unity of God. God wants Abraham to maintain faith even when there are challenges to it.

---

[10]See Proverbs 14.

[11]*Menachot* 53b.

MIDRASH AND OUR OWN SPIRITUAL DEVELOPMENT

What does Abraham's life as a Seeker have to say about his relationship to God and his spiritual development? Using a model for archetype identification in our tradition, we can analyze Jewish texts, building a description of archetypes present in traditional and modern sources, and then see how this description fosters our understanding of God and spirituality.

Abraham's life is a constant search for *kedushah* (holiness). The most fertile source of holiness for Abraham is found in his significant relationships. This is not to say the relationships always look or feel holy. There are, however, lessons in each interaction that Abraham has that teach us about the potential for holiness in the world.

Abraham teaches us that a small child can identify with God. Children have a simple intuition that helps them view the world in a sensitive way. As a child, Abraham's perception opened his senses to the presence of God. He also instructs us by his word and deed that, as adults, we often must change our lifestyle, including the relationships we keep, if they do not foster spiritual growth or a greater connection with the holiness in the world. As we grow older, our material needs slow down that intuitive creative spiritual energy that flows more freely in childhood. It is important to recognize the emotional limitations of our materialism and rededicate ourselves to spiritual living.

Abraham gives us several strategies for how to achieve this transformation. First, he converts the negative energy of his anger about and disappointment over his father's idolatry into a positive desire for spiritual exploration and discovery of his own faith. Second, he communicates with God. Abraham is special enough to be able to converse with God through vision and word. But so are we, in a metaphoric sense.

Through prayer, we can articulate thoughts directed to God and, in effect, communicate with God. Abraham's communication with God is predicated on his deep trust that the Holy One cares. We have to proceed with similar faith if

the communication is to impact us in a profound and meaningful way.

With respect to discerning God's presence, it can feel awkward or inauthentic to utilize biblical models as our spiritual paradigms. However, when we look around us, we can see situations in our lives that transcend the ordinary. It is in this transcendence that we can recognize the hand of God at work. Arguably, this heightened awareness is similar to that which occurs in the lives of archetypal figures in the Bible.

Third, the Rabbis teach us that Abraham stands up for the wayward in a compassionate and loving way. In helping the vulnerable, Abraham strengthens his self-perception that he is a servant of God. God also sees Abraham as a servant, dedicated to teaching others about God's holy Presence. Thus that self-perception and the divine perception are very close to being one and the same. In serving in the ways of God and believing in God lovingly, Abraham's dedication helps him to preserve the spirit and dignity of his relationship with God. This relationship mirrors who Abraham is and who he is to become. In essence, God's Presence helps Abraham identify that God is near and his course of action draws him closer. This sense of proximity builds up Abraham's faith. In his relationship with God, Abraham engages in self-reflection, which continually renews his learning about himself and his purpose in life.

BIBLIODRAMA: AN EXERCISE IN SPIRITUAL IMAGINATION

The human imagination can bring powerful creative energy and spirit to any educational endeavor. Through imagination, we take our rational minds to spiritual truths that go beyond simple facts and proofs. Faith in God requires some imagination. So does understanding the function of primeval archetypes in our daily lives. To understand better how archetypal characteristics inform our spiritual development, psychologist Peter Pitzele developed a technique called "bibliodrama."

Bibliodrama is a psychodramatic, improvisational style of role-playing that focuses on biblical characters. We can extend this technique to our study of *midrash*, since bibliodrama is in itself a *midrashic* enterprise.

One's imagination is critical in drawing out archetypal thoughts and feelings from one's unconscious. Imagination is important because it is a function of one's spontaneity, and spontaneity flows forth from "the unreflective, prompt expression of our unconscious minds."[12] Pitzele says that, oftentimes, "the unconscious connection, the reason why one person chooses a certain character, can open up deep places in our souls."[13] An example of bibliodrama is described below using texts about Abraham, the Seeker.

An Interview with Abraham

Have participants read the *midrash* from *Menachot* 53b found in Example Two above. Ask them to "become" Abraham for a moment and talk about the nature of his conversation with God. (Not all participants will feel comfortable in role-playing. Those who are not can simply observe.) The facilitator will play the role of interviewer, asking many questions so as to evoke various feelings, thoughts, and explanations from the participants about the scene and its characterization. Some suggestions for questions follow.

- How did it feel to approach God regarding the fate of your people? Were you scared? Were you hopeful?

- What made you feel you could approach God with your concerns? Why should God have listened to you?

- What did you think when God told you that your children were sinners and seemingly deserved their exile?

- What do you see in your people that God should be patient with them?

- Why did you remind God about the covenant of circumcision?

- How did it feel when heaven's voice guaranteed that your children Israel would flourish at the end of time?

- Pitzele also employs a technique he calls "using empty chairs." In this case, an empty chair is placed in the center of the room to symbolize God. Participants must stand as close or as far from the chair as they feel represents their relationship with God. To warm up, the facilitator can ask the participants various questions about their feelings toward and their history with God. Next, have the participants act as Abraham in the context of the *midrash* from *Menachot* 53b. Use the questions above or create new ones.

Pitzele emphasizes the importance of not probing too far or questioning too intensively. The facilitator's role is to help participants tell stories while in their roles. There may be situations in which the facilitator feels a participant's ideas and feelings can be expanded upon. Perhaps the participant's unexpressed emotions could be more fully expressed. However, it is crucial that the facilitator let whatever stories come out to stand as they are told. Pitzele assures that this expression is enough and that it will "demonstrate the vitality and richness of this [*midrashic*] method."[14] Moreover, participants will come to identify this imaginative and spontaneous enterprise as a means to uncover some of the deeper feelings they have for God.

The use of bibliodrama is an excellent, contemporary alternative to more classical approaches to the study of *midrash*. However, it is not the only way one should approach text in order to understand the impact of biblical archetypes on our lives. Bibliodrama can serve as a complement to more traditional methods of analysis. It can be a bridge to help students of *midrash* better understand themselves in relation

[12]N. Zion and D. Dishon, *A Different Night* (Jerusalem: Shalom Hartman Institute, 1997), 36.

[13]Ibid.
[14]Ibid.

to text. Through greater self-knowledge, one becomes better equipped to relate to classical texts, their complex historical meaning, and their potential to inform our own lives.

CONCLUSION

Archetypal modeling can provide us a creative and inspiring alternative to more rational modes of theological reflection and spiritual development. To be sure, embracing archetypes will represent for many of us a new and challenging paradigm. After all, as human beings, we tend to rely heavily on palpable facts, ideas, and emotions to inform our realities. Archetypal paths depend more on the power of our imaginations. Affirming the significant impact of

archetypes, Jung writes:

> If we consider the tremendous powers that lie hidden in mythological and religious sphere in [humankind], the aetiological significance of the archetype appears less fantastic . . . The human of the past is alive in us today.[15]

Archetypes represent intuitive, spiritual truths, which exist deep inside us. Archetypal characters reflect our most basic dreams and desires, our most essential fears and frailties. The patterns of their lives mirror the activity of our souls and bring to light the primordial nature of our spiritual instincts, paving the way for a more evolved and imaginative understanding of our relationships with God.

IMPLICATIONS

1. Spirituality has dimensions that are neither conscious nor rational, but rather intuitive, subconscious, and instinctive.

2. Archetypes are spiritual mythological models that are useful for connecting one to God.

3. People, real and fictional, embody archetypes.

4. Using one's imagination is an important way of exploring archetypes and our spirituality.

QUESTIONS FOR CRITICAL INQUIRY

1. How is spirituality something other than a rational, conscious process? What other ways do we have of experiencing and sensing God?

2. How is your relationship to God, your spiritual journey, most like Abraham's?

3. In what ways is Abraham's life a search for *kedushah*, holiness, as Marantz contends?

4. Abraham was a seeker and patriarch. What spiritual qualities does he embody?

5. Think about a person whom you consider to be very spiritual. What archetype would you associate with this person? What qualities does this archetype possess that make him/her spiritually rich?

6. What other educational techniques besides bibliodrama can be used to explore archetypes?

ACTIVITIES

1. Find and read three narratives from Tanach, such as Miriam leading the celebration at the Sea of Reeds, Elijah in the desert cave, and King Solomon deciding what to do with the child claimed by two mothers. Identify the archetypes that each person represents. What are the characteristics of that archetype as portrayed in the narrative. What other char-

---

[15]Jung, 65.

acteristics would you associate with the archetype? What are the major Jewish values embedded in each of these archetypes? Make pictures something like those on Tarot cards for each of the archetypes.

2. Close your eyes and clear your mind. Focus on the word "Jew." Allow visions, images, and pictures come to you. Reproduce (draw, paint, etc.) what you saw. Share your pictures. What subconscious images of a Jew came to your mind? How does this connect to how you live your life today?

3. Identify a symbol that provokes a visceral reaction that is for the most part not intellectually or rationally understandable. For example, a yellow star, boxcars on a train, a Torah held high, a large *tallit* over a person's head, Simchat Torah flags, a *mezuzah*. What is the symbol you identified? How do you react when you see it? What is the relationship between your reaction and your subconscious, the deep spiritual connections buried in your being?

4. Find and read examples of dreams in the Bible. Interpret each dream by identifying the symbols and archetypes embedded in it. In what ways does the dream reflect either the wishes of the dreamer or God? What is the role of God in the dream? Now consider Herzl's dream as represented in the words of

"*Hatikvah.*" Sing and read the words. What are the symbols used to express the dream? For what are the Jewish people really longing? How has this been a dream for Jews throughout history? Other songs can be similarly analyzed, such as *"Sakhi, Sakhi"* (or the English version, "Laugh at All My Dreams"), *"Al Kol Eleh," "Eli, Eli."*

5. Light is a symbol that evokes thoughts and feelings in the subconscious. In Germany, it was a custom for the women to make candles that burned during Yom Kippur. They burned one candle for the living and one as a *yahrzeit* candle for the souls of the dead. While they dipped the wax, they thought about their deeds, thus making the candles became an act of *teshuvah*. Make different types of candles — for Shabbat, Havdalah, Chanukah, *Yahrzeit*, Yom HaShoah, or any other Jewish occasion. While they burn, reflect on the symbolism of light and the thoughts and feelings it evokes.

6. Draw pictures of the patriarchs and matriarchs that emphasize the archetypes each represents. Instead of making pictures of these individuals as human beings, depict them by identifying symbols or words that represent their archetypes. For example, you might depict Rebecca with a picture of a pitcher or a well.

APPENDIX A

Other Masculine Archetypes

In order to expand an appreciation for archetypes beyond that of the Seeker, the following descriptions of masculine archetypes are provided. Descriptions of feminine as well as additional masculine archetypes can be found in *About Men & Women: How Your Great Story Shapes Your Destiny* by Tad Guzie and N. M. Guzie (New York: Paulist Press, 1986).

The Patriarch

When one takes responsibility for a group of people as if he was their own father he evokes the archetypical Patriarch. The Patriarch provides fatherly support to those orphaned by their fathers. He gives support and guidance to those in need of positive direction. Arguably, the Patriarchal *persona* compensates subconsciously all of us who have tragically lost our own fathers through death, illness, or moral failure. The extent to which the Patriarch compensates us seems relative to the impact of his *menschlichkeit* on our lives. His *menschlichkeit* characterizes the various roles he plays as a father figure.

The Patriarch typically understands his identity in terms of his sense of obligation toward others. So well-defined are his functions and responsibilities, one commonly assumes the Patriarch has ready access to his identity. He knows very clearly who he is and what he values. This knowledge remains vital to the Patriarch as he strives to hold constant his self-identification.

The Patriarch is disciplined in his general duties as father. He leads by example. He fulfills his own obligations in a highly responsible way, and he expects a strong sense of discipline and duty from those in his care. While his expectations are high, they are not overbearing.

The Patriarch consistently provides to his children "emotional stability, sturdiness, firm correction, world-wisdom, constructive criticism, moral principles, and a sense of fun."[16]

The King

The King is a great leader. He makes difficult decisions and leads us to places "we must, but do not wish to go."[17] His leadership is both political and spiritual. His actions are marked by a sense of dignity and responsibility. He is generous and creative. He thrives on seeing others succeed. He is not threatened by the success of those around him. In fact, his personal glory is enhanced when people flourish around him. He is a patron of the arts and fosters intellectual activity. He faces criticism and defeat with composure.[18]

The Prophet

The Prophet fights for truth that people often find too painful to embrace. He exposes lies people tell and seeks deeper truths that people ignore when acting falsely. The Prophet is honest to a fault, even when his power to tell the truth puts his personal welfare at risk. Sometimes the Prophet's negativity is mistaken as cynicism. However, the Prophet is driven by the hope that society can discard its illusions and achieve greater morality. The Prophet desires to energize our consciences. The Prophet sees the potential in people and institutions that others do not see.[19]

The Healer

The Healer cures illness and restores people to wholeness.[20] The compassion of the Healer origi-

---

[16]Arnold, 38.

[17]Ibid.

[18]Ibid.

[19]Ibid., 149.

[20]Ibid., 134.

nates from internal healing, from personal wounds and struggles. To foster healing, the Healer assembles "a strong community of committed, compassionate fellow human beings, who join the ill person in a bond of affection, love, physical touching, supportive conversation, hope, and prayer."[21]

The Warrior

The Warrior in us not only fights military wars, he also battles evils such as disease, poverty, and ignorance that afflict society. He fights for what he believes. His Warrior-spirit stands on bravery, self-sacrifice, and heroic detachment.[22] The Warrior trains diligently and works beyond fatigue as he battles for the fulfillment of his ultimate goals. He is disciplined in his struggle for success. The Warrior knows how to defend himself physically from those who would bring

him harm. He also protects himself from people who violate his psychological boundaries — privacy or personal space. Finally, the Warrior within is the archetype of "emotional resolve and mental stamina, technical skill, and vocational competence."[23]

The Trickster

The Trickster is the archetype of irreverence and change. He pokes fun at us and makes us laugh at ourselves. When individuals, society, or its institutions become too self-righteous or complacent, the Trickster "pops pretensions and deflates us back to proper human size."[24] Just when we think we have everything about life figured out, the Trickster "pulls the rug out" from under us, preparing us for new and improved ways of thinking.[25] When humor or fun are scarce, the Trickster brings comic relief.

---

[21]Ibid., 137.

[22]Ibid., 101.

[23]Ibid., 103.

[24]Ibid., 160.

[25]Ibid., 161.

BIBLIOGRAPHY

Primary Texts

The Babylonian Talmud. I. Epstein, trans. London: Soncino Press, 1948-1952.

The Jerusalem Bible. Jerusalem: Koren, 1997.

Midrash Rabbah. H. Freedman and Maurice Simon, trans. 10 vols. London: Soncino Press, 1961.

Tanakh: A New Translation of The Holy Scriptures According To the Traditional Hebrew Text. Philadelphia, PA: The Jewish Publication Society, 1985.

Selected Secondary Texts

Arnold, Patrick. *Wildmen, Warriors, and Kings: Masculine Spirituality in the Bible.* New York: Crossroad/Herder & Herder, 1992.

> An introduction to biblical archetypes and their relationship to the spiritual development of masculinity.

Borowitz, Eugene B. *Choices in Modern Jewish Thought: A Partisan Guide.* New York: Behrman House, 1995.

> A survey of the great modern and contemporary Jewish theologians.

Guzie, Tad, and N. M. Guzie. *About Men and Women: How Your Great Story Shapes Your Destiny.* New York: Paulist Press, 1986.

> An introduction to how mythological archetypes inform our life experiences.

Hopcke, Robert H. *A Guided Tour of the Collected Works of C.G. Jung.* Boston, MA: Shambhala, 1992.

> A primer on the works and thought of Carl Gustav Jung.

Jung, Carl Gustav. *The Portable Jung.* Joseph Campbell, ed. R.C.F. Hull, trans. New York: Penguin, 1971.

> A collection of writings by Carl Gustav Jung.

Marantz, Craig. *Applying the Universal Archetypes of Seeker and Patriarch To Abraham as He Is Portrayed in the Midrash: A Study in Masculine Identity Development.* Thesis submitted in partial fulfillment of requirements for Rabbinic ordination. New York: Hebrew Union College-Institute of Religion, Graduate Rabbinic Program, 1999.

> Application of two universal, masculine archetypes to *midrashic* characterizations of Abraham, in order to shed light on the complex nature of his identity and faith as it develops throughout his life.

Pitzele, Peter. *Our Fathers' Wells: A Personal Encounter with the Myths of Genesis.* San Francisco: HarperCollins, 1995.

> Teaches about the art of psychodrama (or bibliodrama) and its applications to the archetypal stories of Genesis.

———. *Scripture Windows.* Los Angeles, CA: Alef Design Group, 1997.

> A continuation of the discussion of bibliodramatic techniques and their role in the *midrashic* enterprise.

Zion, Noam, and David Dishon. *A Different Night: The Leader's Guide To the Family Participation Haggadah.* Jerusalem: Shalom Hartman Institute, 1997.

> A fine explanation of bibliodrama and its various techniques.

CHAPTER 10

EDUCATING THE SPIRIT

Michael J. Shire

INTRODUCTION

Many Jewish educators would like to develop the spiritual life of their students. But they do not know how to do it. Some educational programs actually claim to be designed to provide spiritual experiences, but then they fail to measure success. Trying to define spirituality proves to be an elusive task, and there are even those who would deny that there is such a thing as Jewish spirituality! All of this led me to investigate what young people say about their own spirituality and how it is influenced by their Jewish educational programs. I will describe the way in which I investigated Jewish educational programs and their impact on teenage spirituality (Shire, 1996). I will then present a portrait of adolescents reflecting on their own religious lives. Finally, I will suggest a curricular approach to enhancing religiosity in Jewish education.

METHODOLOGY

Wanting to hear from young people themselves as to how they understood spirituality and how they expressed it in their daily lives, I interviewed teenagers aged 14 and 15 who had the ability to reflect on their own thought processes.

Since I was interested in how an educational program might impact on their spirituality, I interviewed students enrolled in Jewish educational programs. I particularly wanted to investigate what was the impact of a number of different types of educational programs on each student's spirituality. I therefore looked at four settings that are the norm for teenage Jewish education: the Day School, Religious School, Jewish summer camp, and educational Israel experience. Previous research (Resnick, 1993) suggests informal education is a powerful force in affecting the lives of students, so I was particularly interested in the difference between formal and informal programs. Since Jewish education is not merely a process of schooling and does not take place just in the classroom, it was important to see how different educational environments affected spirituality in students.

For each program, an educator was chosen to be interviewed who was known to affirm the goals of Jewish religious education. Semi-clinical interviews were conducted in their homes and each was observed in a teaching capacity. Methods of observation included field notes, classroom interactions, investigation of the school ethos through conversations, and observation and participation. The educators of the different institutions selected students who reflected a religious commitment and spiritual awareness.

The students were observed in their educational setting and interviewed at school or home using a projective picture interview and semi-clinical interview. The purpose of the student interview was first to generate notions of spirituality through projective associations and then to relate those spiritual associations to the student's own experiences. In this way, the interviewer obtained descriptions of student's religiosity, the meaning it has for them, their experience of Jewish education, and the factors that contribute to it. Students were shown pictures in a projective image method in order to obtain spontaneous associations between the individual and the projected meanings of the photographs.

A series of categories was generated from the data. Units of thought taken both from the response to the projective pictures and the personal reflections were sorted into coding categories. These codes were generated as the data were analyzed and sorted. Therefore, the codes were derived from the respondents themselves. Following this sorting, correlations were made between categories. The categories were then interpreted using the Formal and Instructional Curriculum data collected for each setting and educator.

Investigating the Curriculum

Using the Goodlad (1979) and Klein (1979) "Study of Schooling" model (1979), I investigated four aspects of curriculum in selected educational programs. This model enables a researcher to investigate different aspects of the curriculum of an educational program and works just as well for schooling as for informal educational programs. Most educational programs contain a number of the four aspects of curriculum — formal, perceived, operational, and experienced.

The "formal" domain of curriculum is the stated goals of the program as evident in the written curriculum, syllabus, or parent handbook. The "formal" domain provides a picture of what is intended to be taught in the school, summer camp, or Israel experience. I studied the written material available for each program, searching for what was stated about enhancing spirituality or for what it defined as the goals of religious education.

The "perceived" domain of curriculum refers to the intentions of the educators in carrying out the educational program. The perspective of the educators is key to understanding how the goals of the program will be implemented in comparison to what is supposed to happen through the written "formal" curriculum. To gain an understanding of the perceived domain, I interviewed Rabbis, teachers, and summer camp counselors about their aims in enhancing spirituality and influencing their students' religious growth.

The "operational" domain of curriculum is defined as that which goes on in the classroom or informal educational setting. It takes into account the changes that may occur in the "perceived" curriculum as educators actually engage with students. I observed educators in their programmatic settings in order to see what actually happens while they teach or facilitate.

Finally, the "experienced" domain refers to the educational experience from the viewpoint of the learner. I interviewed students to obtain insight into their perceptions of how the "operational" curriculum impacts on their notions of spirituality and their inner lives. The findings also shed light on unintended outcomes of the curriculum that otherwise remain hidden.

These four domains of curriculum allow the researcher to understand the processes of decision making in planning the program, the intentions of the educators, and the experiences of the learners, so as to explore the strategies that educators use in order to enhance spirituality and the impact of those strategies in different educational programs.

DEFINING RELIGIOSITY IN JUDAISM

Torah, Mishnah, and Talmud define the religious requirements of the Jew. However, the mere performance of these *mitzvot* does not necessarily ensure a spiritual attitude. Performing *mitzvot* can become routine and perfunctory. In the eleventh century in Spain, a book was written dealing with precisely this concern about religious performance. It became one of the most popular and influential books of spirituality in Judaism. Written by the Jewish philosopher Bachya ibn Pakuda in Arabic (and only later translated into Hebrew), it is called *Duties of the Heart*. Bachya uses the following story to introduce a discussion about Jewish spirituality:

A king wishing to test the intelligence of his servants, distributed among them skeins of silk. The diligent and sensible one among them, sorted the portion allotted to him, again and again, and divided it according to its quality into three parts — superfine, medium, and inferior. He did the best that could be done with each of these — he had the material made up by skilled workmen into gala dresses of different styles and colors, which he wore in the royal presence, selecting the garments suitable to the occasion and place. The fool among the king's servants made out of all his silk that which the wise servant had made out of the worst sort, sold it for whatever it would fetch, and hastened to squander the proceeds in eating and drinking. When these things came to the king's knowledge, he was pleased with the conduct of the zealous and intelligent servant, promoted him to a position near himself, and raised him to the rank of one of his favorites. But he was displeased with the actions of the fool, drove him forth, and had him transported to the desolate parts of his realm to keep company with those who had incurred his royal anger. (Bachya Ibn Pakuda, 1970, p.17)

Bachya uses this story to illustrate the relationship between God (the King) and those who can distinguish between the different purposes of the commandments. He explains the metaphor by stating that the wise person understands the difference between the science of the inward life, which Bachya calls the "duties of the heart," and the knowledge of practical duties, which he terms "duties of the limbs." The wise person is able to sort out that which is fitting and weaves it appropriately into a life devoted to God. The fool lumps it all together and loses sight of the fine distinctions between the requirements of an inner life and outer practical duties.

For Jews, spirituality does consist of acts made obligatory by the Torah, such as ritual and ethical commandments. Rabbi Abraham Joshua Heschel commented (Heschel, 1976 and 1962) that in doing *mitzvot*, a Jew meets God. The inner dimension of fulfilling the commandments, encountering God, is obligatory as well. If the inner dimension is not nurtured, then the external commandments cannot be properly fulfilled. It is necessary therefore to have intention, *kavanah*, to carry out the commandments.

For Bachya, duties of the heart were paramount in providing an intentionality to religious commitments. Without them, the commandments could not be fulfilled. These duties of the heart included the awakening to awe and wonder, the building of hope, developing trust and love as foundations of religious awareness, finding meaning and order within and outside the self, and obtaining the knowledge to communicate all this through a religious language and culture.

These vital spiritual virtues were incomplete, however, without expression through "duties of the limbs." Religious commitment and spiritual awareness are therefore two sides of the same coin in Judaism. They are interdependent and together form a wholehearted approach to religious life.

The work of faith development in the United States and Switzerland, coupled with the work of spiritual development in the United Kingdom as part of the Religious Education National Curriculum, has prompted much debate about the nature of spirituality. This has resulted in philosophical reflections on the nature of spirituality and psychological approaches to learning for the development of spirituality. This bringing together of theology and developmental psychology marked the innovative uniqueness of the faith development school.

However, the approach of James Fowler of the United States (Fowler, 1981) and Fritz Oser of Switzerland (Fowler, Nipkow, and Schweitzer, 1992), Canadian scholar Clive Beck (Beck, 1994) and British scholar Kevin Mott-Thornton (Mott-Thornton, 1998) all attempt a universalist approach to the nature of spirituality. This approach widens the definition of spirituality so as to allow those without a religious heritage or affiliation to accept the notion that one can be spiritual without being religious. Such a universalist and syncretistic approach blurs the significant differences between religious traditions and often assumes a Western Rationalist position.

Jews have been uncomfortable with the usage of the word "spiritual" when it has related merely to a series of spiritual virtues. For Jews, spiritual awareness without explicit religious expression is incomplete. I therefore prefer to use the word religiosity instead of spirituality. According to Rabbi Arthur Green, religiosity is "striving for the presence of God and fashioning a life of holiness appropriate to such striving" (Green, 1987, p. *xiii*). Jewish spiritual life is thus a continual task of creating holiness even in the most mundane of daily acts.

Jewish education today is concerned with the transmission of knowledge, the development of ritual skills, the appreciation of Jewish identity, and the affirmation of values. It deals little with the nature of religious experience, the development of religious growth, or the field of spirituality in general. It has found this area of religious education difficult to promote in a modern secular society with teachers and parents ambivalent about their own spirituality, let alone about transmitting it to others. Jewish education has primarily been concerned with the outer dimensions of religion; the historical, social, and theological forms of religious expression. It has rarely been concerned with elements of spiritual experience, such as trust, awe, and love. Where it has focused on inner dimensions, it has not considered the relationship between inner and outer. Rather, it has seen them as separate entities.

However, religiosity is a vital component of Jewish life and experience. There is, therefore, uncertainty as to how it can be translated into educational objectives in order that the goals of a Jewish religious education can be incorporated into the curriculum of Jewish educational settings.

CURRICULUM PHASES

A comparison of the impact of the strategies for the enhancement of religiosity results in an examination of curriculum theory in which three phases of curriculum are newly identified from my research. A phase of curriculum is a component of the operational and experienced curriculum that can be discretely identified.

The three curricular phases that emerged from my research, I term Encounter, Reflection, and Instruction for Religiosity. I develop a description of each of the three phases by pro-

viding examples of statements from the learners about their spiritual experiences, as well as my own analysis.

Encounter

There are several specific elements that appear in curricula that educators and students perceive as significant in their religious development. Taken together these elements can be understood as contributing to or expressing the phase of Encounter. The students in Jewish educational programs experienced these elements in a variety of educational programs. Encounter involves evoking intense feelings of contemplation, peacefulness, wonderment, and concentration.

Experiences in Israel led to a flow of emotions at many holy sites. David, an Israel program participant, reflected on the experience of visiting the Western Wall. The experience precipitated his being able to articulate a certain understanding of what belief in God actually meant to him:

> I don't know if there's a God or not. My ideas have changed over the years. I used to and now I don't know. The reason that made me think if there was a God, was because of the message that I wrote at the Wall. I didn't want to ask anything of God. I began by saying "I'm writing this letter on the off-chance that You exist, because if You don't, then there's not much point, otherwise I'm writing it for myself." I didn't want to ask for anything because everyone else asked things, and if I was a God and everyone asked for things all the time, I'd get pretty annoyed. I started thinking what would I say, what can I write, and then examined the way I felt about life and the way life was and that, for me, was very spiritual. I've got a bit of the letter that I wrote . . . "If You're out there, whoever, whatever You are, I wonder if this is how you intended life to be." I thought it was a pretty odd life that I've already had, so what kind of a mind or being or entity would create a life like this? And I said that

just because I'm friends with certain people, they shouldn't be blessed over other people simply because I'm friends with them. So I asked for everyone to be happy, that they should be given encouragement and be blessed. But the whole time I was writing this I was aware that I didn't actually believe in a God. There was a philosopher who said you might as well believe in God because if you're wrong, then nothing is going to happen, but if you don't, then what happens when you die?

Another common experience of Encounter for Israel participants is the walk up Masada in the early dawn. This organized activity has its impact on the internal life of the students as this participant reflected on his experience. Mark described the experience this way:

Masada was amazing. We had to get up at something like 2:30 a.m. . . . we were all too excited to sleep before. We got up. It was pitch dark . . . We started walking up there and it was getting lighter and lighter as we got up and everyone was exhausted and everyone else was encouraging them and saying come on, we can do it. The tiredness sort of disappeared, changed actually into physical exhaustion rather than mental tiredness when we got to the top, and then we waited for the sun to rise and everyone was really excited. We thought first of all that it would be a boring sunrise because of the clouds, but they were going to clear and then the sun began to rise above the clouds which made it even more amazing because it lit up the clouds around it. I was just watching it in amazement, incredible. I was thinking that the tour so far had been amazing and that it's going to go on and this looks beautiful and everything around me was stunning and I'm with all my friends and everything was just brilliant. I was trying to be calm and patient. It was just knowing that we walked all the way up this mountain to come to this. It was like an amazing challenge, it was incredible. You're standing in the middle of

the desert on top of a piece of rock and you're seeing the sun rise. There's nothing particularly Jewish about that. But this is a particular rock in a particular country with a particular group of people. I felt very Jewish at the time and I was aware also that being at the top of Masada was a place where a tragedy happened and many Jews before me were there. I can't describe exactly why I feel Jewish at those kind of times, but I just do. It's like we're meant to be together, we're supposed to have these experiences.

These feelings of spiritual awareness are elements of Encounter.

Encounter is that which Martin Buber describes as spiritual preparation for a personal confrontation with the Absolute (Buber, 1979 and 1948), the I-Eternal Thou relationship that is transitory. As a result of Encounter, students express a closeness to God and a sense of God's presence. Students reflected on the nature of spirituality in their lives, as an emerging realization. Rebecca, a summer camp participant, profoundly philosophized:

There's two kinds, it's a feeling of being in touch with either oneself or God. It's up to personal belief if you believe in God or not. Normally, the feeling is supposed to be a good feeling. Being spiritual should be a feeling of contentment. It's like opening a door of perception. It can be a road to somewhere else, another way of thinking, another plane of awareness — that's very deep.

It was shown in this study that the opportunity for spiritual Encounter is paramount in forming spiritual attitudes in teens. The study demonstrated that students experience a great deal of Encounter in educational programming. This is predominant in programs in which there is time and space for spiritual qualities to be experienced, such as contemplation, awe, quest, and heightened moments. It was found that most of these experiences take place outside of the classroom. This seems to occur spontaneously in natural settings such as sites in Israel, rural camp environments, and the synagogue sanctuary. Sam, a summer camp participant points out the connections between nature and the spirit:

> There are times here I feel glad to be alive, in the loveliness of the countryside and the fresh air. Here we share with Jewish people; there is no discrimination. No one thinks we are out of the ordinary. You feel special here when you get info about the Jewish people and about the Jewish religion. Everything is done with Jewish intentions in a relaxed environment. People enjoy it. Going to synagogue can be a bit dry, but here everyone goes and joins in and the spirit is really lifted.

Music, ritual, the creative arts, prayer, and meditation were also catalysts for such experiences. Katie, who was studying guitar at camp, begins to understand the connection between Jewish music and her spirituality:

> Then I get my guitar out and stop and think while playing. Music is a trigger for me and has a calming effect. I go more into myself, into an inner world. It's a time to think and to contemplate, a time for myself, which I never get unless I force myself.

During the phase of Encounter, educators acted largely as facilitators, structuring experiences and affirming students' perceptions. This is the confirming influence that Buber encourages teachers to practice. The Religious School Rabbi offers a unique ritual to provide such an experience:

> I do this thing with the *"Shema"* during the family services. I have everybody draw a circle around themselves and stand in the circle quietly and imagine that God is standing in the circle with them. It's just them and God and there is nobody else with them and that's their moment to feel held and to feel close and to feel warm and to say whatever they want, be it anger or asking or just talking or just a moment of quiet within themselves. And I suppose that is my attempt to help them feel enclosed and strong and safe.

Similarly a *madrichah* at summer camp described her perceived role in facilitating children's experiences:

> I would like them to learn that you can perform Jewish rituals to help touch various parts of ourselves, that Jewish spirituality is not something divorced from who we are and that we can use that spirituality to help understand ourselves and feel better about ourselves. I want to pass on to my 15 and 13 and eight-year-olds the sense of what I felt when I was that age. So I use informal education techniques within the setting of my Religious School to try and give them that sense.

The experience of Encounter leads to a willingness to learn and acquire knowledge and skills in religious life. The elements of Encounter are feelings of spiritual awareness that take place in locations of spiritual significance. This results in a perceived closeness to God in which prayer can be communicated. Repetitive rituals, music, or the beauty of nature trigger spiritual qualities of contemplation, awe, and peacefulness. Rebecca, a summer camp participant, explicitly defines her spirituality in these terms:

> I believe that spirituality for me is much more of a sense of connection with other people, with God, with myself. A meeting between myself and other people, with family, nature, things like that.

Encounter prompts a questioning in students, enabling them to verbalize spiritual feelings. An element of historical connection is felt in religious sites where hope, protection, and awe are felt. A group experience heightens the sense of Encounter, including affirmation of belonging to the Jewish people, though Encounter can also be experienced alone. The experience of Encounter in educational settings contributes to the acquisition of religiosity.

Reflection

Elements of curriculum that are expressions of religiosity form the phase of Reflection. Opportunities for thinking about God and prayer characterize an element of Reflection. Reflection motivates students to question and prompts them to seek answers to issues of personal meaning. Reflection is the ability and opportunity for students to contemplate and deliberate on religious experiences by drawing upon their imaginations. This takes the form of imagining aspects of God and pondering God's role in the world and the place of the individual in it.

Reflection is characterized by discussion, meditation, prayer, or conversation. Articulation of questions concerning spiritual experiences is a characteristic of this phase. Reflection often involves sharing deliberations with others when close bonds are formed. The bonds that are made enable the student to reflect critically on his or her experiences. Mark, a Religious School student, reflects on his thoughts and feelings about God:

> I feel there's something which maybe now I know you can call God, but I don't know how strong it is. He would just be everything around, but I don't feel that I can pray to it in the way that is formalized prayer, but there are other ways of getting through. I have developed my own way of thinking about things. When I think hard enough, then I suppose it's a bit like praying. That's why synagogue helps you in that it's somewhere you go and you know what you're supposed to be doing. I think synagogue doesn't instill spirituality in Judaism, but it is a center for it to happen.

The questions that are raised by students concerning God, good and evil, creation, hope in the future, lead to seeking answers in their religious tradition. Reflection is an intimate, imaginative, highly personal activity in a supportive environment that allows speculation, exploration, personal discovery, and affirmation. Leah thinks about how her Day School environment allows reflection to occur:

> It's not going to affect everyone every week, but quite often there will be something internal that you haven't talked about. You're

introspective, thinking about yourself and that's an eye-opener.

Mark also describes his inner thoughts as part of his synagogue experience:

> I know when we go to synagogue, we do the silent prayer. I always think then; I've always done that, and sometimes reading passages, I think about God. Sometimes when I've got something to do and it's really important, I think "I just need some hope and strength."

In this mode of Reflection, educators act in what is essentially a counseling role. This involves encouragement of discussion, active listening, and sharing of experiences of Encounter with peers, families, and teachers.

The study demonstrated that the presence of peers was important in identifying strongly with religious individuals and providing close connections between one another. This is evidenced in the close bonds formed especially at schools and other educational settings. The bonds made during Reflection enable the students to articulate their experiences. Debbie was nervous about revealing too much of herself in her Religious School classroom, but was encouraged by the openness of others and her teacher:

> We used to talk about what we thought God was and aspects of Judaism. Sometimes you don't want to express yourself too much because there's people around you, but you definitely air your main thoughts. You don't go that deep into it though. Some things I wouldn't say. I thought what I think might sound silly, but I definitely could talk about it.

Articulation of spiritual experiences is a vital part of this phase. However these experiences will remain purely implicit if they are not interpreted in a religious context. It is important therefore that students reflect on their reactions to experiences and that educators provide the supportive environment to allow Reflection to occur. This concurs with the understanding of religiosity that sees spiritual experiences as normative in human development:

Religious Truth is an experience understood at its fullest depth: what makes truth religious is not that it relates to some abnormal field of thought and feeling but that it goes to the roots of experience which it interprets. (Madge, 1965, p.8)

Reflection allows students to translate their spiritual moments into Jewish religious language and experience. Sherry Blumberg (1991, p.11) has written, "the challenge of educating for religious experience is to help learners identify spiritual experience as religious experience." As one Religious School student poignantly remarked:

It helps to package some of the spirituality so that it is tangible. You do this certain thing and you know it has a meaning, whereas worship without words and thinking [doesn't] quite [make] it, but with rituals you can [get the meaning]. It's more straightforward.

School assemblies are an important part of this process, since they provide a time for Reflection in a religious context. Responses from learners in this study suggest that creative prayer experiences were important for such Reflections. These moments tended to occur in schools in which leaders and students plan such experiences together. Havdalah at summer camp is the classic example of creative ritual making a spiritual connection for many:

We did Havdalah, which was very spiritual. We were in a long line and then wound into a spiral, close to each other and sat down. It was dark and there were candles and guitars playing. Everyone was singing the *niggun*. It was very spiritual, very nice.

It is also prevalent in special places chosen by the leaders to enhance the experience. Educators are often capable of providing prayer experiences within educational programs that enable students to Reflect on their spiritual Encounters. This was the case during *tefilah* on the Israel experience, which is often held outside and overlooking holy sites:

In peaceful surroundings, prayer is peaceful;

thinking and communication are linked to prayer. If you are able to pray, you have to have faith that prayers will be answered. Prayer is a sign of hope that God can help in ways to communicate with you.

Ritual also has a vital role to play in this phase, in that it provides a channel for spiritual experiences on a regular basis. These are the "deeds of wonder" that Abraham Joshua Heschel describes as a response to God's call (Heschel, 1976). John Westerhoff recognizes that "repetitive symbolic actions expressive of the community's sacred narrative" is the key to religious formation (Westerhoff, 1987, p. 10).

Few educators in any of the formal or informal Jewish educational settings initiated moments for Reflection as part of the program. Where Reflection does occur, it is initiated by the student after particular heightened moments. This occurs more frequently when the student is "living in" an educational environment such as a summer camp, a retreat, or an Israel stay, and has the opportunity to interact with an educator whenever the student has a question or a thought. Such settings also allow Reflection to occur over time. As experiences are mulled over, Reflection emerges in the same educational settings and with the same educators. Reflection is also evoked when a particularly strong relationship between educator and student is present. Reflection aids in naming and understanding the experiences of students and providing critical reflection on their Encounters in a supportive environment.

Instruction for Religiosity

A third phase of the enhancement of religiosity perceived by educators and students is that of Instruction for Religiosity. A number of elements mark this phase. Knowledge/a sense of connection to Jewish history is an element of Instruction for Religiosity. The teaching of Jewish texts from the Bible and the close reading and interpretation of these texts in schools provides an opportunity for students to confront their personal beliefs about God.

There are those who express uncertainty and confusion about their belief and what God means to them. Janis, a Day School student, has studied comparative religion at school, but has not yet found a foundation for belief:

> I really don't know how I feel about God. I mean I know all the Jewish ways and I know the science ways and I know the Christian ways and the Catholic ways and I really can't tell you which is right. I mean I know I am a Jew and everything, but I haven't got any proof to know that this is right, so I can't really say anything yet, because I don't really know . . . no one really knows for sure.

Then there are those students who are beginning to find their own meaning in what God means because of some personal experience. In a long and revealing conversation with Rachel, who attended Religious School, it emerged that synagogue life has been enormously significant in the struggle to make meaning in her life:

> That's really hard because to me, God is not a thing . . . I couldn't really say what God is, but God is something that you can't see, or maybe you can through natural things like trees and stuff like that, but you see a sort of power that no one knows about. So I can't really say, I just know there's something there. If there's no one else around, and no one else to turn to, then you think you need someone else to be able to say how you're feeling and if no one else is there for you, you want to know that the energy of God would be there to reassure you — almost put an invisible hand round you. I went through depression and I felt that no one else was there for me. That's definitely when I felt close to God and I think the Rabbi helped me see that. If there's no one else, there's God, and that's really my spirituality. Now every day I pray to God. I mean, at different times during the day, I think of God, whereas before I wouldn't have, only when I went to a service or before an exam or something. So that's the difference.

Students use their creativity to explore visual images of God in order to compare contrasting views of Jewish belief. The use of the arts expresses religiosity though creativity as students depict the characteristics of God in imaginative form. Instruction in Religiosity includes the element of creativity in expressing religiosity.

The knowledge and application of new skills in Jewish life is another element in Instruction for Religiosity. For some, carrying out Jewish ritual automatically confers a spiritual awareness. As one Day School student remarked:

> For me, Judaism is in my everyday life. It's all an integral part of my life. Judaism gives me my spirituality in the *mitzvot* I carry out.

Instruction for Religiosity provides the theoretical underpinnings for students' spiritual experiences. Varying conceptions of God are taught that allow students to place their experiences in a theological context. God then guides this student's life when decisions need to be made:

> I think He's someone who protects and gives you advice, even if you don't know it. I think that when you make a decision, God helps you to make the decision.

This is education for knowledge and character that develops images and concepts enabling students to grapple with issues and experiences:

> The emphasis should not be on teaching children correct or orthodox doctrine about God. Rather the emphasis should be on enriching children's vocabulary and through conversation developing images and concepts which will enable children to grapple at their own level with the issues and experiences involved in God-talk. (Hull 1990, p. 15)

Instruction for Religiosity is observed in schools. It remains on the cognitive level, however, as it avoids connection with student's personal Encounters. Religious thought, texts, and concepts of God may be taught and expressed by teachers. Teachers, however, are reticent to open up their own experiences of Encounter, let alone hear them from students. Instruction for

Religiosity forms a critical consciousness and stimulates a need to know and do.

CONCLUSION

The spiritual awareness found in Encounter and the verbalizations that emerge from it can lead to articulation of questions in Reflection. These questions are responded to by the Jewish context offered in Instruction. The three phases of Encounter, Reflection, and Instruction for Religiosity are not sequential, but operate concurrently. All three influence each other as Instruction for Religiosity opens up students to new Encounters. Reflection is a crucial phase, however, in that it allows articulation of spiritual awareness to be connected to explicit religiosity in instruction. Reflection allows others to hear experiences and possibly encourage a future disposition to such Encounters or a questioning attitude that places the Encounter in a religious context. The sharing of Reflections is as important for the individual as it is for the educational group. As Buber has posited (Buber, 1948), it is in the asking of questions by students and the subsequent learning in the teacher that a mutuality of education takes place.

The study showed that students experience an enormous amount of Encounter in educational programming. They also receive a great deal of Instruction for Religiosity. However, the two were not connected. It is therefore important that Reflection on experience takes place and that Instruction for Religiosity is then based on those experiences. The enhancement of religiosity is promoted through the presence of all three phases in the curriculum.

IMPLICATIONS FOR CURRICULUM

1. The identification of the three phases of Encounter, Reflection, and Instruction for Religiosity allow Jewish educators to understand the processes at work in enhancing religiosity in any educational environment. All three phases are needed, and educators will need to plan for them when formulating their programs. In each phase the role of the educator changes, and it is therefore important to understand these differing roles and develop a repertoire of skills to be used in differing phases.

2. The educator sets up the right environment for Encounter. He/she must be able to be sensitive to the moment and know when the time is right for silence or speech, ritual or routine. Choosing the right moment to recite a *brachah* with students when something significant has happened in the classroom can be a vital contribution to Encounter. Location is vital in this phase. Will you choose to go outside, into the sanctuary, onto the roof, or sit in the classroom sunlight? Can you allow your class or group to be silent, simply wondering about a challenging idea or following a poignant moment? Be aware of the qualities that engage the student, such as contemplation, calmness, and wonderment.

3. During the phase of Reflection, the educator facilitates the verbal expressions of students, encouraging them to ask questions, wonder, and deliberate about their own experiences. Questions such as "I wonder how you felt at your Bat Mitzvah" can be crucial opportunities for spiritual reflection. Here a supportive environment is needed and the educator needs to know his/her students well so that he/she can challenge or sustain them as needed. It is also vital that the educator can manage the group process so that students listen to one another with respect and in a nonjudgmental way. Learning in this phase comes from peer-peer relationships.

4. The educator guides and inspires in the third phase, Instruction for Religiosity. Here he/she provides answers to questions, but most importantly poses new questions as well. Knowledge of the tradition and its application to young people's lives is vital. Providing access to the texts of our tradition and demonstrating the methods of interpretation will enable young people to seek answers to their questions of meaning within Judaism. It is also crucial to be honest and open. Encouraging questions about God and faith may be difficult, but it is the only way to make explicit the spiritual journey. The educator may not know it all, but is prepared to say that he/she will treat students seriously enough to search for an answer. After all, what can you say immediately when a student asks "Where was God in the *Shoah*?" The important thing in this phase is to open students up to the possibility of further Encounter, as well as deeper Reflection.

5. Nothing is more important in all three phases than listening actively to your students. They will express their fears and hopes and doubts only when they are being truly listened to and affirmed. I have often advocated that teachers should meet with every student before the start of the academic year to get to know him or her as an individual. The full classroom is often not the place to get to know each person's unique potential. This is the time to build a relationship, empowering the students to see the educator as a spiritual guide and sponsor. However, the classroom community or any other learning community needs its set of rituals to mark the moments that are experienced together. Whether it is prayer, meditation, music, appreciations, or sharing time, these are significant and memorable moments for a group of learners.

These identified phases of curriculum assist the school or educational institution in planning for the enhancement of religiosity in a purposeful way. The results of this study demonstrate the vital role that the multifaceted educator plays in enhancing the religiosity of students.

QUESTIONS FOR CRITICAL INQUIRY

1. Shire develops his approach to educating the spirit by first interviewing teens. Thinking about your students, regardless of their age, what questions about their spirituality would you ask them if you were developing a theory on educating the spirit?

2. Recalling the educational experiences of your own students, describe experiences that fit into the categories of Encounter, Reflection, and Instruction for Religiosity.

3. For what reasons should we require teachers to study and clarify their own religiosity?

4. In what ways does your current educational program provide for times of Encounter, Reflection, and Instruction for Religiosity? In what ways could you enrich these elements within your setting?

ACTIVITIES

1. Explore popular songs that reflect spiritual questing for God, such as "From a Distance" by Bette Midler, "One of Us" by Joan Osborne, or "Blue Cars" by Dishwala. What is each songwriter seeking? How does God fit into his/her search? If you were writing a song or movie about God, what would be the main theme? Advanced students might analyze the spiritual search in such films as *Dogma* (1999, rated R, 125 min.), *Stigmata* (1999, rated R, 103 min.), *Keeping the Faith* (2000, rated PG-13, 127 min.), *Oh, God!* (1977, rated PG, 104 min.).

2. Study a text about trust. One example is Genesis 24, in which Abraham sends Eliezer, his servant, to select a wife for his son, Isaac. Look at all the different aspects related to trust including: Why does Abraham select

Eliezer? Why does Abraham send him to Nahor, his brother? After completing this discussion, form pairs. One member of the pair is blindfolded, and the other takes him/her on a trust walk. Switch roles. Then talk about the experience, focusing on the various aspects of trust involved. How is being on this trust walk, during which you cannot see the person who is leading you on the path, like trusting in God? Sing *"Esa Aynai El HaHarim,"* Psalm 121:2. What does this Psalm have to do with what you have learned about trusting in God?

3. Read a selection from Job (chapters 1, 2, 3, and 19). Then act out Job talking to God about what has happened to him or read a section from the play about Job, *J.B.* by Archibald MacLeish. Why does Job get angry at his friends and not get angry at God? Spend five minutes writing: How do the friends feel about what God did to Job? Has anything happened in your life to make you angry with God? For the next two or three weeks, keep a journal of things that happen to people, yourself, or others that seem unfair or unjust. In class, tell how you or others responded to these situations. How were you and each of these people like or unlike Job? What do you think it takes to resolve one's anger with God? Revisit this issue one more time in the class, several weeks later. What does Job teach you about how to deal with anger with God and anger in general? What have others taught you about how to deal with anger with God and anger in general?

BIBLIOGRAPHY

Alexander, Hanan. *Reclaiming Goodness: Education and the Spiritual Quest.* South Bend, IN: University of Notre Dame, 2001.

Spirituality, according to Alexander, is discovering our best selves in learning communities devoted to a higher good. This "good life" is ultimately the purpose of religious education and, as such, gives us a means to integrate ethical and spiritual values with critical thought and intelligence.

Bachya ibn Pakuda. *Duties of the Heart.* New York: Feldheim, 1970.

Eleventh century treatise of devotional duties in Judaism. The introduction, written 1,000 years ago, is a wonderful statement about Judaism's need for an inner discipline!

Beck, Clive. *Better Schools: A Values Perspective.* New York: Routledge, 1989.

Clive Beck provides a list of what he holds to be key spiritual characteristics independent of their religious "language." This taxonomy is a tentative attempt to delineate the area of spirituality, and can be used to indicate the goals educators might have for the growth of their students.

Blumberg, Sherry H. *Educating for Religious Experience.* Ph.D. Dissertation, Hebrew Union College, 1991.

This work analyzes various philosophical implications for spiritual education.

Buber, Martin. *Between Man and Man.* London: Fontana Books, 1979.

This collection of essays includes two significant ones on education.

———. *Israel and the World.* New York: Schocken Books, 1948.

This collection of Buber's essays focuses on the encounter between the historic perspective of the Jewish people and the world.

———. *Pointing the Way.* New York: Harper and Bros., 1957.

Another of Buber's writings that gives insight into his I-Thou theology and its significance for living as a Jew.

Fowler, James. *Stages of Faith.* New York: Harper and Row, 1981.

The foundational work in the field of faith development. Highly readable and significant in its worldwide influence in the 1980s and 1990s.

Fowler, James; Karl Ernst Nipkow; and Friedrich Schweitzer. *Stages of Faith and Religious Development.* London: SCM Press, 1992.

An international collection of many of the key thinkers and researchers in faith and spirituality, the book includes a critique of the work of Fowler, among others.

Goodlad, John. *Curriculum Inquiry.* New York: McGraw Hill, 1979.

A report of his research into the domains of curriculum.

Green, Arthur, ed. *Jewish Spirituality.* New York: Crossroad Publishing Co., 1987.

A collection of scholarly articles depicting aspects of Jewish spirituality throughout history. This collection became "volume one" when a second collection of articles was published.

Harms, Ernest. "The Development of Religious Experience in Children." In *American Journal of Sociology* 50 (1944).

Harms was the first researcher to use projective picture techniques to elicit attitudinal responses from children.

Hay, David, with Rebecca Nye. *The Spirit of the Child.* London: Fount, 1998.

The best description of children's spirituality, including a research study that replicates Dr. Shire's work, except in a secular context. Highly recommended reading!

Heschel, Abraham Joshua. *God in Search of Man: A Philosophy of Judaism.* New York: Farrar, Straus and Giroux, 1976.

Heschel lays out his theology of Jewish life, dealing directly with questions about God and such theological concerns as revelation, Torah, *kavanah, mitzvah,* and sin.

———. *The Insecurity of Freedom.* New York: Farrar, Straus & Giroux, 1966.

Heschel confronts directly the issues of trying to maintain one's Jewish convictions while living in a free society. He devotes a chapter to Jewish education.

———. "The Values of Jewish Education." *Proceedings of the Rabbinical Assembly 26,* 1962.

This address to the Rabbinical Assembly focuses on Jewish education.

Hull, John. *God-Talk with Young Children: Notes for Parents and Teachers.* Birmingham Papers in Religious Education No. 2. Philadelphia, PA: Trinity Press International, 1991.

A small booklet describing the author's conversations about God with his children.

Klein. M. Francis et al. "A Study of Schooling: Curriculum." *Phi Delta Kappan,* December 1979, p. 245.

An article describing the domains of curriculum and the ways in which it can be used by researchers investigating curriculum in a variety of educational settings.

Madge, V. *Children in Search of Meaning.* London: SCM Press, 1965

An empirical study of the religious and scientific thought of children in the primary school grades.

Mott-Thornton, Kevin. *Common Faith: Education, Spirituality and State.* Brookfield, VT: Ashgate 1998.

An exploration of the way in which there can be a common approach to the spiritual development of students in state schools. Mott-Thornton sets out a characterization of "common spirituality," and produces a framework for testing assumptions about policy on spiritual education.

National Curriculum Council. "Spiritual and Moral Development: A Discussion Paper." April 1993.

The current state of thinking in the UK about spiritual development and its implementation and assessment in all state schools.

Resnick, David. "What If Formal Jewish Education Is Really Informal?" *Agenda,* 1993, 9-14.

A challenging article about the nature of formal Jewish education and the ways in which it doesn't really exist.

Shire, Michael J. *Enhancing Adolescent Religiosity in Jewish Education: A Curriculum Inquiry.* Ph.D. Dissertation, Hebrew Union College, 1996.

This chapter in this book is based on Dr. Shire's dissertation.

———. "Faith Development and Jewish Education." *Compass,* July 1987.

This article provides a concise explanation and critique of Fowler's stages of faith for Jewish educators.

———. "Jewish Sources for a Definition of Faith." *Jewish Education News* 16:1, Winter 1995.

How we understand the concept of faith as defined by Fowler and within Jewish tradition.

Westerhoff, John. "Formation, Education, Instruction." *Religious Education* 82:4, Fall 1987.

Interesting article by one of the leading Christian educators. Provides a challenging perspective on the contribution of religious education to a nation.

TEACHING AND LEARNING ABOUT GOD: CONSIDERATIONS AND CONCERNS FOR ADULTS

Betsy Dolgin Katz

INTRODUCTION

"AMERICANS' FAITH IN GOD IS GROWING" WAS THE headline on page 3 of the *Chicago Tribune*. The opening paragraph read: "This holiday season, the largest percentage of Americans in a decade profess a belief in God and the existence of miracles."

The week before, in an article on the 72 percent of American adults who in a Gallup Poll revealed they believed in angels, Peter Kreeft of Boston College described "a kind of hunger for the supernatural, for contact with something greater than the self." Carla Johnson, assistant professor of communication at Notre Dame and a scholar of marketing and popular culture wrote, "With today's breakdown of the family, both Baby Boomers and GenXers long to find someone to protect them . . . . " Marya Smith, in "A Wing and a Prayer: Soaring Angels Lead a Resurgence of Interest in Spirituality," adds, "Women especially, as society's nurturers and caretakers, have a heightened sense of 'Who's going to take care of me?' and who better than someone above this world?"

And what of our Jewish community? The growth of interest in spirituality, healing, *Kabbalah*, books, speakers, and workshops on finding God are the manifestation of this hunger for the supernatural. It is the same quality that has led Rabbi Lawrence Hoffman (at the Great Lakes Region, UAHC Biennial, 1994) to describe the present generation as a "generation of seekers" in contrast to the "generation of rescuers" which preceded them. In the Jewish community, reasons as diverse as the arrival of the millennium, the influx of Jews with non-Jewish backgrounds, the backlash from the age of information and technology, and the search for beauty

and meaning in life have driven interest in adult courses, classes, retreats, and seminars on searching for God.

Regardless of the reasons, the need exists. It becomes the responsibility of Rabbis, Cantors, educational leaders, and teachers to respond to this pressing need. The purpose of this chapter is to address those issues to be considered when creating meaningful learning experiences for adults so that they can deepen their knowledge of theological matters and explore and develop their relationship to God.

WHO ARE THE ADULT LEARNERS?

Searching, Growing Individuals

It may seem simpleminded to begin a discussion on the nature of the adult who comes to learn by addressing the fact that this adult is searching and growing. However, until the middle of the twentieth century, adulthood was considered to be merely the end product of childhood and adolescence. Once through with high school or college, the adult was a fully formed and functioning individual. There was no academic field called "adult development," let alone a subject area sophisticated enough to be subdivided into physical development, cognitive development, moral development, and faith development.

We today have benefitted from recent research and information in the area of adult development and learning. Pioneering work by Erik Erikson, Lawrence Kohlberg, James Fowler, Jane Loevinger, George Valillant, and Daniel Levinson has opened up new vistas for exploration. (For a discussion of the theories of Kohlberg and Fowler, see Chapter 7, "Nurturing a Relationship to God and Spiritual Growth." For theories of Erik Erikson, see Chapter 8, "Psychosocial Resources for a Spiritual Judaism.") Yet, each classroom teacher has an opportunity to contribute to the growing body of knowledge. For us in the field of adult religious and spiritual development, there are questions to answer and much yet to be learned. In our Jewish community, we can gain from the writings on religious education of Linda Vogel, Leon McKenzie, John Elias, or Kenneth Stokes, but believing that faith like politics is local, we need to develop our own literature, our own educational assumptions, and our own effective strategies. Our learners are unique. They are searching and growing *as Jews*.

Self-Directed Learners

Those who come to learn as adults come of their own free will. Granted, they are sometimes motivated by a zealous spouse, an insistent friend, or a concerned Rabbi or teacher, but it is an individual's choice to participate in a learning experience. Participants must have interest in the subject and have questions to pursue. They have the potential to be the students we always want in our classes, highly motivated, curious, and cooperative. To varying degrees, they are taking responsibility for their learning.

On the other hand, as they come voluntarily, they can also change their minds and lose their motivation. There are events in their lives that can take away the time that they have set aside for learning. Because they lead lives full of many distractions, adult attendance can be irregular. If what is pulling them away from the class is stronger than the attraction of what they find in the class, they will drop out. Teachers find themselves faced with the dilemma of teaching something eternal and deeply serious in a setting that is often episodic and discontinuous.

Varied Knowledge and Experience

The nature of student bodies can be compared to an inverted pyramid with classes made up of the youngest children on the bottom point and the

adult classes being the broad top of the structure. Variation within groups becomes greater in proportion to the age of the students. Differences among adult learners reflect their great differences in life experiences and in their Jewish learning experiences. It becomes the responsibility of the teacher of any class, but even more importantly a responsibility of a teacher of adult students, to become acquainted with the nature of the individual students that come to learn.

Adults enter the classroom possessing different levels of Jewish knowledge. Their exposure to Bible, Talmud, and other texts, theology, prayer, ritual, Jewish history, and Jewish culture can range from the most limited to the most refined. Some enter the classroom with no prior formal Jewish education and others have advanced degrees in Jewish studies. Because the study of theology and the exploration of a relationship to God are subjects only recently appearing in adult education listings, few people have had the opportunity to focus on these as formal areas of study. They have rarely been included as a subject of study even in the preparation of Rabbis, Cantors, educators, and other Jewish professionals. Having been taken for granted in traditional circles, and of less professional interest than other subjects in liberal communities, these subjects have remained a subject little explored and little understood.

It is, however, important to keep in mind that although students may be unsophisticated in the area of theology, they can be very sophisticated in areas such as philosophy, psychology, literature, and logic. Their backgrounds in other educational categories can prepare them to deal with the subject of God.

Implied in the approach to this subject is the understanding that learning about God can be pursued from two directions. The study of theology is the study of religious faith, action, and experience. Individuals in the class will have had varying educational exposure to the study of theology. A few will be conversant with major Jewish texts on God and the philosophers who dealt with God questions. On the other hand, knowledge of God can be gained through personal experience and from thinking and talking about one's ongoing relationship with God. In this area, formal education has little to do with knowledge and insights. Anyone in the learning group can be an expert, and yet no one can be the sole authority, including the teacher. This is an area of learning in which participants in a class share experiences and insights and grow together.

Diverse Learning Styles

At all levels of schooling, teachers are becoming more aware of the varied learning styles of their students. Each adult learner has a favorite way of learning. Much of one's learning style is based on previous learning experiences. Although the average learner over 40 is more familiar with text-oriented learning, the text can be presented orally or visually. Many younger adults were exposed to frequent use of video, computers, and interactive learning strategies. They are accustomed to being taught utilizing experiential strategies and technology. These differences in learning experiences support the teacher's use of a variety of strategies. The teacher who varies his/her approach from lesson to lesson is more exciting than the one who does the same things each and every class. Whether it be using lecture, discussion, text explication, small group work, videos, music, drama, or experiential activities, variety adds spice to the classroom. This variety helps in reaching people through ways of learning that are comfortable and familiar.

Special Interests

Adults frequently come to classes with specific needs in mind. Their particular goals and perspectives become the prism through which they perceive the subject matter. Parents want to learn for themselves, but also to look for the ideas that will engage their children and for the language by which they can communicate with them about God. An individual having suffered a recent personal loss brings difficult questions to class about good and evil and God's role in

life. Some older students will look for the Jewish perspective on life after death, resurrection, heaven and hell.

OBSTACLES TO ADULTS LEARNING ABOUT GOD

Research in general adult education (Valentine and Darkenwald, 1990) places obstacles to learning in three categories: physical, content, and psychological. There are physical reasons, such as the time of classes, location, cost, or availability of child care that impede adult learning. The nature of the teacher and the makeup of the class can also be an issue for some.

Other obstacles relate to the content of the course. Even if we take for granted that those who come to the class want to learn about God and their relationship to God, many of these students would opt out of the experience if the class was too difficult or too easy, if the perspective was too fundamental or too liberal, too spiritually-oriented or too philosophically-oriented. Most classes incorporate the perspective that there are many ways to perceive and relate to God. However, there are students who come to class looking for the right answer. They expect to find clear answers as to what Judaism teaches about God. The fact that there are no "right" answers, no one Jewish way to know God, can be a pleasant surprise to some, but a discouraging discovery to others. The awareness that it is the journey that is important in Judaism, not the arrival at a destination, can be exciting to one person and frustrating to another. The difficult questions surrounding theology and involved in examining one's relationship with God can be obstacles to some and challenges to others. Those issues that are considered to be obstacles to belief are important issues that a class needs to address. Does God speak to us today? Does God hear our prayers? How can we describe God in human terms? Are there still miracles? If God is good, why is there so much evil in the world? What really happened at Sinai? What do we do when science conflicts with our beliefs?

The third category of reasons why adults do not participate or continue to be part of adult learning is a category of psychological blocks. Many of these come from students' prior experiences in Jewish settings. Adults bring "baggage" to learning experiences. There is information that will anger them, frustrate them, or confuse them. Many adults must go through the difficult process of unlearning something that is "known," something that has influenced their lives and beliefs for many years. Adults may resist the process of change and, therefore, drop out rather than incorporate their new learning. Another sensitivity that adults bring to class is hesitancy to talk openly about personal spiritual matters. This may arise out of shyness, feelings of inadequacy, or lack of desire to share personal thoughts and feelings. Such reticent students may not return to the learning situation. Also, one who has experienced tragedy and never confronted the ultimate questions connecting that tragedy with beliefs, may find the learning experience too painful to stay in the class.

IMPLICATIONS OF THE QUALITIES OF ADULT LEARNERS

Create a Safe, Open Environment

One of the primary principles of adult learning is that the experience must be learner-centered. This means that planners and teachers must know and respond to the students. Having established some of the qualities of the students who come to learn about God and to explore their relationship with God, the next step is to look at the practical outcomes from that knowledge.

The learning, changing adult needs to study in a setting that provides a culture for exploration and growth. Considering some of the obstacles to effective learning, the setting must provide a safe, nonjudgmental environment in which individuals are welcomed and affirmed. Such an environment is open to all ideas and experimentation with those ideas. Asking questions is encouraged, testing out opinions is the standard, and changing one's mind and making

mistakes are expected. Particularly when talking about God, there is respect for everyone's effort to wrestle with the difficult, elusive questions and answers. There is no one right answer. Doubt is a norm. A person's perceptions of God will change not only throughout one's life, but also through the duration of the class.

Teachers' practices vary according to the ideology of the class sponsorship and their own views as to whether non-Jewish positions are to be discussed in the class. Some settings welcome the non-Jew who wants to explore Judaism. This student will challenge the Jewish perspective and frequently influences the direction of the discussion. Once the non-Jewish student enters the class, that person cannot be told that his/her opinions are out of bounds. More often, the non-Jewish student becomes part of the class only when considering the possibility of adopting a Jewish identity or supporting and understanding someone who is Jewish. Other classes are only for those who are exploring their own Jewish beliefs.

The other question to be addressed by individual sponsors and teachers is whether or not an atheist, a person who denies the existence of God, can be accepted in the same nonjudgmental open way that the doubter, the questioner, or the one who is angry with God can be. There are those who come to study in order to hear a "second opinion," but they are willing to suspend their disbelief and are open to learning. The question to be decided is whether there are limits to what can be affirmed or vociferously denied in a Jewish classroom.

Be a Guide for Your Students

As indicated above, a teacher of this subject may be knowledgeable in the area of theology, but when it comes to experiences in relating to God, we are all equal. This is a kind of teaching that is not telling. Teachers are gatekeepers and guides. They provide the setting and direction of the journey by shaping the class environment, by structuring the discussion with their selection of learning material and questions, and by modeling their own searching and supporting the search of others. Teachers challenge their students and set certain boundaries, advising caution when necessary. Students do their own thinking, discovering, and creating as they move forward, but they do so with a competent guide and in the company of other travelers.

Respect Students' Time and Commitment

When adult learners, like all students, set aside precious time to study, they deserve high quality, well planned learning experiences. There will always be the teacher who walks into a classroom unprepared who can just talk on any subject off the top of his/her head. The fewer of these, however, the better. Even the most charismatic teacher must provide an opportunity for learners to feel a sense of accomplishment, something that results from the clear movement of a lesson from its starting point, through specific key ideas, to its conclusion. Teachers need to be responsive to the questions and needs of students as they arise in class, but, except in rare circumstances, these should not deflect the class from working toward its end goal. Unless students are there strictly to be entertained (and there are many subjects other than the subject of God that lend themselves better to an entertaining evening), a group must not feel as if they have wasted their time. Each lesson must be an opportunity to learn something new. One of the most common reasons given for why students drop out of class is that the expectations created by publicity, titles, and discussions about the class were not met.

Pluralism

To create a culture for growth, it is necessary to teach theology to illustrate the point that numerous great Jewish thinkers have conceived of God in different ways. Judaism encompasses many perceptions of God. Even within a synagogue representing a particular denomination, there are many ways to describe the nature of God and many paths to finding and expressing a relationship with God (see Chapter 1, "The Changing Perceptions of God in Judaism"). This presentation of multiple perspectives gives individual learners permission to find their own meaningful answers within the framework of Judaism. This, rather than an approach that dictates answers, allows the adult learner to find an answer full of personal meaning that links him/her to other Jews, as well as to God. It is liberating to allow the individual to find his/her own place within the system of Jewish belief and Jewish living. A pluralistic environment also serves in a very direct way to model and teach understanding and tolerance of all who make up our diverse community.

One of the valuable aspects of the Jewish practice of studying in a learning community or in *chevruta*, is the exposure one gets to the ideas of others. Learners question and support one another. In the ideal adult setting, differences create an opportunity for exploration and collaboration, not competition. Students may hold diverse opinions and they may experience God in different ways, yet they are part of the same community.

SETTINGS FOR ADULT LEARNING

Because adult learners have so little discretionary time, and because that time allowance is frequently tied to their age and stage in life, it is important to offer opportunities to learn in a variety of settings. Too often in the past, adult education has been limited to Tuesday night at the synagogue. Many congregations are realizing the limitation of this perspective and are broadening their offerings. They are joined by other adult education providers in planning adult learning in a wide variety of additional time slots, settings, and formats. All of the following are occasions that could lend themselves to the study of God and one's relationship to God:

- Sunday morning or any evening (while the children are in Religious School)

- Shabbat morning before or after worship services

- Learning *minyan*
- Home *havurot*
- Take home learning boxes/packages
- Study sessions prior to committee meetings
- Brief study sessions at meetings related to the work of committees
- Social action projects integrating study
- Synagogue skill tutorials
- Book discussion groups
- Lunch and learn
- Early morning (before work) semester
- Weekend in-city retreats
- Weekend out-of-town retreats
- All-day study marathons
- Internet classes
- Computerized learning
- Field trips: Museums, Jewish cemeteries, social service agencies, synagogues
- Educational travel: Holocaust Museum, New York, Israel

GATEWAYS TO STUDYING GOD AND RELATIONSHIP TO GOD

The most common method of teaching God and one's relationship to God is the organization of a class with these topics as the focus. As implied above, however, there are many opportunities to approach the subject as it is integrated into other aspects of Jewish learning. God is part of all aspects of Jewish life. The study of God can also be part of all that we do. What follows is an annotated list of gateways through which one can walk as one studies and searches for God.

Learning Minyan: The *Siddur* can be studied as a book of theology. How is God represented in our prayer book? How do we communicate with God? How can we find God through our prayers?

Social Action Projects: Abraham Joshua Heschel wrote in *God in Search of Man* that we meet God when we perform *mitzvot*. What are the classical Jewish sources for caring for the elderly, helping the poor, dowering the bride, clothing the naked, welcoming guests, and other *mitzvot*? What do these activities have to do with being created in the image of God?

Committee Work: Work in the community, the synagogue, or other Jewish organizations should also be viewed as doing God's work and as perpetuating the image of God. There are links between every committee and God — even fundraising and building committees.

Leadership Development: There are ways to lead that reflect the Jewish ethical system based on belief in God and respect for others. There are Jewish models of leadership inspired by biblical characters whose relationship to God was reflected in how they led and lived their lives.

Educational Travel: As the story tells us, "the phone call to God from Israel is a local call." One can travel to Israel for many reasons, but one of the more important is the opportunity it gives one to discover Jewish roots, to link up with the source of much of our spiritual heritage, to see the land chosen by God for the Jewish people.

Field Trips: God can be studied in synagogue architecture, in the objects in museums, in the kosher butcher shop or *mikvah*, and other Jewish stops around one's home or community.

Text Study: When we pray, we talk to God. When we study our sacred texts, God talks to us. Whether we look at biblical narrative and its commentaries, our legal texts, or the beautiful poetry of the Bible, God is there to be discovered.

Storytelling: Putting us in touch with our own past is part of our search for God. Our personal stories are waiting to be learned, heard by others, and retold. These lead to an examination of family, community, and national stories, all of which create connections with God.

Personal Prayers: *Brachot, Techinot, Kavanot* are formal types of prayers. Formal prayer is one path for relating to God. Looking at personal prayers and meditation and trying one's hand at writing them is another. There are formulas to be learned and models to look at, but much that remains to be done is deeply personal.

Holiday, Life Cycle Rituals: Holidays and life cycle events can be observed because that is what Jews do. We can also look at these occasions as what we do because we are commanded by God. The rituals serve to bring out our God-like qualities and enable us to connect with God throughout the year and throughout our lives.

CONCLUSION

Teaching theology or talking with Jews about their relationship with God is a unique aspect of Jewish learning. It nurtures the souls of students and teachers alike. There are facts to be learned and past experiences to be shared, but the real achievement arises from participating in the process itself. We deepen and grow from sharing the journey, not in reaching a fixed destination. The wandering, like that of our ancestors in the wilderness, enables us to feel the possibilities of the sacred in the world around us, the harmony in our relationships with family, friends, our own community and that of others, and the presence of God in our lives. To be a teacher of this — a spiritual guide for seekers — is indeed a blessing.

IMPLICATIONS

1. Adult education needs to be in tune with the social context of the times. We are seeing an age of seekers for whom we need to generate a response that reaches them as individuals and strengthens their connection to the Jewish community.

2. Adults are varied in their experiences, learning styles, backgrounds, interests, motivation, and schedules. Therefore, those planning learning experiences about God need to consider and respond to these differences.

3. The instructor needs to come to class prepared with a variety of teaching methods included in the lesson plan. Adults do not thrive solely on lecture and discussion. In fact, given the voluntary nature of much of adult education, educational offerings need to be well thought-out and planned, even more perhaps than for children, for whom education is often mandatory. Moreover, teachers of adults need to be trained in andragogy (the study of adult education) as teachers of children are trained in pedagogy.

QUESTIONS FOR CRITICAL INQUIRY

1. For what reason are you interested in studying about God? What interests have adults in your setting expressed as reasons for wanting to study about God? Overall, what is going on in society that has a heightened interest in adult learning in general and about God in particular?

2. Since adults come with such varied backgrounds, learning styles, expectations, interests, levels of commitment, etc., what are ways of your getting to know the adults who come to study? What are the ways of getting to know the adults who are part of your setting, but may not yet be partaking of educational offerings?

3. When planning to teach for children, we would take into consideration such theories and methods as multiple intelligences, learning styles, portfolio assessment, and the like. How might these educational trends be applicable to teaching adults about God?

4. What are the obstacles that Katz mentions about studying about God with adults? What

are any additional obstacles? In what ways can these obstacles be addressed?

5. Katz mentions several gateways for teaching adults about God. What are some of the gateways for teaching about God in your setting?

ACTIVITIES

1. Invite an adult to class, someone who is viewed as a spiritual person and is comfortable talking about God. Interview the person about his/her God experiences, touching on such things as: moments or times that they felt close to God, and ways or images of thinking about God throughout their lifetime. Have the person comment on how his/her views of God have changed over time. What important insights about God have stayed with the person throughout his/her life?

2. Use the Internet or other resources to explore different organizations in the community. First, identify the organizations. Find out what images of doing God's work are the foundation of each organization. Then look at your own setting to explore the ways in which it supports the spiritual searching of adults.

3. Pray alone using the *Siddur*. Then pray with a group. What are the similarities and differences between praying alone and praying as part of a community? How does the liturgy help connect you to the other people in the group? How does praying as a group help connect you to God?

4. Consider the phrase, *"Kadosh, Kadosh, Kadosh."* Think of various ways to express the meaning of these words (e.g., through sculpture, dance, music, painting, debate, writing, videotaping, paper cutting, etc.). How do these different modalities help you to understand the phrase better? For example, dance helps show how being *kadosh*, holy, helps us stretch and reach out and up to God.

BIBLIOGRAPHY

Heschel, Abraham Joshua. *God in Search of Man: A Philosophy of Judaism*. New York: Noonday Press, 1997.

   Any one of Heschel's books could serve as an entryway into discussion and understanding of adult spirituality. This book addresses the places where God and human beings meet, and describes the beauty and awe of that encounter.

Merriam, S. B., and R.S. Caffarella. *Learning in Adulthood*. San Francisco, CA: Jossey-Bass, 1984.

   This is a good introduction to adult development and learning. It summarizes and organizes basic research in the field in a thorough, accessible manner.

Ochs, Carol, and Kerry M. Olitzky. *Jewish Spiritual Guidance: Finding Our Way To God*. San Francisco, CA: Jossey-Bass, 1997.

   There is a new responsibility for Jewish leadership, for Rabbis, Cantors, teachers, and lay leaders, to be spiritual counselors. This book describes that role, the processes, and the resources that support it.

Roof, Wade Clark. *A Generation of Seekers*. San Francisco, CA: Harper & Row, 1993.

   The baby boomers change the climate of every decade they enter. This book explores the spiritual journeys of this rebellious generation, as it looks at the boomer culture and focuses on what members of this cohort believe.

Schulweis, Harold. *For Those Who Can't Believe: Overcoming the Obstacles To Faith*. New York: Harper Perennial, 1994.

   The title says it all. This book is written for those who are seeking serious but non-fundamentalist answers to the ultimate questions in Judaism, such as as the nature of God, revelation, miracles, and prayer.

Smith, Marya. "A Wing and a Prayer; Soaring Angels Lead Resurgence of Interest in Spirituality." *Chicago Tribune*, December 21, 1997.

This is a sample of the plethora of articles appearing in the popular press on the growth of interest in spirituality. Although focused on angels, the article paints a broad picture of the search for the transcendent.

Valentine, Thomas, and Gordon G. Darkenwald. "Deterrents To Participation in Adult Education: Profiles of Potential Learners." *Adult Education Quarterly* 41, no. 1, Fall, 1990, 29-42.

How do we identify the obstacles that prevent adults from entering adult learning programs? How do we help them overcome them? The article discusses six factors and the specific nature of the adults who experience them. It touches on practical implications for program planning and implementation.

Vogel, Linda J. *Teaching and Learning in Communities of Faith*. San Francisco, CA: Jossey-Bass, 1991.

Although written primarily about Christian religious education with reference from time to time to the Jewish community, this book provides some unique insights into religious education, particularly that aspect that deals with spirituality and community.

Wicket, R.E.Y. *Models of Adult Religious Education Practice*. Birmingham, AL: Religious Education Press, 1991.

This book provides a rationale for variety and interaction in religious education. It includes a wide inventory of workable instructional procedures for vitalizing the religious education of adults.

CHAPTER 12

CURRICULUM APPROACHES FOR TEACHING ABOUT GOD

Sherry H. Blumberg

MANY PEOPLE — JEWS INCLUDED — NEED AND very much want to talk about God. Faced with a highly complex and seemingly relativistic world, most people are — at one level or another — looking for something of enduring value, importance and sanctity that will give their lives a sense of direction and meaning. They need to explore their understanding of and their relationship to that which is sacred. To meet this legitimate and real need, Jewish educators need to teach about God. Fortunately, our tradition has an abundant and diverse supply of resources for this exploration.

What Jewish sources can we use to help these seekers answer their questions about existence and purpose of life itself? What curricular approaches will enable students to find hope in the midst of sorrow and tragedy? What values inspired our traditions? Why have the Jewish people always been optimistic and involved in this world? What are the ways Jewish educators can help students learn about the mystery of life, and the Source of life itself?

When I and many others like me think about our lives and reflect on what has given us the courage and stamina to live in this world, we arrive at one answer: our faith in God has given us a Jewish affirmation of life. It is that faith — that *emunah* — a sense of trust and truth — that gives us hope, courage, values, and the link to all other persons in time, especially to other Jews. Our faith sanctifies our lives and raises our lives above the profane, while still allowing us to accept and respond to the responsibilities of living.

For myself, the faith that sustains and nourishes me comes from my Jewish education, as well as my life experience. For people like me, our faith adds depth to the rational and intellectual content of our Jewish studies. Yet that faith is neither blind nor unquestioning. Doubting,

questioning, and dialoguing are integral parts of a Jewish study of and encounter with God. From Abraham's time to the present, we have engaged in dialogue and argument among ourselves and with God. Torah study, prayer, and our daily actions inspire the dialogue, which is at once both a statement of faith and a sign of a relationship. But, just as any relationship that has not been challenged docs not know its own strength, the strength and quality of a relationship with God can be assessed only when challenged. For this reason, it is important to speak about God in a trusting and nurturing environment, one in which we can safely raise our doubts, explore our questions, and pursue our quest. This is why I believe that the Jewish school must be a place where children can go for answers and guidance while testing or affirming their faith.

In this chapter I answer the fundamental educational question of how best to structure this dialogue for students within a school's curriculum, depending upon the goals of the school and the ages of the students.

DESIGNING A CURRICULAR APPROACH TO TEACHING ABOUT GOD

Key Elements

Turning Jewish schools into places where God is encountered and discussed requires well thought-out curricular approaches. How best to approach teaching about God in our Jewish schools evokes many questions: (1) What conception or idea of God should we present? Is there an authentic Jewish God concept? (2) What if the teacher is unsure about his or her own conception or feelings about God? Can an atheist or agnostic Jew teach about God? (3) When do we begin to teach about God? What concepts or ideas are appropriate for each age? (4) Are some teaching techniques better suited than others for teaching about God? (5) With the vast amount of material available, where, as teacher and educator, do I begin, and where end?

These questions translate into five key elements in designing a curricular approach to teaching about God: (1) philosophy and goals, (2) the teacher, (3) age appropriateness of the curriculum, (4) teaching techniques, and (5) the materials. Below, I answer the questions associated with each key element.

Philosophy and Goals

What conception or idea of God should we present? Is there an authentic Jewish God concept? Normative Judaism has no doctrinal statement about the definition and conception of God. Rather, it concentrates on the relationship between God and human beings. God is One, but there are multiple understandings of what that one God is. Therefore, a variety of Jewish God concepts, ideas, and experiences should be provided to learners so they can latch onto that perspective that most strongly resonates with them. As Fritz Rothschild puts it: "Teaching about God in Jewish education must draw on the variety of formulations and approaches which have emerged in the history of Israel's religion."[1] On the other hand, this multiplicity of authentic expressions about God does not mean that everything is acceptable. Some parameters are needed in defining a Jewish God concept in order to maintain a collective understanding, a connection to the Jewish people. (For a further discussion of these parameters, see Eugene Borowitz's discussion in *A Layman's Introduction To Religious Existentialism*.)

The Teacher

What if the teacher is unsure of his or her own conception or feelings about God? Can an atheist or agnostic Jew teach about God? A person who is going to teach about God needs to have examined his or her own belief, and tested it in the light of Jewish criteria, namely, metaphors, concepts, and views of God found in texts or expressed by Jews throughout the ages. For example, a person questioning why bad things happen to good people could examine, among other things, views on the concept of free will, the Book of Job (the biblical classic text on theodicy), or the responses of Holocaust survivors to that horrifying experience.

Perhaps thinking about the agnostic or the atheist teacher raises the deeper question of whether or not a doubter or a non-believer, can or should teach about God. The best teacher to teach about God is one who has a deep religious faith, and yet doubts, questions, and struggles with his/her understanding of God. This person exemplifies the Jewish seeker, one who is actively engaged in a relationship with God. Therefore, I would rather choose the agnostic teacher who can honestly search with the students, than the confirmed atheist, or even a person with a conception of God that doesn't allow for any disagreement or flexibility.

Age Appropriateness of the Curriculum

When do we begin to teach about God? What concepts or ideas are appropriate for each age? In my view, we should begin to teach about God as soon as a child begins asking questions about God. From then on, such teaching should continue throughout one's formal religious education. Hopefully, the curiosity that sparked that first question about God will continue for a lifetime. Some studies, such as one printed in *Compass* magazine,[2] identify the questions about God that most concern each age group from kindergarten through high school. Responding to questions and concerns that students themselves raise is one way of assuring that the curriculum is age appropriate.

[1] Rothschild, Fritz A., "The Concept of God in Jewish Education," *Conservative Judaism* 24:2-20 (Winter 1970), 6.

[2] Bernard Zlotowitz, "Teaching God To Kindergarten and First Grade," *Compass* 38 (March 1976), 1.

Teaching Techniques

What teaching techniques are best to use in teaching about God? In a certain way, teaching about God is like teaching about any other subject. The choice of technique should be guided by what will reach the students. However, teaching about God does present its own challenges in choosing a technique. The authors of *Teaching Basic Jewish Values*, Azriel Eisenberg and Abraham Siegel, warn not to discourage inquiry and not to confuse doubt with disregard for religion. While questioning and doubt challenge tradition, they do not necessarily lead to its breakdown.[3] To me, this means that any teaching technique that is honest, of interest to the students, and provides for open-minded, open-ended discussion, and takes the learner from the "known to the unknown" will work.[4]

Connecting technique to goals and purpose is particularly critical in making teaching about God relevant and effective in Jewish schools. Fritz A. Rothschild (1970) pointed out that for several reasons there is often opposition to the study of theology in Jewish schools no matter what technique you use. The Orthodox usually seek to avoid intellectual ferment and doubt, while the Conservative and Reform are afraid of a limitation of freedom and of the idea that there is one correct belief. Culturalists and secularists, on the other hand, find God study old fashioned and not applicable altogether.

Materials

With all the materials now available, which to begin with, and where do I go from there? Perhaps the best answer on what to use in beginning teaching about God is start with any text, Bible, *Midrash*, *Siddur*, or Hasidic tale. Begin with any question, concept, or idea that seems appropriate for the age group. As for what comes next, the more one seeks, reads, or learns about God, the more there is to know and experience.

Magazine articles, newspaper reports, history books, nature accounts, scientific discoveries, medical reports — all of these are fertile ground for God-talk. A mix of current and classic Jewish texts can also be extremely effective.

CURRICULAR APPROACHES TO TEACHING ABOUT GOD

Thus far, we have focused on the five elements that are part of any curricular approach to teaching about God. Below you will find a typology of common curricular approaches to teaching about God. One must plan and carefully consider how "God" will be a part of the Religious School curriculum. I agree with Rothschild that any discussion of God that comes about appropriately in the classroom can and should be integrated into the curriculum, and that the teacher needs to capture and respond to those special moments that present themselves as well suited for teaching about God. Still, "God" needs purposefully and explicitly to be included as part of the formal, planned curriculum.

In presenting this typology it is important to note that this is not about teaching techniques used to present content, but rather about the conceptual framework that undergirds how we teach about God, and the philosophical underpinnings that shape the content.

None of the five curricular approaches outlined here is generally used exclusively, nor are any of these approaches entirely discrete entities. For ease of discussion, I have divided them as follows: Theologians' Approach, Emotions Connected with God Approach, Conceptual and Question Approach, Historian Approach, and Integrated Approach.

The purpose of this section is to enable the educator or teacher to make an intelligent choice of curricular approach that is consistent with the

---

[3]Azriel Eisenberg and Abraham Siegel, *Teaching Basic Jewish Values, A Teacher's Guide To the Confirmation Reader*. (New York: Behrman House, 1954).

[4]Robert B. Nordberg, "Ideas of God in Children," *Religious Education* 66 (September/October 1971), 376-379.

goals and philosophy of his or her school. Each of these approaches has its strengths and weaknesses. Each is a legitimate method of approaching the content. Each will be examined with regard to its philosophy and goals, arrangement of content materials, the materials available, and age level appropriateness.

Theologians' Approach

One of the most likely approaches to teaching the idea of God is through the writings of those individuals who attempt to explain the concept or experience of God, namely the theologians. The strength of this approach and its underlying philosophy is that committed thinkers, those who live by their philosophies, struggle with exploring and articulating their ideas about and relationship to God. Their theologies reflect both their insights as scholars and their experiences as human beings. In an approach such as this, the lives of the theologians are intertwined with their thinking about God.

The use of text materials from theologians such as Philo, Saadia, Maimonides, Martin Buber, Abraham Joshua Heschel, Mordecai Kaplan, Eugene Borowitz, Milton Steinberg, Eliezer Berkovits, Robert Gordis, Judith Plaskow, and others, make the ideas vibrant, since these materials are not just impersonal abstractions, but are part of the lived experiences and convictions of these thinkers as Jews.

One of the problems in using this approach is that the learner must confront several concepts at a time. While this is an excellent approach for the older adolescent learner who can compare and contrast and see a total *gestalt* of a person's thoughts, such materials might be confusing for the younger student.

There is overlap between this approach and the Historical Approach if the theologians are considered in chronological order. Many of these theologians have created a chronology of theological ideas in their attempts to explain and develop Jewish theology for and in their age. This

theological chronology serves to connect them to those who came before them, while positioning them to address the issues of their time. Placing the theologians in their historical context is important, as often they are responding to the problems of their generation or era. Overlap also exists with the conceptual and emotional content areas, but the initial structuring in this first approach is around the theologians themselves, their writings and thoughts about God.

The materials available for use in teaching through this approach are *Living as Partners with God* by Gila Gevirtz (1997) for elementary students; and *Finding God: Ten Jewish Responses* by Rifat Sonsino and Daniel B. Syme for teens and adults.

Emotional Approach

Perhaps the most difficult of the approaches to explain or define is the Emotional Approach. Here, the human emotions which move us to experience God, such as awe, wonder, fear, love, reverence, humility, curiosity, and even anger, are the focus. Source materials are collected around these emotions. The philosophical underpinnings of such an approach stem from the affective elements of the curriculum (faith, hope, etc.) and the desire to make these the primary entry points into an exploration of God. The experience of God becomes magnified in importance beyond mere theological reasoning or explanations.

Why is the "experience of God" important? Eisenberg and Siegel state, "the experience of God must precede attempts at defining [God] and not vice versa."[5] Experience precedes knowledge in their estimation. Similarly, Rabbi Zlotowitz advocates for the primacy of focusing on experiencing God because of its connection to belief, conviction, and commitment:

Children need to relate to God so that God becomes a meaningful experience in their lives. Religious belief is not an intelligence

[5]Eisenberg and Siegel, op.cit.

test, but an emotional experience that affects our lives and gives meaning to our existence.[6]

Fritz A. Rothschild's work describes what is involved in experiencing God. He presents five fundamental experiences which are basic to a religion's understanding of God: change, dependence, order, value, and imperfection.[7] David Cedarbaum goes further in identifying levels of experiencing God. Each one of these levels helps lead to a more mature concept. The levels of experiencing God are: beauty of nature, beauty of people, forward movement of humankind, law and order in the universe, and an understanding of the moral law.[8]

I believe that any approach to God would be incomplete without an attempt to share, relate, and explain the experience of God. The Emotional Approach is one that overlaps with each of the other approaches in some ways, but it is possibly the best approach to use as one begins teaching children about God. Young children in particular often have an instinctual knowledge of these emotions.

Materials for this approach include *Hello, Hello, Are You There, God?* By Molly Cone (1999) for early childhood; *The Book of Miracles* by Lawrence Kushner (1987) for elementary age students; *Judaism and Spiritual Ethics* by Niles E. Goldstein and Steve Mason (1996) for teens; and *God Whispers: Stories of the Soul, Lessons of the Heart* by Karyn Kedar for adults. The Book of Job is also an especially good resource, and, of course, the Psalms are a rich resource that should not be overlooked.

Conceptual Approach

The Conceptual Approach is the most commonly used approach for teaching children about God. It deals with concepts and ideas about God and theology, which stem from basic questions about God and our relationship to God. Ideas such as Covenant, omnipotence, omnipresence, omniscience, qualities of God, monotheism, naturalism, pantheism, revelation, and redemption are just a few of the concepts that one can study. Questions such as what is evil, why do we pray, does God answer prayer, how can we know God, and the like are the outgrowths of exploring these concepts.

The underlying philosophy of this approach is that through ideas and through questions, we confront the concept of God. Materials are arranged around a specific idea and questions that relate to it. This method of organization is used in many modern texts. Source materials from many different religions may be brought in, since the questions are often similar in many religions. Some ideas, unique to Judaism, such as chosenness, will require Jewish materials.

The Conceptual Approach is effective for every age, as long as the materials selected are age appropriate in terms of activities and level of abstraction. There are ways of simplifying concepts, but a better method would be to let wording and questions for each concept fit the age. For example, adolescent learners and adults can grapple with the concepts of mysticism and gnosticism, while even the youngest preschool learners can understand the idea of creation. It is through the use of the conceptual approach that the conflicts between science and religion, secularism and religiosity, and many other intellectual controversies can be raised and discussed.

Materials for this approach are plentiful. Some suggestions are: *Because Nothing Looks Like God* by Lawrence and Karen Kushner (2001) for early childhood students; *How Do You Spell God?* by Marc Gellman and Thomas Hartman (1995), *Partners with God* by Gila Gevirtz (1996), and *Let's Discover God* by Marlene Thompson (1998) for elementary age students; *God: The Eternal Challenge* (see the Appendix on p. 000 for a reprint of this mini-course) by Sherry Bissell

---

[6]Zlotowitz, op.cit, 1.

[7]Rothschild, op.cit., 6.

[8]David Cedarbaum, "Developing God Concepts with Children," in *What Is the Answer?: A Guide for Teachers and Parents To Difficult Questions*, ed. by Stuart A. Gertman (New York: Union of American Hebrew Congregations, 1971) 9-15.

[Blumberg] with Raymond A. Zwerin and Audrey Friedman Marcus [1980]), and *The Invisible Chariot* by Deborah Kerdeman and Lawrence Kushner (1986) for teens and adults; and *What Do Jews Believe?* by David Ariel (1995), *Sacred Fragments* by Neil Gillman (1990), and *Innerspace* by Aryeh Kaplan (1990) for adults.

Historical Approach

The easiest approach to define in the study of God is the Historical Approach. In it, ideas about God are traced chronologically from the primitive to Abraham through the present day. "History is the laboratory of Jewish theology," asserts Rabbi Eugene Borowitz.[9] The Historical Approach is well suited for schools that present Judaism as an evolving religion or that focus on the presence of God in history.

The arrangement of source materials is done chronologically. Concepts come up when they are confronted in history. The Historical Approach provides an emphasis on cognition. Note that this approach is ineffective with younger students whose sense of history is not yet developed. This approach is best used starting in middle grades and continuing through adulthood.

Tools for the Historical Approach are not plentiful. Some of the books previously mentioned as focusing on Jewish theologians present their views in chronological order. Both *Living as Partners with God* by Gila Gevirtz (1997) for elementary students, and *Finding God: Ten Jewish Responses* by Rifat Sonsino and Daniel B. Syme (1987) for teens, are organized chronologically. Chapter 1 in this book, "The Changing Perceptions of God," and the book *Four Centuries of Jewish Women's Spirituality* by Ellen M. Umansky and Diane Ashton (1992) for adults also reflect an Historical Approach. Additionally, teachers can pull materials from the Bible, Talmud, *Midrash*, *Siddur*, Medieval thinkers, and modern philosophers without too much difficulty.

Integrated Approach

As previously stated, I believe that the best way to teach about God is by integrating the questions, experiences, and emotions connected with God throughout the whole curriculum, whether the topic of study is Prayer, Bible, History, Life Cycle, or Hebrew. The philosophical underpinning of the Integrated Approach is that "all authentic religious ideas relate to the idea of God."[10]

What is the specific definition of an Integrated Approach to God in the curriculum? How do we relate God to the other subjects and materials? In this approach, God is talked about and explored in every class of the school. For example, God should be discussed in relation to God's role in the Bible, beginning with Bible tales and continuing with each new course in Bible. God should also be discussed relative to the *Siddur*, the textbook of Jewish theology and prayer, with such questions as: What do we mean when we say *"Baruch Atah Adonai Elohaynu . . . "*? What is *Adonai or Elohim*? In a course on Ethics or *Halachah*, God may become the standard, the judge to whom we are answerable, the righteous one who is our model as in *"Da Lifnay Mi Atah Omed"* (Know before whom you stand). God is tied into history because of the traditional belief that God is present not just at creation, but throughout history. A connection between just about any topic and God can be made.

The topic, God, and the child are all integrated. The questions and challenges about life in all realms — physical, social, emotional, and spiritual — which the child confronts at each step of his/her development become part of this curricular integration. In order for the Integrated Approach to be used in the school, a commitment to developing the relationship between God and the child, in addition to teaching knowledge about God, must be a top priority.

David Cedarbaum, in his article about developing God concepts with children, states: "A cardinal principle is that we must relate God to the

---

[9]Quoted in Personal Interview with Eugene Borowitz, Summer 1975.

[10]Nordberg, op.cit., 378.

experience of the child at each step of his development as we encourage him to think about the great mysteries of the universe."[11] To go one step further, we must be conscious not only of each step of the child's development, but also of each kind of subject matter. In this way, "God" does not become a subject of discomfort, but rather becomes an important part of our living as a human being and as a Jew.

The following resources are available for the Integrated Approach: *How Does God Make Things Happen* (2001) and *What Does God Look Like?* (2001), both by Lawrence and Karen Kushner, for early childhood students; *When a Jew Prays* by Seymour Rossel (1973) and *God's Top Ten* by Roberta Louis Goodman (1992) for elementary age students; *When I Stood at Sinai* by Joel Lurie Grishaver (1992) and *Test of Faith* by Roberta Louis Goodman (1985) for teens. That the Integrated Approach is popular for adults can be seen in the abundance of available resources, including *The Busy Soul: Ten-minute Spiritual Workouts Drawn from Jewish Tradition* by Terry Bookman (1999); *Soul Judaism* by Wayne Dosick (1999); *The Extraordinary Nature of Ordinary Things* by Steven Z. Leder (1999); and *Jewish Paths Toward Healing and Wholeness* by Kerry M. Olitzky (2000). In addition, the Integrated Approach will or can at other times include all of the other approaches, so that all of the materials relevant to teaching about God become usable here, too. This broad, all-encompassing approach to teaching about God requires planning, a little imagination, and a deep concern for the development of children's relationship with God.

CONCLUSION

This chapter has provided a brief overview of several curricular approaches to teaching children and adults about God. The educator may follow a single approach or use a mix of approaches. The key is selecting an approach that matches the school's philosophy and goals. Whatever curricular approach is selected, the paramount concern is the need for Jewish schools to enable learning about God to occur explicitly and with intent and careful planning.

IMPLICATIONS

1. There are many ways to teach about God within the curriculum.

2. Although there are many curricular approaches to teaching about God, the approach used should reflect the goals, purpose, philosophy, and style of your institution.

3. Curriculum on God, theology, and spirituality needs to attend to the same curricular components (philosophy and goals, teacher, age appropriateness, teaching techniques, and materials) as any other curricular topic.

4. It is not enough just to address learners' God questions as they arise. Rather, "God" needs to be an explicit part of the curriculum.

QUESTIONS FOR CRITICAL INQUIRY

1. From your experience, at what age have most children started asking questions about God? Share what you remember of the questions that they were asking or what they were saying about God?

2. Thinking about your own spiritual quest, which of the approaches in this chapter might be most effective in helping you grow?

---

[11]Cedarbaum, op.cit., 10.

3. What does each of the five approaches outlined by Blumberg accomplish in terms of the messages it transmits about God?

4. In your opinion, what are the strengths and weaknesses of each of the five approaches?

5. Which of the five approaches is closest to how you teach about God in your educational setting?

6. Make a chart of the different curricular approaches for teaching about God. Include in this chart all the books or published materials that you could use for teaching about God through this approach.

7. Design a lesson on a concept about God (for example, *B'tzelem Elohim* — human beings are created in the image of God) for each of the different curricular approaches. Compare and contrast these curricular approaches in terms of (a) what they communicate about the concept, (b) their effectiveness in communicating about the concept, (c) their ability to evoke thoughtful consideration by the learner, and (d) any other highlights or observations.

8. Which of the curricular approaches for teaching about God comes closest to how you were taught in Religious School or Day School? How did that approach affect your exploration of God? What influence do you think the approach of your Religious School/Day School has on the learners in terms of their exploration of God? What could you do to strengthen the approach?

ACTIVITIES

1. Gather questions about God that the class or others in the setting have about God. Identify two or three theologians, such as Maimonides, Buber, etc., for teams of 2 to 4 to study. Present the questions to each group to answer. Have the audience vote on the response to the question that they most agree with in order to identify the most popular theologian of our time.

2. The Torah service is a reenactment of the giving and receiving of the Torah on Mount Sinai. In this reenactment, you are tying together the text of revelation at Sinai from the Torah, a lot of *midrashic* interplay, and the text from the Torah service liturgy. It would be best to be in a sanctuary or have an Ark or at least a Torah scroll accessible. Assign people to be God, Moses, Aaron, Miriam, and some "common" Israelites of different ages and genders. As you read the Torah narrative from Exodus 19 and 20, have the person facilitating the program interject questions as would a newscaster:

   • What does this mean to you?

   • How is this event different from the splitting of the Sea of Reeds?

   • What is it that you think you were accepting?

   • What do you think is the most important for your grandchildren to know about this experience?

   End with a celebration of receiving the Torah. Have each person come up with a sound bite of what they would want to convey to the next generation about this seminal experience.

3. Give students definitions of six to eight concepts or terms related to God (see the glossary, p. 469). In small groups, have them (a) come up with a sentence that uses the word correctly, (b) identify a story from the Bible that incorporates or exemplifies this term, (c) identify a movie that incorporates or exemplifies this term, and/or (d) develop a clever way of remembering the word and what it means.

4. Look at all the stories connected to the different Jewish holidays — the Book of Ruth for Shavuot, the *Akedah* for Yom Kippur, Chanukah and the Maccabees, etc. Discuss the roles of God and then of human beings in each of these events.

BIBLIOGRAPHY

(Note: For additional resources, see "Resources for Learners, Teachers, and Parents" on p. 473.)

For Adults

Ariel, David. *What Do Jews Believe? The Spiritual Foundations of Judaism.* New York: Schocken Books, 1995.

> Chapters in this book address key theological concepts and questions about God, human destiny, good and evil, chosen people, meaning of Torah, *mitzvot*, prayer, Messiah, and why be Jewish.

Artson, Bradley Shavit, et al. *I Have Some Questions about God.* Los Angeles, CA: Torah Aura Productions, 2002.

> This book features 12 questions about God from children in Grades 3-4 and responses from Rabbis Bradley Shavit Artson, Ed Feinstein, Elyse Frishman, Joshua Hammerman, Jeffrey Salkin, and Sybil Sheridan. Some examples of questions are: How do we know there really is a God? Does God know what I am thinking or what I will do? Does God really make miracles? Does God punish people? The book was created to help teachers and parents feel comfortable talking with children about God.

Bookman, Terry. *The Busy Soul: Ten-Minute Spiritual Workouts Drawn from Jewish Tradition.* Woodstock, VT: Jewish Lights Publishing, 1999.

> This guide presents easy to do spiritual exercises that focus on holiday themes. For example, Purim includes themes of risk taking, *mazal* (luck), and self-esteem and self-reliance.

Borowitz, Eugene. *A Layman's Introduction To Religious Existentialism.* Philadelphia, PA: Westminster Press, 1965.

> Borowitz examines existentialism — the philosophical movement begun by Camus and Sartre — and places it in a religious context for Jews. His discussion of the limits of a Jewish God concept is still among the clearest delineations of these boundaries that I have found.

Dosick, Wayne D. *Soul Judaism: Dancing with God into a New Era.* Woodstock, VT: Jewish Lights Publishing, 1999.

> In this do-it-yourself approach to spiritual living, Dosick provides exercises and suggestions for enriching daily life that draw upon Jewish meditation, mysticism, and *Kabbalah*. He provides several practical approaches for deepening personal relationships with God, including praying and meditating, performing rituals and following observances, and utilizing the arts — song, stories, and dance.

Gillman, Neil. *Sacred Fragments: Recovering Theology for the Modern Jew.* Philadelphia, PA: Jewish Publication Society, 1990.

> Each chapter of Gillman's book addresses a critical issue in Jewish theology today. Some examples are: revelation, knowing God, proving God's existence, encountering God, why God allows suffering. Gillman uses classic and modern texts and his own views as he responds to these essential theological questions.

Goldstein, Niles E., and Steven S. Mason. *Judaism and Spiritual Ethics.* New York: UAHC Press, 1996.

> In an attempt to identify spiritual ethics of Jewish conduct, behaviors that reflect our devotion to God, the authors present an exploration of the thirteenth century text, *Sefer Ma'alot Hamidot* (Book of Virtues and Values).

Kaplan, Aryeh. *Innerspace: Introduction To Kabbalah, Meditation and Prophecy.* Jerusalem, Israel: Moznaim Publishing Corp., 1990.

> This source provides a thorough and accessible description of the soul and *sephirot* in mysticism.

Kedar, Karyn D. *God Whispers: Stories of the Soul, Lessons of the Heart.* Woodstock, VT: Jewish Lights Publishing, 1999.

Through interviews and stories about ordinary people and her own life experiences, Kedar shows that the joy and pain in our lives have purpose and meaning. Some of the themes she deals with include: the divine in each of us, hope, patience, acts of loving-kindness, forgiveness, learning from death, surrender, and balance.

Kushner, Harold S. *When Bad Things Happen To Good People.* New York: Schocken Books, 2001.

Explores the problem of evil and suffering from a Reconstructionist point of view. Kushner presents, from his own personal experience, the struggles with classic theological positions, and proposes that suffering and illness are not caused by God, but are, rather, just a part of life. Appropriate for high school students and adults.

Nordberg, R.B. "Developing the Idea of God in Children." *Religious Education* 66:376-379 (September/October 1971).

Describes key elements in approaching the teaching of God in a religious educational setting.

Olitzky, Kerry M. *Jewish Paths toward Healing and Wholeness: A Personal Guide to Dealing with Suffering.* Woodstock, VT: Jewish Lights Publishing, 2000.

Olitzky provides a Jewish framework for understanding healing and suffering. The healing rituals, psalms, and prayers that are featured can be used to precipitate or enrich the dialogue with God.

Rothschild, Fritz A. "The Concept of God in Jewish Education." *Conservative Judaism* 24 (Winter 1970), 2-20.

In this article, Rothschild identifies problems in teaching about God. He argues that in formulating an educational approach in modern times, we need to examine and consider the diverse ways in which Jews have viewed God throughout the ages.

Umansky, Ellen M., and Diane Ashton. *Four*

Centuries of Jewish Women's Spirituality: A Sourcebook. Boston, MA: Beacon Press, 1992.

This volume is a collection of writings by over 100 women that reflect their Jewish, religious self-identity. The material draws on a wide range of sources, including letters, sermons, essays, Responsa, *midrashim*, diaries, poetry, ethical wills, and speeches. These sources help capture and reclaim Jewish spirituality from a woman's perspective.

Zlotowitz, Bernard M. "Teaching God To Kindergarten and First Grade." *Compass* 38 (March 1976), 1-3.

Provides practical wisdom on how to approach teaching God to young children in Kindergarten and Grade 1.

For Students

Bissell [Blumberg], Sherry, with Audrey Friedman Marcus and Raymond A. Zwerin. *God: The Eternal Challenge.* Denver, CO: A.R.E. Publishing, Inc., 1980.

A mini-course for Grades 7 up that considers frequently asked questions about God, including: Where do you live, God? How shall I speak with you? Why do you need me, God? Each question is followed by a combination of activities, Jewish sources, and responses that address each question. The relationship between God and each individual is discussed, and different ways that God can be part of our lives are presented. (See the Appendix, p. 435, for a complete reprint of this mini-course.)

Cone, Molly. *Hello, Hello, Are You There, God?* New York: UAHC Press, 1999.

This collection for Grades K-3 incorporates the stories about God found in the series *Hear, O Israel: The Shema Story Books.* These original stories convey concepts such as learning, belonging, and love of God. The Teacher's Guide contains background materials, activities for the classroom and the family, objectives, and questions for discussion.

Gellman, Marc, and Thomas Hartman. *How Do You Spell God? Answers To the Big Questions from around the World.* New York: William Morrow and Co., 1995.

Each chapter of this book begins with a universal question, such as theodicy (why do bad things happen to good people?). Answers to these questions are explored from different religious traditions. A teacher guide is available.

Gevirtz, Gila. *Living as Partners with God.* West Orange, NJ: Behrman House, 1997.

A second volume that builds on *Partners with God* by the same author, this book focuses on helping students formulate an understanding of community and the Jewish people's Covenantal relationship with God. Concepts are presented by focusing on role models — important Jewish figures from ancient to modern times — who have fulfilled the Covenant by living as partners with God. Their insights and actions give glimpses into ways that we can live as partners with God in today's world. A Teacher's Edition is available.

———. *Partners with God.* West Orange, NJ: Behrman House, 1996.

Gevirtz addresses children's profound questions about God by introducing a Jewish vocabulary for thinking and talking about God. The book fosters a personal search for God. The Teacher's Edition includes commentary on the concepts presented in the textbook, as well as strategies that accommodate different learning styles.

Goodman, Roberta Louis. *God's Top Ten.* Los Angeles, CA: Torah Aura Productions, 1992.

Based on narrative theology, which focuses on the use of stories to convey an understanding of God, this book presents a story from classical or modern sources to help students explore and explain the meaning of each of the Ten Commandments. Interspersed questions raise significant issues about life. A Teacher's Guide is available.

———. "Test of Faith: An Instant Lesson on Faith Development." Los Angeles, CA: Torah Aura Productions, 1985.

This Instant Lesson for teens and adults is perhaps the first piece published that uses faith development theory in a Jewish setting. It challenges students to think about how they make meaning out of their lives. Activities include: trying to figure out what stage the learner is at and interpreting a story by answering significant meaning making questions.

Grishaver, Joel, et al. *When I Stood at Mt. Sinai.* Los Angeles, CA: Torah Aura Productions, 1992.

Written with a class of sixth graders, this volume invites students to tell their own stories about revelation and what it means to receive the Torah at Mt. Sinai. The material can be used with sixth graders through adults.

Kerdeman, Deborah, and Lawrence Kushner. *The Invisible Chariot: An Introduction To Kabbalah and Jewish Spirituality.* Denver, CO: A.R.E. Publishing, Inc., 1986.

This workbook on Jewish mysticism for Grades 9-adult strives to connect mysticism and spirituality to the students' lives. It presents major ideas and concepts about *Kabbalah* in an accessible, but rich way. Learners explore and reflect on their place in the universe, the roles they can play in repairing the world, and how their lives can be connected to God. A Leader Guide is available.

Kushner, Lawrence. *The Book of Miracles: A Young Person's Guide To Jewish Spirituality.* New York, NY: UAHC, 1987.

Midrash, storytelling, and evocative illustrations are used to impart the connections between God and Torah and every element of creation. Best suited to junior high school students.

Kushner, Lawrence and Karen. *Because Nothing Looks Like God.* Woodstock, VT: Jewish Lights Publishing, 2001.

Real-life examples help children and parents explore possible responses to the questions people have about God. Stories revolve around fear and hope, happiness and sadness, and other spiritual matters. Appropriate for all ages, but especially younger students.

———. *How Does God Make Things Happen?* Woodstock, VT: SkyLight Paths Publishing, 2001.

The story line in this book gives concrete examples of how God daily gives us ways to change the world for the better. Geared to babies and preschoolers.

———. *What Does God Look Like?* Woodstock, VT: SkyLight Paths Publishing., 2001.

Filled with colorful illustrations and real-life examples from a child's everyday world, this book draws parallels from what is all around us in our daily lives to God's being omnipresent — everywhere. This awareness creates a sensitivity to that which makes our lives holy and special. Geared to babies and preschoolers.

Leder, Steven Z. *The Extraordinary Nature of Ordinary Things.* West Orange, NJ: Behrman House, 1999.

In a poetic fluid style, the author presents the connections between the ordinary events of our lives to God and spirituality. Crunching on *matzah*, pulling weeds in the heat of the summer, and even a roller coaster ride become extraordinary events when viewed from a Jewish perspective. Leder's essays are enriched by texts from *Midrash*, Talmudic excerpts, and passages from Torah. Geared to high school students and adults.

Rossel, Seymour. *When a Jew Prays.* New York: Behrman House, 1973.

Texts and stories help illuminate the art of praying and the meaning of the prayers. Geared to upper elementary students.

Sonsino, Rifat, and Daniel B. Syme. *Finding God: Ten Jewish Responses.* rev. ed. New York: UAHC Press, 2002.

While there is only one God, views about God have not been monolithic. Sonsino and Syme present ten different views of God from biblical through modern times in an accessible, yet sophisticated way. Some of these are collective views of the Bible and the Rabbis; others are the individual views of such philosophers as Philo, Maimonides, Luria, Spinoza, Buber, Steinberg, Kaplan, and Fromm. The book helps people connect to Jewish sources and perspectives on God that are more complex than their own childhood views of God. Geared to high school students and adults.

Thompson, Marlene. *Let's Discover God.* West Orange, NJ: Behrman House, 1998.

Basic concepts about God are presented in eight four-page booklets for Kindergarten through Grade 2. These include our Covenant with God, why we perform *mitzvot*, how we can act in God's image. Poems, photographs, activities, discussion questions, prayers, and blessings enrich the series. A Teacher's Edition is available.

CHAPTER 13

TEXT, TEACHER, AND STUDENT: ENHANCING SPIRITUAL DEVELOPMENT

Jeffrey Schein

WE ALL KNOW HOW CRITICAL RELATIONSHIPS ARE IN the development of a spiritual, Jewish human being. Our first healthy instinct as educators is to value the relationship between a student and a teacher as the primary source of that spirituality. If life is with people, spiritual life is with the people who have enough spiritual presence to draw us into a meaningful relationship. In valuing this element of spiritual dialogue, we might legitimately call ourselves the children of Martin Buber, the master of human and religious dialogue.

For a strict Buberian, though interestingly not for Buber himself, the raw materials for spiritual growth are present in the persons of the student and the teacher, a potential "I" and a potential "Thou." Buber himself, however, understood that the world of education is a world of mediation. Character is built through the effective selection of the material and cultural worlds in which we live, as well as the unmediated dialogue between human beings (Buber, 1967).

In Jewish tradition, the mediating force between human beings, or between the individual and the community, is often a Jewish text. A triangle among teacher, student(s), and text is formed when two or more people engage in study. This dynamic triangle unleashes spiritual potential. Yet, the role of text within this dialogue is itself multi-faceted and complex. The proper use of Jewish texts presupposes an awareness on the part of the teacher of overarching spiritual purposes.

In this chapter, I will:

1. suggest that there are at least three valid, distinct, and irreducible goals of education for

Jewish spirituality. These three goals can be subtitled as: narrative and peoplehood, Jewish values and ethics, and relationship to God. Spirituality has both communal and individual dimensions. Spiritual potential is unleashed in the encounter among the three parts: teacher, learner(s), and text. This occurs through:

   a. linking teacher and learner to a narrative in which the Jewish story and its many chapters or sub-stories unfolds [narrative and peoplehood].

   b. challenging the teacher and learner to discover the values which make Jewish/ human living worthwhile [Jewish values and ethics].

   c. pointing the teacher and learner to *Makor HaChayim*, the Source of Life, the source of one's spiritual connection to God [relationship to God].

2. surprise the reader by turning to the centrality ascribed to "texts" by two Christian educators instead of drawing on expected quotations from our own Jewish tradition.

3. offer two extended examples of teaching with a view toward addressing each of the three purposes of education for nurturing Jewish spirituality. One example is of a communal spirituality that arises from *Shirat HaYam*, the song at the Sea of Reeds, and the other focuses more on individual or personal spirituality in connection with *teshuvah*, turning or repentance.

4. conclude with a few suggestions about how teachers can strive toward educational *shlay-*

mut, completeness, in regard to teaching Jewish texts and promoting a Jewish child's spiritual development.

Much of what I describe in this chapter is based on my own experiences in preparing teachers on how to promote spiritual growth.

THE TEXT IN THE TRIANGLE

Text-centered Jewish learning has much greater currency today than in the recent past. One can see this most clearly in regard to adult Jewish learning. When I began my teaching of Jewish adults several decades ago, aside from *Parshat HaShavua,* studying the weekly Torah portion, it was rare to see text courses offered. Great Jewish ideas, history survey courses, Judaism and contemporary dilemmas, were far more common foci for adult Jewish learning.

The rediscovery of the text as central to the Jewish enterprise has led to our own share of clichés and banalities. The leap, for instance, from making texts a "central feature" of Jewish study to the "most authentic form of Jewish learning" is a significant and often unexamined one. Rather than recycle the obvious or clichéd, I find it helpful to look at the role of text anew from the perspectives of two Christian educators.

Parker Palmer, in his book *To Know As We Are Known,* reminds us that texts create a bounded space in which teacher and students can dwell. He writes at length:

Where schools give students several hundred pages of text and urge them to learn speed reading, the monks dwell on a page or a passage or a line for hours and days at a time. They call it *lectio divina,* sacred reading, and they do it at a contemplative pace. This method allows reading to open, not fill, our learning space.

When all students in the room have read the same brief piece in a way that allows them to enter and occupy the text, a common space is created in which students, teachers, and subject can meet. It is an open

space since a good text will raise as many questions as it answers. It is a bounded space since the text itself dictates the limits of our mutual inquiry. It is a hospitable, reassuring space since everyone has walked around in it beforehand and become acquainted with its dimensions. Too often we fail to capitalize on this space-creating quality. We hold students individually accountable for what they read on texts, but seldom allow their reading to create a common space in which the group can meet in mutual accountability for their learning. (Palmer, 1993, p. 76)

The Christian scholar and educator, Walter Brueggemann, suggests that the triangle creating capacity of the text allows for fruitful argument and debate. Borrowing from the work of family systems theorists, such as Murray Bowen and Edwin Friedman, Brueggemann (1990) writes:

Consider what happens in such a conversation when it is seen to be a triangle. There are, in fact, in most church situations of interpretation three voices, that of text, of pastor, and of congregation, three voices creating a triangle. The text continues to be present, but it has been usurped by the pastor. Our standard practice is for the pastor to triangle with the text against the congregation, that is, to make an alliance so that the voice of the pastor and what is left of the voice to the text gang up on the congregation and sound just alike. This process automatically generates controversy because, completely aside from the substance of theological or ethical conflict, nobody wants to be the lone one in a triangle. Predictably, the third party, the congregation, becomes a hostile, resistant outsider who will undertake reckless, destructive action in such a triangle where one is excluded by the other two.

If, however, the text is as scandalous as we suspect it is, then we need an alternative strategy. We are aware that the text is in fact more radical and more offensive and more dangerous than any of us, liberal or conservative. As a result, it is not honest to ally with the text, because the dangerous text is not any one's natural or easy ally. I suggest, then, let the pastor triangle with the congregation against the text, so the text is the lone member of the triangle, and then see how the text lives as the odd one in such a triangle. I believe that the textual conversation in the church would be very different if pastors were able to begin with the awareness that the text is too offensive for the people, but is also too offensive for the pastor, because it is the living Word of God, and it pushes always beyond where we want to go or be. Such a posture honors the great authority of the text. It also acknowledges our restless resistance to the text and lets us enter into dangerous textual conversations with some of our best friends as allies.

The proposal for alternative triangling requires, however, that the text be permitted its own voice, apart from our creedal impositions or critical reductionisms. There can be no genuine triangle unless the text is permitted a voice other than our own. Thus, this strategy calls for some interpretive distance between pastor and text.[1]

One notes only somewhat parenthetically that in Jewish education, teacher and text also triangle against the learner. A teacher angered or frustrated with the lack of Jewishness or *meschlichkeit* of his/her learners can always find a text that will underscore their shortcomings. The intimacy and energy of being jointly held to a higher standard — the text, tradition, or God — is then replaced by platitudes and recriminations from the teacher and can result in students shutting down, withdrawing from the learning process.

THE TRIANGLE AND THE THREE GOALS OF EDUCATION FOR JEWISH SPIRITUALITY

As mentioned before, three distinct goals exist for promoting the Jewish spirituality of our

students. These involve: (1) narrative and peoplehood, (2) Jewish values and ethics, and (3) relationship to God. The three goals are presented here.

Narrative and Peoplehood

The Jewish "story" has a life of its own. The primary actors in this story — God, the Torah, and the Jewish people — play unique roles within the master stories that link Jews to one another and their tradition. Before critiquing and analyzing these narratives, we need to step inside them sympathetically. One goal of Jewish spirituality is to acculturate the learners, to invite them to live as participants in the narrative. "Peoplehood" is a good shorthand term for this educational purpose. Whether "belonging" is more central to Jewish life than "behaving" and "believing" is an interesting but academic question. What is important is the awareness that Jewish children and adults in spiritual formation rarely ask questions of behaving or believing until they feel themselves belonging to the Jewish master stories.

Jewish Values and Ethics

Jewish life is values centered. Many a *midrash*, interpretation, begins to make sense only when we switch from the *mashal*, the ongoing story being told, to the *nimshal*, the value being strengthened through the story. The ongoing Jewish struggle to understand and actualize these values and remake the world in a Godly image is a significant second goal of Jewish spiritual education.

We sense some of the complexity of this goal in the *"Ahavah Rabbah"* prayer of the Shacharit service, which speaks of the revelation of Torah to the Israelites as a sign of God's love for us. In regard to the teachings of Torah, we are exhorted in this *tefilah*:

le-havin – to understand

le-haskil – to distinguish its different applications

---

[1]Walter Brueggemann, "The Preacher, the Text, and the People," *Theology Today* 47 (1990), 239. Reprinted with permission.

lishmor – to treasure

la-asot – to act on the words

le-kayem – to make them realities in the world

Each word seems to demand a different teaching/learning process. If this is correct, then the gifted spiritual educator will need to be nearly as long in pedagogic repertoire as he/she needs to be deep in personal commitment to Jewish spirituality. We will return to this point near the end of the chapter.

Relationship To God

The third goal of Jewish education for spirituality is to facilitate the learner's search for the source of his/her own spirituality. In a Jewish context, this inevitably points us to God. The wide array of understandings of God and godliness in Jewish tradition, from supernatural to transnatural, from person to process, from imminent to transcendent, and so forth, is a rich resource for this teaching. The questions here are ultimately very personal: When in my life have I encountered forces greater and grander than myself? What experiences are so touched by "holiness" that I recognize them as emanating from God? When has God entered my life?

The strategies appropriate to teaching in this third domain of Jewish spirituality range from gentle coach to prophet or social critic. The gentle coach approach is the strategy employed by Lawrence Kushner when he teaches with a mystical orientation, and by Harold Kushner when he urges and guides from a more rationalist orientation. Lawrence Kushner (1987) uses storytelling and a poetic style of writing simultaneously revealing and concealing the mysteries involved in seeking and encountering God in our lives. Harold Kushner's theology (1985) of "when is God" rather than "where is God" leads to intricate correlations between the child's exclamation of surprise "I've grown in knowledge, caring, etc.," and traditional Jewish *brachot* that sanctify moments in time. Sandy Eisenberg

Sasso (1992 and 1994) utilizes the same gentle coach approach as she encourages children's imaginations to picture the colors and names of God's presence in the world.

Finally, Buber sees the role of teacher as a combination of prophet and social critic. In his famous essay on the education of character (1967), he counsels educators that the only possible way to move people away from the grip of conventional wisdom and the "collective idols" to a life of God and spirituality, is to hold a mirror up to them [one's students] and allow them to see the distortions in their own images of God.

EDUCATIONAL AND SPIRITUAL SHLAYMUT: TRYING TO TEACH IN ALL THREE MODES

Below are two lessons or unit plans of topics and texts that I have felt are particularly central to Jewish spirituality. One example, *Shirat HaYam*, the Song at the Sea, focuses on the communal dimension of Jewish spirituality. The other, on *teshuvah* (change and repentance), focuses on the individual dimension of Jewish spirituality.

In both, I have been guided by the challenge of working in all three domains simultaneously. Yet, I have deliberately not labeled each domain within the lesson or unit plan. I imagine that many readers will approach the material at the level of *assiyah*, wise practice; therefore, labeling the domains would be an impediment. For those who understand it at the level of *beriyah/yetzirah*, creative thought, the labels are probably unnecessary anyway.

Shirat HaYam: The Communal Dimension of Jewish Spirituality

The curricular outline of materials developed on *Shirat HaYam*, the Song at the Sea includes three distinct lessons, each of which is described below.

Lesson 1: The Song Itself

Activity #1: Explore *Shirat HaYam* in a *Sefer Torah*

— a Torah scroll. Invite students to comment on the shape of this poem as written in the Torah scroll. Why is it not lined up evenly as other sections of the Torah? If the words in the *Sefer Torah* are thought of as objects, of what do they remind you? (While it is said in a traditional *midrash* that the columns look like the bricks of slavery, a common suggestion is that they look like the waves of the Sea of Reeds).

Activity #2: Read and chant *Shirat HaYam*, Exodus 15: 1-23. Begin to discuss what emotions particular phrases from the song fill you with (e.g., awe, terror, disgust, joy). According to the text, Moshe and the children of Israel did the singing. Why is it significant that Moshe did not do this alone? At the conclusion of the song, Miriam and the Israelite women break into dance. Does this mean that they were not singing?

Activity #3: Play "Miriam's Song" by Debbie Friedman on the recording *You Shall Be a Blessing*, which is about Miriam and the Israelite women. If yours is a particularly spirited group, invite people to join in the dancing.

Activity #4: Create a handmade *midrash* in response to the phrase or verse from *Shirat HaYam* that people find most moving. Handmade *midrashim* are pictures interpreting a text. Jo Milgrom, who originated the technique, recommends tearing, not cutting with scissors (hence "handmade"), construction paper, and other materials. (For more details on the technique, see *Handmade Midrash* by Jo Milgrom (Jewish Publication Society, 1992.).

Lesson 2: Responding To the Splitting of the Sea

Activity #1: Explore three different theories of how the splitting of the sea might have occurred. It is important to keep people open to the possibilities inherent in the other explanations. So I create a challenge for each group.

Theory #1: Students who choose the explanation that attributes all that happened to God's power must write about this question: Why if God is all powerful could God not save the Israelites without drowning the Egyptians?

Theory #2: Students who choose the *midrash* about Divine/human partnership, God waiting to split the sea until Nachson jumps in, are asked to write about: What was going through Nachson's mind the moment he jumped into the sea?

Theory #3: Students who prefer the more naturalistic explanation of the Sea of Reeds must write about how to explain the "timing" of the splitting of the sea. How can something so "natural" be so well-timed in terms of the needs of the Jewish people?

Lesson 3: My Own Yam Suf/Sea of Reeds

Activity #1: Identify times when you were witness to a "miracle." A miracle is when there was a victory moment so important to you, your family, or your community that you might have broken out in song or dance. The range of possible responses is always uneven, with some people focusing on victories over cancer and others on the time they scored an "A" on a test or their team won the Little League championship. Draw a picture or make a collage of the "miracle" moment and calligraph *"Mi Chamocha"* in Hebrew or English at the bottom. Have each person share their event and picture with the group. After each person has described their victory or moment of deliverance, the group calls out *"Mi Chamocha."*

Teshuvah: The Personal Side of Jewish Spirituality

The curricular unit on *teshuvah* includes four lessons. This set of lessons was originally developed for teachers as part of a conference on teaching Jewish spirituality.

Lesson 1: Teshuvah: Getting Started on Change

Activity 1: Each participant writes a journal about the nature of changing oneself for the better. Each journal entry consists of the completion of the following phrases:

The most meaningful "I'm sorry" (not my own) I ever witnessed was ____ .

The most meaningful act of *teshuvah* (turning, repentance) I ever did was ____ .

The older I become, the more *teshuvah* ____ .

Like Maimonides, I know that *teshuvah* is never complete until I have been challenged by the same situation and respond differently (see "Laws of Repentance," *Mishneh Torah*, Chapters 3 and 4). The hardest thing for me about completing the cycle of *teshuvah* is ____ .

Like Rav Kook (see *Lights of Repentance*), I know that the yearning for return is deeply implanted within my soul. I feel the impulse to return to God most powerfully when ____ .

Activity 2: Tell the following story about the Chafetz Chayyim (Rabbi Israel Meir HaKohen) interspersed with discussion about key issues. The inspiring, but enigmatic character, the Chafetz Chayyim, was a late nineteenth, early twentieth century Rabbi, educator, and codifier of *halachot* surrounding *lashon ha-ra*.

The story goes like this. An ordinary Jew was traveling in Poland to Radnetz to visit the great Chafetz Chayyim. He happened to sit down on the train next to him. When he began sharing his excitement about seeing the honored sage, the Chafetz Chayyim said that the man really was not so great at all, too much was being made of him. The ordinary Jew flew into a fit of rage and slapped this fellow traveler across the face. How can you speak in such a way about a *tzadik*?

Question A: If you were the Chafetz Chayyim, how would you respond?

The story continues. The ordinary Jew eventually shows up at the door of the Chafetz Chayyim. When he sees that the *tzadik* and the person on the train whom he had slapped are the same, he immediately drops to his knee and begs for forgiveness.

Question B: How should the Chafetz Chayyim respond now?

The story ends in this way. The Chafetz Chayyim thanked the person who had slapped

him saying: "You have taught me an important lesson. The laws of *lashon ha-ra* also apply to oneself. It is forbidden to speak falsely or in a degraded way about oneself even if it is to preserve humility."

Question C: What does this story say about the process of *teshuvah*? How might one relate this teaching to the better known one of Hillel's in *Pirke Avot*: "If I am not for myself who will be? If I am only for myself, what am I? And if not now when?"

Lesson 2: Forgiveness

Activity 1: Study the selection about *teshuvah* by Maimonides in *Mishneh Torah,* Chapters 3 and 4, on whether an individual is commanded to accept a person's request for forgiveness.

Activity 2: View and respond to the Ray Bradbury film *All Summer in a Day*. Focus on the last scene, which brings to a close the *teshuvah* drama between the protagonist Margaret and her rival William. Margaret is an earthling from Ohio who has seen the sun before. None of her friends on this "other planet" have. They are doubtful that the sun will appear as forecast. William is particularly cynical. William takes the lead in playing a joke on Margaret, locking her into a closet. When the sun actually does come out, William leaves Margaret in the closet in his excitement to get outside to witness the sun. Thus, Margaret, who most passionately believed in the sun's appearance and wanted most to re-experience the light, is the one deprived of the opportunity to enjoy the sun.

When the rain resumes, other friends help Margaret out of the closet, but she has missed her opportunity to see the sun. Unrelenting gray and rain have returned. Billy is repentant and approaches Margaret on two different occasions, asking for her forgiveness. The film is particularly poignant because the request is nonverbal, in the form of a bouquet of flowers which he picked when the sun appeared.

The film is an eloquent visual *midrash* on the suggestion in *halachah* that "one need not accept a person's apology immediately, but must by the third time." Connect the dilemma of the film to the *halachah,* exploring the ways in which the *halachah* might help us either understand or critique both Margaret's and William's actions.

Lesson 3: Forgiveness and Compensation

Activity 1: Study the selections about forgiveness and monetary compensation from the *Book of Legends* by Hayim Nachman Bialik and Yehoshua Hana Ravnitzky, page 647, entry 47.

Activity 2: View and respond to the movie, *The Unforgiven,* directed by and starring Clint Eastwood. Rated R, this film is especially appropriate for mature teens and adults.

The *teshuvah* focus is the two individuals who were involved in the beating of a prostitute when she teased one of the men about his sexual prowess. The particular scene that relates to the Jewish text presented occurs when the two men return to pay their debt in the form of horses, which the sheriff mandated as adequate repayment. Is this *teshuvah*? Of the two men, the one who stood by at first and eventually stopped his more brutal partner is the one who is most repentant. He brings in a particularly beautiful horse as an expression of his sorrow. The prostitutes respond as a group with great anger. The woman who was beaten never has a chance to respond. But whether or not she should have accepted the payment is a question worthy of exploration.

The film and the text can be highly interactive. For Jewish purposes, the film illustrates how complex *teshuvah* can become when multiple characters are involved.

Lesson 4: Looking Ahead

Activity 1: Reflect in writing on what you have learned about *teshuvah* from the previous three lessons. Try to connect them to your own struggle to return to God, holiness, and righteousness. Put the reflection in an envelope marked "Elul." Return to your reflections early in the month of Elul.

REFLECTIONS ON THE ROLE OF THE TEACHER

There are two frequently heard assertions about teaching that *al achat kama v'chama* (how much the more so) apply doubly to the teaching of spirituality. They are: (1) that good teaching is more often "caught" than "taught," and (2) you cannot teach what you do not believe. To these aphorisms I would like to add the absolute imperative of teacher self-awareness in the domains of both Jewish thought and educational philosophy. In regard to the former, I am much indebted to my own teacher, Rabbi Ira Eisenstein *(z"l).*

Rabbi Eisenstein believed that there indeed are many different ways to understand the spiritual topics of God, Torah, and Israel. One could employ naturalistic, transnaturalistic, or supernatural strategies for teaching any of the concepts. The key challenge, he taught, is congruence of the three concepts. A supernatural God is congruent with the notion of a divinely revealed Torah and a chosen people Israel. An equally congruent example from a natural or transnatural perspective is that of a people Israel who searched for the Divine and developed the Torah out of that search. When a teacher is reasonably "congruent" in his or her beliefs (which is not the same as fixed or static or without ultimate contradiction) about these three related and fundamental Jewish ideas, good teaching can take place. When, however, incongruent concepts about God, Torah, and Israel are employed (e.g., Torah is the product of human wisdom, but God must have revealed it), teaching often becomes either contradictory or insipid.

In regard to pedagogic assumptions, I would like to return to the opening of this chapter. A teacher must be self-aware, whether his or her goal in relationship to a given Jewish text is to promote Jewish belonging and peoplehood, teach particular Jewish values, or help a student explore his/her relationship with God. As I hope I have shown in the lesson plans regarding *Shirat HaYam* and *teshuvah,* these goals are not mutually exclusive. But to be taught effectively, there needs to be a "bracketing" off of the two other goals in order to focus on the third.

What happens when a teacher crosses rather than separates these pedagogic purposes? I offer now as testimony the story of "Aaron and the Wrath of God" (Appendix A, p. 161). The story portrays a father who as the informal, bedside teacher of his son has crossed his pedagogic wires as he presents the God of the *"Shema"* and its blessings, the succeeding three paragraphs, to his son. Aaron's father starts out by treating the second paragraph as narrative for a bedtime story. The telling itself is all bound up with the narratives of peoplehood: "this is something I remember my parents doing with me." The father wants to initiate the son into the same Jewish traditions that were part of his childhood.

Ninety nights out of a hundred, Aaron, the seven-year-old son would simply have processed *"VaHayah Im Shamoa"* as part of the Jewish initiation as well. This paragraph from Deuteronomy connects the Israelites' listening and following God's commandments to God causing natural things to occur, such as rain and the growth of plants, and the Israelites' ignoring of God's words and commandments to precipitating God's wrath. But on this night, Aaron processes the

God of the second paragraph of the *"Shema,"* the God who rewards and punishes, who shows generosity and anger, through the more intimate and vulnerable sense of spirituality. Aaron's Dad must then sort through the different modes of experiencing God, in order to teach his son. Since his son has perceived God in the values and spiritual modes, the father, too, moves the story into the mode of seeking God as the divine support behind the values of compassion and justice.

We learn from the story that good insight can come out of our naïveté about teaching God if we (1) roll with the punches as lovingly and openly as does Aaron's father, and (2) distinguish between "primary" and "secondary naïveté" in our own teaching, "primary naïveté" being the result of not having confronted rational contradictions in our own understanding of prayer, while "secondary naïveté" is a commitment to surprise and wonder once such a rational examination has actually taken place.

Although these lessons are of great value, I trust that teachers might avoid such dilemmas if they develop congruent Jewish understanding of related conflicts and greater awareness of how they relate to the three goals of spirituality discussed in this chapter.

IMPLICATIONS:

1. The three sides of the triangle — teacher, student(s), and text need to be present for each individual, yet having them all present is difficult.

2. Fostering a personal relationship to God is necessary, but not sufficient for educating for spiritual development.

3. The text should be allowed to speak to the learner directly. The teacher need not always mediate the relationship, but rather should assist the learner in understanding how to approach the text.

4. We as Jewish educators have much to learn from Christian educators and those of other religions. These others have done significant work in the area of spirituality and education.

QUESTIONS FOR CRITICAL INQUIRY:

1. In what ways are the three parts of the educating for spirituality triangle (narrative and peoplehood, Jewish values and ethics, and a personal relationship to God) connected?

2. What happens if spiritual teaching focuses on one of these three goals to the exclusion of the other two?

3. Think of a program or lesson that you have used in nurturing spiritual development. In what ways did it incorporate the three goals? How would you have to adapt the program to draw on all three goals?

4. What does it mean that a text has to have its own voice?

5. Palmer's quotation suggests that texts should open, rather than fill, our learning spaces. What happens when a text opens a learning space? Contrast that to what happens when a text fills a learning space.

6. Brueggemann talks about the three sides of interpretation: text, Rabbi or teacher, and congregation or learners. He suggests different alignments in order to open people to the text. Can all three sides be aligned — text, teacher, and learner? What happens if they are all aligned?

7. Schwab identifies four irreducible common places for the educational experience: teacher, learner, content, and milieu. Compare and contrast these four to Schein's three goals for spiritual education.

ACTIVITIES

1. Draw a triangle. Write "learner" in the lower left-hand corner, "text" at the top, and "teacher" in the right-hand corner. Put your answers to the following questions in the specified corner: Learner: In what way are you connected to God? Text: What is your favorite text about God? Teacher: Who taught you something important about God? What did they teach you?

2. Schein says that the text should be able to speak to the learner without the intermediary of a teacher. Pick your favorite text about God (for example, the *"Shema"* or *"Mi Chamocha"*). Pretend that you are that text. Have a "cocktail party" at which people circulate, talking about the text that they are. At the end of the cocktail party, the "hostess" brings the group together. Each person shares something that they learned about the text.

3. A *midrash* teaches us that when human beings stamp a coin, every coin comes out the same. However, when God stamped the image of God into every human being, each one came out different. How great is God! So, too, each human being understands and relates to God in Whose image he/she was created in different ways. How do you think views of God are the same? How are they different? Are there any ideas that all people need to share in common?

4. Make a list of three values important to you. Share all participants' lists. In what ways, if at all, is each value connected to our being made in the image of God? In other words, how does each value reflect how we are like God?

APPENDIX A

Aaron and the Wrath of God[2]

Ninety nine nights out of a hundred, the seven-year-old son would have processed the *va-hayah im shamoa* — a symmetrical affirmation in Deuteronomy of just and unjust rewards as a consequence of the observance or flaunting of the *mitzvot* — in a narrative acculturation mode. But on this particular night, Aaron processes the God of the second paragraph of the *"Shema"* through his more intimate and vulnerable sense of spirituality.

"Who's going to punish us?" he asked, his voice and gaze still far away?

"What?" said his father.

"You said if you're bad you get punished. Who?" He seemed a little annoyed by my apparent dullness.

"Now let me see if I understand your question. You mean . . . "

"Daddy! Who Punishes us? The Police?"

"No, son take it easy. God says that . . . "

"God punishes us? God does it? God? . . . " He was actually huddled up in a ball and his eyes were welling with tears.

Aaron's Dad must then sort through the different modes of experiencing God in order to teach his son. Since his son has perceived God in the values and spiritual modes, the father, too, moves the story into the mode of seeking God as the divine support behind the values of compassion and justice as embodied in the story of Abraham, God, and the cities of Sodom and Gomorrah.

"Dad, can you argue with God?"

"So, what could I say? I told him briefly the story of Abraham arguing for the cities of Sodom and Gomorrah. I've never seen such an enraptured audience for that tale, either before or after."

Spirituality is as much hard work as it is an effortless appreciation of God's gifts, so Aaron must work all these thoughts over . . . in his mind and in his dreams. Before going to bed that evening, Aaron announces that he plans to argue with God.

"What are you going to argue about with God, Aaron?" I asked seriously.

"About this business of punishments. I'm going to tell him to stop it."

"Why don't you ask him to stop it? That seems a lot more polite."

"Okay. But if he says no, I'm going to argue."

"Aaron?"

"Yes, Daddy?"

"Why shouldn't God punish? I wanted to hear what God would be up against?"

"Because it's just not fair. God is too big to be punishing people. People get too afraid of God for that. It's not good. God is too smart for that. God can think of something else to do instead. I'm going to tell God that."

I listened and I knew. God had no chance in this argument. God was clearly outmatched. "You'll let me know what the answer is?"

"I'll tell you in the morning. Good night, Daddy." And he left.

"Good night, little prophet," I called after him.

The next morning, Aaron came downstairs a little draggy, but clearly happy.

"Well?" I asked.

"God said yes!" he told me brightly.

"God won't punish anymore?"

"He promised more."

I sat beholding him over the corn flakes. My small giant was ready in the name of justice and mercy to take on anyone, including the Almighty. Tears welled up in my eyes. "Aaron," I said, "you are the best."

"I know," Aaron said.

I kissed him. I watched him as he walked off to school. And despite my will to disbelieve, despite my wish to laugh at this childish nonsense, despite my strong desire to attribute it all to an overactive seven-year-old imagining a voice in his head, despite all this, I found myself feeling incredibly good and very much at ease knowing that at least in one small part of the universe such a promise had been returned to such a request.

---

[2]Reprinted with permission from the Jewish Reconstructionist Federation.

BIBLIOGRAPHY

Bialik, Hayim Nachman, and Yehoshua Hana Ravnitzky. *Book of Legends: Sefer Ha-Aggadah.* New York: Schocken Books, 1992.

Available both in Hebrew and English, this brilliant collection of *midrashim* is organized thematically. The authors compiled these texts from Talmud and *Midrash*.

Brueggemann, Walter. "The Preacher, the Text, and the People." In *Theology Today* 47 (October 1990), 237-247.

A Christian theologian, Brueggemann has made significant contributions in the area of understanding and teaching biblical text. This article presents his view of the interrelationship among clergy, text, and people in the teaching, interpreting, and learning dynamic.

Buber, Martin. *Between Man and Man*. New York: MacMillan Publishing, 1985.

Buber's two essays "Education" and the "Education of Character" provide insight into the educational philosophy cited in this chapter by Schein. Most famous for his "I-Thou" concept, Buber contributed greatly to Jewish adult education in Germany and Israel.

Fitzpatrick, Jean Grasso. *Something More: Nurturing Your Child's Spiritual Growth*. New York: Viking, 1991.

This author of several children's books and guides for parents and teachers, writes here about nurturing children's spiritual growth. Although he writes as a Christian, his insights about children's spiritual development are helpful and useful in reflecting about the spirituality of Jewish children.

Fowler, James. *Stages of Faith*. San Francisco, CA: Harper Collins, 1981.

This is Fowler's seminal work in which he describes faith development theory and its stages in detail.

Kook, Abraham Isaac. *Abraham Isaac Kook: The Lights of Repentance, Lights of Holiness: The Moral Principles, Essays, Letters and Poems*. New York: Paulist Press, 1978.

Rav Kook served as the Ashkenazic Chief Rabbi of Palestine in the early twentieth century. He wrote many philosophical works that displayed a balance between modernity and traditional Judaism.

Kushner, Harold. "The Idea of God in the Jewish Classroom." In *Creative Jewish Education*, Jeffrey Schein and Jacob L. Staub, eds. Philadelphia, PA: Reconstructionist Rabbinical Press and Chappaqua, NY: Rossel Books, 1985.

Kushner raises questions and provides responses to how and why one should make God part of the Jewish classroom experience.

Kushner, Lawrence. *The Book of Miracles*. New York: UAHC Press, 1987.

Although published as a textbook for Grades 4-6, this book presents its material in an alternative style. The book is a young person's reader of Kushner's mystical approach to life. It combines *midrash*, storytelling, and illustrations to relay ways of connecting God and Torah to life and creation.

Maimonides, Moses. "Laws of Repentance." In *Mishneh Torah*, Chapters 3 and 4.

The *Mishneh Torah* is a major work on Jewish law by Maimonides. He was a scholar and a physician who wrote in the twelfth century.

Milgrom, Jo. *Handmade Midrash*. Philadelphia, PA: Jewish Publication Society, 1992.

Artist and scholar, Jo Milgrom presents a unique combination of using art and paper-made *midrash* along with text study. Paper is used as a medium to draw out people's ability and capacity to explore and interpret texts.

Parker, Palmer. *To Know As We Are Known: Education As a Spiritual Journey*. New York: HarperCollins Publishers, 1993.

Parker Palmer is a Christian theologian (Quaker) and educator who integrates theological issues into his educational philosophy. His style of writing is poetic and inspirational, as well as accessible and insightful. In this book he presents his theory on the "spirituality of education."

Sasso, Sandy Eisenberg. *God's Paintbrush.* Woodstock, VT: Jewish Lights Publishing, 1992.

Story and illustrations illuminate this encounter of God for the reader and listener. Sasso shows ways of finding God in the experiences around us. She punctuates the story with questions for the reader and/or listener to consider. The storybook lends itself to discussion between parents and children about experiences of God.

———. *In God's Name.* Woodstock, VT: Jewish Lights Publishing, 1994.

Sasso writes in myth form about how God was named. Beginning with the Genesis creation story about how every creature was named, the human beings set out on a quest to determine God's name. It is this search that is the focus of Sasso's cleverly laid out story, which is enriched by beautiful illustrations.

Schein, Jeffrey. "Aaron and the Wrath of God." In *Windows on the Jewish Soul.* New York: Jewish Reconstructionist Federation, 1994.

The full version of "Aaron and the Wrath of God" is cited in Appendix A. It is a story about a bedtime conversation between a father and his son about God, spurred on by the recitation of the nighttime *"Shema."*

CHAPTER 14

EDUCATION FOR SELF-TRANSCENDENCE

Sherry H. Blumberg

INTRODUCTION

REALLY GOOD EDUCATION, BOTH PUBLIC AND religious, is transcendent in nature. It enables the learner to reach beyond the self and the immediate moment and connect with the universal and the timeless. Unfortunately, self-transcendence seldom comes intuitively, and many educators today have forgotten that students need to learn how to transcend themselves. Students need guidance in exploring, understanding, and ultimately connecting with eternal truths about life, the universe, and God. I propose that we must return to education for self-transcendence as a primary aim, especially for Jewish education.

In this chapter, I will first examine what is meant by self-transcendence and briefly trace some of the valuable scholarship in the field — the work of philosophers who have contributed immeasurably to our understanding of the phenomenon. From what these philosophers suggest, I will also derive some logical implications for religious education in general, and Jewish education in particular. Second, I make an argument for self-transcendence as a vital, principal aim for Jewish education. Third, I share an initial description of how this aim might be applied in a Jewish educational context.

WHAT IS SELF-TRANSCENDENCE?

Walter Conn, a Christian theologian well versed in developmental psychology, provides a good, generally applicable definition of self-transcendence. He defines it as "moving beyond oneself at the cognitive, moral, and affective levels."[1] Experiencing self-transcendence, then, is a process that integrates thinking, moral reasoning, and feeling. Self-transcendence is an inner process, a personal experience that may grow from the content and process of a lesson or from other personal or group experiences of everyday life.

William James, an influential American philosopher and psychologist of the early twentieth century, in his seminal work, *The Variety of Religious Experience*, suggested the need for making self-transcendence an integral part of religious experience. He wrote about how a person's inner life and the experiences of the world outside can relate to one another, and that when they do, it is as if the energies combine synergistically.

> . . . the conscious person is continuous with a wider self through which experiences come . . . . The whole drift of my education goes on to persuade me that the world of our present consciousness is only one out of many worlds of consciousness that exist, and that those other worlds must contain experiences which have a meaning for life also; and although in the main their experiences and those of this world keep discrete, yet the two become continuous at certain points and higher energies filter in.[2]

Self-transcendence, then, involves exploring the deep reaches of one's mind, soul, and psyche as a way of connecting to forces outside and beyond oneself.

Whereas James and others have utilized the methods and theories of the humanities — the

[1] Walter Conn, *Christian Conversion: A Developmental Interpretation of Autonomy and Self Surrender* (New York: Paulist Press, 1986), 19.

[2] William James, *The Varieties of Religious Experience* (New York: Collier Books, 1961), 99.

"softer sciences" of psychology, philosophy, and theology — to delve into the problem of how human beings reach self-transcendence, modern research on the brain has used the techniques, instruments, and theories of the biological and natural sciences. One theory from the brain research of Virginia Ross argues that there is a transcendent function in the brain that integrates the conscious and unconscious elements of the human mind.[3] Interestingly enough, James arrived at a similar conclusion about transcendence using his own methods. Another finding of note made by Ross was that the transcendent function of the brain usually works in a relaxed mood.[4] This has implications for the use of meditation and other techniques that release tension in an educational context. Finally, brain research has shown that transcendence is related to creativity in both the arts and sciences.[5]

Both Conn and James view self-transcendence as central for human development, as well as for living a religious life. Both believe that self-transcendence can be nurtured, acquired, cultivated, and taught. Brain research affirms the human capacity and proclivity for seeking the transcendent. So, how does education connect with self-transcendence as a goal of human development?

Drawing on one's own experiences as well as those of others is a theme that runs through educational philosophy. Nahum M. Waldman is a Jewish educator who focuses on the role and importance of experiences. He defines education as: " . . . involv[ing] the effort to construct a realistic and integrative view of the world, based upon what is learned (drawing from the experience of others) and upon what is personally experienced."[6] In this case, what is learned from the great body of traditional knowledge and texts (i.e., from the teacher) needs to be balanced with what is personally experienced. In that balance, a student's ability to transcend both the self and the present are crucial.

Other educators go further in connecting experience, education, and religious life. Alfred North Whitehead, a distinguished educator, stated that, "the essence of education is that it be religious."[7] He is referring to a religious education that inculcated duty and reverence. Both duty and reverence require the individual to go beyond one's self interest, by acknowledging and affirming powers and truths that are greater than the self.

Dwayne Heubner, a religious educator, elaborates on Whitehead's statement by drawing on Genesis, Leviticus, and Deuteronomy[8] to suggest that by "duty" we mean humanity's responsibility for the earth and for other human beings, while "reverence" is linked to the idea of an eternity or God. In his argument he moves toward suggesting that education is "the lure of the transcendent that which we seem is not what we are, for we could always be other." Heubner builds on this role of education as connecting us to God — the Transcendent, the Other:

> Education is the openness to a future that is beyond all futures. Education is the protest against present forms that they may be reformed and transformed. Education is the consciousness that we live in time, pulled by

---

[3]Virginia Ross, "The Transcendent Function of the Bilateral Brain," *Zygon* 21:2 (June 1986).

[4]This relaxed mood has resonance in James Macdonald's need for "centering." See James B. Macdonald, "A Transcendental Developmental Ideology of Education," *Heightened Consciousness, Cultural Revolution and Curriculum Theory*, William Pinar, ed. (Berkeley, California: McCutchan, 1978), 85-116.

[5]Ross, op.cit.

[6]Nahum M. Waldman, "Tradition and Experience in the Book of Job," in *Studies in Jewish Education and Judaica in Honor of Louis I. Newman*, eds. Alexander M. Shapiro and Burton I. Cohen (New York: KTAV, 1984), 157.

[7]Alfred N. Whitehead, *The Aims of Education and Other Essays* (New York: Macmillan, 1929), 14.

[8]See Dwayne Heubner, "Religious Metaphors in the Language of Education," *Religious Education* 80:3 (Summer 1985): 461-472. He uses Genesis 1 and 2 to demonstrate that man had to subdue and serve the earth, and Genesis 19:18 and 19:33-34 to show that human beings had to be "response-able" for other human beings, including the stranger. He uses the "*Shema*" declaration in Deuteronomy 6:4-5 to explain the concept of reverence.

the inexorable Otherness that brings judgment and hope to the forms of life which are but the vessels of present experience.[9]

Education seeks to cultivate a dynamic tension between the self and the Other, the present and the eternal.

Another educator, James B. Macdonald,[10] a curriculum theorist, views transcendence as a central educational function. Macdonald uses the term "centering" to refer to his understanding of transcendence. He defined centering as a process in which the human being draws power and energy from sources that are not completely explicable (such as God or a spiritual power) in order to help the person create meaning out of perceptions and reality. Centering is often connected to spirituality, meditation, and self-transcendence.

The thoughts of Heubner, Whitehead, and Macdonald about education suggest that good education must either be linked to the transcendent or be transcendent in nature. Writing about this link, Heubner states that "the source of education is the presence of the transcendent in us and in our midst. We can transcend ourselves, go beyond ourselves."[11] This assessment is especially true for religious education in general and for Jewish education in particular, since one of the primary goals of Jewish education is to enable the student to develop a relationship with a transcendent God.

WHY MAKE SELF TRANSCENDENCE A PRIMARY AIM OF JEWISH EDUCATION?

An educational aim is a statement that reflects an underlying philosophy of education and points the educator in the direction of developing more specific goals that are consistent with and that will further that philosophy. Education for self-transcendence is a vital aim for religious education, since our relationship with God — a major concern for religious educators — is one of transcendence (experiencing God as eternal, beyond, and greater than ourselves) as well as of immanence (experiencing God as close, personal, within us). Indeed, as described above, self-transcendence is vital to human development, and all good education is transcendent in nature. As such, education for self-transcendence should be a primary aim of Jewish religious education.

The ideas of transcendence and immanence are not mutually exclusive, but rather mutually determinative. All theologies and metaphysical systems that posit an ultimate reality must address this dual aspect of the nature of God and the sacred. This inclusion of one with the other fits very well with the ideas of such American Jewish theologians as Eliezer Berkovits, Eugene Borowitz, Abraham Joshua Heschel, and Mordecai Kaplan.[12] While these are modern theologians, Jewish views of God throughout the ages have dealt with these two characteristics, some emphasizing transcendence (biblical and Rabbinic) and others immanence (*Kabbalah* and Hasidism).

Jewish theologians such as these would agree that good Jewish education must include self-transcendence as an aim. I mention these four theologians specifically, because each one is a major exponent of each of the four major movements in American Jewish life: Berkovits is Modern Orthodox, Borowitz is Reform, Heschel is Conservative, and Kaplan is Reconstructionist.

[9]Heubner, 463.

[10]Macdonald is considered to be one of the founders of the educational reform movement called "reconceptualist." See descriptions of that movement and Macdonald's role in it in the introduction to his "Curriculum Theory" in *Curriculum: An Introduction to the Field*, eds. James R. Gress with David E. Purpel. (Berkeley, California, McCutchan, 1974), 41-44, and also William Pinar, "Currere: Toward Reconceptualization," *Curriculum Theorizing*, ed. William Pinar (Berkeley: McCutchan, 1978), 396-414.

[11]Heubner, 463.

[12]The author's doctoral dissertation (and much of her work before and since that dissertation) was a cross-movement educational study of Jewish religious experience, based on the theological positions of Berkovits, Borowitz, Heschel, and Kaplan, who would all agree with the need for education for self-transcendence. For a more complete discussion, see Sherry H. Blumberg, *Educating for Religious Experience: An Analysis of the Definition of Four Major American Theologians and the Implications of Their Thoughts for Jewish Education Curriculum and Practice* (Ann Arbor, MI: University Microfilms International, 1991), D.A.I. No. 9210472.

For Borowitz, Berkovits, and Heschel, transcendence is related to the concept of a transcendent God. While Kaplan believed in godliness — a naturalistic view of religion, he leaves a place for self-transcendence as well, since identification with the peoplehood of Israel is, as Kaplan has suggested, an act of self-transcendence. If we are to educate for Jewish religious experience, then self-transcendence becomes a primary educational aim.

While much of Jewish education in recent years has begun to address experiences of immanence and of God as immanent — the personal, spiritual journeys that bring the experience of God close to us — a need still exists to help our learners explore transcendence and the transcendent aspects of God. Without the ability to transcend themselves and to connect themselves to the past, present, and future of our religious traditions and to our sacred stories, our students will not be able to develop deep and intensive relationships with God. They will not be able to develop a commitment to the values that both sustain them and enable them to pass tradition on to the next generation.

Education that focuses solely on experiencing immanence and the immanence of God can lead to narcissism, individualism, and isolation, since it over focuses on the immediate, the present, the personal, and on direct experience only. Ironically, such a highly personalized educational focus further serves to cut off the individual Jew from the community, from our history, and from our texts — often the very problem that it seeks to remedy. If our educational goals are not encouraging transcendence, then our philosophy of education (which gives rise to those goals) is lacking.

Education for self-transcendence is as important as the aims that lead religious educators to create programs for commitment and participation. It certainly is equal to the aim to educate for knowledge, especially with the current call for a core knowledge of the values, sources, and

traditions. And, it is as important as the need to educate for character growth and development. Self-transcendence that enables the learner to connect to God enables all of these other aims to be effective.

Formal Jewish education has not specifically educated for self-transcendence in most contexts or environments.[13] With a few notable exceptions, most mainstream North American Jewish education has emphasized other aims.

HOW CAN WE TEACH FOR SELF-TRANSCENDENCE?

How then, can education for self-transcendence and centering be translated into a Jewish context? What environment, what techniques, and what relationship between the learner and teacher can encourage and model self-transcendence? What is the appropriate content, the curricular approach, and the proper context if one has self-transcendence as a major aim? To answer these questions, I divide the presentation of educating for self-transcendence into two distinct areas: curriculum, including activities; and the teacher. For each of these areas, I will present both concerns and suggestions related to how one actually implements Jewish education for self-transcendence.

Curriculum and Activities

A curriculum that leads to self-transcendence involves finding a midpoint between the development of self and the individual's responsibility to the Jewish tradition. Cultivating the development of the self and the personal domain are very important, but not sufficient, to achieve self-transcendence. Teaching the learner to move beyond the self is a critical component of educating for self-transcendence. In this regard, the self must be developed in the context of the values and expectations of the Jewish community

---

[13]Because Torah study and meeting communal needs have been dominant activities of the North American Jewish community, the primary and explicit educational aim of formal Jewish education has been national and ethnic survival.

and in relationship to God or godliness. Hence, the introduction of Jewish tradition in its broadest sense must be balanced with these more individually oriented aims.

Michael Rosenak writes about the need for education to address this dialectic — the development of the self and the responsibility to Jewish tradition. He uses the terms "normative-ideational" and "deliberative-inductive" to describe this tension between kinds of teaching.[14] Normative-ideational refers to "explicit religion" — that which concerns itself with what is imposed on the learner and teacher by tradition and authority. The deliberative-inductive aspect of religious life are "implicit religion," focusing on subjective spirituality and individual discovery. He asserts that Jewish religious education needs to attend to both dimensions.

Combining these two concerns, another educator — William H. Schubert — presents the fundamental curriculum question as: "What knowledge and experience are most *worthwhile* [to teach]?" He uses the question of worth as an organizing center around which all curricular and teaching processes should be coordinated.[15] Certainly this question is vital to teaching for transcendence and for Jewish religious experience, especially since it involves integrating a blend of knowledge and experience — Rosenak's explicit and implicit religion. Schubert recommends a curricular approach that leads the learner on a path toward self-transcendence. This approach involves group process activities that encourage the student to reflect in community on core questions.[16] Enabling learners to discuss collectively questions of ethics, observance, and other spiritually challenging situations that can arise throughout their lives can lead to moments of self-transcendence, particularly if the questions are addressed from a variety of per-

spectives, including those presented in classical texts and other Jewish sources.

Another aspect of curriculum development that needs to be transformed is the subject matter orientation. In order to educate for self-transcendence, alternative approaches to curriculum and curriculum development must be blended with some traditional elements. This reorientation involves a greater focus on the individual and the inner life of the learner as participant in the Jewish tradition. Although this reorientation may sometimes mean that the traditional subject-oriented curriculum with behavioral objectives will be used when teaching Hebrew language, a broader curriculum theory that concentrates on the individual and the group and their spiritual and religious development will be called for when teaching other subjects.

The selection of activities to educate for self-transcendence would also involve a change of focus from some traditional or typical types of activities. In this curricular shift, more attention would be placed on the connection between the student's inner life, the student's relationship to the group, and the subject matter. The types of questions that would be asked in the selection of activities include: What kinds of activities encourage a student to "open up" to such perceptual experiences? What kinds of activities facilitate the process of sensitizing people to others and to their own inner feelings and intuitions? What kinds of activities provide experiences for developing close-knit community relationships? What kinds of activities encourage and facilitate religious experiences? In what ways can we organize knowledge to enlarge human potential through meaning? All of these are key questions in designing curricula for self-transcendence.[17]

While the shape of the "total curriculum" may vary from school to school, there are some

---

[14]Rosenak, *Commandments and Concerns* (Philadelphia, PA, Jewish Publication Society, 1987), 17-25.

[15]William H. Schubert, "The Question of Worth As Central To Curricular Empowerment," in *Teaching and Thinking about Curriculum: Critical Inquiries*, James T. Sears and J. Dan Marshall, ed. (New York: Teachers College Press, Columbia University, 1989), 211-227.

[16]Shubert's questions include: (1) What kind of life should I create for myself, and how can I do so?, (2) What is the impact of my life on others and society?, and (3) How can I improve my life in needed or desired directions?

[17]See these and other questions in Macdonald's article, "A Transcendental Developmental Ideology of Education," (1978).

common elements that should be present. Activities such as pattern making, playing, meditative thinking, imagining, creating art, fostering aesthetic appreciation, and educating for perception are crucial and would aid in self-transcendence. (Examples of some of these activities may be found at the end of this chapter.) This must include a kind of physical education that allows us to be as much at home in our bodies as we are at home with our minds and emotions. Each of these categories of activities has a real potential to be used with Jewish content and in Jewish education. For example, learning experiences that involve patterning could include exploring the patterns or rhythms of Jewish life that are meaningful to the student, comparing his or her patterning to those of others and to the history of the Jewish people. Activities that involve imagining could include having the student imagine that he or she was a biblical character (e.g., Moses or Sarah) experiencing God. Playing or role playing activities could include playing at creating a Jewish home with young children and, for older children, role-playing that they are the Jewish community leaders.

Other learning activities include a balanced use of silence, meditation, thinking, and journal writing with active projects for Jewish living. Students must experience Jewish life in its fullest extent. That is, they must participate fully in study, meditation, worship, life cycle events, community action involvement, *gemilut chasadim* (deeds of loving-kindness), and then reflect upon their experiences. The learning must be and must be perceived as social (communal) as well as individual: it must be interactive, continuous, unbounded, and transcendent.[18] The learner is learning and experiencing life and, it is to be hoped, experiencing God in that life in many places, with many different people, and at many different times. Care must be taken within the curriculum to be aware of the many different ways that students learn and come to "know."

One means of educating for self-transcendence in a Jewish context is through the study of texts. A teacher who is very excited by the text, who knows how to excite the students by examining interpretations of commentators throughout the centuries, exploring its meaning for today, and perhaps even extrapolating its meaning for the future, can begin the process of self-transcendence through study. If the teacher adds a moment of meditation on that text during the class for centering the student, and combines the moment of meditation with information about how that text helps the individual and group to reach toward God, that might lead to a moment of self-transcendence for the student.

Another means of education for self-transcendence involves the use of prayer and worship — and not just in the synagogue or home. A nature walk to collect beautiful things (a virtual nature walk using film or CD-ROM, an actual outdoor experience, or a guided imagery drawing on memories) followed by the recitation of the blessing said when one sees beauty, perhaps group singing of a song about the beauty and goodness of the world, and then reflection and writing about beauty might stimulate self-transcendence in some students.

There are many other possible ways to incorporate self-transcendence in a Jewish context.[19] It is especially important in developing activities to prefer those that require the use of creativity, that foster a sense of accomplishment or fulfillment, and that create feelings of being needed, loved, and special. For some students the emotions of love, peacefulness, and timelessness will be important components of learning environments that are conducive to self-transcendence.

---

[18]See Nel Noddings and D. Scott Enright, "The Promise of Open Education," in *Theory into Practice*, 22:9 (Summer 1983), 182-189.

[19]I believe, as one of those who helped design the Union of American Hebrew Congregations Schuster Curriculum (1981), that it was designed with an attempt at self-transcendence. It was structured with five clusters, including connection of the present, past, and future, with the self and others. The attempt at teaching for self-transcendence was never stated explicitly, however. As a consequence, the attempt was often lost amid the process of carrying out the activities and objectives of the curriculum.

The Teacher and the Learner

Teachers, too, are experiencing and learning. As they share with the students their excitement about learning Jewish texts, traditions, values, history, and other subjects, they are modeling for their learners how they perceive these experiences as part of Jewish religious experience. While being models of committed Jewish living, teachers also need to model a sense of vulnerability and openness as they experience other people, ways of being and knowing, and God. This demonstration of vulnerability and openness will help make the learners see that their teachers are both approachable and willing to explore and listen to alternative viewpoints and experiences different from their own.

Macdonald[20] also comments on the need for the teacher to really "see" him/herself in relationship to the other person with both an explicit awareness of the other and a sincere attempt to understand the other. This empathic orientation involves dialogue based on the content of the course and the inner workings of the person, and is based on centering as well.

Also of great importance are activities that help the learner to explore the concepts of "paradox" and "metaphor." The use of literature, fine arts, autobiography, and critical thinking techniques are applicable. Much of the material for these activities can be drawn from the everyday lives of the students and the teachers.

One educator who speaks about the importance of drawing upon the learner's experience of everyday life is Edward Robinson. The implications of his studies of children's religious experience suggest that long buried experience may germinate when the child is allowed to reflect upon it.[21] Robinson also explores the idea that religious experience gives the individual the feeling that there is "something more" to life, and that many experiences of childhood may have been religious. His works contribute strongly to my conclusion that reflective thinking about past experience is vital, and that relating common everyday experience to religious thought and values is one of the methods that must be used. Therefore, all events of everyday life are experiences for reflection. Activities of reflective thought, journal writing, sharing feelings and perceptions, and critical feedback from the teacher and the group should all be a part of curricula that attempt to teach for self-transcendence.

Besides the kinds of activities used, the learning environment also plays an important role in creating conditions that would foster and nurture religious experience. It is vital that synagogues, schools, and the family join in seeing themselves as teaching for self-transcendence. In a Day School or even in a one-day-a-week setting, it is not impossible for the educator to plant the seed (a seed that is to be nourished by the individual and the family) that it is easier to learn all that must be learned in a supportive, practicing family and community. While it is possible that a person could, over time, learn what is needed on his or her own, in truth, the whole community needs to be involved in education for self-transcendence.

CONCLUSION

While this is by no means a complete discussion of this rich topic, this chapter has described what is meant by education for self-transcendence, drawing upon the work of Jewish, Christian, and secular educational philosophers and theorists. They all underscore the importance of making self-transcendence an aim for education in general and Jewish education in particular. This aim can be translated into a Jewish context by extrapolating from their general principles and adding specifically Jewish activities.

The ability to help our students transcend themselves may allow us to help move them and ourselves into new understandings of what God

---

[20]Macdonald (1974, 1979).

[21]Edward Robinson, *Original Vision: A Study of the Religious Experience of Childhood* (New York, Seabury Press, 1983), 145.

wants of us as we strive to live and work together on this small planet. The hope is that through such education we may be able to transcend the things that divide our world and to focus on those aspects of life that we all share in common.

———◆———

IMPLICATIONS

1. Self-transcendence can be nurtured, taught, and acquired.

2. Self-transcendence needs to be taught.

3. Among the various ways of developing a relationship to God, relating to God as both transcendent and immanent are important to a whole understanding of God. The transcendent connects us to tradition and to others, moving us beyond ourselves.

4. Transcendence is not just a Jewish educational issue or problem, but one for all good education.

QUESTIONS FOR CRITICAL INQUIRY

1. Why should we be concerned about Jewish education for self-transcendence?

2. Thinking about Jewish texts and tradition, what images of God as transcendent exist? In what ways is God as transcendent expressed in your community or home — your environment, practices, ritual objects, etc.?

3. What are the shortcomings of focusing only on teaching a transcendent God? on teaching an immanent God? What of importance does each aspect of these ways of relating to God bring you?

4. Brainstorm how you can integrate education for self-transcendence into your setting.

ACTIVITIES

1. Make a list of the different techniques that people use to help them focus or concentrate on prayer (e.g., singing, meditating, deep breathing, sitting quietly). Try one that you do not normally engage in. What was the experience like? How was it different from the way that you would normally focus or concentrate on prayer? Would you try this approach again? How is this focusing or centering a way of transcending the world around you and bringing you to a different spiritual awareness? In what ways is concentrating or centering connected to the idea of *kavanah* (intention)?

2. Imagine scenes from movies or cartoons that depict a situation that affects you personally — relationships with others, things we do, events in our life. In small groups, act as the "transcendent voice," the voice that uplifts the ordinary into the realm of the spiritual. Identify ways in which the scene or cartoon points to the sacred in our lives or our relationship to God.

3. Pick a household chore that you dislike doing. Think about ways to infuse the chore with spiritual meaning (e.g., grocery shopping is a way of ensuring the health of the family, doing homework is a way of honoring parents, recycling is a way of caring for the planet). Practice the chore with this thought in mind. In what ways is doing the chore different now?

4. On one half of a shield, draw something that symbolizes your connection to your family and to the past. On the other half, draw something that symbolizes your connection to the future. What are the transcendent values that are found in both representations?

5. What do you do that totally absorbs your attention and makes you forget about time (reading, playing video games, singing, listening to music, putting together a puzzle, playing ball)? What happens to you during this activity? How does doing this make you feel? What is it about the activity that holds your attention?

6. Each learner creates a puzzle of the thing that holds his/her attention. Give the puzzle to someone else to do. Without making a race of it, time how long it takes for that person to put the puzzle together. Then ask that person how long he/she thinks it took. When we are absorbed in an activity, time seems to "slip away." When concentrating on something, what happens to our sense of what is going on around us? What don't we notice? What do we seem to notice more deeply? Is this focus maintained when we pray to God?

BIBLIOGRAPHY

Blumberg, Sherry H. *Educating for Religious Experience: An Analysis of the Definitions of Four American Theologians and the Implications of Their Thoughts for Jewish Educational Curriculum and Practice.* Ann Arbor, MI: University Microfilms International, 1991. D.A.I. No. 9210472.

This is Blumberg's Ph.D. dissertation, in which she surveys the relevant literature, proposes a definition of "Jewish Religious Experience," and presents her theory of educating for religious experience.

Conn, Walter. *Christian Conversion: A Developmental Interpretation of Autonomy and Self Surrender.* New York: Paulist Press, 1986.

Conn presents his model of personal development as self-transcendence, drawing on the works of Erik Erikson, Jean Piaget, Lawrence Kohlberg, James Fowler, and Robert Kegan.

Heubner, Dwayne. "Religious Metaphors in the Language of Education." *Religious Education*, vol. 80, no. 3 (Summer 1985), 461-472.

Heubner draws upon biblical sources in connecting religious metaphors to the language of education. He uses Genesis 1 and 2 to demonstrate that human beings had to subdue and serve the earth, and Genesis 19:18 and 19:33-34 to show that human beings had to be "response-able" for other human beings, including the stranger. He uses the *"Shema"* in Deuteronomy 6:4-5 to explain the concept of reverence.

James, William. *The Varieties of Religious Experience.* New York: Collier Books, 1961.

Written in the early 1900s, this book presents the empirical work on religion and religious life of one of the foremost American philosophers.

Macdonald, James. "A Transcendental Developmental Ideology of Education." In *Heightened Consciousness, Cultural Revolution and Curriculum Theory*, William Pinar, ed. Berkeley, CA: McCutchan, 1978, 85-116.

Macdonald presents his concept of "centering," which stresses the necessity for the brain to be in a relaxed mode in order to experience the transcendent.

———. "Curriculum Theory." In *Curriculum: An Introduction To the Field*, James R. Gress and David E. Purpel, eds. Berkeley, CA: McCutchan, 1974, 41-44.

A description of Macdonald's role in the re-conceptualist educational reform movement.

Noddings, Nel, and D. Scott Enright. "The Promise of Open Education." In *Theory into Practice*, vol. 22, no. 3 (Summer, 1983), 182-189.

Noddings is best known for her writings on the ethic of care. In this article, she and Enright trace the philosophical tradition of open education prior to the 1960s. Open education is viewed as an ideal description of education practice and beliefs, and not as bodies of perspective rules and principles.

Robinson, Edward. *Original Visions: A Study of the Religious Experience of Childhood.* New York: Seabury Press, 1983.

Presents research on the religious experience of childhood.

Rosenak, Michael. *Commandments and Concerns: Jewish Religious Education in Secular Society.* Philadelphia, PA: Jewish Publication Society, 1987.

Presents the distinction of aims between explicit educational theology, which is the norm and tradition-oriented, and implicit educational theology, which is responsive to encounter, deliberation, and social conditions.

Ross, Virginia. "The Transcendent Function of the Bilateral Brain." *Zygon* 21:2 (June 1986).

The findings about the ways in which people's brains and systems are "wired" for religious experience provide scientific evidence about intuition, the unconscious, the inner life, and the varieties of religious experience that heretofore have been viewed as subjective, personal, and plausible at best. Ross looks specifically at the issue of the ability to experience transcendence.

Schubert, William H. "The Question of Worth as Central To Curricular Empowerment." In *Teaching and Thinking about Curriculum: Critical Inquiries.* James T. Sears and J. Dan Marshall, eds. New York: Teachers College Press, Columbia University, 1989, 211-227.

Presents Schubert's challenge to design curriculum that focuses on subjects that are of worth or worthwhileness to the learner.

Waldman, Nahum M. "Tradition and Experience in the Book of Job." In *Studies in Jewish Education and Judaica in Honor of Louis I. Newman* by Alexander H. Shapiro and Burton I. Cohen. New York: KTAV Publishing House Inc., 1984, 157-168.

In this chapter Waldman views the Book of Job as a collection of views on human suffering and the justice of God, and explores these different views.

Whitehead, Alfred N. *The Aims of Education and Other Essays.* New York: MacMillan, 1929.

A prominent twentieth century educator, Whitehead describes education as being religious in nature.

CHAPTER 15

WRITING A PERSONAL THEOLOGY

Neil Gillman

APPROACHES TO TEACHING JEWISH THEOLOGY

THERE ARE TWO WAYS TO TEACH JEWISH THEOLOGY: as an academic discipline or as existential testimony. This applies to the classroom for all ages, whether one is teaching in an explicitly secular setting such as a university or in an identified religious setting such as a seminary, synagogue, Jewish school, or Jewish Community Center. Some Jewish settings choose not to teach theology explicitly or systematically at all. In those that do teach theology, the choice is not always existential testimony.

Teaching theology involves looking at the range of issues related to the relationship between God and human beings. Some of the concerns with which both theologians and individual Jews have struggled over the years include: Covenant, life after death, the nature of good and evil, free will, theodicy (when bad things happen to good people), creation, redemption, revelation, and so forth. Both approaches seek to address these concerns.

Teaching Theology As an Academic Discipline

The first approach, teaching theology as academic discipline, views theology as one more subject for scholarly inquiry, not intrinsically different from physics or economics. The material can be taught either historically — the evolution of Jewish theological thinking from the Bible to our own day — or thematically — by focusing on specific issues such as the nature of God, revelation, the problem of evil, and eschatology (end of days). The approach throughout is dispassionate and critical.

The personal theology of the instructor is irrelevant to this inquiry. Indeed, the instructor may not even be Jewish, and certainly need not be a "religious" or practicing Jew. Whatever criticisms are advanced should reflect the inherent inadequacies of the position, not the instructor's personal beliefs. That distinction may be subtle, but it is real and profoundly important, and the instructor will surely appreciate the difference. The goal of the course is to have the students acquire certain bodies of knowledge and methods of inquiry, and the achievement of these goals can be tested by objective exams or research papers.

Teaching Theology As an Existential Testimony

The second approach, teaching theology as an existential testimony, assumes that theology is not like economics or physics, that it deals with the most fundamental issues involved in living a human life, with what we call "meaning of life" issues. The goal of the course, here, is to help the student formulate and defend a personal theology, one that enables the student to function as a religious Jew in the modern age, that is, to worship and practice as a Jew. True, this personal statement should be grounded in the age-old teachings of Judaism concerning theological issues. But this is an interim step in the process of engaging a student explicitly in reflecting on theological issues; the ultimate goal is to have the student integrate the source material in a personal way. The only way to test this is to have the student write a personal theological statement. In this classroom setting, the personal theology of the instructor is crucial. It serves as a model for what the students should be able to develop on their own. It must, then, be articulated in the classroom and subjected to a searching critique by both students and instructor.

Comparing the Two Approaches

The first approach presents no monumental educational challenge. Every academician, trained in an American graduate school, has been exposed to multiple examples of this kind of teaching. It is the bread and butter of American academia, embodied both in class teaching and in publications, the gateway to tenure and promotion.

The second approach is far more complicated, largely because it makes different demands of the instructor, demands that have not been made during the entire course of his or her education. In our current educational culture, meeting these demands brings few academic rewards.

Overcoming a Crisis Regarding the Teacher's Role: A Personal Statement

My personal education in theology and philosophy prepared me very well to teach Jewish theology as an academic discipline. I simply had to reproduce the model my teachers had employed, and I did that with reasonable success in my early years of teaching at The Jewish Theological Seminary.

But even then, I must have experienced a subliminal discomfort with this approach. That early teaching was confined to introductory undergraduate classes in Jewish thought. I always gave my students an objective test on the course material at the end of the semester, but I also asked them to write a personal theological statement which, I assured them, would be totally confidential, would not affect their grade, and could be reviewed in a personal conversation at the end of the semester, if they wished.

But the real crisis in my teaching career came when I was asked to teach similar courses to Rabbinical students. The crisis was two-fold. First, I realized that Rabbinical students were different from undergraduate or typical graduate students, that they would be expected to serve as religious role models, not mini-professors. They should, then, have a personal theology, and they should properly be expected to articulate that theology in their teaching and preaching. Second, I understood that if I wished to help my students develop their personal theology, I would have to articulate my own, front and center, in the classroom. As I began to do that, I quickly realized that what I claimed to believe could not withstand even my own critical examination, and that, in fact, I did not really believe any of it any more.

Every religious Jew has a rudimentary theology; it will remain rudimentary until it is examined. But it will not be examined until it is articulated. I distinctly remember spelling out my belief system in those early classes, seeing the words dangling in the air before me, confronting and challenging me, daring me to make some sense of what I was saying, and realizing that I simply could not continue to teach as I had been. That process of articulating my personal belief system was crucial to the future evolution of my teaching style.

I then had two choices: either to stop teaching, or to get to work and begin to clarify what I really did believe. Of course, I did the latter. The eventual result was my book, *Sacred Fragments* (Gillman, 1990). But even then, it was the late Gerson Cohen, chancellor of The Jewish Theological Seminary, who insisted that the book should not simply review traditional and modern Jewish options on a series of theological issues, but should include my own personal positions as well. The afterword to that book, entitled "Doing Your Own Theology," in which I urge readers to write personal theological statements and describe how to structure that exercise, was indeed an afterthought.

Applying Existential Testimony To the Classroom

I subsequently incorporated this method into my Rabbinical school classes. I divided the course material into four units: revelation, God, the problem of evil, and eschatology, assigning two units to each semester. I spent the bulk of class time doing frontal teaching on each issue, tracing the various options presented to us by past thinkers, and asking the students to do a good deal of reading on their own. My own personal position on the issue was incorporated each step of the way. The students were then asked to write personal statements. I copied and distributed four of the most interesting for class review and critique at the last session of the unit. I sat in the back of the room, and allowed the class to speak to the four students and to each other. Only in the last ten minutes of the class did I introduce my personal reactions to the four papers.

More recently, I have altered the balance between frontal teaching and personal writing in an even more radical way. I now teach a course entitled "Advanced Theology Writing Workshop." I devote only three sessions (out of 13) to frontal teaching on the issue (again based on extensive readings), but the bulk of the semester is devoted to the critique of the personal statements. Class size is limited to ten students.

Using Existential Testimony with Adolescent and Adult Learners

Finally, I took the further plunge and began to use this method outside the Seminary as well. I have conducted workshops of this kind at the CAJE Conference, at Rabbinical Assembly retreats, subsequently in adult education programs, more recently with teachers in congregational and Day Schools, and even with their students in Grades 7-12.

To be as effective as possible, a workshop of this kind demands time, and some of my colleagues in the Rabbinate have generously allotted me a number of evening class sessions so that every member of the group may have an opportunity to share his or her thinking with the group as a whole (usually, not more than 15-20 members).

But at other times, I have used a rudimentary form of the method for a one evening session. Again, I limit the size of the group, I ask for a

rather large home with many rooms so that the students can find a private space in which to write, along with drinks and munchies to ease the inevitable tension.

I begin by setting the tone: I describe the method, tell them what I will ask them to do, explain how it can be helpful to them, urge them to be honest, to maintain confidentiality, to keep the room "safe," to be gentle and charitable with each other, and to work alone.

I then present a few leading questions just to stimulate their thinking. On revelation: What "really" happened at Sinai? Is the historicity of Sinai (as described in Exodus 19-20) important to them? Whatever it is they feel obligated to do as Jews, what is the source of that obligation? Does God want women Rabbis? On God: No human being has a "fix" on God, so when you think of God, what image comes to your mind? Describe a moment when you felt particularly close to God. On Prayer: When you pray, is it important that you be praying "to" some other reality? Are the words of the prayer book important, helpful, a hindrance? Is community (a *minyan*) important, helpful, a hindrance? Are fixed times and places for prayer, helpful, a hindrance? On eschatology: What do you believe will happen to you after you die? I insist that none of these questions is from Sinai, that they are designed to help not to hinder, and that they may all be ignored.

What follows is the most magical part of the whole evening. Students scatter to different parts of the house and begin to write. Twenty-five adult Jews are gathered in a house, yet total silence reigns. I rarely give them more than 20-25 minutes, explaining that people usually take up whatever time they are given to complete an assignment.

Then we come together again and I ask for volunteers to read what they have written. I anticipate the extended silence that ensues, and I let it be. Eventually someone will take up the challenge, and then the dam is broken and hands fly up. I take a back seat because my primary purpose is to allow the participants to talk to each other. I will add a few personal reactions at the end of each statement, refining, clarifying, extending, identifying a position as very Buberian, Heschelian, or Kaplanian, and suggest further readings in one of these authors.

These discussions are inevitably very powerful. Masks are shed; people get to know each other on a far deeper level than in the past; sometimes tears flow. In short, what began as a more or less random assemblage of Jews becomes a community.

These groups are clearly self-selected, but I am astounded at the sophistication I encounter. I have not done any frontal teaching here, but these people have been listening to sermons and attending adult education lectures and classes for years, and they clearly have been thinking about theological issues. They may not know as much as my Rabbinical students do, but they can think. Their professional lives make serious intellectual demands on them, and they can apply their minds to other issues as well — when challenged to do so.

One note for teachers and group leaders. Since I often do not know who is in the room, and I must allow anyone who wants to read to do so, from time to time, I get a clearly disturbed or inappropriate statement. I distinctly remember the paralysis that crept over me the first time one such statement was read. What do I do now? To my immense good fortune, I did not have to do or say a thing. The group took care of the problem. It had as much stake in preserving the integrity of the process as I did. Gently, but firmly, the other participants distanced themselves from the statement, and we went on with the evening.

Finding a Balance between the Two Approaches

My main issue, today, is adjusting the balance between the two approaches. The seminary setting in which I teach is explicitly a modern, Western academy. That model exercises its own none too subtle demands on me. But even beyond this, I feel a responsibility to teach the material and to do so thoroughly and rigorously.

I do want my students to know what they should know about the history of Jewish thought. I most emphatically do not want the class to deteriorate into a touchy-feely exercise. Besides, my students need to ground their personal theologies in the Jewish theological tradition as a whole. Only then can they decide what of that tradition they want to appropriate for themselves. In short, their statements must be authentically Jewish.

Of course, the issues of authenticity and authority in Jewish theology pose their own problems, which are always addressed. But putting these issues aside, how can I balance the claims of objective knowledge and personal appropriation? I would love to believe that my students do all of the assigned readings before coming to class, and some do, but others do not. And the difference is usually perceptible in what they write. So I cannot avoid a certain amount of frontal teaching. The question is: how much? And how to balance that part of the course with the class discussion?

The point remains that teaching Rabbinical and Cantorial students, and also students in our School of Education is qualitatively different from teaching undergraduates and graduate students. The former need to go beyond the dispassionate review of the data and to address their personal theological agenda. To deprive them of this challenge is to deprive them of the preparation they must have to function successfully in their chosen careers. Anything less would be educational malpractice. And this additional task must not be confined to the periphery of their educational experience in the school, to extracurricular symposia or self-learning. It must take place in the classroom and at the heart of the curriculum.

The enterprise as a whole presents distinctive educational challenges. First, the instructor is far more exposed than in the usual academic setting, and second, standards for successful teaching and student achievement are far more difficult to define. (How does one grade a personal theological statement?) But the broader issue relates to our educational goals. If our goal is to do Jewish *religious* education, to educate for mature religious commitment, as opposed to just teaching *about* Judaism, we simply have no choice. So the same is true if we are teaching theology to adolescents or adults. While the class is not directly aimed at helping them function in their chosen careers, it is intended to educate them to live vibrant lives as Jews.

IMPLICATIONS

1. Although Gillman emphasizes the need for Rabbis, Cantors, and educators to clarify their own theologies in preparation for becoming Jewish role models, in fact, all people would benefit from examining their own theological stance. This self-examination would enrich their lives, deepen their understanding of and relationship to God, and better prepare them to share their views with others.

2. In teaching theology, it is important to present some combination of studying Jewish texts, traditional or modern, on theological issues with a sharing of personal perspectives.

3. Having a balance between asking probing questions and being compassionate is essential to helping people in this process of examining their own views. Not all statements have to be taken at their face value. If people are to move and strengthen their views, they need to think critically and examine their own assumptions. Yet, this needs to be done in a way that validates their views and sense of self.

4. As people practice expressing their viewpoints on theology, they are likely to become more comfortable and capable at doing so.

5. People of all ages have a theology. How they are able to express it and critically examine it differs. Some age groups are better at being self-critical and systematic. (See Chapter 7, "Nurturing a Relationship To God: A Developmental Approach.")

6. Gillman uses an approach in teaching his semester-long courses that focuses on a few areas of theology. He mentions four areas: God, evil, revelation, and eschatology. Concentrating on a few issues allows the learner to examine in-depth sources from Jewish authors, traditional and modern, and his/her understanding of these sources.

QUESTIONS FOR CRITICAL INQUIRY

1. Gillman makes the teaching of theology an "either/or," either an academic discipline or an existential testimony. In what ways do you agree with the portrayal of approaches as being a dichotomy? In what ways do you disagree with the portrayal of approaches as being a dichotomy? Are there ways of teaching theology other than the two he has described?

2. Recall an educational experience when the class was taught as an academic discipline. Recall an educational experience when the class was taught as an existential testimony. What did you get out of each experience? How did you feel about each experience?

3. Gillman does not talk explicitly about the role of life experience in formulating one's personal theology. Describe one life experience that you have had that affected your view of God.

4. In what ways can Gillman's approach to the teaching of theology be adapted to the Religious School or Day School classroom? Consider age appropriateness, setting, curriculum, role of teacher, etc.

5. What suggestions does Gillman make about creating a classroom that is conducive for encouraging people to share their personal theologies? What other suggestions do you have?

6. Gillman says that the personal sharing of theological statements leads to a sense of community. For what reasons do you think this happens? For what reasons is the creation of community an important outcome of education?

ACTIVITIES

1. Keep a spiritual journal for three weeks. In addition to writing, you can use pictures, newspaper articles, songs, poems, prayers, arguments with God, cartoons. Reflect on how it felt to keep this journal. Did it get easier or harder? What were the main theological themes that you expressed in your journal?

   Using the glossary of theological terms on p. 469, match the themes that you identified with concept(s) or term(s) that best describe them. In what ways, if any, did this raise your awareness of spiritual issues or matters around you?

2. Consider some theological questions such as: Why are we here or what is our purpose in life? Why is there evil? How do we experience the ongoing revelation of God's presence? What do you think happens after we die? Each person should pick one of the questions, find a comfortable place, and write his/her response. After writing about the question for ten or 15 minutes, participants swap writings with another person. Then each person reflects on and writes more about what thoughts the writing provokes in relation to the question. Finally, the pairs can talk to one another about why they chose their question and their responses to it.

3. Bring together a panel of people, each of whom has experienced tragedies, crisis, or life changing events. Have each explain how he/she understands theodicy: why do bad things happen to good people? Have each comment on where God was in their lives at during this time and how this experience affected their spiritual path.

4. If God had an 800 number and you could dial up God, what would you talk to God about? Role-play this dialogue with God. When it is over, pull out the theological concepts that you covered. Use the glossary of theological terms on p. 469 as a guide.

5. Watch a segment from the film *Oh God!* (1977, rated PG, 104 min.). Discuss the images of God presented in the film.

BIBLIOGRAPHY

Gillman, Neil. *Sacred Fragments*. Philadelphia, PA: The Jewish Publication Society, 1990.

   The book's subtitle, *Recovering Theology for the Modern Jew,* indicates both the focus and audience for this work. Each chapter presents a fundamental theological question and a survey of responses to it throughout the ages. For example, the first chapter is "Revelation: What Really Happened?" The material is presented in a way that supports each Jew's journey in finding answers to these difficult questions today.

CHAPTER 16

TELL ME A STORY ABOUT GOD

Sandy Eisenberg Sasso

As children we longed for narrative. "Tell me a story before I go to bed" was a rhyme I used to chant to coax my parents into one more bedtime story. We all remember sitting in rapt attention at story hour in school and drifting off to sleep in the embrace of a good book. The stories we received were gifts we continued to unwrap as life events called them forth to memory once again.

Stories helped us find our place in the world and invited us to imagine new possibilities. Belden Lane, Professor of Theological Studies of Saint Louis University, writes about the uncommon power of story to change the status quo. " . . . (Hearing) stories of what 'might be,' the reality of 'what is' can never be the same."[1]

A most striking biblical example is the Exodus narrative. Generations, having read this powerful account of a small group of slaves and their escape from bondage, have imagined their own freedom and acted to overthrow oppression. Story is never "just a story." Why else would governments and movements seek to burn and censor books if it were not for the extraordinary ability of narrative to plant the seeds of change?

If religion seeks to help us move beyond ourselves, to enter a place we never imagined we could be, to look at reality in a new and redemptive way, then story is the first language of religion. Religion begins in a moment of revelation, a spiritual experience. That encounter is expressed through story. The story is then dramatized through ritual and liturgy and ultimately reflected upon in theology. Theology is the abstract religious language of the scholar-philos-opher; story is the concrete religious language of the person of faith.

Moses heard God's voice at the burning bush calling him to lead his people out of bondage. Exodus relates the episode in the following manner:

> . . . When God saw that he (Moses) had turned aside to see, God called to Moses, " . . . Put off your shoes from on your feet, for the place on which you stand is holy ground." (Exodus 3:4)

One can only imagine how many others had walked by the burning bush and had not "turned aside to see." But Moses' attentiveness established a unique relationship to a particular set of circumstances. What Moses had that others did not was not more knowledge about desert foliage, but a greater awareness of the ineffable.

Teaching religion is not primarily about transmitting information, but about evoking wonder. It is not in understanding the essence of God, but feeling the presence of God. Good narrative allows the reader to "turn aside to see." It evokes, as close as any words can, the world of experience. Story ought to be at the heart of all religious education.

To appreciate a story, the reader must do the work that the spirit demands. The spiritual life requires that the self be silent, humble in the face of circumstances it cannot always control. Recognizing all as being created in the image of God, the religious person apprehends the interconnections of all life. Listening to a story requires the same characteristics. First, it is nec-

---

[1]Belden Lane, "Fantasy and the Geography of Faith," *Theology Today* 50 (October 1993), 403.

essary to quiet the self, to relinquish control. The characters of a narrative invite the readers into their story not as directors, but as witnesses. But if the readers are open enough, silent enough, the soul of the characters will touch their own. They will laugh and weep aloud because the story has enabled them to empathize with the people whose lives they have entered. The religious life is precisely about making those connections and sensing wonder. Stories teach us to listen, to be more filled with awe than answers.

Not only does reading or listening to a story require the same qualities necessary for spiritual development, the narrative allows readers to better understand themselves. In a good story, readers confront individuals who struggle with the same existential problems they do. The characters are loving and hateful, arrogant and humble, compassionate and indifferent. They struggle to make sense of their lives, to create meaning, to find a way through despair. Their story helps readers imagine the same possibilities for themselves. They offer a path to redemption.

The use of biblical narrative is a normal component of religious education. But there is a reservoir of good literature that can provide a pathway to the spirit that we often relegate to the secular world. Stories that wrestle with ultimate questions are religious stories whether or not they mention the Divine. The biblical books of Esther and Song of Songs contain no reference to God. They tell tales of courage and identity, love and relationship. Nonetheless, they are holy books.

A story about a character who finds a path to forgiveness is far better than a sermon or treatise about forgiveness. Preaching about religious truths is never as effective as facilitating the discovery of those truths. Stories, close as they are to the events that gave them birth, provide the ground for that revelation.

What is true for adults is even more so for children whose primary language is story. So often we believe that children are incapable of theological thought because they cannot understand abstract concepts. We presume that adults are the serious God seekers and children are the

empty vessels into which those older and wiser must pour a religious spirit. What a tragic mistake. Children already have a deep spiritual life, and the role of teachers and parents is to help them give expression to what is already inside. Children are often reluctant to speak about their spiritual experiences for fear of being embarrassed, not taken seriously, for lack of a way to name the experience.

Story is the concrete language that can help children give voice to that inner life. The extraordinary quality of narrative is that it invites the reader into dialogue. No one can tell another what a story means, for its meaning is dependent on the reader and the experiences he/she brings to it.

I used to tell stories to my congregation during family services and conclude by explaining what those narratives meant. As a storyteller, I came to realize that I was communicating what the story meant to me and was depriving the children of the spiritual work they needed to do. By allowing children their own relationship to the narrative, we offer them an environment in which they can freely struggle (in a way in which they are able) with their religious questions.

Stories that challenge our understanding of what it means to be a human being are sacred stories. They leave lasting impressions on our brains that influence how we respond to life; they provide a narrative context for our personal and communal searching. The spiritual life is best nurtured through experience and its first language, story. We cannot manufacture sacred experiences, but we can become more attuned to seeing the holy in the ordinary. Far more than theological abstractions and religious pronouncements, story helps foster that awareness.

WHY I WRITE STORIES FOR CHILDREN

I have written numerous children's books, because I believe strongly in the power of story to encourage the religious imagination of children. I write for children because it matters what children believe. If they grow up believing that they are better than anyone else, they may just act that way, finding "religious" sanction for intolerance. If they grow up believing that fortune is deserved and misfortune a sign of divine disfavor, they may reject religion in times of hardship instead of allowing their faith to carry them through difficulty.

I tell stories about faith that encourage youngsters to imagine not what they can get from God, but what they can do because of God.

> Sometimes I think God is just like my Dad when he holds the back seat of my new two wheel bicycle just long enough for me to catch my balance. Then he lets go, and I ride all by myself! But it's nice to know he's running alongside me.

> Sometimes I think God is just like my Mom when she helps me look both ways in crossing the street and then she lets me go — all by myself! But it's nice to know she's still watching me at the corner. *What makes you feel big enough to do something, all by yourself, for the very first time?*[2]

I write for children about issues of theological concern because they ask. They have the same religious questions that adults do. They seek to make meaning of their world. They experience hurt, failure, loss. They want to know why life is not always fair, why they cannot live forever. Too often we have not taken their questions seriously. In my writing I try to honor the spirit of the child and to give them a language to express what is already on the inside.

When I wrote my first book, *God's Paintbrush*, I wanted to focus on everyday events in children's lives. Spirituality is about noticing the extraordinary in the everyday. Learning to ride a bicycle for the first time, getting lost in a large store, losing a tooth, moving to a new city are all ordinary experiences of childhood. I want children to see these as windows into the sacred, to see God's presence in their growing, in a

teacher's wisdom, in music that makes them dance, in the changing seasons, in love that lifts them up, in courage that carries them through the hard times, and in themselves.

Most of all I want them to be able to talk about God. Many religious books seek to give absolute, simple answers to complex questions. The more I work with children, the more I realize that they want to converse about religious matters. Too often, they are met with pat responses or silence. *God's Paintbrush* is a source of vignettes, each ending with a question. When children talk to me about what they like best about the book, they unanimously say, "The questions." One parent related to me an incident of reading *God's Paintbrush* to her child. One night, the child's father wanted to hurry the bedtime reading ritual. He read the vignettes, but left out the questions. But his child insisted, "No, Dad, read the questions!"

In part, I wrote both *God's Paintbrush* and *In God's Name* to offer a variety of divine images to children, to paint a picture which moves beyond the "graying grandfather." All God-talk is a set of metaphors, approximations. If we are going to say something about God, we need to use human language. If we are not going to say anything about God, then God is irrelevant. We help our children most by offering a multiplicity of images. Too often the stories we tell our children offer just a single image. Yet a single image becomes not a model, but the only description of God, an idol. Various images help our youngsters to call God out of their place and to understand that all images are incomplete, that each image is only a partial knowing.

Before I read *In God's Name* to the children, I ask them what is their favorite name for God. They usually respond with traditional terms, "Father," "*HaShem*." *In God's Name* is a story about people's search for the true name of God. Everyone calls God out of his or her experience. The farmer calls God "Source of Life." The woman who nurses her baby calls God

---

[2]Sandy Eisenberg Sasso, from *God's Paintbrush* (Jewish Lights Publishing, Woodstock, VT, 1992).

"Mother." The soldier who is tired of too many wars calls God "Maker of Peace." The lonely child calls God "Friend." In the end, they decide that all the names for God are good, no name is better then another, and together they call God "One." After reading the story, I ask the children again what their favorite name for God is. Invariably, they respond "Mother" and "Friend." I ask them of what prayer the story reminds them. Without hesitation, they sing the *Shema*.

In God's Name is based on a Rabbinic teaching that God is like a mirror, and everyone who looks into it sees a different face. What we see depends on who we are, our age and our experiences. We need to give children stories that will enable them to look in that mirror and tell us what they see.

I write stories for children because of the questions they ask and because of the questions I ask myself. I ask myself questions about faith, where it comes from, where do I seek it. In writing *God in Between*, I explored that journey. A man and a woman seeking to solve a Chelm-like town's problems go to find God. They venture to all the traditional places of revelation — a mountain, the desert, the sea. It is only when they come together that they find God in their relationship, "in between." Their encounter enables them to do things that they never thought possible. In many ways, this book is my way of making Martin Buber's *I and Thou* into a story for children. Children may not be able to articulate this theology of dialogue in the abstract, but they can understand it in a story.

For Heaven's Sake tells of a similar journey. In this case, a young boy seeks heaven. His family and the people he meets give him the traditional answers about heaven, but he remains unsatisfied. He insists on finding the place where everyone tells him his grandfather, who has died, has gone. Finally, he and his grandmother go to look for heaven together. Their journey helps him find the place in their hearts where heaven is. The story provides a catalyst for an important conversation. It is not about telling youngsters what is the right way to believe, but about encouraging them to think about questions of faith.

Both *But God Remembered* and *A Prayer for the Earth — The Story of Naamah, Noah's Wife* are *midrashim* for children. They give voices to women who have no voices, names to those with no names, and stories to those with no stories. They help children see women in strong leadership roles. It is one thing to tell young girls that they can become whatever they choose. It is another thing to allow them to grow up with characters who face some of the same problems they do and who find a way through them. It is essential for boys and girls to grow up with sacred stories about men and women in which women are also heroes and shapers of history.

God Said Amen is a fantasy tale about pride and stubbornness, about peace and reconciliation. It raises questions about the meaning of prayer. It helps children consider the ways in which prayer is meant not to change God, but to change us.

Cain and Abel: Finding the Fruits of Peace takes a fresh look at the biblical story of sibling rivalry and the first act of murder. The book imagines a world without violence and helps readers think about how they can direct their own anger at life's unfairness in constructive ways.

READING WITH CHILDREN TO ENHANCE THEIR SPIRITUALITY

When you sit in a quiet place with children and give them your full attention, when you put aside the frenetic schedule of an ordinary day and read them a story, you are doing more than just improving their language skills. The closeness between you and them, the quiet space in a busy day becomes a spiritual experience.

On Shabbat, we replicate this experience as we read the Torah before the entire congregation. God's love for us is manifest through the gift of Torah. And so we pause in our weekly routine, open a book and read the narratives of the Torah and prophets, the stories of our people. In this act, we renew our relationship with one another, our people and our God. From the stories we tell, we learn who we are and we begin to live in our story. On a smaller scale, we can do this every time we open a book with children.

Even as our children or students grow older and learn to read on their own, they will appreciate your reading to them. Katherine Patterson, a well-known children's author, once said that to be asked to read is to be given an assignment; to read to someone is to give a gift. With great love we give our children the gift of story. Our children will be exposed to increasing amounts of information. They will know many facts and figures, but stories are what they will remember.

The best stories to read to children are ones that capture the imagination. If they are not intrinsically interesting, they will be boring to our children. Just because a book teaches a valuable lesson does not make it a good narrative. Good books have real life characters with flaws. They do not preach or talk down to children. They have a story to tell; they leave room for conversation and wonder. They can talk about difficult and tragic situations, but they always give a child hope.

How to Use Story in a Classroom

When you are using a story in a classroom, introduce the reading with the focus you want to develop in discussion. For example, if the story is about anger and forgiveness, begin by asking your class if anyone has ever been really angry at someone. Spend some time letting the students talk about personal experiences. If the students are reluctant to talk, have them share an experience with a partner and then ask if anyone would share his or her story.

After the discussion, read the story. Don't think that picture books are too juvenile for older students. The stories in some picture books are powerful for adults. Students who have just graduated to middle school novels might bristle at being read a picture book. Just read the story and don't show the pictures.

At appropriate ages, pictures are an important complement to the narrative. Sometimes they simply enrich the plot and at times they tell a story all their own. Looking at pictures in a storybook is a wonderful way to connect younger children to the narrative. Children may create their own responses to the reading through drawing the part of the story that is meaningful to them.

After reading a story, you may encourage a discussion through a variety of other methods.[3] It is most important that you don't tell the students what the story means. Let them develop their own relationship to the narrative, find their own place in the story. Don't violate the searching that they need to do.

You may encourage a discussion through questions. Give students a few minutes to think about what they are going to say. It may help to ask them to write down a sentence about what they are thinking, or to have them share their ideas with a partner. This will make the subsequent conversation more thoughtful. Ask open-ended questions, not ones that require one or two word responses. Don't ask questions that have right or wrong answers. "Wondering questions" enable students to connect their lives with the characters in the story. For example, you might ask: I wonder who you are in the story? I wonder what your favorite part is? I wonder what it must have felt like to be . . . ? I wonder if you have ever felt like that? You might ask what the students want to talk about or what made some difference to them. What are they curious about, what do they think happens next in the story?

I tell a story in Bar/Bat Mitzvah seminars about a shepherd who prayed everyday a simple prayer to God until a Rabbinic scholar came along and told him that he needed to pray the fixed liturgy. The scholar proceeded to teach the shepherd the correct order of the prayers. When the scholar left, the shepherd promptly forgot everything that he had learned and stopped pray-

---

[3]My gratitude to Shirley Mullins, owner of Kids Ink Bookstore in Indianapolis, and a teacher of children's literature, for her suggestions of ways to use story in the classroom.

ing altogether. When the shepherd's prayer was no longer heard in heaven, God asked the angels to find out why. The shepherd told them that his simple prayer was foolish; the scholar told him so. The angels showed him that the way he prayed was the way the angels prayed in heaven. The shepherd resumed his prayer of the heart.

After the story, I asked the students who they were in the story, the shepherd or the scholar. The majority of students said that they were the shepherd. They told me they were learning the fixed prayers in preparation for becoming B'nai Mitzvah, but they yearned for the shepherd's prayer of the heart. Over the years, I have taught prayer in many ways, this was the most enthusiastic response I had ever had.

There are many other techniques aside from questions to encourage conversation. Ask students to write a letter to one of the characters in the story. Let the students role play in partners and have the characters speak to one another. Students can write a letter to the author. You might ask the class to tell the story from the point of view of one of the lesser characters in the narrative. This is especially helpful in telling biblical stories when you want to encourage the students to imagine what the women might have been thinking and feeling.

Certain exercises encourage critical thinking skills. Draw two overlapping circles and ask the class to brainstorm what the characters share in common and how they differ. Place the similarities in the overlapping part of the circle. You may choose to discuss and list the benefits and burdens of living a certain way or making the decision of one of the characters.

Remember that there is not just one interpretation to a story. Solomon is said to have known 3000 stories for every verse of Scripture. You can be creative in allowing your students to develop their unique relationship to the text. If you allow them to read themselves into the narrative, the story will become their own.

Stories should not be relegated to a library

session or special class time set aside from the rest of the curriculum. Consider fashioning your curriculum, whether it be history, ritual, prayer, holidays, or ethics, around stories. Make them the centerpiece of your teaching. In addition to beautiful Jewish folklore, *midrashim*, and religious stories, there is outstanding "secular" literature that addresses the themes and values we seek to transmit. A good story from any source will make a lesson come alive and help students to remember.

I have often fantasized about developing a holiday or ethics curriculum based on good children's literature. For example, instead of reading a text book about the rituals and customs of Sukkot, read a story about thanksgiving. Use this as a focus for discussing the meaning behind the festival. Instead of sharing a collection of essays or definitions of *tikkun olam, tzedakah*, and *gemilut chasadim*, find stories of people who live out these values. The moral life grows through grappling with morally challenging stories; they provide the contextual situations for critical decision making.[4]

In addition to the classroom, the home is the perfect place to develop a ritual of storytelling. Encourage parents to set aside a part of the day, perhaps bedtime, to read to their children. Longer books can be read over several nights. Just as we begin and conclude our Torah reading in the synagogue with prayer, so a bedtime story ritual could be framed with traditional Jewish prayer ("*Shema*" and "*V'ahavta*"). Consider asking what prayer a character in the story might offer. Even nature prays. Let younger children make up a prayer that an animal or natural object in the story might say. If a daily ritual is impossible, it can be made part of Sabbath celebration.

When we read to children, we not only give them a gift of story, we give them the gift our ourselves. We encourage not just the accumulation of fact, but the cultivation of the imagination, of the soul.

---

[4]Paul Vitz, "The Use of Stories in Moral Development," *American Psychologist* 45 (June 1990), 709-720.

Rabbi Menachem Mendel of Kotzk, a leader in Hasidism, said he became a Hasid, a "lover of God," because he met a man who told stories about the righteous. "He told what he knew, and I heard what I needed." We, too, should tell the stories we love and know so that our children will hear what they need. It is in the intersection between story and child that the spirit grows.

IMPLICATIONS

1. Spiritual learning requires space for the learner to struggle, question, explain, and explore.

2. The learner needs to help shape and form the spiritual learning that occurs.

3. Story or narrative is central to relating to God and learning to speak about God.

4. The writing and telling of stories is a spiritual activity. The listening to and interpreting of stories is a spiritual activity.

5. Children as do adults have rich and deep spiritual lives. They ask religious questions, seek meaning, and confront situations of a spiritual nature, e.g., loss, hurt, and joy.

QUESTIONS FOR CRITICAL INQUIRY

1. What are some of the stories that, as a child, connected you to God?

2. What advice about reading stories with children to enhance their spirituality does Sasso offer? What advice would you add?

3. How does Sasso show how story evokes wonder? In what other ways does she indicate how story or narrative and spirituality are linked?

4. How can stories be used in deepening and enriching the exploration of God in worship services, Torah study, and social action efforts?

5. What type of spiritual work does Sasso suggest that children and adults need to do?

How does the telling of stories help them do this spiritual work? What is the importance of asking questions in nurturing spirituality?

6. Writing stories about God is a passionate spiritual activity for Sasso. What activity evokes spiritual passion for you?

7. Why do you like stories? Why do your children like stories? Why do your learners — young and old — like stories? How are these reasons similar to the reasons that Sasso presents that stories are good ways of fostering spiritual growth?

8. How does the *Seder* help us relive the Exodus from Egypt? How does the Torah service help us act out revelation? How do Friday night blessings over candles, wine, *challah*, and children help us act out creation? Think of another ritual, prayer, or prayer service. How does this ritual, prayer, or prayer service help retell a story of our people's relationship to God?

ACTIVITIES

1. The beautiful illustrations in Sasso's books add an additional understanding of God. Using your favorite prayer, psalm, or song about God, create your own "illustrated" book or, if desired, create a videotape or "MTV" version of it. You could also "illustrate" the prayer by using a camera to take pictures.

2. Ask people to close their eyes. Read to them one of Sasso's books. Have them concentrate on the images of God that emerge. Then, as a

class, discuss the images and make abstract drawings depicting them.

3. Create a poster for each of Sasso's books that reflects the understanding of God that emerges from each.

4. Sasso's books teach us that God and godliness can touch our daily lives if we only pay attention. Draw a poster of yourself, or make an outline of your body on butcher paper. Then indicate how each part of your body can connect you to God (e.g., your eyes see the beauty of creation in nature, your heart reaches out to a loved one).

BIBLIOGRAPHY

Adult References

Bausch, William. *Storytelling, Imagination and Faith*. Mystic, CT: Twenty-third Publications, 1995.

This book is rich in stories, and discusses the power of narrative in nurturing the spiritual imagination.

Lane, Belden, "Fantasy and the Geography of Faith." *Theology Today* 50, October 1993, 397408.

In this article Lane discusses the importance of story and imagination in helping to fashion new worlds, to see alternative realities.

Berryman, Jerome. *Godly Play: An Imaginative Approach To Religious Education*. Minneapolis, MN: Augsburg, 1991.

Berryman provides the philosophical basis for his innovative and popular approach to teaching the biblical narrative. While his narrative method has primarily been used in church settings, he offers important insights for the Jewish storyteller and teacher of the Bible.

Buxbaum, Yitzhak. *Storytelling and Spirituality in Judaism*. Northvale, NJ: Jason Aronson Inc., 1994.

The author introduces the rich traditions of Hasidic storytelling and describes its value in nourishing the life of the spirit.

Hay, David, with Rebecca Nye. *The Spirit of the Child*. London: HarperCollins, 1998.

This book is the result of a three-year study of children's spirituality. It underscores the innate spirituality of children, the essential moral value in nurturing that spirituality, and the social forces that often undermine it.

Lewis, Richard. *Living by Wonder: The Imaginative Life of Childhood*. New York: Touchstone Center, 1998.

A delightful journey into the many languages of childhood, this book offers a glimpse of the imaginative world of the child.

Sasso, Sandy Eisenberg. "Tell Me a Story." *The Catechist's Connection* vol. 15, no. 3, November 1999.

The first part of this chapter is drawn from this article.

———. "When Your Children Ask — A Jewish Theology of Childhood." In *Spiritual Education: Cultural, Religious, and Social Differences — New Perspectives for the 21st Century* by Jane Erricker, Clive Erricker, and Cathy Ota. Brighton, England: Sussex Academic Press, 2001.

Using the *Seder* meal as a primary example, this article talks about how Judaism understands the spiritual voice of the child, and how it honors that voice by encouraging imagination and questions.

Vitz, Paul, "The Use of Stories in Moral Development." *American Psychologist* 45, June 1990, 709-720.

Addresses how stories contribute to a person's moral development.

Children's Books

Sasso, Sandy Eisenberg. *But God Remembered: Stories of Women from Creation To the Promised Land*. Woodstock, VT: Jewish Lights Publishing, 1995. (Ages 8 and up)

Four stories about women that invite children to explore the biblical text and to use their own imagination to become a part of it.

———. *Cain and Abel: Finding the Fruits of Peace.* Woodstock, VT: Jewish Lights Publishing, 2001. (Ages 4-8)

This book takes a fresh look at the biblical story of sibling rivalry and the first act of murder. The book imagines a world without violence and helps the reader think about how they can direct their own anger at life's unfairness in constructive ways.

———. *For Heaven's Sake.* Woodstock, VT: Jewish Lights Publishing, 1999. (Ages 4 and up)

Isaiah and his grandmother try to find out where heaven is. After seeking answers from people of different faiths and backgrounds, he discovers that heaven isn't so difficult to find after all. In this charming, award winning story, Sasso reminds us that heaven can be found within ourselves and those we hold dear.

———. *God's Paintbrush.* Woodstock, VT: Jewish Lights Publishing, 1992. (Ages 4-8)

This beautifully illustrated book presents different thoughts that provoke thinking about God and experiencing God in everyday life and the world around us. For example, thinking about rain as God's tears and an ice cream soda that makes a person laugh, are ways of getting children to think about what makes God cry and laugh. Every two pages has a reflection and questions for children to discuss.

———. *God in Between.* Woodstock, VT: Jewish Lights Publishing, 1998. (Ages 4-8)

This story teaches that God can be found where we are: within all of us and in the relationships between us.

———. *God Said Amen.* Woodstock, VT: Jewish Lights Publishing, 2000. (Ages 4-8)

Two royal rulers are too stubborn to ask each other for help, so they turn to God. In the process, they learn that they need only reach out to each other to find God's answers to their prayers. Children learn that by working together we can work with God to create a better world.

———. *In God's Name.* Woodstock, VT: Jewish Lights Publishing, 1994. (Ages 4-8)

A modern fable about the search for God's name that celebrates the diversity and unity of all the people of the world. Each seeker claims he or she alone knows the answer. Finally, they come together and learn what God's name really means.

———. *A Prayer for the Earth: The Story of Naamah, Noah's Wife.* Woodstock, VT: Jewish Lights Publishing, 1996. (Ages 4 and up)

When God tells Noah to bring the animals onto the ark, god also calls on Naamah, Noah's wife, to save each plant on earth. Naamah goes to every corner of the world, discovering and gathering a fabulous array of growing things.

———. *What Is God's Name?* Woodstock, VT: Jewish Lights Publishing, 1999. (Baby-Preschool)

An abridged board book of Sasso's *In God's Name* for the youngest of children.

Sasso, Sandy Eisenberg, and Donald Schmidt. *God's Paintbrush Celebration Kit: A Spiritual Activity Guide for Teachers and Students of All Faiths, All Backgrounds.* Woodstock, VT: Jewish Lights Publishing, 1999. (Ages 4-8)

Inspired by Sasso's book *God's Paintbrush*, this kit enables children to study, play, and learn through Activity Sheets that feature crafts, games, and other indoor and outdoor activities. Suitable for a variety of settings, including a Sabbath morning children's service, Religious School and Day School, and/or retreats.

(The first part of this chapter is drawn from Rabbi Sasso's article "Tell Me a Story," which appeared in *The Catechist's Connection* vol. 15, no. 3, November 1999.)

CHAPTER 17

PARENTS AS JEWISH SPIRITUAL GUIDES FOR CHILDREN

Julie Greenberg

By ENCOURAGING PARENTS TO EXPERIENCE THEIR OWN spirituality in as many Jewish contexts as possible, we set the stage for helping them nurture their children's spirituality in Jewish ways. Parenting is a sacred task that links the generations. It begins before conception, and, therefore, so should our spiritual programming. From the moment parent(s) undertake the intricate, magical, demanding, ultimately rewarding process of rearing a child, their receptivity to the value of Jewish community and to the values of Judaism begins to expand. As Jewish educators, we have many resources to support parents in this most significant undertaking.

We know that isolated family units can be connected, not only to other families, but also to a tradition that roots them securely in four thousand years of development. We also know that in a world of material greed and ostentation, the spirit of love, connection, and being is what ultimately matters. Through our commitment and our presence, we validate and consecrate the deeply moving moments of a family's life cycle: bringing children into the world, nurturing them as they grow, marking their coming of age, celebrating their unions, and mourning the loss of loved ones. For families in this day and age who are vulnerable, stressed, and at risk for disintegration, what we Jewish educators and clergy have to offer can be a lifeline.

Given all this, why wouldn't parents "get it" — that Judaism is worthwhile for their children? Somehow we do not always manage to connect what we offer to the deeply felt passions of parents. They feel awe, humility, confusion, challenge, fear, hope, and passion in relation to being parents. They are having religious experiences; we have religious institutions. Somehow we need to connect the two. How do we do that? How do we show that we provide a framework, a Jewish framework, for the most meaningful moments and important issues in a person's life? Through this Jewish framework we can connect to God, to higher purpose, to meaning, to what is good and growing. In addition, we connect ourselves to one another.

There are two aspects to constructing a relevant Jewish framework for families. One aspect has to do with how and when we relate to families, and the other has to do with the content of what we offer and the degree to which it empowers parents as guides.

WHEN ARE FAMILIES AVAILABLE FOR JEWISH SPIRITUALITY?

As Jewish educators we need to think about the developmental tasks faced by families with young children and then structure Jewish experiences around those tasks. Organized Judaism "catches" some of those moments, such as welcoming a baby into the community or having a coming of age ritual. Extending the wisdom of consecrating these sacred junctures communally, we need to consider when else families can meaningfully intersect with the Jewish community. From preparation for birth or adoption through the play group and child care years and on through the parenting life cycle, our Jewish institutional offerings need to connect with the felt needs and likely spiritual openings relevant to a family's life.

Some synagogues sponsor "Baby University" and Lamaze classes, which prepare parents for childbirth and for early Jewish child rearing. Some synagogues have hosted adoption or Stars of David groups, the Jewish network of adoptive Jewish families. Starting with some of the earliest moments of pre-parenting and then parenting, the object is to bring the synagogue's message to the family in the making: "This is what we do with you and for you. This is what we care about, and you are what we care about. This is why we are here."

These groups can include synagogue members, non-members, and even non-Jews. They can be synagogue sponsored only, or they can be cosponsored with other agencies in the Jewish community — the JCC, Jewish Family Service, other synagogues, and the like. Since we want parents to learn to make any time Jewish time, remember at each such event to have the leader or the participants tell a Jewish story, do a Torah *drash*, lead a song, or teach a text. Open every session with participants contributing to *tzedakah*, discussing what in the world/community needs fixing, and reciting a *brachah*. Ask each participant to take turns opening a session with a brief poem, story, or teaching. Let them research and "own" their findings, again linking another powerful experience to our heritage.

Probably the most spiritual experience my nine-year-old son has is the ecstasy of soccer. He prays he will make a goal. He thanks God when he intercepts a ball. He wholeheartedly shouts "*halleluyah*" for his team. Much of my social life, it seems, takes place on the sidelines of a soccer field. What if this team were associated with the synagogue? What if my son's experience was connected to the Jewish community? As it is, many Shabbat prayer services compete with soccer/baseball/basketball on Saturday morning. Instead of competing with these sports, why not get into the act and join children and families in finding God through what they love most? A synagogue sponsored Sunday morning or afternoon league could be open to the whole community.

Torah is read on Mondays and Thursdays because in the times of the Temple in Jerusalem, those were market days when people congregated in the city. In other words, the Torah was taken to the people, not the people to Torah. What are our "market times and places"? Are they not where people congregate — the day care center, the sports field, the after school program, birthday parties, children's performances,

driver education classes, and the like? The challenge is to figure out how to bring Torah and Jewish values to the people, wherever and whenever they gather. They in turn will "get it." They will pass it on to their families.

WHAT HELPS PARENTS TAKE ON JEWISH SPIRITUAL LEADERSHIP?

Some parents have trouble being Jewish spiritual leaders for their children because of a struggle with either the term "Jewish" or the term "spiritual." Parents raised with a solid Jewish education often had the experience of Jewish ritual performed by rote at high speed with little understanding, reflection, awareness, or sense of God. While they may be very comfortable with the forms of Judaism and with Hebrew, it does not feel spiritual to them. Some parents have a commitment to universal values and little experience with Jewish ritual or with Hebrew. Furthermore, there is a gap between what Jewish professionals know and what the average Jewish community member knows and is comfortable with concerning "Jewish" and "spiritual." Jewish professionals in love with Judaism, sometimes forget how tentative and uncomfortable some Jews feel when it comes to religious practices. Many Jews identify strongly, yet have few skills, little information, and little confidence with regard to "doing Jewish." Even those with excellent Jewish education typically are not empowered to lead.

How can parents pass on a passionate commitment to Judaism when they feel that they do not have the knowledge, tools, or competence to do so? As Jewish family educators have been saying for years, we will not be successful in raising Jews without the input and modeling of parents. To accomplish our goals, we need to make this "Jewish thing" work for parents. Parents have to be seen by their children as capable guides for their heritage.

The way we structure Judaism for families can enable this to happen. Hebrew can be daunting and disempowering for parents. In fact it has even come to be referred to as "the *sefer* barrier." However, we have precedent for using the language of the day as our primary means of Jewish expression. After all, the Talmud is written mostly in Aramaic, because that was the daily language of the people when it was being written. The Rabbis did not abandon Hebrew, but they had most important conversations in the language that the people understood. While Hebrew can add depth, nuance, and resonance to every Jewish experience, Judaism does not equal Hebrew. Therefore, let us not forfeit potentially elevating Jewish experiences by getting hung up on the academic acquisition of blessings and vocabulary and recitation of Hebrew in ritual. Let us do whatever we must to enable parents to understand and connect with the inner meaning of our ritual — be it solely in English or in a combination of English with Hebrew. There is always time for Hebrew learning and Hebrew can be an inspiring and enriching part of Judaism, but we may need to back away from Hebrew as long as it is viewed as a barrier to Jewish experiences.

What does it mean to find the inner meaning or purpose of ritual? When people feel connected and confident, their curiosity emerges. They will be eager to learn more about Jewish tradition, about Hebrew, about Jewish acts and observances and celebrations. For example, in teaching parents to lead a Shabbat ritual in their homes on Friday night, I would present candles, wine (or grape juice), and *challah* in this way:

- Light candles together, sending light to loved ones and to those who need healing all over the world. (You might mention people living in troubled places as broadcast on the news.) Sing songs about light, such as "This Little Light of Mine." My favorite memory of Shabbat light was when my earnest five-year-old sent Shabbat light "to all the aliens in the universe."

- Pass the *Kiddush* cup around and share something special about the past week, something that you look forward to in the days ahead. This intergenerational "check-in" keeps family members up on what each other is thinking and doing. "I'm glad I got an A on my math test," says my 11-year-old, while our guest of the week says, "I'm looking forward to being finished with a huge work project and having time to play with my niece."

- With hands on the *challah,* say thank you and express appreciation to each other. "I appreciate Zoe for picking the toys off the floor. I appreciate Rosie for taking care of Jonah while I cooked dinner. I appreciate Jonah for learning how to skip. I appreciate Raffi for being a good friend when Michael needed help." In this way, you are noticing your family members and also communicating your values about their growth and behavior.

If the Hebrew blessings are a comfortable or desired part of this ritual, that is fine. If not, a beautiful Shabbat ritual has taken place in English.

WHAT ABOUT GOD?

In many cases, parents want guidance from Jewish professionals in responding to children's questions about God and in shaping their own teachings about God. The best approach to supporting parents as spiritual leaders is to create situations in which parents themselves can be active in the spiritual quest. A discussion group on "What to say when children ask about God" is sure to attract interest.

In one such group, parents were asked, "What is the hardest part of teaching about God for you?" One parent started by saying, "I talk with my kids about God as a spirit or force of life. And then we read these very particular Bible stories in which God is a persona, a character in the story. And I just can't make the connection in my own mind between the God I believe in and the God in these stories." This opened the agenda for a deep discussion of how we each encounter God, the relevance of our legends, what it means to be part of a people, and levels of meaning and metaphor.

In another group, one mother said, "I'm not sure how much *bad stuff* to share with my kids. I want them to feel trusting and safe, yet the world isn't perfect. We have this book about Noah and the flood. It shows all the animals that are left behind drowning. I always skip over that part. It just seems too intense." Another parent responded, "Oh, I have that same book, and we always talk about the animals that were left behind and how sad and angry they felt. I think it's an important part of the story." "But how do you explain how God could have left some creatures behind?" asks the first parent. "It's part of life. Bad things sometimes happen," responds the second. As we can see, learning and insight sometimes happen, too.

Here are some questions that could be used in parent groups to generate discussion:

- When have you encountered God in your life?

- How do you see God acting through your life?

- In what ways are you doing God-work?

- Share an experience in which you felt fully alive, present, and aware.

- What were you taught about God as a child?

- If God could give you a list of priorities for your life right now, what would it look like?

- What is the easiest part about helping your child(ren) discover God? What is the most confusing part for you?

- In what ways are you the hands of God, the eyes of God, the lips of God as a parent?

- What are the questions about God that you imagine your child(ren) might someday ask?

A hard issue for parents to deal with is when children blame God or question God's existence because of tragedies that have happened. "God must not like my family," said one girl who had experienced a series of major losses. Another child decided, "There can't be a God, because God wouldn't have allowed six million Jews to die in the Holocaust." An important Jewish teaching is that human beings are partners with God in the ongoing work of creation. We have to learn to make a world that is safe and healthy for everyone. We are the ones who can comfort, mourn, and join together when times are hard.

For specific Jewish teachings on God there are some useful resources that should be in any Jewish library. The books by Harold Kushner, *When Children Ask about God* (Schocken Books) and *When Bad Things Happen To Good People* (Summit Books), help parents deal with theological questions by looking at experiencing God through helpfulness, growth, kindness, healing, and goodness.

In addition to enabling adults to engage on God issues, educators can encourage families to find some time each week for God-talk. My seven-year-old daughter Zoe invented a bedtime ritual during which she tells me what was "God-ish" about her day: "Playing with Theresa, Mrs. Netzky telling me my handwriting is nice, eating raspberries for desert." One week when the whole family had head lice and I was a raving maniac washing heads, laundry, and everything else in proximity, I challenged Zoe at bedtime, "What is God-ish about lice?" She pondered for a moment and then responded, "What's God-ish about lice is that we will be finished with them soon." Appreciating the blessings of life is what spirituality is all about.

There is no right or wrong answer to these God issues. It is important to provide a Jewish context in which parents can talk about God, talk about our relationship with God, and our children's emerging sense of God. By doing so, we give tacit and emotional support to parents and enable and empower them to become their child(ren)'s Jewish spiritual leaders.

Parents need to know that the spirit of Judaism is not some esoteric thing out there — "It is not in heavens above . . . nor is it beyond the sea, but it is right here in your heart and on your lips" (Deuteronomy 30:12-13). Spirituality is being awake to everyday life. As Jewish institutions help parents embrace the meaningful moments in parents' lives, we create a context in which parents can become confident guides to their offspring — the next generation. We give permission for parents to nurture their child's sense of awe, pride at growth, feelings of connectedness, and belonging to the Jewish people.

We become partners with parents in creating a Jewish community that recognizes connection to the beyond, intimacy and belonging, caring, and meaning.

IMPLICATIONS

1. Parents need to be spiritual guides for their children.

2. Parenting is a sacred task.

3. The comfort level of parents with their own spirituality affects their comfort in guiding their children's spiritual growth.

4. Parents and teachers can learn to be more spiritual themselves, and thus become more involved in guiding their children's spiritual development.

5. Synagogues and Jewish communal institutions need to go where the families are most likely to gather and teach Judaism and spirituality. Families are often most receptive to learning about spirituality in the comfort of their own home or in settings such as parks, soccer fields, or bookstores.

QUESTIONS FOR CRITICAL INQUIRY

1. When Greenberg says that "parents need to know the spirit of Judaism," what does that phrase mean to you?

2. From your experience, how much of family education helps parents become spiritual guides to their children? What barriers exist to moving family education in this direction? What about family education makes it well suited to introducing this concept of helping parents become spiritual guides?

3. In what ways is your institution currently helping parents to fulfill their role as spiritual teachers of their own children? In what other ways might Jewish communal institutions, such as Religious Schools, Day Schools, preschools, and JCCs, help parents see themselves as facilitators of their children's spirituality?

4. Greenberg takes the symbols of Shabbat evening and suggests ways of connecting the ritual objects to the experiences of family members and to the world around them. Do you have a "family tradition" that connects rituals, sacred times, and the lives of others? Can you create ways of connecting another set of ritual objects and a sacred time with people's lives, e.g., Havdalah, dwelling in a *sukkah*, Chanukah candle lighting?

ACTIVITIES

1. In what ways have your parents been or are spiritual mentors to you? Write a letter to your parents thanking them for what they have taught you and for how they helped you grow.

2. Joel Lurie Grishaver wrote a book about 40 different ways to save the Jewish people. He invites people to think simply, but creatively, about how they can do things in their own homes or places that they frequent that help make them Jewish. Make a list of 18 different things that you could do in your home or in the places that you frequent to make your life more spiritually meaningful.

3. Make a *mizrach* (a design to go on the facing-east wall) that shows your family's connection to God and Israel.

BIBLIOGRAPHY

Fuchs-Kreimer, Nancy, *Parenting As a Spiritual Journey*. Woodstock, VT: Jewish Lights, 1998.

This exquisite book is a gem for parents in its validations of the sacred within the day-to-day responsibilities of parenting. Parents will enjoy the many anecdotes and agree with the affirming perspective that parenting can be holy work.

Kushner, Harold, *When Bad Things Happen To Good People*. New York: Summit Books, 1985.

How can evil exist in a world made by a good God? How can disease, war, and other tragedies be reconciled with a belief in God? While preserving God's positive attributes, Kushner teaches that God is all-knowing and all-present, but not all-powerful.

————. *When Children Ask about God*. New York: Schocken Books, 1971.

Kushner redirects the attention of parents away from "what is God?" or "who is God?" to the question of "when is God?" God is . . . when there is love between people. God is . . . when there is growth, beauty, understanding, and so forth.

CHAPTER 18

GOD AND SPIRITUALITY IN PRAYER AND PRAYING

Roberta Louis Goodman

WHY DO WE NEED TO TALK ABOUT GOD AND spirituality in regard to prayer and praying? After all, to whom are we praying if not God? We create special, often beautiful spaces in which to worship. We fill them with magnificently crafted ritual objects and artistic expressions that acknowledge these are places of spiritual searching, in which human beings encounter their Creator. We have trained clergy and skilled lay *sh'lichay tzibor* to lead services. We have an array of songs an melodies, inspirational liturgy, innovative rituals, and committed worshipers. Taking all of this into account, aren't we safe in assuming that God is present when we pray? And how could prayer services be anything but uplifting and spiritually satisfying?

Yet, even our liturgy suggests that God and spirituality do not come automatically, but rather that we must intentionally seek out God and strive for spirituality. At the beginning of the *"Amidah,"* the worshiper recites: *"Adonai s'fatie tiftach u'phi yagid tehilatecha"* (Eternal God, open up my lips that my mouth may declare Your glory). We pray that we can pray, that our prayers will be directed to and focus on God. Neither the importance of the person praying to be ready and focused nor the aim of the prayers, glorifying God, are taken for granted. Addressing God and spirituality in the context of prayer and praying is necessary and expected.

How does one approach the teaching of God and spirituality through prayer and praying? This chapter addresses that topic in four ways. First, it describes three elements that should be part of every curriculum that teaches about God and spirituality through prayer: mechanics, meaning, and encounter. Second, major problems in the teaching of prayer from a developmental perspective are presented, with specific

reference to four groupings (early childhood, elementary school, middle and high school, and adulthood). Responses or solutions to these problems are included. Third, some thoughts on the tension between personal and communal aspects of finding God and spirituality through prayer and praying are discussed. And fourth, some thoughts on the importance of addressing the question of "why pray" are shared.

TEACHING PRAYER AND PRAYING: MECHANICS, MEANING, ENCOUNTER

Prayer and praying are often part of the curriculum of both formal (Jewish schools or classrooms for children and/or adults) and informal educational opportunities (camps, youth groups, Israel experiences, retreats, and family education). A well-balanced curriculum contains the teaching of three parts: mechanics and skills, meaning, and encounter (Holtz 1993, Shire 2002). All three parts need to be present to teach about God and spirituality effectively. Together, these parts or elements result in outcomes, competence, confidence, comfort, relevance, and renewal that contribute to establishing a relationship to and understanding of God, and a sense of spirituality for both children and adults. One aspect without the other two, or two without the third, can leave prayer and praying redundant, irrelevant, empty, or unconnected to God and/or Jewish life.

Obtaining the mechanics and skills of prayers and praying involves mastery of reading the prayers with fluency, singing the appropriate *nusach* or melodies, learning the order of the prayers, knowing the choreography of the service, and translating words, phrases, or paragraphs. Major goals of many programs are learning how to lead portions of services in a synagogue for Bar/Bat Mitzvah or rituals at home, everything from Shabbat blessings to the Pesach *Seder*. This aspect of a prayer curriculum generally aims to help socialize the learner as a participant and to some extent, as a leader, into the worship *minhag* (customs) of a particular setting, movement, or community. It can lead to a feeling of *k'lal yisrael*, of connection to Jews throughout history and around the world today.

What does the mechanical or skill side of learning about prayers have to do with connecting one to God and spirituality? To be specific, it can convey the names of God, present ways of addressing God (as with the *brachah* formula), and provide glimpses into how to establish a relationship between individuals and God or the community and God. Focusing on these mechanics and skills grounds the worshiper in a Jewish framework for connecting with God and enriching one's spirituality.

A popular approach to the teaching of prayer is focusing on key concepts. Prayers are filled with concepts about God and spirituality. Jewish liturgy is a microcosm of Jewish theology that explores the relationship between the Jewish people and God, shares insights about the nature of God, and seeks answers to life's most significant questions. As such, it deals with important ideas, such as theodicy, omnipresence, resurrection, peace, purpose, Covenant, healing, sin, compassion, and more. Concepts emerge from the prayers that relay the story of the relationship between the Jewish people and God, the struggles of Jews throughout the ages. For example, the prayers surrounding the *"Shema"* focus on the concepts of creation, revelation, and redemption, among others. Most prayers are filled with expressions that are conceptual in nature. Although it is brief, the *"Shema"* presents key concepts including God's oneness, hearing or listening, the people Israel, and being commanded. Prayers are filled with metaphoric references to God, such as Rock, Shield, Protector, Savior, and Ruler, which themselves are concepts.

Concepts lend themselves to being interpreted. People of all ages can understand concepts and ascribe meaning to them. Even young children can have a sense of what is meant by God's loving-kindness because of their experience of love and care from their own parents. As contrasted to the skills and mechanics of prayer that are about information and often memorization, concepts help the learner explore the deeper theological questions about living in a covenantal relationship to God. For those searching for meaning and seeking spirituality, the theological concepts presented in prayers are a rich source of expanding awareness about, understanding of, and relationship to God.

Teaching encounter, the experience of God's presence, is perhaps the most desired and probably the most difficult of the three parts of a prayer curriculum to tackle. How can one ensure that a person will connect to God or have a spiritually fulfilling experience? Is spiritual encounter really something that can be taught or is it cultivated? Schon (1990), in his writings on educating professionals, suggests that this task be seen not as purely a science of conveying knowable skills and information, but as being akin to the apprentice in the artist's shop who learns by watching, doing, critiquing, discussing, imitating, and experimenting. Many do go and study with individuals identified as spiritual people themselves for a weekend retreat, a course, or in a *yeshivah*. Schon's approach is compatible with that of Ochs (2002) who, in Chapter 26 of this book, "Spiritual Mentoring," presents the role of the spiritual mentor as a guide and advisor to the seeker on his or her spiritual journey — the quest for God and *kedushah* (holiness). Others, would suggest that spirituality is a discipline that can be acquired through tools such as meditation (Bookman, 1999 and Kaplan, 1990); routines such as regularly reading Psalms, poetry, or inspirational writings (Olitzky 2000, Olitzky and Forman, 1999 and 2001); or settings such as nature (Biers-Ariel, 2000) or Israel experiences. These tools, routines, and settings can help facilitate connecting to God and experiencing moments of spiritual fulfillment.

COMMON TEACHING MISTAKES: INSIGHTS FROM DEVELOPMENTAL THEORIES

Over the years, I have observed some mistakes that too often occur in the teaching of God and spirituality through prayer and praying. By nature, humans are spiritual beings. They are continually searching for meaning in their lives, raising ultimate questions about their existence and the world, examining the values that shape their lives, and striving to connect to something transcendent beyond themselves — to a power or force, often God. Therefore, the teaching of God and spirituality through prayer and praying needs to tap into this energy, this natural predisposition, to draw it out and open it up for reflection and review, to share the wisdom and beauty of Jewish liturgy, and to present ways for deepening and strengthening spiritual quests.

The experience and spirituality of prayer and our understanding of and relationship to God change over the life span, growing and evolving. Developmental theories give us insights into these changes and demonstrate how educators can adapt curriculum and programs to address more fully the needs of the worshiper. In particular, Fowler's theory of faith development, how people making meaning out of their lives (see Chapter 7, "Nurturing a Relationship To God and Spiritual Growth: Developmental Approaches"), offers an important glimpse into the ways in which people at different points in their lives might be more receptive to a certain approach (Fowler, 1981). In other publications, I have looked at developmental theories and written about their Jewish educational implications (Goodman, 1996 — focusing on prayer, and Goodman, 2002). For this chapter, I identify the major developmental mistakes that are often made in each of four grade levels, and offer some suggestions or responses that emerge from an understanding of the educational implications of these developmental theories concerning the teaching of God and spirituality through prayer and praying.

Early Childhood

While most Jewish preschools include rituals and celebrations that involve prayers and praying, they too often forget to combine how children learn best with this particular content, namely imitating and playing. Dressing up and imitating others are favorite early childhood activities. Yet, when was the last time that you saw a child get dressed up as the Sabbath Queen and have classmates welcome this bride and celebrate a festive meal with her? Some early childhood programs do have dress up corners that include ritual objects used for blessings and prayers. These ritual objects can be used in more structured explorations that involve imitating parents, clergy, Torah readers, or even God. For example, can children carry or dance with the Torah, pretend to be parents blessing their children, imagine God's reactions to a Shabbat service, and so on?

In general, teaching about God and spirituality needs to be an intentional part of the early childhood curriculum. This is the age of awe and wonder when children are receptive to the mystery and majesty of the universe. Even the most simple of things, seeing a butterfly or a rainbow or lighting candles, brings delight and joy to these children. Most Jewish early childhood programs integrate prayers and praying into holiday and Shabbat experiences and curricular units. However, they tend to stop short of teaching about God and spirituality in an explicit way that these children can comprehend. Young children can understand such concepts as holiness, God as a Rock, God as Creator, blessing, and much, much more. They can master the words and even blessings and songs about God and sacred times. They can understand stories that address the longings and hopes that led to the writing of these prayers in the first place. They can even practice looking for the mysteries in God's creation, and they can understand that this searching and appreciation constitute some of the skills and perspectives that lead to a rich spiritual life.

Elementary School

Supplementary Religious Schools and Day Schools tend to teach a great deal about prayer and praying in the elementary years. This is especially true in Grades 2 to 6, when the students become realists and rationalists, replacing the awe and wonder of the early childhood years. A very common approach to teaching about God and spirituality with this age level focuses on mastering to read, chant or sing, and translate prayers. This age group is well suited to the task. They like to learn and master new skills, information, and content. The problem is that too many curricula stop there, teaching, as Barry Holtz (1993) says, about the prayer book — and not about prayer and praying. This is equally applicable to the issue at hand of teaching about God and spirituality through prayer and praying. However, by overemphasizing the reading, chanting, singing, and translating, these curricula ignore some of the other attributes of these learners that would lead to learning about God and spirituality through prayer and praying.

These children like to know about the extraordinary, the unusual, and the extremes. Think about coin collectors or baseball statistic mavens. What name for God is used the most in a section of the prayer service? How many different tunes are there to the "*Shema*"? These are concrete learners for whom symbols or concepts have few meanings. They can design bulletin boards about God, *kedushah*, blessing, and other spiritual concepts. They want to feel capable and industrious. They are candidates for taking care of the ritual objects in their homes, school, or synagogue. They can polish silver objects, change Torah covers for the festivals, set the Torah for the weekly *parashah* reading, serve as ushers for services, watch to make sure that the Eternal Light does not go out, organize the *Chumashim* on shelves or in pews, and the like. The moral order that comes from studying prayer concepts adds to their sense of right and wrong in the universe. They can link rules and regulations to God. They can learn to explain how *tzitzit* are related to God as Commander,

how rules in society help bring peace in the world, how saying a blessing can get people into patterns of good behavior.

Middle School and High School

Too often, schools neglect teaching about God and spirituality through prayer and praying after Bar/Bat Mitzvah. Since, often, too much time and energy is directed toward preparing the children to become Bar/Bat Mitzvah, the focus shifts away from anything having to do with prayer and praying. This is unfortunate, as adolescents especially are often searching for a personal relationship to God and answers to questions about the future, and their own future in particular.

Adolescents truly come of age when they begin to express independent views and to make choices about behavior and the direction of their lives. These choices are often different from the choices of parents and different also from their own childhood understandings. Such young people look to mentors, adults who show an interest in them, to listen to their struggles, to help explore their questions, and to give them direction. They are emotive and can get stuck on a feeling, experience, or relationship. Sometimes there is the sense that no one can know or understand their inner thoughts or struggles. Some write diaries or poems to express their feelings, some talk to friends or mentors, and others remain dangerously silent.

Children in middle school and high school are more capable of exploring the longings and feelings found in the prayers and more interested in having a relationship with God and discussing life's significant questions than the younger children who receive a heavy dose of prayer education. Standing on Masada, touching the Western Wall, praying outdoors in a naturally beautiful setting, or swaying arm in arm with peers and counselors in the light of a Havdalah candle are all spiritual experiences that teens often savor. This receptivity to God and spirituality through prayer and praying needs to be tapped before they go to college and are exposed to the larger world and different religious approaches. They need to feel captivated or engaged by Judaism's struggles with many of the same questions, thoughts, and feelings about prayer and praying that they have themselves.

Adulthood

Adulthood is the most complex of the age groupings, as there is more variety among adults than the three other age groupings identified. In reality, most development theorists identify multiple adult stages or phases rather than just one. The aging process in itself brings about a multitude of changes. Life is filled with events, relationships, experiences, and conditions, both local and worldwide, that can affect our spiritual seeking:

- Life cycle changes – marrying, turning 40, or retiring

- Events in one's life – job promotion, the death of a relative or colleague

- Relationships and interactions with colleagues, neighbors, strangers, friends, and foes

- Surrounding issues of race, religion, politics, or values

- Events in one's community or the world – loss of a communal service, changes in Institutional leadership, or a tragedy, such as September 11, 2001

Any of these can open a person to seeking God and spirituality through prayer and praying.

Two common mistakes are seen in the teaching of God and spirituality through prayer and praying for adults. First, educators and learners alike too often act as if they should have learned all that they need to know about God, spirituality, prayer, and praying when they were in their youth. They feel that they are deficient in some way because they do not know it all. In some cases this is true, for example, if they cannot read Hebrew or participate in a service. Still, for the most part, they have learned many important things about God and spirituality through prayer and praying either through schooling or attending services. Often the important ques-

tions about God and spirituality, the rationale for prayers, the meaning of prayers, or the hows of encountering God are not emphasized enough and take second place to the mechanics of prayers and praying. In part, the problem is less about what was taught in childhood and more about the expectations adults have about their learning as children and the ways in which they view lifelong learning and lifelong engagement with prayer and praying.

It would be far more helpful to realize that practice and growth throughout one's lifetime with a sport, art, or even a subject, is needed to maintain, much less expand, a certain knowledge base. For example, I was a good math student in high school and can read a balance sheet and interpret statistical data. Yet, I fear the day my child brings home an algebra or geometry problem. I have not practiced; I have lost the information and much of the conceptual thinking that goes with it because I do not use those skills, concepts, and knowledge. My math SAT taken in high school was significantly higher than my math GRE taken after I had left college; already the lack of practice was evident. In contrast, while I took tennis lessons throughout my childhood beginning at age six and competed in tournaments even in college, my tennis game has not diminished. It has actually improved because I have continued to learn (taking lessons, doing drills, and reading a tennis magazine) and continued to practice. I can do some things now that I could never have done as a teenager. The reasons for this are intellectual and emotional. This progress can also be attributed to the availability of new types of tennis equipment. With my tennis, I built on the foundation that was established when I was a child. Currently, it is my math ability and not my tennis ability that is the model of how people think about learning about God and spirituality through prayer and praying. As we come to understand better the values and ramifications of lifelong learning, then hopefully my "tennis" and not my "math" experiences will become the model for thinking about our learning and growth as Jews throughout our lifetimes.

The second mistake that we often make is that while we know with adults to focus on the meaning of God and spirituality in prayer and praying, we underestimate the importance of building competence. Competence involves knowledge, familiarity, and ability with skills and information, as well as being able to interpret the prayers, discuss theological questions, and deepen one's relationship to God. Compe-tence has to do with developing feelings of comfort and confidence while, often, overcoming a sense of embarrassment and deficiency. Adults are used to being and feeling knowledgeable and skillful in their professional fields, volunteer work, and family/household matters. Fostering a sense of confidence is crucial in teaching adults about God and spirituality through prayer and praying.

PERSONAL AND COMMUNAL ASPECTS OF PRAYER AND PRAYING

To experience God and spirituality through prayer and praying involves both personal and communal aspects. For some prayers, a *minyan* of ten individuals is required; for others, prayers or blessings, different numbers are required — two witnesses for marriage vows and three for the introductory section to "*Birkat HaMazon,*" the prayer after eating a meal. Why the need for others when one can communicate personally with God? The key is the concept of being an "*ayd,*" a witness, the combination of the letter *ayin* at the end of the word "*shema*" and the *dalet* at the end of the word "*echad,*" in the "*Shema.*" It is about sharing an experience, reaffirming and reliving the Covenant with God. The whole history and purpose of the Jewish people is based on the covenantal relationship with God. Prayers and praying in the Jewish worship tradition heavily reflect this communal aspect.

Personal prayer is valued, too. King David is viewed as the great psalmist who sang God's praises. The *piyyutim* were written as expressions of one author's understanding of and relationship to God. Jews are encouraged to recite a hundred *brachot* a day, often over very mundane acts, in order to elevate the ordinary and make their lives

sacred. Jews can pray directly to God; no intermediary is necessary as in some other religious traditions. Prayer can be spontaneous, too. Even in the midst of the fixed prayer service, time is set aside for individual meditations at the end of the "*Amidah.*" These are all evidence of the personal or individual paths to God and spirituality that one can take through prayer and praying.

Spirituality is not synonymous solely with individuality within Judaism. Cohen writes: "Spirituality in Judaism involves corporate effort as well as individual initiative. The individual remains spiritually unfulfilled as long as the community is spiritually wanting" (1997, p. 33). Redemption is not fundamentally about the individual, but rather about that of the entire Jewish people.

One of the challenges of teaching about God and spirituality through prayer and praying is to help those who are uncomfortable with the fixed prayer services, rituals, and blessings to find their place within Jewish life. Many of these seekers are comfortable meditating on their own. Perhaps we should begin by teaching them the meditative practices and texts found within Jewish tradition. This will create a sense of comfort. If they can augment their own meditative practices, they may find a spiritual home within liturgy and practices of Jewish prayer and praying. While the goal may be to help make a Jewish framework fit these individual seekers, it means that those who are seemingly comfortable with the prayers and with praying must be prepared to change their worship experience, too. Those comfortable with worship services need to be God wrestlers too, struggling to strengthen and deepen their spirituality through prayer and praying. As such, they must constantly be reviewing their prayer and praying practices, liturgy, and experiences in order to heighten individual and communal spirituality.

WHY PRAY: A CHALLENGE FOR ALL

Finally, all teaching about God and spirituality through prayer and praying must address the question of "why pray." We should not assume that the answer to this fundamental question is obvious. In a postmodern world, explanations need to be made explicit as to why anyone should care about any particular thing, including prayer and praying. To make prayer and praying relevant and meaningful in one's life is something that must be worked at. It is not an inherent trait.

The liturgy is filled with hints of the answer to the question of "why pray." Each student needs to explore these hints throughout his/her lifetime. The different types of prayers are suggestive of the reasons we pray to God. We praise or bless, thank, and petition. We express our highest ideals, our deepest thoughts, our dreams, hopes, beliefs, and aspirations. We seek comfort for our greatest sorrows, losses, defeats, disappointments, and despair. We confess our wrongdoings, the ways in which we have strayed, and ask for forgiveness. We pray to become more forgiving and compassionate. We show God our love and hope to be recipients of God's lovingkindness, God's unconditional love. Our prayers acknowledge the Covenant between God and the people and recognize the grandeur, majesty, and wonder of the universe. The prayers humble us, reminding us of our humanity, our faults, foibles, and failings, and our responsibilities and potential, and the paths to righteousness. In prayer we meet our Creator, Redeemer, Savior, and Protector.

The experience of praying these prayers provides us with an ongoing opportunity to reflect on our lives, to make us introspective, to do our own *cheshbon nefesh* (personal review) of our purpose in life, our place in the world, and our fulfillment of the Covenant. Praying helps us turn and return to God. A condensed version of the theology of the Jewish people, prayer and praying lead us on paths to God and spirituality.

CONCLUSION

Prayer and praying are rich sources for teaching and learning about God and spirituality. Yet, teaching about God and spirituality needs to be an explicit part of a curriculum on prayer and praying. Just because one is focusing on prayer and praying does not mean that God and spirituality are addressed. Including God and spirituality explicitly in the curriculum sends a message to learners that their spiritual growth matters.

IMPLICATIONS

1. God and spirituality are not automatically the focus of prayer curricula. An effort needs to be made to incorporate them into prayer curricula.

2. Educators should regard the teaching of spirituality as a discipline that has its own skills, vocabulary, texts, and concepts that are transmittable from one person to another. The inner life can be nurtured and encounter can be fostered.

3. Mechanics, concepts, and encounter are essential elements in enriching people's spirituality and knowledge of and relationship to God. One without the other affects a person's ability to deepen his/her spirituality.

QUESTIONS FOR CRITICAL INQUIRY

1. Thinking about your own and another prayer curriculum with which you are familiar, what does it teach about mechanics? about concepts? about encounter? How would you recommend adjusting the curriculum to balance all three?

2. Goodman identifies common mistakes in the teaching of God and spirituality through prayer and praying. Based on your experience, describe problems or difficulties that

you have encountered in teaching about God and spirituality through prayer and praying. Do these support, refute, or not affect Goodman's observations?

3. In what ways do you consider spirituality and your relationship to God to be personal? communal?

4. If your students asked the question, "Why do you pray?" — what would you answer?

ACTIVITIES

1. Teach the prayer *"L'cha Dodi"* using all three elements — mechanics, concepts, and encounter. For the mechanics, include teaching different melodies. For the concepts, focus on the concept of the Sabbath Queen. Discuss who is the bride and who is the groom in this prayer. For the encounter part, consider an outdoor prayer worship experience with someone dressed as the Sabbath bride or queen. Be certain to debrief and also to reflect on the encounter prayer experience.

2. Write a paragraph about a prayer experience you found to be particularly spiritual. Describe the experience. Include details such as: when it occurred (about how old you were or your phase of life), where it happened, who was present — people you knew, did not know, youth group event, etc. Was it a prayer service or a personal prayer? What was it that made it particularly spiritual? In what ways, if any, did it connect you to God? How did it make you feel? Ask people who are comfortable to share their experiences. Begin to develop a list of themes of what makes for a spiritual prayer experience.

3. Do a synectics exercise to get at the multiple understandings of God. Introduce the idea that names for God are metaphors that help us understand what God is like. It is difficult to know God. Maimonides believed that we could not know what God is, only what God is not.

Go through the prayer book and write down names you find for God. Then, for one of the names, write: God is like (name for God, e.g., Shield, Rock) because _____. Then identify objects in your home. Write how God is like one of those objects, e.g., God is like a television because _____. Share responses. Then flip the exercise and write why God is *not* like those items, e.g., God is not like a Rock because _____, God is not like a television because _____. Based on these metaphorical writings, what is God like? Again, share responses.

BIBLIOGRAPHY

Biers-Ariel, Matt; Deborah Newbrun; and Michael Smart. *Spirit in Nature: Teaching Judaism and Ecology on the Trail.* West Orange, NJ: Behrman House, 2000.

This book blends nature, Judaism, and spirituality. The activities in the book stress the miracle and wonder of God's creations, the divine spark found in the natural world around us. It presents Jewish sources and traditions that show how to sanctify God's creation.

Bookman, Terry. *The Busy Soul: Ten-Minute Spiritual Workouts Drawn from Jewish Tradition.* Woodstock, VT: Jewish Lights Publishing, 1999.

This guide presents easy to do spiritual exercises around the cycle of the year that focus on holiday themes. For example, Purim includes themes of risk taking, *mazal* (luck), and self-esteem and self-reliance.

Cohen, Martin. "What Is Jewish Spirituality?" In *Paths of Faithfulness: Personal Essays on Jewish Spirituality*, Carol Ochs, Kerry M. Olitzky, and Joshua Saltzman, eds. Hoboken, NJ: KTAV Publishing House, Inc., 1997, 27-34.

Cohen presents a review of how Jews have viewed spirituality throughout the ages, suggesting it differs from the way in which Christians view spirituality.

Fowler, James W. *Stages of Faith: The Psychology of Human Development and the Quest for Meaning.* San Francisco, CA: Harper & Row Publishers, 1981.

This is Fowler's seminal work, in which he describes in detail faith development theory and the stages.

Gates of Prayer. New York: Central Conference of American Rabbis, 1975.

This is the prayer book of the Reform Movement. It is currently being revised.

Goodman, Roberta Louis. "Nurturing Students' Spirituality and Prayerfulness." In *Connecting Prayer and Spirituality: Kol HaNeshamah As a Creative Teaching and Learning Text*, Jeffrey L. Schein, Editor-in-Chief. Wyncote, PA: The Reconstructionist Press, 1996.

Goodman explores how to nurture the spirituality of learners through Fowler's theory of faith development.

Holtz, Barry. "Prayer and Praying: Teaching the Inner Life." *The Melton Journal* 27, Autumn 1993, 14.

Holtz asserts that much of the teaching about prayer that occurs in our schools is really about teaching the prayer book, and not teaching the inner life.

Kaplan, Aryeh. *Innerspace: Introduction To Kabbalah, Meditation and Prophecy.* Jerusalem, Israel: Moznaim Publishing Corp., 1990.

This source provides a thorough and accessible description of the soul and *sephirot* in Jewish mysticism.

Olitzky, Kerry M. *Jewish Paths toward Healing and Wholeness: A Personal Guide to Dealing with Suffering.* Woodstock, VT: Jewish Lights Publishing, 2000.

Olitzky provides a Jewish framework for understanding healing and suffering. The book includes healing rituals, Psalms, and prayers that can be used to precipitate or enrich the dialogue with God.

Olitzky, Kerry M., and Lori Forman. *Restful Reflections: Nighttime Inspiration to Calm the Soul, Based on Jewish Wisdom.* Woodstock, VT: Jewish Lights Publishing, 2001.

As in its companion volume, *Sacred Intentions*, this book first presents a quotation. This is followed by a reflection of a spiritual thinker, which is aimed at enriching one's daily life and spiritual path.

———. *Sacred Intentions: Daily Inspiration to Strengthen the Spirit, Based on Jewish Wisdom.* Woodstock, VT: Jewish Lights Publishing, 1999.

For each day, following the secular calendar, an inspirational quotation from a Jewish source is followed by a reflection on the text.

Schon, Donald. *Educating the Reflective Practitioner.* San Francisco, CA: Jossey-Bass Publishers, 1990.

Schon proposes that professional education should lead toward creating the reflective practitioner. He suggests that this involves thinking of learning about a profession as akin to study in the artist's workshop, the relationship between expert and apprentice.

CHAPTER 19

GOD DWELLS IN THE STORY

Steven M. Rosman

ONCE UPON A TIME

A TALE: LONG AGO, WHEN TRAGEDY THREATENED THE Jewish community, the Baal Shem Tov retreated to a special place deep in the surrounding forest. There he lit a fire and directed a prayer to Heaven. And tragedy was averted. In the next generation, the Magid of Mezritch went to that same place whenever the community was in danger. Though he did not know how to kindle that fire, he directed a prayer to Heaven. And tragedy was averted. In the next generation, Moshe Leib of Sasov he did not know the prayer nor how to kindle the fire, but he went to that place and that was sufficient to save the community. And in a time after that, Rabbi Israel of Rizyhn would sit in his chair. He did not know the place. He did not know the prayer. He did not know to how to kindle that special fire. He knew only how to tell the story. And that was enough. The story reached God.

We Jews have known the sacred power of stories since "In the beginning . . . " Jotham told fables to the citizens of Shechem (Judges 9:8-15). Hillel told stories to teach his pupils (*Soferim* 16:7). Stories fill *Aggadic* sections of the Talmud and permeate the *Midrashic* literature, and they are found throughout the esoteric tomes of the mystics. *Badchanim*, the medieval Jewish jesters, spun tales at weddings and other celebrations. Hasidim told parables to teach Torah and electrify the souls of their disciples. We Jews have written fairy tales, folktales, tales of morality, and tales of intrigue. We have our own versions of "Cinderella" and Aesop-like fables, and even of "Frankenstein." Sometimes we have adapted material of the surrounding culture, and sometimes we have created tales out of whole cloth.

Once upon a time, stories abounded. The greatest spiritual masters used them to conjure paradoxes to fool the logical minds of their disciples, and thereby share the mysteries of the universe. They knew that the most entrancing words a language holds are, "Once upon a time . . . " Once a listener passes through that gateway, the soul is in charge, not the brain, and the soul knows the way to its Source.

IN A LAND FARAWAY

Historically, cultures around the world have turned to stories and their storytellers when it came time to teach a new generation about the values, the wisdom, and the spiritual truths of their people. These kinds of stories might be called myths, legends, parables, or fables. In Judaism, the stories might be about young Abraham's first intuitive encounter with God, or Moses' awesome encounter with God in the cleft of the rock atop Mount Sinai. Of all the literature of all the great spiritual masters of our Jewish tradition, story might be the form most chosen to convey the wonder of revelation and the mysteries of spirituality.

Though Joseph Campbell may have mourned the modern neglect of what he called the "literature of the spirit," over the last decade or two, storytelling has been "rediscovered" by professionals of all disciplines. Bibliotherapy and guided imagery (or visualization) are popular psychotherapeutic and holistic healing aids. Professors, such as Paul Vitz of New York University, advocate storytelling as a primary means of moral education, and the popularity of William Bennett's best-selling *The Book of Virtues* underscores the wisdom of that viewpoint. Storytelling is used in school districts to teach pre-reading and encourage more reading, to enhance receptive language skills, to enrich public speaking skills, to excite children about history, science, literature, and even mathematics, to increase self-esteem, to bridge cultural gaps and promote interpersonal tolerance, and to make abstract principles easier to digest when exposition and lecture have failed to do so.

In addition to these gifts, storytelling can inspire and penetrate to touch the soul. I think it does so because, during genuine storytelling, the storyteller and the listener are engaged in a Buberian "I-Thou" experience. Others think so, too: Robert Coles, the eminent psychiatrist and popular scribe of children's stories about morality and spirituality, has observed that "the *sine qua non* of storytelling is human mutuality." And, as Buber taught, every I-Thou moment grants us a window through which to experience the Eternal Thou, The Holy One, God.

What is it about the relationship of storyteller and listener that engenders this spiritual experience? Perhaps it is what King Solomon called a *layv shomaya*. Torah tells us that long ago, when Solomon had finished the construction of the Temple in Jerusalem, God offered him any reward he would name. With the gifts of the universe spread before him, Solomon asked for a *layv shomaya* — the wisdom of a "listening" heart. A heart that listens is the basis of "I-Thou" spirituality. Children are born with it. Storytelling cultivates it. Adults, if they are fortunate, rediscover it — often through storytelling interaction with children.

THERE LIVED A STORYTELLER

Once upon a time, every people had its own master storytellers; for example: the Irish had their *ollahms* and *shanachies*, the Jews had their *maggidim*, the Africans had their *griots*, the Norse had their *skalds*, the Anglo-Saxons had their *gleeman*, and the French had their *troubadours*. Today, for the sake of our children and ourselves, we must become storytellers. In some magical, mysterious way, everyone has the capacity to be a storytelling master.

Everyone can be a storyteller, and everyone

can find a comfortable style for sharing stories. For some, it is most natural to create their own stories; for others, it might be most comfortable to recall incidents from their own lives or stories they heard in younger days. Some people like to read stories rather than tell them without a text in hand. Your own sense of what is right for you is the only guide you need.

Here is some of my own storytelling advice based upon personal experience and the insights I have gained over the years from my workshops:

- The Medieval Spanish Jewish sage, Moses ibn Ezra taught that "words that come from the heart enter the heart." So, delight in your stories, assemble children close to you, read through the story before you tell/read it so that you can become familiar with it, of course, but more importantly so it can enter your heart.

- Use your words. Do not concern yourself with sounding like one of the Brothers Grimm or Mother Goose. *Tell* a story. It is a conversation, a sharing with your children.

- Choose stories that you like. It helps to transmit the spirituality, the wonder, the mystery, insights, and wisdom of your story if you are enchanted by it, too.

- When possible, go to library storytelling sessions or to local/regional meetings of professional storytelling associations so that you can watch others. If you are so fortunate as to have the time and opportunity to do so, listen for the warmth and affection in the storyteller's tone and watch the open, embracing, welcoming body language as much as you pay attention to the actual words of the stories themselves.

- Contact the Jewish Storytelling Center (212-415-5544) and the Jewish Storytelling Network of the Coalition for the Advancement of Jewish Education for general information, for recommended book lists, and for information about local/regional storytelling associations that provide resources, mentors, and a safe, secure place to do your own storytelling. (For name and phone number of network coordinator, call CAJE at 212-268-4210.)

- Form your own parent, grandparent, teacher, or clergy storytelling club or group to enable you to swap information and tell stories.

- Like the old bromide, "How do you get to Carnegie Hall?" ("Practice, practice, practice"), I truly recommend that the best way to improve or feel comfortable as a person who tells stories is to practice, practice, practice whenever you can and in front of whomever you can (or to yourself, alone).

- If possible, find a fixed time and a special place for your storytelling and, thus, ritualize it daily for your children and yourself.

- Though the resources I have listed include some tales specifically about God, there are many other kinds of tales that will help children search for God in their own ways. In my book *When Your Jewish Child Asks Why* (co-authored with Rabbi Kerry M. Olitzky and David Kasakove), distinguished professors Louis I. Newman and Ellen Umansky respond to children's questions — "Is there really a God?" and "Where can I find God?" — with this advice:

One of the strongest indications that a God exists can be found in the order of nature . . . Many people also find God in their relationships with others . . . The wonder and depth of human life itself leads many people to believe that God really exists. (Newman, pp. 38-39)

God wants to be discovered. Because our relationship is one of partnership, because we need one another to constantly recreate the world, both literally and figuratively, God reaches out to us, providing us with signs, or clues, that can help us. When I look up at the sky and watch the clouds slowly pass by in endless, glorious configurations, or gaze at butterflies fluttering in my yard, I think to myself, "These could not have been created

by natural forces alone. They have been created by God and are a sign of God's existence." When I witness even the smallest acts of kindness and compassion — when my five-year-old asks the mother of the boy whose birthday party he's attended whether he can have an extra balloon to bring home for his brother — I am struck by the fact that to be human means so much more than simply to inhabit the world. And again, I feel the existence of God. The world is filled with such signs — what Religious School teachers called "the hand of God" (Umansky, p. 53).

So, I recommend that you tell stories about God, about the search for God by others, and about the "hand of God" that leaves clues for us in nature, in relationships, and in moments of awe and wonder. Stories actively engage listeners in drawing their own conclusions, and children will draw their own inferences about God from all these various tales. Simply include your tales as part of larger lessons about personal searches for God and the many paths of those searches. The children will do the rest.

Tell stories everywhere. Tell them outside and inside. Tell them in living rooms and sanctuaries. Let the room and the mood of your children lead you to the type of story you wish to tell. And when it is time to begin, simply say "Once upon a time . . . " and permit the story, itself, your love of the story and the children, and their soulful imaginations do the rest.

Let it be, and it will be fine.

EPILOGUE

Once upon a time, the great sage Menachem Mendel of Kotzk was asked how to find God. He replied that God is found wherever we let God in. God may enter the lives of our children through stories. Perhaps God dwells in the tale.

In *Souls on Fire: Portraits of Hasidic Masters*, Nobel Prize winner Elie Wiesel writes: "My father, an enlightened spirit, believed in man. My grandfather, a fervent Hasid, believed in God. The one taught me to speak, the other to sing. Both loved stories. And when I tell mine, I hear their voices whispering from beyond the silenced storm . . . 'God created [human beings] because [God] loves stories.'"

———— ••◆•• ————

IMPLICATIONS

1. People can come to know God effectively and deeply through story.

2. Stories are fundamental not just to Jewish tradition, but all traditions.

3. Within stories are answers to spiritual questions, paths to spirituality, and ways of connecting to God.

4. Stories appeal not only to the intellect, but to the emotions.

5. God can be experienced through stories.

6. Stories are a form of narrative theology. Stories use and evoke metaphorical ways of knowing. They help us to explore the mysteries of God and life.

QUESTIONS FOR CRITICAL INQUIRY

1. In what ways is there a different spiritual experience for the teller and the listener when a story is told rather than read?

2. Rosman says that with stories, the "soul is in charge, not the brain." Why do you agree or disagree with this statement?

3. What is one of your favorite stories about God? Why do you like it? What makes it meaningful to you?

4. Take a look at textbooks that teach values. How many of them use stories? How do you explain the pattern that you found?

ACTIVITIES

1. Hold a "God Story Fest." Have people share stories from tradition, modern sources, and personal sources about finding God and experiencing the sacred in our lives.

2. It is a tradition to recite the *"Shema"* at bedtime. Find a story that is connected to concepts presented in the *"Shema"* and share it at bedtime.

3. Have each participant bring a ritual object or two to class (or have each think about ritual objects in his/her home). Give the group time to write stories about the ritual objects. Stories should in some way show how the objects are connected to the writer's spiritual journey.

4. Review the story of Esther, in which God is never mentioned. In small groups, create *midrashim* about what God and the angels thought about the events in Shushan.

BIBLIOGRAPHY

Jewish Parenting

Bell, Roselyn, ed. *The Hadassah Magazine Jewish Parenting Book.* New York: The Free Press, 1989.

> A collection of articles about Jewish parenting stemming from Hadassah's commitment to Jewish education.

Donin, Hayim Halevy. *To Raise a Jewish Child.* New York: Basic Books, 1991.

> A useful book that aids parents in helping their children find meaning and satisfaction in Jewish customs and a strong Jewish identity. Provides practical wisdom for tasks such as selecting a Jewish school, dealing with peer pressure, and planning home observances.

Greenbaum, Avraham. *Under the Table & How to Get Up: Jewish Pathways of Spiritual Growth.* New York: Tsohar Publishing, 1991.

Using the Nachman of Bratslav tale about the prince who thought he was a rooster or turkey, Greenbaum applies the steps taken in the prince's recovery to spiritual growth steps for Jews today.

Grishaver, Joel Lurie. *40 things You Can Do to Save the Jewish People.* Northvale, NJ: Jason Aronson Inc., 1993.

This book is filled with doable suggestions for how to bring Judaism into the lives of families.

Hoffman, Edward. *Visions of Innocence: Spiritual and Inspiration Experiences of Childhood.* Boston, MA: Shambhala, 1992.

An author with an eclectic background, Hoffman combines psychology, *Kabbalah,* and spirituality in his varied writings.

Kurshan, Neil. *Raising Your Child to Be a Mensch.* New York: Atheneum, 1987.

Kurshan emphasizes the importance of raising one's child to be a *mensch* in today's world. He provides suggestions on how to do so.

Kushner, Lawrence. *God Was in This Place and I, I Did Not Know: Finding Self, Spirituality, and Ultimate Meaning.* Woodstock, VT: Jewish Lights Publishing, 1991.

This book presents a combination of Jewish sources and soulfulness in guiding people's spiritual quests. It presents the lives of Jews who provide insights into Jewish spirituality.

Reuben, Steven Carr. *Raising Jewish Children in a Contemporary World.* Rocklin, CA: Prima Publishing, 1992.

The focus of this book is the question of how non-observant Jews can raise their children as Jews in an assimilated world.

Rosman, Steven M. *Spiritual Parenting: A Sourcebook for Parents and Teachers.* Wheaton, IL: Quest Books — The Theosophical Society Publishing House, 1994.

A practical book for parents of all religious traditions, it suggests ways to bring spirituality into family life.

Rosman, Steven M.; David Kasakove; and Kerry M. Olitzky, eds. *When Your Jewish Child Asks Why: Answers for Tough Questions.* Hoboken, NJ: KTAV Publishing House, Inc., 1993.

Over 40 different difficult questions about God, religion, Judaism, and Jewish identity are answered by educators, Rabbis, and professors.

Siegel, Danny. *Gym Shoes and Irises: Personalized Tzedakah* (Books 1 and 2). Pittsboro, NC: The Town House Press, 1982, 1987.

Presents inspirational stories and many ideas for doing *tzedakah.*

———. *Mitzvahs.* Pittsboro, NC: The Town House Press, 1990.

Presents inspirational stories and ideas for doing *mitzvot.*

Wolpe, David J. *Teaching Your Children about God: A Modern Jewish Approach.* New York: Henry Holt and Company, 1993.

Rabbi Wolpe provides practical advice to parents about how to bring God into family life. In the first chapter, he addresses parents, encouraging them to rediscover their spiritual roots. He goes on to describe how children view the world, including God, and in the remaining chapters, he presents questions about life that lead us to God. Each chapter includes spiritual exercises or activities for family members and discussion questions, all of which heighten awareness of God in our lives.

Lists of Jewish Books

Jewish Book Council, 15 East 26th Street, New York, New York 10010, 215-532-4949.

Jewish Books in Review, 15 East 26th Street, New York, New York 10010, 215-532-4949.

Musikant, Ellen, and Sue Grass. *Judaism through*

Children's Books: A Resource for Teachers and Parents. Denver, CO: A.R.E. Publishing, Inc., 2001.

> Provides an annotated listing of Jewish books for children in seven categories. Main ideas, discussion starters, and easy to implement creative activities are provided for featured books in each category.

Books for Children

Bogot, Howard I. *My First 100 Hebrew Words: A Young Person's Dictionary of Judaism.* New York: UAHC Press, 1993.

> Provides Hebrew vocabulary to help the child see the world through Jewish eyes.

Bogot, Howard I.; Joyce Orkand; and Robert Orkand. *Gates of Awe: Holy Day Prayers for Young Children.* New York: Central Conference of American Rabbis Press, 1991.

> Beautifully illustrated *Machzor* for use with young children.

Cone, Molly. *Who Knows Ten? Children's Tales of the Ten Commandments.* rev. ed. New York: Union of American Hebrew Congregations, 1965.

> These original tales use stories to convey the core ideas of each of the Ten Commandments.

Fisher, Leonard Everett. *The Seven Days of Creation.* New York: Holiday House, 1981.

> A prolific author who retells the tales of many different cultures, this book provides a delightful version of the creation story.

Frankel, Ellen. *The Classic Tales: 4,000 Years of Jewish Lore.* Northvale, NJ: Jason Aronson, Inc., 1989.

> Presents 300 stories from classic sources including Bible, Talmud, Midrash, Hasidic tales, Sephardic culture, and more.

Gellman, Marc. *Does God Have a Big Toe?* New York: Harper & Row, 1989.

> A collection of original *midrashim* that address some of life's big questions.

Gellman, Marc, and Thomas Hartman. *Where Does God Live?* New York: Ballantine Books, 1992.

> The book's premise is that it is important for parents and children to talk to one another about God and not to rely just on clergy. Authored by a Rabbi and a priest, the book supports these conversations between parents and children by presenting an important theological question, answering it, and then giving pause for parents and children to respond. The theological questions are ones that the parents and children are likely to have considered such as: What does God look like? Does God make miracles? When my pet hamster Elmo died, did he go to heaven?

Goldin, Barbara Diamond. *A Child's Book of Midrash.* Northvale, NJ: Jason Aronson, Inc., 1990.

> Classical *midrash* is presented in age appropriate language.

Kushner, Lawrence. *The Book of Miracles: A Young Person's Guide To Jewish Spirituality.* New York: UAHC Press, 1987.

> The author uses *midrashic*, Talmudic, and biblical stories as a basis to present his own comments on the importance of maintaining one's awareness of the world around us.

Rosman, Steven M. *Sidrah Stories: A Torah Companion.* New York: UAHC Press, 1989.

> A collection of stories connected to each Torah portion.

———. *The Twenty-Two Gates To the Garden.* Northvale, NJ: Jason Aronson Inc., 1994.

> A collection of fanciful tales.

Rosman, Steven M., and Peninnah Schram. *Eight Tales for Eight Nights: Stories for Chanukah.* Northvale, NJ: Jason Aronson Inc., 1990.

> A collection of Chanukah tales.

Sasso, Sandy Eisenberg. *God's Paintbrush.* Woodstock, VT: Jewish Lights Publishing, 1992.

This beautifully illustrated book presents different thoughts that provoke thinking about God and experiencing God in everyday life and the world around us. For example, thinking about rain as God's tears and an ice cream soda that makes a person laugh, becomes a way of getting children to think about what makes God cry and laugh. Every two pages has a reflection and questions for children to discuss. A separate activity kit with teacher and student activities is available. (For a listing of Sasso's other children's books on God, see the bibliography for Chapter 16, "Tell Me a Story about God.")

Scharfstein, Sol. *Let's Do a Mitzvah*. Hoboken, NJ: KTAV Publishing House, Inc., 1986.

Presents ways for children to do *mitzvot*.

Schram, Peninnah. *Chosen Tales: Stories Told by Jewish Storytellers*. Northvale, NJ: Jason Aronson Inc., 1995.

A collection of favorite stories from many talented Jewish storytellers.

———. *Jewish Stories One Generation Tells Another*. Northvale, NJ: Jason Aronson Inc., 1987.

An anthology of Jewish tales.

Schwartz, Howard. *Elijah's Violin and Other Jewish Fairy Tales*. New York: Harper & Row, 1983.

An anthology of fanciful Jewish tales.

Sfer, Patricia. *Chag Sameach: A Jewish Holiday Book for Children*. Berkeley, CA: Tabor Sarah Books, 1985.

A tale about Jewish holidays.

Siegel, Danny. *Tell Me a Mitzvah: Little and Big Ways to Repair the World*. Rockville, MD: Kar-Ben Copies, Inc., 1993.

Combines stories of real life Jewish heroes and suggestions for action.

Audiotapes and Videotapes with Jewish Stories

Ganenu: A Child's Garden of Judaism. An Educational Video Systems, Inc. Production,

9595 Wilshire Blvd., Suite 502, Beverly Hills, CA 91202.

Jewish Tales of Magic and Mysticism. Gerald Fierst, 222 Valley Road, Montclair, NJ 07042.

Joseph the Tailor and Other Jewish Tales. Syd Lieberman, 2522 Ashland, Evanston, IL 60201.

The Rooster Who Would Be King and Other Jewish Folktales. The Telling Tale, Inc., 837 West 34th Street, Chicago, Illinois 60608.

Sidra Stories: A Torah Companion. UAHC Press, 838 Fifth Avenue, New York, NY 10021.

Stories in the Park. Cloudstone Productions, 10 Patchin Place, New York, NY 10011.

The Secret in Bubbie's Attic. Ergo Media Inc., P.O. Box 2037, Teaneck, NJ 07666.

Waiting for Elijah. Judith Black, 33 Prospect Street, Marblehead, MA 01945.

Worldwide Jewish Stories of Wishes and Wisdom. Cherie Karo Schwartz, 996 S. Florence Street, Denver, CO 80231.

Publishers and Booksellers

1-800-JUDAISM: The Catalog for a Jewish Lifestyle, 2028 Murray Avenue, Pittsburgh, PA 15217.

A.R.E. Publishing, Inc., 700 N. Colorado Blvd. #356, Denver, CO 80206, 800-346-7779.

Behrman House, 235 Watchung Avenue, West Orange, NJ 07052, 800-221-2755.

Breslov Research Institute, P.O. Box 587, Monsey, NY 10952, 914-425-4258.

Jason Aronson Inc., 230 Livingston Street, Northvale, NJ 07647, 201-767-4093. (Call for information about The Jewish Book Club 610-437-2159.)

Jewish Lights Publishing, Sunset Farm Offices, Route 4, Woodstock, VT 05091, 802-457-4000.

Jewish Publication Society, 1930 Chestnut Street, Philadelphia, PA 19103, 215-564-5925.

Jonathan David Judaic Book Guide, 68-22 Eliot Avenue, Middle Village, NY 11379, 718-456-8611.

KTAV Publishing House, Inc., 900 Jefferson Street, Box 6249, Hoboken, NJ 07030, 201-963-9524.

Kar-Ben Publishing, a division of Lerner Publishing Group. Orders to 1251 Washington Ave. N., Minneapolis, MN 55401, 800-452-7236. Editorial inquiries to 6800 Tildenwood Ln., Rockville, MD 20852, 301-984-8733.

The Source for Everything Jewish, Hamakor Judaica, Inc., P.O. Box 48836, Niles, IL 60714, 800-426-2567.

The Tree of Life Book Club, P.O. Box 115, Boston, MA 02258, 617-558-7651.

Tora Aura Productions/Alef Design Group, 4423 Fruitland Avenue, Los Angeles, CA 90058, 800-238-6724.

UAHC Press (Union of American Hebrew Congregations), 838 Fifth Avenue, New York, NY 10021, 212-249-0100.

Vaad Hanochos Hatmimim (a foundation dedicated to perpetuating the teachings of Rebbe Menachem Mendel Schneerson), 788 Eastern Parkway, Suite 303, Brooklyn, NY 11213, 718-774-6448.

CHAPTER 20

ART THERAPY AND THE SPIRITUAL ENCOUNTER

Nadine Cohen

My INITIAL INTEREST IN EXPLORING WAYS OF integrating spirituality and the creative art experience within the everyday arose from my journey — my own experiences of having emigrated. Having left a culture where my place was relatively secure, I was forced to reexamine much of my identity, as well as to look afresh at many of my relationships. The process of looking at myself in relation to a new culture led to an absorbing interest with transformation and metamorphosis and what it might mean to maintain separateness, and at the same time relatedness, within the context of a spiritual life.

To follow this journey backwards, my conscious awareness of a process that became very significant began to dawn upon me in the fall of 1991. I associate fall, a season filled with so many of our Jewish holidays, as a rich time of harvesting, and of new beginnings. As I listened to Rabbi Levi Meir sharing insights and different layers of meaning about the *parashah Lech Lecha*, something of Abraham's response to being called to "go toward himself," to trust in his own process as he accepted to leave everything that was familiar and known to him, resonated deeply. In an act of deep faith, when he was called to an as yet unknown place that God would show him, Abraham knew what it was to be still, and to listen to the voice of God.

As the question was answered about how we, too, could enter into dialogue with God, I knew that our sacred texts reverberated with both a contemporary and existential significance for me. My connection with the stories of our ancient people was both beyond and within the language of *midrash* and mythology, with all the transmission of values that implies. I learned on that day that these stories are replete with layers of meaning that could be a mirror to my own

life, and that as I "lost" myself in biblical text, my own story was being woven, and I emerged knowing both myself and the text differently.

I did not yet know that this experience would years later lead me to do a study on the effectiveness of using an art therapy modality in facilitating spiritual growth in our Jewish tradition.

WHAT IS ART THERAPY?

Art therapy implies the use of art media to explore and express different parts of the self within the context of a therapeutic relationship. Essential to all those relationships that affect us profoundly, are elements of deep listening and dialogue that lead us into partnership. The art encounter has an additional element of presentness in that we are called on to engage directly and spontaneously with the art materials. Using art as a more abstract form of expression may help us to transform and symbolically understand our experiences and the worlds we live in. As our daily experiences are so much more than verbal, it becomes impossible to reduce to words the myriad of sensations and emotions we experience. Artistic activity and expression can become a vehicle for existential communication, leading to deeper levels of knowledge and awareness.

Art making in this context does not focus on art as "fine art," but on the process of engaging with all of our senses. As we enter into dialogue with the materials on different levels, this can act as a passageway for dialoguing with different parts of ourselves. No background in art is necessary for this kind of experience. There is no critical eye or judgment for correctness of style, technique, or an accurate representation of any form or ideology. Rather, what is stressed is a desire to understand what motivates the life force in people, on both the conscious and unconscious levels, and how this energy can be directed and channeled with increased awareness.

The paradigm that I use focuses on an insight-oriented approach that incorporates my love and appreciation of story with Jewish text learning.

THE ROLE OF STORY, MYTH, AND METAPHOR IN THIS PROCESS

Both art and religion are processes of forming and integrating metaphor into our lives. In entering intimately into biblical textual study and looking closely at the challenges of the character's lives in a larger-than-life way, deep and personal metaphors may be elicited. Story in all its layers of meaning, and the art process, share this language. Metaphor and symbol in its most generous expression, shows us indirectly how we live our lives. When we learn to live outside of ourselves, and to incorporate knowledge and meaning from stories that hold truths, there is an ancient resonance and connection within us.

Archetypal Images

Every culture uses myth and story to convey truths. When we are able to open ourselves and resonate on the deepest of levels with the mystery and truth of a language greater than our own, we expand all possibilities of connectedness. Each one of us reads and tells our story differently as we travel our paths. To be able to be a part of this process, and to witness storytelling in other people, is a privilege in human encounter. As Martin Buber (1995) wrote, it is then that you are " . . . nothing but an ear that hears what the universe of the world is constantly saying within you" (Buber, 1995, p. 60).

I look at the experience of grappling with sacred text as part of the experience of sharing story, and preserving a "living myth" that connects the individual to the community. It is through these unique symbols that deep cultural values are conveyed, and universally, each cul-

ture's "living myth" acts as a source for informing and binding people. There is a great deal of feeling in this arena that moves beyond the thinking level. The importance of using text as a basis for informing and enriching learning may be seen in the context of the universal importance of using story and myth to transmit deep cultural values, while inviting personal participation in the act of storytelling. The notion of ritual and hearing stories over and over again as we grapple with different layers of meaning, engages us in the experience of this myth. The essence of all religions, from the most primitive to the most highly developed, has always been expressed in stories and images, both literary and visual.

Jewish tradition teaches that in response to the great *midrashic* stories of our religion (and these include interpretations of biblical verse and history, as well as esoteric and mystical Jewish tradition), one can begin to find one's own individual story. The symbolic meaning behind our own fate is expressed as we gain deeper consciousness and awareness of the motives that determine the day-to-day choices of our lives.

Much of the literature reviewed in the area of art and spirituality seems to suggest the importance of integrating one's religious and spiritual experience from a place that is both deeply personal and at the same time transcendent of oneself, and beyond what is rational. While Jung has written that the psyche is by nature religious, there is the recurring suggestion that we are able to integrate and deeply connect with something far larger than an individual truth and that we can in fact find ourselves mirrored in different contexts and places over time. Using the religious story as a metaphor and vehicle for conveying these spiritual truths and cultural values suggests a unique way of complementing an art therapy modality as a way of gaining spiritual insight and personal meaning. As we open ourselves through moments and encounters that are intrinsically mindful and contemplative, we allow for relationships that have the potential to be expanding and co-creational. Daniel Goleman (1997) has shared the importance of deep contemplation, suggesting that creativity coming from this place teaches us how we can sacralize the ordinary, and give spiritual meaning to our everyday encounters (Preface to *Gifts of the Spirit: Living the Wisdom of the Great Religious Traditions*, p. *ix*).

In this sense, there is a parallel between the creative art process, and the creative reading of text as we apply it in reframing different aspects of our lives.

THE PROCESS AND CHILDREN'S PLAY

The creative process seems to parallel the experience of play, which is key to active imagination. Children who constantly create, destroy and remake new worlds know the innocence and pure relief of being able to express themselves without value judgment. Many unexpected things happen in a process like this, and like the child in play, a state of disequilibrium can often result from seeing things in new ways for the first time. It can be exciting, it can be alarming, and it can surely test one's sense of reality. In the suspended reality of play, and creating, we are transported in active imagination.

To enter into the experience of play as children know it, we empty ourselves of preconceived ideas and immerse ourselves in this experience with a disregard for conventional boundaries. We free ourselves to make connections in the fullest sense of the word. We learn to pay close attention to themes and motifs as they are presented in the different layers and literary echoes implicit in sacred text, as we learn to listen for "meta-messages." In a similar way, when we learn to pay attention to our own personal inner images that emerge in the art process, we begin to discern recurring themes and symbols specific to our own life stories. This experience, which parallels play in the deeper sense of the word, is key to active imagination. Children know only too well what it is to play, to create, to destroy and to reenvision new worlds.

Often before change and resolution settle in to the transformational aspect of this process,

people experience a state of conflict. In workshops that I have given, I have inevitably been witness to people's pain and their joy. This is a powerful process, which is deceptively simple. There is often an aspect of tapping into unconscious images when we surrender to this process. While people might feel self-conscious about what emerges and is unexpectedly expressed in their artwork, they should be encouraged to pay attention without judgment, to all images that surface. This is part of the process of honoring and bringing different parts of the self to consciousness.

PLANNING A LESSON

This art encounter of which I am speaking is interactive, and the process itself suggests immediacy and spontaneity. In facilitating this process for other people, several aspects of preparation are important to keep in mind. The kind of art process that is developed is always linked to the study of sacred text. The creative process that follows text study moves us from the text to a personal experience of some aspect of the essence that has been distilled prior to the learning experience.

Whatever visual images appear, be they undefined shapes, or expressive lines that have not been consciously planned, it is the artist who imbues them with meaning.

In this process, our focus is on paying attention to the unconscious images that emerge, on both an individual level, and within the larger context of cultural truths that are conveyed through images that are both timeless and universal in their appeal. In creating dialogue with sacred text, parts of us begin to resonate with archetypal images (see Chapter 9, "Archetypal Pathways To God: Exploring the Role of the Subconscious in the Development of Faith"); we see echoes of our own spiritual and emotional lives in the images that emerge for us. It is in this process, and experience of deep play, that we allow a creative process to transform us as we encounter possible contradictions of images in our worlds. Art becomes important not as art for art's sake, but as a way of giving form to our inner symbolic lives. The art externalizes and concretizes to some degree our symbolic lives, giving us the possibility for greater understanding and connectedness in the world as we engage in dialogue and therapeutic encounter.

Choice of Art Materials

How structured or unstructured the art experience will be is in part affected by participants' background and level of comfort with art materials, what their needs are, and how comfortable they are with being self-directed or not in this process. Materials are evocative in subtle ways, and will elicit certain responses in people, often on unconscious levels. What kinds of reactions does working in clay have as opposed to a cleaner air-drying mixture that is less consuming as an experience? Do participants need the fluidity and tactile experience of paint and watercolor, or will this be too unstructured? What different effects might be evoked from providing precut forms, as opposed to allowing people to create their own work right from the beginning? Will providing mask molds, as opposed to making individualized and fitted face masks, be freeing or inhibiting to the creative experience? Responses to these kinds of questions in the planning stages of facilitating these kinds of workshops will greatly impact on the experience.

The emphasis in this kind of art experience is clearly on process; in essence, we are attempting to give form to our own inner images and symbols. A playful dialogue can emerge between the art materials and us no matter how rudimentary or untutored we are in our art backgrounds. Entering fully into this kind of process requires no background or training in art, but rather a willingness to suspend judgment, and an openness to experience and observe whatever emerges without expectation of outcome.

Creation involves a relaxing of control, and a kind of surrender which has more to do with flexibility and the ability to change direction than with defeat and destruction. By way of

example, in doing my own artwork, I often experienced an integrating of random and opposing perceptions. At times, I would feel as though something inside of me was reordering itself through an experience that was beyond my rational planning and control. I knew strongly and instinctively which materials were calling to me, whether it was the organic nature of wood that I needed to battle in reshaping and reforming, or the clear perspex that would talk to me of centering. I let go enough that I was willing to experience the surrender of this encounter. I recognize now, how on this level of creating, there is a process that takes on a life force of its own. In yielding to what this is about, we enter into a time space that suggests almost a time outside of time, a perceptual kind of integration of responses that I can only describe as a deep and respectful dialogue.

The art object and the materials concretize and objectify some of these inner images that may otherwise not have come to consciousness and awareness. Through such a creative experience, we tap into unconscious thoughts more in keeping with our dream worlds. It is equally important to remember how much of a spiritual component there is in this process. Essentially, hands and heart give voice to a rich inner symbolic life. Our senses become windows to deep parts of our soul life if we allow this kind of dialogue to emerge.

Understanding the evocativeness of different materials, and the effects that they elicit even on subtle levels, is part of the process of developing sound principles before implementing this approach. Appreciating how comfortable participants are with art materials would also impact on how structured or unstructured the art process might be.

Choosing Text

In choosing text that is appropriate for any particular course of study, I would, as with any teaching or therapeutic goal, establish a theme. As we extend ourselves to engage meaningfully and grapple with biblical texts, we explore something of an interplay of recurring problems and patterns in our texts. Avivah Zornberg (1995) reiterated the need for us to pay close attention to themes and recurring motifs as they appear and weave their way through our literature, suggesting multiple layers of meaning. Is our objective to invite us to look for parts of ourselves that resonate with seasonal events as they return again and again to inform our lives with new meaning? Or, is it to look for contemporary meaning as we teach about a Torah portion, or perhaps *teshuvah*, and how we bring ourselves to the process of repentance? It is a challenge to look for ways that our texts may echo aspects of our own lives. If we are able to look at ourselves in relation to possible paradoxes and contradictions that might emerge, we can begin to take what we have, to learn to look and to relook at it, and to envision our lives in new ways.

Facilitating This Creative Process

While this process can challenge and enrich people's insights, it is important as a facilitator to understand what it is to provide safety and support for participants. I believe that every nurturing and growth promoting experience contains both therapeutic and educational components. While there are overlaps between these two paradigms and the contexts in which these experiences take place, it is also important to be sensitive to several differences in these settings. There may be more of an agenda to one's approach in an educational setting, with key concepts that one wants to convey and teach, while the process tends to be more open-ended and client-directed in the framework of therapy. Boundaries are more clearly defined in a therapy setting, with a stricter adherence to the symbolic nature of both time and place. In therapy, all issues that emerge tend to be addressed, while in more of a teaching context, it may be deemed inappropriate to explore certain issues that emerge. Issues are not addressed with the same degree of anonymity as they are in therapy. In all cases, it is important to develop and maintain a clear framework with boundaries in which work is

processed and shared at the end of sessions. If participants are to feel safe enough to express themselves in uncritical and nonjudgmental ways, the facilitator, as witness to this process, needs to ensure an atmosphere of acceptance and encouragement.

Participants need also to understand what it is to be a witness to other people's experiences, to be dispassionate, reflective and yet involved as they encourage and respond to one another's work, without either judging or analyzing what they see. Guidelines for questions that could be given as people view and respond to one another's work are presented in the following section.

There will be a difference in relationship or level of involvement among the participants and facilitator, depending on whether this is a one-time workshop or if it is an art process that continues over a period of time. If the workshops form part of a series, the facilitator is able to develop a different level of intimacy with each participant as they come to understand and share their images over time. There is also a difference between a teacher or a facilitator who sees participants on a consistent and regular basis. By virtue of a more consistent involvement over time, the facilitator will come to know and understand the participants and what issues they bring to the process. Artwork that is done with regularity begins to assume a life and inner rhythm of its own. What we have created becomes something of a journal for us. We can hold onto this experience, and later gain new insights when we look at our work in different contexts. This can happen during the process, or even years later. Something new surfaces at each level.

Wrap-Up: Processing and Evaluation

The final part of having worked in a group involves processing the experience together. This reflective part of the experience, is as important as the more active and creative aspect of the experience, and provides necessary closure to an experience in which participants may have been open in their willingness to explore meanings on different levels. It is important to be able to honor the safety that sharing in an intimate group evokes, and to guard against participants feeling exposed in their openness and willingness to explore and express unknown and deep parts of themselves.

In essence, it is a privilege to bear witness to another's creative expression when it is done in this kind of authentic and deeply spontaneous way. In appreciating this, it is important not to analyze other people's work, or to judge it in any way, but to offer reflections about what is visually perceived. While the emphasis in this kind of experience is placed on the art making process rather than on the end product, the artwork is an important component of an art therapy experience. Like a journal, it becomes a concrete and tangible expression of an encounter in which sacred space and time have been created and honored.

In encouraging observation and not analysis of one another's work, the following are possible questions to guide the group processing of sharing, and offering feedback. Participants can ask each other to describe what they see in each other's work. Attention should be drawn to the sizes of pieces and their proportion in relation to one another. Participants could be encouraged to look for connections with what they have expressed in their work, and aspects of their personal lives. People could also be encouraged to look for balance between feeling, form, and concept. Does one figure or shape dominate or emerge from the background, and does the total configuration obscure any of the parts?

Depending on the setting, and whether this is a retreat or an ongoing workshop, the process could be documented in words and photographs, and evaluated for its effectiveness over time in terms of the original goals and expectations.

(For examples of workshops based on the process described herein, see Appendix A, p. 219, and Chapter 45, "Your Link in the Chain of Jewish Tradition" by Nadine Cohen, p. 370.)

CONCLUSION

The art therapy modality, especially image making, has been invaluable in personalizing a religious experience for me. While in this process there is a reverence for all images that emerge, both learning and art making take place with a devotional attitude, and are deeply grounded in spiritual practice, faith, and supportive relationships. Wherever these ideas take root, and are used in different educational, religious and therapeutic settings, homage is paid to the richness of this experience.

While this experience is understood to be partly about joining with the community, in the deepest sense it suggests a reintegration of self. By letting go of preconceptions and attachments, we allow ourselves to experience and see things beyond the intellectual. We enter into the process of not-knowing with more comfort and acceptance, and learn to engage and dialogue with the deepest parts of ourselves. The most valuable part of this approach is to arrive with questions, and within that, to look at our relating, with either text, our own image making, or other people who may be part of our group, and to begin the dialogue. As inner dialogue is stimulated, we see mirrors and reflections of different parts of ourselves. The strength of this approach is to arrive with not-knowing, and to leave with knowing differently. We learn to be still within ourselves, and to hear with our beings what our inner voice is saying. We prepare for our journey. The experience is total. It embraces us, and every part of us begins to respond differently, renewed.

IMPLICATIONS

1. Experiences with God happen. Art is one way of opening ourselves to that experience and uncovering the meaning of those experiences.

2. Imagination plays an important role in deepening spirituality.

3. It is in the interaction among the art process, the text, and person that deepens the spiritual experience.

4. Extrapolating on the principles of art therapy that are applicable in a normative Jewish educational setting, art is a powerful tool because it focuses on connecting, interweaving, and examining the relationship among the body, imagination, text, experiences, and spirit. This process is interactive and playful.

QUESTIONS FOR CRITICAL INQUIRY

1. Why, for adults and children, can playing with clay be such an evocative spiritual process?

2. Cohen argues that it is important for a conversation to take place among participants regarding the art that they create as part of deepening and enriching the spiritual experience. What is the distinction that she makes between judging and analyzing another person's work as opposed to describing what is visually perceived? Why does this matter?

3. How does art help connect the creator and the observer to texts?

4. How does art help give order and meaning to mystery, discomfort, and chaos?

ACTIVITIES

1. Study a passage from the Bible. Using micrography, share your interpretation of the text. (Micrography, an art form used by Jews for more than a millennium, is the scribal practice of employing minuscule script to create abstract shapes or figurative designs. For examples of micrography, see an exhibit at the Jewish Theological Library called "The Hebrew Word As Art" at www.jtsa/edu/library/exhib/microg/ index.shtml. Click on "Enter the Exhibit.")

2. Each participant chooses a favorite song about God, either a familiar one from worship services such as *"L'cha Dodi"* or *"Adon Olam,"* or a popular modern one such as Debbie Friedman's *"L'chi Lach"* or *"Miriam's Song."* In a cartoon style, design one frame (draw, make a collage, etc.) for each phrase or set of phrases from your song. Everyone can explain his/her "cartoon" to other group members. Then, together, sing each song.

3. Using different translations of a prayer, use items from nature or wilting Shabbat flowers to make a collage interpreting the prayer. See how the different interpretations provide new insights into "God wrestling," nurturing our relationship to — and knowledge of — God.

4. Cohen speaks about the role of metaphor in helping us imagine God. Choose a name of God (e.g., Shield of Abraham from the *"Avot"* prayer) or a metaphor for God (e.g., God as Shepherd from the High Holy Day liturgy). Create a picture of the metaphor. Then identify all the characteristics of the metaphor and discuss how God demonstrates these qualities.

APPENDIX A

I Am Again in Your Presence — Hazarti Lefanecha
A Workshop Presentation

(Note: The following workshop outline is an example of the art therapy approach to deepening spiritual encounters described above. The workshop, in which we explored the process of atonement, and the experience of *teshuvah* was presented presentation at the CAJE Conference in Columbus, Ohio in August, 1999. (See also Chapter 45, "Your Link in the Chain of Jewish Tradition," p. 370.)

INTRODUCTION

This Thursday night is Rosh Hodesh Elul, the month that leads us directly into Rosh HaShanah, the cycle of a new year, and another beginning. I would like to use this opportunity to look at this as a window into how we can see ourselves in sacred time and sacred space.

In the wisdom of ancient Greek writing and thinking, there are two words that are used to describe time. *Kronos*, or chronological time, is linear, and time as we know it to structure the everyday. (How long will this workshop be? Where am I going next . . . ?) Then there is *kairos*, real time, God's time, sacred time. *Kairos* has been described as "time that is beyond time, time in which we become what we are called on to be, and when we feel our creativity as though we are co-creators with God" (Campbell, 1949 and 1988).

The creative process that I would like to share with you involves creating *kairos* moments through play, surrender, and bringing to consciousness different parts of ourselves that ask to be heard. It is essentially about dialoguing with our inner questions with the attitude of both mindfulness and play. Children easily lose themselves in moments of *kairos* as they play, feeling the freedom constantly to create, destroy and recreate new worlds.

In creating mindfulness, and alertness, we create moments that weave in and out of our everyday lives, and give integration to our everyday experiences. We bring to consciousness different parts of ourselves. Daniel Goleman has written that "contemplation, in its most profound sense, connotes awareness directed toward a sacred end," reiterating that what many of us are looking for today, is "a way of weaving these contemplative modes into the fabric of daily existence, of bringing the highest aspects of the spiritual into the ordinary moments of life" (Goleman, et al).

I want to share with you a way of looking at the art process, a process Jo Milgrom has described (Milgrom, 1992) as creating "Visual *Midrash*." This is a way of not only creating *kairos* moments for ourselves, but of engaging in deep play and dialogue that can satisfy our spiritual needs beyond what is academic and intellectual. This experience is not about art for art's sake, but creating form for the sake of symbol. In that, we learn a visual and perceptual literacy that helps us tell our own story.

David Whyte, English poet and storyteller, has written that "the way we tell our stories has a lot to do with the way we see ourselves in the world, with our identity" (Whyte, 1994), and that the story is magnificent only when we touch on our essential connection with the world, our creativity. When we learn to tell our stories in a profound way, and reach a certain depth in the telling, the word destiny belongs to us as much as it does to anyone who has shaped history. "The word destiny, even as it falls from our mouths, demands a maturity that stretches our sense of ourselves" (Whyte, 1994). So, I invite you to lose yourselves, to bring your questions to this encounter, and so to experience your storytelling in a deeper way.

There is a teaching out of the Northwest Native American tradition that would be told by an elder to a young girl or boy who asked the question, "What do I do when I'm lost in the forest?" which is really, as David Whyte has written, "What do I do when I forget who I am?" David Wagoner has translated this response into modern English. Here is the answer the elder gives:

> Stand still. The trees ahead
> and bushes beside you
> Are not lost. Wherever you are is called Here.
> And you must treat it as a powerful stranger.
> Must ask permission to know it and be known.
> The forest breathes. Listen. It answers.
> I have made this place around you.
> If you leave it you may come back again, saying Here.
> No two trees are the same to Raven.
> No two branches are the same to Wren.
> If what a tree or a bush does is lost on you,
> You are surely lost. Stand still.
> The forest knows
> Where you are. You must let it find you.
> (Whyte, 1995, pp. 259-260)

I have learned from different people how Rav Kook has written of *teshuvah* as being the natural process of the soul, and a way of finding ourselves back from being lost. It is not about forcing ourselves to come back to a certain way, but about bringing to consciousness different parts of ourselves that ask to be heard. It is about integrating, and it is about understanding what it is that will create harmony between our inner worlds, and our outer worlds. It is about finding and reconnecting with the divinity within each of us, and it can be an extremely emotional experience. In essence, each individual's motivating center must be in harmony with the spiritual essence of the world.

We learn that there is always an opening for us to engage in the process of at-one-ment, and that we will always be received. Like Yonah, it is about understanding what our destiny is, and how we face ourselves rather that run away. It is about learning to listen to the voices that are God's agents, and finding how "I am again in Your presence, *Hazarti Lefanecha* . . . "

THE WORKSHOP

Following is an outline of the actual workshop.

Movement (15 min.)
Explore desire and fleeing with our bodies
Directed movement, spontaneous movement

Text of Yonah (20-30 min.)
Yonah's escape from his destiny, from God, and essentially from himself. I draw on this book as a significant metaphor which helps us understand the process of *teshuvah*, and at-one-ment.

God sends many *messengers* to Yonah; some are revealed, while others are hidden:

- "And the Lord appointed a fish . . . " (2:1)

- "And the Lord God appointed a plant . . . " (4:6)

- "And God appointed a worm . . . " (4:7)

- "And God appointed a strong east wind . . . " (4:8)

All of these messengers come from different elements in the world; the land, the sea, and the air. Implicit in this reading, there is a parallel process for us, and it is only through a process of real openness and listening that we are able to absorb and respond to our own personal messengers. Take a few moments to think of what your messengers/agents might be. Look at key words, and their repetition (some examples follow):

- *Going up*, how many times the key word "*kum*" is used

- "Get up" and "call" are both verbs expressing awakening and movement.

  "And Yonah got up . . . " (1:3)

  "I have called . . . to God . . . " (2:1-3)

- *Going down*, through the use of the keyword "*rayd*," also used as a spiritual metaphor.

  "And Yonah descended into the recesses of the ship . . . " (1:5)

  Yonah was "escaping from before God, for he had told them" (1:10)

"Lift me up and lower me into the sea . . . " (1:12)

Yonah's movement involves descent after descent, leading to an escape from his understood reality and destiny. While for prophets, destiny and mission may be clear and un-equivocal, for us, this process is surely more complex, and filled with hidden elements.

- Hidden in the word Nineveh, is *"neveh"* (home), and *"nun"* (fish in Aramaic).

   "And Nineveh was a great city to the Lord, measuring three days journey." (3:3)

   This is where Yonah was supposed to have gone to fulfill his destiny and his mission.

   In 2:1-2 we read that " . . . God appointed a great fish to swallow Yonah, and Yonah was in the bowels of the fish three days and three nights." In exploring the word "Nineveh," there is an intriguing parallel process, suggesting that the way we try to escape our destiny, is the way we come back to it . . .

The Art Process (20-30 min.)

David Nativ has written that when we flee from our destiny, we assume a "limited perception of reality" (Nativ, see bibliography). While we are by nature full of doubt and internal struggles, the clarity of our journey is determined by the perception of our goal and our destiny. It is with this understanding that I have chosen the questions for the art experience that follows. It is important to keep in mind that this is about process. Rather than creating "fine art," we are attempting to give form to our inner symbols, and so understand them better.

Free associate, allowing images and thoughts to surface and be expressed.

Using three different pieces of colored construction paper, create forms and shapes in a free-hand way by tearing, in responding to the following questions.

1. What is your destiny; what is a key question with which you are grappling?

2. What are the agents/voices that are telling you this?

3. How have you avoided facing yourself, and meeting that part of yourself?

Once you have responded to these questions with the different forms you have created from the construction paper, find another paper which will be the background to these questions. Your work can be laid out in two or three dimensions.

With a Partner, Discuss and Share Your Work (10 min.)

A certain intimacy is created. In your listening, it is important not to analyze each other's work, or to judge what you see. What is most important, is to be able to bear witness to each other's process.

These are some questions to guide you in your observations, and your sharing.

- Ask each other to describe what you see in your work.

- Look for a balance between feeling, form, and concept.

- Does one shape dominate from the background?

- How do the parts relate to one another?

- How do the parts interact to form a whole?

- Share what was the hardest or the easiest form to make, and why.

- Discuss the role that color plays.

- What about sizes, proportion, and movement?

More Artwork and Final Processing (10 min.)

If you could add a piece, how would you bring resolution to your work; how would you put yourself in the process of at-one-ment, and bring yourself back to yourself?

Wrap-up/Evaluation of This Experience (5-10 min.)

Reflect on the most important thing that happened to you in the process. Please take a few moments to give feedback about this workshop experience.

BIBLIOGRAPHY

Ben Shalom, Y. *Poetry of Being*. Tel Aviv, Israel: MOD Books, 1990.

> Gaining an in-depth understanding of Abraham Isaac Kook's philosophy and interpretations is difficult, in that the philosophy is "organic" and "holistic," and the truth can be recognized only within the framework of an overall and comprehensive overview. This book presents aspects of that complex whole in a way that makes several pieces more easily accessible. It concentrates on the metaphysical aspects of Kook's views, primarily as they relate to determinism and free will, and the nature of the physical world.

Bolen, Jean Shinoda. *Crossing To Avalon: A Woman's Midlife Pilgrimage*. San Francisco, CA: Harper Collins Publishers, 1994.

> The author traces the history and significance of sacred sites she visited on pilgrimage. She links her own inner journey of The Spirit to her travels and to women's primal knowledge of The Sacred.

Breytenbach, Breyten. *The Memory of Birds in Times of Revolution*. New York: Harcourt Brace & Company, 1996.

> Breytenbach, a South African born painter and poet, has lived in Paris for many years. He has written about different aspects of living in exile from one's homeland. He has extended this metaphor to represent the existential state of aloneness, the duality and complexity of living separate, and at the same time, connected. In his poetry and writing, he explores the effects this can have on one's psyche.

Buber, Martin. *Ten Rungs*. New York: Carol Publishing Group, 1995.

> Buber includes Hasidic sayings and teachings that emphasize a spiritual approach to a path of enriched awareness.

Campbell, Joseph. *The Hero with a Thousand Faces*. Princeton, NJ: Princeton University Press: Bollington Series, 1949.

———. *An Open Life*. New York: Larson Publications, 1988.

> Campbell has written extensively on comparative mythology, sharing themes and motifs common to all cultures. He draws on universal and archetypal symbols to convey how ancient legends have historically been recreated to inform and impact the fabric of both community and personal life.

Campbell, Sarah. "Encountering the Creator Within: Art Therapy as a Vehicle for Spiritual Growth." Denver, CO: American Art Therapy Association, National Audio Video, 1997.

> In this presentation, Campbell discusses the rationale underlying her forming a group seeking religious and spiritual growth. Group members' experiences are also discussed. This particular group was grounded in Christianity, yet the principles can be universally extended and applied.

Edinger, Edward. *The New God-Image*. Wilmette, IL: Chiron Publications, 1996.

> Edinger traces a parallel of Western cultural development with the history of how a "God-image" is defined. He draws on Jung's phenomenological understandings of a collective self that defines a sense of religious, and spiritual identity. He posits that this process is dynamic as it develops and undergoes transformations.

Edwards, Betty. *Drawing on the Artist within Us*. New York: Simon & Schuster, Inc., 1986.

> This practical guide explores avenues that tap creative thinking, thereby demystifying the role of the artist and returning different forms of expression to the domain of the everyday.

Goleman, Daniel. "Preface." In *Gifts of the Spirit: Living the Wisdom of the Great Religious Traditions* by Philip Zaleski and Paul Kaufman. San Francisco, CA: Harper & Row Publishers, 1997.

> In the preface to this book, which is a compendium of different religious traditions informing the everyday, Daniel Goleman

advocates for a contemplative and spiritual life that emotionally enriches both the personal and the communal.

Metzger, Deena. "A Traveling Jewish Theater." In *Everyday Sacred* by Sue Bender. San Francisco, CA: HarperCollins Publishers, 1996.

Here is an article written with simplicity and elegance about making the everyday sacred. The author shares experiences and examines what makes up both inner and outer journeys that are undertaken at different points in people's lives.

Milgrom, Jo. *Handmade Midrash*. Philadelphia, PA: Jewish Publication Society, 1992.

Milgrom uses an innovative and interdisciplinary approach, connecting biblical study to personal growth and expression. Art and related literature are used to stimulate participants' thoughts and emotions, which are then expressed through different visual media. This process is then followed by discussion and processing of participants' work.

Nativ, David. "Yona's Flight from Destiny." The Israel Koschitzky Virtual Beit Midrash, at www.vbm-torah.org/roshandyk/yona.htm.

In his analysis of the book of Jonah, Nativ adds literary depth and cohesiveness to the concept of destiny. *Midrashic* allusions from both the Hebrew and Aramaic texts convert a literal reading of the biblical prophet's story into a metaphor for seeking to embrace

rather than escape confrontation and knowledge with the unconscious forces informing our intentions.

Whyte, David. *The Heart Aroused: Poetry and The Preservation of the Soul in Corporate America.* New York: Currency/Doubleday, 1996.

Whyte writes how infusing our work lives with poetry and metaphor is akin to balancing the material and the light with the spiritual and the dark. He argues not for superiority of one over the other, but rather necessity, complementarity, and wholeness if we are to live as integrated and soulful people.

Zobel, Gerry. "Images of the Psyche." Unpublished master's thesis, Southern Illinois University at Edwardsville, IL, 1992.

In her collation of various images, Zobel develops her thesis that the workings of the psyche incorporate forces beyond our conscious knowledge and control.

Zornberg, Avivah Gottlieb. *Genesis: The Beginning of Desire.* Philadelphia: The Jewish Publication Society, 1995.

Incorporating her strong academic background in English literature, Zornberg adds a sophistication and depth to our understanding of the complexity of the human workings portrayed through the stories of Genesis. She argues for faithfulness to Hebrew text within a Rabbinic tradition of literary analysis.

CHAPTER 21

AWAKENING SPIRITUALITY THROUGH ART EXPERIENCES

Lynn Lutz Friend

INTRODUCTION

VISUAL ART IS A NATURAL AVENUE TO EXPLORING God and spirituality. Jewish, Christian, and other religious artists have been using this means of expression for thousands of years. If you look at art through time, a great majority of it has been in response to spiritual or theological themes. The first Jewish artist of course was Bezalel, the artisan of the Tabernacle. God gave him the appointed task to create a beautiful place to house the Tablets of the Law. Many years later, Michelangelo was attracted to this powerful moment in history and painted his interpretation of God's words, God's giving of the Law.

Artists create inspirational art as an expression of their spirituality. Their products awaken a sense of awe and provide the viewer with a spiritual encounter. At the same time, we can also assume that during the process of creation the artists experience a spiritual awakening and journey. In this chapter the process of exploring is the important factor, for it reveals the hidden within us. Bezalel, Michelangelo, Chagall, Agam, and many others were able to have their artistic product reveal their spirituality, but our goal here is simply the process of awakening within ourselves and our students our spirituality.

When focusing on the process itself as the goal, no artistic talent is needed. The actual process allows an individual to reach deep within him/herself to discover hidden understandings of God and spirituality. When an individual is faced with a new artistic task, they must search for avenues to solve the task. For most people, the last time they had to "do an art project" was in elementary school. Most likely, it was a very structured, prescribed project, such as, "Draw the vase of flowers." Other types of exercises can help individuals tap into the creative and expressive domains that reach into their spirituality. Betty Edwards in her book, *Drawing on the Right Side of the Brain* (1989), describes exercises much like those presented in this chapter that focus on the process of creating itself, rather than on the final product. The process allows an individual to reach deep into parts of themselves often hidden by the verbal world in which we live. Edwards states, "Your drawings can show you how you see things and feel about things" (1989, p. 222). The awakening of spirituality is possible when we remove the verbal and access the nonverbal. We hold our spiritual selves deep inside, and — in this fast paced society — we are reluctant to allow them to surface. Art experiences are one way to allow that inner spirituality to surface and become a part of us.

No discussion of Jewish art would be complete without reference to the second commandment, "You shall not make for yourself a sculptured image, or any likeness of what is in the heavens above or on the earth below, or in the waters under the earth. You shall not bow down to them and serve them" (Exodus 20:4). Jo Milgrom in her book *Handmade Midrash* (1992), solves the puzzle by interpreting the text to mean not that images cannot be created, but rather, that one cannot create images to bow down to as with idol worship. Bezalel certainly had to create images and in fact created *cherubim*, angel-like creatures, with faces and wings (Exodus 25:19). Following in this broad interpretation of the second commandment, ancient art on old mosaic synagogue floors, such as at Bet Alpha in Israel, included influences from the cultures surrounding them at the time including, in this example, faces and zodiac images. Others chose to circumvent the second commandment as in the case of micrography, the creation of images through the use of small writing.

Historically, most Jewish art is ceremonial in nature. It expressed the artist's desire to make beautiful the objects with which we perform the ceremonial rituals, thus enhancing the spirituality of our Jewish lives. Jewish artists have also used illuminated manuscripts to make beautiful the sacred texts of our people.

There are many Jewish artists who are not only Jewish, but choose to create Jewishly based pieces of artwork. Worthy of mention, but surely not an exhaustive list are, Peter Freudenthal, Marc Chagall, Louise Nevelson, Eva Hesse, Yaacov Agam, Ben Shahn, Judy Chicago, Shalom of Safed, and others. They have developed styles that present the visual arts that speak to an array of themes about life that Jews and humanity have confronted throughout history, rather than just creating ceremonial objects. Taking time to look at the work of these artists gives one insight into their spiritual journeys and that of Jews throughout history.

ART EXPERIENCES FOR THE CLASSROOM

Our own spiritual awakening can begin with exercises based on the work of Jo Milgrom. She developed the suggestion to start with a discussion of text, then move to an art experience, and then return once or even twice to discussion and writing about your art experience. Doing these nonverbal visual art exercises can free us, allowing us to enter into new places in our hearts and souls. For example, Milgrom described the journey of one poet who was experiencing writer's block. However, at the end of the exercise, the poet was able to create a verbal representation of the artwork she had created.

In the remainder of the chapter, I will describe various art exercises that can be used with students of all ages. On one family retreat at North Shore Congregation Israel, Glencoe, Illinois, we gave the same exercise to both the parents and the children. They were in separate rooms and asked to respond to the same text and create a torn paper *midrash* (Milgrom, 1992). The children were given a simpler text, but on the same theme. We then brought the group together and had them explain their *midrashim* to each other. The children were able to create and interpret their work as well or sometimes even better than the adults. It is possible that the children feel freer in their thinking and are not bound by societal pressure to produce the "right answer" or the "right appearance." Helping to make people comfortable and opening them up, especially adults — intellectually, creatively, and emotionally — will deepen the process.

The exercises that follow are presented in order of their complexity, but don't be fooled into thinking that complex is better; it is not. Often the simpler the exercise, the more one is forced to reach deeply into the meaning of the encounter. The entire process involves turning the experience around and inside out until a new reality and understanding becomes apparent.

Basic Recipe

As a group, read together any Jewish text. (There is a text suggested with each exercise, but feel free to use whatever material is appropriate to your needs. Each text evolves into its own visual *midrash*. Using the same text again with the same or a different exercise can result in enhanced and new spiritual experiences.) The text can be a piece of a prayer, a verse of Torah, a line from *Pirke Avot*, or a line of Talmud. I have found that using a few lines of a prayer (not the whole thing, as that would be too much material) in Hebrew or in English often helps an individual to create a new *kavanah* — a connection to or understanding of that particular prayer, thus awakening their spirituality. Passages from Torah describing an encounter with God such as: Moses at the burning bush (Exodus 3:1-6), Jonah's adventures (Jonah 2: 8-10), or Abraham's argument with God (Genesis 18:24-32), can be a catalyst for exploring one's own feelings about God.

1. Discuss the material at whatever level is appropriate for the participants. With young children, it is often helpful to explain the literal meaning of the text. With adults, the discussion can become more interpretive.

2. Explain to the group that the art experience is *not* meant to produce a piece of artwork, but rather a new way of looking at the text and discovering hidden meanings and understandings. In fact, they will be asked to do things in ways that most of them have not done before, even those who have "taken art lessons."

3. Set down the "rules":

   • You are free to use the materials in anyway you feel comfortable.

   • Work quietly and respect the work of others.

   • Allow yourself to explore the material. There is no "right or wrong" response.

   • Allow the feelings and work to follow its own path; it will take on a life of its own.

   • What is shared and created here remains the property of the person who created it (unless the group agrees at the conclusion to share their work and insights with others).

   • Explain the procedure and steps to the particular exercise.

   • Give the participants time to create their artwork.

   • Instruct the participants to write about the process and the product.

   • Begin a discussion by displaying the artwork and allowing participants to discuss what they feel is involved in each piece.

   • Encourage individuals to explain the process they went through and the artwork they created.

   • If time permits, encourage participants to write about the experience.

   • Obtain permission, if desired, from individuals to share their work with others, i.e., to display it or use it in other settings. You do not have the right to use any material created or insights gained without the permission of the participant.

   • This process is very personal and many people do not want to share with others. This should be respected.

Exercise 1: Basic Drawing of Lines

Materials:

White paper

Pencils

Procedure:

1. In advance, choose eight words, feelings, or phrases from the material to be discussed.

2. Have participants fold a sheet of paper into eighths, creating eight separate sections (see Figure A below)

Figure A

3. Ask each participant, without removing his/her pencil from the paper, to create a continuous line to represent each of the eight words or phrases from the text, one word or phrase per box. Encourage participants to create a line that represents the word, not that *is* the word. In other words, they should try to avoid drawing a heart for love.

   For example, if you choose to interpret Exodus 3:1-6, Moses and the burning bush, the following words and phrases could be used:

1. Moses

2. Fear

3. Wilderness

4. Holy

5. Bush

6. Fire

7. Blazing

8. Here I am

Each square represents one of the eight words or phrases (see Figure B below).

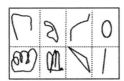

Figure B

4. The second sheet of blank white paper is then used to create an interpretation of the text discussed, using the line drawings of the words or phrases as a springboard. Participants do not have to use all eight of the lines they created from the first sheet. They can use a line more than once. They can vary the size and orientation of the line as well, and are free to add whatever additional images they choose to represent their interpretation of the text.

5. Some questions you might ask: What images are brought to mind when you think of these words? How does this text make you feel about your ability to communicate with God? What impact do these images have on your relationship with God? One interpretation of Moses and the burning bush might look like Figure C below:

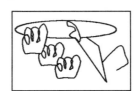

Figure C

6. Optional: Mount artwork on a piece of black or colored construction paper. Doing so really enhances the finished product.

7. Continue with the discussion and processing of the experience (see Basic Recipe above).

Exercise 2: Wire Sculpture

Materials:

Pencils

White paper

Wood bases (approximately 4" x 4" x 1" pieces of wood. These can easily be cut from standard 1" x 4" pieces of lumber. A lumber yard will cut these to size. Often they will sell bags of scrap lumber of various sizes that can also be used. As an alternative, substitute small pieces of self-hardening clay for the bases.)

Sandpaper

Tacky Glue

Drill

Wire, size 14-16 gauge, in various colors (telephone wire comes coated in various colors, or you can use copper, black, and steel wire)

Wire cutters

Pliers

Optional: In advance, sand the rough spots on the wood and pre-drill five or six 1/8" holes on top of each piece of wood (see Figure D below). Have the drill available to drill more holes as necessary. If this step is not done in advance, participants may sand and drill their own wood pieces.

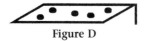

Figure D

Procedure:

1. As in Exercise 1 above, each participant chooses eight words, feelings or phrases from the material to be discussed.

2. Each participant folds his/her paper into eighths, creating eight separate sections.

3. Without removing the pencil from the paper, each participant creates a continuous line to represent each of the eight words or phrases. Again, encourage participants to create a line that represents the word, not *is* the word.

4. *Pirke Avot* 2:21 would be an appropriate text for this exercise: "It is not your duty to complete the work, but neither are you free to desist from it." Ask participants to envision their partnership with God. Encourage them to create their view of this partnership or their view of the world itself and God's presence in the world.

5. Each participant chooses as many colors of wire as desired and bends the wire into shapes to match his/her interpretive lines. (They can use as many or few of their line shapes as they wish, and can repeat their line shapes as many times as they feel necessary to create their sculptures.)

6. Each participant pokes one or both ends of each piece of wire into the holes of their piece of wood and secures them with glue. More than one wire will usually fit into each hole. (See Figure E below.)

Figure E

7. Discuss and process the experience (see Basic Recipe above).

Exercise 3: Geometric Abstracts (in the Style of Peter Freudenthal)

Materials:

White 12" x 18" tag board, one for each participant

Construction paper in various colors, whole pieces

Construction paper of various colors (including black), cut into squares, triangles, and rectangles of various sizes

Scissors, one for each participant

Glue sticks, one for each participant

Optional: 12" x 12" pre-cut mat boards

(available from arts and crafts catalogues, such as Beckley Cardy, www.junebox.com)

Copies of paintings by Peter Freudenthal (available online at www.everybuy.com/cgi-bin/webc.cgi?st_main.html?catid=19&sid=396s0AKS or ww.bronett.com/galleriet/freudenthal)

Procedure:

1. Explain that Peter Freudenthal is a Swedish Jewish painter born in 1938 in Norrköping, now living in Stockholm, Sweden. Pass around copies of his paintings. Freudenthal uses geometric shapes to convey his message, always including a black rectangle in his work. Ask participants to interpret what these shapes might represent. He explores the use of color and how its appearance seems to change when placed next to another color. For example, blue next to red appears to look different from the same blue placed next to black. Have the participants look at the shapes in front of them and place them next to each other in different color combinations. Freudenthal's paintings appear as if the shapes are layered one on top of another. This technique lends itself well to visual *midrash* because the participants are able to move and layer the shapes as in a puzzle. The final product is varied and rich in symbolism.

2. The prayer *"Ma'ariv Aravim"* from the *"Amidah"* would work well with this exercise. Ask participants to envision God's creation of light and dark, day and night. Encourage them to express their feelings about the miracle of creation and what impact this has on their understanding of God's awesomeness. The shapes lend themselves well to this concept because you can place them in many different relationships to one another, and can make them of many colors and in many sizes.

3. Each participant uses a glue stick to attach the shape of his/her choice to the white tag

board (see Figure F below). Remind them that they are free to layer the shapes and cut them as necessary.

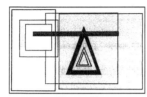

Figure F

4. If using pre-cut mat boards, each participant attaches the finished work with tape to the mat board.

5. Discuss and process the experience (see Basic Recipe above).

Exercise 4: Chagall-style Watercolor Washes

Materials:

White paper, suitable for use with watercolor paint, one piece for each participant

Watercolor paint (the kind in a tray used in schools works well)

Brushes

Water cups

Colored chalk or pastels

Optional: Pre-cut mats to frame the finished pieces (available from arts and crafts catalogues such as Beckley Cardy, www. junebox.com)

Tape (if using the mat frames)

Copies of paintings by Marc Chagall, such as "The Creation of Man" or "Paysage Bleu" (These paintings are available as posters or prints from most art museums and many Judaica shops. There are also many web sites with pictures of Chagall's work, such as www.discoverfrance.net/Frane/Art/Chagall/Chagall.shtml.)

Procedure:

1. Tell participants that Marc Chagall (1997-1985), a Jewish artist, used his imagination to create bright surrealistic paintings, prints, posters, and stained glass. This style lends itself to visual *midrash* because it allows each person to explore freely the imagery of the text without feeling weighed down by having to create a "realistic" image. Show examples of Chagall's work. Ask participants to pick out the various images they see. Reinforce the idea that Chagall used many hidden forms, and that these are not necessarily realistic images. Note that he also placed images within other images.

2. Jonah 2:8-10 describes Jonah's struggle to accept and understand God. This text is well suited to this watercolor exercise. Ask participants to envision themselves in Jonah's place, and to describe the images and feelings this evokes. What kind of struggle did Jonah have? What understandings of God's presence did Jonah discover?

3. Ask each participant to cover his/her entire piece of white paper with the watercolor paint, blending the colors to create a pleasing all-over watercolor wash with no particular form (see Figure G below).

Figure G

4. Each participant then uses chalk to outline the shapes in the watercolor wash that remind him/her of the text discussion (see Figure H below).

Figure H

5. If desired, place each finished work into a pre-cut mat and use tape to secure it.

6. Discuss and process the experience (see Basic Recipe above).

CONCLUSION

These are but a few ways to using art as an interpretive and expressive process to stimulate spiritual exploration and growth. All four approaches are based on the idea of examining texts and reaching into ways of viewing and experiencing the world that for many remain untapped or underutilized. Using art as a process can provide new insights into our minds, hearts, and souls.

IMPLICATIONS

1. The visual arts can be used to uncover ideas and emotions about God and spirituality that rest deep within our minds, hearts, and souls.

2. The visual arts offer a different way of seeing and experiencing the world and our relationship to God.

3. Tapping into our artistic intelligence emphasizing process over product can lead to understandings that might not otherwise surface.

QUESTIONS FOR CRITICAL INQUIRY

1. What is the difference between creating a beautiful ritual object and creating a beautiful piece of visual art as with Marc Chagall, Ben Shahn, Yaakov Agam, Shalom of Safed, etc.? How can each contribute to our spiritual journeys?

2. Gardner and others talk about multiple intelligences. What can an art exercise achieve that a discussion may not be able to accomplish?

3. Friend suggests following the process that Jo Milgrom models: studying a text, doing an art exercise, and discussing the exercise. What happens if you do only two of the parts, but not all three? How does each part of this model contribute to spiritual exploration? How does each part contribute to spiritual exploration as an individual pursuit? How does each part help connect you to the Jewish people, your community, other people, and God?

ACTIVITIES

1. Put the words of a prayer on strips of paper. Hebrew or English can be used, but it is important that the participants are able to understand what is written on each strip. Organize the strips on poster board or butcher paper in sequence or randomly. Use string to connect the ideas that are related. Attach the string with sticky tack or clear tape. Using a marker, write the ideas that emerge from the connections. What do you learn about the prayer's meaning? What do you learn about God?

2. Do a tour of Jewish art in your institution. Identify what Jewish sources are depicted. What images of God or ideas about God are presented? Other variations of this activity would be to visit a local Jewish museum, to have participants bring in a piece of Judaic artwork, or to obtain and study catalogues with Judaica artwork.

3. Many *Haggadot* are beautifully illustrated as a way to help interpret the text. Give people either the same or different illustrated *Haggadot*. Have them write an interpretation of different pictures or drawings in the text. Share insights.

4. Close your eyes and listen to music for prayers or those related to a text. Based on

the music alone, use the Chagall technique described and create an interpretation of the prayer or text. Explain your creation. Then read the prayer or text. See what new insights and questions emerge.

BIBLIOGRAPHY

Edwards, Betty. *Drawing on the Right Side of the Brain.* New York: Jeremy P. Tarcher/Putnam, 1989.

Edwards teaches an individual, even one who is art-challenged, how to draw by looking at things in a new way. She uses a series of exercises to enable students to shift their visual and perceptual system, forcing them to come to a new understanding of what they see.

Milgrom, Jo. *Handmade Midrash: Workshops in Visual Theology.* Philadelphia, PA: The Jewish Publication Society, 1992. (Also available at www.dfscott.com)

Milgrom provides an in-depth view of "Visual *Midrash*," a term she coined to mean a piece of artwork that represents the interpretation of a piece of text. She presents a clear plan that leads the reader step-by-step through the study of text and the creation of his/her own Visual *Midrash*.

CHAPTER 22

ENCOUNTERING GOD THROUGH DANCE

JoAnne Tucker

"SOME OF US ARE BORN MOVERS," POINTED OUT Carolyn Adams, a member of Juilliard's dance faculty, in an address to alumni. Wow! That sure makes sense to me! I am one of those born movers. It is through physical action that I learn about the world.

I have been exploring my Jewishness and wrestling with a personal God definition as a dancer and a choreographer since I was a teenager. As artistic director of The Avodah Dance Ensemble for the past several decades, I have worked in a collaborative setting with dancers, composers, and visual artists, creating repertory on Jewish themes. It is from my work with Avodah that ideas and curriculum have developed for educational settings.

BACKGROUND

When I was 14, I attended a prominent performing arts camp, Perry-Mansfield, in Steamboat Springs, Colorado. It was thrilling to be selected as one of two young campers to work with college students on a piece that faculty member Helen Tamiris was choreographing. Tamiris, a pioneer modern dancer and choreographer of Broadway shows, was an inspiring role model. The challenge of new dance ideas and the reinforcement of my abilities cemented my decision to be a dancer.

Perry-Mansfield's location in Steamboat Springs provided another unanticipated surprise. I found myself surrounded by lush green mountains, colorful wild flowers, and tall, quivering aspen trees. Sometimes, between classes, I would hike up a hillside just beyond my cabin. There, with a breathtaking valley below, I would dance a personal prayer — a thank-you to God for creating such majestic places, for my being able to

be surrounded by such beauty, and for having given me dance abilities. Perhaps you remember such moments, too: spontaneous outpourings of heartfelt enthusiasm. The link of expressing my spiritual feelings through dance was formed.

Fifteen years later, now with carefully honed skills, I would return to using dance as religious expression. Gaining these skills included years of theater training and dance study, especially two challenging years at Juilliard, and culminating in a Ph.D. in creative dramatics and movement.

While living with my husband and two young children in Tallahassee, Florida, I began working on an interpretation of several prayers for a dedication service. With a local composer, Irving Fleet, we looked at four prayers: *"Barechu," "Shema," "May the Words,"* and *"Alaynu."* In discussions with Irving, I shared that I did not easily relate to these prayers. I suggested that maybe if we explored the prayers through our talents of dance and music, we could make deeper personal sense of them. Careful research preceded long hours of sharing and tentative creating.

The idea we developed and expressed in music and dance for the *"Barechu"* was an acknowledgment of God by seeing God in nature, in love between individuals, and love between parent and child. In many ways, I was back at the hillside in Colorado, but now personal expressions were combined with research in the context of a key Jewish prayer. My dialogue with God through dance continued now rooted in traditional prayers. Since this early work in 1973, I have continued to create dances exploring liturgy, Torah, and Jewish history.

I have chosen to introduce this chapter with some autobiographical background before setting out the educational implications of the work that I do because it is important to keep in mind that "finding God" is a highly personal experience. How I function as a teacher, guiding others to express their spiritual feelings, is directly characterized by my own personal experiences. I have been blessed with teachers and colleagues who encouraged and reinforced my abilities, enabling me to develop my uniqueness. Each of us is unique! I connect this uniqueness to God. As a teacher, I have a responsibility to reinforce the uniqueness of my students. In doing so, I may possibly be helping them on their journey to encounter God.

When I reflect on the work that I do, I find that in two specific areas dance activities are avenues to finding God. These are: (1) teaching Torah through the process of "Dance *Midrash*," and (2) experiencing liturgy in a physical manner. Creating Dance *Midrash* and choreography based on liturgy are integral parts of the Avodah Dance Ensemble repertory. So, as an educator, I not only guide others in finding God through movement, but continue actively on my own search in this same way. My journey takes many surprising turns and twists and my God definition often changes, reminding me that flexibility is a guiding principle in working with students.

Rabbi Lawrence Kushner once asked a group of students, "What is The Torah?" After several typical responses, he took in his hand a copy of *The Torah: A Modern Commentary* by W. Gunther Plaut and offered it to a student saying, "Imagine that I am God." The student reached for the book. We saw Kushner holding onto one corner and the student holding onto the other. The two were linked together by the book.

That image continues to resonate in my mind. Torah is a link to God. It is through Torah that God reveals God's self to us. *Midrash* is a 2,000-year-old process through which we fill in the gaps in Torah. By explaining, searching out, and questioning, the text is elaborated upon and clarified. Biblical events and people may be linked in new ways. A biblical story may be related to contemporary issues. There are many different *midrashim* for each story and personality. These *midrashim* often reflect the time in which they were written. It is important to note

that for a specific event in Torah, there are many different responses to it in the *midrashic* literature. What a wonderful reminder to us as teachers. The very *midrashic* process promotes creative thinking. By using movement activities to interpret text, we can encourage each student to express his/her ideas in a unique way.

Walt Whitman (1971) wrote this in his famous collection of poems, *Leaves of Grass*: "There was a child went forth every day; And the first object he look'd upon, that object he became." Whitman is reminding us of several things: the innate curiosity of the child, how the child can be quickly attracted to something, and the total way in which a child responds by being the object.

Dance *Midrash* activities and the creative interpretation of liturgy through movement give the young and young of heart an opportunity "to be" the prayer or Torah verse. We are able to satisfy our curiosity by engaging ourselves totally in the moment of prayer or Torah interpretation. Physical learners have an avenue to enter into study in a manner that suits their abilities.

DANCE MIDRASH AS AN AVENUE TO FINDING GOD

When leading Dance *Midrash* activities, I have become aware of a variety of different opportunities in which to encounter God. As we dance the diverse biblical texts, we are able to: (1) experience a direct action of God, (2) become a biblical character following the instructions of God, (3) portray angels of God delivering messages, (4) become a biblical character directly dialoguing with God, (5) react to experiencing the presence of God, and (6) dance metaphors or symbols for God.

Following are some sample texts with a brief description, illustrating how Dance *Midrash* can be encounters with God. For more detailed information on how to lead activities like these in educational settings, see the book *Torah in Motion: Creating Dance Midrash*, which I co-authored with Rabbi Susan Freeman.

Experience a Direct Action of God

"And God separated the light from the darkness" (Genesis 1:4).

Participants begin moving in pairs, mirroring each other. At a cue from the leader, they separate, one person portraying light and the other darkness.

"And the Israelites went into the sea on dry ground, the waters forming a wall for them on their right and on their left" (Exodus 14:22).

Participants explore, in movement, the following events: seeing the sea in front of them while hearing the sound of the Egyptians approaching from behind, watching the waters part, and moving through the dry land with a wall of water on each side.

Become a Biblical Character Following the Instructions of God

"God said to Abram, 'Go forth from your native land and from your father's house to the land that I will show you'" (Genesis: 12:1).

Participants explore the different emotions that Abram feels as he leaves his home. Some possibilities are: reluctance to leave, excitement about the unknown, fear of becoming a stranger in a strange land, and inner strength as a result of being chosen by God. Participants may also be guided to portray Sarai's experience at the moment when God spoke to Abram. Perhaps Sarai heard God at the same time as Abram, or she may have heard God speak before Abram did and encouraged Abram to follow God's instruction. Maybe Sarai did not hear God at all and was told what happened by Abram.

"Remove your sandals from your feet, for the place on which you stand is holy ground" (Exodus 3:5).

Participants imagine they are Moses, and illustrate in dance how he reacted after taking off his shoes.

Portray Angels of God Delivering Messages

"He (Jacob) had a dream; a stairway was set on the ground and its top reached to the sky, and angels of God were going up and down on it" (Genesis 28:12).

Have participants dance the messages that the angels are bringing to or carrying from Jacob.

"God drove the man out, and stationed east of the garden of Eden the cherubim *and the fiery ever-turning sword, to guard the way to the tree of life"* (Genesis 3:24).

Participants dance the energy of the *cherubim* with the fiery ever-turning sword. Then ask them to contrast this with portraying the nurturing quality of the *cherubim* to be carved "with wings spread out above, shielding the cover . . ." of the Ark (Exodus 25:20).

Become a Biblical Character Directly Dialoguing with God

"And he (Abraham) said, 'Let not God be angry if I speak but this last time: What if ten should be found there?' And God answered, 'I will not destroy for the sake of the ten'" (Genesis 18:32).

Participants become Abraham arguing with God not to sweep the innocent of Sodom and Gomorrah away with the guilty. Show how Abraham's energy changed during the argument. (Note: at first, he starts with 50 innocent in verse 24.)

"And as Moses came down from the mountain bearing the two tablets of the Pact, Moses was not aware that the skin of his face was radiant since he had spoken with God. Aaron and all the Israelites saw that the skin of Moses' face was radiant and they shrank from coming near him" (Exodus 34:29-30).

Divide the participants into two groups. One group portrays Moses as he comes down from the mountain with his radiant face. As Moses, participants are to show how their actions reveal the experience of having just spoken with God. The other group is the Israelites reacting to the radiance. How do they shrink away? Is it in fear or awe or a combination of both?

React to Experiencing the Presence of God

"Fire came forth from before Adonai *and consumed*

the burnt offering and the fat parts on the altar. And all the people saw, and shouted, and fell on their faces" (Leviticus 9:24).

Have participants be the Israelites reacting to seeing God's presence during the dedication of the sacred place they helped to build. Encourage them to shout as they are doing the falling movement. Depict the emotions they are feeling.

"God went before them in a pillar of cloud by day, to guide them along the way, and in a pillar of fire by night, to give them light, that they might travel day and night" (Exodus 13:21).

Participants are the Israelites leaving Egypt with God's help. Have them imagine they are following the cloud and the fire. Focus on whether movement quality changes if following God as the cloud as contrasted with God as the fire.

Express Metaphors or Symbols for God in Dance

"Like an eagle who rouses its nestlings, gliding down to its young, so did God spread wings and take (Israel) along, bearing (Israel) on God's pinions" (Deuteronomy 32:11).

Have half the group be Israel (the nestlings) and the other half be forces that are nurturing and strong (the eagles). Show in movement how the two groups interact together. Switch roles.

"Some time later, the word of God came to Abram in a vision, saying 'Fear not, Abram, I am a shield to you; Your reward shall be very great'" (Genesis 15:1).

Participants are to be Abram becoming aware that God is a shield to him. How does Abraham's movement change? Encourage the group to expand on that quality.

Summary of Examples of Interpretation

The above examples of how biblical text can be interpreted in dance show six different ways that dance participants can gain insights into finding God by doing "Torah study" through movement. Using these types of Dance *Midrash* activities, we are able to explore God's relationship to our Israelite ancestors and make connections to how the text can relate to our lives today.

LITURGY: A DIALOGUE WITH GOD

It is through liturgy that we have the opportunity to acknowledge, praise, and petition God directly. One of the first important ways that I encourage students to learn more about a particular prayer is to experience whatever ritual gesture might accompany the prayer. By focusing on the gesture without words, new insights are possible for a particular prayer. For example, a bowing movement accompanies the *"Barechu."* Two possible reasons we might bow are to greet someone, particularly royalty, and to show humility. Incorporating these two ideas into the *"Barechu"* reinforces the role that this opening prayer plays in our liturgy. We are entering into prayer with God. Therefore, bowing is an appropriate action for greeting God while acknowledging our smallness.

The gestures that accompany the *"Shema"* are traditional movements which enable us to come closer to God. First, we gather together the corners of the *tallit*. Then we cover our eyes, often bending the head down. It is as if we are gathering in all of our energy to affirm God's oneness as we find a place within ourselves to relate to God. After the *"Shema,"* for the *"V'ahavta"* we open back out, uncovering our eyes, letting go of our *tallit* fringes as we say the prayer about "teaching these things to our children." Our movement now echoes the intent of the prayer; we become action-oriented, open and outgoing.

Besides approaching a prayer by learning, experiencing, and understanding the ritual gestures, we can interpret the meaning of the prayer through creative movement. For example, the paragraphs between the *"Barechu"* and the *"Shema"* acknowledge God for creating nature, for creating love between people, for Torah, and for Shabbat. Each of these topics provides wonderful opportunities for exploration in movement for all ages. Young children delight in creating different images related to nature, from pretending they are a bright shining sun to "becoming" a shooting star. Older groups may want to develop choreography related to ushering in Shabbat, or holding the Torah to acknowledge and praise God.

The "*Mi Chamocha*" provides another immediately accessible opportunity of exploring a prayer through movement. Foremost, the prayer recalls our ancestors thanking God for the miracle of the Exodus. In Torah, we read that Miriam and the women celebrated in dance after crossing the Sea of Reeds. This is the first time dance is mentioned in our history. What did Miriam's dance look like? What fun it is to create movement imagining we are Miriam at that moment. The prayer reminds us that we were once slaves and now are free. Often, I guide a group in bound or slave-like movement, then ask them to progress to free-flowing movement. Another approach to take is to think about other groups beside the Israelites who have gone from slavery to freedom, then to create modern day improvisations related to their journeys of becoming a free community.

As we explore ritual movement and creative interpretation of various prayers, we find that a variety of images and insights occur. Each encounter has the potential to help us build our God definition.

CONCLUSION

As a teacher and choreographer, I am continually refreshed and renewed on this ever-changing and sometimes startling journey of finding God through dance. From the teenager's "aha" on the hilltop in Colorado to my role as artistic director of The Avodah Dance Ensemble and leader of workshops for all ages, dance is my avenue for expressing spirituality. Just as movement ranges from stillness to exploding leaps and falls, so, too, is it a diverse journey to finding God through movement.

As an educator, I am ever mindful of keeping an atmosphere of flexibility present in my workshops. Whether relating to God by creating Dance *Midrash* or interpreting liturgy through movement, each participant's personal expression is encouraged and welcomed.

Rabbi Richard Jacobs, a member of The Avodah Dance Ensemble in the early 80s and now Senior Rabbi of Westchester Reform Congregation, eloquently reminded an audience gathered for a program on liturgy and dance, "May the movements of our body be acceptable, O God . . . "

IMPLICATIONS

1. Dance can uncover the symbolic meanings of metaphors. The metaphors in prayer and Torah are excellent vehicles for encountering God through movement.

2. Movement, dance, physical activity, are significant ways of knowing and experiencing God. The use of all five senses allows learners to access God in all the ways that are available. For some, movement may be the most important avenue for understanding and relating to God.

3. The fullness of education involves teaching the whole person — body, mind, emotions, and spirit.

QUESTIONS FOR CRITICAL INQUIRY

1. Why is the physical so powerful a vehicle for teaching about God through Torah and prayer?

2. Tucker describes a spontaneous outpouring of heartfelt enthusiasm when she expresses her spiritual feelings. Can you recall and describe similar moments in your life?

3. Tucker presents different ways of using dance to interpret Torah and prayer. How would you use dance to interpret: (a) the reunion of Joseph and his brothers? (b) the *motzi*? (c) a biblical text or prayer from your curriculum?

4. How can you as a teacher enable and encourage students to find God in their own way, using all the senses?

ACTIVITIES

1. Use your bodies to express different questions and views of God. In a room with sufficient space, have the class stand in a circle in pairs. The students in pairs are to do the following exercises that involve their touching one another: wrestle with God as did Jacob, show your love for God, question God, bless God, thank God, be God as a Rock, be God as the Creator, and more!

2. Find a prayer that has many different melodies. Choose a different melody for every 3 to 5 people in the class. Give each group a copy of the prayer and a tape with their particular melody. Using ribbons, banners, exercise balls, or other appropriate equipment as in an Olympic gymnastic-like event, choreograph an interpretation of the prayer paying close attention to the music. Compare and contrast the spiritual interpretations this activates. Discuss what you learned about praying to God.

3. Put up a white sheet with lights behind it so that you can see through it and the people behind the sheet cast shadows. The teacher gives each person a vignette from Torah that involves God directly (e.g., creation, Moses and the burning bush, the giving of the Torah at Mount Sinai). Then each participant creates a movement interpretation of the story. If desired, someone can act as narrator. Have the others guess what the scene is. Describe what you learn from this exercise about being in the presence of God.

BIBLIOGRAPHY

Plaut, Gunther W. *The Torah: A Modern Commentary*. New York: Union of American Hebrew Congregations, 1981.

This Torah commentary is easy to follow with the Hebrew text on the top of the page and the English after it. There are excellent introductions to each book and to specific topics. Thoughtful quotes from sources throughout the ages follow each section.

Tucker, JoAnne, and Susan Freeman. *Torah in Motion: Creating Dance Midrash*. Denver, CO: A.R.E. Publishing, Inc., 1990. (Available from http://www.E-Reads.com as a print on demand book or for downloading via the Internet.)

This book provides movement activities for each week's Torah portion.

Whitman, Walt. *Leaves of Grass*. New York: Madison Square Press, 1971.

This book is a collection of Walt Whitman's poems.

CHAPTER 23

SPIRITUAL SEEKING THROUGH DRAMA AND MUSIC

Shawn Israel Zevit

INTRODUCTION

"Praise God with harp and lyre . . .
Let every Soul praise God" (Psalm 150)

THE HEBREW BIBLE BEGINS WITH A GRAND SERIES OF creative acts. Out of a soup of divergent energies, competing elements, and lack of distinctions, the Spirit of God washes over creative potential. With the words "Let there be," the unformed is transformed into the manifest. Out of a "no-thing" comes a "some-thing." The soundscape begins immediately with the crashing of waves on the newly formed shores of land. Birds are soon chirping, all variety of creeping things are creeping, and the music of life plays on. Long before the Psalmist details the instruments of the Temple "band" in Psalm 150, there is chorus of creation declaring its very existence.

Before the script is committed to parchment, music and theater are intertwined into the very fabric of creation itself, heightened by the original oral storytelling tradition of the Jewish people. The entire first chapters of Genesis are high drama of the first order, filled with interesting character development, poetic dialogue, birth, and death. Throughout, God is a key player with the capacity to respond to unfolding realities in the biblical drama — the exploration by Adam and Eve of the forbidden fruit, the killing of Abel by Cain, and humanity not living up to pre-flood expectations. Far from being confined to a preordained script, God is portrayed as the Cosmic Improvisationalist, dancing with the twists and turns of the very human characters that have been let loose on the world stage to search for their purpose and identity. The foundational religious value of Judaism views the creation of humanity as reflecting the Divine in each of us (*B'tzelem Elohim*). This prime directive

should not go unnoticed in our own creative expression.

The Jewish people as a nation are born in no less a dramatic fashion. In one of the earliest "plays," the Exodus, scripted for rehearsal on an annual eternal reminder of the power of liberation from oppression, God's actions in Jewish history and our acting out of a core-value story play a profound role in keeping spiritual and cultural identity alive (see Exodus 12).

If we believe that the classroom, the sanctuary, the community center, the home, are places in which we engage in lifelong learning, then to live a God-centered life is actively and consciously to express and participate in the sounds and music, the spontaneous and rehearsed dramas in which we are constant players. As Psalm 150 describes, some of us may be able to express our divine potential with an actual instrument. Others of us can strum the chords of our own voices. Still others of us can be expressive actors for Jewish values and spiritual insights. Regardless of how trained or skilled we may be in our own or others' perceptions, every soul can express itself. Music and theater, or sound and self-expression (scripted or unscripted) are both powerful ways to do this.

I approach the subjects of music and drama from an integrative perspective. My background is in commercial scripted theater, ensemble work in educational and social theater, improvisation, Playback Theater (see *Acts of Service: Spontaneity, Commitment, Tradition in the Nonscripted Theater* by Jonathan Fox), Bibliodrama (see *Scripture Windows: Toward a Practice of Bibliodrama* by Peter A. Pitzele), and psychodrama. It is my practice to blend these with my work in voice, leading prayer services, singing, and composing. Rarely is my creative work in either of these areas devoid of influences or use of the other modalities. While I strive to find the truth in artistic and educational expression, I am by no means a purist in either of these fields. In fact, the more I work in a variety of settings, the more I realize that sacred values are best served by finding the modality, or combination of modalities, that suits the message and the group best. Process and outcome, form and content, become mutually enhancing and interdependent ways of being *B'tzelem Elohim*.

The intersection of theology and creativity invites us into a relationship with the Divine that is a dynamic process, not a static conceptualization. During my years in Toronto, Canada, I was part of an ensemble that did, among other social, historical, and educational plays, performances based on biblical narratives. These were often a combination of narratives taken straight from the Hebrew Bible and brought to life by improvised images and anecdotes inspired by the texts. What struck me was how audiences on the street, in schools, synagogues, or churches, would quickly gravitate to and be inspired by the universal messages and human journeys of the biblical stories. God's "role" was often of particular interest, though the key to engaging the audience who did not pay for seats in a theater was engendering a connection to and belief in the ideas being communicated. The interest and access that theater and music gave to the deep questions in people's lives was tremendous.

My experience with the ensemble taught me that the search for God in artistic life was no longer remote or as formal as in past centuries. Ellen Schiff (1982) reflects this understanding when she says, "On the twentieth century stage, God becomes not necessarily less holy or powerful, only infinitely more approachable." This can be seen quite clearly in Jewish writers such as Sholom Aleichem, Arthur Miller, and Woody Allen, to name a few. In some cases, it is drama itself that has become the new liturgy for many

people today, whether they are regular worshipers or alienated from Jewish communal life. This dramatic exploration of the human-Divine encounter, or trying to give voice to new *midrash* about God, whether bibliodramatically from sacred texts, or through improvised and scripted new plays, should be handled with some sensitivity. Peter Pitzele the creator of Bibliodrama, spells out some of the parameters in his book *Scripture Windows*:

> There are times when a bibliodramatic scene cries out for the presence of God. Directors should be guided by their own theological scruples as to whether they will or will not bring God onto the stage. Some may rightly fear the reduction of the *mysterium tremendum* to the scale of play; others may feel that the personification of the Divine offends their own sense of religious decorum or may offend members of the group. Others may feel that God needs to be brought into the drama so that people can find ways of being in dialogue with the Divine.[1]

Pitzele also points out, "The Bible affirms that there is a mystery working in human experience that has Divine origins and designs. As that design unfolds, we may unknowingly prove to be God's agents. Moreover, even if we are mistrustful of providence or skeptical about a personal God, we can find, in the Bible, stories of dignity, faith, and perseverance in the face of ordeals and the unknown."[2]

For those not as familiar with more improvisational work outside the traditional theater and music, it is important to remember that it is only in the last century or so that Jewish dramatists found voice again in scripted works. Jewish composers found renewed expression in music through traditional cantillation, or new compositions for liturgy and folk music, while still staying connected to their Jewish roots and identity. Even though the performance of standard plays

[1]Peter A. Pitzele, *Scripture Windows: Towards a Practice of Bibliodrama* (Los Angeles, CA: Torah Aura Productions, 1997/8), 163.

[2]Ibid., 92.

and musicals can be wonderful artistic experiences and community-building activities, we must also keep our focus on one of the core reasons for the development of theater and music in the ancient and modern world. Those core reasons were to express, challenge, mirror, entertain, and inspire us to our fullest humanity and potential.

Peter Brook, an English director, describes this in his analysis of Polish director Jerzy Grotowski's ensemble work that explored a number of religious themes from a radically new perspective:

> Jerzy Grotowski, a Polish theater director, felt drama had a sacred aim. 'The theater, he believes, cannot be an end in itself; like dancing or music in certain dervish orders, the theater is a vehicle, a means for self-study, self-exploration, a possibility of salvation . . . This theater is holy because its purpose is holy; it has a clearly defined place in the community and it responds to a need . . . [3]

IN THE BEGINNING: GOD AS THE CREATIVE FORCE IN ALL

To express insights into the Divine-human relationship, reconcile conflicting texts and traditions, and develop new understandings and rituals is to create *midrash*. The rhythms of the psalmists in the Bible, and oral storytelling of the Rabbis (later compiled in written form as *aggadah* in the Talmud and classical *midrash* in other collections), could be described as the Jewish people's initial musical and dramatic forays. Using *midrash* in its broadest sense, music and creative drama gives us inroads across the ages to the cultural legacy of the Jewish people, expression of our current experience, and visions of where and what we may yet be. The music our voices give to our souls, and the scripted and improvised narratives we develop, are core educational means of embodying and conveying

theological perspectives in artistic form. As Rabbi Mordecai Kaplan writes:

> The liturgy speaks of God as "renewing daily the works of creation." By becoming aware of the fact, we might gear our own lives to this creative urge in the universe and discover within ourselves unsuspected powers of the spirit. The belief in God as creator, or its modern equivalent, the conception of the creative urge as the element of Godhood in the world, is needed to fortify the yearning for spiritual self-regeneration.[4]

Kaplan's thought might lead us to develop a theology of creativity[5] in which we do not only see music, theater, and all the arts as wonderful creative skills we possess, but the very ongoing expression and reflection of the Source of all. While this has general implications in every culture, there are specific implications in Jewish cultural life. However, this necessitates a playfully serious approach to music and creative drama. We need to do more than put on plays for the various Jewish holidays (though these are important and wonderful opportunities to draw young people and adults into the religious and cultural aspects of Jewish peoplehood). We need to look for opportunities to invite spontaneity, personal stories, melodies, vignettes, role-plays, interactive video, etc., into interactions beyond the art classes or year cycle celebrations. Marilyn Price, an educator and puppeteer, expresses the importance of this Jewish spiritual endeavor:

> There are those who fear the Jewish arts are "arts and crafts" from the days of lanyard key rings and bottle cap *menorahs*. If that is the case, we must rethink the ways we connect arts to Judaism in meaningful and substantive ways . . . the arts are basic in helping nurture our Judaism. They make understandable the often wordy and intricate concepts of Judaism. They make pleasurable and mem-

---

[3]Peter Brook, *The Empty Space* (London: Penguin, 1980), 66.

[4]Mordecai M. Kaplan. *The Meaning of God in Modern Jewish Religion* (Detroit, MI: Wayne State Press, 1994), 62-63.

[5]Liz Bolton, "Toward a Jewish Theology of Creativity," *The Reconstructionist* 62:1, Spring/Fall 1997, 21.

orable the ways we pray and the way we learn. They might help an artist whose art is Jewish just because she was born a Jew be transformed into a Jewish artist who does Jewish art.[6]

There may be no more powerful way for people in a generation of spiritual seeking to experience the possibility of a Divine Presence in their lives than in the intersection between creative expression, Jewish identity, religion, and culture.

ALL THE WORLD IS A DIVINE STAGE — CREATIVE DRAMA

There are many ways to interact with our sacred texts and weave in how we experience the Divine working through us now. One method I have used with young people and adults is to ask them to write a "Dear God" letter, or Dear Source of Life, Friend, etc. . . . This may be on their behalf or on behalf of a biblical or historical Jewish personality. This exercise provides an avenue to voice what is not in a text, but is informed by it, or voice what is in our hearts, though not conventionally expressed. These may be written from the perspective of the character, e.g., "Sarah" writes: "Dear God, Abraham and Isaac have been gone for days now. I had a foreboding feeling about this trip and now I feel my worst fears may come true." Or they may be personal: "I have been learning the prayers lately, but have been wondering if You can hear me." A letter in a similar fashion could be written back to the character or to the participant with God's response. These can be woven together to make a contemporary *midrash* on a biblical story, to give voice to an event in Jewish history, or simply to stir the creative thinking in relationship to God in our lives. This exercise can be done by interviewing the group as a whole and asking them to be like Moses in the Torah and "take on the role of God" for the exercise, or go into small groups and craft their

own "conversations with God." The suspension of judgment, and deep listening to the words beneath the words, are very important in any of these exercises.

The role creative drama can play in the classroom or sanctuary is also an extension of how God was represented to a community at large over many millennia, including the roles of Temple priests, prophets, Sages, Hasidic masters, and so on. The oral telling of a values-based story, whether rehearsed or spontaneous, has always been part of the role of connecting God's presence to humanity in sacred community.

We can approach this transmission of values through oral storytelling in our own contexts in a variety of ways. Groups of children or adults can discuss the values that they feel are important to living a Jewish life, or the values that they experience as Godly, or that God asks of a human being. Smaller groups or pairs can then choose the value they are most attracted to and can develop and present to the group a monologue for the value they chose (compassion, *tzedakah*, justice, humility, etc.). For example, "*tzedakah*" might tell us why it is central to being a holy person, how it affects the person giving and receiving it, how it impacts the whole community. There can even be a dialogue between the values, or a panel discussion. If you have more than one session for the exercise, the pairs or groups can do some research about the value concept in Judaism to add to their narrative. If music is involved, songs or words with instrumental backing can be created in any style to communicate the same material.

The groups can also create sculptures around a certain Jewish value or *mitzvah*. One person begins by striking a pose and, one by one, others take silent positions in relation to them. The observers may try to guess what Jewish values, practice, or quality is being demonstrated. Different people in the sculpture can be interviewed by the teacher as to what aspect of their chosen value they represent. The different mem-

---

[6]Marilyn Price, "Fine Arts — Fine Schools," *Gesher Vekesher* 6:1, January 1997, 1.

bers of the sculpture can even dialogue among themselves (e.g., if *tzedakah* is the chosen value, people create a *tzedakah* sculpture and each says a line telling what aspect of *tzedakah* they represent). If desired, Jewish values or practices can be replaced by ritual objects — Havdalah ritual objects, the *Seder* plate, *tallit*, *tefillin*, and so on. The objects can tell what they represent and what God-awareness or spiritual quality each strives to evoke in us.

Telling the story or creating vignettes of the history of one's congregation, school or organization, and the Jewish values it stands for, can help a group realize how it can live in, and create sacred community. I have even used the mission statement or articulated sense of what a community stands for as a contemporary sacred text to be explored for its support of and inconsistencies with what the lived reality is for the members of the group. You might even focus on a single line, e.g., when the Israelites are leaving Egypt "and a mixed multitude (*erev rav*) went up with them." This can make for a variety of vignettes or creative interchanges about who was in this mixed multitude and what were the stories behind their leaving. This example speaks to the importance of those who are teaching or in a religious leadership role and of pointing out the drama inherent in our sacred texts themselves.

The act of embodying and/or telling the story (whether with lines or improvised encounters) is itself the "hooking up" to the divine impulse of creation and creativity. This can also occur by having someone give voice to God's unspoken words in a similar text, or what they imagine to be God's response to a current situation in the world. One of the most powerful experiences I have had using such creative drama techniques is in using the first chapter of Genesis. Again, I have found this equally moving for groups of children, teens, and adults. Begin by taking people backward in time, preferably with their eyes closed, finding a comfortable place in their seat. Have them think back to when they woke up the day before, then go back weeks, then years, to past events in the world and in Jewish history. Guide them all the way to

before the beginning. Then read the first line of the Torah, preferably without the indefinite article as the Hebrew suggests, "In beginning God created . . . " You might then pause and remind people they are back before time, and have permission to speak freely. Say: "Now I want to ask You this question God. Why did You begin to create? What came before?"

The responses are often fascinating and quite inspiring. If desired, continue one day at a time through the first seven days of creation, exploring each day from God's perspective and from the perspective of the element or beings created. Ask God why God had a need to create human beings. Interview the birds, animals, fish, and creeping things as to how they feel and what they expect of humanity. Since the text is in the plural, "Let us create human beings in our image," it gives rise to very interesting perspectives. Finish with God resting from the work of creation on the seventh day, rather than collapsing from the "work week." This presents another opportunity to examine the balance between creativity and compassion, doing and being.

Of course, there are different comfort levels when setting up scenarios such as those described, or when giving voice to God. Do only what you and your students are comfortable with. I have done these exercises with interfaith and multi-faith groups, with Orthodox and self-professed atheists, all with moving and stimulating results. Both children and adults are able to express and reflect on the beliefs they hold about a Higher Source in the universe, how that does/does not align with their actions in the world, and what it tells them about who they long to be Jewishly and as a human being. Biela Lepkin puts it succinctly:

Creative drama . . . deals with developing personality and character, allowing children to use their own inner resources to develop their talents and sense of individuality and originality. Creative drama guides and encourages children to express and "give out" their interpretation of what has been "put into" them. In addition, it offers techniques that can be used in the teaching of factual subjects. Serving as it does both aspects of education, the "putting in" and the "giving out," creative drama then becomes a necessity and not a luxury.[7]

Viewing creative drama in this fashion reinforces the necessity of a shift from an emphasis on production to integrating creative dramatic moments in prayer, educational settings, board meetings, and so on. Any place a spiritual consciousness can be reflected can itself be a time to realize creative potential.

SINGING A NEW SONG — SOUND AND MUSIC

"Shiru L'Adonai shiru shir chadash"
Sing to God a new song[8]

Ilu Finu Maleh Shirah Kayam
Were our mouths filled with song . . .
We would never have sufficient praise for You
Abundant one, our God . . . "[9]

With the first words of Genesis, God is portrayed as bringing the creative idea into manifestation by giving voice to it. Everything needs a "let there be" to leap off the drawing board into being. It is not just human beings who create by giving voice in sounds, words, and song as we respond to being alive and to our varied experiences. As we sing a new song, we express the infinite wonders of the universe, and we become part of the "soundtrack" that accompanies life.

Similarly, expressing our voices in song, chant, poetic reading, humming a note, choral singing, prayer services, etc., provides many opportunities to find our place in the soundscape of the community. This is true for all of us — the gifted singer, composer or musician, as well as the less vocal or more musically challenged.

When we give voice to the musical score of Jewish tradition, and when we become involved in creative contemporary interpretations and

compositions, we find that there are many options for bringing music into any learning situation. For example, a *niggun* can begin a text study session. A piano or guitar can underscore a reading or meditation. A choral piece can serve as a group building exercise. It is also important to remember that the Jewish way of transmitting wisdom and spiritual truth from generation to generation was aided by chant, *trop* (cantillation for the Torah and Haftarah), and *nusach* (melody lines for liturgy).

The Psalms, themselves musical poetry, can be a wonderful tool for seeing the breadth and depth of thought and emotions expressed about God in our tradition. Create new melodies for Psalm 145, known as the *"Ashrei."* Use the Hebrew acrostic formula to create an English acrostic based on what participants feel most grateful for. Or chant the line that begins with the same letter as their Hebrew or English name. These are all ways of creating personal connection with an ancient gift. One can also use an existing Psalm or prayer as a foundation for writing a new version that reflects our own experience of God. You can then add a traditional, contemporary, or new melody, chant, or vocally created soundscape. The following is an excerpt from my interpretation of Psalm 27, which I then set to music. It uses both translation and interpretation interchangeably:

> When pressures and perspectives of a cynical world
> Threaten to bring me down
> I ride the wave of undying faith
> And its lies that finally drown
> For one thing I ask
> For one thing I long
> To build Your house with my life
> To see the beauty in every smile
> And the light in every night
>
> You are my light and my salvation
> Of whom shall I fear

---

[7]Biela Lepkin, *Creative Drama in the Hebrew School* (Haifa, Israel: Pinat Hasefer, 1978), 25.

[8]Isaiah 42:10; Psalms 96:1.

[9]Morning service, translated from *Kol Haneshamah: Shabbat Vehagim* (Elkins Park, PA: Jewish Reconstructionist Press, 1996), 236-237.

You are the stronghold of my life
Of whom shall I be afraid
I will look to You
My God[10]

Another suggestion is to sing Psalm 150, which is a list of ancient musical instruments and sounds used to praise God, adding of all the sounds and instruments children or adults associate with inspirational song today. Still another idea is to rewrite a contemporary song that most inspires us or has emotional memory attached to as a song that reflects a moment of sensing God's presence.

Rabbi Bob Gluck, a contemporary composer, states: "Premodern Jewish music is substantially folk tradition. Inherent in the life of folk traditions, is its oral means of transmission."[11] Even when there are traditional melodies or notated scores, we are still asked to find our own voices in relation to the present moment of bringing the notes of a composition, or the sounds and songs of praise and longing, challenge and loss. Jonathan Fox has this to say on the subject:

Paradoxically, even though the singer endeavors to sing his tale the same way every time, it is impossible. This makes sense if we remember that the tale is not a "text" that has been memorized, but the experience of an auditory moment which cannot be objectively recalled or referred to . . . A particular story exists in all its variations as voiced by all its tellers in all their recitations. In oral culture the story is constantly being recreated.[12]

Music was intimately tied to the ancient Temple. Even after the destruction of the Second Temple in 70 C.E., the very chanting of the Torah, prayers, *niggunim* (wordless melodies), the mantra-like intonation of Talmud study, reflected the Jewish people's yearning to express musically an individual and collective response

to the acts of hallowing life. The musicologist Judith Eisenstein wrote:

The people gave the music life, and the music in turn pulsated in the people, passing from parent to child, and from land to land. The joys and triumphs, the tenderness and warmth, the agony and sorrows, the prayer and protest, which were shared by Jews and made them one, were poured into music; and where they are still felt, that process continues today. When we live for a moment with that music, we are touching the pulse itself, and our own is quickened in turn."[13]

Bringing a musical expression into every learning situation helps to deepen the remembrance and transmission for the generations to come.

MIDRASHIC MOMENTS — PUTTING ART AND SPIRIT INTO ACTION

The following exercise makes use of the Book of Ruth to put creative drama and music into action. Through such exercises, we can become co-creators of new expressions, even as we embrace our our heritage of old. In the Book of Ruth, God is not actually present as a character. This enables us to bring God's voice into the scene. We can discuss where we think a Higher Source is operating — behind the scenes or through the characters themselves, who see no burning bushes, hear no voices, and make no cultic sacrifices. We can also open discussions throughout the creative process regarding how we experience and understand God in our own lives.

The Book of Ruth is traditionally read during Shavuot, the spring Festival of Weeks, a first fruit and harvest festival that was later linked by Jewish Sages to the revelation of the Torah. It is one of the most beautiful and richly woven wisdom stories in the Hebrew Bible, and is one of

---

[10]Shawn Zevit, "Heart and Soul" (Philadelphia, PA: Radioactive Productions, 1998).

[11]Bob Gluck, "Jewish Music or Music of the Jewish People," *The Reconstructionist* 62:1, Spring/Fall 1997, 44.

[12]Jonathan Fox, *Acts of Service, Spontaneity, Commitment, Tradition in the Non-scripted Theater* (New Paltz, NY: Tusilata Publishing, 1994), 14.

[13]Judith K. Eisenstein, *Heritage of Music* (New York: Union of American Hebrew Congregations, 1972).

the few biblical texts that sets women explicitly at the forefront of the story. It is also a story about faith across many cultures and religious expressions.

A creative drama and music process can work well for any size group, though groups of more than 12-15 should probably be broken up into smaller size groups with parallel or different assignments. You may want to write some lines down, have texts available as aids in discussion, and have available a variety of instruments, percussion pieces, even household or classroom items that produce sound.

Preparation

The following are the necessary steps to follow as you prepare for this exercise:

1. Spend time familiarizing yourself with the text, even if you have studied it in the past.

2. Prepare handouts of the text ahead of time. (Be sure to have more than enough copies available. This will avoid scrambling for more materials at the last minute and interrupting the flow of the process.) Divide the book into narrative sections. The number of sections will depend on the time you have, the number of sessions, and the size of the group.

3. Plan your introduction. If the group is not already familiar with improvisation, take a few minutes to explain the process. Be sure to let participants know that they control their level of participation and that they may choose to be an observer instead of a participant at any point. You may also want to provide some context, especially if the program is to be used as part of a holiday celebration.

4. Plan your warm-up exercises. Most groups will require some warming up. This can be done in a variety of ways. For example, you may want to ask the group if they are familiar with creative drama or music, the Book of Ruth, or the festival of Shavuot. Other ways to warm up are: (1) engage in simple improv-

isational games, such as asking participants to say their English or Hebrew names along with a gesture, (2) adopt a pose of a biblical character with whom they are familiar, (3) create a story by having each participant add one word or sentence can be helpful. (In the latter case, the musicians and/or vocalists can add their soundtrack to the images.)

5. Be sure to check out the set-up of the space in advance. You will need space for break-out groups, as well as a space in which the whole group can convene and watch each other's presentations.

The Program

Here is an outline of the actual program:

1. Welcome the group and introduce them to the process. Take time to answer any questions or concerns that the participants may have.

2. Do the warm-up exercises that you have selected.

3. Divide the group into break-out groups of a minimum of three people each, and provide each participant with a copy of the text.

4. Instruct each break-out group to develop a scenario with enacted scenes, dialogue, and soundscape from one of the narrative points. For example, you could ask each group to develop three or four tableaux (still images, like embodied photographs) and present them in sequence, with perhaps one line spoken by a member of the tableau, and others singing a song or playing instruments that support the context of the scene. The group might also create a short scene around the narrative, and provide the dialogue. This does not have to be limited to the setting of biblical text. For example, a group may decide to present their scene as a newscast: "This just in: Ruth and Naomi sighted at the border of Israel!" Allow only 10 or 15 minutes for this work. I like to avoid lengthy

time periods that create a "production" mentality and rob spontaneity. This is not about being "stellar"; rather, it is about being present. If there are not enough participants for the number of groups you want, or there are participants who do not want to be up in action, you can simply read the missing moments from the text provided.

5. Reassemble all the participants. Have each group present their work in sequence. In this way, the entire story is reenacted and can be experienced in a more creative way than in a straight reading.

6. Take the time to debrief afterward. Ask: What insights did you get from the text? Where was God in this story? What Jewish values and beliefs about God's unfolding in our lives does the text convey? If you were to give God the last word, what would God's message be? How did the creative drama, music, and/or song bring the story to life, convey new meaning, and engage you in the message of the Book of Ruth?

You may also want to revisit the text. Analyze what the spontaneous encounter brought to the understanding of the text, and process what the creative approaches unlocked in the participants about God and human beings in our sacred texts and tradition.

CONCLUSION

An important thing to remember is that creativity is the art of self-expression, but creativity is not the possession of artists. Each human being, a spiritual being in his/her own soul journey, is a creative spark awaiting more kindling. These approaches, with some encouragement and clear, simple directions can be made accessible to young and old, novice and veteran alike.

Whatever approach you take, do your homework before, and trust in the development of your own style of leadership. We may have a strong bias in favor of a particular interpretation of a passage and what we hope or want people to get from the experience. These are important considerations, but in the moment of the creative encounter, as in any artistically alive and spiritual moment, it is our task as facilitators to be present to the relationships and dynamics in the room. The insights, healing, enjoyment, and challenge people will receive depends on this "teaching of presence."

May these words and thoughts help inspire and support you to move beyond the page into the plays and sounds of the Soul of all Creation that waits within each of you for expression.

IMPLICATIONS:

1. Drama and music are aspects of the ways in which the relationship between God and the Jewish people get played out in the Bible.

2. The use of drama and music are useful tools in exploring and deepening our understanding of and relationship to God.

3. Music and drama can awaken spiritual insights and our souls.

QUESTIONS FOR CRITICAL INQUIRY:

1. Zevit describes God in the Bible as the "Cosmic Improvisationalist." In what ways is God the "Cosmic Improvisationalist" then and now?"

2. According to Zevit, in what ways has music connected Jews to God throughout Jewish history and tradition?

3. What are the reasons that Zevit presents for

viewing music and drama as powerful tools for exploring our relationship to and understanding of God?

4. From your perspective, how can music and drama strengthen our connection to God?

ACTIVITIES:

1. Choose a Psalm, prayer, and episode from Torah involving God. Form three groups. Using a variety of instruments, create a musical interpretation. Discuss what you learn about relating to God from these interpretations.

2. Zevit calls God the "Cosmic Improvisationalist." Ask the participants to write down the questions that they would like to answer. Then give a pair of participants the questions and act away — one person as him/herself and the other as God.

3. Play *Charades*, and act out the different names of God.

4. Every religion, people, culture has its master story. The Exodus/Revelation is sometimes viewed as the Jewish Master Story, which describes the relationship between God and the Jewish People. Read segments from Exodus and the *Haggadah* and watch excerpts from the video *Prince of Egypt*. See how each builds upon your understanding of the relationship between the Jewish people and God.

BIBLIOGRAPHY

Bolton, Liz. "Toward a Jewish Theology of Creativity." *The Reconstructionist* 62, no. 1, Spring/Fall, 1997.

Bolton is a congregational Rabbi, Cantor, voice teacher, and opera singer, as well as the Director of Liturgy and Music for the Jewish Reconstructionist Federation.

Brook, Peter. *The Empty Space*, London: Penguin, 1980.

One of the world's most famous directors gives us the distillation of his knowledge and experience of theater. He took a variety of approaches from the high-end productions on Stratford-on-Avon to spontaneous street performances.

Eisenstein, Judith K. *Heritage of Music*, New York: Union of American Hebrew Congregations, 1972.

Eisenstein, author of this classic, was a leading Jewish composer and champion of music in Jewish congregational and cultural life in the twentieth century.

Fox, Jonathan. *Acts of Service: Spontaneity, Commitment, Tradition in the Non-scripted Theater*. New Paltz, NY: Tusilata Publishing, 1994.

Playback Theater is totally improvisational. The objective is to act out or play back the personal stories of the audience through mime and music, as well as spoken scenes. Developed by Jonathan Fox, the first performance took place in 1975.

Gluck, Bob. "Jewish Music or Music of the Jewish People." *The Reconstructionist* 62, no. 1, Spring/Fall, 1997.

Rabbi Gluck composes in electronic media, often working with archival sounds from traditional Jewish music as raw material.

Kaplan, Mordecai M. *The Meaning of God in Modern Jewish Religion*, Detroit, MI: Wayne State Press, 1994.

Kaplan (1881-1983), ideological founder of Reconstructionism, was a towering figure in North American Jewry. This work presents his unusual combination of theology and common sense that led him not only to construct new approaches to Judaism geared to our time, but to devise practical expressions as well. He was a champion of creating dynamic Jewish art and developing Jewish artists as one of the highest expressions of Godliness in the world.

Kol Haneshamah: Shabbat Vehagim. David Teutsch, ed. Elkins Park, PA: Jewish Reconstructionist Press, 1996.

This prayer book, with its morning service, translations, transliterations, commentary, and explanations of the various prayer services, is helpful in regard to the understanding and development of creative responses in worship.

Lepkin, Biela. *Creative Drama in the Hebrew School*. Haifa, Israel: Pinat Hasefer. 1978.

Published with the help of the Multiculturalism Program of the Secretary of State, Canada, Biela's book was a forerunner of books on creative expression in teaching that moved beyond arts and crafts to see creative drama and music as core expressions of the divine spark in every human being. It is a practical book with games and exercises for a multiplicity of Jewish settings and holidays.

Pitzele, Peter A. *Scripture Windows: Towards a Practice of Bibliodrama*. Los Angeles, CA: Torah Aura Productions, 1997/8.

Peter Piztele, a therapist and psychodramatist, developed the structured process called Bibliodrama as a form of role-playing in which the roles are taken from biblical texts. It is a form of interpretive play or *midrash-making*.

Price, Marilyn. "Fine Arts — Fine Schools." *Gesher Vekesher* 6, no.1, January 1997.

Price is a puppeteer, storyteller, school principal, consultant. *Gesher Vekesher* is the newsletter of the education department of the Jewish Reconstructionist Federation.

Schachter-Shalomi, Zalman. *Paradigm Shift*. Northvale, NJ: Jason Aronson Inc., 1993.

Reb Zalman is one of the most innovative and inspiring Rabbis in the Jewish world today, and a founder of the movement for Jewish Renewal. This book is a record of his major teachings that includes contemporary thinking about God.

Schiff, Ellen. *From Stereotype To Metaphor: The Jew in Contemporary Drama*. Albany, NY: State University of New York Press, 1982.

A comprehensive study of the Jew in modern theater, tracking the evolution of the Jewish persona on stage from the Middle Ages to the twentieth century.

Zevit, Shawn. "Heart and Soul." Philadelphia, PA: Radioactive Productions, 1998.

A collection of 15 original songs based on the psalms, liturgy and life. (Available by e-mailing Mazel@erols.com or Tara Publications.)

CHAPTER 24

GOD AS TEACHER: JEWISH REFLECTIONS ON A THEOLOGY OF PEDAGOGY

Hanan A. Alexander

IN JUDAISM, GOD IS THE ULTIMATE ROLE MODEL. "You shall be holy," says the Priestly Code, "for I, the Lord your God, am holy" (*Leviticus* 19:1).[1] If the followers of *Adonai* are to be a "kingdom of priests and a holy people" (*Exodus* 19:6) that "walks in God's ways" (*Deuteronomy* 10:12), then to adhere to the divine word involves *imitatio Dei* — imitation of the Deity. When the Torah depicts God as creator of the universe, we learn that creative activity is sanctified (*Genesis* 1). From the description of God resting on the seventh day, worshipers derive that they, too, are to rest (*Exodus* 19:8-11). God adheres to a moral code, so Abraham adopts this code (*Genesis* 18:20-33). God redeems the oppressed in Egypt, from which Israel is to understand never to oppress the powerless (*Leviticus* 19:9-37). "Just as God is merciful and gracious," states the *Midrash*, "so, too, you be merciful and gracious" (*Sefré Deuteronomy, Ekev*).

It is instructive, therefore, that the Rabbis envisioned God in their own image as a *Talmid Chacham* — both a student and teacher. As Simon Rawidowicz put it:

God in *midrashic* Judaism is the *eternal student*. He learns *with* Israel, learns always and everywhere. He learns with the sages, in the academies of Palestine and Babylonia. He learns with the learners of Yavneh, Sepphoris, Sura, and Pumbeditha. The creator

of the world studies the *halachah*.[2] As judge of the world, God also teaches. Rawidowicz continues:

When the sages in Israel cannot agree on the settling of a controversy on *halachic* problem, they call for a heavenly decision . . . Rav, an *Amora* of second the century, went even so far as to describe exactly the daily agenda of God Almighty: The first three hours . . . God learns *Torah*; the second three hours, He judges all the world; the third three hours, He feeds all the world.[3]

Study and teaching, in this tradition, are holy acts; and the teacher of divine wisdom is a revered personality. The Rabbinic teacher represents God both symbolically, by imitating Divine behavior, and pedagogically, by leading students to understand and embrace divine teachings.[4] This is why the Rabbis taught that if you must choose between saving your teacher or your parent, save your teacher first, for your parent "brings you into this world, but your teacher introduces you to the world to come" (*Mishnah, Bava Metzia* 3:11).

It should come as no surprise, then, that the Rabbis referred to the tradition they received from God at Sinai as "Torah," which literally means instruction or teaching. In revealing Torah to the Israelites in the desert, God also disclosed a pedagogic aspect of the divine personal-

[1]Unless otherwise noted, translations follow *The Torah: A New Translation of the Holy Scriptures According To the Masoretic Text* (Philadelphia, The Jewish Publication Society of America, 1962).

[2]Simon Rawidowicz, *Israel: The Ever Dying People and Other Essays*, B.C.I. Ravid, ed. (Rutherford, NJ: Farleigh Dickinson University Press, 1986), 135.

[3]*Ibid.*, 136.

[4]On theology and symbolic language, see Neil Gillman, *Sacred Fragments: Recovering Theology for the Modern Jew* (Philadelphia, PA: The Jewish Publication Society, 1990), 79-108, and Paul Tillich, *The Dynamics of Faith* (New York: Harper Torchbooks, 1957).

ity. Since God is our ultimate teacher, to study Torah is to worship God; and to worship the Divine is to engage in the study of Torah.[5] Nowhere are educational images of God more pronounced, therefore, than in Jewish liturgy.

WORDS AND DEEDS

At the heart of the Rabbinic worship service is the recitation of a citation from *Deuteronomy* (6:4-8):

Hear, O Israel! The Lord is our God, the Lord Alone. You must love the Lord your God with all your heart and with all your soul and with all your might. Take to heart these words with which I charge you this day. Impress them upon your children. Recite them when you stay at home and when you are away, when you lie down and when you get up. Bind them as a sign on your hand and let them serve as a symbol on your forehead; inscribe them on the doorposts of your house and on your gates.

This passage encapsulates an educational orientation.[6] Faith in God is to be taught by means of recitation of sacred texts at home and away from home, and by means of actions — binding holy words on our hands, doors, and gates. What is the origin of this pedagogy? It is the very method that God used to instruct the Israelites. To adhere to the words of the *"Shema"* is not only to follow God's teaching, but also to imitate God as teacher. Thus, the Deuteronomist introduces this passage with the words: "This is the instruction — the laws and the norms — that the Lord your God has commanded [me] to impart to [teach] you (6:1)."[7]

To drive this divine pedagogy home, the biblical text continues after rendering the *"Shema"* with a response to a query (6:20-25):

When, in the time to come, your son asks you, "What mean the exhortations, laws, and norms which the Lord our God has enjoined upon you?[8]" you shall say to your son, "We were slaves to Pharaoh in Egypt and the Lord freed us from Egypt with a mighty hand. The Lord wrought before our eyes marvelous and destructive signs and portents against the Egyptians, and against Pharaoh and all his household; and us. He freed from there, that He might take us and give us the land that He has promised on oath to our fathers. The Lord commanded us to observe all these laws, with reverence for the Lord our God, for our lasting good and for our survival, as is now the case. It will be therefore to our merit before the Lord our God to observe faithfully this whole Instruction, as He commanded us."

Our observance of divine instruction is predicated upon God's deeds — the redemption from Egypt — and words — the revelation at Sinai. Just as God taught us to observe the Torah with actions and with verbal explanations, so we are to teach our children and students God's message by example and study.

DIALOGUE AND INQUIRY

Two aspects of this instructional method are worth noting. First, *it is dialogical.* The father's actions and explanations respond to the son's questions. We see this question and answer format in *Exodus* as well. "And when your chil-

---

[5]Max Kadushin, *Worship and Ethics: A Study in Rabbinic Judaism* (New York: Bloch Publishing, 1963).

[6]See H.A. Alexander, "Education," in David L. Lieber, ed., *The Humash: A Conservative Commentary* (Philadelphia and New York: Jewish Publication Society and the Rabbinical Assembly) and "A Jewish View of Human Learning," *The International Journal of Children's Spirituality*, forthcoming.

[7]The new JPS translation renders this as God commanding Moses to "impart" the laws and norms. However, the original Hebrew states: *asher tzivah Adonai Elohayhem lelamed etchem* (that the Lord your God commanded to teach you). God here is our teacher.

[8]The new JPS translation rightly notes here that in the Septuagint (the first Greek translation of the Hebrew Bible) and in Rabbinic quotations, the text reads "enjoined upon *us*."

dren ask you, 'What do you mean by this rite?' you shall say, 'It is the Passover sacrifice to the Lord, because He passed over the households of the Israelites in Egypt when He smote the Egyptians, but saved our houses' (12:26-27)." Similarly in relation to the eating of unleavened bread, the text states, "And you shall explain to your son on that day, 'It is because of what the Lord did for me when I went free from Egypt.' (23:8)." Finally, in connection with the redemption of the firstborn males, the Bible relates (13:14-15):

> And when, in the time to come, your son asks you saying, 'What does this mean?' you shall say to him, "It was with a mighty hand that the Lord brought us from Egypt, the house of bondage. When Pharaoh stubbornly refused to let us go, the Lord slew every firstborn in the land of Egypt, the firstborn man and beast. Therefore, I sacrifice to the Lord every first male issue of the womb, but redeem every firstborn among my sons."

The Rabbis were so enamored with this dialogical pedagogy that they constructed a typology of both questions and those who would ask them in the well-known *midrash* of the Four Sons (*Milchilta Bo*, 18; *Talmud Yerushalmi, Pesahim*, 10:4; *Yalkut Shimoni*, 226) that appears in the Passover *Haggadah*:

> The Torah has four children in mind: one, intelligent, a second wicked, a third simple, and a fourth, a child that does not yet know how to ask. *What does the intelligent child say?* "What mean the testimonies and statutes, and ordinances which the Lord our God hath commanded you?" (*Deuteronomy* 6:20) And you shall instruct him in the precepts of Passover, to wit: "One may not conclude after the Paschal meal (by saying), 'Now to

the entertainment!'" *What does the wicked child say?* "What is this service to you?" (*Exodus* 12:26) To you, and not to him. Since he removed himself from the group, and so denies God, you in return must set his teeth on edge, and answer him: "It is because of that which the Lord did for me when I came out of Egypt" (*Exodus* 13:8). For me, not for him; had he been there he would not have been redeemed. *What does the simple child say?* "What is this?" (*Exodus* 13:14). And thou shalt say to him: "By the strength of hand the Lord bought us out from Egypt, from the house of bondage" (*Exodus* 13:14). *And with him who does not know how to ask*, you must open and begin yourself. "And thou shalt tell thy son on that day, saying: It is because of that which the Lord did for me when I came forth out of Egypt" (*Exodus* 13:8).[9]

The asking of questions became so essential to this pedagogy that the liturgy for Passover eve was built around four questions that are mandatory even if it might be supposed that all present know the answers. The *Mishnah* (*Pesachin* 10:4) prescribes that the son asks his father, just as depicted in the Bible. Current practice is that the youngest child asks. However, if only husband and wife are present, the wife asks the questions; and if one is alone, he or she must read them. "Even two scholars who know the laws of Passover ask one another the questions" (*Pesachin*, 116a).

The dialogue of the Passover *Seder* is illustrative of the entire Rabbinic pedagogic tradition. The whole of the Talmud is built around the *shaklia vetaria* — give and take — of asking questions and positing answers among students and teachers.[10] Indeed, the idea that Torah study should be conducted in a dialogue of questions and responses became so rooted in the Rabbinic

---

[9]Nahum N. Glatzer, ed., *The Passover Haggadah* (New York: Schocken Books, 1979), 29-35. Note that the biblical translations in the *Midrash* follow Glatzer's translation rather than the new JPS version used above.

[10]See, for example, David Halivni, *Midrash, Mishnah, and Gemara: The Jewish Predilection for Justified Law* (Cambridge, MA:

Harvard University Press, 1986), Michael Fishbane, ed. *The Midrashic Imagination: Jewish Exegesis, Thought, and History* (New York: State University of New York Press, 1993), and H.A. Alexander, *The Critical Temple in Judaism* (Los Angles, CA: University of Judaism Occasional Papers, 1985).

tradition that when the eleventh century scholar, Rabbi Solomon Yitzhaki (Rashi) wrote his classical Bible commentary, he assumed that the questions were understood. His job was to supply answers.[11]

In addition, both the *Midrash* the Mishnah show a sensitivity to the developmental and intellectual circumstances of those who ask. The simple question is taken no less seriously than the intelligent one, and even the so-called wicked (I prefer "rebellious") child is afforded a response. Indeed, the *Mishnah* (*Pesahim* 10:4) teaches that if children do not know how to ask the Passover questions, their parents are to teach them, and the answer is to be given according to their abilities.

The point to be emphasized is that parents and teachers are not expected to invent this dialogical pedagogy out of whole cloth. Rather, *when we take seriously the questions our children and students ask, we are acting in the image of God.* Dialogue is the essence to the divine human encounter. God models this dialogical pedagogy, for example, when Abraham hears of plans to destroy the cities of Sodom and Gomorrah because their sinfulness. Abraham asks God: "Will You sweep away the innocent along with the guilty? Shall not the judge of all the earth deal justly?" (*Genesis* 18:22, 25) Each time Abraham asks if the city can be saved for some number of innocent people — 50, 45, 40, 30, 20, ten — God responds that He will not destroy the city for the sake of so many innocents.

Moses also questions God, challenging the Divine to live up to God's own principles and promises. When God's anger seethes after the Israelites have betrayed Him by worshiping a golden calf, God seeks to destroy the whole people as He had done to all of humankind in the generation of Noah, but Moses intervenes (*Exodus* 32:11-14):

Let not Your anger, O Lord, blaze forth against Your people, whom you delivered from the land of Egypt with great power and with a mighty hand. Let not the Egyptians say 'It was with evil intent that He delivered them, only to kill them off in the mountains and annihilate them from the face of the earth.' Turn from your blazing anger, and renounce the plan to punish Your people. Remember your servants, Abraham, Isaac, and Jacob, how you swore to them by Your Self and said to them: I will make your offspring as numerous as the stars of the heaven.

God responds to Moses' entreaties as God did to Abraham, "And the Lord renounced the punishment He had planned to bring upon His people" (*Exodus* 32:14).

The biblical God is also aware of the situational needs of those who receive revelation. "I am the Lord," God said to Moses (*Exodus* 6:2-3), "I appeared to Abraham, Isaac, and Jacob as *El Shaddai*, but I did not make Myself known to them by my name YHWH." To know one's name in the Bible is to grasp one's essential nature. For God to be revealed by one name to the Patriarchs and by another to Moses and Aaron suggests that God discloses aspects of divinity according to the needs of the recipient.

Caring and Covenant

A second aspect of this pedagogy worth noting is that it is grounded in love. "You must love the Lord your God with all your heart and with all your soul and with all your might. (*Deuteronomy* 6:5)" The form of this passage is perplexing. We are commanded to love God. But can one love on command? Can love be rooted in coercive power and uncompromising obligation? An answer to these queries lies in the fact that this command must be understood in the context of a covenental relationship between God and the Israelites. Put differently, *divine pedagogy is not only dialogical, it is also relational.* The command

---

[11]See Ezra Zion Melamed, *Bible Commentaries* (Jerusalem: The Magnes Press, 1978), 353-448, and Chaim Pearl, *Rashi* (New York: Grove Press, 1988), 24-62.

to love God should be understood as responding to God's caring, which is offered first, like that of a parent or a teacher.[12]

The redemption and revelation were unsolicited acts of love that preceded the expectation of reciprocity. God's love is not calculated or utilitarian. It is unconditional and spontaneous. "It is not because you are the most numerous of peoples that the Lord set His heart on you and chose you," wrote the Deuteronomist (7:7-8), "indeed, you are the smallest of peoples; but it was because the Lord loved you." We are expected to love God much as a child loves her parents, or a student his teacher, because we have received unsolicited and unconditional love that confirms our very worth, even when we feel ourselves to be unworthy.

The Rabbinic morning liturgy captures this sentiment beautifully in its introduction to the *"Shema"*:

> With great love hast thou loved us, Lord our God; great and abundant mercy hast thou bestowed upon us. Our Father our King, for the sake of our forebears who trusted in thee, whom thou didst teach laws of life, be gracious to us, teach us likewise. Our Father, merciful Father, thou who art ever compassionate, have pity on us and inspire us to understand and discern, to perceive, learn, and teach, to observe, do, and fulfill gladly all the teachings of thy Torah; attach our hearts to thy commandments; unite our heart to love and reverence thy name, so that we may never be put to shame.[13]

The point is repeated in the evening service with greater emphasis on Israel's reply. God has demonstrated God's concern for Israel by the gift of Torah. In response, Israel is obliged to receive that gift and reciprocate by adhering to divine instruction and observing the commandments:

Thou hast loved the house of Israel thy peo-

ple with everlasting love; thou hast taught us Torah and precepts, laws and judgments. Therefore, Lord our God, when we lie down and when we rise up we will speak of thy laws and rejoice in the words of thy Torah and in thy precepts evermore. Indeed, they are our life and the length of our days; we will meditate on them day and night.[14]

OBLIGATION AND AUTHORITY

It is important to understand the nature of the obligation implied in this relational context. God's authority is not coercive as is often supposed. Whether or not God could force the Israelites to observe the commandments, God chooses not to do so because to enforce compliance externally would be to deny the very idea of Torah as both law and instruction. Maimonides clarified this when he explained why freedom of will on the part of each human is a prerequisite for any law or instruction:

> . . . the human species had become unique, there being no other species like it in the following respect, namely, that man of himself and by the exercise of his own reason knows what is good and what is evil and there is none who can prevent him from doing that which is good or that which is evil . . . . This doctrine is an important principle of the Torah and the commandments, as it is said, "See, I set before you this day life and good, and death and evil" (*Deuteronomy* 30:15); and again it is written, "Behold, I set before you today a blessing and a curse" (ibid. 11:26) . . . If God had decreed that a person should be either righteous or wicked, or if there were some force inherent in his nature which irresistibly drew him to a particular course . . . how could the Almighty have charged us through his prophets: "Do this and not that, improve your ways, do not follow your

---

[12]In Hebrew, the word for parent and teacher share a common root with the word "Torah." They are related to teaching or instruction.

[13]Philip Birnbaum, trans., *The Daily Prayer Book* (New York: Hebrew Publishing Co., 1997), 76.

[14]Ibid., 192.

wicked impulses," when from the beginning of his existence his destiny had already been decreed, or his innate constitution irresistibly drew him to that from which he could not set himself free. What room would there be for the whole Torah?[15]

God's authority is not coercive but moral, born of an ongoing relationship with Israel. Parker Palmer points out that we often confuse coercive power with moral authority. But the two are not the same:

> Power works from the outside in, but authority works from the inside out. We are mistaken when we seek authority outside ourselves . . . This view of teaching turns the teacher into a cop on the corner, trying to keep things moving amicably and by consent but always having recourse to the coercive power of the law . . . . Authority is granted to people perceived as *authoring* their own words, their own actions, their own lives, rather than playing a scripted role at great remove from their own hearts. When teachers depend on the coercive power of law or technique, they have no authority at all.[16]

Exercising coercive power is a good way to loose authority. This is why parents or teachers who engage in power struggles with their children or students, have already lost. When we resort to coercive power, we leave children with little choice but to rebel in order to exercise their own autonomy and forge their own identities. On the other hand, moral authority grows, in Franz Rosenzweig's words, as a "power from within,"[17] or to use Thomas Green's terminology, in the educational formation of conscience.[18]

Because it is cultivated from within, moral authority is fostered in the context of relationships in which feelings are shaped by the caring of one person for another. Martin Buber notes that relation calls for reciprocity. "One should not try to dilute the meaning of relation," he writes, "relation is reciprocity."[19] This does not mean, however, that every participant in relation plays the same role. Clearly, God's position as teacher of Israel creates an asymmetric relationship. As with any caretaker, God's caring for Israel does not call for an equivalent act of caring toward God by Israel in return. It calls for another kind of response that is appropriate to the one cared-for.

By teaching Torah, God sets us free to become who we might be, who we ought to be. Torah offers a framework — a vision of the good — within which it becomes possible to formulate ideals to live by. *Mitzvot* come to speak with Rosenzweig's "inner power" or Green's voice of conscience when Israel as one cared for reciprocates God's love with its own. By seeking — often struggling — to discover our best selves within the context of the ideals set forth in divine instruction, we acknowledge and confirm God's love. In response, God delights in our achievements. Just as the student reaffirms the relation with the teacher when he/she learns what is being taught, every commandment that we fulfill reaffirms the covenant God made with Israel at Sinai.

TEACHING AND TRAINING

As we have seen from the emphasis on dialogue and questioning, this by no means implies blind or unthinking acceptance of God's commandments. Indeed, it is hard to imagine how one could internalize any teaching mechanically, without the investment of intelligent understanding. For a teaching to become mine, for me to "own it," I must understand it and be

[15]Moses Maimonides, "Laws Concerning Repentance," in Isadore Twersky, *A Maimonides Reader* (New York: Behrman House, 1989), 77-78.

[16]Parker L. Palmer, *The Courage to Teach: Examining the Inner Landscape of a Teacher's Life* (San Francisco, CA: Jossey-Bass Publishers, 1988), 32-33.

[17]Franz Rosenzweig, *On Jewish Learning* (New York: Schocken Books, 1965), 72-92.

[18]Thomas F. Green, *Voices: The Educational Formation of Conscience* (Notre Dame University Press, 1999).

[19]Martin Buber, *I and Thou*, Walter Kaufman, trans. (New York: Charles Scribner's Sons, 1970), 60.

able to adopt it, interpret it, and apply it according to the circumstances I face. This is the very essence of Rabbinic hermeneutics.

The idea that God intended for us to follow Torah blindly is antithetical to the very meaning of divine authority as conceived here. Hence, "the classical doctrine *na-aseh v'nishmah,* "We will do and (then) understand" *(Exodus* 24:7) is not best understood as preferring mindless practice to religious understanding. Rather it asserts that . . . the trusting relationship between God and God's students calls ultimately for understanding based on learning rather than blind obedience."[20]

This is not to say, of course, that there is no role for rote learning in divine pedagogy. On the contrary, the *"Shema"* states clearly that its precepts are to be recited, even if they are not understood, night and day, at home and away. The role of such rote recitation in this connection can be explained in light of distinctions between unintelligent and intelligent behavior and belief, training and teaching, and mechanical and genuine learning.[21]

Unintelligent behaviors and beliefs are mechanical. To do or believe them, we need not form intentions, make decisions, attribute or interpret meaning, or draw conclusions. On the other hand, *intelligent* behaviors and beliefs require us to do one or more of these mental acts. Our heart beats mechanically, but feelings of love or anguish require interpretation and understanding. Spelling is routine, writing poetry intelligent.

We *train* people to behave and believe mechanically, but *teach* them to do so intelligently. We train students to count, but teach them to do algebra; we train them to recite the alphabet, but teach them to read. Teaching, in other words, always involves mental activity — forming intentions, making decisions, attributing or interpreting meaning, or drawing conclusions. It requires an attempt to communicate understanding to a student. Teaching entails intelligence.

Mechanical or rote learning is generally accomplished by means of training. Since training requires little understanding, no investment of will or mind is required on the part of the trainee to get the point. Training can fail, but the trainer always has the option of external control — reward, punishment, manipulation of the environment — to produce the desired behavior.

Genuine learning, on the other hand, requires the sort of understanding associated with teaching. For this reason, teaching and learning always involve the risk of failure. The student can miss the point. If he/she chooses not to learn, or lacks sufficient preparation or capacity, he/she can get it wrong. Teaching and genuine learning entail the possibility of criticism.[22]

Because it involves understanding, teaching is a moral activity, not in the sense that it entails a particular ethical doctrine, but in the sense that it empowers students to make moral choices more intelligently on their own. Genuine learning is likewise a moral activity; it involves acquiring the skills necessary for moral decision making.

In contrast, training is not a moral issue; it is mechanical and does not require the sort of understanding necessary for moral discourse. Although the line between them is not always easy to discern, teaching often relies on prior training in order to achieve the desired understanding. To do algebra, one must be able to count; to read, one must know the alphabet.

[20]H.A. Alexander, "Teaching Theology in Conservative Ideology: Historical Judaism and the Concept of Education," *Conservative Judaism* 49,4 (1006), 52. See also H.A. Alexander, "On the Possibility of Teaching Theology," *Panorama: International Journal of Comparative Religious Education and Values* 7,2 (1995).

[21]See H.A. Alexander, *Reclaiming Goodness: Education and the Spiritual Quest* (Notre Dame: University of Notre Dame Press, 2000).

[22]See Thomas F. Green, *The Activities of Teaching* (New York: McGraw Hill, 1971). Also H.A. Alexander, "What Is the Power of Jewish Education: Lipset's Analysis in Philosophical Perspective?" in Seymour Martin Lipset, *The Power of Jewish Education* (Los Angeles, CA: Wilstein Institute of Jewish Policy Studies, 1994).

When training leads to teaching, it participates in the process of moral development.

However, if training continues when teaching is in order, it is sometimes called indoctrination; for instead of empowering students with the capacity to act independently on the basis of their own understanding, we continue to require unintelligent, mechanical responses. Under these conditions the process of moral development is thwarted. Indoctrination is an a-moral activity because it undermines the capacity of students to act as responsible moral agents.[23]

The rote recitation called for in the *"Shema"* can be understood as a form of religious training that is an important step on the road to understanding divine teaching. It, therefore, enables us to receive and reciprocate God's love through the observance of *Mitzvot*. The danger lies, however, in the possibility that the instructional process never moves beyond training to teaching. In such an instance, God's loving Torah is transformed into religious indoctrination. This is an anathema to God as a student and teacher of moral vision, for training without teaching — indoctrination — undermines the very intelligence and free will upon which moral responsibility relies.

REWARD AND PUNISHMENT

With love and relationship comes disappointment, anger, and consequences. As in all relationships, the parties do not always do what is expected of them. Israel does not always keep God's commandments. The Rabbis emphasize this point in the citation from *Deuteronomy* (11:13-17), which they chose to accompany the first paragraph of the *"Shema"*:

> If, then, you obey the commandments that I enjoin upon you this day, loving the Lord your God and serving Him with all your heart and soul, I will grant rain for your land in season, the early rain and the late; you

shall gather in your new grain and wine and oils, and I will provide grass in the fields for your cattle, thus you shall eat your fill. Take care not to be lured away to serve other gods and bow to them. For the Lord's anger will flare up against you, and He will shut up the skies so that there will be no rain and the ground will not yield its produce; and you will soon perish from the good land that the Lord is giving you.

This passage is often understood in terms of a simplistic conception of reward and punishment. If we do God's will, we will be rewarded, and if not, there will be a price to pay. However, consider the relational context of which we have been speaking. God has undertaken to care for Israel as a teacher, and the people has understood that this calls for a reciprocal obligation to follow divine instruction. God's anger is not best understood as that of a dictator who has been disobeyed. Only a morally weak and insecure God would be riled at the defiance of so minuscule a people. It is the ineffective teacher indeed whose emotions are so easily aroused by his/her students.

According to an alternative reading, God's anger is not that of an insecure despot. It is rather that of a caring but disappointed teacher. God is stung by the rejection of the one cared for, and recognizes that the path of other gods leads naturally to a self-destructive course. In this interpretation, reward is viewed as a natural consequences of the path of Torah, which affirms life, freedom, and the possibility of goodness. Punishment, on the other hand, follows from the self-destructive behaviors that flow from viewing human conduct as determined by history, society, chemistry, or fate.

God does not seek to impose the commandments on Israel by means of external rewards and punishments. This would confuse coercive power with moral authority. God's aim, rather, is to internalize the *Mitzvot* so that they can be-

---

[23]H.A. Alexander, "Teaching Religion," *Religious Education* 89,1 (1994), 4-7.

come the inner ideals from which Jewish identity is formed. Thus, the Deuteronomist continues (11:18-21):

> Therefore impress these My words upon your very heart[24]: bind them as a sign on your hand and let them serve as a symbol on your forehead, and teach them to your children — reciting them, when you stay at home and when you are away, when you lie down and when you get up; and inscribe them on the doorposts of your house on your gates — to the end that you and your children may endure, in the land that the Lord swore to your fathers to give them, as long as there is a heaven over the earth.

Does not this consequentialist account of reward and punishment conflict with the Ten Commandments? Consider the third commandment *(Exodus* 19:5-6, *Deuteronomy* 5:9-10) which is also repeated when God reveals the 13 divine attributes to Moses *(Exodus* 34:6-7): "I the Lord your God am an impassioned God, visiting the guilt of the fathers upon the children, upon the third and upon the fourth generations of those who reject me, but showing kindness to the thousandth generation of those who love me and keep my commandments."

This passage can be read as God punishing children for the sins of their parents. However, this contradicts the entire biblical thrust of self-determination and moral responsibility. As the Deuteronomist put it, "Parents shall not be put to death for children, nor children be put to death for parents, a person shall be put to death only for his own crime. (24:16)"[25] Consider an alternative account. It is well known that families governed by anger and hate create patterns of compulsion and abuse that carry on from one generation to the next. Children of parents who abuse substances such as drugs, alcohol, or food,

tend themselves to be substance abusers; and the sons and daughters of parents who abuse their children are at much greater risk than the norm of themselves becoming child abusers. The pain and suffering of those whose lives are grounded in hate is a natural consequence of that hatred, and it is transmitted from one generation to the next — at least until the third and fourth generations.

However, the God of Torah teaches not enslavement to compulsion or caprice, but freedom grounded in self-control and personal responsibility. So, for example, divine instruction places limits on dietary consumption and sexual pleasure which have the capacity to take control of our lives, and enjoins us to rest on the seventh day so that we do not become slaves to our labors. To love God, on this account, is to live within a communal and moral framework that enables the freedom to become our best selves. The natural consequence of reciprocating God's caring with a tender embrace of the commandments is a love that outlasts hate by nearly a thousand generations.

DIVINE FALLIBILITY

We are accustomed to thinking of God in terms of absolutes: omniscience, omnipotence, omnipresence, benevolence, as Anselm of Canterbury put it, "that than which a greater cannot be conceived."[26] Yehuda Halevi refers to this as the God of the philosophers. Halevi points out that the God of Abraham, Isaac, and Jacob (to whom we should add Sarah, Rebecca, Rachel, and Leah) is not an abstract concept, but a living being Who strives to teach a moral path.[27] The biblical and Rabbinic deity is not a perfect, but a learning and teaching God. God models in deeds the very behaviors the Torah expresses in words. Since these are fundamentally moral activities,

---

[24]Literally, "heart and self."

[25]See Ezekiel 18.

[26]Anselm of Canterbury, *Prosologian*, in John H. Hick and Arthur E. McGill, *The Many Faced Argument* (New York: Macmillan, 1967), 3-8.

[27]Yehuda Halevi, *The Kuzari*, in Hans Levy, Alexander Altman, and Isaak Heineman, eds. *Three Jewish Philosophers* (Philadelphia, PA: Jewish Publication Society, 1961), 113-121.

God as student and teacher is a moral agent; and moral agency requires fallibility.

The fallibility inherent in moral agency follows from the requirement of free will. If I am to be held responsible for my actions, it must be supposed that I am the agent of those actions. It must be me who decided to enact them and who, in fact, caused them to happen. If the behaviors in question are the consequence of some other agent, say the gods, or my chemistry, or the forces of history, or the society in which I grew up, or the culture whose values I inherited, or the family in which I was raised, then it is not I, but these other agents who are accountable for my behavior.

If this were the case, as Maimonides points out, why bother with moral instruction altogether, since it is not I who requires instruction, but the gods, or my chemistry, history, society, culture, or family.[28] The very idea of moral discourse is predicated on the fact that I, and not these other forces, am the agent of my actions; and so it is I who should be called to account when these actions have missed the mark.

But what if I were infallible? Suppose that it was part of my very nature, inherent in the logic — so to speak — of my essence, that I could make no moral error. In that case, it would not be I who was the agent of my actions, but "my very nature" or "the logic of my essence." This is no different than supposing that the gods, or chemistry, or history, or society, or culture, or family determine my actions. In this case, it is the "logic of my very nature" that does the determining; and it is this logic or nature that needs to be addressed in order to affect a change in behavior. Moreover, if this is a necessary nature — if it could not be otherwise — then change would be impossible. For me to be a moral agent, I must be capable of behaving badly and of changing my behavior. This is why I can benefit from instruction in goodness. If

God as student and teacher is a moral agent, therefore, God, too, must be fallible. The Hebrew Bible is full of examples of divine fallibility. This God admits mistakes, such as flooding the world; God argues with humans, such as Abraham; God changes course, as in the case of Sodom and Gomorrah: God gets frustrated and angry; as in the case of the golden calf; and God relates to people, sometimes as with Moses, even face to face. Why would a God who was all-knowing and all-powerful make a mistake, or change course, or argue, or get angry? Why would such a God not create a world as perfect as God is?[29]

Divine fallibility does not follow only from the logic of moral agency, however, but from other aspects of divine pedagogy as well. First, a learning God, as Simon Rawidowicz points out, "indicates want, a need to fill a gap, a desire to improve one's mind, to widen one's understanding, to make up for deficiencies, to free one's self from ignorance."[30] Rawidowicz emphasizes the intellectual deficiencies implied by a learning God, but moral inadequacies are equally important. A learning God implies the desire to improve one's ways in addition to one's mind, to broaden one's capacity to care for others based on wider and deeper understanding, to free one's self not only from ignorance but also from wrongdoing.

Moreover, if God is all-knowing, then it would not be possible for students to discover anything new. There would be no reason to challenge or question God as teacher, because it would be supposed that God had the truth in God's pocket. There could be no genuine dialogue between teacher and student under these circumstances, nor any real relationship. Questions could only be for purposes of clarification, never discovery; and no form of reciprocity would be possible since there is nothing God requires in return from the learner.

[28]Moses Maimonides, "Laws Concerning Repentance," in *A Maimonides Reader* by Isadore Twersky (New York: Behrman House, 1989), 77-78.

[29]H.A. Alexander, "Teaching Theology in Conservative Ideology: Historical Judaism and the Concept of Education," *Conservative Judaism* 48, 4 (1996).

[30]Simon Rawidowicz, *Israel: The Ever-Dying People*, 135.

Faith in God as a teacher grows . . . not merely as a conclusion to an argument, but also as a product of sustained learning, of real engagement between teacher and student. The biblical term for faith, *emunah*, is better translated as faithfulness or trust. To have such trust in a teacher is not a cognitive state alone, but an emotional one as well. For such a trusting relationship to be real, God as teacher must be fallible, so that God's students can become genuinely independent learners without artifice.[31]

A THEOLOGY OF TEACHING

Thomas Green has argued that teaching is a norm, rather *than* a rule governed activity. Rules, on this account, are mechanical principles that dictate proper practice with limited flexibility. They require little understanding on the part of teachers, and when properly implemented, produce outcomes that can be explained by the statistical generalizations upon which they are based. Norms, on the other hand, are intelligent guides to practice that are rooted in traditions of educational and moral thought rather than experimental laws. Whereas rules provide explanations of student behavior caused by particular teaching techniques, norms provide reasons upon which teachers decide to pursue one course of action rather than another. Teaching, in this view, relies more on traditions of pedagogy than on the behavioral sciences.[32]

A theology in which the metaphor of God as teacher is taken seriously can be understood as the basis for a significant tradition in which to ground the norms of teaching. God, in this theology, is the ultimate role model who enacts in deeds the words of God's Torah. God's pedagogy is not didactic, but dialogical, in which questions are encouraged, challenges embraced, and discovery is possible. God's relationship with the student is that of one caring, in which instruction in a vision of the good life is lovingly offered.

The appropriate response from the one cared for is to endeavor to discover one's best self — the person one was meant to be — within the communal and moral framework provide by God's Torah. Although this response relies on training and mechanical learning at the outset, it must strive to transform this training into an understanding of God's teaching that can be owned by students and internalized as a voice of conscience speaking with the inner power of moral authority.

The rewards of adopting this way of life are a natural consequence of the fulfillment we feel when we recognize that we are free to achieve our potential. The punishment of following other gods is a result of the frustration and rage we experience when our independence is thwarted and our potential denied. To transmit this message, God as teacher must be a good, not a perfect being, who is able to teach us by example how to learn from our mistakes, turn away from our anger, and return to the right path.

When we follow this model, we realize that what each of us thinks and does matters. The directions of our lives are not determined by external forces outside of our control, but by decisions we make and values we embrace. If we make the wrong decisions, we can learn from our mistakes, we can change, we can redirect ourselves to a new and better course. We can take hold of our lives in this way because we experience the confirmation of God's caring; and when we do so, we demonstrate our own love for God by embracing God's teaching and reconfirming our covenant with God. The Rabbis called this process *teshuvah*, or repentance. That we can learn from our mistakes and chart the course of our own lives is probably the most radical of all Jewish ideas. It is a precondition for any coherent account of teaching and learning, and should stand at the heart of all educational theory.

---

[31] H.A. Alexander, "Teaching Theology in Conservative Ideology: Historical Judaism and the Concept of Education," *Conservative Judaism* 48, 4 (1996).

[32] Thomas F. Green, "Teaching, Acting, and Behaving," *Harvard Educational Review* 34,4 (1964): 416-446.

IMPLICATIONS

1. *B'tzelem Elohim*, being created in the image of God, implies that being a teacher is an important God-like activity. Therefore, both study and teaching are holy acts.

2. Traditional sources give us an indication of how one is to be a teacher by considering the relationship between God and the people.

3. The principles of educational practice that God models include: learning through both words and actions; facilitating learning through use of dialogue and inquiry; grounding teaching in caring, covenant, obligation, and authority; distinguishing between teaching and training and using them appropriately; using reward and punishment; and being willing to make mistakes and asking for forgiveness.

4. God's authority is not coercive, but a moral authority which similarly should apply to teachers.

QUESTIONS FOR CRITICAL INQUIRY

1. In what ways has God been a teacher to our forebearers? In what ways has God been your teacher?

2. What makes study a holy act?

3. Is being a learner a holy act? Why? How is that related to teaching being a holy act?

4. Think about your own Jewish education, what has been the role of dialogue? inquiry? love? How does this agree with or differ from Alexander's views?

5. Alexander identifies principles of educational practice that God models: learning through both words and actions; facilitating learning through using dialogue and inquiry; grounding teaching in caring, covenant, obligation, and authority; distinguishing between teach-

ing and training and using them appropriately; using reward and punishment; and being willing to make mistakes and asking for forgiveness. What would it mean for you to follow these principles of educational practice? How would you have to change your style to fulfill these principles?

ACTIVITIES

1. Think of a favorite teacher. Using the 13 attributes of God found in *Exodus* 34:6-7 (also found in the prayer book in the Torah service on *chagim*), write about how your teacher is/was like God. For example, my teacher showed her godliness by being long suffering and endlessly patient as she prodded me and gave me the support I needed to do — and remember to turn in — my homework.

2. Write a story or poem about a great lesson that God has taught you.

3. Looking through the Bible, find examples of times when God acts as a teacher. Identify the main characteristics that God shows as a teacher and describe what God teaches. For example, at the end of Jonah's travails, he rests in a booth in the shade of the gourd, then complains to God when the gourd dies. God teaches Jonah through a life experience. Using an analogy, he teaches about the importance of caring and forgiving.

BIBLIOGRAPHY

Alexander, H. A. "Education." in David L. Lieber, ed., *The Humash: A Conservative Commentary.* Philadelphia, PA and New York: The Jewish Publication Society and the Rabbinical Assembly, 2001.

An appendix to the new Conservative commentary on the Pentateuch that examines the relation between education and the good in the Hebrew Bible.

———. "A Jewish View of Human Learning." *The International Journal of Children's Spirituality*, forthcoming.

This article explores how the Bible views the process of initiation into a community of meaning and memory.

———. *Reclaiming Goodness: Education and the Spiritual Quest*. Fort Wayne, IN: University of Notre Dame Press, 2000.

This book explores the relation between spirituality and education in democratic society. It develops a theology of education in which God is viewed as a loving parent and teacher.

———. "Teaching Religion." *Religious Education* 89, 1 (1994), pp. 4-7.

An editorial to an issue of *Religious Education* on the theme of "teaching" that explores the role of critical thinking in religious education.

———. *The Critical Temper in Judaism*. Los Angeles, CA: University of Judaism Occasional Papers, 1985.

A monograph exploring the role of critical thinking in Jewish tradition.

———. "Teaching Theology in Conservative Ideology: Historical Judaism and the Concept of Education." *Conservative Judaism* 48, 4 (1996), 35-52.

This article asks whether ideology can be taught and develops a non-indoctrinary way of thinking about Jewish theology and education.

———. "On the Possibility of Teaching Theology." *Panorama: International Journal of Comparative Religious Education and Values* 7, 1 (1995), 83-93.

This essay asks whether an authoritarian concept of God can be taught and develops a non-indoctrinary biblical theology. A different version of this essay has appeared in the *Journal of Beliefs and Values* 22:1 (2001), 5-17.

———. "What Is the Power of Jewish Education." In Seymour Martin Lipset, *The Power of Jewish Education*. Los Angeles, CA: The Wilstein Institute of Jewish Policy Studies, 1994.

This introduction to a monograph by sociologist Seymour Lipset argues that there is a conceptual link between Jewish education and continuity.

Birnbaum, Philip, ed. *The Daily Prayer Book*. New York: Hebrew Publishing Company, 1997.

A standard edition and translation of the traditional Jewish prayer book based on modern scholarship.

Buber, Martin. *I and Thou*. Walter Kaufman, trans. New York: Charles Scribner's Sons, 1970.

Buber's classic discussion of human relations as a basis for knowledge and theology.

Fishbane, Michael. *The Midrashic Imagination: Jewish Exegesis, Thought, and History*. New York: State University of New York Press, 1993.

A compendium of research on the role of *Midrash* in Jewish thought and history, edited by a leading contemporary Bible scholar.

Gillman, Neil, *Sacred Fragments: Recovering Theology for the Modern Jew*. Philadelphia, PA: Jewish Publication Society, 1990.

This clear and accessible summary of Jewish theology argues that God can be understood by interpreting our theological metaphors and symbols.

Glatzer, Nahum. *The Passover Haggadah*. New York: Schocken Books, 1979.

A clear translation of this classical Rabbinic text based on modern scholarship, with excellent notes connecting the *Haggadah* to Rabbinic sources.

Green, Thomas F. "Teaching, Acting, and Behaving." *Harvard Educational Review* 34, 4 (1964).

An early essay by a leading philosopher of education that explains the intelligent and creative aspects of teaching.

———. The Activities of Teaching. New York: McGraw Hill, 1971.

A classic of analytic educational philosophy that explores the logic and wonder of teaching.

———. *Voices: The Educational Formation of Conscience.* Fort Wayne, IN: University of Notre Dame Press, 1999.

The most recent contribution of this preeminent educational thinker that reconsiders the concepts of conscience and norm acquisition in moral education. Of particular interest is Green's critique of the concept of values.

Halevy, Yehuda. "The Kuzari." In Hans Levy, Alexander Altman, and Isaak Heineman. eds., *Three Jewish Philosophers.* Philadelphia, PA: The Jewish Publication Society, 1961.

This classic of medieval Jewish thought posits that the God of the philosophers is not the same as the historical God of Abraham, Isaac, and Jacob.

Halivni, David. *Midrash, Mishna, Germara: The Jewish Predilection for Justified Law.* Cambridge, MA: Harvard University Press, 1986.

Written by one of the foremost Talmudists of our time, this book explains how Rabbinic ideas are justified through a process of questions and answers.

Hick, John. *The Many Faced Argument.* New York: Macmillan, 1967.

Edited by a leading philosopher of religion, this collection of theological essays asks whether God's existence follows from divine perfection.

Kadushin, Max. *Worship and Ethics: A Study in Rabbinic Judaism.* New York: Bloch Publishing, 1963.

Kadushin argues that Rabbinic worship transmits ethical concepts through metaphors, symbols, and rituals.

Melamed, Ezra Zion. *Bible Commentaries.* Jerusalem: The Magnes Press, 1978.

A Hebrew review of methods used by medieval Rabbis to interpret the Bible.

Noddings, Nel. *Caring: A Feminine Approach To Ethics and Moral Education.* Berkeley, CA: University of California Press, 1984.

A classic of feminist ethics that is heavily influenced by Martin Buber by a leading philosopher of education.

Palmer, Parker. *The Courage to Teach: Examining the Inner Landscape of a Teacher's Life.* San Francisco, CA: Jossey-Bass, 1998.

A personal exploration of the inner life of a teacher written in a graceful, poetic style.

Pearl, Chaim. *Rashi.* New York: Grove Press, 1988.

A popular introduction to the eleventh century giant of Franco-German Jewish scholarship, Rabbi Shlomo Yitzhaki.

Rawidowicz, Simon. *Israel: The Ever-Dying People and Other Essays*, B.C.I. Ravid, ed. Rutherford, NJ: Farleigh Dickinson University Press, 1986.

A collection of essays by a pioneer of contemporary Jewish scholarship who understands the Rabbinic deity as a learning God.

Rosenzweig, Franz. *On Jewish Learning.* New York: Schocken, 1965.

A collection of short essays on Jewish education by this influential German Jewish existentialist philosopher which argue — contra-Buber — that God can be encountered in Jewish ritual.

Tillich, Paul. *Dynamics of Faith.* New York: Harper Torchbooks, 1957.

An important work of modern existentialist theology that understands faith in terms of an ultimate concern that entails doubt.

Twersky, Isadore. *A Maimonides Reader.* New York: Behrman House, 1989.

A collection of the most essential legal and philosophical writings of Maimonides, translated and edited by today's leading Maimonides scholars.

CHAPTER 25

A SPIRITUALITY FOR JEWISH TEACHERS: WORKING WITH GOD, FOR GOD, AND THROUGH GOD

Jeffrey K. Salkin

WHILE WALKING THROUGH A NEIGHBORING VILLAGE one night, the Rebbe met a man who was also walking alone. For a while, the two walked together in silence. Finally, the Rebbe turned to the man and asked, "So, who do you work for?" "I work for the village," the man answered. "I'm the night watchman." They continued on in silence.

Finally, the night watchman turned to the Rebbe and asked, "And who do you work for?" The Rebbe answered, "I'm not always sure. But this I will tell you. Name your present salary and I will double it. All you have to do is walk with me and ask me, from time to time, "Who do you work for?" (Buber, 1948, p. 93).

Many of us ask ourselves the same question. We work hard. We know our job title, we know our job description, we know who our boss is (if you're a Rabbi or a Jewish educator there may be a thousand bosses, or at least it seems so). But the unfinished, barely begun spiritual task of our time is this: We want know for Whom we really work.

The word for "work" in Hebrew is *avodah*. The word for "worship" in Hebrew is also *avodah*. Most of us feel a distance between these two realms. Our work is one thing; spirituality is another. We lead fragmented lives. There is the Monday to Friday piece. And then, we Jews who come to synagogue on Shabbat have the Friday/ Saturday piece. We keep two file folders for our reality. We do our best to keep religion insulated from the rest of our life and the rest of the week. But as a Baptist preacher once said: "A religion that ain't good on Monday, also ain't much good on Sunday," or Saturday.

The author John Updike is reported to have said: "We may live well, but that cannot ease the suspicion that we no longer live nobly." We want to live nobly. And to live nobly is to know that there is more to life than just working and getting and spending and consuming. We yearn for something deeper and higher. We long, many of us, for that great intangible that religion can and should and traditionally does offer.

Every question about ultimate meaning is a religious question. To paraphrase the Jewish theologian, Franz Rosenzweig, "Religion has to be smuggled into life" (Rosenzweig, 1965). Religion also has to be smuggled into our work, even perhaps especially, into our work as Jewish educators. The original meaning of "career" is "that which you carry." What spiritual meanings do we, as Jewish educators, carry into the world?

Let us consider the "big three" of Jewish spirituality — creation, revelation, and redemption. Where does the Jewish teacher find a "home" within these rubrics?

CREATION

I have always believed that the imitation of God — doing what God does — is the highest and headiest form of imitation. This principle often underlines Jewish ritual. Consider: One interpretation given for lighting two candles on Shabbat is that we light one for the sun and one for the moon. We remember that God created the two great lights of the heavens, and so, at that moment, our hands become the hands of God.

The highest form of God — imitation is creativity. As God creates, so do we create. It is true of artists, composers, and architects. It is also true of the Jewish teacher. How do we imitate God's creativity in our work? The first thing that we Jews created for ourselves after the liberation from Egypt was the Tabernacle. Yet, God was constantly implicated in that human act. God gave explicit directions regarding its design, even to the extent of showing Moses a blueprint of how it should look. Just as God rested from the labors of creation, so, too, construction on the Tabernacle ceased on Shabbat.

To have a place to worship God, we Jews had to mimic God's creativity. According to the ancient Rabbis, God's presence dwelled among us only after we had engaged in that creative work. This was God's way of saying that the Jewish people had come of age, that we were ready to have a place for the beginning of a long and intimate conversation with God.

The chief architect of the tabernacle was Bezalel, a name which means "in the shadow of God." Jewish educators might come to see themselves as living descendants of Bezalel. The tabernacle — and ultimately, the Temple in Jerusalem — come from God's instruction to us — God's gift to us. But the synagogue is our gift to God — our way of keeping up the conversation with the Holy One even and especially after the *Churban* — the destruction of the Temple. The synagogue metaphorically is the dwelling place of the *Shechinah* on earth.

Therefore, our creativity in Jewish education — teaching, planning, and administration — is a holy act. It is (if I may coin a Yiddish term) *Bezalelkeit*. Our role can be to remind leadership that God held aloft a model of the *Mishkan* for Moses to see. The Jewish educator can — and must — point to the reflection of that model in the synagogue for which we work.

Think of what we do. The well executed lesson plans, the dynamic curricula, the planning and administration that can be so frustrating, even and especially the learning games we create (playfulness is also a sign of God's presence in the world) — all of these are earthly intimations of God's creative power working through us.

REVELATION

The next step in the Jewish spirituality of teaching is revelation — the sense that as teachers, we stand in a line of teachers that goes back to Sinai itself. It is our understanding that what we teach and say in the classroom has echoes within it of the original moment of revelation, that in our words there are sparks of the original fire of God's word.

This does not require a literal interpretation of what happened at Sinai. It merely (merely!) requires that we see ourselves as links in a chain, as those who know that our teachings do not spring forth *de novo* from our lesson plans, but that our lesson plans find their authenticity in our people's ancient voice. "Every day a voice goes out from Horeb (Sinai)" (*Brachot* 17b) — and we will hear it if we can train our ears to listen for it. How do we bring that sense of spirituality into our classrooms? Sometimes, a simple *brachah* — " . . . *la-asok b'divray Torah*" (. . . commands us to wrestle with words of Torah) — can suffice. It reminds us that our study is a matter of Divine commandment, not merely of secular studies. So, too, our sense that we are teaching Torah, Judaism, and the like, and not merely teaching *about* Torah or Judaism, connects us to the sacred.

And there is yet another way. As the Hasidic master, Rabbi Elimelekh of Lizhensk, once said, "I not only remember the moment at Sinai, I also remember who was standing next to me" (Agnon, 1994, p. 161). That's our real job description: to teach about what happened at Sinai, and to teach every Jew about who was standing next to them.

REDEMPTION

But what if our words are not yet heard or heeded? How do we, as teachers, deal with the ever present potential of burnout — struggling as we do with student apathy and parent disinterest? Here, too, the tradition has something powerful to teach us.

Why, it is asked, does the "*V'ahavta*" speak of God's words being "*al levavecha*" — upon your heart, and not "*bilvavcha*" — in your heart? Menachem Mendl of Kotsk suggests that there is a lesson about Jewish education in this. The teacher must take holy words and place them *upon* the students' hearts. The message to students is this: "Even if you feel that your heart is shut tight and words of Torah do not penetrate it, or because you are weary or inattentive or preoccupied or simply dull, do not despair. Do not cease your efforts even if you feel that your heart is securely locked against the transcendent message of the Divine. Just let the words rest upon your heart. Be confident that in due time your heart will open up, and when it does, inspiration will come. Then, all that has been gathered in, lying patiently upon your heart, will tumble into your newly opened heart . . . " As Professor Norman Lamm writes, "At that time, all previous efforts will be vindicated" (Lamm, 1998, pp. 152f.).

We can never know what it is in our work and in our daily existence that will be remembered and that will become holy. It has everything to do with the faith and the vision and the love that we bring to it. While Mother Teresa was working with people who were starving in Ethiopia during the famine of the 1980s, there were people dying all around her. "How can you tend to the sick and the dying," an interviewer is reported to have asked, "knowing that you will not be successful with everyone?" "We are not here to be *successful*," she answered. "We are here to be *faithful*."

Know that what you do survives you. During the Middle Ages, it was common to chisel on tomb stones insignias of the professions of the deceased. When people were buried, the casket was often constructed from the wooden table upon which the deceased had worked. So too, even after death, our work is part of who we are, and what we carry into eternity. We study Maimonides; his words are his immortality. We read Shakespeare or see one of his plays performed; his place in time is in them. Hearing Mozart's music means that he has, in one sense,

conquered death. So, too, with the designer of the classic Mustang, the doctor who saves lives, the lawyer who helps a defendant, the secretary who creates an efficient filing system, the architect who designs a building — all are immortal because their work survives them.

My friend who owns a bookstore told me, "Every time I recommend a book to a child, and that book had been recommended to me by Mrs. Cohen, my fourth grade teacher, that's Mrs. Cohen's immortality. That's her *"Kaddish."*

When our children sing the Sulzer *"Shema,"* that becomes his *"Kaddish."* When our children read the words of Heschel, that becomes his *"Kaddish."* Every young woman who becomes Bat Mitzvah creates a new *"Kaddish"* for Judith Kaplan Eisenstein, the first Bat Mitzvah.

I will never forget the Yizkor service last year on Shavuot. I asked everyone in the congregation to name a teacher who had influenced them. Some named public school teachers and college professors. My teacher and congregant, Professor Eugene B. Borowitz, was present at that service. He mentioned the name of the late Reform Jewish theologian Samuel Cohon. At that moment, I felt Professor Cohon's presence, though I had never met him. He was present in Professor Borowitz who in turn taught me, and . . . so it goes — that chain of immortality, that is the chain of Torah. Which is why we call it *"Torat chayim,"* the Torah of life — the Torah that guarantees that who we are and what we teach lives forever.

Whenever a departed teacher is quoted, the Sages say that his/her lips move in the grave. To be a Jewish teacher and to feel the spiritual moment is to hear the lips moving from the beyond. It is to feel the presence of our departed teachers who to this day continue to shape who we are, and continue to teach lessons through us in ways that we cannot begin to imagine.

IMPLICATIONS

1. While being a Jewish educator is a holy act, it still remains difficult to keep ourselves connected to the spiritual sacredness of what we do. In addition, it may be difficult to attend to our own spiritual needs as well as those of our students.

2. Through acts of creation, revelation, and redemption, we as educators do God's work.

3. We work for God. God is our C.E.O., even though we may have other bosses.

4. Recognizing that our work is sacred elevates what we do.

5. Since our work is sacred or holy, our tasks involve the whole of the person, his/her spiritual, emotional, intellectual, and social needs. This holiness also means that we need to view and imbue the settings, tools, and approaches that we use in educating with a sense of this sacredness.

6. Our immortality is the work that survives us.

QUESTIONS FOR CRITICAL INQUIRY

1. What is the connection that Salkin makes between *avodah* as work and worship? In what ways, do you connect the two concepts of *avodah* as work and worship in your Jewish educational practice? In what ways do the two concepts converge and diverge? How does experiencing your Jewish educational practice as *avodah* bring it into the realm of the spiritual?

2. What does Salkin suggest are the rewards for doing God's work?

3. Why don't we always feel like we are doing God's work?

4. Salkin uses Rosenweig's explicit theological categories of creation, revelation, and redemption to demonstrate ways in which he connects his work to his spiritual life. What theological concepts other than cre-ation, revelation, and redemption can be used to describe our work as holy?

5. Salkin gives examples of people whose work exemplifies each of the three categories: creation, revelation, redemption. Think about all the things you do as an educator. Which aspects mirror creation, revelation, or redemption?

6. What about this chapter do you find comforting or inspiring?

ACTIVITIES

1. Make a collage of people working for God. Did you include teachers? Why or why not? In what ways are teachers doing the work of God?

2. Draw a line down the middle of a page on a flip chart. One side represents what you consider to be God's work, and the other side represents what you do not consider to be God's work. List 20 things you did during the past year (e.g., went to school, paid taxes, tutored a child, voted). Then write each activity on your list on one side or the other of the chart. In the large group, each person explains and discusses the placement of the activities. According to Salkin, everything moral that we do is doing God's work. Discuss whether you agree with him or not.

3. Create a "Dear God" column (something like "Dear Abby") about things you do not like to do (e.g., taking out the garbage, carpooling, taking tests). Swap letters and answer the letters of one of your classmates. Share the responses.

BIBLIOGRAPHY

Agnon, S.Y. *Standing at Sinai*. Philadelphia, PA: Jewish Publication Society, 1994.

Agnon is a Nobel Laureate, and one of the great Hebrew writers.

Buber, Martin. *The Tales of the Hasidim: Later Masters*. New York: Schocken Books, 1948.

Buber was an early anthologizer of Hasidic tales. The tale cited in this chapter is ascribed to Reb Naftali of Ropschitz.

Lamm, Norman. *The Shema: Spirituality and Law in Judaism*. Philadelphia, PA: Jewish Publication Society, 1994.

This work, by one of the most highly regarded modern Orthodox Rabbis of his time, combines his understanding of God and Jewish law.

Rosenzweig, Franz. *On Jewish Learning*. Nahum N. Glatzer, ed. New York: Schocken Books, 1965.

This is a collection of Rosenzweig's writings and speeches on Jewish education and learning.

CHAPTER 26

SPIRITUAL MENTORING

Carol Ochs

INTRODUCTION

WHAT PREPARES ONE TO BE A SPIRITUAL MENTOR? Becoming a mentor begins with examining one's own spiritual journey. It comes from answering questions such as: How do I describe my relationship to God? Who has helped shaped my journey? What events in my life have contributed to my spiritual growth and development? What texts have I studied that most influenced my views?

The spiritual mentor benefits from discussing his/her own spiritual path and relationship to God with others. These discussions are the basis of practicing to help others engage in exploration of their own spiritual journeys. The discussions can revolve around Jewish texts, as well as personal experiences. Hopefully, this type of interchange with others will lead to the recognition that not all journeys nor all seekers are the same. The spiritual mentor is not leading the person on a path, but rather helping the person uncover his or her way; not shaping the person in his or her image, but rather in the image of God.

Studying Jewish texts is essential to becoming a spiritual mentor. Below I highlight the centrality of Jewish texts in encountering the holy, knowing God and ourselves, and making moral choices. The spiritual mentoring aimed for here is one that deepens, enriches, and strengthens one's connections to God and the Jewish people. Familiarity with Jewish texts will serve the mentor well as he/she tries to match Jewish texts with the issues, concerns, and questions of the seeker.

Spiritual mentoring is an art with its own techniques, theories, and experts. Many books and articles exist about spiritual growth, faith or human development, spiritual mentoring, and mentoring in general that can prepare and inform the approach that a spiritual mentor takes. These resources come from Judaism and other religious traditions, psychology, general education, and a variety of other disciplines. It is possible to identify and consult with people who are models of good spiritual mentoring. The spiritual guide can learn important lessons from all of these sources that will help improve the mentor's effectiveness.

The spiritual mentor must continue to search and seek, change and grow, and learn and question as part of his/her own spiritual quest. By doing so, the mentor can authentically speak to the seeker and act as a guide.

OUR RELATIONSHIP WITH GOD

Our relationship with God is the subject matter of spiritual mentoring. These key words — our relationship with God — are deceptively simple.

Our relationship with God: Ours. Not the Israelites' relationship with God. Not all of humanity's relationship with God. Ours. Ours alone — and yet we learn through this relationship between God and the Israelites that we are never alone. We all left Egypt. We ourselves, together, collectively as a people. We ourselves, each one of us individually, personally — in relationship with God.

Our *relationship* with God: We know about relationships. As teachers and learners, we must now apply that knowledge to God. We know that relationships require constant contact. In order for us to have a relationship with someone, we need to meet them, see them, speak to them, communicate with them — on a regular basis. If this relationship is to work, then we must not consider God as an explanatory principle, a historical idea, a cognitive construct. God has to be the God we meet in our personal journey through life. Is it really possible for an ordinary person to experience God? Yes. It is not only possible, the life of the ordinary provides the foundation for genuine religious experience. In our human relationships we can ask, "What, in addition to contact, is required for a relationship?" Martin Buber taught that our human relationships should reflect the Divine relationship we are trying to maintain (Buber, 1970, Part III). Buber described such relationship as "I-Thou" and distinguished it from superficial relationships, which he named "I-It."

Our relationship with *God*: clearly, God is not something we can ever fully understand or articulate. We can at best get only glimpses, brief insights. But each glimpse, each image must be examined and confronted. A "god-image" is one of the means through which we come to understand God. Our God images can change over time.

Focusing on our relationship to God has one aim — to bring us into closer relationship. To achieve this focus often takes help — a tutor or guide, a spiritual mentor. Spiritual mentoring is a practice between *peers*. The guide merely opens the way to the relationship between the guided and God. The guide, when most effective, simply gets out of the way and lets God's being emerge. What that feels like is effortless assurance. When spiritual guidance is done correctly, the guide has no sense of strain, no second guessing, just clarity, calmness, and confidence. After the seeker goes home, the guide may wonder how those questions came to be asked that took the seeker where the seeker needed to go. Then the guide may suddenly experience fatigue, but during the actual session there is no weariness. As with a well practiced musical recital, all the effort precedes the performance; the analysis goes on after the performance, but during the performance, there is only music.

There really is "music" when the guide, after personal practice of prayer and attentiveness, is able to be open to God's guidance during the actual session. The guide also helps the seeker recognize the many things that may obstruct the relationship. But spiritual mentorship is not psychotherapy, counseling, or judging.

TANACH AS A SPIRITUAL GUIDE

For spiritual mentoring to be *Jewish* spiritual mentoring, a basic worldview must be shared by the guide and the guided. We are committed to the Tanach, which names and shapes the world in which our encounter with God takes place. One of the major goals of spiritual guidance is to lead us to recognize that God still speaks to us. The Tanach gives us two "maps" to help us along the spiritual way. The standard journey model for Jews has always been the Exodus from Egypt across the wilderness to the Promised Land. That journey is instructive for the spiritual life because like the Israelites, we, too, have been enslaved, even if we are not immediately aware of it. When we can affirm that we are enslaved, we can begin our spiritual exodus from slavery.

A second model which depicts a relationship with deepening intimacy, the kind potentially developed between the individual and God, is described in the Song of Songs. The text, a collection of passionate love poetry that commentators have understood to refer to the love between God and Israel, reminds us that Covenant is central to our lives. Love is not only nourishing, it is also painful; it can, indeed, be its own kind of desert.

PRAYER AS A STARTING POINT FOR A RELATIONSHIP TO GOD

Our starting point is prayer. What happens when we pray? It seems like a simple question. Yet we realize that before we can answer any question about prayer, we need to ask ourselves about our own prayer life. Living a spiritual life includes establishing a dialogue with the Divine. This dialogue is what we call prayer. We soon realize that there are other questions to consider: How do we pray? When do we pray? Why do we pray? What is prayer for us?

Although we could come up with an anthology of answers, our emphasis will be on remembering that spiritual mentoring begins with our own experience.

Prayer is about relationship. So often, we discover this truth along the path of prayer. We were created to live in relationship with God; prayer is an intrinsic part of that relationship. Since prayer is part of a relationship, we naturally assume that prayer is not a monologue and that one of the things we need to learn how to hear or discern is God's response.

The first step in learning how to hear or discern God's response or will is learning how to wait. In our fast paced society, it is not surprising that we experience waiting, which is a requirement of spiritual growth, as a form of testing and trial. We want to storm the heavens outwardly and immediately, rather than gradually grow in our openness and trust toward God. When we love God, we are presented with many occasions to wait. One of the tasks of the spiritual mentor is to guide us through periods of uncertainty and encourage us to endure them, and help us to learn how to wait.

LOVING AND LISTENING TO GOD

But hearing, listening, discerning require more than patience. Listening implies a relationship and is also part of it. Our capacity to understand is related to the nature and quality of our relationship. The more we know someone, the better is our understanding of what they are trying to say. This is knowing in the sense of love. When a child first learns to speak, a person unfamiliar with the child's attempt to form specific words or word groups may have no idea of what the child is trying to say. Yet the parents of the child readily understand what is being said. The parents do not *hear* better. The parents understand the words of their child because of the ongoing relationship they share. We learn to hear because we love. The same principle holds true for our relationship with God. Learning how to listen to God is learning about our rela-

tionship with God. We grow in our capacity to listen because we love.

The greater our attentiveness to the world, the greater our love for God, the more aspects of reality will speak to us of God and, thereby, convey God's instruction to direct our lives. God speaks through things, events, words, and texts. God speaks through other people we encounter. And God speaks in our own voice, in our own deepest emotions.

While discernment is, in some ways, very subtle, in one respect it is much simpler than we might imagine. There is really only one subject: our relationship to God. Where is God in what is happening? This commitment to the one subject changes our reaction to all that happens to us. Instead of the accusatory, "Why me?" when facing adversity, we ask, "Where is God in this experience?" Hearing is grounded in God's promise throughout the Torah: "I will be with you." That is the heart of all discernment. The more we look back, with the help of a sensitive mentor, the more we see God's presence and caring throughout our life. It is indeed a warrant for hope and trust.

INTIMACY WITH GOD AND FEAR OF GOD

We want intimacy with God and we also fear it. Our fears takes many forms: we fear our own unworthiness; we fear claiming our own knowledge and giftedness; we fear expressing anger; we fear being wrong or inadequate; we fear the loss of autonomy; we fear the unknown; we fear that approaching God will mean that God will see us and maybe reject us; we fear that *we* will really see ourselves and judge ourselves harshly. In general, there is a fear of intimacy and that fear is compounded when the subject of our intimacy is God. Above all, we fear the rejection that is potential in all dimensions of love. We are afraid of the very same things we desire. We fear knowing and being known, loving and being loved. Love enables us, fills us, nurtures us; it is also what makes us vulnerable. Spiritual mentoring helps us to recognize and understand these feelings. We may not be conscious of our own fear, or the fear may be disguised. We are not always aware that we are afraid or why we are afraid. Instead, we think that — because of our busy lives — we are merely unable to find time to pray, to be with God, to seek solitude. But is our busy-ness a means of delaying or hiding from a relationship with God?

Fear of the unknown is really part of our fear of death. The unknown life is seen as the end of life as one knows it. Regardless of how we live or what we do, death awaits us. We cannot escape our fear of death by refusing to commit to the spiritual path or to a relationship with God. On the contrary, such a commitment will lessen that fear . . . as the spiritual mentor helps us confront it.

For some, the fear of death is at its base a fear of life. In order to transcend this fear, we have to distinguish a fear of death from a fear of dying. Furthermore, we have to distinguish between a fear of death and a fear that loss of life includes a loss of self. Leaving behind the life and self as we knew them leads us into a new life and a new self.

Fear of God can represent an ambivalence to the nearness of the holy. We have an impulse to withdraw from God's possible displeasure even as we are drawn toward God's splendor. Yet, as we have learned from human relationships, the best way to heal fear is through a deepening relationship. So, too, concerning a fear of God. With a supportive mentor and sacred texts, we can discover that others have safely traveled where we now go in order to achieve this relationship. A mentor can also help us examine which fears require further exploration, and which fears simply need to be avoided so that we might gain distance from them.

GOD IMAGES

One great source of fear is our image of God. God-images are formed in earliest child-hood not by explicit teaching, but by the way we have felt in relating to the significant people in our lives. The God-image is an amalgam of our father, mother, sibling, grandparent, teacher, police, and others who have cared for us or exerted power over us. Our God-image can grow as our experience grows. It is essential for a spiritual mentor to help the guided continue to be open to an ever expanding image of the people who were and are significant in his/her life from the earliest childhood days to the present.

If nothing initially attracted us, we would not begin the process of coming into relationship with God. In other words, we begin with a provisional theology that is modified by our actual encounters with God. Long before we employ academic terms like "theology," we have images of God, not quite ideas or theories, but some pastiche of experiences we have had with adults we revere or love, who we find have power over us or who frighten us. We are taught songs, told stories, all of which are usually uncritically absorbed and integrated into the early formulation of our "God-image." It is all too rare a phenomenon that the unconscious process becomes conscious and we begin to reflect on our "God-image" and modify it in terms of our mature consciousness. More common is the experience that we form the God-Image, do not look at it again until a crisis hits (death of a loved one), and then are embarrassed by its resemblance to the moth-eaten teddy bear we embraced at the same age as we formed our God-image. Under the crisis condition, we may be tempted to discard God, rather than just the inadequate God-image. God-images, if they are sufficiently attractive, are self-correcting. That is, if we are attracted to a relationship to God, then our growing experience of God's presence will transform our earlier images.

This self-correcting aspect of God-images is one reason why we can comfortably allow those we mentor to start from their own position — however seemingly unconventional. Our agenda is not to modify their view or bring it to conform with some acceptable notion. Our goal is to help bring them into relationship with God.

They must grow themselves; we cannot grow for them. Over the years, we have seen people start from radically different positions and still arrive at a sense of love, trust, and caring concern.

STUDY AS AN ACT THAT GIVES RISE TO JEWISH SPIRITUALITY

Study is at the heart of Jewish spirituality. It functions on many levels. It increases our understanding of our own lives, as well as of the story of our people. It gives us tools for making responsible moral decisions. It opens us to an encounter with the holy. We do not study the text in order to learn more about the text; we study the text in order to learn more about ourselves.

There are three forms of knowledge: knowing *that* — we know that there are five books in the Torah; knowing *how* — we know how to read Hebrew. The first two forms of knowledge are the forms usually addressed by institutions of learning. But the third form of knowing, is a knowing that engages all of our being and is transformative. This is the greatest educational challenge. The purpose of religious study is to pass on the third kind of knowledge. We do not succeed by rote learning or by mimicking certain behaviors. How can one, who really has succeeded in experiencing the *Shechinah*, the Presence of God, transmit the methods that have worked and the insights that have been attained?

Sometimes a question, a "cognitive concern," can begin us on our way. The question becomes more than an abstract intellectual concern — it becomes the riddle that leads us to wonder about our origins and our ultimate destination: Why do our lives move from dependency to self-reliance and then back to dependency? What meaning can that unchanging pattern have? What is the meaning of all we do and suffer here? Why were we born into our family — what does our lifelong engagement with this family mean to teach us? So many aspects of our being raise compelling questions: that we are created

mortal, that we develop and age, that we are simultaneously part of a social structure — born in community, reared and formed by society, and, yet, existentially alone and individual.

We meet the text the way we would meet anyone with whom we want to have a relationship. Initially, it may be significant to pile up facts about the one we are meeting: How old are you? What are your interests or concerns? To whom are you related? But in any serious relationship, the facts about someone recede in importance as the real encounter takes place. Ultimately, we do not want to know *about* X, we want to know X. So it is with Tanach. We learn theories about how it came to be written and preserved and transmitted. We learn about a codex, the Dead Sea Scrolls, *genizah* fragments. We learn about higher and lower biblical criticism. We learn comparisons of one book to another. Then the distance fades. Now we are not outside studying the size and shape and history of the text. We are inside of it and seeing the world from its perspective. What does the world look like from the perspective of Ruth or Job? But even that question fades as we move deeper. The distance between ourselves and the text is gone. *Our* questioning ends, and it is *we* who are being questioned. It is no longer about the text or even about the world of the text. It is about us! The book has become a place of encounter. We are addressed. We experience the power of the text — a power to transform our lives. What does it mean to be questioned by a text? How does it feel?

Our awareness of our own reaction to the text becomes one of the tools we bring to hearing another person's doubts as they come for spiritual mentoring. We hear them speak of a moment of profound closeness with God's presence and then they immediately switch to discussion of an abstract theological concern. We know that move — we have done that ourselves. It is the move from heart to head. As educators, teachers, scholars — we are almost too skilled in the cognitive domain. That domain we have mastered and control. But a spiritual mentor listens for the moment when a seeker is touched in the emotional domain, and encourages him or her to go back to that experiencing of God's presence and not to think about it, but to feel it. The experience of feeling and attending to their own emotions will do all the education that needs to be done. Our commentary is not needed, but our own awareness of the ways we express resistance helped us to recognize that in our seeker.

Study is a model for our way of relating to others in the world. We need to have this relationship of knowing that we have to the text with all the people we meet in our world. Each person is a sacred text (we are in the image of God and that is not just a saying, it is the essential premise for all of our ethics). So each person must be approached with reverence, with quiet, patient waiting, with openness to surprise and transformation.

ADDRESSING SIN ALONG OUR PATHS TO GOD

A great obstruction to intimacy with God is our sense of our own unworthiness because of sin. Too often, we focus on sins — deeds that are less than worthy of us. But spiritual mentors are most concerned about repeated patterns of sin: sins that cut off our life with God. The working assumption is that virtue is not a cause of blessings and sins a cause of suffering, but rather, virtue is a form of blessing. We are not good in order to be blessed, but we are blessed by being able to be good. So the objective of the spiritual mentor is to hearten and encourage us so that nothing slows or stops our spiritual way, or leads us to "settle in a land that falls short of the Promise." The *essential* sin is despair: giving up on yourself and your relationship to God and the Jewish people.

Temptations are real. But we are not unprepared. Despair is idolatrous: if God is God, no situation is hopeless. But what is the nature of our hope? Not that the situation will be different, but that the situation will be *meaningful*. We are not blessed because we are virtuous, but our virtue *is*

our blessedness. The sin we must avoid is to grow a carapace or to harden ourselves (and our heart). The prophet Amos reminds us (Amos 3:1-8) of our special relationship to God in order to soften us and bring us back to God's healing love.

THE NEED FOR SPIRITUAL MENTORING THROUGHOUT OUR LIVES

What is at stake is a lifelong relationship and not a single goal. So spiritual mentoring does not end. We may need it less frequently and it may serve — for long periods — just to keep us sensitive, alert, awake, and not on automatic pilot. Things go along and then, suddenly, we are at a different place in life and a whole new set of questions arise. Just as we learn that the adventure need never end once we have made the choice of profession, spouse, location in which to live, so we are repeatedly surprised and refreshed by the newness of life. Sometimes the changes are large, demanding, scary, and then there can be a quiet, integrative time. And then, suddenly, a lot of questions arise. We are used to seeing on film or reading in novels or newspapers about the heroic, single dramatic encounter: winning the game, racing to the top, facing a villain, enduring a trial. But in the spiritual realm, heroism involves resiliency, abidingness, daily faithfulness to a lifelong Covenant.

We learn to fall. When we learn to ride a bicycle without training wheels, the first lesson is how to fall. We will fall, the only question is how to fall with minimal hurt, and how to get up again. The physical fall of the novice bicycle rider has its spiritual analogue in our falls — into doubt and discouragement. We, too, need to learn how to fall with minimal damage. The spiritual guide will help us prepare for falls in times of comfort and fervor. We learn to develop habits and structures of practice that will support us through difficult times. We will not always be at the moment of our greatest insight, but we can make covenants, retain the memory (we are encouraged to keep journals so we can actually read descriptions of our times of deepest intimacy with God — not for the sake of nostalgia, but for making present now that prior experience of Presence). We learn to fall and rise again. Falls are not indicators of weakness on our part. They are part of the normal systole and diastole of the spiritual way. One of the great tasks of the spiritual guide is to encourage.

Just as falls are inevitable, so are occasions of rising. Surprisingly, rising, our highs can be as challenging as falls. We may grow overconfident and grow lax in our habits of faithfulness; our focus may shift from the relationship to the phenomenological accompaniments to the relationship. We may become careless. Relationships develop out of carefulness and attention. We are involved in an ongoing lifelong relationship. It never becomes automatic.

The spiritual life is an entire life, and not just a stage along the way. We may grow weary, impatient. We have to learn that this is the shape of our entire life. The test of the spiritual life is the life. We are not our own ends. We are intrinsically valuable, but all the energy we put into growing closer to God makes us better able to transform the world.

SPIRITUAL GUIDES FOR TEACHERS: A CONCLUDING THOUGHT

It is obvious that the job of a teacher is to guide; it is less clear that they are guided. In those areas of life that are most significant, including our spiritual growth, none of us is an expert, and even an astute five-year-old can ask the question that refreshes our perspective and takes us further on our own journey. The values students learn in class are not merely the facts of history or the mastery of a language, they are, more significantly, the process of encounter between two human beings, which is often the place we encounter God. All teachers, whether teachers of adolescents or preschoolers, need to have a peer relationship in which they can talk about what happened in class. And, above all, they need to give someone permission to give them advice and even correct them.

When I was in graduate school studying ethics, a classmate and I were appalled to discover that a number of our professors were less than ethical in the way they treated their students. We wondered if they had always been that way or if something had occurred over the years of teaching that had made them insensitive, sarcastic, and even cruel to their students. We lost time speculating on them, and agreed to serve as watchdogs for each other so that we would never fall into the patterns we observed in our teachers. Now, 30 years later, we still have regular conversations about our teaching. We still remind each other to return papers on time, keep appointments, and rejoice as our students surpass us. Teaching is a sacred task. As teachers, we need a partner to help further our growth professionally and personally, skill-wise and spiritually.

IMPLICATIONS

1. Being a spiritual mentor is an important role for teachers.

2. A teacher who wants to be a mentor to another must also be aware that they, too, are on a spiritual journey and are learning all the time.

3. Relationship to God is the essential ingredient of a spiritual life. Prayer and study are vehicles to nurturing that relationship to God. Therefore, the curriculum of the school and congregation should allow learners of all ages to seek spiritual guidance.

4. God-images change as we grow. We grow out of certain images. In growing out of these

images we run the risk of rejecting God, rather than the old and inadequate image. Being able to leave behind images that we have outgrown is an important part of spiritual maturity.

QUESTIONS FOR CRITICAL INQUIRY

1. Compare and contrast the two spiritual maps that Ochs presents as arising from Tanach: (1) the Exodus from Egypt and journeying toward the Promised Land, and (2) the covenantal relationship between God and the Israelites as presented in Song of Songs.

2. How does one come to know a text? In what ways does a text come to help us know ourselves?

3. What are the barriers to having a relationship with God?

4. Does everyone need a spiritual mentor? Explain your answer.

5. Think of someone who has been a spiritual mentor to you. What qualities stand out for you? How do the qualities that you identified compare to the ones that Dr. Ochs identifies?

6. In what ways is being a teacher the same or different from being a spiritual mentor? How can a teacher be a spiritual mentor?

ACTIVITIES

1. Make a road map of the places where you have journeyed in your life (e.g., where you have lived, traveled, gone to school or camp), and/or make a map of your day-to-day journeys (e.g., go to school, synagogue, places to eat, places you play, friends and family you visit). Indicate special points of spiritual connection on the map (e.g., my favorite place to be alone, where I come into contact with nature, where I like to pray). Share your maps.

2. Watch a short excerpt from the film *Joseph*

and the Amazing Technicolor Dreamcoat (2000, unrated, 78 min.), or listen to selections from the original cast recording. Create a chart of the sequence of the major events in the Joseph story. Identify the parts of the story that were most important to you at different ages or the parts of the story to which you most closely relate. How has what was important to you in the story changed over time? What are the reasons for these changes? Why do you relate to certain parts of the story more than others? Ochs talks about the ways that coming to know a text help us to know ourselves. Based on what you have learned about your connections to the Joseph story, how is this true for you?

3. Ochs indicates that a person who wants to be a mentor to another has to be aware that he or she is on a spiritual journey and learning all the time. In pairs, consider whether at this time in your life you would be a good spiritual mentor for someone. Give reasons for why or why not. If not, what would you need to learn or do to become a spiritual mentor? Do you have, or have you had, a spiritual mentor? Describe how you came to be in this relationship. What do you do to help mentor someone spiritually? What does — or could — a spiritual mentor do for you?

BIBLIOGRAPHY

(Note: For Jews, our basic source text is the Tanach. There have been books on spiritual guidance in the Hasidic manner, but they are in the main hierarchical and, therefore, not after all is said and done particularly helpful. Spiritual mentorship — called spiritual direction in the Roman Catholic tradition — has a long history in Christianity. The sources below include both Jewish and Christian perspectives.)

Barry, William A., and William J. Connolly. *The Practice of Spiritual Direction*. San Francisco, CA: Harper & Row, 1992.

This is a major resource for people interested

in spiritual direction/guidance. Since its publication, Barry has written other books that explore the theology behind spiritual direction, as well as on issues such as how we learn to discern God's will through prayer.

Buber, Martin. *I and Thou.* Walter Kaufmann, trans. New York: Charles Scribner's Sons, 1970.

Buber's seminal work in which he describes his well-known theology of relationship.

Fischer, Kathleen. *Women at the Well: Feminist Perspectives on Spiritual Direction.* New York: Paulist Press, 1988.

Fischer remains an urgent voice for the contribution of women's experiences and insights and spiritual perspectives. This book offers enriching new ways of imaging God.

Ochs, Carol, and Kerry M. Olitzky. *Jewish Spiritual Guidance: Finding Our Way To God.* San Francisco: Jossey-Bass, 1997.

This book elaborates in detail the points described in this chapter.

CHAPTER 27

GOD, PULPIT, AND PRAXIS

Morley T. Feinstein

INTRODUCTION

Teachers and educators within and outside the congregation need to think about the ways in which the Rabbi or Cantor can assist their efforts to nurture people's spirituality and relationship to God. The connections between the *bimah* and the classroom, between worship and study, are critical. Multiple opportunities exist for making these connections: (1) providing a context in which learning about God and the sacred are useful and meaningful, (2) communicating messages about the importance of Jewish learning for one's spiritual journey, (3) serving as a forum for learning about God, and (4) motivating and inspiring people to search for God through prayer and study. I will deal with all of these issues in this chapter on nurturing spirituality from the pulpit.

The prayer service provides a context in which much of the knowledge and skills learned in the classroom in terms of reciting prayers, reading Torah, and connecting with God are utilized. Students learn to read, translate, and interpret a prayer, enabling them to participate in a service and navigate their way through the service. They must have opportunities to use these competencies so as to reinforce the significance of their achievements. A combination of skills, knowledge, and understanding can lead to making prayer a spiritual, fulfilling experience. Learning not only how to "do the prayers and Torah reading," but also gaining insights into the meaning of those prayers and passages adds to the experience of the sacred, and deepens our relationship to God.

The pulpit is an important place for sending messages about what is important. Many topics are dealt with from the *bimah*. God and spirituality need to be among those topics highlighted.

Ironically, while one would expect God to be continually on people's minds since God is on people's lips during the prayer service, unless God and the sacred are intentionally and explicitly addressed, their importance is diminished in comparison to the other concerns presented. Clergy need to spend time consciously and purposefully considering how the prayer experience connects us to God while challenging and strengthening our spiritual journeys.

The pulpit can be used to advance learning about God and spirituality. I will therefore present several strategies for incorporating learning about God and spirituality into the worship service. These include highlighting a different prayer each Shabbat, providing commentary from traditional and modern scholars, and pointing out insights into the prayer's relevance for our lives today. The intentional use of instruction, of raising understanding of the liturgy, reminds us that study itself is viewed in Jewish tradition as an act of worship. Learning is a form of prayer, a way of communicating with God.

Finally, the leadership that emanates from the *bimah* can motivate and inspire people to search for God. I speak below about the catharsis that occurs when a Rabbi speaking from the pulpit shares his questions, doubts, and struggles in searching for and relating to God. This gives others permission to have similar thoughts and feelings, while encouraging them to continue their spiritual quests. Rabbis and Cantors, through music, interpretation, education, orchestration, and participation, can unlock gates and doors to finding God for even the most skeptical worshiper.

Two men on a plane began a conversation. "What do you do for a living?" one asked. "I am a Rabbi," came the response. The first man turned away for a moment, thought, and turned back. "Gee, I don't really know much about religion, but I know that all of religion can be summarized in that famous phrase, 'Love your neighbor as yourself.'"

The Rabbi was somewhat upset by the man's high degree of generalization. He asked his neighbor, "What do you do?" The man said, "I am an astrophysicist." The Rabbi turned away for a moment, then turned back and said, "Gee, I don't really know much about astrophysics, but I know that the entire discipline can be summarized in that famous phrase, 'Twinkle, twinkle, little star!'"

Pithy phrases are easy to use when we want to avoid a subject completely. Many of us feel uncomfortable grappling with the essence of our religion. And we have the most difficulty talking about God. We are awkward in describing our views. For generations, many felt that God was too awesome, too holy, for us to make contact. Rabbi Harold Kushner suggests that we can feel at ease when religion is about coming to services, reading the prayers, or signing a petition, as long as we don't have to get too close to God. We're not annoyed when religion avoids God and in its place uses the language of psychology — about liking yourself better, conquering stress, or having honest relationships. We are more comfortable hearing a speaker, reading a book, going to a meeting, or giving *tzedakah*, than confronting God. In fact, the word God makes many uneasy.

For years, we spoke little if at all about God. Why the silence? And, what led to breaking that silence, to our people turning inward, seeking and searching for the sacred, for God in their lives? What can I as a Rabbi, teacher, and Jewish professional do from the pulpit, in the classroom, and at other places in my setting to foster and inform people's spiritual quests? These are the questions that I attempt to answer by sharing my own experiences and praxis as a Rabbi and educator for the past 20 years.

THE SILENCE ABOUT GOD

The Reasons Why

Why was there such silence about God for so

long? Rabbis in North America did not focus on God in their sermons; their emphasis was on other matters. Worries about the outer world, both Jewish and secular, were so great that the inner life was left as if without a shepherd to attend it. Rabbis and congregants alike were preoccupied with concerns about Jews behind the Iron Curtain and in Ethiopia, about the survival of Israel, about civil rights, the war in Vietnam, equal rights for women, and the environment. Such social and political issues set the Jewish agenda for decades, relegating God, the inner reaches of our souls, or the experience of *kedushah* (holiness) to a back burner in our personal lives, in our communities, and in our synagogues.

Not only was spirituality not a prime issue in the 1960s, it was rarely even discussed. Indeed, some then declared that "God is dead." In an article in the *Journal of Reform Judaism* (1986, p. 18), my teacher, Rabbi Jakob Petuchowski (*z"l*) noted:

> There has not been too much talk of God in Reform circles within recent years. Indeed, the most recent edition of American Reform Jewish liturgy even contains "services" that are meant to make atheists and agnostics feel comfortable. Apparently one no longer has to believe in God in order to be a Reform Jew — or even a Reform Rabbi — in good standing.

God's absence was to be tolerated or even expected.

Rabbis themselves used to be hesitant to speak about God. In the Reform seminary in the 1970s, we dealt with the grammar of the names of God, learned the Aramaic of the "*Kaddish*," read about God in the Talmud, but rarely talked with our professors or asked one another our thoughts or feelings of God. In my course on theology at the Hebrew Union College, never once was there a formal opportunity to share personal beliefs of God with my future colleagues. My experience in the Reform Movement was not unlike that of my Rabbinic colleagues in other movements.

What Broke the Silence?

Spirituality is a word which came into vogue in

the Jewish community within the last decade. This is reflected in the countless books on the subject. As people have been able to open up to their faith and inner spiritual life, so, too, have Rabbis begun to speak on the subject, and as they do so in classrooms and from the pulpit, more ears are attuned than ever in recent times. Moreover, many Jews have embarked on their own spiritual journeys, and are creating memoirs about them. There is a hunger for understanding the details of people's spiritual life. From Maimonides to the Baal Shem Tov to Paul Cowan and Stephen Dubner, Jewish authors have helped others find God everywhere, in reflections on abusive situations or the blessings of family life. Baby boomers are focusing more and more on the meaning of life, and on their own spiritual sparks.

Ironically, the expansion of scientific knowledge has helped foster a boom in religiosity and spiritual inquiry. The world is rapidly changing due to the growth of new knowledge in technology and biotechnology. For the first time, we are able to manipulate the process of creation in plants, animals, and humans — a heretofore god-like power. The ethical decisions that arise from genetic manipulations, the medical advancements that prolong life, and the technological changes that create an instantaneous global community, just to name some, have us looking for answers and perspective to these perplexities. Ultimate questions lead to the search for ultimate answers — for a certain wisdom that might provide a framework of values, a sense of purpose, and a relationship to the transcendent.

When information was finite, an educated person could be knowledgeable enough in various subjects and adept in discussing them. Today, knowledge grows exponentially. A seemingly infinite number of messages are transferred (as if mystically and magically) from one computer to the next — everything from business data to scientific theorems to gossip to Torah study are channeled through the Internet. Change is instantaneous and constant. And suddenly, thanks to all we know, we know that we know less and less about all that is and can and

will be. Yesterday, the earth was huge and expansive and countries and people were separated if not isolated; today, the globe shrinks as planes and wireless communications and CNN merge us all into one global community.

Yet, virtual proximity leads to a push, a need for face-to-face community. A high-tech life, seems to require a high-touch response. So people have returned to synagogue life, to the life of the spirit, to the ineffable qualities which nurture our souls, to the God who created all. Even though the desire for spirituality has changed from previous decades, we still struggle with how to articulate our relationship to God.

A few years ago, I wrote to a colleague who had published an article in a Jewish magazine describing his experiences and encounters with God. He talked about his feelings both at the moment of his ordination as a Rabbi at the historic Plum Street Temple in Cincinnati and, years later, the wonderful emotion shared with a Bat Mitzvah when both stood before the open Ark. He spoke of prayer and peoplehood, but most of all, he spoke of his relationship with God. I complimented him on his fine article and on how well he echoed some of my own feelings. To me, his response was astounding: "How many people have written me, flabbergasted that I, a Rabbi, would write about my own personal relationship to God!" I was surprised that they were stunned, and awed by his honesty.

Why is it so difficult to speak of God? Where is God? How does God interact in our lives? If we are looking for God, is God also looking for us? A Hasidic master remarked, "Where is God? Wherever we let God in!" Perhaps we do not focus enough attention on our own personal view of God, as Rabbis, educators, and Jewish professionals. Is it not our responsibility to attempt to answer these questions not only for ourselves, but also to explore them with our congregants?

We have to search for whatever we mean by God, to enable us to experience God's nearness and presence. Not only do we need to help our congregants in their searches, we need to bring God-talk into our own family discussions; we need to invite God to the dinner table. What do our parents believe about God, or our brothers or sisters? A child asks about God at age three. Will we continue the discussion at age 13 or 30? Have we queried a friend about a God-view lately, if at all? Rabbi Al Axelrad asks why so many young Jews, driven by a thirst for God, desert our people and carry out their speculation through all sorts of non-Jewish channels, including cults. How can we best use the pulpit, the classrooms, the social hall — the spaces and the times in the Jewish year and in people's lives — to encourage the quest for God? I write about how I have accomplished this in my Rabbinate in the sections that follow.

WORSHIP SERVICES

Prayer

Worship and study are indeed intertwined in the traditional Jewish prayer service. Commenting on the liturgy is a way of heightening one's awareness of the prayers and of God and enhancing the worship experience. The Rabbis taught that prayer should not be a fixed or routine duty, but should always be enhanced in a spontaneous way. So much God-talk is limited to the rote recitation of prayer. Interpreting and explaining can get to the heart of a prayer and can lend relevance and raise the level of our spiritual connection.

When I pray with the congregation, it is my custom to stop and draw attention to a word, pattern, phrase, relationship to another prayer or text, or to explain the linkages about God in the prayer. I use classical texts and commentaries, personal experiences, poetry and stories, and modern interpretations to explore the meaning and mystery within the prayers.

For example, with the short *brachah* for lighting the braided Havdalah candle, *"Baruch Atah Adonai, Elohaynu Melech HaOlam, Boray M'oray HaAysh,"* I draw attention to the four different names we use for God — *Adonai*, our God, Sovereign of the Universe, Creator of the lights of the fire. To refer to the Eternal as *Adonai* and

as *Elohim*, draws us to Exodus 6, in which God hears the groans of the Israelites and reveals the divine self to Moses as *Adonai*/the Eternal, who was the God of Abraham, Isaac, and Jacob. At Exodus 6:2, *Adonai* and *Elohim* are distinctive. But by Exodus 6:7, instead of proclaiming *"Ani Adonai"* — I am *Adonai*, the phrase used is *"Ani Adonai Elohaychem"* — I am *Adonai* your God. There is already a confluence, so subtle and yet so important, that the God to whom Moses shows deference is indeed *Adonai*. The same liturgical continuity occurs in our simplest *brachot*.

Immediately, this phrase is followed by *Melech*/God as Sovereign, or Ruler. And only after we refer to God through these three names, do we find out the particular reference at this moment, that God is the Creator, a genuinely universal attribution. God is known as *Boray*/Creator from Genesis and the Book of Isaiah, and appears as Creator in the *"Yotzer"* morning prayer, which immediately precedes the *"Shema."*

Allowing congregants to become privy to the theological issues, the messages about God that prayers give, the communicative style of the liturgy, helps the worshipers become more fluent in their own personal prayers. In providing background, context, and history about the prayer, the communal prayer experience is enriched. It has an intellectual appeal for both the learned and the learning Jew. At the same time, the process of interpreting prayer challenges a worshiper to explore, respond, and relate to the prayers and to God on a personal, emotional level. It highlights the wonder, connection, and majesty of the prayers, the prayer service, and God, all within the context of an ongoing Jewish tradition.

Prayer is also a time for me to bring a teaching from Abraham Joshua Heschel, a story of the Hasidic masters, a quote from *Masechet Brachot* of the Talmud, or a poem that will highlight a theme I want to accentuate during the service. Such a reading may also connect the prayer to the reading from the weekly *parashah*. For example, the words of Ruth Brin or Marsha Falk can express a point of view about God and also enhance the mood of prayer. Such additions complement the prayer service and make prayer more lively. Such insertions are not repeated by me more than once during a calendar year. Thus, every prayer service has something unique both for me from the pulpit and for the congregant who is praying.

I know that some people may relate to God through song or dance, meditation or mantra, speech or silence. In many congregations, opportunities for any or all of these techniques are incorporated into the normative worship experience. Or, some synagogues offer Alternative Services — usually a Kabbalat Shabbat service in which these elements form the style and/or the basis of the worship experience.

Congregants, as well as the Rabbi, are given opportunities for sharing their interpretations of the prayers. Each Bar/Bat Mitzvah student creates a personal prayer to God. After studying over 90 names of God culled from the Bible, Rabbinic literature, and modern texts, students explain why a particular name of God is meaningful to them. Through Socratic dialogue, the students end up writing about God and then speak their words during their Bar/Bat Mitzvah service. Likewise, Confirmation students journal their feelings about God and/or prayer, and often these thoughts are woven into their Confirmation service. As students (and adults) express their feelings about God, they engage in the process of bringing God into their lives.

Prayer and Our Relationship To God

Where does prayer fit into the relationship we have with God? Prayer is the medium through which God and people interact. To pray is to overcome distance, to heal the breech between God and the world, to reduce our pain and increase our joy. Prayer, for Abraham Joshua Heschel, is a doorway where the finite meets the Infinite, where people meet God.

> God is unwilling to be alone, and man cannot forever remain impervious to what He longs to show. Those of us who cannot keep their striving back find themselves at times

within the sight of the unseen and become aglow with its rays. Some of us blush, others wear a mask. Faith is a blush in the presence of God (Dresner, 1985, p. 5).

If we do not attempt to pray, we may never know if God cares. And if we do not remind ourselves of the pressing needs of life, are we capable of caring?

Heschel taught that God's handiwork was each human being. He taught that the Bible regards only one thing as the symbol of God, not a synagogue nor a tree, a statue nor a star. "The symbol of God is each individual person. God created us in His image, in His likeness" (Dresner, p. 49). Each of us has a moral possibility to act as if worthy of being God's symbol, worthy of the gift of life. God stands in a passionate relationship to us. We have to nurture God's presence in us and in those we love.

The Torah Reading

Another portion of the service that is very important in communicating ideas about God is the reading from the Torah itself. My colleague and former senior Rabbi, Samuel Stahl, taught me that reading the Torah requires a modern *Meturgeman*, a recreation of the position of translator to the congregation. Instead of merely offering the English of Torah as it is being read or chanted, I follow Rabbi Stahl's model by offering commentary. This may be from the *Mefarshim* of ancient days or from modern scholars. Especially in those passages containing narrative about the relationship between God and our ancestors, this is a ripe field in which to harvest meaning. The commentary might focus on God's intention to destroy the Jewish people after the golden calf, and how Moses intervened to create and forge a new relationship. Likewise, after the sin of the spies, Moses quotes back to God the divine attributes in order to sway God and change the divine decision. Thus the reading from the Torah and the *D'var Torah* preceding the reading or chanting are unique opportunities to explore the profundity of God and

God's unfolding interaction with our people in ancient days.

Divray Torah: Sermons

Sermons are often seen as the key vehicle for teaching about God. As a way of bringing the voices and views of great Jewish thinkers to the congregants, I have spoken on major theological issues of our times such as, "Where was God in the Holocaust?" I have reviewed books on theology, such as *Evil and the Morality of God* by Harold Schulweis. I often focus on a theological event, concept, or issue that is in some way connected to each holiday: creating a new theology of miracles at the High Holy Days, concern for the environment on Sukkot, God's giving us freedom of choice on Pesach, and the concept of God's choosing us as a special people for Shavuot.

Congregants also have spoken about their own spiritual quests on a variety of different occasions. Often the services and ceremonies that welcome Jews by Choice include moving statements about their journeys and commitments.

More than the sermon's message is the role modeling that comes from the pulpit. If I have preached a sermon that being created in the image of God involves caring for the needy, then I work with our Social Justice Committee to act upon that concern. Serving the needs of the hungry and the outcast at the South Bend Center for the Homeless is one way in which this important aspect of being in the image of God was acted upon in our congregation. The experience of becoming a Bar/Bat Mitzvah, accepting the yoke of the commandments, standing before the Ark in the presence of the congregation, is followed up by the young adult's participation in our annual Mitzvah Day. A sense of godliness flows from pulpit to congregation to community, from moments of worship to moments of action.

Storytelling

A special opportunity in lieu of sermon is story-telling, especially during Family Services or Tot Shabbat Services. Whether on a Shabbat morning or during a holiday, stories are fun and creative opportunities to teach about God. Young children sit on the edge of their seats as I come off the pulpit and tell the story, walking through and among the congregants. Their parents and grandparents also grasp the story's meaning and may take it to heart.

A favorite story I tell every few years is, "The Princess Who Wanted to See God." Found in Molly Cone's book *Who Knows Ten?* (UAHC Press), a somewhat bratty, insensitive princess desires to see God, and no one in the kingdom can help her. She always got everything she wanted, and had never shed a tear. Her father (the king), the chief of law and order, the chief of the treasury — none of them could show her God. Then, an older Jewish man who brings her face-to-face with a poor, tattered, handicapped girl of her age. By forgetting about herself for the first time in her life, and caring about another's needs, the princess realized that she could grow and change. She finally shed a tear, and in the process realizes that she has seen God. This story resonates deeply with children, parents, and grandparents, for it concretizes through a child's eye the I-Thou relationship described so beautifully by Martin Buber.

Worship Services in the School

Praying within a Religious School setting is also a unique opportunity to teach about and to connect students with God. Such services are opportunities for learning and creativity. Sometimes students lead their service and try to express their own feelings about God. Teachers may work with students in the classroom helping them prepare their prayers, which are then included in the Religious School service. This is also a format utilized in camp and retreat settings.

Family education programs are ripe opportunities for orienting families to prayer and God. Since the Religious School year begins around the time of the Jewish New Year, parents can come into the classroom, create prayers or meditations with their own children on the themes of the High Holy Days, and then share such writings during a Religious School service. Such prayer moments can also create an opportunity to learn about a particular prayer, elicit questions from students about the prayer, study in a focused way, and then continue on with the service. The essential aspect is to try to make prayer come alive, connect it with the individuals, and bring God verbally and consciously into the discussion.

PASTORAL COUNSELING

Following a sermon that may touch someone, there is always time to connect in a personal way, privately and confidentially. In my office, I can help an individual relate text and teaching to his or her personal life, problems, or family situation. Sometimes a congregant needs a listening ear and turns to the Rabbi.

It is often in a counseling situation that someone will address an issue of healing or abandonment, pain or worry, suffering or response to tragedy. When the moment is right, a text of prayer may be meaningful for an individual. I urge the person to attend services and take a text that we have looked at together and pray it as part of our community during our time for *Tefilah*. This certainly applies to family members who may have a loved one in the hospital, who may want to have a *"Mi Shebayrach"* prayer recited at bedside in the hospital or may wish to pray it with the community.

CONCLUSION

As the Hasidic tale advises: God is present wherever we let God in. That can occur while examining spirituality in a classroom setting, in private meetings in my office dealing with an individual's questioning, in studying with a candidate for conversion, or in using prayer to help a person find support and *shlaymut* (wholeness). What is most necessary is the

desire to express God in every aspect of synagogue life, from the pulpit to the hospital bed to the hospitality offered a guest to the honesty expressed in dialogue.

There certainly are risks in seeking to be open and honest about how we relate to God. But if we say *"Baruch Atah Adonai Elohaynu Melech HaOlam . . . ,"* and have not considered who our God, our Creator, our Maker, or Eternal Sovereign is — then those words lack meaning, and become merely a hodgepodge of syllables, incantations. We need to discover times, places, and ways of talking about God, so that people with questing souls can find an opportunity to connect with God.

In closing, I share this anonymous story: There was a woman who loved opals. Over the years, she collected a treasured set of opal earrings, a magnificent opal ring, and a gorgeous opal necklace. The woman placed her opal jewelry in a safety deposit box. She decided to wear the opals only on special occasions. Many years passed. No occasion was deemed just right — special enough to wear the opals. Finally, the wedding of her own daughter drew near, and the woman decided that the time had arrived. With great excitement, she took the box containing the jewelry. As she removed the necklace, earrings and ring from the box, the opals crumbled in her hands. She had been so busy collecting her jewelry that she had failed to learn that opals need to be worn; they need the oils of the skin in order to retain their luster and their integrity. It is the warmth of the body, the touching, which gives them life and beauty.

We cannot keep God hidden away in a safety deposit box, expecting the Holy One at moments of crisis or tragedy. We cannot manipulate God to be a cosmic bellhop, ready at our beck and call. When we connect with God on an ongoing basis, when we infuse our God belief with fresh meaning and insights, when we learn to sense God in our relationships and in our prayers and our study and in the experiences of our lives, then we will be on a path to finding God.

IMPLICATIONS

1. Silence about God was prevalent for a long period of time in both Jewish and American culture. Our modern life has provided the initiative for changing this.

2. God-talk can be promoted by clergy on and off the pulpit in many different ways, including through worship experiences, sermonizing, teaching opportunities, counseling, storytelling, and programming.

3. Clergy need to share their views and experiences of God and provide opportunities for others to do the same.

4. What is taught about God in the classroom needs to be connected to what occurs on the *bimah*.

5. The reverse of this is also true: the messages about God and spirituality that are presented on the *bimah* need to be explored in the classroom.

QUESTIONS FOR CRITICAL INQUIRY

1. Feinstein relates Heschel's image of prayer as a gateway or doorway to spirituality. How is study also a gateway or doorway to spirituality?

2. Why do you think clergy struggle with sharing their perceptions of and the nature of their relationship to God?

3. What are the practical suggestions for nurturing spirituality and a quest for God that Feinstein suggests? In what ways would these approaches be helpful in meeting the goal of connecting a person's spiritual quest to a Jewish framework? What other techniques or approaches could be used?

4. Feinstein contends that the high-tech age demands a high-touch response. What do you think he means by that? What are the implications of both high-tech and high-touch for Jewish education in your setting, and globally?

5. What is your favorite story for teaching about God?

ACTIVITIES

1. Interview your Rabbi, Cantor, and education director about their views of God. Here are some questions that you might want to ask: (1) How do you connect God to your work? (2) How have your views of God changed over time? (3) Do you have a favorite theologian who guides your understanding and relationship of God? (4) What do you struggle with in terms of God? (5) How do you make your life holy? (6) What is your favorite story about God — either one that you experienced or read?

2. Think of a story that your Rabbi told about God that you really like, or find a story about God in a book of Jewish folktales. Act out or illustrate the story. Share the story with younger children and get their responses to it.

3. What music in your prayer service connects you to God? What do the words of the prayer mean? How do the words and the melody help you think about God? Ask your Rabbi or Cantor why they choose to use that particular melody. Then create a music video about the prayer.

BIBLIOGRAPHY

Cone, Molly. *Who Knows Ten? Children's Tales of the Ten Commandments.* rev. ed. New York: UAHC Press, 1999.

This classic book has been revised, and includes one values-laden tale for each of the Ten Commandments.

Dresner, Samuel H., ed. *I Asked for Wonder: A Spiritual Anthology: Abraham Joshua Heschel*. New York: Crossroad/Herder & Herder, 1983.

A student and friend of Abraham Joshua Heschel, Rabbi Dresner draws upon ten of Heschel's published works in English. The book is grouped around the themes of Heschel's spirituality: God, Prayer, Sabbath, Religion, People, Bible, and Holy Deeds.

Petuchowski, Jacob J. "Reform Judaism's Diminishing Boundaries: The Grin that Remained." *Journal of Reform Judaism* 33:4, 135, Fall 1986, 15-24.

A leading expert on liturgy and theology, Rabbi Petuchowski, a professor at the Hebrew Union College-Jewish Institute of Religion, was known for his vast erudition and his outspoken views.

Schulweis, Harold M. *Evil and the Morality of God*. Cincinnati, OH: Hebrew Union College Press, 1984.

A leading Conservative Rabbi, Schulweis taught theology and liturgy at the Hebrew Union College in Los Angeles. Here he proposes a predicate theology to reconcile the coexistence of God and evil.

CHAPTER 28

THE ROLE OF VOLUNTEER LEADERS IN EDUCATING ABOUT GOD AND SPIRITUALITY

Roberta Louis Goodman and Daniel S. Schechter

INTRODUCTION

EDUCATORS AND BOARD MEMBERS NEED TO JOIN together to create a shared institutional vision promoting *kedushah* (holiness), nurturing people's spiritual journeys and relationships to God. What we teach about God and spirituality needs to be reinforced throughout the institutions in which we work, particularly in the boardroom, in order to be most effective. If spiritual growth occurs only in pockets or sections of an institution, but not its entirety, then people learn that it is not serious or important. Nurturing spiritual growth needs to be pervasive, infused throughout an institution.

What happens in the boardroom can reinforce the most important lessons that educators, parents, and clergy are trying to send about engaging in a quest for God. Values and ideals modeled in the boardroom reflect those of the institution. The boardroom contains the organizational leaders who send out messages, both symbolic and real, about what is most important in an institution. The personal sense of God and spirituality of the board members affects seeing their work as holy and the institution's goals as those of promoting a sense of spirituality and God.

Educational programs aimed at nurturing the spiritual growth of board members and considering how their relationship to God affects board operations and decisions is a critical step toward enhancing spirituality in an institution. The board members' viewpoints are critical factors in creating an institutional culture attuned to nurturing a relationship to God and a sense of spirituality. Those viewpoints are based in part on their knowledge and learning.

Leadership development programs focusing on increasing Jewish learning, and synagogue change efforts aimed at reaching individuals within congregations in meaningful ways, underscore the power and significance of enhancing people's engagement with Jewish life. These programs promote the importance of expanding people's knowledge, strengthening their connection and commitment to living as Jews, and deepening their spiritual quests. Educators should have a role in developing and implementing programs that foster seeking God and *kedushah* among board members. The spark ignited in one lay leader can inspire and propel others on their spiritual journeys.

There is no better statement on leadership responsibilities than that written by Dr. Eugene Borowitz:

> God called us all to be holy not in some general, spiritual way but in the humdrum of making money and spending it, of working with some people and against the designs of others, of loving and hating and being indifferent, of the situations we are stuck with and those we create to our will. Our Judaism seeks to make us realists who are not cynics, idealists who are not fools. (Borowitz, 1987, pp. 61-62)

This chapter addresses two questions about making volunteer leaders partners and promoters in the quest for God and spirituality: (1) How does the involvement of volunteer leaders enrich the process of seeking God and spirituality, in a congregation, community, *havurah*, healing service, or home? (2) In the place and role where we expect to find volunteer leaders expounding their views, how can the boardroom and the operation of Jewish organizations be infused with a sense of *kedushah*?

UNDERSTANDING THAT WE ARE ALL JEWISH SEEKERS

All Jews seek answers to spiritual concerns. Some people are wiser, more knowledgeable, deeper, more skillful seekers and articulators of their spiritual quests, but all are seekers nonetheless. Spiritual questing, like sports, arts, and most disciplines, requires a balance of skill abilities, knowledge, and conviction. No one can be a seeker for another. Guides, advisors, and teachers can teach us, but they cannot lay claim to our personal story.

Dr. James Fowler, a minister and theologian at Emory University, offers a rationale for understanding the importance of spirituality and God in peoples' lives today. In his theory of human development, Dr. Fowler sees making meaning of one's life as the defining activity of human beings. Part of this meaning making activity, according to Fowler's conceptualization of Faith Development (Fowler, 1981; see also Chapter 7 of this volume, "Nurturing a Relationship To God and Spiritual Growth: Developmental Approaches" by Roberta Louis Goodman, p. 69) involves making allegiances and loyalties to values, institutions, people, and even to God. These allegiances guide every aspect of human life, including thoughts and commitments. People are constantly raising value-laden questions about their existence, the purpose of their lives, the way they should spend their money, raise their children, support their community, and choose their professions. People find answers to these questions by responding to the symbols and rituals that surround them, the signs and wonders that captivate their imaginations, the values that the culture provides, and the stories and values that their family and community convey. Spiritual questing occurs whether or not any professional enters into that conversation, whether or not one is a member of a congrega-

tion, and whether or not one studies texts or participates in worship services.

PUTTING GOD AT THE CENTER OF JEWISH ORGANIZATIONS

The challenge to lay leaders is to draw Judaism to the center of their own lives and to help their constituency to do the same. Furthermore, the responsibility of synagogue board members — like those of the Rabbi and Cantor — do not end in the sanctuary. They include defining how to help the trustees themselves, their families, and their fellow congregants to grow Jewishly, both within the synagogue and in their daily living.

Jewish values should be at the heart of all congregational decisions. (Such values are frequently derived by attempting to translate God's vision into human terms in the form of *mitzvot*.) Volunteer leaders are urged to look at the agenda for their next meeting — or the minutes of the last — and check all the items pertaining to worship, study of Torah, or religious commitment. How much time was allocated for these matters in comparison with all other matters? As Dr. Neil Gillman, professor of philosophy at the Jewish Theological Seminary of America, emphasizes:

> Every single decision that a congregation reaches in what transpires within the walls of a synagogue and within the parameters of congregational life must be seen as encouraging or discouraging specific models of Jewish expression. . . . In short, it is simply omnipresent. (Schechter, 2000, p. 5)

The premise of this chapter is that if we are going to work toward becoming a holy people (*am kadosh*), we need to examine the role of boards of trustees in every synagogue (and in Jewish organizations and agencies). In synagogues the trustees are frequently the missing link in making decisions on the spiritual life of the community. Furthermore, they frequently lack the knowledge to make such decisions. It may sound strange to point to the board — the highest policy group in the congregation — as an underserved educational population. But the demonstrated fact is that synagogues and Jewish denominations have historically shown minimal commitment to the governing body as a targeted educational audience. When they have offered educational programs, these have generally been on management oversight matters. The role of the board in the spiritual oversight of a congregation has only begun to be addressed.

CHANGING PERCEPTION AND ROLES OF LAY AND PROFESSIONAL LEADERS IN SUPPORTING SPIRITUAL QUESTING

Educating about God and spirituality has long been seen as the province of Rabbis, and more recently, also of other Jewish professionals. It is not uncommon for them to be viewed as *klay kodesh*, holy vessels. (Ironically, this reference comes from a term used in Rabbinic times to refer to things rather than people. *Klay kodesh* were the items or implements that the priests used, and not the priests themselves.) In any event, the expression is meant to convey a sense of holiness, a proximity to God, or special status accorded to those who convey it. Therefore the work of clergy in conducting services, providing pastoral care, teaching sacred texts, confronting life's major questions, and officiating at life cycle events is viewed by many as a path to a spiritual life and connection to God.

In synagogues today, the relationship between volunteer and professional leaders is changing and becoming more collaborative as they work toward enriching spirituality and involvement in Jewish life. (Expectation of such collaborative involvement is emerging in other types of Jewish organizations, in which practices are also changing). Initiatives such as Synagogue 2000, which seeks to expand the spirituality experienced in synagogues, and the Experiment in Congregational Education (ECE), which seeks to create communities of learners in synagogues (Aron, 2000), emphasize the importance of collaboration between volunteer and professional leaders in designing and fulfilling these visions.

Volunteer and professional leaders are sitting down together, studying texts, sharing their views, and planning for ways of engaging more individuals actively in Jewish learning and spiritual seeking. Those involved in and advocating for synagogue transformation attest to the need for reaching and involving more people in significant ways, particularly relating to the spiritual life of the congregation and its members.

Spiritual Workshops

An outstanding example of how lay leaders can help make discussion of spiritual pursuits acceptable among laity was developed in Atlanta more than a decade ago by Gary Metzel (z"l), a lay leader, who took an idea he had heard from Dr. Eugene Borowitz to bring conversations about God to his Reform community. Dr. Borowitz had spoken of the need for Rabbis to speak about their views of God as a way of breaking the silence about God. Metzel organized annual spirituality conferences that began with a national keynote speaker and moved into smaller groups led by local Rabbis. The critical element of the program was the series of workshops featuring local congregational Rabbis sharing their views of God. It was a cathartic experience for those present. It allowed the laity present also to speak about God, to share their struggles, as well as encounters and quests. These spirituality conferences became a forum, a safe space in which it was permissible for the typical Reform Jew to come, explore, and speak about God. (See Chapter 43, "Jews in Search of Spirituality: A Spirituality Conference," p. 362, for the full program description.)

Empowering Lay Leaders

Another change found in many congregations is the expressed desire of volunteer leaders and members to be empowered to take responsibility for their Judaism. As congregations have physically and symbolically lowered the *bimah*, brought the Torah into the congregation to be touched or kissed, people have shown that they want more connections to the sacred, a greater sense of the sacred and God in their lives. People who are competent in their professions, volunteer work, family life, and other aspects of their lives, want to increase the level of skill and engagement in their Jewish lives. They want to experience the sacred directly. What people willingly relegated to clergy at one time, they are now beginning to reclaim as their own — everything from leading *Tefilot* in the congregation on weekdays and Shabbat to designing liturgy for special occasions such as a *Brit Milah* or *Brit Bat* to giving *Divray Torah*. People do not want Bar or Bat Mitzvah to be the only time they lead or participate in a service. Some congregations limit the role of clergy, preferring to oversee and implement worship on their own. As one observer has suggested, Judaism makes for a poor spectator sport, but it is a great participatory experience. More and more congregations are following this adage.

While the tendency may exist in modern life to view Jewish professionals as set apart from others when it comes to spirituality and God, Judaism does not require an intermediary in order to reach God. Spiritual guides — Rabbis, Cantors, and educators — have long labored to open Jews to the possibility of connecting with God, but Jews have learned that this cannot truly succeed without their taking responsibility for their own commitment. It has been said that we cannot love God with our father's or mother's heart; and likewise, we cannot love God through the experience of another. We must come to it in our own lives. Some have sought God in prayer, study, and *mitzvot*. Others have found their approach through good works. For example, they have continued the Jewish focus on social justice, and are slowly reestablishing the connection between social action and its religious underpinnings. They realize that there can be no Judaism without moral indignation, and that a synagogue must work to alleviate the anguish of the suffering. As Rabbi Eric Yoffie, President of the Union of American Hebrew Congregations, has pointed out:

"Now more than ever we embrace ritual and prayer and ceremony; but like the prophets, we never forget that God is concerned about the everyday and that the blights of society take precedence over the mysteries of heaven." (Yoffie, 1997)

To the extent that this "do it yourself" Judaism increases, it to some degree changes the role of clergy from the "doers" to the "trainers of the doers." Sidney Schwarz, a Reconstructionist Rabbi and Jewish institutional innovator, writes extensively about synagogue transformation and the far reaching changes that need to be made in terms of what professionals and lay leaders each need to do in order to reach and engage Jews in meaningful ways. While he wrote for a Reconstructionist audience, what he says about the art of empowerment, of making congregations participatory, is valid for all congregations:

If Reconstructionist congregations mean more by the term "participatory congregation" than an occasional English reading done by a layperson at services, then Rabbis must invest time in helping Jews learn how to create synagogue-communities. This involves getting congregants to take maximal responsibility for all the tasks that, in many congregations, are ceded to the Rabbi: teaching synagogue skills; reaching out to new and marginal members; leading services; creating a study group or teaching a course; providing for pastoral needs of members; spearheading social action projects, etc. It is the art of empowerment — taking power that would normally be invested in a given office and sharing it with others in the system in a supportive way. I used to say that this agenda amounted to a Rabbi putting himself/herself out of a job. I was wrong; this is the job . . . . It is the way that a Rabbi can emerge as a true spiritual leader. (Schwarz, 1999, p. 28)

An example of this spiritual empowerment is found in a congregation that already has a high level of lay participation. Before its only Rabbi and clergy person went on sabbatical leave, he established workshops on how to write a *D'var Torah* so that congregants would be prepared to do so. The Rabbi did not expect congregants just to fill a void. He prepared them for a high level of performance and involvement. An even greater challenge is having the Rabbi prepare lay leaders to write and deliver the *Divray Torah* when the Rabbi is present in the congregation.

The subject of the dynamics of such change cries out for early, friendly, full conversation among the Rabbi, Cantor, educational director, administrator, and the board of trustees. It is a sensitive subject, the implications of which must be understood and agreed upon by all parties involved. Synagogue boards and Rabbis inevitably see the world from different perspectives. These differences can give rise to different approaches on issues, and even to conflict. However, the shared dissatisfaction of some Rabbis and volunteer leaders with their relationship provides an opportunity for a redefinition of synagogue leadership as partnership (*brit*) and sacred duty (*mitzvah*). It offers a chance for Rabbis, Cantors, educators, administrators, and volunteer leaders all to view themselves and each other as *klay kodesh*, people with the common objective of helping congregations to discover the holy. When professionals and volunteer leaders exhibit a partnership and a shared commitment to the content of Jewish life, this role modeling should have dramatic results in the quality of the religious life of the congregation. Rabbi Peter Knobel of Beth Emet The Free Synagogue, Evanston, Illinois, states:

> If the leadership of the synagogue is truly an observing community, . . . it will have a "trickle-down" effect on the synagogue. This is not accomplished by making rules for how many services board members must attend or what programs they must attend. The transformation takes place only if worship and study can be shown to improve the quality of the "business" of the synagogue and touch the members of the board in the process." (Knobel, 1999, p. 139)

All synagogue trustees share a common responsibility: to build a vision and to assemble the means to carry it out. Board members must join in planning a sound financial future for the congregation. Most programs with which the board deals have financial implications. But if the board can move beyond "business as usual" into the experience and demonstration of an active and energized faith, it has the potential to affect the whole congregation. The definition of responsible synagogue trusteeship includes being Jewish role models, whose example will encourage their peers to live richly textured Jewish lives in which worship, study, and *gemilut chesed* are central, and Jewish value-based decision making becomes normative.

CONCLUSION

A new paradigm is needed for decision making in synagogues and other Jewish organizations and agencies. It combines Jewish value-based decision making with the exercise of governance on management issues. Questions that need to be addressed in the context of the new paradigm include: How well is the board serving the religious mission of the synagogue? To what extent would an increase in attention to religious matters in the content and context of a board meeting increase the satisfaction of board members? Is it possible to include biblical and other text study in the actual decision making of the board? What should be the role of individual or group prayer (other than the customary opening and closing prayers) in the context of board meetings? In what way is concern for the religious life of the congregation demonstrated in the planning of the agenda and the conduct of board meetings? What do board members really value, and how is this demonstrated in board actions and activities?

IMPLICATIONS

1. While much of the language in this chapter is addressed to synagogues, all Jewish institutions should be attending to the spirituality of their members or clients.

2. Lay leaders need to be brought into the process of bringing God and the sacred into all aspects of institutional life including, but not limited to the boardroom.

3. New types of partnerships between lay and professional leaders will need to be forged to help make this transition or transformation in institutional life possible.

4. The role for professionals, including clergy, will be to teach and guide the lay leaders to be able to lead and inspire others in terms of God, spirituality, and *kedushah*.

QUESTIONS FOR CRITICAL INQUIRY

1. From the perspective of the authors, what are the motivating factors precipitating the need for involving lay leaders in the quest for God and spirituality? From your own experience, what, if any, are the motivating factors? What are the benefits of involving lay leaders in the quest for God and spirituality?

2. What are the obstacles or barriers to lay leaders being greater advocates for spiritual seeking?

3. In what ways is God found in your boardroom? How are these ways similar to or different from ways that God is found in the classroom? Who or what is at the center of your boardroom? What does this mean in terms of messages given to your key lay leaders and professionals and those who come in contact with your institution — members, clients, other institutions, and other stakeholders?

4. In what ways have lay leaders in your institution taken an active role in the search for God and spirituality? In what ways have the professional leaders, including teachers, in your institution helped engage the lay leaders in the search for God and spirituality? What would be the next steps in your institution that would help move along the process of encouraging and preparing lay leaders to aid spiritual seeking?

5. In what ways do teachers, parents, and lay leaders interact around spiritual issues, sacred acts, and God? What additional interactions could be instituted?

ACTIVITIES

1. List the organizations in which you belong (e.g., school, health club, synagogue, Jewish community center, political organization). Indicate on the list what you get from belonging to each of these organizations. Then star the organizations that are spiritual (connect you to God) and the ones that are religious (connect you to a tradition). Compare and contrast the lists. In what ways does each of these organizations enrich your life? In what ways does each make you feel a sense of *kedushah*?

2. Pretend that you are on your synagogue board and are asked to design a leadership training course. What texts or stories (e.g., stories about Moses, Miriam, Hasidic tales, great teachers) would you use to help the participants understand how theirs is a sacred role?

3. Watch a video about a social service or environmental organization such as Jewish Federation, United Way, Jewish National Fund, etc. Based on the video, in what ways are the leaders of these organizations trying to do God's work? What signs, symbols,

words, music, etc., do the videos use to communicate these sacred messages?

BIBLIOGRAPHY

Aron, Isa. *Becoming a Congregation of Learners: Learning As a Key to Revitalizing Congregational Life.* Woodstock, VT: Jewish Lights Publishing, 2000.

Aron wrote this book based primarily on her experience in working with congregations through the Experiment in Congregational Education at Hebrew Union College-Jewish Institute of Religion. The goal of that project was to transform Jewish education through developing learning congregations and communities. Her book conveys the significance of cooperation between lay and professional leaders, and presents ways that these leaders can work together to energize their spiritual communities.

Borowitz, Eugene. "Co-Existing with Orthodox Jews." *Journal of Reform Judaism*, vol. 34, no. 3 (Summer 1987), 61-62.

Borowitz, a professor of Jewish philosophy and theology at Hebrew Union College-Jewish Institute of Religion in New York, has written extensively about theology and leadership.

Knobel, Peter S. "Recreating the Narrative Community Or It's Hard to Do Mitzvot by Yourself." In *Duties of the Soul, the Role of Commandments in Liberal Judaism*, edited by Niles E. Goldstein and Peter S. Knobel. New York: UAHC Press, 1999.

In this chapter, Knobel, a congregational Rabbi, presents his views on the role of God, *mitzvot*, study, and spirituality in forming religious community.

Olsen, Charles M. *Transforming Church Boards into Communities of Spiritual Leaders.* Washington, DC: Alban Institute, 1995.

In Olsen's vision of leadership, work on the church board is part of the religious experience and development of lay leaders. He shares vignettes and examples from his work with his own congregations and those of others. His book is published by the Alban Institute, which offers resources "for people who care about congregations."

Schechter, Daniel S. *Synagogue Boards: A Sacred Trust.* New York: UAHC Press, 2000.

Schechter, a lay leader in the Reform Movement and past congregational president, presents his views on how to bring the sacred into the work of synagogue boards. This volume is a handbook and a guide for those interested in integrating values, *kedushah*, and God into the organizational life of synagogues and other Jewish institutions.

Schwarz, Sidney. "The Rabbi As Spiritual Leader." *The Reconstructionist*, vol. 63, no. 1 (Fall 1999), 24-33.

Schwarz has written extensively on the role of synagogue transformation in reaching spiritual seekers, many of whom find synagogues lacking in spirituality. In this article, he focuses on the role of the Rabbi as a spiritual leader and the implications of this conceptualization on the role of congregational lay leaders and members in both fulfilling their spiritual quests and supporting that of others.

Yoffie, Eric. "Renewing the Covenant: Our Reform Jewish Future." Presidential Address to the Sixty-fourth General Assembly, Union of American Hebrew Congregations, Dallas, Texas, November 1997.

Rabbi Yoffie is President of the UAHC, the synagogue organization of the Reform Movement.

INTRODUCTION TO PART II
Teacher Training

Roberta Louis Goodman

EDUCATORS APPROACH TEACHING ABOUT GOD AND spirituality with different experience and comfort levels. For some, teaching about God and spirituality is a new "topic." Others have been teaching about God and spirituality in their classroom settings, but have not been engaged in professional development. Both groups would benefit from professional development offerings on the theories, skills, techniques, and content related to teaching about God and spirituality. Those planning professional development offerings need to normalize presenting about God and spirituality, focusing on this subject as they would focus on any other subject.

Preparing Jewish educators, parents, and clergy to nurture people's spirituality and relationship to God is critical in making God an explicit part of the curriculum of Jewish educational programs. Before Jewish educators can nurture the spirituality of others, they need to examine their own path. Such awareness becomes coupled with increasing familiarity about the paths that others are taking both within and outside Jewish frameworks. This understanding aids teachers in determining how to respond to the variety of learners and journeys they are likely to encounter. Jewish educators need to be comfortable and capable to talk about God within Jewish tradition. As with any other subject, they need the content knowledge, skills, approaches, and techniques that come from the research, theories, and experience of experts. Attending to their own ongoing spiritual growth through study, prayer, and exploration sets a good example for the learners whose lives they are trying to reach. While one's views about and relationship to God may be personal, it is important to break the silence, putting God on the communal agenda in Jewish education.

Presented in this section are actual, successful professional development programs, both one-time and multiple sessions. The programs were selected as models by the editors because of their quality. Examples of good programs were not hard to find, as many Jewish educators have begun preparing their faculty to nurture people's spirituality and relationship to God. These programs model the ability of educators to design and implement compelling, engaging programs that prepare teachers to teach others about God and spirituality. Professional development programs on this topic are doable and worthwhile.

Those programs presented here are written in such a way as to facilitate replication and adaptation. However, a program should be used only when it meets the goals of an educational institution, and not just because it is a good program. When replicating or adapting a program, consideration needs to be given to the different organizational cultures and systems of operation found in the institution. Hopefully, these programmatic examples will stimulate the development of other outstanding programs.

FORMAT OF PROGRAMS

A uniform format was devised to provide consistency and ease to the reader. The programs are described in detail. Please note: In the case of programs with multiple sessions, the topics covered in all sessions are listed, but only one session is outlined in full.

For each program, a brief description of each element is provided:

Title: Program's title

Topic: God or spirituality thematic focus

Target Audience: Population or group for which the program is intended

Time Frame: Program frequency, schedule, and length

Staffing: Listing of professionals and volunteers and their roles in the program

Overview: Succinct description of the entire program or curriculum

Purpose: What the program, curriculum, or lesson is trying to accomplish

Objectives: What the participants will do and learn

Content: Major concepts covered

Learning Materials: All books, supplies, and other materials needed to execute the program

Learning Activities: Step-by-step description of how to implement the program

Evaluation: Presents ways of evaluating the program

Watch Out For: Concerns to consider in implementing the program

DESCRIPTION OF CHAPTERS

In Chapter 29, "Teaching about God: Where I Stand," contributor Janice P. Alper encourages her faculty to talk about God in their classrooms and to accept different perceptions of God as expressed by the students. In order to accomplish this, she helps the teachers articulate in their own words a personal view of God. She engages them in text study and helps them develop a vocabulary for class discussions that deal with concepts of God.

Dr. Sherry H. Blumberg contributes Chapter 30, "'Jewish Religious Experience' Workshops for Teachers." This program combines Jewish content, personal sharing, and classroom applications to enable teachers to identify their own relationship to God and spirituality in order to be able to apply the material to their particular grade or setting.

Finally, Chapter 31, "God in the Classroom," describes an eight-session program by contributor Rabbi Isaac Serotta. The program is geared to help teachers become comfortable with their own understanding of and relationship to God so as to be comfortable talking about God and spiritual issues with their students.

CHAPTER 29

TEACHING ABOUT GOD: WHERE I STAND

Janice P. Alper

TOPIC:

Various perceptions of God as depicted in Torah and liturgy

TARGET AUDIENCE:

Faculty of any Jewish school setting

TIME FRAME:

2 to 2-1/2 hours

STAFF:

One facilitator

OVERVIEW:

This program is designed to help teachers understand that there is no one way to perceive God. This is an age-old tradition as depicted in Jewish literature, which includes the Torah and *Siddur*. It is designed to help the faculty reflect on their own views of God.

PURPOSE:

The purpose of this program is to encourage the faculty to talk about God in their classrooms and to accept different perceptions of God as expressed by the students. In order to do this, it is important for the faculty members to know how they themselves view God. Open-ended questions, a review of texts from *Chumash* and *Siddur*, and interactive reflection are all employed to accomplish the program objectives.

OBJECTIVES:

Participants will be able to:

*   articulate in their own words a personal view of God.

*   recognize that God, as depicted in "sacred" Jewish texts, takes on many different characteristics.

*   develop a vocabulary for class discussions which deals with concepts of God.

CONTENT:

Facts: There are many different ways God is depicted in our sacred writings. We view God in different ways, depending on our own background and knowledge.

Concepts: Everyone in a Jewish setting should have a perception or view of God that is consistent with the rest of his/her belief system.

Values: The teacher, as facilitator and role model, should encourage discussion and questions about God in the classroom. The teacher should be comfortable with his/her own personal view of God and be willing to accept the views of others, even if these views do not agree with his/her own.

Feelings: Awe, confusion, frustration, satisfaction, love.

LEARNING MATERIALS:

*   Copies of the prayers *"Ahavah Rabbah"* and *"Avot"*

*   Copies of Genesis 22:1-19 — the *Akedah* (Binding of Isaac) - Genesis 22:1-19

• Index cards or paper

LEARNING ACTIVITIES:

1. Introduction

   Ask participants to complete the sentence, "For me, God is . . . " on an index card or piece of paper. Instruct them to fold it in half and put it away.

2. Distribute copies of the three texts — "Ahavah Rabbah," "Avot," the Akedah.

   Divide the group into three smaller units. Ask each sub-group to focus on one text. Have each group answer the following questions about their text:

   • What words are used to describe God in this text?

   • What kind of relationship does God have to you, the community, and humanity as described in this text?

   • If you were teaching this text to your class, what concepts would you want to get across?

   • Other comments about the text.

   Bring everyone back together and ask each group to report on their answers to the questions listed above. See if you can determine similarities and differences among the three texts in regard to the questions and answers given.

   In a group discussion, talk about what these texts tell us about God. Are there other texts which describe God in other ways? If so, what are they, and how is God described?

3. Talking with Our Students about God

   In pairs, ask participants to develop a lexicon for talking about God by doing the following:

   Make a list of questions you might ask children in your classes in order to encourage discussions about God.

Think about responses you might make to children when they talk about God.

Think about what you will say if children ask you about your own level of belief in God. The pairs report back to the entire group.

4. Closure:

   Once again, each person writes down a response to "For me God is . . . "

   Have the participants look at the responses that they wrote at the beginning of the session and now at the end. Ask for feedback from the participants. Is what you wrote the same or different? What has/has not changed? What other comments about the program do you want to make?

Here are some alternative suggestions for the in-service session:

• Select any number of texts other than the three cited above. This is a particularly relevant discussion when talking about Megillat Esther, Sodom and Gomorrah, or the wars of Gog and Magog.

• Once this workshop is completed with teachers, encourage those who engage in the study of synagogue skills to apply the same principles to looking at some of the blessings in the various services. This works particularly well with students in Grades 6 and 7.

• Try other ways of personalizing God, such as an art project to "draw what God does" or writing a letter to God.

EVALUATION:

Encourage faculty to plan lessons in which there are discussions about God. Ask each faculty member to write a paragraph describing the lesson and the results. Discuss these at a future faculty meeting.

WATCH OUT FOR:

If the session is done with teachers from different settings, participants may be used to different versions and translations of the prayers. This is especially true for the *"Avot"* prayer, for which many congregations include the Matriarchs and their relationship to God, as well as the Patri-archs. These differences in the content of the prayer can alter what is learned about God from these prayers. Help the groups affirm different views and the significance of the language used in the prayers, rather than engage in a divisive argument over the differences in perspectives.

CHAPTER 30

"JEWISH RELIGIOUS EXPERIENCE" WORKSHOPS FOR TEACHERS

Sherry H. Blumberg

TOPIC:

What is the meaning of "God" for me? What is the Jewish concept of holiness? How can we teach about God and holiness? What are the paths to Jewish spirituality?

TARGET AUDIENCE:

The educator and faculty of a Religious School.

TIME FRAME:

2-3 hours each session, 3-4 sessions

STAFF:

One facilitator

OVERVIEW:

These programs are designed to enable the teachers to identify their own relationship to God and spirituality. The programs combine Jewish content, personal sharing, and classroom applications. Participants meet over breakfast or lunch in a relaxed atmosphere. They engage in discussions, text study, and project development — so as to be able to apply the material to their particular grade or setting. Often staff that works with similar age groupings join together to work on the assigned projects. In addition to sessions with the teachers, meetings are held with the educator and Rabbi to work toward consistently integrating Jewish religious experience into the Religious School curriculum.

PURPOSE:

The overall purpose is to encourage the teachers to begin to talk about God and to introduce God into all aspects of the school's curriculum. For this reason, values clarification techniques, open-ended questions and discussion, art projects, and metaphoric projects are combined with text study (mostly in English). In one group (with whom this project has been ongoing since 1991), the turnover in teachers was seen as a problem, and so packets of materials from past workshops were made available.

OBJECTIVES:

At the end of these sessions, participants will be able to:

- explore the meaning of God in their own lives and discuss how God as an idea and experience may work in the lives of their students.

- define God and holiness as they understand the concepts and hear how others define the terms.

- examine and share feelings about texts in Tanach, *Siddur*, and other Jewish texts (such as *Orchot Hayyim* by Asher ben Yehiel, the Rosh, 1250-1327) that discuss God, holiness, piety, wonder, etc.

- experience several techniques for teaching about God and religious experience, including the use of metaphor, music, art projects, meditation, text study, dance, theater, etc.

CONTENT:

Facts: There are many different Jewish concepts of God and holiness. Some questions have no "absolute answers." Jewish tradition speaks about God in its texts.

Concepts: God, holiness, piety, religious, transcendent, immanent, *Brit* (Covenant), metaphor.

Values: The Jewish teacher is the role model for students and needs to be comfortable exploring ideas and feelings about God with them. The struggle with, love of, and relationship to God is, and has been, central to Jewish thought and religious tradition.

Feelings: Joy, wonder, love, confusion, anger, frustration, longing, gratitude, fear

LEARNING MATERIALS:

- Blumberg, Sherry H. *Educating for Jewish Religious Experience.* University Microfilms, 1991.

- *Orchot Hayyim* by Asher ben Yehiel.

- Various texts on holiness: *"Kedushah"* and *"Mah Tovu"* from the *Siddur*; Leviticus 19; Psalms; Genesis 28:16 ("Surely God was in this place"); Exodus 2 (The burning bush); songs about God: *"Eli, Eli"; "Adonai, Adonai"* (by Beged Kefet); other songs that people like.

LEARNING ACTIVITIES:

Discussion, debate, guided fantasy and imagining, journaling, brainstorming (translation of ideas into classroom), making Visual *Midrash* (Jo Milgrom); Values Clarification and experiential exercises, such as nature walks, trust walks, mirroring, continuum, forced choice; singing; movement.

EVALUATION:

These questions are asked orally at the end of the sessions and in writing: Is it easier or harder now to talk about God with your students? What did you learn from the workshop that was of value to you about (God, holiness, theology)? What did you find troubling? What classroom techniques and suggestions made the most sense to you? Which ones will you try? What else do you want to/need to know? What would you change about this session?

EXAMPLE OF ONE PROGRAM:

I. Introductions (name, grade they teach, and a statement as to the meaning of holiness for them at this time.)

II. Opening: Make a Midrash

A. Hand out black and white construction paper, glue, and two texts, "Holy, Holy, Holy is the Lord of Hosts" and "You shall be holy because I, *Adonai*, am Holy." Ask participants to make a collage of their interpretation of their *midrash*.

B. Participants make their *midrash*, then present it to the others. What did they learn about themselves as they made it? What did they learn about holiness as they listened to one another?

III. Discussion

A. Discuss a line in Hebrew with English from the *"Yotzer Or"* or *"Ma'ariv Aravim."* Or, use the text from *Gates of Prayer*: "We walk sightless among miracles." Discuss the following questions:

- How do you find God in nature?

- Do you find God in nature through the order of life and the universe?

- Do you find God in nature in the natural beauty?

- How do the changing seasons affect you?

- What if you couldn't see?

- How do we find God in ourselves?

- How are we each different, yet the same?

- When are you acting as if you were God's partner?

- What role does love and friendship play?

B. Text: "Surely God is in this place and I did not know it" (Genesis 28:16)

Participants are asked to see if they can find holiness in their daily actions during the next week. They may choose one of the following:

- Take something you don't like doing and try to find a spiritual reason for doing it.

- Relate something you love to do to a blessing or create a blessing for it.

IV. Brainstorming: Ways to Help Students Experience the Holy

A. Work in grade groupings (PK, 1-3, 4-6, 7-8, high school). Brainstorm ways that you can bring experiences of the holy into your classroom — for example, begin each day of school with a *brachah,* each student shares a special thing for which he/she is grateful, make a God's partner bulletin board (each student shares ways he/she has acted as God's partner during the week, such as visiting an elderly relative or friend, cleaning up a park, etc.).

After the brainstorming in grade groupings, each group of teachers can share their ideas for bringing experiences of the holy into the classroom.

V. Closure: Sing a New Song unto God

A. Conclude by singing favorite songs about God: *"Yedid Nefesh," "Mi Pi El,"* etc.

CHAPTER 31

GOD IN THE CLASSROOM

Isaac Serotta

TOPIC:

Aiding teachers in the process of being comfortable with their own understanding of and relationship to God; helping to prepare teachers so that they are comfortable talking about God and spiritual issues with their students.

TARGET AUDIENCE:

All teachers in the supplementary school Grades Kindergarten through 10.

TIME FRAME:

Eight one-hour sessions.

STAFF:

Education Director of the congregation.

OVERVIEW:

This program was originated and taught as a course by the congregation's Education Director (author of this chapter). The sessions were held Sunday mornings before school. They were conducted on four consecutive Sundays in late fall, then continued with four consecutive sessions after winter break.

Each session had a particular theme or focus, such as finding one's spiritual path, experiencing God, etc. The sessions tended to follow a pattern of: (1) set induction of a practical, experiential activity, (2) text study (traditional or modern), and (3) application by examining a question from a student.

Each session began with a set induction of a practical idea related to the day's topic. The set induction modeled an activity that each teacher could use in his/her own classroom. It was then followed by discussion of one page of a story or article. The sources included: Hasidic tales, Torah narrative, writings by Jewish authors and non-Jewish authors, and reporting on significant conversations. Teachers discussed the sources in dyads and triads. Small groups were used to encourage interaction among the teachers and an exploration by each teacher of his/her own spirituality. The instructor ended the session with a question from a student which related to the day's focus. Sometimes teachers role-played ways of responding to the question.

PURPOSE:

The instructor recognized that what motivated teachers initially to attend these sessions was that they learned something that they could apply immediately in their own classrooms. Yet what kept the teachers coming back session after session was that they personally got something out of the experience.

The course was designed to model a classroom setting conducive to examining one's own spirituality. The intent was to model an approach that the teachers could incorporate into their own classrooms. One underlying assumption of the instructor was that they would be more influential and powerful as teachers if they were able to show and share the kind of person that they are, specifically the ways in which they personally approached different questions related to God. It was important for the teacher to share his/her own spiritual journey, even if the teacher was unsure or ambivalent about some aspect of his/ her understanding of or relationship to God.

OBJECTIVES:

The course focused on two objectives:

1. To enable the teachers to become comfortable with their own spirituality. I had adequately screened the teachers in the hiring process so that there would not be a problem with the appropriateness of any teacher's spirituality or belief system.

2. To give the teachers a chance to interact with one another.

CONTENT:

Different aspects of understanding and relating to God are presented in this course, including: finding a spiritual path, communicating with God, experiencing God, and recognizing God's presence.

LEARNING MATERIALS:

The texts are the main materials needed for each session. Each text is listed below.

LEARNING ACTIVITIES:

My role as instructor was to facilitate, as it was an important goal to get the teachers to examine their own ideas and feelings about God. I selected texts that were substantive in that they had something important to say about spirituality. I also conveyed my own knowledge in the areas of philosophy and theology, my own life experiences, and my knowledge of texts. It was important for me to model my own journey, and to be willing to share experiences that brought me to where I am on that journey. As a means for modeling how individual Jews have answered for themselves certain issues related to God, I

shared stories about myself and about others (such as Franz Rosenzweig's decision not to convert to Christianity).

The eight sessions are outlined below. The outline includes the theme or focus of the lesson, the text used, and the question asked by a student. As a more complete example of a session, Session #3 is described in slightly more detail than the other sessions.

Recommended reading for all faculty members was: *Finding God: Ten Jewish Responses* by Rifat Sonsino and Daniel B. Syme (Union of American Hebrew Congregations, 1986). Other readings were recommended to individuals as their interests emerged.

Session #1: Seeing God

Text: Exodus 33:17-23 in which Moses sees God's back.

Key Points: No one knows what God looks like, but Jewish tradition and texts make suppositions and hint as to the appearance of God. What are the boundaries to knowing what God looks like?

Student Question: What does God look like?

Session #2: Finding God in Every Letter

Text: "*Yud*" in *The Book of Letters* by Lawrence Kushner (Jewish Lights Publishing, 1990), pp. 44-45.

Key Points: In addition to *gematria*, a spiritual message can be found in all the letters of the *alef-bet*. *Yud* is most often used for God's name.

Student Question: Why do we have to study Hebrew?

Session #3: Broadcasting and Receiving

Text: "*Tet Zayin* (16)," *Honey from the Rock* by Lawrence Kushner (Harper & Row Publishers, 1977), pp. 32-33.

Key Points: In this text, Kushner makes the analogy between God and a television set. God is always broadcasting, but we are not always receiving. He suggests turning on the mute button on the television so that there is no sound, then playing with the buttons so that there is no picture. Although there is no sound and no picture, somewhere someone is talking. God is like this TV set, on but no one is necessarily paying attention to see or hear God. Perhaps with the right attention, we could hear.

Set Induction: This exercise is adapted from Sherry Blumberg's suggestions for nurturing religious experience (see Chapter 30, "'Jewish Religious Experience' Workshops for Teachers" by Sherry H. Blumberg, p. 298). Set up one bottle of water with sugar in it and one without it. Set up a taste testing experiment. Have several people taste the water. Ask them: "What is the difference between the water in the two bottles? How did you know that they were different? What made them appear to be the same? How is God like the two bottles of water?" Essentially, the idea behind the exercise is that you cannot see or smell the sweetness until you taste it. You cannot see or sense God in the conventional way until you experience God.

Student Question: If we can't see God, how do we know that God is there?

Session #4: Getting Connected

Text: *I and Thou* by Martin Buber (Charles Scribner's Sons, 1970), p. 160.

Key Points: Buber's concept of the "Eternal You" — the idea that the Eternal You cannot become an It. The Eternal You cannot be measured and is without limit. This means that one cannot know everything there is to know about God, so we must not be afraid of saying what we think we know about God.

Student Question: If God is there, why doesn't God talk to me?

Session #5: Missing God's Sign

Text: "The Fish That Looked for Water" in *Hear*

O Israel: About God by Molly Cone (UAHC Press, 1973), pp. 13-15.

Key Points: The story is about a fish that unsuccessfully searches for water. The analogy is between water being everywhere and God being everywhere. At the end of the story is the prayer *"Kadosh, Kadosh, Kadosh"* that tells us of God's presence everywhere. In another text in the Torah, after Jacob dreams of a ladder with angels going up and down, he awakens and exclaims, "God was in this place and I did not know it." We do not always acknowledge when God is. We need to try to recognize the moments when God is present.

Student Question: Where is God?

Session #6: Exercising Your Free Will

Text: Talmud, *Baba Metzia* 59b

Key Points: This texts presents the Rabbis arguing with Rabbi Eliezar. Rabbi Eliezar says if I am right, then let this tree be uprooted as a sign of God's support of my argument. The tree is uprooted. The story continues with Rabbi Eliezar using many such signs and the Rabbis holding their ground. Finally, the Rabbis comment that God gave them free will to interpret the laws according to their own understanding. God concurs.

As partners with God, we continue to interpret God's laws. What we know today and what we will know ten years from today is not the same. It is okay to stand up and say that this is what I think today. Growth and change in our understanding of and relationship to God are supported and affirmed.

Student Question: What am I supposed to do? What does God want me to do?

Session #7: Journeying

Text: "Franz Rosenzweig" in *Contemporary Jewish Philosophies* by William E. Kaufman (Reconstructionist Press and Behrman House, Inc., 1976), pp. 29-31.

Key Points: The text presents Franz Rosenzweig's decision not to convert to Christianity as he had planned to do. Rosenzweig attended a High Holy Day service in Berlin, and his life was transformed.

Student Question: How can I believe in God?

Session #8: Getting To Where You Want to Go

Text: "Playing Checkers," in *Tales of the Hasidim: The Later Masters*, edited by Martin Buber (Schocken Books, 1948), p. 73.

Key Points: This Hasidic tale draws the analogy between the rules of checkers and the path to a spiritual life. Background on Hasidism adds to this discussion.

Student Question: How does one get close to God?

EVALUATION:

These are some questions that the teachers should be able to answer: (1) In what ways did this course affirm your views of God? (2) In what ways did this course challenge your ideas and relationship to God? (3) Describe your approach to bringing God into the classroom.

FEEDBACK ON THE PROGRAM:

I made certain that everyone in the group spoke at some time during each session. The teachers like the program. A few teachers used some of these activities in the classroom. Two of the teachers of Hebrew/prayer made certain that part of their lesson plans included having the students explore the views of God presented in the text. They also talk about what the prayers meant to them personally. Sometimes, these teachers asked me to address questions about God that students asked based on a particular prayer.

The course ignited something in the mid-week Hebrew program. It triggered rewriting curriculum as the teachers started asking: What are the spiritual lessons that come from each of the prayers? The teachers added goals and objectives of spiritual lessons that emerge from each of the prayers. A core of four or five Hebrew teachers met regularly to make these changes occur in the curriculum. In addition, they put together a prayer book for the year.

WATCH OUT FOR:

It is important that the facilitator not talk more than the learners.

FOLLOW-UP:

The eight-session course in the following year was based on a text study of the book *Sabbath* by Abraham Joshua Heschel. This topic also helped people become comfort able in talking about their spirituality, and got them to think about experiences of Shabbat that they could bring into the classroom. The teachers ran the full gamut of Shabbat synagogue observance — regular, occasional, and attendance at other congregations. Reading Heschel was an aid in focusing the religious perspective of our congregation and movement. Although Heschel taught for the Conservative Movement's seminary, he focuses more on the spirituality than on the *halachic* aspects of Shabbat. The teachers worked in pairs to present each chapter of the book to the group. There was dialogue and discussion following the teachers' presentations.

INTRODUCTION TO PART III
Lessons, Curricula, Programs

Roberta Louis Goodman

LEARNING ABOUT GOD AND SPIRITUALITY SHOULD begin at an early age and continue throughout one's life. It is our responsibility as Jewish educators, clergy, and parents, to nurture people's spirituality along the way. How do we do this? What are some approaches? What can we learn from others who have experience in this area? This section presents programs that model a variety of ways to teach about God and spirituality.

As with the programs geared to train teachers in Part II, examples of good programs were not hard to find. The programs chosen for this section demonstrate the ability of educators to design and implement compelling, worthwhile, and engaging programs that prepare learners of all ages in different settings to strengthen their relationship with God and develop their spirituality.

The programs described here are actual programs that have been used successfully. Targeted at diverse age groups, they cover a range of concepts and content, such as names of God, *Kabbalah*, a person's relationship to God, prayer, and holidays. The programs utilize a variety of approaches, including the study of Jewish texts, the visual arts, discussion, writing, movement and dancing, music, storytelling, and more. The different formats of the programs range from one-time programs to conferences, retreats, at home activities, and programs in Jewish educational institutions. Please note that in the case of programs with multiple sessions, the topics covered in all sessions are listed, but only one session is outlined in full.

All of these programs are written in a way to facilitate replication and adaptation. However, it is important that a program be used only when it meets the goals of an educational institution, and not just because it is a good program. When replicating or adapting a program, consideration needs to be given to the different organizational cultures and systems of operation found in the institution. Hopefully, these programmatic examples will stimulate the development of other outstanding programs on this topic.

In order to provide consistency and ease of access, the same format is used to describe programs in Part III as in Part II. Below, a brief description of each of the elements is provided.

Title: Title of program

Topic: God or spirituality thematic focus

Target Audience: Population or group for which the program is intended

Time Frame: Program frequency, schedule, and length

Staffing: Listing of professionals and volunteers and their roles in the program

Overview: Succinct description of the entire program or curriculum

Purpose: What the program, curriculum, or lesson is trying to accomplish

Objectives: What the participants will do and learn

Content: Major concepts covered

Learning Materials: All books, supplies, and other materials needed to execute the program

Learning Activities: Step-by-step description of how to implement the program

Evaluation: Ways of evaluating the program

Watch Out For: Concerns to consider in implementing the program

DESCRIPTION OF CHAPTERS

The chapters in Part III are divided according to age groups: Early Childhood, Elementary, Teens, Adult, and Family Education.

Early Childhood

Max Segal Handelman's contribution, Chapter 32, "Rosh Chodesh: The Jewish Timekeeper," leads off the early childhood section. Through learning about and celebrating Rosh Chodesh, children become attuned to God's role in setting nature in motion. They bless and thank God for all that has happened in their lives from one month to the next.

Chapter 33, "To Be Thankful: A Spirituality Havdalah," contributed by Dr. Sherry H. Blumberg, describes an experiential program in which the celebration of Havdalah is the framework for exploring a way in which we talk to God. The content focuses on thankfulness, gratitude, and awe as emotions we might feel when we speak to God.

Chapter 34, "HaMotzi: Thanking God for Bread," shows how contributors Rena Rotenberg, Rachel Meisels, and Nancy Rubin use as a reason for thanking God the sense of awe and amazement that accompanies turning things of nature into food.

Elementary

Chapter 35, "Psalms Alive: A Musical Presentation," contributed by Linda Kaufman and Carla Silen, describes a 20-minute musical that provides a look into the life of King David in his youth. The play focuses on the Psalms as an expression of King David's relationship to God. The script and original music are included.

The program described in Chapter 36, "Talking To God," contributed by Rabbi Marcia R. Plumb, gives students a chance to reflect on and discuss praying to God — what we say and why we say it.

Chapter 37, "Moving Metaphors for God: Enriching Spirituality through Movement," contributed by Kate Mann, presents ways of using the human body as an insightful teacher in order to awaken and deepen spiritual awareness. When the body is flowing with energy, Mann asserts, it embodies the whole person — body, mind, and soul.

Chapter 38, "Where in the World Is Adonai Echad?," outlines a course taught at UAHC Joseph Eisner Camp Institute that immerses learners deeper and deeper into the *Pardes* (orchard) of God. *Pardes* stands for the four levels of study in Judaism.

Chapter 39, "Poetry and Prayer: The 'V'ahavta,'" demonstrates how contributor Dr. Cathleen Cohen taps into the tools and techniques of poetry in order to help the learner interpret prayers, to make connections to their own lives, and to relate to God. The *"V'ahavta"* is used here as a model; the approach can be applied to almost any prayer.

Teens

Chapter 40, "Does God Know? Does God Care?," contributed by Dr. Sherry H. Blumberg, describes a program of text study and discussion. The program explores the relationship of meaning and purpose in our lives and connects that meaning to our relationship with God. Blumberg finds this program to be appropriate for teenagers, who are often confused about their identity and about God.

Chapter 41, "Whose Body Is It, Anyway?," was contributed by Kyla Epstein Schneider and Rabbi William Dreskin. The program reframes many teenage issues, such as appearance, clothing, alcohol/drugs, piercing, tattooing, and suicide in light of the essential concept that we are made *B'tzelem Elohim*, in the image of God.

Rabbi Jordan Millstein, contributor of Chapter 42, "What's God Got to Do with It?," contends that the religious experience has been central to Jewish existence. The intent of this program is to bring to the surface the students' own experiences, identify them as connected to God, and validate them within a Jewish environment and tradition.

Adults

Chapter 43, "Jews in Search of Spirituality: A Spirituality Conference," describes an annual day-long conference in Atlanta for members of area Reform congregations. The Conference provides an opportunity for laity and Rabbis together to discuss and explore their spirituality and their understanding of and relationship to God.

Chapter 44, "Searching for God," describes a *kallah* program contributed by Dr. Betsy Katz and Rabbi Alan Bregman *(z"l)*. The *kallah* provides an opportunity over two or more sessions for participants to explore their personal feelings, reflections, conflicts, yearnings, experiences, and encounters with God.

The course outlined in Chapter 45, "Your Link in the Chain of Jewish Tradition," contributed by Nadine Cohen, combines principles of textual analysis and interpretation with those of art therapy. Women explore their spirituality through text study and artistic expression.

Family Education

In Chapter 46, "Kesher L'Adonai," contributor Janice P. Alper uses a series of interactive strategies to move participants toward a greater connection with God.

Alper also contributed the program described in Chapter 47, "God around Us." In this program, parents and children explore together their perceptions of God, how they can talk to God, and what they think about God.

Chapter 48, "Light: A Family Kallah," contributed by Harriet M. Levine, describes a family *kallah* in which participants explore the importance of light in Judaism and the meaning of light in their lives and in the lives of all Jews.

The "Family Sukkot Retreat" in Chapter 49 was contributed by Michelle Shapiro Abraham, Dr. Sherry H. Blumberg, and Rabbi David Wechsler-Azen. Families gather for an extended period of time to enjoy the celebration of Shabbat and Sukkot in community and to explore concepts and feelings connected with God.

Chapter 50, "Ba'bayit: Parent and Child Exploring God, Prayer, and Spirituality Together," contributed by Michelle Shapiro Abraham, contains a series of Family Books for children in Kindergarten through Grade 2 and their parents or grandparents. The books are meant to be used at home as a follow-up to a classroom unit on prayer, God, and spirituality, or to be part of a family education program.

Bev Fox contributed Chapter 51, "God As a Topic for Family Conversation," a weekend retreat for nearly 200 hundred parents, fourth graders, and their siblings to dialogue about God. The retreat provides time for parents and children to sit together, talk about God, and learn more about Jewish views of God.

Chapter 50, "God Is in *This* Place: A Family Treasure Hunt," contributed by Ben Zion M. Kogen and Julie Jaslow Auerbach, outlines one part of a series of programs, primarily for parents, that focuses on bringing God and spirituality into family life.

ROSH CHODESH: THE JEWISH TIMEKEEPER

Maxine Segal Handelman

TOPIC:

Recognizing and acknowledging the New Moon is a way of helping preschoolers understand cyclical changes. Doing so also helps them view God as the Creator Who sets the natural order into motion, and gives them an opportunity to pray for the blessings in our lives that each month brings.

TARGET AUDIENCE:

Preschoolers in a weekday or weekend program

TIME FRAME:

Once a month for 15-30 minutes

STAFF:

Teacher or adult leader

OVERVIEW:

The program introduces celebrating Rosh Chodesh with song, blessings, stories, food, and reflection. The key concept is the moon as the Jewish timekeeper. This program, when done on a monthly basis, helps the preschoolers mark time as they see changes both in the order of nature and in their lives. They become attuned to God's role in setting nature in motion. They bless and thank God for all that has happened in their lives from one month to the next.

PURPOSE:

The program gets children from the earliest ages into the rhythm of the Jewish year. It creates in them a sense of the passage of time, how their lives change, how the world around them changes, and reinforces their thankfulness to God for the cycles of time and life.

OBJECTIVES:

The preschoolers will be able to:

*   state how the world around them and their lives have changed from one month to the next.

*   identify Rosh Chodesh as the celebration of the New Moon and new Jewish month.

*   share their reasons for being thankful to God from New Moon to New Moon.

CONTENT:

The main concepts that the preschoolers learn are:

*   The moon is a Jewish timekeeper.

*   The moon changes. It grows bigger, becomes a full moon, and gets smaller.

*   This cycle of the moon happens over and over again.

*   When the sliver reappears in the sky, we celebrate Rosh Chodesh, and a new Hebrew month.

*   God set in motion cycles, such as the changing of the moon and the seasons.

*   We are grateful to God for the changes in our lives that each new month brings.

LEARNING MATERIALS:

Since this program occurs monthly, some of the materials (e.g., the story that is read or the supplies for an art projects) will differ each time. Other materials will be the same from month to month: moon-shaped cookies (almond cookies are a favorite of our preschool), calendar of the Jewish year with the months and holidays visible, picture of the cycle of the moon, other decorations.

A copy of the Rosh Chodesh blessings (in abbreviated form is recommended) and song sheets should be available to all teachers.

LEARNING ACTIVITIES:

The key learning activity for the monthly Rosh Chodesh program is the "Rosh Chodesh spot." At the beginning of each school year, each preschool classroom chooses their own Rosh Chodesh spot outside: a tree, a hill, a garden. Each Rosh Chodesh (regardless of the season, so tell students to dress appropriately for an outdoor activity, especially if they live in a cold climate), the class visits the spot. Thus, over time, this gives them a sense of ownership. They may bring to their spot other activities for the program, such as stories and songs, or they may come there to make observations. These observations may be catalogued in a book or on a bulletin board; the children may draw pictures or create art work with things from their "spot." Another option is to take a picture on site each month.

The basic concept is that everything changes. Over a year, children will be able to observe one spot in nature die and be renewed. (Even in warmer climates, plants go through cycles of blooming, dormancy, and trimming even if there is not the great "fall" of leaves. For example, the city of Santa Monica, California trims their palm fronds every fall in coordination with Sukkot.) By tying this cycle of nature to Rosh Chodesh, itself a holiday of cycles, the children may come to relate nature to Judaism, and, as

they grow and mature, a groundwork may be established to further their understanding of the cyclical nature of Judaism. In the case of catastrophes, such as floods, earthquakes, hurricanes, or tornadoes, which happen all too frequently, the students have a regular way of making sense out of the power of nature and the way it affects their lives. (Obviously, because they visit the spot during the school day, the children will not be able to view the moon while they are there.)

The time in the "spot" is an opportunity for the preschoolers to share what has changed in their lives from month to month. For example, Shoshana got new shoes because her feet grew, Jacob's family welcomed a new baby, Zoe's grandma who was sick got better, Paul was new to the class, and the class learned three new letters of the alphabet. In this way, the students begin to chart their own growth and changes in their lives. They can learn to appreciate the cycles and changes in life and express their gratefulness to God for setting in motion the order of the universe through their blessing of the new month.

Remember that children of this age are just gaining a sense of time, so sometimes they will share things that happened longer than a month ago. Referring to the previous times that they met, to some memorable aspect of that meeting (e.g., leaves were turning colors, we saw a red cardinal in the tree, Jacob showed us a picture of his new baby sister) might help them remember and mark the passage of time as they come to understand the concept of a month.

The First Month

The first month, it is important to introduce Rosh Chodesh as a special Jewish celebration and the moon as the Jewish timekeeper. One activity to help the children become more aware of the moon and its cycle, is to give the families a chart to complete. The chart looks like a regular month's calendar at a glance. The calendar should follow the Hebrew month with "1" being for day 1 of the Hebrew month. In the box for each day is a circle representing the moon. The families are to draw what the moon looks like each day. If possible, somewhere on the page, draw a picture of a new or Rosh Chodesh moon as a thin, white crescent bulging to the right with the rest of the circle colored in black, and a full moon left completely white.

Discuss with the students how the moon changes over the course of a month. Tell them about how Jews used to watch for the New Moon, and once two people saw it, *shofrot* would be sounded and torches lighted to inform people of the New Moon. Tell children to watch with their families for the New Moon and report it to the class the next day. Be certain to have a loud celebration at the sighting of the next New Moon.

All Months

The rest of the program involves telling stories about the moon or cycles in nature, singing songs, saying a Rosh Chodesh blessing or two, hearing the name of the new month and any Jewish holidays that occur in that month, eating moon-shaped cookies (a full moon-shaped cookie is obviously the easiest to find, but baking your own cookies in different moon phase shapes is fun, too), and doing an art project with materials gathered from the class spot, or any other topical project make for a complete program.

Children's Books

Here are some suggestions for age appropriate books about the moon.

Asch, Frank. *Moongame*. New York: Scholastic, 1984.

———. *Mooncake*. New York: Scholastic, 1983.

———. *Happy Birthday, Moon*. New York: Scholastic, 1982.

———. *Moondance*. New York: Scholastic, 1993.

———. *Moonbear*. New York: Simon and Schuster, 1993.

Banks, Kate. *And If the Moon Could Talk*. New York: Farrar, Straus & Giroux, 1998.

Carle, Eric. *Papa, Please Get the Moon for Me*. New York: Scholastic, 1986.

Fowler, Susi G. *I'll See You When the Moon Is Full*. New York: Greenwillow Books, 1994.

Rosenfeld, Dina. *Why the Moon Only Glows*. New York: Hachai Publishing, 1992.

Schaefer, Carole Lexa. *Sometimes Moon*. New York: Crown Publishers, 1999.

Whitcher, Susan. *Moonfall*. New York: Farrar, Straus and Giroux, 1993.

Parent Education

Parent education is an important element of incorporating Rosh Chodesh into the preschool curriculum. For many parents, Rosh Chodesh will be a newly discovered holiday, so educating parents as to what Rosh Chodesh is all about is the first step. Beyond that, parents can be educated about Rosh Chodesh from their children's point of view, so they can come to understand the concepts involved in their children's developmental levels.

A parent bulletin board, or bulletin board and table, can be designated as a spot to help parents become oriented to the new month and Hebrew calendar. Use the calendar to inform parents about happenings and holidays in the school. This is an ideal way to educate parents as they drop off and pick up their children at the classroom door. Bold captions with brief explanations will catch the eye and communicate in the brief time slot allotted by most busy parents. Topics such as "What is Rosh Chodesh?," "Why celebrate the moon?," "How to celebrate the moon," and holidays coming in the new Hebrew month are appropriate and achievable. Basic information about Rosh Chodesh can be repeated every month for the first several months of the school year. Rosh Chodesh can be mentioned in monthly newsletters, and handouts can be sent home with activity ideas for families. Parents can be invited into the classroom for the monthly Rosh Chodesh celebration and trip to the Rosh Chodesh spot.

After their children have been celebrating Rosh Chodesh for several months, parents can be invited to the school one evening for an adult celebration of Rosh Chodesh. The ceremony could include stories, song, prayer, study, and, of course, food. Not only might the experience help parents understand why their children have become so taken with the moon, but it will help Rosh Chodesh add a little significance to the lives of the entire family. If it is dark out, everyone can, of course, go outside to see the moon.

Adult Resources

The following are some references for adults on the subject of the moon.

Adelman, Penina. *Miriam's Well.* New York: Biblio Press, 1990.

Agus, Arlene. "This Month Is for You: Observing Rosh Chodesh As a Women's Holiday." In *The Jewish Woman: New Perspectives*, edited by Elizabeth Koltun. New York: Schocken Books, 1986.

Burstein, Chaya. *The Jewish Kid's Catalog.* Philadelphia, PA: Jewish Publication Society, 1993.

Berrin, Susan, ed. *Celebrating the New Moon: A Rosh Chodesh Anthology.* Northvale, NJ: Jason Aronson Inc., 1996.

Solomon, Judith. *The Rosh Chodesh Table: Foods at the New Moon.* New York: Biblio Press, 1995.

Umansky, Ellen, and Dianne Ashton, eds. *Four Centuries of Jewish Women's Spirituality.* Boston, MA: Beacon Press, 1992.

Blessing for Rosh Chodesh

This blessing is adapted from *Kiddush Levanah*, the sanctification of the new moon, which is recited while looking at the new moon, usually the Saturday night after the new moon. This version, which is age appropriate for preschoolers,

uses the familiar blessing formula, which helps children relate to the blessing:

Baruch Atah Adonai, M'Chadaysh Chodashim.
Thank You, God, for renewing the months.

A Song for Rosh Chodesh:

Here are the words to "Twinkle, Twinkle, Little Moon" (inspired by Jeremy Levin), which is sung to the tune of "Twinkle, Twinkle, Little Star."

Twinkle, twinkle little moon,
I wonder if I'll see you soon.
Up above the world so high,
Like a crescent in the sky.
Twinkle, twinkle little moon,
I wonder if I'll see you soon.

EVALUATION:

The following questions can be used with preschoolers to make certain that they are comprehending and incorporating into their lives the main concepts associated with Rosh Chodesh: (1) What is something special that happened to you since the last time we welcomed the new moon? (2) What changes do you see outside in nature since the last time we welcomed the new moon? (3) How does the moon change? (4) What happened during the month for which we want to thank God?

WATCH OUT FOR:

The circle, or reflection time, when children talk about the changes in nature and in their lives, is the crux of this program. Sometimes preschoolers can bring up some very painful experiences or act out because something that makes them uncomfortable happened during the month. The teacher needs to be prepared for dealing with sadness and discomfort. Some children's experiences may therefore require follow-up with the teacher, social worker, other resource person, or parents.

CHAPTER 33

TO BE THANKFUL: A SPIRITUALITY HAVDALAH

Sherry H. Blumberg

TOPIC:

Thankfulness, gratitude, and awe in the context of *Havdalah*; ways of talking to God

TARGET AUDIENCE:

Preschool, Kindergarten, and/or Grade 1. This may also be used as a Family Education program.

TIME FRAME:

Saturday evening, 45-50 minutes

STAFF:

One leader, aides and assistants (approximately one for each 5-8 children)

OVERVIEW:

This is an experiential program in which celebrating Havdalah is the framework for exploring a way we talk to God. The content focuses on thankfulness, gratitude, and awe as emotions we might feel when we speak to God. The program can be done in different formats, including having the younger children go through the activities while the adults are studying, or as a family program.

PURPOSE:

Havdalah presents itself as a powerful ceremony in which the senses are heightened and the symbols and rituals create a mystical mood. All of this is utilized to help us explore the emotions of thankfulness, awe, wonder, and gratitude as part of our lives as Jews. The young children are given the opportunity to respond to the symbols and emotions in their own language, illustrating one way of talking to God. Values voting, discussion, role-playing, and guided fantasy are integrated into the Havdalah ceremony.

OBJECTIVES:

The participants will be able to:

*   recall times in their lives when they were very happy.

*   find ways of saying "thank you" to whomever or whatever made them happy.

*   show happiness in their face and body.

*   celebrate Havdalah.

*   role-play different ways of talking to God and share these with the group.

*   imagine a place where everyone is happy and grateful.

*   sing the *"Shehecheyanu"* together.

CONTENT:

Concepts and feelings, such as happiness and gratitude, are connected with God. Havdalah is presented as a way of saying "thank you" to God at the end of Shabbat.

LEARNING MATERIALS:

*   A Havdalah service that the leader likes (it should include the four blessings — wine,

spices, candles, and Havdalah/Distinction, and end with singing *"Eliyahu HaNavi," "Shavuah Tov,"* and *"Shehecheyanu"*)

- Havdalah candle
- spice box
- wine cup
- wine
- matches
- a "drip plate" for the candle wax

LEARNING ACTIVITIES:

Set Induction: Values Voting

- Leader asks the following questions, and participants put thumbs up or down:
- Have you ever had a birthday party?
- Have you ever been really happy, such as when you came into a warm place after being really cold? (This question can be adapted as necessary for the group.)
- Have you ever been really glad to see someone?
- Have you ever been sick and then got better?
- Have you ever seen or heard something so funny you couldn't stop laughing?
- Have you ever gotten something you really wanted?

Processing the Values Voting

- Think about the questions just asked. How did you feel at each of these times? (Prompt with some of the things listed above — birthday party, getting over a sickness, etc.)
- Did you want to say thank you for these things?
- Who did you thank?
- Who do you want to thank now for these things?

Activity #1: Magic Circle

In groups of 5-8 children, have each child share with the group how they felt. Tell about one time when they felt happy.

Transition: Each group leader says, "Happiness can also be called gratitude or thanks. Jews show gratitude or thanks to other people and to God. We say blessings as a way of showing our thanks. We are going to share a ceremony that ends the Sabbath. It is called Havdalah."

Activity #2: Havdalah Symbols

With all the participants in the circle, bring out the symbols used for Havdalah. Ask children to hold the symbols. Begin the Havdalah ceremony. Before each blessing, tell what it is we are being thankful for:

Wine: drink, sense of taste, tongues and mouths to do the tasting, joy in our lives

Spices: food, sense of smell, noses to do the smelling, variety in life, good smells that fill our homes on Shabbat

Candles: light and warmth, sense of sight, eyes to see with, wisdom, an additional soul

Hamavdil ben kodesh l'chol (prayer separating the holy and the ordinary, separating Shabbat from the other days of the week): sense of touch, comfort and closeness, kisses and hugs to mark sharing Shabbat with others, time to be with family, time to enjoy one another, time to think about the week

The leader says: "Before we end our Havdalah, we want to imagine . . . what would a world be like if everyone was happy and felt that they had a lot to be grateful for? Close your eyes and imagine it."

Leader adds: "At the end of Havdalah we sing a song and hope for a time like you imagined." Sing *"Eliyahu HaNavi,"* and end the ceremony with *"Shavua Tov."*

Activity #3: Role-playing

Divide into groups of 6-8. If the entire group is not larger than 12, you can stay together.

Group leader says: "Now let's see what we have learned. Let's role-play. Someone is going to play God, and we will try to say 'thank you.' Do you only do this using words? Can you pray? sing? give *tzedakah*?" etc. (Note: You may want to rotate the part of God among the children.)

Closure: Shavua Tov: Thanking God during the Week

Leader comments: As we go into the new week, remember to say "thank you" to God when you feel happy or grateful.

EVALUATION:

Ask the children the following questions: (1) How might you talk to God? (2) How and when do you say thank you to God?

WATCH OUT FOR:

The leader should watch to see that the children are involved and that they are able to express thanks. Make certain that one child does not dominate, and that the assistants or aides do not do most of the talking.

CHAPTER 34

HAMOTZI: THANKING GOD FOR BREAD

Rena Rotenberg, Rachel Meisels, and Nancy Rubin

TOPIC:

What does God have to do with the making of bread? Why do we say a blessing over bread? We thank God for helping us turn nature (grains) into food.

TARGET AUDIENCE:

Preschool/Primary Grades

TIME FRAME:

For the most part, the activities from this curricular unit can each be done in 20 minute time slots over several days.

STAFF:

Classroom teaching staff. One optional activity involves a field trip for which drivers will be needed.

OVERVIEW:

Children in preschool and primary grades are naturally curious and inspired by the world around them. Yet part of nurturing their spiritual growth involves presenting concepts in very concrete terms. This curricular unit connects the sense of awe and amazement of human beings turning things of nature into food as a reason for thanking God. The curricular unit succeeds in presenting this concept through three main activities: identifying types of grains, turning grain into bread, and growing plants.

PURPOSE:

The methods used are kinesthetic, drawing on the five senses, and interactive.

OBJECTIVES:

The preschool and primary school child will:

- consider the care needed to grow a plant.

- watch the steps involved in turning grain into bread.

- connect the wonder of human beings turning nature into food with thanking God for bread.

- identify the foods for which the blessing *"HaMotzi"* is said.

- practice reciting *"HaMotzi."*

LEARNING MATERIALS:

- a plant

- watering implement

- pictures of fields of grain

- samples of grains in their original forms (pictures can be substituted)

- poster board

- different types of breads (crackers, bagels) and cereals (rye, whole wheat, white, cracked wheat, oatmeal, pumpernickel)

- plates and napkins

- camera and film

A bakery or bagel shop where the preschoolers can see how bread is made is one option. A second option is making bread from scratch using the ingredients of your favorite *challah* or bread recipe, principally, water, flour, honey/sugar, and yeast. Another possibility is to go to a Lubavitch *matzah* making factory if you include *matzah* in the learning activities.

LEARNING ACTIVITIES:

The curricular unit has three parts: identifying types of grains, turning grain into bread, and growing plants. Following are activities for each.

Identifying Types of Grains:

• Spread the strands of grain and breads, crackers or bagels, out on the table. Place the strands of grain next to the grain in its bread, cracker, or bagel form. For example, put the strand of rye next to the rye bread, cracker, or bagel. Put the strand of wheat next to the varieties of wheat breads, crackers, bagels (white, cracked wheat, and whole wheat), or *matzah*. Cut or break the breads, crackers, bagels, and *matzah* into pieces for taste testing.

• Have a tasting party of the different kinds of breads, crackers, bagels, and *matzah*. Recite the appropriate *brachah* before eating the bread, crackers, etc.

• Connect the pictures of the fields of grains with the individual grains.

• Point out that grains are usually grown in big fields.

• Ask if the students have ever seen fields of grains growing.

• Point out that the people who grow the grain are called "farmers." Go over the things that farmers do to help grow the grain.

• Connect the strand of grain with the bread food product.

• Explain that we do not eat grain straight from the field. The grain has to be prepared to use in the making of bread.

• Review the types of grains, both their differences and similarities.

• Did all the breads taste or smell alike? Connect different grains with different tastes.

• Did all the breads look or feel alike? Go over the different colors, textures, and properties.

• Explain that the breads are different, depending on the grain from which each came. Yet, despite all these differences, they are all called grains. Grains are the main ingredient used in making breads, crackers, bagels, cereals, and *matzah*.

• When eating bread, say or sing *"HaMotzi."* If eating crackers, recite *"Boray Minay Mizonot."* Translate the Hebrew into English. (If desired, transliterate it as well.)

• Discuss saying *"HaMotzi"* or *"Boray Minay Mizonot"* when eating foods made with grains in order to reinforce the connection between these *brachot* and such foods.

Turning Grain into Bread

(Note: Be certain to take pictures. You will need them for the third lesson.)

Option #1 - Tour a bread or bagel factory. Show the students the different steps taken in turning grains into breads. Be certain to eat some samples and to recite to *"HaMotzi"* before doing so.

Option #2 - Use your favorite *challah* or bread recipe to show the steps involved in making bread. Remember to let the students do as much of the measuring and mixing as possible. Continually discuss what it is that you are doing. You will probably have to spread out this activity over a morning or afternoon in order to show all the steps. Have all the ingredients available for the preschoolers to touch and taste. Compare the strand of grain or its picture with the flour. Ask children if the ingredients taste like bread. Have them carefully watch all the steps that it takes to make bread. Be certain to eat the finished product and to recite *"HaMotzi"* before doing so.

Additional Element: Options #1 and #2 above trace the turning of flour into bread. This additional element traces the steps of turning wheat grains into flour. If you include this additional element, do it prior to the other two options. Either take the preschoolers through a Lubavitch *matzah* making factory or ask the Lubavitch if they can do this "off season." The *matzah* making factory involves turning the wheat grain into flour. Be certain to have a five pound package of flour to show the students so that they can connect the flour that they make in the *matzah* factory with the flour in the bag that they see in the grocery store or at home.

For both options #1 and #2, discuss:

- What are the steps taken to turn grains into bread?

- Who is involved? What does the person do? How long does it take?

Connect the wonder of all these steps involved in turning grain into bread as a reason that we thank God for our food.

Growing Plants

Make a chart on which you can graph the process and progress of each plant.

Day #1 - Bring two plants that require a lot of water to the classroom. Tell the students that you are going to conduct an experiment. You want to see what happens when someone takes care of one plant and no one takes care of the other plant. Ask the students if they have any experience helping take care of plants inside or outside. Ask if their parents have any experiences helping take care of plants inside or outside. What do they do to make the plants grow? Suggest that you will water only the one plant to see what happens to the two plants.

Day #2 - See how the plants look. Note the differences between the three plants. Water the one plant, and keep one plant out of sunlight.

Continue this procedure until one plant looks nearly dead. Discuss the differences with the children. Why did the one plant grow well? Why is the other plant dying? How do we know what has to be done so that the plant will grow well? You can refer to the chart on a daily basis.

Show the children the grains and pictures of the bread making. Show them the pictures of the fields of grains. Why do the grains in the field grow well? What would happen if there is too much rain? (Include other conditions: bugs, no sunshine, no rain, etc.) We are glad when things go just right so that the grain can grow, so that we can have our food. We thank God for the rain, sun, and all the things in nature that make the grains grow.

What would happen if there was not enough rain, or if the farmer did not water the fields? What would happen if the farmer decided for a whole week not to water the fields? God helps us to know what the plants need to grow well. God helps the farmer to know what the plants need to grow well.

Remember how the bread was made. (Show pictures of the process.) You start with the raw ingredients like grain. Someone turns the grain into flour. God helps the person know how to grind the grain to make it into flour. (Show pictures if you went through that process.)

Then we stir the ingredients and bake them to turn them into bread. God helps the person who makes bread, crackers, or bagels know how to make them.

We were made in God's image. We are like God. God gave us a mind to think and create and make special things like bread.

Before we take a bite of bread, a cracker, bagel, or *matzah*, we say or sing a prayer, a thank-you to God for helping the farmer take care of the seed, the person who grinds the grain, the baker who bakes the bread. We say thank you to God, and we think about the many things that have to be done so that we can eat the bread. Jewish people all over the world say this same prayer in Hebrew when we eat bread. When we say or sing this prayer, we are saying thank you to God for this bread. Who knows what prayer I am talking about? Let's sing *"HaMotzi"* together. Eat some bread, crackers, bagels, or *matzah*.

As the preschoolers settle in with their snack, read the story "Thanks for Bread" from *When a Jew Prays* by Seymour Rossel (Behrman House) When a boy finished lunch, he thanked his mother. She said, "You should not thank me alone, for I only prepared the food." The boy sets out to find who else he should thank. He visits the grocer, the bakery, the miller, and the farmer. Each told the boy he should not thank him alone. The boy could not figure out who else to thank, until the farmer invited him to eat with his family. Each person took a piece of bread, and together they recited *"HaMotzi."* Then the boy discovered that it was God whom he needed to thank.

Two other good books are: *Bread* by Beverly Randell (Glendale, CA: Bowman Publishing Corp., 1969), and *The Little Red Hen* by Harriet Ziefert and Emily Bolam (New York: Puffin, 1995).

EVALUATION:

(1) Sing or say the prayer for eating bread. (2) What do people have to do to turn wheat into flour, and flour into bread? (3) How does the farmer help a plant grow? (4) Why do we thank God when we eat bread?

WATCH OUT FOR:

The three lessons are spread over a period of time. Try to keep the preschoolers interested in the topic. Serve a snack as often as possible for which *"HaMotzi"* should be recited. Add songs, stories, and art projects to the curricular unit. Remember that young children learn better in small groups. You can bring a large group of preschoolers to a bakery all at once, but be certain to divide them into smaller groups for the tour. Although this approach is time-consuming and repetitive for the teachers and presenters, it allows the preschoolers to experience firsthand the process leading to *"HaMotzi."*

(This curricular unit is based on "The Prayer Curriculum Guide: Early Childhood Level" by Rena Rotenberg, Rachel Meisels, and Nancy Rubin, a work of the Center for Jewish Education of Baltimore. The curricular adaptations for this chapter were made by Roberta Louis Goodman.)

CHAPTER 35

PSALMS ALIVE: A MUSICAL PRESENTATION

Linda Kaufman and Carla Silen

TOPIC:

The young (King) David and his Psalms.

TARGET AUDIENCE:

Grades 3-6

TIME FRAME:

Actual performance time of this musical is 20 minutes. The material can be used for a single classroom session or as a play that a class performs. The choice of format will affect the amount of time needed.

STAFF:

A classroom teacher with an accompanist or a music specialist. (The music is written for piano or guitar.)

OVERVIEW:

Psalms Alive is a musical that provides a look into the life of King David in his youth. The play focuses on the Psalms as an expression of King David's relationship to God. The play is adaptable for use in a variety of contexts within the school or communal setting. It can be used in a classroom as a lesson for a unit, as a curriculum for a music or drama class, or as a play performed for others as part of a theater or music club. In terms of content, the play can be used to focus either on the Psalms as a form of expression connecting people to God or on the relationship between King David and God.

PURPOSE:

Art is a vehicle for interpreting texts, and forging an understanding of and relationship to God. Moreover, the Hebrew for Psalms, *Tehillim*, means "songs." As songs, they were a form of worship, a way of communicating with God. A play is a participatory way of presenting material to learners.

OBJECTIVES:

The students will be able to:

- relate information about the life of King David in his youth.

- discuss the meaning of the Psalms presented.

- discuss the relationship between the young David and God.

- begin to see oneself as a worshiper.

- experience worship through Psalms and songs.

CONTENT:

The Psalms (*Tehillim*), which represent expressions of the relationship between Jews and God, are a central focus of this curriculum. The young David's relationship to God, especially his love and devotion to God, is another focus. Concepts included are: praise, loneliness, comfort, angels, guarding or watching.

LEARNING MATERIALS:

- copies of the play for students (see Appendix A, p. 321, for the script of the play and Appendix B, p. 323, for the music)

- music

- piano or guitar

- hand-sized harp, real (if possible) or imaginary

- costumes and props as desired

- copies of Psalms 92, 91, and 34

LEARNING ACTIVITIES:

Anywhere from 5 to 45 students can participate in this performance. The fewer the students, the more doubling up on the narration parts is needed. While it adds greatly to the learning experience, the pantomime is an optional part of the play. In addition, if necessary because a musical accompanist is not available, the songs can be recited as poems, rather than sung as songs.

The core of this curriculum is the play. The following activities can augment the learning experience:

Questions for Study:

- What do you learn about David's life from this play?

- What is a Psalm?

- What did David write about in his Psalms?

- For what reasons does David praise God?

- What do the Psalms tell us about David's views of and relationship to God?

- If you were writing a psalm, what would be the main theme? How would you address God in your psalm?

- In what ways is a Psalm a prayer?

Other Activities:

The students can:

- make collages depicting the Psalms in the play.

- write psalms.

- research the life of King David.

- read other biblical texts about King David.

- look at Psalms in the prayer book to see how they are used in the liturgy.

EVALUATION:

The questions for study can serve as a good way of evaluating the students' grasp of the material presented in this lesson.

WATCH OUT FOR:

Any time a play is part of a school program, it is important to make certain that the performance portion does not overtake the learning function.

APPENDIX A

Psalms Alive! A Musical Presentation from the Psalms[1]
By Linda Kaufman and Carla Silen

Director's Notes

The following script is designed to be used by upper elementary students under the direction of a classroom teacher with an accompanist or by a music specialist.

The number of students that can be involved can be expanded to 35-45 or more, as there are three distinct performance groups: (1) Narrators, (2) Choir, and (3) Pantomime actors. At least ten voices should be in the student choir. It is possible to eliminate the pantomime of the story if there are not enough students to participate. Performance length is approximately 20 minutes. As with any creative project, it may be necessary to adapt the script to the needs of your students.

The Script

(Choose students to pantomime the story as told by the Narrators.)

Narrator 1: Once upon a time, many years ago, there lived a boy named David. He would one day grow up to be the king of Israel.

Narrator 2: David's father, Jesse, used to tell David and his seven brothers stories about God.

Narrator 3: Of all the boys, David loved these stories the most.

Narrator 4: As the youngest son, David's job was to watch his father's flock of sheep. Even at night, he had to stay in the fields to make sure that none got lost or hurt.

Narrator 5: David would sit alone on the side of a hill and enjoy the beautiful sky all filled with stars. And he would think about God.

Narrator 6: Often he would take his harp and sing songs to God — songs that he had made up himself.

CHOIR:
Psalm 92 (See Appendix B, p. 323, for the music.)

I sing for joy at the work of Your hands
The sky filled with stars
The shore filled with sand

I lift up my harp and I sing You a song
And promise my heart
Only to You belongs

And I will praise You
I will praise You
Each time that I sing
I will praise You, O Lord

I will praise You
I will praise You
Each time that I sing
I will praise You, O Lord

Narrator 7: At times, David was cold and lonely out in the fields at night all by himself. But when he was afraid, he would sing a song that reminded him that he was never alone.

CHOIR:
Psalm 91 (See Appendix B, p. 325, for the music.)

Listen, hear
Have no fear
To this special song
God has sent his angels
To guard you all week long

They will lift you up with their hands
So you will not hurt your feet
They're always right around you
Each day of the week

So, listen, hear
Have no fear
To this special song
God has sent you angels
To guard you all week long

Narrator 8: When David was still a young man tending the sheep, Saul, the King of Israel, became very sad and upset, and his head hurt. Nothing seemed to make him feel better.

Narrator 9: Then one of his servants said, "David, the son of Jesse, knows how to play the harp. Maybe he could help."

Narrator 10: And so they sent for David. He picked up his harp, sang a song, and took away Saul's sadness and headache.

CHOIR:
Psalm 34 (See Appendix B, p. 326, for the music.)

Whenever you're feeling lonely
Whenever you're feeling blue
Just lift up your heart with music
That's what you ought to do

If you'll give praise to God
Your troubles will fade away
If you'll give praise to God
Your troubles will fade away

Whenever you're feeling grumpy
Whenever you're feeling sad
Just lift up your heart with music
And things won't seem so bad

If you'll give praise to God
Your troubles will fade away
If you'll give praise to God
Your troubles will fade away
Yes, your troubles will fade away

Narrator 11: All through his life, David sang to God with his harp and lyre. He made those instruments himself.

Narrator 12: The songs that he wrote are called Psalms.

Narrator 13: There are 150 Psalms in our Bible. David wrote the Psalms to praise God and remind himself of God's mighty power and goodness.

Narrator 14: He knew that God was always with him.

Narrator 15: Just like David, we can write our own psalms. It's always easier to remember important things if we sing them.

Narrator 16: And it is important for us always to remember that God lives in our hearts.

All join in the final song. (See Appendix B, p. 328, for the music.)

All:

There's a little piece of God in me
God in you, God in me
There's a little piece of God in me
That's how it's supposed to be

When we come together
Each brings our God inside
So many godly pieces
Make our god big and wide

There's a little piece of God in me
God in you, God in me
There's a little piece of God in me
That's how it's supposed to be

It's our little secret
That God lives in our hearts
We never can be lonely
If God's there from the start

There's a little piece of God in me
God in you, God in me
There's a little piece of God in me
That's how it's supposed to be
That's how it's supposed to be
That's how it's supposed to be

APPENDIX B

Psalm 92: I Sing for Joy

© Linda Kaufman, 1998

Psalm 92: I Sing for Joy *(cont.)*

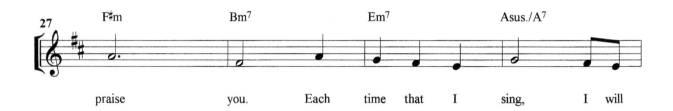

praise you. Each time that I sing, I will

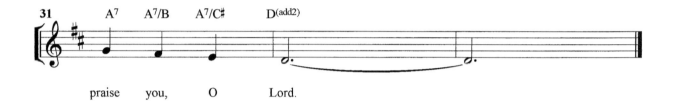

praise you, O Lord.

Psalm 91: God Has Sent His Angels

© Linda Kaufman, 1998

Psalm 34: Lift Up Your Heart With Music

© Linda Kaufman, 1998

Psalm 34: Lift Up Your Heart With Music *(cont.)*

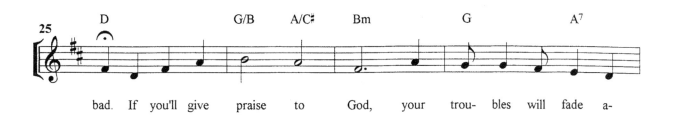

bad. If you'll give praise to God, your trou- bles will fade a-

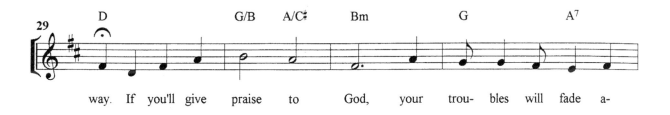

way. If you'll give praise to God, your trou- bles will fade a-

way. Yes, your trou- bles will fade a- way.

There's a Little Piece of God in Me

© Linda Kaufman, 1998

There's a Little Piece of God in Me *(cont.)*

It's our lit - tle se - cret that God lives in our hearts. We

ne - ver can be lone - ly if God's there from the start. There's a

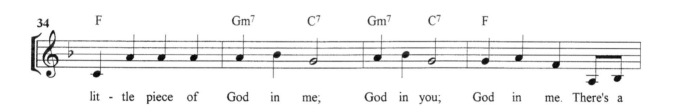

lit - tle piece of God in me; God in you; God in me. There's a

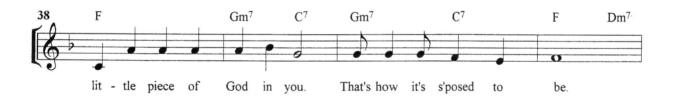

lit - tle piece of God in you. That's how it's s'posed to be.

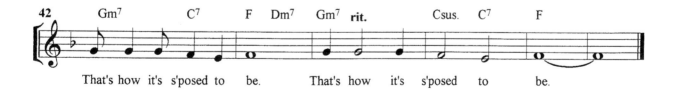

That's how it's s'posed to be. That's how it's s'posed to be.

CHAPTER 36

TALKING TO GOD

Marcia R. Plumb

TOPIC:

When and where do we pray to God, and the role of *kipot* in prayer

TARGET AUDIENCE:

Religious School children in Grades 1-6

TIME FRAME:

30 minutes

STAFF:

Teacher

OVERVIEW:

This program was designed to help the students reflect on and discuss praying to God — what we say and why we say it. Students will discuss the role of *kipot*. The children and teachers sit in a circle on the *bimah* for a discussion. The structure is one of questions from the teacher and responses from the students. The students also help each other think about the issue. There is a relaxed atmosphere, and students are given time to think about their answers in a nonjudgmental environment.

PURPOSE:

The first purpose is to introduce the wearing of a *kipah* by all children. The lesson sets the stage for a follow-up lesson in which children make their own *kipot*. The second purpose is to help the children understand a liberal perspective that boys and girls can pray to God, study equally, and wear *kipah, tallit*, etc. The third purpose is to allow the students the opportunity to share their prayers to God, and to remind the students that God is available to them all regardless of their gender and movement affiliation. The fourth purpose is to encourage students to value their ability to make personal choices about how, where, and when they pray to God and what they say or their beliefs.

OBJECTIVES:

Students will be able to:

- express their belief in God.

- discuss their prayers to God.

- ask questions and share responses about prayer, God, gender differences in worship, and the wearing of *kipah* and *tallit*.

- reflect on the liberal practices regarding prayer and prayer clothing.

CONTENT:

The content is divided into facts, concepts, values, and feelings.

Facts: Both girls and boys can talk to God. There are different views regarding gender, prayer, and prayer garments for liberal Jews and for traditional Jews.

Concepts: Prayer, God, equality.

Values: Each person's view is valued. Each person has the right to question and be honest about his/her feelings and ideas. All can approach God at any time and any place.

Feelings: Love, hope, confusion, sadness, anger.

LEARNING MATERIALS:

- *tallitot*
- *kipot*
- *tefillin*

LEARNING ACTIVITIES:

The teacher and students sit in a circle on the *bimah*. The teacher asks: Raise your hand if you love your parents. [Students raise their hands.] How do you show you love them? [Hugging them, kissing them, saying I love you.] How many of you feel that your parents love you? [Students raise their hands.] How do your parents show their love for you? [Hugging us, telling us they love us, setting rules for us, trying to keep us safe.] How does God show that God loves us? [Giving us Shabbat, making things beautiful around us.] How do we show that we love God? [By keeping *mitzvot*, going to synagogue, keeping Shabbat.] How do we tell our friends that we love them? [By telling them, asking them to play with us, etc.] So how do we tell God that we love God, or that we are angry with God, just as we might be angry with our friends or parents? [We tell God, we say prayers, we pray, etc.] Where do we pray? [In synagogue, at services, etc.] Do we only talk to God in a worship service? How many of you talk to God outside of the synagogue? [Raise hands.] The teacher continues: Sometimes we might talk to God before a test, and say how worried we are, and we want help. Other times we might complain to God if something did not go well. Or we might be angry with God if something made us sad or angry, like if someone we loved died. [Watch for nodding heads.] The teacher asks: What are other reasons we might talk to God? What might we say? [Wait for responses.] So, the

teacher concludes, we can talk to God anywhere, at any time, right? Now hold that thought and we will come back to it.

How many of you have ever seen the President/Prime Minister/Queen? Can anybody see the President/Prime Minister/Queen? [They can catch a glimpse, but need a special invitation to meet him/her.] What do people do when they see the leader of our country? [Bow, curtsy, say hello, give flowers, etc.] What do people wear when they go to meet him/her — would they wear an old outfit? [No, people dress up.] Why do they dress up? [Out of respect.]

So, now back to God. What do we wear when we talk to God? [If we are playing at home, we wear jeans; if we are going to services at synagogue, we dress up; if we are going to sleep, we wear our pajamas. We also wear special coverings — *kipot* and *tallitot*.] Right. Why? [Out of respect for our religion and for God.]

[The teacher asks and pauses for raised hands after each question.] Can anyone talk to God? [Yes.] Can only boys talk to God? How many think that only boys can talk to God? How many think only girls can talk to God? How many think we can all talk to God? How many think that only boys can like or show respect to God? How many think that only girls can like or show respect for God? How many think anyone can like or show respect for God? How many think that only boys can wear a *kipah* to show respect for God? How many think that everyone can wear a *kipah* or a hat to show respect or talk to God?

A child says: But you do not have to wear a *kipah* to show respect or talk to God. [If no one makes this comment, then the teacher can ask it as a question.] The teacher answers that this is true. Sometimes a *kipah* is not for God, it is really for us, to help us concentrate on what we are saying to God. How many of you have ever had a conversation with a friend, but you were not really paying attention? You heard what the friend was saying, but at the same time you were thinking about the test you had in the next class, or thinking about an argument you just had with another friend. How many have done that? [Students raise their hands.] Well, we do not want to do that when we talk to God. Talking to God is special, and we want to pay attention. Putting on a *kipah* reminds us to pay attention to this conversation, and not to let our minds wander. How many think that both girls and boys should pay attention when we talk to God? [Students raise their hands.] How many think that both boys and girls should wear *kipot* to help us pay attention? [Students raise their hands.]

Another child asks why some people wear a *kipah* all the time, and should we not wear a *kipah* all the time if we want to pray to God at any time? The teacher replies, yes, some people do wear a *kipah* all the time. Wearing a *kipah* all the time reminds us that God is always with us, no matter where we are or what we are doing. Some also wear a *kipah* to show respect for God all the time. Can you think of other reasons for wearing a *kipah* all the time? [To show that we are Jewish and proud of it.] Yes, some people wear *kipot* to show that they are proud to be Jewish. Some people in the liberal movements, including some of the founders, think that we do not need external or outside signs to show that we are Jewish. They believe that it is what is in your heart and how you behave that matters. How many think that you might like to wear a *kipah* all the time? Why? [Show respect to God.] That would be fine if you decide to wear a *kipah* all the time.

A student shares that they have been with Orthodox girls and women who do not wear *kipot* when praying. The teacher asks the students why they think that Orthodox Jews do not allow or encourage women and girls wear a *kipah* when praying? [Students give their responses.] The teacher makes certain that the students know that married Orthodox women cover their hair with wigs, scarves, or other head coverings at all times as a sign of modesty. What practice are you most comfortable with — females wearing *kipot* or not wearing *kipot*? [Students answer.] Teacher reinforces that it is important that we show respect for people who have different views from ours.

The teacher ends the lesson by displaying various *kipot*, *tallitot*, and *tefillin*. The children look at them and try them on. They also identify which *tallitot* and *kipot* are their favorites. The teacher then asks the children, "Who wants to go and make his or her own *kipah*?" The follow-up lesson is having the students make their own *kipot*. One method: Purchase white *kipot*, and have students decorate them with fabric markers, glitter, felt pieces. For this project, you will also need scissors and glue.

EVALUATION:

(1) How do we show our love for God? (2) Who can pray to God? (3) When do you pray to God? (4) For what reasons do people wear a *kipah*?

WATCH OUT FOR:

Make certain that you foster an environment in which the students are comfortable sharing their experiences, questions, and feelings.

CHAPTER 37

MOVING METAPHORS FOR GOD: ENRICHING SPIRITUALITY THROUGH MOVEMENT

Kate Mann

TOPIC:

The focus is on using movement to nurture spiritual development. This lesson presents three examples, each of which focuses on a metaphor or name for God: God as Source of Life, God as Ruler, and God as Protector.

TARGET AUDIENCE:

Grades 3-6

TIME FRAME:

Flexible. Each movement activity takes a minimum of 10-15 minutes. Add 10-15 minutes for follow-up discussion. Any of the activities could be expanded into an entire class period if the teacher wishes to extend the time for movement, group sharing, and discussion.

OVERVIEW:

The human body is an insightful teacher, for when it is flowing with energy, it embodies the whole person — body, mind, and soul. Nonverbal expression is key to verbalization, and verbalization is key to learning.

Kinesthetic learning triggers a person's mind and emotions by activating their breath, pulse, muscles, and bones. Teacher directed improvisations work by engaging children in a literal interpretation of a word through movement. The process begins as simply as that! The teacher's task becomes guiding or coaching students to realize that their personal movement responses are a

means to discovering or uncovering their inner spiritual thoughts and feelings.

The approach in the following sections, was developed over many years of incorporating dance and educational theory with texts, prayers, concepts, and metaphors. Three curricular examples are used to illustrate this approach to using movement to nurture spirituality.

PURPOSE:

These movement activities are offered to provide teachers with simple kinesthetic activities that will engage students holistically in exploring their own spirituality. These short improvisations are meant to open new doors in fostering the students' ability to articulate their own spirituality. These activities are designed for use in tandem with other teaching or learning modes.

FORMAT:

Each lesson is titled with one metaphor or name of God: God as Source of Life, God as Ruler, God as Protector. A movement activity is listed first, followed by a specific prayer that includes that particular image of God. For instance:

Name or Metaphor: God as Protector

Movement Activity: Building and Dwelling in a *Sukkah*

Prayer Connection: *"Hashkivaynu"*

A movement activity could be an icebreaker to stimulate discussion on the names of God or on images of God in prayer. The Teacher Script tells you what instructions to give your students. Some of the instructions are in question form and are intended to be answered by the students with their bodies. For example: Can you show me a *sukkah* with your whole body? Have you ever felt protected by God?

The movement experience is the first half of the lesson. The second half is the follow-up discussion, or possibly a time for journal writing. Each activity has a list of questions for discussion to pose after moving. Or, you may be using movement to prompt students to find personal meaning in a specific prayer. Giving physical expression to the words of a prayer can help students make meaning out of poetic language. These activities can be done with the whole group, small groups, or even partners.

OBJECTIVES:

- Students will have a physical experience that enables them to give words to a spiritual feeling or idea about God, either orally or in written form.

- Students will come to recognize and value how they are spiritual beings with a body, mind, and soul. of poetic language. These activities can be done with the whole group, small groups, or even partners.

LEARNING MATERIALS AND SETUP:

- open space in which to move

- music and a boom box if you choose

LEARNING ACTIVITIES:

    I. God as Source of Life

    II. God as Ruler

    III. God as Protector

I. GOD AS SOURCE OF LIFE

Movement Activity #1: Breath awareness meditation

Prayer Connection: *"Elohai Neshamah"* . . . the soul You have given me

Vocabulary:

Neshamah/Soul
Ruach/Breath or Spirit

Teacher Script:

Invite students to sit or lie down on the floor so that they have a personal space and are not touching anyone or anything. Guide them to focus on the rhythmic sound of their own breath. Say: The Hebrew word *"ruach"* means breath and spirit. Each of us is born with *ruach*. Notice how your rib cage enlarges and contracts with every breath you take. Your lungs are like two balloons inflating and deflating with every breath you take. Allow your belly to fill like a balloon on each inhale and empty out on each exhale. Listen to your breath, the body's *ruach*, in constant motion. God breathed a pure soul into each of you. As you inhale, bring in all of God's goodness: love, forgiveness, healing, compassion. As you exhale, send out all the things you don't want, such as sadness, anger, pain, or disappointment. In your imagination, send the goodness to your lungs, and then blow out what you don't want. Inhale, sending God's love to your feet (or any other body part you choose). Exhale anything you don't want to carry inside of you. Your breath is purifying and refreshing your body.

To close, read aloud *"Elohai Neshamah"* in English. Or sing Laura Berkson's song, *"Ruach Elohim,"* which may be found on the recording *Vzamru: And You Shall Sing.*

Questions for Discussion:

- Where does our soul come from?

- What new ideas about your own breathing do you have after this meditation?

- Why do you suppose there is a special prayer thanking God for our soul?

- Can listening to your breath help you pray? help you hear yourself think?

Movement Activity #2: Meditation on the heartbeat (5-10 minutes)

Prayer Connection: *"Asher Yatzar"* (Who has made our bodies with wisdom)

Teacher Script:

Begin by focusing on your breath. Now notice another of the body's involuntary rhythms, your heartbeat. Focus on the steady beating of your heart muscle, which is busy pumping blood throughout your body. Consider the miraculous wonders of your body: your heart beating and pumping blood throughout your arteries and veins, your breath bringing oxygen into the bloodstream to nourish every cell. God, Ruler of the universe, has created the human body with wisdom. On your head alone, think of the miracle of each of your senses, and what information and pleasure they bring you — your eyes for seeing, ears for hearing, nose for smelling, your mouth for tasting. Just imagine if any one of these openings were blocked or shut down. Then think about how your body heals when you get a cut or bruise. Think about how your body mends itself. Our bodies are truly a wonder of God.

Questions for Discussion:

- If you keep in mind that God is the Creator the universe, including the complicated human body, how does this change your view of your own body?

- How do you suppose God wants us to take care of our body?

- How did you feel when a part of your body didn't work?

- How can we be partners with God?

Movement Activity #3: Exploring personal space with different body parts (10 minutes or more)

Prayer Connection: Try moving to Debbie Friedman's version of *"Asher Yatzar,"* found on the recording *Renewal of Spirit.*

Teacher Script:

(Note: Finding personal space is a helpful way to start any movement activity because it defines every person's boundaries.)

Sit in a space all by yourself, so that you can move freely without touching anyone or anything. Everyone needs his/her own personal space or "bubble" in which they can move safely. Slowly reach out, limb by limb, in all possible directions. Reach and stretch with one arm, then the other, one leg then the other, an arm and a leg. As you stretch, sense the shapes that your body is making in space. Gradually make your way to a standing position and continue to explore all the space around you. Staying in your spot, experiment by stretching your limbs to make big shapes, twisted shapes, curved shapes, pointy shapes, etc.

Additional Prayer Connection: Psalms 35:10 . . . "All my limbs shall say, who is like You?"

Prayer Connection: Play *"Mi Chamocha"* by Craig Taubman, found on the recording *Friday Night Live.*

Teacher Script:

Using one arm, ask, *"Adonai,* who is like You?" Try asking with two arms. Now add a leg. Both legs. With your whole body, "God you are awesome!" or *"Adonai,* You are the Almighty One." In what direction do you move when you ask questions? when you praise God? Where do your eyes naturally go? Let's look at each other's gestures of praise. Let's try copying one another's movements to see what they feel like.

Questions for Discussion:

- What do you think David really means in his Psalm when he asks God, "Who is like you?"

- When David declares, "all my limbs shall praise You," do you think he was talking about doing a dance? What else could David have meant? Does this suggest that physical expression is a form of prayer?

- Have you ever felt close to God when you were being physically active?

II. GOD AS RULER

Movement Activity #1: Interpret the opening line of *brachot* in movement.

Prayer Connection: The beginning of all *brachot*: Praised are You, *Adonai* our God, Ruler of the universe . . . *Baruch Atah Adonai Elohaynu Melech HaOlam.*

Vocabulary:

Berech/knee
Adon/Lord
Melech/Ruler

Teacher Script:

The first words in a *brachah*, a blessing, are "*Baruch Atah*" . . . Praised are You.

To whom are we speaking? Interestingly, the root of *baruch*, b-r-ch, is the same as for the word *berech*, knee. What connections can we find between giving praise and the knees? How could you use your whole body to communicate praise for *Adonai, Elohaynu, Melech HaOlam*? Who are we praising or blessing? Explore with your body different ways you might show praise for a ruler. Notice what your knees are doing. Would anyone like to share the motions about praise for us to try? Let's see, and then try several of your ideas.

Questions for Discussion:

- After moving, what new information did your body give you that might help explain why *berech* and *baruch* share the same Hebrew root?

- When we bend or bow before a ruler, what does our body language communicate?

- What do you suppose is the purpose of always beginning every *brachah* with these same words?

- What is the spiritual value in reciting these words with every *brachah*?

III. GOD AS PROTECTOR

Movement Activity #1: Building and dwelling in a *sukkah*

Prayer Connection: "*Hashkeevaynu*"

Teacher Script:

Before we talk about God as Protector, let's do some investigating with our bodies to get ready. What is a *sukkah*? Yes, a kind of shelter that we build on Sukkot. Yes, the kind of portable huts the Jews lived in while they wandered in the desert and when they were farmers in the land of Israel. Using just your hands, show me a tiny *sukkah*. What could be sheltered in your hands? Try making a *sukkah* with your whole body. What would fit underneath? Build a shelter to protect a person underneath. Try building a *sukkah* with four or five other people.

Questions for Discussion:

- How did you feel being sheltered inside the *sukkah*?

- How did you feel being the *sukkah*?

- We know that God does not have a body, then why do we call God our Protector?

- How does that help us know God?

- What kind of relationship does a protector have with others?

- Have you ever been a protector of someone? How did that make you feel inside?

- When have you felt protected by God?

- When in history have the Jews been protected by God? How did we express our gratitude to God then?

Movement Activity #2: Scarf dance

Prayer Connection: Play Craig Taubman's version of *"Hashkevaynu,"* found on the recording *Friday Night Live.*

Teacher Script:

In the *"Hashkevaynu"* prayer, we ask God, "Spread over us the shelter of Your peace." Try a movement improvisation using big scarves or pieces of flowing material. Have students work with a partner. One person goes down to the floor, sitting or lying down. The other person takes the big scarf and experiments with different ways to spread over them a shelter of peace. Then the partners switch parts. Ask a student to read the *"Hashkevaynu"* prayer in Hebrew and/or English while the others move with the scarves.

Questions for Discussion:

- What did it feel like being under the scarf?

- How did you feel when creating a shelter of peace with the scarf?

- After doing this exercise, can you describe a "shelter of peace" in your own words?

OVERALL EVALUATION:

(1) What new insights did you gain into the three names and metaphors for God — God as Source of Life, God as Ruler, and God as Protector? (2) How can you use your body to pray to God?

WATCH OUT FOR:

The use of movement to explore concepts and metaphors in general and spirituality in particular may be a new experience for many of the students. Some will relate more to the physicality of the experience, and others will relate more to the artistic and dance aspects. Using movement can bring out the kinesthetic learner who often has difficulty in a visually and verbally driven classroom setting. Children who are uncomfortable with their bodies may need some encouragement and support to participate freely. Most important, it is central to create an emotionally safe environment in which all feel comfortable to explore their spirituality through movement. Setting rules, following directions, and respecting others will serve to make this a rich experience for all.

BIBLIOGRAPHY

Joyce, Mary. *First Steps in Teaching Creative Dance.* Mountain View, CA: Mayfield Publishing, Co., 1973.

This handbook for teachers of children in Grades K-6 presents 26 structured lessons covering the elements of dance. Easy to fol-

low, it also explains to teachers how to structure their own ideas for exploration through movement.

(Note: For additional references on movement, see the bibliography for Chapter 22, "Encountering God through Dance" by JoAnne Tucker, p. 232.)

CHAPTER 38

WHERE IN THE WORLD IS ADONAI ECHAD?

UAHC Joseph Eisner Camp Institute

TOPIC:

Encountering the many faces of *yud hay vav hay*, the One God of the Jewish people; "letting God in." This camp curriculum is part of a three-year cycle of studying God (the architect of the world), Torah (the blueprint of how to live in the world), and Israel (the builders in the world).

TARGET AUDIENCE:

Although it was written for campers in Grades 3 through 8, the program is most appropriate for Grades 6 and 7.

TIME FRAME:

A series of one-hour sessions used over a four-week period of time; a total of 21 sessions are part of the curriculum.

STAFF:

Most of the sessions require a facilitator and group leaders. Group size influences the total number of staff needed. A good ratio is one adult to 10-15 youth. Some of the sessions have stations, each of which also needs to be staffed.

OVERVIEW:

The course seeks to immerse the learners deeper and deeper into the *Pardes* (orchard) of God. *Pardes* stands for the four levels of study in Judaism, and follows this sequencing.

    p = *peshat*, the simple meaning of a text
    r = *remez*, a clue, connecting one text to another

    d = *drash*, interpretation of a text
    s = *sod*, secret or mystical meaning of a text

During the first week, the campers encounter God on the *peshat* level. They explore the simple signs of God around them; God in nature, song, places, etc. In the second week, they explore the *remez* of their experiences and seek to understand the nature of the God they have begun to encounter. In the third week, they attempt to *drash* the world around them, using their developing ideas to wrestle with God, themselves, and some difficult issues around us. In the fourth and final week, the campers seek the *sod*, discovering that God is within each of us, wherever we "let God in." On the final day of each week, a different section of *Tefilah* (prayer) is addressed: "Shema," "Amidah," "Kaddish," and "Alaynu."

PURPOSE:

The methods are experiential, learner-centered, and active, making them well suited to a camp setting. The variety of methods and their playful nature allow the learners to break through inhibitions in how they experience and express their understanding of and relationship to God.

OBJECTIVES:

The primary objectives are:

- Campers will have the opportunity to explore their understanding of and relation ship to God. They will examine how their lives are connected to, informed by, and imbued with a sense of God.

- Campers will be exposed to different ways of thinking about paths to God from biblical, Rabbinic, medieval, and modern sources.

CONTENT AND LEARNING ACTIVITIES:

The entire outline of the 21 sessions is presented here. The content focus and the main learning activity are listed below for each session.

Week One: Peshat — Encountering God in the Most Simple Ways

Session 1: Many Paths To One God
God is in the simple places: inside you, inside me, and inside all of us. Participants went on a treasure hunt for the many paths. Different clues, including biblical, Rabbinic, and modern texts, all lead to the same treasure.

Session 2: God-talk
Learners begin to articulate personal ideas about God and affirm the legitimacy of every learner's thoughts. Learners explain how their God ideas are similar to common objects drawn from a paper bag.

Session 3: Leap of Faith
Trust exercises are used to explore faith in a God whose face we can never see.

Session 4: God in Nature
Participants go on a "God Walk," a hike with stops for different *Birchot HaNehenin* (blessings of things we enjoy).

Session 5: Shema
Hearing God and prayer are the foci. At a "Shema Festival," stations include wrapping *tefillin*, listening to different melodies, learning sign language, writing, calligraphing letters, and more.

Week Two: Remez — What Clues Do I Have about the Nature of this God I am Encountering?

Session 6: Amidah
The learners create a mural depicting each of the *brachot* in the *"Amidah."* At the service that evening, they pray the full *"Amidah."*

Session 7: Names of God
Participants play a version of *Family Feud*, and act out the meanings of the names.

Session 8: God in the Bible
Each group of campers develops a dramatic presentation of Torah texts about creation, revelation, and redemption.

Session 9: God in Rabbinic Literature
Four Rabbinic "Godiators" (Jackie the Judge – Judgment, The Enforcer – protection of Israel, Mr. Rogers – the presence (neighbor) of God on earth, and Mr. Mom – the Parent) each takes a corner where they explain a text related to their metaphor. In the end, the Godiators battle it out to a chorus of original cheers from the group.

Session 10: Medieval and Modern Theologians
The theologian's God concepts are introduced through DonaJew and HolyGod Squares.

Session 11: Developing a Personal God Concept
Campers go shopping to the Temple Mall stores where they obtain their God concept sayings for the price of a decent explanation. The learners attach their God concept sayings to their shopping bag as a way of assembling their personal God concept.

Week Three: Drash — How Can I Interpret My World with My New Understanding of God?

Session 12: God Wrestling
The campers watch Jacob and the angel wrestle. Then they have their turn to wrestle with an angel about one of their own challenges.

Session 13: Challenging the Justice of God's Actions
The campers examine biblical texts in which God punishes or seems to act unfairly. They hold trials over the *Akedah,* Korach, the golden calf, and Noach.

Session 14: How Can I Believe When . . . God's Role in Current Events (in Our Lives Today)
The campers wear a God T-shirt for two minutes while they are asked questions related to current events, such as a massacre in Ireland, a baby girl rescued from a well, and flooding in Georgia.

Session 15: Kaddish
This session continues to explore God's role in human events, especially death. God comics (e.g., Fred Flintstone coming home from work and slipping on a banana peel and later a piano dropping on his head) are the springboard for discussion. The themes in the *"Kaddish"* as they relate to God and our lives are examined.

Week Four: Sod — What Is the Secret of What God Wants from Me?

Session 16: The Gifts God Gave Me — B'tzelem Elohim
The campers trace themselves and label all the gifts and talents that God gave them that makes them special.

Session 17: Putting God on the Guest List
Campers explore the role of God in their upcoming Bar/Bat Mitzvah by going through stations of the different parts of the celebration.

Session 18: God in My Cabin — Does God Care If I Short-sheet my Bunkmate's Bed?
Campers examine an ethical dilemma such as stealing, respect, cooperation that is relevant to their bunk. The question of where God fits into this dilemma is posed.

Session 19: When God Calls — The Prophet As One Who Is Called
Campers act out God calling prophets (Abraham, Moses, and Jonah) based on biblical texts provided. In the end, campers write letters to God and then write their own answers as if they were God.

Session 20: What Do I Believe?
As part of a moderated panel, representatives from the campers and staff share their beliefs about God and how they have grown in their thoughts and beliefs.

Session 21: Alaynu Prayer — Bayom Hahu: On that Day, God's Name Shall Be One
Through singing, text study, discussion, letter writing, and enscribing a symbol on a plaque, the campers develop a vision of God for the future.

SAMPLE SESSION

The following is a detailed description of one session.

Session 11: Developing a Personal God Concept

Campers go shopping to the Temple Mall stores where they obtain their God concept sayings for the price of a decent explanation. The learners attach their God concept sayings to their shopping bag as a way of assembling their personal God concept.

OBJECTIVES:

Campers will:

- use knowledge from previous sessions.

- encounter different God options and make personal choices about the nature of God.

- articulate their view of God based on the choices they make at the mall.

CONTENT:

Metaphors of God; beliefs about God

LEARNING MATERIALS:

Decorations and items needed to turn facility into a mall — art supplies, glue, mall map, shopping list, shopkeeper costumes, cutouts of items with statements on them, one plain bag per learner

LEARNING ACTIVITIES:

Outside a large program space, the principal will announce that there's a new program at school. Students were complaining that there wasn't enough to do at the synagogue, so he/she built the Temple Mall. Learners then move into the "mall" in the facility. (5 minutes)

As campers enter, they're handed a "shopping list"/map of the mall that instructs them to visit every store. They're also given a shopping bag in which to put their God concept. There are nine mall stores: "Swatch-maker," "Chess-King," "The Disney Store," "The Sci-Fi Store," "Sam Goody," "The Nature Company," "Bible Store," "Rabbinic Republic," and "Barnes and Noble," each representing a different God concept. At each store, campers can buy cutouts of items (store logos or shape) with statements about God written on them (see list). One idea about God is written on each slip of paper. For example, Swatch-Maker shape with "God created the world" on one slip of paper, another with "God is not involved in our lives today," and so forth. By visiting every store, campers will build their own God concept. Shopkeepers should act as salespersons, encouraging campers to "shop around." Shopkeepers and mall security guards should make sure campers know what they're buying. Before they purchase an item, the campers should give a rationale for their product choice. Though everything is free, learners must pay with their analysis. Each store has its items on a different color of paper. (25 minutes)

Campers get into groups and decorate their bags with art supplies. They should paste their items (products with sayings) all around their bags. Group leaders explain that these will be used for decorations so they should look nice. (10 minutes)

Campers go around in groups to share what they picked and why. (10 minutes)

Wrap-up: Campers answer how similar or different were everyone's shopping bags? (5 minutes)

Mall Stores and Items for God Shopping:

Swatch-Maker — God as Watchmaker (cutouts in watch shapes)

- God created the world.
- God is not involved in our lives today.
- God doesn't cause bad things to happen to good people.
- God is there, but God is silent.
- God depends on us to maintain creation.

Chess-King — God as the Ruler of the universe (chess pieces)

- God plays an active role in our lives.
- God protects and cares.
- God rewards good people and punishes bad people.
- God hears my prayers.
- God works miracles.
- God gives order.
- God is just and fair.
- God holds us up in times of trouble.

The Disney Store — God as Jiminy Cricket (Disney Character)

- God is my conscience.
- God is inside of everyone.
- God is the still, small voice within me that helps me make decisions.
- God talks to me.
- God lets me know what is right and wrong.
- God helps me to be just.

The Sci-Fi Store — God as the Force (Science Fiction Objects)

- God is everywhere.
- The beauty of nature represents God.
- The patterns in the world are evidence of God.
- God does not deal with me personally.
- God is found in science.
- God is order.

Sam Goody — God as Goodness, Love, Dreams, Ideals (records and CD's)

- God is everything possible.
- God is "doing the right thing."
- God is a hero worthy of praise.
- God acts through my actions.
- God is in being the best I can possibly be.
- God is our dream for a united humanity.

The Nature Company — God as our Partner in Creation (trees and plants)

- God gave human beings free will.
- We are made in the image of God.
- God depends on us to repair the world (tikkun olam).
- God recreates the world continually.
- I am God's partner; we are both fulfilling an agreement.
- I can argue with God.
- God helps us to hold ourselves up in times of trouble.

Barnes and Noble — God as the Author of Life and Death (books)

- God is responsible for all that happens in the world.

- Reward and punishment are given out in the afterlife.
- God has reasons for doing things that we will never understand.
- I cannot argue with God.
- God can bring people back to life.

The Bible Store — God as Creator, Revealer, Redeemer (Torahs)

- God created the universe.
- God gave us the Torah at Mount Sinai.
- God freed us from Egypt.

The Rabbinic Republic — God as Protector, Parent, Neighbor, Judge (clothing)

- God is the protector of the Jewish people.
- God is our parent.
- God is present on earth.
- God is the judge all of humanity.

EVALUATION:

The campers should be able to answer these questions: (1) Which view(s) of God are closest to your view of God? (2) Why did more people pick a combination of views rather than a single view? (3) How similar or different were everyone's views of God? (4) In what ways is thinking about God as a metaphor (God is like an author, parent, creator, etc.) helpful in talking about God?

FEEDBACK ON THE PROGRAM:

The program received a resounding response from the campers. The felt they accomplished something — they identified and developed their own God concept that was not just based on their opinions. They were able to apply their God model in the last two weeks of the program.

WATCH OUT FOR:

The staff consciously worked hard at not portraying God using a voice. They wanted the campers to form their own images. They intentionally did not use a voice of a man or woman to portray God. Throughout, the staff struggled with trying to allow the campers' images, metaphors, and formulations dominate, rather than any particular image, metaphor, or formulation found within Judaism.

Some of the metaphors in the program might need to be changed to be more relevant to the students' lives.

In adapting the programs to another setting, one needs to remember that this camp setting was resource rich. There were dozens of staff and faculty readily available to fill the multiple roles needed.

(Those involved with the program "Where in the World Is Adonai Echad?" included: Jonah Pesner; Zach Shapiro; Aaron Katersky; Rabbi Jeffrey Sirkman, Chairperson, Program Advisory Committee; Dr. Sherry H. Blumberg, Educational Consultant; and David Friedman, Camp Director. A full copy of this curriculum can be obtained by writing or calling Camp Eisner, 633 Third Avenue, New York, NY 10017, 212-650-4130.)

CHAPTER 39

POETRY AND PRAYER: THE "V'AHAVTA"

Cathleen Cohen

TOPIC:

Using poetry as a tool and lens for interpreting prayers

TARGET AUDIENCE:

Day School or supplementary school classroom for Grades 4-8

TIME FRAME:

One session of 60-75 minutes, or two sessions of 35-45 minutes

STAFF:

In supplementary schools – Jewish studies or Hebrew teachers are both well suited for teaching this class. For Day Schools – secular studies or English teachers could be effective teachers of this lesson.

OVERVIEW:

Prayer shares much in common with poetry. Like prayer, poetry seeks to articulate the ineffable. It speaks from the heart to the heart, and shares with prayer the impulse to express deep feelings. Both take up such themes as love, pain, awe, forgiveness, praise, ecstasy, petition, and thanksgiving. This lesson taps into the tools and techniques of poetry in order to help the learner interpret prayers, making connections to their own lives and relating to God. While a lesson only on the "V'ahavta" is presented here, the approach can be applied to almost any prayer.

PURPOSE:

Ironically, prayer is not always a spiritual experience that brings one closer to God. Studying prayer often focuses on skill acquisition rather than making meaning and enriching spirituality. Learners need to spend time interpreting prayers, searching for meaning, and seeking God.

BACKGROUND:

Poetic expression is part of our heritage. The Bible is a repository of poetic language such as lyrical phrasing, metaphors, and repetition. Many prayers in the *Siddur* are actually liturgical poems, for example, *"Shir HaKavod," piyyutim,* and hymns or songs.

It is a natural step to link poetry writing to a prayer curriculum. Children can deepen their understanding of prayers by writing poems based on themes from the prayers. They can interact with fixed texts in personal ways, and bring *kavanah* to the experience. Writing taps the inner self. It is a vehicle through which children can observe and articulate their own beliefs about God and the world around them.

In the approach presented here, prayers are coupled with certain poetic elements such as line breaks, lists, repetition, symbols or metaphor, and narratives. Key words and prayer concepts are provided for each prayer.

OBJECTIVES:

The students will:

* use poetic devices to identify and investigate spiritual questions.

- explore the meanings of the *"V'ahavta"* prayer using poetic devices.

- learn to be careful readers of prayers.

CONTENT:

This lesson was originally presented as a year-long supplementary school curriculum on using poetry to examine prayer. The elements of the prayer service covered included: *"Shema"* and its blessings, *"Amidah"* (*"Avot,"* *"Gevurot,"* and *"Birkat Shalom"*), *"Kaddish,"* *"Shalom Aleichem,"* *"Lecha Dodi,"* *"Tzadik Katamar,"* Psalm 150 (*"Halleluyah"*), and *"Kiddush."*

For the *"V'ahavta"* Prayer

- Prayer concepts: loving God, God as Commander, teaching our children about God

- Poetic Devices: repetition, sequencing

- Key Words: love, remember, *levav* (heart), *nefesh* (soul), *me'od* (very much)

MATERIALS:

- *Siddurim*

- paper

- pens

- 4" x 6" index cards

- markers

LEARNING ACTIVITIES:

1. Let the students know that the class will use some poetic tools and poetry writing to interpret prayers. Here is an example of what one student wrote:

   A prayer is said.
   The words stay in my head
   Long after it ends,
   Leaving footprints on my heart.
   Like the flames of the Shabbat candles,

The prayer flickers in my mind
Just as flares flicker in my eyes
Long after they burn out.

Julia Spieler, Grade 8

In her poem, what ideas about prayer are expressed?

2. Have students read, chant, and/or sing the *"V'ahavta"* in Hebrew and/or English.

3. Have students look up the *"V'ahavta"* prayer in Deuteronomy 6:4-9. Mention its placement in the story of Moses and the receiving of the Covenant, the Ten Commandments and the entire Torah, at Mount Sinai. The *"V'ahavta"* is filled with commandments from God. Ask the students to search through the prayer for the commandments. Ask the students to respond to the question: What are the connections between this prayer and Moses and the receiving of the Covenant by the Israelites?

4. Mention the prayer's strong message, almost a demand, that we love God with all our being. Ask the students to underline the words *levav*, *nefesh*, and *me'od* in the prayer. Discuss: At what times does the prayer say to love God? In what places does it say to love God? In what other ways does the prayer instruct us to love God? Why are so many different words and expressions used to show our love for God? What is the connection between loving God and doing God's commandments?

5. Repetition is a poetic device to help identify important ideas in a prayer or text. Have students circle the phrases in the prayer that begin "with all your." Ask the students why people repeat things when they talk. Ask why they think these phrases repeat. Why does the prayer say "your" instead of "our"? Point out that the sequence or order of the three repeated phrases seems important. The word *me'od* (might) gets special emphasis since it comes last. What message does the order of these three phrases send?

Repetition gives the prayer a lyrical, circular feel. Not only do several words repeat in this prayer, but so, too, does the rhythm and phrasing. Read the prayer again. Ask students to circle more word and phrase repetitions. What ideas repeat, as well?

6. Breaking the prayer down into phrases helps us concentrate on the prayer's meaning. Take the first line or two of the prayer and break the line(s) down into phrases in a couple of different ways. For example, *You shall love, love the Lord, with all your heart, your heart.* Suggest that these different ways of looking at phrasing helps open up a prayer to examination, exploration, and interpretation.

7. Ask the class to write down the phrases that communicate the most important messages in the prayer. Using a marker, write one phrase per index card. Then take these phrases and write them in different ways. Examples are:

with all your heart	upon your heart
your soul	when you lie down
your might	when you rise up
take to heart	command you
teach them	upon your gates
to your children	bind them
a sign	

Keep moving the words and phrases around. Identify any new ideas that emerge from changing the word order, indentation, visual arrangement of the prayer.

8. Divide the class into partners or small groups of 3 to 5, and distribute the phrase cards among them. Ask them to try to draft their own poems about the important messages found in the "V'ahavta" using the phrase cards, other phrases, and their own words. Use some repetition. Place God and themselves in the prayer. For students who get stuck, help them brainstorm some ideas and encourage them to write what comes to mind.

As students finish their poems, suggest that they read them over and make any changes, adding in ideas or words that they feel they left out.

9. Ask students to share their prayers either with the group as a whole or in small groups of two to four. Share the poem found in Appendix A. What do these poetic writings teach us about loving God, God as Commander, teaching our children about God?

10. Conclude by reading, chanting, or singing the "V'ahavta" prayer.

EVALUATION:

Ask students to answer the following questions in writing: (1) From the "V'ahavta," what are two or three key words or phrases that convey important messages? (2) In what ways does word repetition help you interpret the prayer? (3) In what ways do you show your love for God? (4) What is one important thing that you have learned about the "V'ahavta" prayer?

WATCH OUT FOR:

Paying attention to poetic devices can help students interpret the prayers and find meaning. The emphasis should be on the meaning making and not simply the poetic devices. The opportunity to explore a familiar prayer in a new way will challenge students and spur their creativity. Some may feel more comfortable writing their own poetry while others may be more comfortable interpreting the prayers. Part of the students' responses to this approach may depend upon their experiences reading, writing, and interpreting poetry in other settings. But, since this lesson uses key phrases and concepts in the prayer, it adds to students' comfort and success.

APPENDIX A

Take To Heart These Words

Take to heart these words
Remember each syllable
Each consonant
Each vowel
So you shall not forget.

Let words serve as symbols
In your mind
Through your eyes
So truth can be seen.
Bind your words with actions
You can not forget.

Remember all I say
And be holy
Because you were born holy
And let each word
Carry your heart
To holiness.
If so
How can you forget?

Let words
Flow through your mind
And off your tongue
When you lie down
And when you rise up.

Let words
Serve as your bridge
Serve as your sight
Serve as your thoughts.

When words are beautiful
When words are true
Then how can My Commandments
Be forgotten?

David Aichenbaum, Grade 8

CHAPTER 40

DOES GOD KNOW? DOES GOD CARE?

Sherry H. Blumberg

TOPIC:

What does God have to do with the meaning of life?

TARGET AUDIENCE:

Teens

TIME FRAME:

2-3 hours

STAFF:

A leader and as many assistants as needed, so that discussion groups will be no more than 8-10 learners.

OVERVIEW:

This is a program of text study and discussion that explores the relationship of meaning and purpose in a person's life and connects that meaning to a person's relationship with God. The teen years are times when adolescents are often confused about their identity and about God in their lives. The question about whether God cares is an important one to consider.

PURPOSE:

This session employs both text study and interpretative activities, such as discussion and art. The rationale for these methods is that the text study exposes the students to Jewish views about meaning and purpose in one's life. The session

models how Jewish texts can provide a framework for exploring values and answering life's significant questions. Text study provides a way of further understanding the role that God plays in finding and creating meaning. The discussion and art activities are a means for the teenagers to share their thoughts and for others to model the importance of learning as a way of growing together.

OBJECTIVES:

The participants will be able to:

*   read short texts about life's purpose from Jewish tradition.

*   read short texts about God and God's relationship to human beings.

*   rank order things that they think give their lives meaning.

*   hear the different rankings that others make.

*   connect their own views and opinions to the textual references.

*   suggest ways in which they might help others who are struggling to find meaning.

*   demonstrate an understanding of their favorite text by using drama, art, music, or dance.

*   share the product of their work with others in the group.

CONTENT:

Jewish texts on the meaning of life and the relationship of human beings to God; Jewish concepts of finding meaning in helping others, serving God, studying, loving, and raising a family, along with popular contemporary ideas such as being happy, famous, popular, wealthy, creative, and enjoying work.

LEARNING MATERIALS:

- one copy per student of "What Gives My Life Meaning"

- one copy per student of Jewish sources (Appendix A, p. 351) on what is important in life and the relationship between God and human beings

- pencils or pens

- art supplies for collage, watercolors, silk painting, or materials for any chosen art form

LEARNING ACTIVITIES:

Set Induction
Have the students work individually filling out the following questionnaire on what things give their lives meaning.

Section A: Questionnaire — What Really Matters To You?

1. Rank order these things that give life meaning 1-13, with 1 being the most important and 13 being the least important.

    ____ I'm happy.

    ____ I help others.

    ____ I become famous.

    ____ I become the best I can be.

    ____ I enjoy my work.

    ____ I serve God.

    ____ I study and learn a lot.

    ____ I'm popular and have a lot of friends.

    ____ I'm wealthy.

    ____ I love someone, and that person loves me.

    ____ I have a family (children) and raise them well.

    ____ I'm creative.

    ____ Other (Fill in:_____)

2. Share and compare your list, first in pairs and then in fours.

    In the group of four, answer: "What do your lists have in common? What was different?"

    Follow up by asking: How many of you ranked anything to do with God or religion as one of your three most important things that gives life meaning? Which items have to do with God or religion? Be certain to discuss those responses that may not obviously be religious or connected to God but which, in fact, have much to do with religiosity and God, such as love, family, creativity, helping others.

Section B: What Really Matters To God: Does God Care about You?

1. Leader begins with the question: Does God care about you? After some answers, the leader adds: According to Jewish writings, God cares about human beings. God's care or love can give life meaning.

2. Leader asks: How do you know when someone cares for you? Then, to move the discussion along, ask: What is it that people do that shows that they care about you? How do you know when God cares about you? How does God show care for you? (e.g., created life, made a beautiful world, gave us commandments, gives us minds to explore and think, gives us the ability to create).

Activity #1: What Judaism Has to Say about Giving Life Meaning

With the entire group, the leader shares a story about what gives life meaning in a Jewish context. Somewhere in the story should be the concept of God caring for us. One such story is "Mother's Night" by Marian McHale, about a teenager who follows her drunken mother to help her. The teenager is inspired by the beauty of the world to have courage and hope. The story may be found in *Legacies: Stories of Courage, Humor, and Resilience, of Love, Loss, and Life-changing Encounters, by New Writers Sixty and Over*, edited by Maury Leibovitz and Linda Solomon (HarperCollins, 1993).

The leader then describes the text study. The texts focus on what gives life meaning and God's relationship to human beings (see Appendix A). Each person is assigned to a small group of up to eight to ten people. The group develops arguments about why their text gives important insights into what gives life meaning.

The group presents their case, attempting to convince everyone else of the text's wisdom. The other participants can ask questions of the group and even challenge their arguments. The group members have a chance to respond. It is important that this part of the activity begin by clearly and explicitly establishing ground rules for safe and trusting participation: no personal attacks, no teasing or making fun of what others say, safety for anyone to ask any question, etc.

Activity #2: Interpreting What Gives Life Meaning through the Arts

Students are asked to express their favorite text in some interpretative art form, e.g., the visual arts, such as a collage or silk print or creative writing of a skit or lyrics for a well-known song.

The students share their project and describe how they used art to symbolize what the text says about what gives life meaning. The leader asks each student to explain what their text and artistic interpretation has to say about God's role in giving life meaning.

Closure: What We Bring To the World

Make a human chain. Participants link arms in a circle as they tell what special gift they bring to this world that gives meaning to their lives, and perhaps to the lives of others.

The leader ends by saying: "God cares about human beings because our lives have meaning and purpose."

EVALUATION:

Leader should observe how the participants are responding and use the art pieces that they produce as a method of evaluation. The final chain is also a way of evaluating. If desired, the teens could be asked to complete the following phrases: (1) Today I learned _____. (2) Today I felt _____. (3) Today I wondered _____.

WATCH OUT FOR:

Some teens cannot handle sharing their personal views and/or doubts about their relationship to God, especially in front of their peers. Teens who are struggling with being candid should be encouraged to get involved in the lesson in physical ways, such as by creating art projects to express their feelings, role-playing, and creating a dance.

APPENDIX A

Jewish Sources on Life and God

Jewish Sources on What Is Important in Life:

Torah is the nutrient of the soul. (*Tanya*, chapter 4)

Hillel said: Be of the disciples of Aaron, loving peace and pursuing peace, loving your fellow creatures and drawing them near to the Torah. (*Pirke Avot* 1:12)

If I am not for myself, who will be for me? If I am for myself only, what am I? And if not now, when? (*Pirke Avot* 1:14)

It is our destiny to live for what is more than ourselves. Our very existence is an unparalleled symbol of such aspiration. By being what we are, namely Jews, we mean more to mankind than by any particular service we render. (Abraham Joshua Heschel)

Because we are human, we are vulnerable to doing wrong; because we are spiritual beings, we are capable of learning from our mistakes and thereby refining our characters. We should not delay this opportunity for character growth. (Abraham Twersky)

Health alone does not suffice. To be happy, to become creative, man must always be strengthened by faith in the meaning of his own existence. (Stefan Zweig)

Simon the Just used to say: "Upon three things the world stands: Torah, worship (work), and on doing deeds of loving-kindness." (*Pirke Avot* 1:2) Rabban Simeon, the son of Gabriel, said: "Upon three things the world exists: on truth, on justice, and peace." (*Pirke Avot* 1:18)

Texts on Relationship of God To Human Beings:

I will be to Israel like the dew, it shall blossom like the lily . . . They who sit in its shade shall be revived. They shall bring to life new grain, they shall blossom like the vine. (Hosea 14:6, 8)

It has been told to you what God does require of you, only to do justly, love mercy, and walk modestly (humbly) with your God. (Micah 6:8)

You shall be holy, for I the Lord your God am Holy. (Leviticus 19:2)

Once, the Baal Shem Tov became so depressed that he thought: I have no share in the world to come. And then he said to himself: If I love God, what need have I of paradise? (Hasidic story)

To seek God is to strive for the good: to find God is to do good. (Leo Baeck)

Talk to God as you would talk to your very best friend. Tell the Holy One everything. Even if all you can say to God is "Help," it is very good. Pray with emotion and God will forgive you. Pray with joy and watch your requests ascend straight to God's chamber. (Reb Nachman of Bratzlav)

God is my Shepherd, I shall not want. God makes me to lie down in green pastures and leads me besides the still waters. God restores my soul, guiding me in straight paths. So even when I walk through the valley of death, I will fear no evil. (Psalm 23:1-4)

CHAPTER 41

WHOSE BODY IS IT, ANYWAY?

Kyla Epstein Schneider and William Dreskin

TOPIC:

Because we are created *B'tzelem Elohim*, in the image of God, there is holiness and sanctity in the human body. This is a response to issues of how we treat our bodies — appearance, tattooing, self-injury, and suicide.

TARGET AUDIENCE:

High school students.

TIME FRAME:

Four study sessions are scheduled for this *Shabbaton*. Each study session is about an hour in duration.

STAFF:

All four study sessions involve text study (close reading of the text) and discussion. Smaller groups of 8-12 are recommended. Staff is needed to lead these discussion groups. Minimal large group presentation is required.

OVERVIEW:

The program's title, "Whose Body Is It, Anyway?" is indicative of the focus. The program reframes many teenage issues, such as appearance, clothing, alcohol/drugs, piercing, tattooing, and suicide in light of the essential concept that we are made *B'tzelem Elohim*, in the image of God. Our bodies are holy vessels. We are responsible for taking care of them. The issues are discussed in light of traditional sources, primarily biblical and Rabbinic, on

B'tzelem Elohim and other related concepts and values.

PURPOSE:

The participants are introduced to texts that help them understand how Judaism views issues that they are confronting in their lives. The texts provide the values, worldview, and framework for helping the individuals make decisions about how to live their lives.

OBJECTIVES:

The participants will:

- read and discuss texts on *B'tzelem Elohim*, appearance, self-injury, and suicide.

- describe what it means to be created *B'tzelem Elohim*, in the image of God.

- explain how we can reconcile our desire to be attractive, desirable, and find real satisfaction and comfort with our mind and body, with how we are.

- explain how the prohibition against harming oneself is related to being created in the image of God.

- explain why suicide runs counter to Jewish values.

MATERIALS:

- booklet of texts and "clothing and jewelry exercise" for each participant

- pencils

- literature or an article about teen suicide

CONTENT AND LEARNING ACTIVITIES:

The *Shabbaton* has four text study sessions. Each participant receives a handbook of texts and worksheets. The instructors are given a curricular outline that lists the key concepts, texts, and discussion questions.

In terms of technique, the text study involves a variety of formats. So for example, sometimes *chevruta* (studying in pairs) is used, sometimes whole group discussion is the preferred format, and sometimes both are used. Other formats are possible too, e.g., trading *chevruta* partners for each new text, going from groups of two to groups of four to groups of eight, large group followed by *chevruta*, *chevruta* followed by large group. Mixing of the groups can be done by gender, age (Grades 9 and 10 together and Grades 11 and 12 together), newcomers and "old-timers," and so forth, again depending on the goals, the content, and the group.

The main concepts, texts, and questions for each of the four sessions follow.

Session I: B'tzelem Elohim — In the Image of God

Concepts:

- miraculous nature of the human body

- tenuousness of life

- "tenants" within our own bodies

Texts and Questions for Study:

- *Beresheet* (Genesis) 1:26-28

- What does it mean to be created in the image of God?

- What is the image of God?

- The passage has God speaking *in* the plural — "our image" and "*our* likeness." Why?

- How is being created in the likeness in the image of the Divine different from the cre-ation of other creatures?

- What are the implications of being created *B'tzelem Elohim* and of having the responsibility of tilling and subduing the land?

Midrash from *The Legends of the Jews*, Volume I, by Louis Ginzberg (Jewish Publication Society), pp. 54-59. (Available for download from www.amazon.com)

- According to the Ginzberg *midrash*, how do the Rabbis view the human body?

- What are the implications of parents and God sharing in the role of the creation of a person?

Ginzberg, p. 35

- What is the significance of the particular parts of a person attributed to who they were?

"Asher Yatzar" (*Siddur* — morning service, *"Birkot HaShachar"*)

- What state of mind do you think the author of *"Asher Yatzar"* was in when writing this prayer?

- Why should this be a *tefilah*?

- Originally said in the privacy of the home, this *tefilah* can now be found in the Conservative and Reform prayer books in the morning service. Why?

- How would a doctor read this *tefilah*? a sick person? a healthy person?

Session II: Appearance

Concepts:

- beauty

- ugliness

- appreciation for that which is extraordinary

- cleanliness/care

- clothing
- modesty

Texts:

- *Shulchan Aruch, Orech Chayim* 225:8
- Talmud, *Avodah Zarah* 20a
- Midrash Rabbah, Leviticus 34:3
- Talmud, *Kiddushin* 30b
- Talmud, *Ta'anit* 4:8
- Mishnah, *Pirke Avot* 4:27
- Talmud, *Shabbat* 50b

Set Induction:

You are what you wear . . . aren't you? On the left side of a sheet of paper, list every article of clothing and jewelry that you are wearing today. On the right side of the sheet of paper, write down what you want these items to say about you.

Questions for Study:

- Why are these *brachot* to be said upon seeing a little person or an albino?

- What are the implications for looking directly at someone to acknowledge the fact that he or she is a little person, an albino, or the like?

- What was Rabbi Gamliel doing when he blessed God on behalf of a pagan woman?

- How do we define "extraordinary looking"? How do we feel in the presence of someone who is "extraordinary looking"? How are extraordinary beauty and extraordinary ugliness defined?

- How does Judaism suggest we respond to extraordinary appearances?

- Why did Rabbi Hillel bother to answer such a question from his students? How is bathing considered a *mitzvah*?

- Why does Rabbi Hillel compare our bathing

to the washing of statues of the king? What is he suggesting?

- Is it possible to overdo the care of our bodies? When do concern and care become obsession?

- North Americans have a distinct and profound response to the care of their bodies. Why do you think this response is so different from Europeans or people from the Middle East?

- How can we reconcile our desire to be attractive, desirable, and to fit in, with *real* satisfaction and comfort with how we are?

Session III: Self-Injury

Concepts:

- uses and effects of alcohol/drugs
- tattoos
- gashing, burning, piercing
- connection between idolatry and self-infliction
- penalties connected to self-injury

Texts:

- Genesis 9:18-25
- Leviticus 19:28
- Deuteronomy 14:1-2
- *Mishneh Torah, Avodah Zarah* 12:11, 13
- Talmud, *Makot* 3:6
- Talmud, *Baba Kama* 90a

Questions for Study:

- We've gone from the care and concern for one's body to the marring of one's body. Why do you think Judaism even speaks to these issues?

- The Torah speaks specifically to the issues of

marring and hurting of oneself through gashing for the dead or idolatry. What are some modern day counterparts? Is today's "modern tribalism" idolatrous? How so?

- Today, tattoos are making a comeback. There are even "little kid" tattoos that come off with water. What is our fascination with painting ourselves? How would you respond to a Jewish kid who wanted a tattoo?

- What were the effects of alcohol on Noah? What was the effect on his children? Was alcohol responsible?

- How can alcohol be considered among that which harms the body when Judaism clearly uses alcohol for celebratory purposes?

- How is the prohibition against harming oneself related to being created in God's image?

- How could the penalty for harming oneself be lashing? Does the punishment fit the crime?

- How is the prohibition against gashing connected to being a "holy nation"— a nation that God has especially chosen?

Session IV: Suicide

Concepts:

- death

- Jewish response to suicide

Texts:

- Talmud, Minor Tractate: *Semachot*, chapter 2: *Halachah* 1 and *Halachah* 3.

- I Samuel 31:1-6

- Deuteronomy 29:11-14, 30:11-16

Set Induction:

- In a sensitive matter, introduce suicide as the extreme extension of self-injury. Read a piece of literature or a news article about a teen's suicide. Discuss:

- Can you conceive of a legitimate justification

for someone ending their life?

- Do you know of friends who have considered, talked about, threatened, attempted to end their lives?

- How does society (modern American) view suicide?

- What do you think is the view of most Jewish sources on the idea of suicide? How do you think Jewish sources would treat one who has attempted and/or succeeded in taking his/her life?

Continuing Activities:

Read aloud the Samuel text.

Discuss:

- Saul, a great and mighty king, honored and revered by Jewish tradition as a warrior and leader, commits suicide. Why is this in our Tanach?

Read aloud the *Semachot* text.

Discuss:

- In light of this text, how do you think Jewish tradition treats Saul?

- What do the Rabbis do with him in retrospect?

- Why does Jewish law make such a big deal out of witnessing a person's intent and subsequent actions to commit suicide before calling it suicide?

- Why does Judaism have such a hard time with suicide in general? (*B'tzelem Elohim* implies that suicide is antithetical to the entire Jewish enterprise, which is based on God creating and blessing life.)

Read aloud the Deuteronomy text.

Discuss:

- What is this text about? To what is it referring?

- Why do you think this text is considered one of the most pivotal and profound of all biblical texts?

- What is the ultimate choice? What is its application in our everyday lives?

Closure:

Final message:

- make-up

- dress

- facial hair

- appearances

- adornments

- beauty/ugliness

- designer whatever

- earrings

- piercing

- gashing

- tattoos

- alcohol

- substance abuse

- suicide

- self-esteem

- You were created in God's image.

- Your body is a holy vessel.

- Treat yourself well and with respect.

- Choose life.

- Choose blessing.

EVALUATION:

The participants will be able to answer the following questions: (1) If we understand that we are created *B'tzelem Elohim*, then how should we treat our bodies? (2) What are some of the key values and ideas coming from the Jewish sources that address issues of appearance, self-injury, and suicide?

WATCH OUT FOR:

Adolescents can be self-conscious, emotional, and reactive. The issues discussed can arouse some strong, personal responses, not all of which may be immediately evident. Be careful to deal with feelings of embarrassment, low self-esteem, and anger. Be prepared to provide support and follow-up to those deeply affected by a review of the issues covered.

CHAPTER 42

WHAT'S GOD GOT TO DO WITH IT?

Jordan Millstein

TOPICS:

Religious experience; God; religious vocabulary; images of God

TARGET AUDIENCE:

Grades 7-12

TIME FRAME:

The unit consists of six lessons, each approximately 50 minutes in length.

STAFF:

A classroom teacher

OVERVIEW:

We often ignore our students' own religious experience. Time that is spent on religious thought usually focuses on beliefs and *mitzvot* and not on the students' experience of God. Jews, including Jewish professionals, tend to be afraid or suspicious of religious experience, thinking that it smacks of Christianity, or even cults. And yet, who can deny that our tradition was founded upon religious experience? From the Patriarchs through Moses, from the prophets through the Rabbis, religious experience has been central to Jewish existence. Judaism as a religion does not exist without God at the center. Unless we educate our students as to the nature and validity of religious experience, the very tradition we seek to transmit may be perceived as alien and unfounded.

This unit does not focus on theology, but rather on the more subjective aspects of religious experience. Its intent is to bring to the surface the students' own experiences, identify them as connected to God, and validate them within a Jewish environment and tradition.

The techniques utilized will be affective and experiential as much as possible. Certain cognitive goals of a more "rational" bent will be considered in order to help place the students' own questions about God and religious thought within a Jewish framework.

PURPOSE:

It is hoped that this unit will help the students to be more open to God and to the religious experiences in their lives, that it will expand their religious vocabulary, and give them the message that being religious is "okay." This is particularly important for the adolescent who is struggling with his/her identity and is experimenting with different experiences and ideas. As adolescents reject those beliefs handed down to them by parents and teachers, we need to give them the opportunity to generate their own thoughts and beliefs about God from their own experiences. They must make God their God. In a profoundly secular world, they are unlikely to see religious experience as a possibility unless we give them that opportunity.

OBJECTIVES:

Each of the six lessons has its own set of objectives. The overall objectives for the unit state that the students will:

- identify their own religious experiences and hear about those of others.

- explore a variety of images of God.

- examine how religious experiences can be or are incorporated into their own identities as Jews.

- examine the nature of religious experience.

- explore ways of becoming closer to God.

- examine how God works in our lives and in the world.

CONTENT:

The unit is made up of six lessons: (1) What is Religious Experience?, (2) God Imagery, (3) God in Nature, (4) Prayer, (5) God in the Personal and Interpersonal Moments in Our Lives, and (6) Doing *Mitzvot*. A detailed description of Lesson #1 follows.

Lesson #1: What Is Religious Experience?

Goals:

- To create a comfortable environment for the students to talk about and question God.

- To recognize that there are many different kinds of religious experiences.

- To consider and extend the range of what is typically considered religious experience.

- To understand that religious experience may have to do with feeling (non-rational), as well as cognition.

- To recognize that religious experience can be both universal or particular (Jewish).

- To recognize that religious experience can be both individual and communal.

- To model that it is permitted to discuss God and God's existence.

Objectives:

- Students will follow the class groundrules, especially for listening and respecting people's experiences.

- Students will identify some of their own past religious experiences by filling out a Values Clarification Sheet.

- Students will be made aware of the variety of experiences by listening to their classmates and the teacher discuss some of their own experiences.

- Students will identify the feelings that accompanied some of the experiences described on the Values Clarification Sheet. They may include a profound sense of appreciation, gratitude, awe, wonder, etc.

- Students will understand that some experiences of God are particularly Jewish or more universal, while some are very individual and others are communal.

- Students will be challenged by the teacher to consider whether some experiences which they never considered "religious" could possibly have been experiences of God.

- Students will discuss the ways in which Jacob's experience at Beth El is a religious experience, and consider Jacob's reaction to the experience.

- Students will distinguish between religious experiences and belief.

- Students will feel that it is okay to discuss God and God's existence by the tone set by the teacher and the impression left by the story of Jacob at Beth El.

Learning Materials:

- Values Clarification Sheet for each student

- tag board of classroom expectations and rules

- copies of Genesis 28:10-22

- sheet of examples of religious beliefs and religious experiences for each student

- pencils

Learning Activities:

Activity #1: The Students' Experiences of God

Hand out the following Values Clarification Sheet entitled "What's God Got to Do with It?" Ask students to fill it out.

Values Classification Sheet: What's God Got to Do with It?

Directions: Please respond to the following questions or statements as honestly and thoughtfully as possible. Do not look at what others are writing or discuss your answers with them.

1. There have been times when I have been outside, in a park or in the woods, when I felt that God was there.

   Yes_____ No_____

   What went through my mind was

   _____.

2. There have been times when I have been talking to someone and really felt "connected" to them. That is, we were so into talking or being together that everything else in the world seemed irrelevant at the time.

   Yes_____ No_____ Explain your answer.

3. There were times when I was up on the *bimah*, for example, during my Bar/Bat Mitzvah service, when I felt close to God.

   Yes_____ No_____

   (If yes, explain when this was, specifically, and how you felt. If no, explain how you did feel during your Bar/Bat Mitzvah service).

4. I think there is a God.

   Yes_____ No_____ Explain.

5. There have been times when I was really afraid that something bad was going to happen, but it turned out okay.

   Yes_____ No_____

   Explain what happened and how you felt afterward. Did you feel someone or something was looking out for you? If yes, what was it like having someone or something looking out for you?

6. There are times when I get really into something, when I am fully focused on that thing or activity.

   Yes_____ No_____ Explain.

7. When I am in services in synagogue, I usually feel

   _____.

   But sometimes I feel

   _____.

8. There have been times when I felt that no one in the world really cared about me.

   Yes_____ No_____

   What got you out of that feeling?

   _____.

9. The last time I prayed to God, _____.

10. There are times I feel there is a God.

    Yes_____ No_____ Explain.

Activity #2: Classroom Expectations

Listening and respecting one another is a key part of being able to explore the students' religious experiences. Therefore, it is important to make it clear from the beginning what the expectations are and what the classroom rules are. Go over the ground rules for the class and post them on tag board:

- Listen to classmates. Speak one at a time.

- Never laugh at or make fun of anyone's ideas or beliefs.

- Don't judge other's experiences, beliefs, and so forth.

- Preface statements with "I believe" or "I feel."

- Do not make assumptions about other people's beliefs, feelings, or ideas.

Activity #3: Students' Religious Experiences:

Sharing the Values Clarification Sheet

Ask students to begin sharing one of the experiences on the Values Clarification Sheet. Make certain that every student has an opportunity to share something from the sheet. As the students share their experiences, try to pull from the students the particular feelings that accompanied their experiences. Let them explain their feelings in detail if they are so inclined. Reflect back to them your understanding of how they felt.

As students begin sharing their experiences, write on the blackboard the words "Universal" and "Jewish" and "Individual" and "Group." As students share their experiences, point out when experiences fit these categories. Go over what is meant by these categories.

When students describe experiences that are "non-religious," ask: "Could God be connected to this?" Discuss: When is an experience religious, and when is it not?

(Note: This is hard to define. Can one have a religious experience and not know it?)

Activity #4: Jacob at Beth El

Read or tell the story of Jacob at Beth El about his dream of a ladder to heaven in Genesis 28:10-17. End with this statement: "God was in this place and I did not know it." Ask: "What did Jacob mean by that? Is it possible that God has done things in our lives and we did not know it?"

(Note: The lesson could end here if time is short.)

Activity #5: Religious Experience: Creative Writing Loops

Explain that this exercise involves writing. Students will be invited to share with the group some of what they write, but will not be required to do so.

Have students write freely for four minutes to get them used to writing. Ask them to write anything that is on their minds. Use any words. Keep the pen moving. Announce when there is 30 seconds left.

Then ask them to describe a place and time when they generally feel most comfortable, at ease. Give them three minutes to write. Ask two or three people to read aloud what they wrote.

Then ask students to describe a time when they were doing something they really enjoyed. Have them describe what they were doing, when it was, who was there, and how they felt. Give them three minutes to write.

Next, instruct students to write a story about a time when they had to make a difficult decision and struggled on a gut level with what they wanted to do. Describe what the issue was, who was involved, when this happened, and what made it difficult for them. Allow four minutes to write. Provide time for sharing.

Ask that students make a list of three or four people to whom they could or did speak about this decision. Allow one to two minutes to write.

Then have them describe the reasons they listed just one of these people. Give them two or three minutes to write. Then discuss: Could God be on this list? Judaism has often understood God in terms of relationships. God is someone upon whom Jews have called for centuries. God is someone upon whom we can depend. A relationship to God is part of religious experience.

Activity #6: The Distinction between Religious Experience and Religious Belief

Explain that Jacob had one kind of religious experience. Ask: What is the difference between a religious experience and religious belief? In order to help illustrate the difference, have students complete statements orally, such as: "I did ____," and "____ happened to me," which are ways of sharing religious experiences. Statements that start "I believe ____" and "I felt ____" are more commonly used to express religious beliefs. Discuss: Can one have a religious experience without having a belief about God? Suggest "yes," and add that sometimes one can experience God and still have doubts.

Activity #7: Closure: Lingering Doubt and Questions

Read or tell the end of the story of Jacob at Beth El in Genesis 28:18-22. The story ends with Jacob still unsure about his belief in God. Ask students if they have ever felt the way Jacob did.

EVALUATION:

The students should be able to: (1) give an example of a religious experience and of a religious belief; (2) provide an explanation of what is meant at the end of the Jacob story by "God was in this place and I did not know it"; (3) answer the question, "In what ways is doubt part of religious experience and belief?" (4) respond to the

question, "How does religious experience fit into living and identifying as a Jew?"

WATCH OUT FOR:

Teenagers can be reluctant to share their views and experiences. They are concerned with how their views will appear to others. It is critical to establish a setting free of embarrassment, in which they feel comfortable enough to share their views.

Another issue is that teenagers can be adamant about the views they express today, even if the next day their views have changed. If you want to be reflective and critical of a view, it is often better not to use one of the student's views as an example to question, Instead, using the views of others from a newspaper article, traditional Jewish text, or some other source works well. For example, raising question of Jacob's religious experience as presented in Torah and *Midrash* is a good way of helping students probe and ask difficult questions about religious experiences in general.

CHAPTER 43

JEWS IN SEARCH OF SPIRITUALITY: A SPIRITUALITY CONFERENCE

TOPIC:

This conference examines a different aspect or question related to spirituality each year. Atlanta was the first site in the Reform Movement to hold a spirituality conference for member congregations. In Atlanta, the program began in 1985.[1]

TARGET AUDIENCE:

The Reform congregations and synagogue council sponsor this adult educational program annually for all interested members of the Jewish community in Atlanta in every movement, as well as the unaffiliated and Jews in the surrounding communities. The latter cover a radius of several hundred miles, including Augusta, Chattanooga, Athens, Columbus, and Macon. The program is for both lay members and teachers. For almost 15 years, this has been an annual professional development program for teachers in the Reform congregations. The program annually attracts approximately 300 attendees, half of whom are teachers.

TIME FRAME:

Annual conference is planned for a Sunday morning, lunch, and early afternoon. Times are generally from 8:00 a.m., beginning with registration, through 2:30 p.m. The conference is always held on the second Sunday in February so that congregations can know not to schedule other programs that might conflict with this annual gathering.

STAFF:

The program is coordinated by a volunteer committee consisting primarily of lay people. This committee meets year round, but goes into "high gear" from after the High Holy Days through the month or so following the conference in February. The following subcommittees are charged with various roles and responsibilities:

Conference Committee – consists of Chairperson and Co-Chairperson (who becomes the next chairperson), all subcommittee chairpeople, and other volunteers. The duties of this committee are:

1. Selecting the keynote speaker, usually done in the fall an entire year and a half in advance of the upcoming conference

2. Working with the keynote speaker in customizing the format to fit the selected topic

3. Assigning a representative to attend the Atlanta Reform Synagogue Council meetings to report on the conference (usually 2 or 3 meetings)

4. Overseeing the work of all committees

Arrangements Committee – works with on-site coordinator (either staff or lay member) assigned by host congregation. This committee is responsible for:

---

[1]Sponsors included Atlanta Reform Synagogue Council, Temple Beth David (Snellville, GA), Congregation B'nai Israel (Riverdale, GA), Congregation Children of Israel (Augusta, GA), Mizpah Congregation (Chattanooga, TN), Temple Kehillat Chaim (Roswell, GA), Temple Emanu-El (Atlanta, GA), Temple Beth Israel (Macon, GA), Temple Kol Emeth (Marietta, GA), Temple Shir Shalom(Duluth, GA), Temple Sinai (Atlanta, GA), and The Temple (Atlanta, GA).

1. Coordinating all on-site logistics

2. Selecting and working with the caterer (breakfast, snack, and lunch)

3. Coordinating facility and staff needs (including custodial services) for setting up, serving, and cleaning up

4. Recruiting guides for hallways to help people locate rooms the day of the conference

5. Arranging for baby-sitting, which is offered at a minimal cost of $5 per participating family

6. Making signs for program areas to help direct people to rooms used

Program Committee – this Committee has the following duties:

1. Finalizing schedule, format, and content

2. Recruiting as speakers/workshop leaders Reform Rabbis, educators, and Cantors from the local and surrounding congregations; often these are individuals who serve in communal positions, such as chaplain, central agency staff, or other non-congregational positions, such as camp or Day School staff.

3. Maintaining ongoing contact with speakers/ workshop leaders about such issues as session titles, materials, and the like

Publicity and Public Relations Committee – this committee is responsible for:

1. Developing press releases and advertisements for local Anglo-Jewish papers and congregational bulletins

2. Developing and distributing registration form to all congregations. These are sent to various leaders within the congregation, including the president, Rabbi(s), educator, adult education chairperson, bulletin editor, and so forth.

3. Arranging for a photographer

4. Arranging for someone from the Atlanta Anglo-Jewish paper to be present to take photographs and/or do a story

Moderator Committee – the tasks of this committee are:

1. Recruiting and assigning moderators for each session

2. Providing moderators with a biographical statement of presenters being introduced and instructions on moderating the session

Note that the host site assigns either a staff person (e.g., administrator, education director, Rabbi, or a lay volunteer) to act as Conference Coordinator. The main role of this person is to help coordinate the logistics for all sessions and needs with the Arrangements Committee.

OVERVIEW:

The annual conference featured here was aimed at congregational members and teachers. The program featured a keynote speaker of national renown. The day was divided into three learning periods, including the keynote. For the other two periods, participants could select from among numerous sessions offered by Rabbis, Cantors, and educators. One of the two periods had special sessions geared for teachers on how to apply the topic of the day to their classroom teaching. The program included introductory and concluding assemblies, sometimes with a worship experience and lunch. Moderators were assigned to each session to introduce the instructor and help moderate the discussion as needed.

After the first conference, the Reform educators decided that the teachers would benefit from receiving exposure to spirituality, to the Rabbis, to the movement's theology, and to the Reform community. The annual gathering of Reform educators in the community has taken place at the spirituality conference ever since.

Currently, a minimal charge of $18 is requested of all participants, regardless of how long they stay or if they eat lunch. Kosher food is served. The main costs are for speaker, food, facility use (generally maintenance costs), and publicity. The program is partially supported by a congregational Endowment Fund in memory of Gary Metzel at Temple Sinai and by the Southeast Council of the Union of American Hebrew Congregations.

PURPOSE:

The spirituality conference was established in 1985 in response to a need of the community. Gary Metzel (z"l), the lay person who established the conference, was influenced by Rabbi Eugene Borowitz, who had expressed the sentiment that until the leaders of the movement shared their own struggles and journeys, the laity would not feel comfortable freely discussing and exploring their spirituality and their understanding of and relationship to God. Metzel started this program as a way initially to bring together the Reform Jews of Atlanta to engage in conversation with the community's Rabbis and one another, studying and talking about God.

OBJECTIVES:

The objectives for the conference are:

- To explore different aspects of God and spirituality.

- To provide a forum that encourages and supports the professional leaders of the congregations sharing their views on and relationship to God and spirituality.

- To give the community members the opportunity to engage in dialogue and study text with one another and the professional leaders of the congregations as a way of exploring their own views of and relationship to God and spirituality.

- To give the teachers the opportunity to hear the professional leaders of the congregations share their views on God and spirituality, to come to know the Reform community better, and to augment their ability to bring God and spirituality into their classrooms.

- To bring together Jews of all movements from the surrounding Jewish communities for a day of study under the auspices of the Reform congregations and the Atlanta Reform Synagogue Council.

CONTENT:

Each spirituality conference has a different theme or focus. These have included: prayer, Covenant — the relationship between God and Israel, life after death, dialogue with God, finding spirituality in your work, God and the Holocaust, and the earth is full of God's glory.

LEARNING MATERIALS:

 instructors provide any texts that they use in their sessions. Music and/or prayer are usually part of the program. Sheets of songs and prayers, including "Birkat HaMazon," are provided as needed.

LEARNING ACTIVITIES:

While the schedules are somewhat similar in their elements, the timing, and sometimes approach, varies from year to year as the format is customized to fit the keynote speaker's style and topic. For example, one year the service was held after the morning sessions. The keynote speaker that year felt that the morning workshops opened up the participants spiritually, and that if they waited for the service to the end when people were more tired, an important teachable moment would be missed. One year, all the first workshops were text study sessions. This modeled how text can inform the way we understand and relate to God rather than leaving it to workshop presenters to decide whether to use text to share their views on the topic. A typical program schedule is outlined below.

Overall Theme: A Dialogue with God

8:30-9:00 a.m.	Registration
9:00-10:30 a.m.	Opening Session Welcome *Niggun* Introduction of Keynote Speaker Keynote Speaker Presentation Questions and Answers
10:50-11:45 a.m.	Workshop I: Personal Communication with God – Sessions for Lay Members Teachers' Workshops
12:00-12:55 p.m.	Lunch *"HaMotzi"* Lunch *"Birkat HaMazon"*
1:00-1:55 p.m.	Workshop II: Seeking God through Community
2:00-3:00 p.m.	Closing Session Commentary by Keynote Speaker *Niggun* Summation

Keynote speakers were predominately from the Reform movement and generally live outside the Atlanta area. Several were associated either with the Union of American Hebrew Congregations, the central office for the Reform movement, or Hebrew Union College-Jewish Institute of Religion. Occasionally, a local speaker, a person from outside the movement, or a university professor was invited. Keynote speakers have included: Rabbi Lawrence Kushner (congregational Rabbi), Rabbi Daniel Syme (then Education Director of the UAHC), Dr. David Blumenthal (professor at Emory University), Dr. Sherry H. Blumberg (then professor at Hebrew Union College-Jewish Institute of Religion), Rabbi Michael Chernick (professor at HUC-JIR), and Rabbi Jeffrey Salkin (congregational Rabbi).

The two sets of workshops open to the laity are led by congregational Rabbis, educators, and Cantors. The instructors are asked to devise a session related to the theme. Sometimes one of the workshop sessions is devoted to text study on the conference theme. Often, the instructors utilize texts as part of their sessions. Others prefer to share their own personal views on the theme. Most encourage dialogue and discussion among the participants.

For one time period, there was a program just for the teachers in attendance. (The rest of the time, the teachers participated in all other aspects of the program with the participants.) The program for teachers has taken two different forms. In some years, the teachers spend time with the keynote speaker, both listening and engaging in dialogue about applying the particular theme to the classroom setting. In other years, the education directors of the congregations teach a variety of sessions on applying the theme to the classroom setting. Other years, the teachers select one of the workshops to attend along with the lay participants. The program for the teachers is set by the local Reform education directors who coordinate their preferences with the Conference Committee.

Special Notes: Jackie Metzel, the widow of Gary Metzel, annually hosts the keynote speaker, the Conference Committee members, and the site coordinator at a dinner the Saturday night before the conference. This is a special way of thanking those who have committed so much time and effort to the program.

Generally, lunch is either a box lunch or a served "family style," with trays of food already on each table. This shortens the time needed for lunch. Buffets are not conducive either to the time frame or to community building.

The teachers are generally paid to attend the conference as one of their professional development days, and this is included in their contracts.

EVALUATION:

Participants responded to such questions as: (1) What was one idea or view about God or spirituality that you found to be provocative, penetrating, or significant to you in some way? (2) What was the main reason that you decided to attend the conference? (3) What is the main reason that you would return next year? (4) What themes would you like to be the focus of a future spirituality conference? (5) In what ways, if any, would you suggest improving future conferences?

FEEDBACK ON THE PROGRAM:

The first spirituality conference had no keynote speaker. It was important for the professional congregational leaders, only Rabbis in this case, to break the silence about God by sharing their own views and struggles. The entire conference was a cathartic experience for all present. Overall, the conferences help the participants explore how to fit God into their lives. It provides them with the opportunity to discuss spiritual issues with people equally interested in pursuing their own spiritual quest and relationship to God.

WATCH OUT FOR:

The session group size should be such that it allows all participants to speak and interact with one another. For the teachers' program, the session with the keynote speaker and the teachers is best received when it focuses on how they can use the topic in their classroom.

(Note: This program outline was prepared with the assistance of Joanne Barrington Lipshutz, former Education Director, The Temple, Atlanta, Georgia, and currently a Hebrew/Judaica teacher at The Davis Academy, and Bernice Lacefield, President of the Atlanta Reform Synagogue Council.)

CHAPTER 44

SEARCHING FOR GOD

Betsy Dolgin Katz and Alan Bregman

TOPIC:

Becoming more aware of our views of and relationship to God.

TARGET AUDIENCE:

Adults are the primary audience. The program has been used for lay and professional leaders, seniors, and CAJE participants.

TIME FRAME:

An extended period of time with the same group of people is needed for this program. The program was designed as a two-day *kallah* with six hours set aside each day. The *kallah* was scheduled on two mid-week days from 10:00 a.m. to 4:00 p.m. Participants had to commit to both days. Since then, the program has been presented at CAJE over a six-hour period and at an Elderhostel over five sessions of one and one half hours each.

STAFF:

The original *kallah* was done with two facilitators, one Rabbi, and one Jewish educator. The co-facilitator approach has certain advantages, especially in modeling that there is no single way of relating to God, no one path to God.

OVERVIEW:

The *kallah* program is an opportunity for each individual to explore his/her personal feelings, reflections, conflicts, yearnings, experiences, and encounters with God. The themes follow a pro-

gression from darkness to light, from confusion to understanding, from doubt to confidence. The techniques include journal writing, a lifeline expression, personal storytelling, partner interaction, and small group and full group discussions.

PURPOSE:

The program grew out of the opinion that too often the approach to the spiritual aspects of our lives is solely through the intellect. We may study texts, or listen to philosophical lectures on what a Maimonides or Martin Buber have to say about God, or we may consider various concepts of God. However, an encounter that considers the possibility that God is a personal force in our lives is rare. Educationally, the *kallah* was based on a belief that powerful, personal, educational experiences are often ones in which we learn to think, feel, and talk in new ways.

OBJECTIVES:

The participants will:

- explore their relationship with God, including the profound, puzzling aspects of life, and what role God plays in these.

- become familiar with Jewish views of God from traditional sources.

- join with others in examining their relationship with God so as to enlighten one another's steps.

CONTENT:

Our relationship to God; pathways to spirituality; journeys; struggles; times of light and darkness; changing images of God; images of the relationship between God and the people or particular person in the Bible; experiencing God; sharing our feelings and fears; building confidence in our spiritual journeys.

LEARNING MATERIALS:

*   *Lech Lecha* (Genesis 12)

*   *Appalachian Spring* by Aaron Copeland, or some other inspirational music

*   tape or CD player

*   Genesis chapter 23 (Jacob wrestling with the messenger)

*   Numbers 6:22-27 (priestly blessing)

*   paper, pens or pencils

*   whiteboard

*   markers

*   flip chart

LEARNING ACTIVITIES:

The *kallah* has several thematic sessions, each of which is described briefly below. These sessions connect a metaphor or concept from traditional text with an aspect of one's spiritual journey and quest for God. Since this program was presented more than once to different audiences, a range of themes and educational techniques are presented here. However, no single program need incorporate all of them.

Thematic Session #1: Introduction — Our Relationship To God

The introduction should include some rules for the sessions:

*   People are encouraged to participate in all aspects of the program, but one's silence or decision not to share will be respected.

*   Everything shared in the room is confiden-

tial and not to be discussed outside of the session.

*   Listen to one another; do not judge people's responses.

*   The introduction should review the purpose and goals of the sessions:

*   To deal with our own experiences and feelings about God.

*   To draw upon metaphors and narratives from traditional sources. These can be used as guides to help apprehend and bring clarity to individual ways of relating to and experiencing God.

Thematic Session #2: Lech Lecha — Starting on a Journey

Read *Lech Lecha*, Genesis 12. Take 15 minutes to write in your journal: Think about a risk that you took in your life. For what reasons did you take the risk? Who, if anyone, was influential in your taking the risk? What was the experience like? How did it feel? In what ways did it affect your relationship with those involved (e.g., family, friends)? What were the results, outcomes, or consequences, both positive and negative? In dyads, share your risk taking experience with a partner. As a large group, discuss: What is it like to start on a journey? In what ways are these risk taking experiences like the journey of Abram and Sarai? How are they like starting on your own spiritual journey?

Thematic Session #3: Journey through the Wilderness

Life can be viewed as a journey with both miracles and pain. Life has moments of light and darkness. Life as it is given has no boundaries. Our choices and what happens to us outside of what we choose, determine the shape of our life, our boundaries. Create an outline of the journey, the miracles and pain, the light and darkness, that occur in Moses' life and journey. What were highlights of the relationship between God and

Moses? What were the highlights of the relationship between God and the Israelites during the journey from slavery in Egypt through reaching the Promised Land? How do you think Moses felt during those times of light and of darkness? How do you think the Israelites felt during those times?

Create a map and time line of events in your life (it need not be a straight time line). Highlight the key moments in your life, both times of light and darkness. In pairs, talk about the events and try to recapture feelings surrounding them. As a large group, discuss: Where was God in your moments of light? in your moments of darkness?

Thematic Session #4: Yisrael: Wrestling with God

Read the story of Jacob and the messenger, Genesis 23. Act out the conversation that could have taken place between Jacob and the messenger after the event. In your journal, take 15 minutes to write about your life struggles: What have been the hard questions with which you have struggled in life? What does it feel like to struggle with them and to prevail? What does it feel like to wrestle alone? What does it feel like to wrestle with help? How did you feel when the struggle is over?

Thematic Session #5: Ehyeh Asher Ehyeh: Changing Images of God

We change, and our images of God change throughout our lives. In groups of 4 or 5, discuss: What did God mean to you at different points when you were child? In what ways, if any, has your perception of God changed since then? What do you think contributes to your changing images of God?

Thematic Session #6: Ya'ayr Adonai Panav Aylecha: Light

The metaphor of God's light shining on us,

bringing light to our lives (dealing favorably or kindly with us), is repeated in different ways throughout traditional texts. The phrase *"ya'ayr Adonai Panav Aylecha"* comes from the priestly blessing, Numbers 6:22-27. Traditionally recited by the priests, and today in some congregations by the *Kohanim*, the priestly blessing is said by parents for their children on Shabbat evening. When Moses ascends the mountain, he sees God's face. Tradition teaches that seeing God's face is far too powerful for most of us to endure. God's light shining on us is itself a moving experience, a "wow" or "ah ha" moment.

Listen to *Appalachian Spring* or other inspiring music. When in your life have you experienced something extraordinary? When did all of a sudden something become clear to you? Share your story. In what ways, if any, did this experience of the extraordinary involve feeling the presence of God? Write a letter to someone containing your reflections on this experience.

EVALUATION:

The participants should be able to answer the following questions: (1) In what ways are you now more comfortable and secure in your search for God? (2) What did you learn about your relationship to and understanding of God?

WATCH OUT FOR:

Make certain that people feel comfortable sharing. This type of sharing and discussion will come more easily for some than for others. You need to be aware that rather than strengthening the relationship to God for some participants, this probing may create a crisis of faith. Be prepared to provide support or recommend avenues of support for those who are in need of help.

YOUR LINK IN THE CHAIN OF JEWISH TRADITION

Nadine Cohen

TOPIC:

Exploring one's own spirituality in the context of learning about the spirituality of women in our biblical tradition.

TARGET AUDIENCE:

The program was originally developed in the context of exploring women's multifaceted roles in the process of forming a more defined sense of self, at the same time examining the struggles and potential conflicts of reconciling feminism within a traditional Jewish framework. This approach can be meaningfully adapted to any audience. Maximal benefit of this kind of approach is derived when the goals and expectations are clearly articulated and mutually agreed upon by all.

TIME FRAME:

The initial program was designed as a two-hour class that met once a week for eight weeks. The eight sessions were interrelated, suggesting and allowing for a degree of continuity and thematic enrichment. Even though each session was essentially discrete and self-contained, regular attendance implied a commitment and encouraged participants to build a sense of trust and openness with one another. Whatever the structure of this program in adapted form may be, it is important to allow time for the experiential art component, as well as follow-up processing to facilitate closure and containment of issues evoked in this kind of expressive work.

In the original program, the first hour was devoted to studying a biblical text and source material. Using original text was regarded as key to directing participants to look for parallels in their contemporary and personal experience. The second hour then focused on an attempt to concretize metaphor and imagery evoked in the preceding learning experience, through visual and creative expression. This related experiential art response ended with a series of questions, either written or discussed, which are designed to help participants process the connections among the text, their interpretive art, and their spirituality.

STAFF:

Two staffing models are possible: (1) The original approach involved using text experts, content specialists, to teach the biblical portion, and an educational specialist with art therapy training to facilitate the art response and process the connections, and (2) The second approach utilizes one person to teach the text portion as well as facilitate the art creation and processing that follows.

OVERVIEW:

This program combines principles of textual analysis and interpretation with those of art therapy in a course for women and men to explore their spirituality. Art becomes a medium for uncovering the ways we interpret texts and connect its meaning to our lives through the structured medium of free association and play. In this way, an attempt is made to create dialogue between the unconscious and the conscious, the symbolic and the rational, the implicit and the explicit, the personal and the communal, all of which affect our spiritual being. A more detailed understanding of the approach is presented in Chapter 20, "Art Therapy and the Spiritual Encounter," p. 212, which I authored.

PURPOSES:

The original purpose of the program was to facilitate women's self-exploration of their spirituality within a traditional Jewish context. It was anticipated that the participating women would be able to identify parts of themselves with the primary themes presented and explored in the learning. It was also expected that women would attain a greater sense of identity with the role models studied, and that their ability to derive spiritual meaning from biblical text would significantly increase. Finally, it was anticipated that these women's sense of identity within the Jewish community would develop, and that they would be able to integrate their Jewishness as an organizing principle into their lives.

OBJECTIVES:

The participants will:

- examine texts about Jewish women's spirituality for what they have to say about the women of the Bible and for what they have to say to us today.

- use art, and discussion of the art, to help explore the meaning of the texts and how they relate to their spiritual lives.

TIME FRAME:

The course met for eight sessions in total. All but the last session focused on a different biblical female personality. The eighth session, Closure, was devoted to processing the whole experience.

CONTENT:

Female biblical persons: Eve, Sarah, Rebekah, Leah, Rachel, Tamar, Yocheved, Miriam, and Esther

LEARNING ACTIVITIES:

The art directive and processing questions emerge out of the texts studied and the concepts emphasized. As each teacher is likely to use different texts in emphasizing various aspects and understandings of the biblical women's spiritual quests, the art directive and process questions will need to be adjusted to fit the key concepts investigated. Session #3 is described in detail below.

SESSION #3: REBEKAH

Texts: Genesis chapters 24 and 25, *midrashim* on Rebekah, and the book *Biblical Images* by Adin Steinsaltz, p. 45

Concepts: Implications of acting and following through on decision making; significance of family origins and lineage

Discussion of Concepts to Be Explored: In Rebekah, we sensed and learned of the implications and strength of prophetic vision, and also the implications of acting and following through on decision making. In this workshop, we explored the notion of acting on the situation in which we find ourselves, and making conscious decisions in relation to our families and ancestry. In so doing, we discover our own strength to reshape and remold what comes our way, and find ways to use this new understanding of our past in living today and in the future.

Midrash relates how Rebekah, in accepting to marry Isaac, had to leave behind her family of origin. In Genesis 25:20, when she is described as "Rebekah, the daughter of Bethuel the Aramean at Padanaram, the sister to Laban the Aramean," there is a significant emphasis on her origins in terms of place, as well as in terms of her relationships as both sister and daughter. Steinsaltz (1984) portrayed her as having a sense of vision, vitality, and purpose strong enough to resist and overcome the negative influences of her family of origin. Of the two branches of the family of Terach from which she descended, Abraham's line is described as powerful, while the "other, that of Nahor, declined, lost its property, and engaged in petty trade" (Steinsaltz, p. 45). She is portrayed as an "atavistic figure, containing within herself the strength and vitality of the great line from which the Patriarchs descended" (Steinsaltz, p. 45). In physically separating herself and entering into an independent relationship of marriage, she was able to transcend the negative influences of her family of origin, and draw on her inner strength to create and form a vital link in the future structure and lineage of the Jewish people. It is from her marriage with Isaac that Jacob and Esau descend.

Art Directive: Using clay, mold yourself as though you were a vessel, a container housing qualities and values that can be transmitted. Participants were encouraged to respond to the malleable properties inherent in clay as they created and felt emerging form.

Materials:
Clay and appropriate tools and work area. (The clay pieces were later fired.)

Processing Question: In learning about Rebekah's stepping into Sarah's tent, and then creating her own home, how do you see yourself impacted by those women in your family background who precede you? In what ways did they affect the forming of your self as a container? How do you see yourself passing on essential values to your own children?

EVALUATION:

The eighth session should serve as an evaluative session of the content and process. You might want to have the participants write a brief response to the following questions before you discuss them as a group. (1) Which was your favorite project? Explain your response. (2) What were the one or two most important insights that you gained about the life of one of the biblical figures? about your own spirituality? (3) In what ways did you find that this workshop series affected your understanding of your own Jewish identity and spirituality? (4) In what ways did the combination of art and text study elicit new understandings for you? (5) What would entice you to sign up for another group of sessions?

WATCH OUT FOR:

While this program utilizes art therapy principles and approaches, it is intended to be an educational program. Help keep the sharing at an appropriate level.

BIBLIOGRAPHY

Steinsaltz, Adin. *Biblical Images*. Northvale, NJ: Jason Aronson Inc., 1994.

Steinsaltz provides insight into the different biblical figures by drawing on *Midrash* and his own interpretations of the text.

CHAPTER 46

KESHER L'ADONAI: CONNECTING TO GOD

Janice P. Alper

TOPICS:

Examining the role of God in one's life; communicating with God through prayer and in individual ways; coming closer to God through study; living in the image of God through *mitzvah* activities; and coming closer to God through creating family heirlooms

TARGET AUDIENCE:

Families of any configuration with children of all ages

TIME FRAME:

2-1/2 to 3 hours

STAFF:

One teacher, music specialist, and an assistant. (If the teacher or assistant can lead music, then the music specialist is not required. The music may also be led by a participant who is given the appropriate materials and instructions in advance.)

OVERVIEW:

This program revolves around a series of interactive strategies that help participants to reflect and react to the experience as individuals, as family units, and as a community. The activities involve an interaction with prayer, group study, and a means to move forward from the specific program to integrate various ways to become more connected to God.

PURPOSE:

The purpose of the program is to help families learn to relate to God in their lives. It is designed to have people of different ages and backgrounds understand that belief in God is central to Jewish life. Through the use of various modalities, participants can begin to see that the Jewish view of God is not linear, and that it can be manifested in many different ways.

OBJECTIVES:

Participants in this program will:

- write down thoughts and/or feelings they have about God and share them in family units or with the entire group.

- examine Jewish prayers, then reflect on how God is presented in these prayers, using words, music, nonverbal methods, art, or combinations, such as poetry, songs, dance, etc.

- articulate how they can continue the act of creation by taking on personal *mitzvot* that are consistent with their lives.

- make an object, such as a *mezuzah* case or prayer book cover, to remind them of their experience at this program and to help them focus on communication with God when they are not in a worship environment.

LEARNING MATERIALS:

This program features many activities. In several cases, alternative activities are suggested. Therefore, the learning materials needed will depend on the activities chosen. The staff should use the following list of supplies to determine what is needed in order to complete all of the activities.

- tape recorder and/or CD player

- Jewish music on cassette or CD

- folder for each family

- name tags

- markers for each family

- outline of the schedule on tag board

- copies of handout "God in My Life" (Appendix A), one per person

- a pencil for each person

- a piece of art paper, butcher paper, or flip chart paper for each family

- "God in our life" pictures (e.g., people praying, tending to the aged, a cemetery, nature scenes, happy faces, sad faces)

- "Shehecheyanu" prayer in Hebrew, transliteration, and translation

- song "Eli, Eli" in Hebrew, transliteration, and translation

- "La'asok b'Divray Torah" prayer in Hebrew, transliteration, and translation

- copies of texts for parallel activities for adults and children (see activity #5 for recommended texts)

- the Mitzvot Contract form (Appendix B), one copy for each family

- art supplies for mezuzah case, wimpel, or other ritual object (see activity #7)

- one copy per family of the Program Evaluation form (Appendix C)

- take-home items about God, including bibliography of books, short stories, personal accounts of experiences of finding God, and articles about talking to children about God, one set per family

Resource Materials:

- God story. Possible stories include: *God's Paintbrush* by Sandy Eisenberg Sasso, or "The Shepherd" found in Eric Kimmelman's book, *Days of Awe*, pp. 32-38 (see the bibliography, p. 382, for complete reference).

- text source materials for activity #5

- "Eli, Eli" in sign language (You will need a sign language book. If the entire song is too difficult to sign, you could do just part of it or a few words in sign language.)

LEARNING ACTIVITIES:

Preparation

As participants come into the room play background music, such as "Oseh Shalom," "Shehecheyanu," "Y'did Nefesh," "Sing Unto God a New Song," or "Eli, Eli." The facility should be arranged so that people can move around freely, yet come together as family units and as a whole group when the need arises. Be sure to provide name tags for each person, folders for each family, and an outline on tag board of what to expect for all the families.

Activity #1: Introduction: God in My Life

The purpose of this activity is to help participants focus and reflect on how God is a part of their lives. You may do this by using one or more of the following:

- Worksheet (Appendix A, p. 379): A large piece of art paper with markers for each family. Instruct them to designate a portion of the art paper (e.g., a corner) for each family member.

- Pictures placed around the room that help people to verbalize God's role in their lives (e.g., people engaged in prayer, tending the aged, at a cemetery, scenery, sun, moon, stars, happy faces, sad faces, etc.).

- Allow time for individuals in the families to reflect on God in their lives. Share these reflections in family groups, then with the whole group present if they so desire.

Activity #2: Communicating with God: A Prayer Experience

The purpose of this activity is to demonstrate that everyone can communicate with God in his/her own way. Do the following:

- Read either "The Shepherd" by Kimmelman or *God's Paintbrush* by Sasso. Take a few moments for the group to discuss the story among themselves, then ask for any reactions. Do not spend too much time on this part of the activity.

- *"Shehecheyanu"* – Teach the *"Shehecheyanu"* blessing and one melody for it. Sing it together.

- Discuss when we say *"Shehecheyanu."* Ask the group to mention some *"Shehecheyanu"* moments in their lives.

- Sing *Niggunim* (melodies without words) – Teach a *niggun*. Encourage participants to use their bodies when singing the *niggun*. Explain that this is another way we communicate with God without using words.

Activity #3: Communicating with God in Our Own Way

- Teach the song *"Eli, Eli"* with words and sign language. (This is a good way to involve a participant who has knowledge of sign language.)

- Ask families to take a few moments to write down a prayer or poem to God or to come up with a *niggun* or a dance of their own in which they communicate with God. This may be done with the whole family, or individual family members may do the exercise separately. Those who wish to do so may share what they wrote with the entire group.

Note: The above three activities introduce the participants to ways of communicating with God. The facilitator can vary the activities to make them more consistent with the philosophy and mission of his/her institution or comfort level. One suggestion is to have everyone experience wrapping themselves in a *tallit* to understand the idea of *kavanah*, preparation for prayer, separating oneself from the world in order to communicate with God. Another suggestion is to use passages from the *Siddur* which reflect God's work in the world, such as *"Ma'ariv Aravim," "Yotzer Or," "Ahavah Rabbah"* or *"Ahavat Olam."*

At this point, you may also want to introduce the concept of a God Journal — keeping track of when you communicate with God or when God is reflected in your life (e.g., *"Shehecheyanu"* moments, blessings of the senses, or simple everyday occurrences).

Activity #4: Talmud Torah — Coming Closer To God through Study

The purpose of this activity is to provide participants with opportunities to share their insights about Judaism and God. Primary texts should be used, as well as sources from Jewish philosophy. For source material, consult *Teaching Your Children about God* by David Wolpe, or the classic, *Debbie and Joey in God's World* by Morris and Lenore Kipper. (See bibliography, p. 382, for complete citations.) Instructions for using each of these resources follows.

Teaching Your Children about God:
This book is a rich resource for teaching about God. Each chapter begins with a *midrash*. There are suggestions on how to respond and several exercises designed to crystallize one's ideas about God. One such exercise in Chapter 3 explores God images. Children are asked to describe things they cannot see. After the discussion, they may draw a picture of what God is like. Questions at the end of each chapter may be used for further discussion. In Chapter 3, Wolpe asks: What other images do you have of God? What is God like? (Is God like a king, a parent, a police officer, a friend, a school teacher?) (Wolpe, 1993, p. 60)

This book is appropriate for families to use together since it formulates questions, addresses issues, and provides a vehicle for learning about how to view God. While the questions are designed primarily for discussions with children, they are also appropriate for participating adults. The questions help adults understand how their own images, conceptions, and relations to God have changed and why their responses may be different from their children's.

Debbie and Joey in God's World:

Each chapter of this book begins with a quotation about God, followed by a story to illustrate a point about how God plays a role in our lives. Most of the quotations come from traditional Jewish sources, such as Tanach and *Midrash*. Others are found in the *Siddur* or are popular phrases or proverbs. The chapter entitled "Learning Tricks" begins with the words of *Beresheet* 2:7: "Then the Lord God formed man . . . and man became a living soul." The story following reminds Debbie and Joey that as we grow, we mature and learn new things. We should be appreciative of the gifts God gave to us, including the ability to learn new things and use them to move forward in the world.

Any of the chapters and the quotes can be used as a vehicle for learning about God. Before reading the written story, ask each participant to articulate his/her original *midrash*, an interpretation, which amplifies the quote. The written story can then be used as an illustration of how the authors viewed it. Another way to use this book is to break the families into several groups and assign each one a different chapter to discuss. A third way is to write out the quotes, then ask participants to share what they think is being said about God.

Activity #5: La'asok b'Divray Torah

Teach the blessing "*La'asok b'Divray Torah*" to everyone present. Another way to introduce the study is actually to take out a *sefer Torah* and pass it around to all participants. You may wish to combine the two as an introduction.

Parallel Learning Activities for This Lesson

Adults and children over the age of 11 meet with the facilitator. Use the portion of the week, a particular prayer, a philosophical essay which reflects a Jewish view of God, or any other material that is appropriate for the setting.

Children under the age of 11 (this may also be subdivided into two or three groups, depending on the number of children and ages) should engage in parallel study about God focusing on the portion of the week, a particular prayer, or a story. Use puppets, a story board, a video, or some other means to engage the children in the discussion.

When the study session is over, bring the group back together and ask them to share the experience with each other before proceeding to the next activity.

In the Image of God: Mitzvah Opportunities and Coming Closer To God: Creating Family Heirlooms

The following are simultaneous activities that provide opportunities for participants to learn about *mitzvah* opportunities in their own community, and to create a family heirloom (e.g., a *mezuzah* case or *wimpel* or other object that reminds them of their relationship to God).

The *mitzvah* opportunity is designed to help participants understand that we are created in the image of God. When we do things to make the world a better place, we are God's helpers in repairing the world and engaging in the act of creation.

Discuss how doing *mitzvot* brings us closer to God. When we perform *mitzvot*, we are helping to complete the act of creation. Put an emphasis on actions that make a difference to people, to their community, or to the world. (Do not encourage children to regard not being mean to their siblings as a *mitzvah!*)

Ask the Social Action Committee or a similar body, to provide you with a list of *mitzvah* opportunities in the community. Also, consult the Rabbi or spiritual leader to see in which *mitzvot* he/she would like to see people engage in order to come closer to God.

Gather as much literature and information possible about each *mitzvah* opportunity. If you are short on time, create posters about the various opportunities. These might include: photographs of families doing various *mitzvot*, such as lighting Shabbat candles, preparing meals at a shelter, working for Habitat for Humanity, cleaning a local cemetery, giving time in the synagogue, reciting a blessing before each meal, etc. If you have extended time, invite speakers to tell about the *mitzvot*.

Provide each family with a Mitzvah Contract form (Appendix B, p. 380) to help them determine the *mitzvot* in which they will engage.

Creating a *mezuzah* case, something we put on our doorposts, helps us to acknowledge God in our homes. Creating a *wimpel*, an object that "hugs" the Torah, helps bring us closer to God when we study. Other items might be prayer book covers, spice boxes, fringes for a *tallit*, a decorative *kipah* or head cover, a blessing wheel, etc.

It is important to provide ample time for families to complete these activities so that they do not feel frustrated. It may be necessary to have some alternative things happening so that those who finish early will still have something to do.

Distribute Program Evaluation forms (Appendix C) for families to complete as they finish this activity. Ask them to bring their evaluation forms to the Wrap-up Circle.

Wrap-up Circle

Bring the group together for one last time in a circle. If there are too many people for one circle, put children in a concentric circle in front of parents.

Sing *"Eli, Eli"* using words and sign language.

Sing two choruses of *"Shalom Chaverim,"* then

hum. As the group is humming, ask them to share feelings, thoughts, ideas about God that they acquired from this program. You may want to provide the line, "For me God is _____"

When everyone has shared their thoughts and feelings, sing a final chorus of *"Shalom Chaverim."*

Send home a set of materials about God. Be sure it consists of materials that will enable families to continue to explore their relationship with God. Examples: bibliographies, short stories, articles about how to talk to children about God, or first person accounts of experiences in finding God.

Alternative Suggestions for This Program:

The program as presented is for one session. Ideally, it should take place during an extended school session on the weekend or an evening. It may also take place at a *Shabbaton* or retreat designed for this purpose. (If the program is a *Shabbaton*, some of the activities may have to be altered to adhere to the *halachot* of your institution.)

An alternative way to conduct this program is in three sessions of 60-90 minutes:

Session I: God in My Life

Communicating with God through Prayer

Introduce God Journals (See explanation below.)

Session II: Reflections about God in My Life from God Journals

Communicating with God through Prayer

Session III: Reflections about Communicating with God from God Journals

In the Image of God: *Mitzvah* Opportunities

Coming Closer To God: Creating Family Heirlooms

In order to maintain consistency, this three-session program should be set up the same way for each session. Music and dance should be a part of each session. Instead of the Wrap-up Circle at the end as described in the program above, have mini-closures at the end of each session, using either open-ended sentences or sharing of the experiences among participants.

Note: God Journals are a wonderful way to involve the families in ongoing reflection about their relationships with God. You may provide each family with a bound notebook that has some quotes or leading sentences to help them reflect about their experiences with God. Encourage them to bring these journals to each session.

EVALUATION:

Each family should complete the Program Evaluation form, which helps them reflect on the session (see Appendix C, p. 381).

In order to determine if the program was effective, use some of the following techniques:

Group follow-up: After a few weeks, contact a few participating families either by phone or letter and ask them to reflect on their relationship with God. Is there anything different about their lives after having had the group experience?

How would they complete the introductory worksheet today?

Request reflections from God Journals that may be reproduced in the synagogue bulletin or a school newsletter.

Teachers provide opportunities for students to reflect about God in their lives, e.g., ongoing interactive bulletin boards, a chart of *"Shehecheyanu"* moments, or moments of reflection during which students can talk about God in their lives.

If possible, bring together a small focus group to reflect on the program experience.

WATCH OUT FOR:

Both families and members within families may differ in their comfort levels with the subject, familiarity with exploring their relationship to God, and interaction among family members. On a subject that is as personal and sometimes as sensitive as this one, the family dynamics are as critical as the content. Be certain to stress that all families and family members are on their own journeys in relating to God and identifying as Jews. Emphasize that finding God often involves joy, hope, light, and peacefulness, as well as struggles, doubts, anger, and fear.

APPENDIX A

God in My Life

1. Circle the words that represent what God is for you:

great	omnipotent	patient	big
a model	power	everywhere	mysterious
with me	beautiful	a woman	a parent
a friend	abundant in goodness and health	forgiving	loving
George Burns	an umbrella	all knowing	a fountain

2. Add some of your own words and circle them:

3. Write down some thoughts or feelings you have about God. For example, tell about times when you feel close to God, or talk to God, or wish God would help you.

APPENDIX B

Mitzvah Contract

We, the members of the _____ family, consisting of

_____

_____

agree to do the following *mitzvah*:

We will begin on _____.

(date)

Signed: _____

_____

_____

_____

Date _____

APPENDIX C

Program Evaluation

Complete these phrases:

1. I/we came today expecting:

2. One new thing I/we learned today was:

3. The best thing about this program was:

4. One thing I/we would change or do differently is:

5. One thing I/we will do as a result of this program is:

Overall, the program was (check all that apply):

____ great   ____ fair   ____ so-so   ____ fun   ____ enlightening   ____ engaging   ____ stimulating

____ challenging   ____ boring   ____ interesting   ____ too intellectual   ____ too simple

Please write down any other comments that are important to you or will help with planning future programs:

Your Name (optional) _____

BIBLIOGRAPHY

Kimmel, Eric. "The Shepherd." In *Days of Awe: Stories for Rosh Hashanah and Yom Kippur*. New York: Viking, 1991, 32-38.

This book, which is meant to be used particularly during the High Holy Day season, includes this story about understanding God metaphorically as a shepherd.

Kipper, Morris and Lenore. *Debbie and Joey in God's World*. New York: Sheingold Publishers, 1968.

Featured herein are stories about two children who explore their relationship to God and the ethical principles of Judaism. Each chapter begins with a quotation about God, followed by a story to illustrate a point about how God plays a role in our lives. Most of the quotations come from traditional Jewish sources, including Tanach, *Midrash*, and *Siddur*.

Sasso, Sandy Eisenberg. *God's Paintbrush*. Woodstock, VT: Jewish Lights Publishing, 1992.

A beautifully illustrated and poetically stated storybook about God's place in the universe and how God touches our world.

Wolpe, David J. *Teaching Your Children about God*. New York: Henry Holt and Company, 1993.

An excellent resource for parents to use with their children as they explore questions and clarify their views about God. Each chapter deals with a major theological issue, often stated in the form of a question such as: What does God want from us? Does God hear our prayers? Each chapter begins with a *midrash* that focuses on a theological issue. This is followed by suggestions on how to respond to children's questions. At the end of each chapter, there are questions for discussion.

CHAPTER 47

GOD AROUND US

Janice P. Alper

TOPICS:

People's views of God, God's blessings; reflecting on God through music and poetry.

TARGET AUDIENCE:

This program was designed for families with children in Grade 2. It may be adapted for families with children in Kindergarten to Grade 4.

TIME FRAME:

1-1/2 to 2 hours

STAFF:

Two people — a teacher/facilitator and someone to assist.

OVERVIEW:

This program is designed to involve families in an interactive process in thinking about God. Together, parents and children explore their perceptions of God, how they talk to God, and what they think about God.

PURPOSE:

This program is appropriate for families with children of early elementary age because it allows all participants to reflect personally, then talk to each other. It encourages children to ask and answer questions, focus on ideas that may concern them, and verbalize their thoughts in a non-threatening environment. For the adults,

this kind of program is a way of introducing them to Jewish concepts of God and to help them reflect about their own thoughts and feelings. The interaction between parents and children enables the adults to confront the often confounding questions which children pose. The program provides a totally non-threatening environment in which parents can react and develop their own ideas about God at an adult level.

OBJECTIVES:

Participants will:

*   explain in their own words how they view God.

*   be involved in an activity during which they determine how we are God's creation and how we use the gifts God gave to us.

*   write prayers/poems/reflections about God.

LEARNING MATERIALS:

This program features many activities. In several cases, alternative activities are provided. Therefore, the learning materials needed will depend on the activities chosen. The staff should use the following list of supplies to determine which are needed in order to complete each of the activities:

*   signs for each station

*   VCR and television

*   video: *god@heaven* or *How Do You Spell God?* (see bibliography)

*   "Thinking about God" sheets, one per person

- pencils, one per person

- large piece of paper, one per family

- catalogues and magazines

- scissors

- glue sticks

- markers

- plain white paper or lined paper

- cassette or CD player

- cassette or CD of songs about God

- take-home items about God, including bibliography of books, short stories, personal accounts of experiences of finding God, and articles about talking to children about God, one set per family

LEARNING ACTIVITIES:

This program consists of a group introductory activity to be followed by three stations. It is designed so that children, no matter how young, may work on their own, then talk to their parents about God. In activities other than the introductory one, families may work at any station of their choice at their own pace. If there is a large number of people, you may wish to set up a procedure for moving from one station to another to be sure that everyone completes each activity.

Activity #1: Introduction

Everyone watches the video. This is followed by a brief discussion.

Alternative Introductory Activities

1. Have a brief service during which families pray together. Provide explanations about the blessings in the service.

2. Read a story, such as *God in Between* by Sandy Eisenberg Sasso, *God's Mailbox* by Marc Gellman, or *Does God Have a Big Toe?* by Marc Gellman. (See bibliography for complete citations.)

Three Interactive Stations

Station Alef: Thinking about God

Two worksheets are presented, one in large print for young children, the other in smaller print for older children and parents. Both contain the same open-ended statements. (This exercise is adapted from *God: The Eternal Challenge* by Sherry Bissell [Blumberg], with Audrey Friedman Marcus and Raymond A. Zwerin.)

- I talk to God when _____.

- God talks to me when _____.

- I feel close to God when _____.

- I think about God when _____.

Adults and children complete these open-ended sentences independently, after which they sit down and discuss their answers as a family.

Station Bet: God's Blessings in Pictures

Each family folds in half a large piece of paper. On one half, family members draw or cut out pictures from catalogs and magazines that show things that only God can make (trees, ocean, stars, people, food items, etc.). On the other half, they cut out pictures that show things that people have made with the gifts God has given to them (e.g., houses, gardens, creating meals). Hang up the pictures around the room. At some point, perhaps at the end of the session, families will talk about their pictures.

Station Gimel: Music Helps Us Reflect about God

Set up a listening center in which participants may quietly listen to a tape or CD of a song about God. Examples: *"Eli, Eli,"* a *niggun*, "Sing Unto God a New Song," etc. Instruct each participant to write a poem or song in praise of God. Collect the poems and songs and put into a booklet that can be used at a later time, such as at a service or at special school, synagogue, or JCC event.

Variations for the Stations:

- Take a nature walk. Look around at all the things God makes. Think about how we use God's gifts to create things to make life better for us.

- Go to a park and collect items from nature. Using the items, make collages or make spice boxes for Havdalah.

- If *Tefilah* is a usual part of your program, use this as an opportunity to talk about how Jews pray to God.

Closure

End the day by bringing everyone together for a moment of reflection and sharing their feelings and thoughts about God. Participants can share information about family pictures, read their poems or prayers, or simply reflect on their own perceptions of God. Have participants complete the evaluation phrases either as families or in the large group (see "Evaluation" below).

Note: Be sure to send home materials that will enable families to continue to explore their relationship with God. These may include bibliographies, short stories, articles about how to talk to children about God or first person accounts of others experiences in finding God. (See the bibliography at the end of this program for sources.)

EVALUATION:

Ask families to complete the following. This will provide input on the program, as well as show how it has influenced their thinking and feelings about finding God:

- I feel _____.

- Prior to today, I _____.

- This session made me think _____.

- I enjoyed _____.

- Finding God _____.

- One of God's blessings that is important to me is _____.

- I have doubts about _____.

- I wish _____.

- I am grateful for _____.

Note: Because it is important to try to get all the members of each family to speak, rather than just a representative, these sentence completions are best done in family groups. Families can then be asked to share some of the highlights of their comments.

WATCH OUT FOR:

The age range for children is broad, although for the most part they are concrete learners. Some of the children will know how to read and write, while others are just beginning to acquire these skills. Make certain that the younger as well as older children have the opportunity to participate fully. Remember, though, the older children need to feel that their responses and ways of doing things are age appropriate and sophisticated.

BIBLIOGRAPHY

For Adults

Gellman, Marc, and Thomas Hartman. *Where Does God Live?* New York: Triumph Books, 1991.

> A Rabbi and a Monsignor answer common questions about God and demonstrate that Jews and Christians, although they worship differently, are nonetheless worshiping the same God.

Kushner, Harold. *Who Needs God.* New York: Summit Books, 1989.

> Kushner examines his own faith and shows how it can enrich and lead to a fulfilling life.

Wolpe, David J. *The Healer of Shattered Hearts: A Modern Jewish Approach.* New York: Henry Holt, 1990.

> Through texts and ancient traditions, Wolpe examines the role of God in our daily struggles, fears, needs, and questions.

For Children

Bissell [Blumberg], Sherry, with Audrey Friedman Marcus and Raymond A. Zwerin. *God: The Eternal Challenge,* Denver: A.R.E. Publishing, Inc., 1976.

> This mini-course provides interactive and challenging ways of viewing one's relationship to God. (For a reprint of this mini-course, see the Appendix, p. 435.)

Bogot, Howard. *I Learn about God.* New York: UAHC Press, 1982.

> Text and illustrations portray Jewish children learning about God as they go about various activities.

Gellman, Marc. *Does God Have a Big Toe?* New York: Harper and Row Junior Books, 1989.

> A fanciful book filled with *midrashim* that focus on our understanding of and relationship to God.

———. *God's Mailbox.* New York: Morrow Jr. Books, 1996.

> A book of *midrashim* that respond to commonly asked questions about God.

———. *How Do You Spell God?* New York: Morrow Junior Books, 1995.

> An examination of the world's religions through their holidays, philosophies, wisdom, stories, and approach to God.

Sasso, Sandy Eisenberg. *God in Between.* Woodstock, VT: Jewish Lights Publishing, 1998.

> When the wise people leave their lonely, confused town to find out if God exists, they make a discovery about where God can be found.

———. *In God's Name.* Woodstock, VT: Jewish Lights Publishing, 1994.

> A modern fable that highlights the spiritual celebrations of all people, and their belief in one God who does many things for us.

Videos

God@heaven. 20 min., color. Ergo Media Inc., P.O. Box 2037, Teaneck, NJ 07666, 1- 877-539-4748, www.jewishvideo.com.

> Seven-year-old Adam sends an e-mail all the way to Jerusalem's Western Wall, an "e-mail direct to God." Days pass without a reply. Then suddenly . . . This contemporary video's mix of theology and technology addresses an age-old question of how we can communicate with God in a new and innovative way.

How Do You Spell God? 20 min., color. An HBO Kids Film. Available from amazon.com.

> Provides a unique perspective on questions every child asks about God, faith, and their place in the world. Children of different faiths come together through animation and conversation to create a provocative discussion on the meaning of God in their lives. Based on the book of the same name by Rabbi Marc Gellman and Monsiegnor Thomas Hartman.

CHAPTER 48

LIGHT: A FAMILY KALLAH

Harriet M. Levine

TOPIC:

Light as a physical reality, symbol, and metaphor is a deeply spiritual connector for Jews. The thematic focus of this family *kallah* is light. A family *kallah* over a Shabbat has its own special goals: to bring families together to observe and celebrate Shabbat, to allow families to spend quality time together in a Jewish environment, to build community among families, and to bring children and adults together for study. In terms of this theme or topic, a *kallah* over Shabbat provides an environment in which the concept of light can be both experienced and studied. Spiritually, this blending of experience with study facilitates the simultaneous blending of traditional views with new understandings, thoughts with feelings, actions with meanings, and perhaps mind with soul.

TARGET AUDIENCE:

Families

TIME FRAME:

Shabbat or weekend (can be adapted for other formats)

STAFF:

Facilitator

OVERVIEW:

Since the dawn of humankind, light has been important to us. It has evoked fear and wonder. It has been mesmerizing, mysterious, and necessary. It has been written and sung about.

Every religion uses light. Our own Jewish sacred writings, starting with the very first sentences of the Torah, speak of light. Not only are we commanded to use light, some rituals and festivals are built around candles and oil lamps. The candle has great significance as a ceremonial object. Almost every festival, celebration, and commemoration involves the kindling of light at some point. Beyond the symbols themselves, light has been a metaphor found throughout Judaism. Light as a metaphor has been used to speak about God and the Jewish people.

Because light is so much a part of our ritual and is mentioned in many of our written sources, it is a subject that is interesting to explore. During Shabbat, or at a weekend program when light is used for religious as well as social purposes, a family *kallah* can be a good way to explore the importance of light in Judaism. In this informal setting, parents and children can learn about light from a Jewish perspective as they experience light in a living, vital context. The family can learn the hows, whats, whens, and whys of the different candles as they use them ritually for Shabbat. They can connect the experiences of natural light, sun, moon, and stars to the words of the prayers on creation. The setting encourages them to interpret, using such sources as *Midrash*, as well as the arts, and to express their views and feelings. Over a campfire, which sets a mood in itself, they can sing songs about light, share stories about light, and create scenarios about what the world would be like without light. For even the smallest child and the oldest adult, during meals, formal study sessions, and recreational opportunities, the family *kallah* encourages examination of the meaning of light in their lives and in the lives of all Jews.

PURPOSES:

This family *kallah* attempts to integrate the theme of light into as many educational, social, recreational, ritual and survival (food, clothing, and shelter) opportunities as possible. The family *kallah* is about heightening awareness of light as found in our tradition (broadly defined) and in our lives as Jews.

The goals of the program are to:

- explore the meaning of light in Judaic tradition using a variety of activities.

- discover and interpret what our sacred literature says about light.

- acknowledge the significance of the creation of light in Judaism.

- explore the physical properties of light and candlelight.

- experience the common bond that emerges when Jews share ritual lights together.

- experience the creation of light out of darkness through the use of our senses.

OBJECTIVES:

The primary objectives are listed here.

Participants will:

- list ways in which light is used in Jewish rituals and in the lives of Jews generally.

- examine what Jewish sources say about light, its uses, metaphors, and meanings.

- read and interpret the verses in Genesis about light and creation.

- explore the physical properties of light.

- interpret the properties and meaning of light through different means including dance, music, and the visual arts.

- create their own *midrashim* and interpretations about the significance of light in their lives and for the Jewish people.

CONTENT:

The *kallah* program covers the following concepts, themes, symbols, and rituals related to light: Shabbat candles and blessings, Havdalah candle and blessings, sunset, sunrise, creation, physical properties of light, Jewish lights, ordinary lights, uses of lights, God and light, fire, and darkness.

FORMAT:

Rather than provide a schedule for a *kallah*, the following is a list of the components of a retreat weekend that can incorporate the theme of light.

- Watch the sunset, gaze at the stars, and wake up for the sunrise. Go on a nature hike at different times of the day and night to see how the plants, animals, and people respond to different amounts of light and darkness. Look at the colors of light.

- During services, highlight prayers that contain images and metaphors about light especially *"Ma'ariv Aravim"* in the evening *"Shema"* and blessings section, and the *"Yotzer Or"* prayer, found in the same section in the morning.

- Highlight the candles used in Shabbat evening blessings and Havdalah at the end of Shabbat. Discuss why traditionally no new lights are lit on Shabbat and how that affects one's life.

- Use story and arts and craft time for children and adults to explore light and lights through different media. Have families make Shabbat candles and/or Havdalah candles.

- Play an afternoon game of lights and shadows, during which people move from one location to the other in a lighted area or a shadow area as instructed by the "caller." If desired, You can add a game of *Tag*. As people move from one place to the other, the caller can try to tag someone else to be "It," and then become the person who calls the next move.

- Include songs on light as part of song sessions after meals or around the campfire.

- Use the evening campfire outside or inside to set a mood. Have the participants think about what the world would be like without light (think about living on a spaceship or about someone who is blind). Sing songs and/or tell stories about light. Have a sing-down using light as the theme. Focus on the smells and tastes that light and fire produce. Roast marshmallows or pop popcorn.

- Games could consist of seeing who can devise the longest list for: general uses of lights, Jewish uses of lights, types of Jewish lights, types of general lights, physical properties of light, metaphors of light, songs about light, movie titles with light in their names.

- Watch and discuss the video *Lights: A Fable about Chanukah*.

- Conduct the formal learning activities described below.

LEARNING ACTIVITIES:

Session #1: Beresheet: Light, God, and Creation (All Ages)

Participants read Genesis 1:3 in which God creates light comes from darkness. After they answer questions about the light, they then create a *midrash* using visual arts.

Session #2: Dawn: Experiencing the Creation of Light out of Darkness (All Ages)

After watching and reacting to the sunrise, participants listen to music composed about the different phases of the day. The music can come from (1) Jewish sources (liturgy or Jewish composers, both traditional and contemporary); (2) classical music or folk songs; or (3) popular music. Participants are invited to dance to the

music. They share feelings and thoughts about how the music interprets the experience of sunrise. The participants create a visual interpretation of the music or their own reactions to watching the sunrise.

Session #3: Light in Our Tradition (Grade 3 and Up)

This session examines ideas and metaphors about light through the lenses of classical and modern Jewish texts. A detailed presentation of Session #3 is provided below.

LEARNING MATERIALS:
(For Session #3):

- Copies for each participant of the pages from the texts listed under "Learning Activities"

- A copy of the actual book from which the source material comes

- One piece of poster board or tag board for each family

- A marker for each family

LEARNING ACTIVITIES:
(For Session #3):

This session is recommended for children in Grades 3 and up, as well as for adults. The session is best scheduled for 60-90 minutes.

Activity #1: Set Induction
Remind the participants that they have been sharing ideas about common experiences. Those experiences, so far, have related to the senses of seeing and hearing, and have drawn on the participants' creativity. Now, we are going to explore the ideas of others related to the same topic of light by reading from some Jewish sources, to discover what our scholars and teachers past and present say about light.

Define mysticism. Here is one definition: The spiritual practice and belief that union with God is possible and desirable. A belief in a reality that is beyond normal perception. Judaism has a mystical aspect called *Kabbalah*.

Activity #2: Ha-Or — The Light of Awareness
Give each person a copy of "Ha-Or — The Light of Awareness" in *Honey from the Rock* by Kushner. Rabbi Kushner, a neo-mystic and neo-Hasid, quotes from various sources to explain his view of light. In small groups of 3 to 6, assign each group a section to read and interpret. (If the number of participants is small, it is more important to pass out a manageable amount of text than cover the whole chapter.) Ask the groups to focus on what the ideas and metaphors have to say about light. Spend time with the groups sharing their ideas.

Divide the participants into groups of 6 to10. Ask half of the groups to read and discuss Rabbi Judah's interpretation of Song of Songs 6:10 regarding light. This verse is found in "*Vayishlach*," *Zohar*, Volume II. The other half of the groups will discuss the phrase from Psalm 97:11, "Light is sown for the righteous." Be certain to discuss what it means to be righteous. Have the groups share the highlights of what they have learned about light.

In family groups, explore the variety of ways in which the prayer book uses light in the Shabbat service. Use the prayer book from your congregation and the service of your preference — either evening or morning. The Reconstructionist prayer book, *Kol Haneshamah*, and the Reform prayer book, *Gates of Prayer*, are cited in the bibliography. (In *Gates of Prayer*, it is recommended to use Shabbat Evening Service III.)

Read through the service looking for references to light in Hebrew or English. Make a list on poster board of at least three ways that light is used in the prayer service. For example, from *Gates of Prayer*, here are some phrases:

- " . . . the awareness of the soul, our light within" (p. 172)

- "We walk sightless among miracles. Lord, fill our eyes with seeing and our minds with knowing; . . . Your Presence, like lightning, illumines the darkness . . . " (p. 170)

- "Oh may we come to see the world in a new light." (p. 158)

Discuss:

- To what does the light refer in each phrase?

- What does each phrase tell us about light?

- How does each phrase compare to Rabbi Kushner's understanding of light?

- Which is your favorite phrase, and why?

- Put up the pieces of poster board around the room. Have everyone circulate around the room reading the phrases that each family found. Among the entire group, discuss the following questions:

- What patterns or common themes are found in the texts?

- How do the texts vary from one another?

- What makes light such a powerful Jewish symbol?

- What makes light so spiritual?

- What does light have to do with God?

EVALUATION:

With everyone present sitting in family groups, ask each family member to share responses to the following: (1) What experience or activity involving light did you like the most?, (2) What is one thing that you learned about light?, (3) What is one way that Judaism connects God and light?, (4) How does light connect you to God? How does light connect you to other Jews?

BIBLIOGRAPHY

Gates of Prayer. New York: Central Conference of American Rabbis, 1975.

> This prayer book for the Reform Movement provides a variety a choices for Shabbat and weekday liturgy. It was revolutionary in its time. The differences among the services include type of translation, theological emphasis, special readings, and length.

Kol Haneshamah: Shabbat Vehagim. 3d ed. David Teutsch, ed. Elkins Park, PA: Jewish Reconstructionist Press, 1996.

> This is a Reconstructionist prayer book, which contains Shabbat and festival services, and features translations, transliterations, commentary, and explanations of the various prayer services.

Kushner, Lawrence. *Honey from the Rock: Visions of Jewish Mystical Renewal.* San Francisco: Harper & Row, 1977.

> One of Rabbi Kushner's early writings that presents a twentieth century liberal Jew's insights into *Kabbalah.* Kushner writes poetically about our connections to God.

Sholem, Gershom. *Zohar.* New York: Schocken Books, 1995.

> This volume features selected passages from the *Zohar,* the central work in the literature of the *Kabbalah,* culled by the greatest authority on Jewish mysticism in his time.

Video

Lights: A Hanukah Fable. 24 min., color. Ergo Media.

> A charming retelling of the Chanukah story — the struggle to maintain religious beliefs in the face of adversity. It also addresses the issue of religious freedom and the right to be different. Features beautiful music.

Music

"Boker Ba L'Avodah"

"Erev Ba"

"Erev Shel Shoshanim"

"Oh What a Beautiful Morning" from the musical *Oklahoma*

"On a Golden Afternoon" from *Alice in Wonderland*

"Some Enchanted Evening" from the musical *South Pacific*

"Sunrise, Sunset" from the musical *Fiddler on the Roof*

All melodies for the prayers *"Ma'ariv Aravim,"* said in the evening service, and *"Yotzer Or,"* said in the morning service

CHAPTER 49

FAMILY SUKKOT RETREAT

Michelle Shapiro Abraham, Sherry H. Blumberg, and David Wechsler-Azen

TOPIC:

God

TARGET AUDIENCE:

Families with children ages preschool through high school

TIME FRAME:

From 8:00 a.m. until 7:00 p.m. on one day of Sukkot, or from Friday night through Havdalah on the Shabbat in the middle of Sukkot

STAFF:

At least five group leaders are needed to work with the different age groups, both children and adults. The children were divided into groups in different ways, depending on the session. Child care was provided for preschoolers during all activities. Assistant teachers of all ages are helpful, especially with the younger learners. A song leader is recommended.

OVERVIEW:

The activities that were done with children and adults together were: building and decorating a *sukkah*, worship services, a family softball game, and a concluding art project. The younger students (Kindergarten through Grade 6) studied about God through song, story, and art, using materials appropriate for each different level. They went on a treasure hunt for signs of God, or took pictures of places at camp where they found signs of God. Grade 7 through Grade 10 students explored the *Sephirot* (the attributes of God) through texts, song, story, and activities on

metaphor. The adults studied Ecclesiastes and Torah readings for Sukkot through discussion and activities. The adults also had an experiential session that included meditation.

PURPOSE:

The program fulfills the following goals:

- To enjoy the celebration of Shabbat and Sukkot in community

- To explore concepts and feelings connected with God in order to encourage thought and discussion among family members and congregants

- To provide quality educational and social experiences for the different ages

- To integrate music, art, and worship with learning

OBJECTIVES:

Participants will be able to:

- identify things in the natural world that are unique, surprising, and beautiful, and connect these things with God.

- discuss different ideas about God.

- compare ideas of transcendence and immanence in songs, poetry, and text.

- experience different views of God as found in nature, text study, music, worship, story, meditation, and fellowship.

- build and decorate a *sukkah* and share meals in it.

- work together on a project that represents their family.

CONTENT:

The main concepts presented in the program are: how God works in the world and in ourselves; how God is portrayed in current North American culture; the presence of God in nature, text, and ourselves; the *Sephirot*, emanations of God according to *Kabbalah*, which come through *Keter* (Crown), *Chochmah* (Wisdom), *Binah* (Understanding), *Chesed* (Kindness), *Gevurah* (Severity or Judgment), *Tiferet* (Truth, Beauty, Compassion), *Netzach* (Endurance, Eternity, or Victory), *Hod* (Glory or Splendor), *Yesod* (Foundation), *Malchut* (Royalty, Sovereignty).

(Note: The content varies according to the age appropriateness of the concepts for the children. Therefore, not all learners will be exposed to exactly the same content.)

FORMAT:

The following is the overall schedule for the retreat:

Time	Activity	Group
8:00 a.m.	Breakfast and introductory games at the synagogue	All Families
8:45 a.m.	Drive to camp site	All Families
9:15 a.m.	Arrive at camp Opening discussion with Rabbi	All Families
9:30 a.m.	Build and decorate the *sukkah* Families choose from the following activities: cranberry and pasta stringing collecting branches for top of *sukkah* popcorn stringing	All Families
10:00 a.m.	Morning worship services: Grades K-10 together with adults Baby-sitting provided for PK	
11:00 a.m.	Content Program I: Different Ideas and	By Age Group

Attributes of God
Adults – Five Views of God
K-6 – Hunt for signs of God
7-10 – The Attributes of God
Baby-sitting provided for PK

Time	Activity	Group
12:15 p.m.	Prayer Wrap-up Students return to the service for *"Alaynu"* and *"Kaddish"*	All Families
12:30 p.m.	Lunch	All Families
1:15 p.m.	*"Birkat HaMazon"* and Songs	All Families
1:30 p.m.	Content Program II Adults - Meditation K-2 – God in Song and Story 3-6 – God in Song, Story, and Art 7-10 – God in Song and Story Baby-sitting provided for PK	By Age Group
3:00 p.m.	Family Softball Game and Free Time	All Families
4:30 p.m.	Content Program III God in Our Family Families put together *shiveetees* (*Mizrach* wall hangings)	All Families
5:15 p.m.	Dinner	All Families
6:00 p.m.	Singing and Havdalah	All Families
6:30 p.m.	Return to congregation	

Activities:

Each age group participated in its own customized program. The Kindergarten through Grade 10 students rotated through the following three activities for each of the first two content sessions: (1) text and stories; (2) songs and movement; (3) either a treasure hunt (Kindergarten through Grade 4), or photography (Grades 5 and 6), or a metaphoric matching activity (Grades 7 through 9). The adults had one text study session and one experiential session that included meditation, movement, and prayer. For the final activity, all families came together and created a family *shiveetee* (a family crest or symbol) about God in their family.

The following is a full outline of one content session.

CONTENT SESSION I: KINDERGARTEN THROUGH GRADE 6

Session Title: A Photo Opportunity

Goal: For students to explore the role of God in the natural world

Objective: The students will be able to identify things in the natural world that are unique, surprising, beautiful, and identify these as signs of God.

Learning Materials:

- 1 Polaroid or digital camera per 3 to 4 students (borrow the cameras to minimize expense)

- film for each Polaroid camera

- 1 clip board for each group of 3-4 students, "Clue Sheet" attached (see Appendix A, p. 397)

- pen for each group

- tape

- story of the little boy who taught that one can find God anywhere, written in large letters on a poster board and attached to a large sheet of butcher paper (see Activities below).

(Note: Leave room on the sheet of butcher paper for students to attach their photographs of where they found signs of God and to write headings for the photographs.)

Activities:
Tell the following story. (Use the large poster with the story written on it as a visual aid.)

Once there was a young boy who wanted nothing more than to study Torah. Unfortunately, his family was poor and they needed him to work on the farm. Day and night, he plowed the fields and cared for the animals, always hoping that some day he would be able to study.

One day, a great Rabbi came to the town looking for a new student. The Rabbi said that he would pay the student's family to allow him to come and study if indeed the student was brilliant. The little boy was so excited and hopeful. However, he heard from the townspeople that in order to quality, one had to answer the Rabbi's most difficult question. Although the little boy was frightened, he was determined to try.

The little boy stood before the great Rabbi. The Rabbi smiled at him warmly, asking: "Tell me son, where can you find God?" The little boy trembled. He thought of the plants that grew in the fields and the animals that lived off the plants. He thought of the sun that heated the earth and the moon and stars that filled the night sky. He thought of his parents, whose love was so strong that he could almost touch it. Then he knew. In a quiet voice, he said, "Rabbi, tell me, where can you not find God?"

At the end of the story, explain to the students that during this program, they will be hunting for signs of God. Indeed, if the little boy is right, God is truly everywhere if we only look. Ask them where they think they will find signs of God. (Answers will probably include in nature, in people, and in prayer.) Explain that they will be looking for signs of God in any place they think is appropriate. They will receive a "Clue Sheet" (Appendix A) to give them ideas.

Separate students into small groups of 3 to 4 students, each with a mixture of older and younger students. Groups can be configured before the program by colors on name tags. Give each group a Polaroid or digital camera and the "Clue Sheet." Establish any rules about where they cannot go, such as outside the camp grounds or where another group is located. Send the groups out for about 20-30 minutes to find signs of God on the camp grounds.

When the groups return, have them write a caption for each picture that explains the rationale of why they found signs of God in that place.

Wrap-up: Congratulate students on their searching. Have each group explain one or two of their pictures. Discuss what they learned about finding signs of God everywhere. (Suggestion: Put up the photographs in the dining area so the entire group can see them.)

CONTENT SESSION I: GRADES 7-10

Session Title: The Manifestations of God in the World According To Kabbalah

Goals:

*   To explore the *Sephirot* as mystical symbols for God's presence in the world

*   To involve the students in active debate and symbolic thinking

*   To share with each other their own understanding of how God works in their lives

Learning Materials:

*   Lots of pictures, magazines, catalogues, nature calendars, and so forth

*   pencils

*   construction paper or tag board

*   scissors

*   glue sticks

*   1 Sephirot Sheet per person (Appendix B, p. 398)

*   1 large piece of poster board or butcher paper with the *Sephirot* drawn on it

Activities:

Opening: Give a short introductory talk (just a few minutes long) on the mystical tradition: the reasons for its emergence, and the concepts of sparks and *Sephirot* (see bibliography for refer-

ences). Share interesting things about the mystical tradition, such as the stricture to be over 40 and married before one studies the *Zohar, The Book of Splendor*.

Hand out the Diagram of the *Sephirot* (Appendix C, p. 401). Go over the diagram, including the terms in Hebrew and English. Acknowledge that different people might interpret the terms in different ways.

*   *Keter* (Crown)

*   *Chochmah* (Wisdom)

*   *Binah* (Understanding)

*   *Chesed* (Kindness)

*   *Gevurah* (Severity or Judgment)

*   *Tiferet* (Truth, Beauty, or Compassion)

*   *Netzach* (Endurance, Eternity, or Victory)

*   *Hod* (Glory or Splendor)

*   *Yesod* (Foundation)

*   *Malchut* (Royalty or Sovereignty)

Break into teams of 2 to 4. Each team looks through the magazines, calendars, old pictures, catalogues, etc., to find and cut out an object or picture that expresses each of the *Sephirot*. Each group then creates its own diagram of the *Sephirot* with objects or pictures in place of the names.

Each group compares their diagram with those of the other groups. A selection is made of one picture or item that best represents each concept. Students should try to come to a consensus if possible, but if they cannot, then a majority can make the decision. One option is to have large piece of poster board or butcher paper on which the "consensus" objects or pictures are placed, next to the term for each of the *Sephirot*.

(If time permits, do the following activity.) The *Sephirot* represent a map of how humanity and God interrelate. In particular, mystic tradition has it that we have a soul, which emanates from God. Stage a debate in which the students agree or disagree with this concept.

Closure: Ask: Based on this exercise, what do you think the *Sephirot* suggest about the relationship between God and the world? between God and human beings?

CONTENT SESSION I: ADULTS

Session Title: Contemplation and Meditation

Goals:

- To explore the *Sephirot* as mystical symbols for God's presence in the world

- To involve the learners in symbolic thinking

- To share with each other their own understanding of how God works in our lives

- To provide an opportunity for learning together to create a sense of share knowledge about the tradition, ourselves, and others

- To encourage the adult learner to grapple with his/her views of God

Learning Materials:

- quotation sheets

- paper and pens

Activities:

Begin with an introduction to the *Sephirot* as one way of understanding God. Provide some historical information about *Kabbalah* in general and the *Sephirot* in particular (see Gershom Scholem's writings as a resource.) Distribute to each person a copy of the Sephirot Sheet (Appendix B), which contains quotations that illustrate three of the attributes — *Hod (*Glory or Splendor*), Gevurah (*Severity or Judgment*)*, and *Chesed* (Kindness). Ask each person to find a comfortable space anywhere on the grounds, one in

which they feel some sense of holiness. (As this was done in a retreat setting, there was a lake, a number of trees, and lots of beautiful outdoor spaces and cozy indoor spaces, too, that were rustic and connected to nature.) Once in their space, participants read the texts and contemplate their meaning and significance as they relate to God, the world around them, and their life. Allow about 20-30 minutes for participants to think about the texts on their own.

In the reassembled group, ask people to share the quotation they found most meaningful, and then explain their connection to and understanding of the quotation. (In some cases, people shared images of God, rather than reacting to the entire content of the quotation.)

Closure: Based on this exercise, what do you think the *Sephirot* suggest about the relationship between God and the world? between God and human beings?

EVALUATION:

In advance, prepare an evaluation sheet for each family. Include the following questions, plus any other about the logistics that are merited:

- What was the best part of the retreat for you?

- What one thing would improve the retreat?

- What did you enjoy most about the family activities?

- How would you rate the balance between study and fun?

- What is one thing that you learned about God? yourself? someone in your family?

- In what ways, if any, has the program enriched your sense of God? being part of a congregation or community?

APPENDIX A

Hunting for God
Clue Sheet

As you look for signs of God, see if you can find:

- something incredibly beautiful
- something very unique
- something very smooth
- something alive
- something spooky looking
- something you have never seen before
- something that doesn't seem real
- something that is frightening
- something that at first seems ugly, but upon a closer look is really amazing!
- something that makes you gasp
- something that has an unusual design

APPENDIX B

Sephirot Sheet on Hod, Gevurah, and Chesed

HOD (GLORY OR SPLENDOR) IN THE BIBLE

God said to Moses: "Take Joshua and give him charge in front of all the priests and people, and you shall put some of your *Hod* upon him, that all the congregation of Israel may be obedient." (Numbers 27:18)

"He shall build the Temple of God; and he shall bear the *Hod* and shall sit and rule upon his throne." (Zechariah 6:13)

"Great is God's honor in your salvation, *Hod v'Hadar* [majesty and splendor] have you laid upon God." (Psalm 21:6)

"Bless the Lord, O my soul, *Adonai*, my God, You are very great. You are clothed with *Hod v'Hadar* [majesty and splendor suited for a sovereign]." (Psalm 104:1)

"*Hod v'Hadar* [majestic and splendor] is God's work, and God's righteousness endures forever." (Psalm 111:3)

"Gold comes out of the north, about God is awesome *Hod*." (Job 37:22)

"God will cause to be heard the *Hod* of God's voice." (Isaiah 30:30)

"And God magnified Solomon greatly before all Israel and bestowed upon him the *Hod* of *Malchut* [royalty] as had never been on any king before him in Israel." (I Chronicles 29:25)

"*Adonai* our Lord, how majestic is Your name in all the earth, who has set Your *Hod* above the heavens." (Psalm 8:2)

"I will speak of the *hadar k'vod Hodecha* (the majestic honor of your *Hod*)." (Psalm 145:5)

"God's branches shall spread, and like an olive tree God's *Hod*, and God's fragrance like the [cedars of] Lebanon." (Hosea 14:6)

"Let them praise the name of *Adonai*, for God's name alone is exalted; God's *Hod* is above the earth and the heaven." (Psalm 148:13)

HOD (GLORY OR SPLENDOR) IN CONTEMPORARY KABBALAH

Schwartz and Haas identify a goal-achieving strategy in which *Tiferet* (reasonable goals) + *Hod* (persistence) = *Netzach* (success)]. "Persistence is key to getting what we want. Persistence is better than luck. Persistence is always in our control. Luck is not." (Schwartz and Haas, pp. 167-168)

"*Hod* represents child, yielding, receptivity, and acceptance, purity and innocence, as well as dependency." (Cooper, p. 90)

GEVURAH (SEVERITY OR JUDGEMENT) IN THE BIBLE

(Note: *Gibor* and *Gevurah* are from the same Hebrew root.)

Moses coming down from the mountain before discovering the golden calf: "It is not the voice of those who shout for *Gevurah*, neither is it the voice of those who shout for being overcome, but the noise of those who shout do I hear." (Exodus 32:18)

"You have an arm with *Gevurah*, strong is your hand, and high is your right hand." (Psalm 89:14)

"Counsel is mine, and sound wisdom, I am understanding, I have *Gevurah* (strength)." (Proverbs 8:14)

"Have you given the horse *Gevurah*, have you clothed his neck with power?" (Job 39:19)

"And Kush begot Nimrod, he began to be a *gibor* (mighty one) in the land, he was a *gibor*-hunter before the Lord." (Genesis 10:8)

"The mighty God, the great, the *gibor*, the awesome." (Deuteronomy 10:17)

"Happy are you, O land, when your king is a man of dignity, and your princes eat in due season, for *Gevurah* and not for drunkenness!" (Ecclesiastes 10:17)

"There was a little city, and a few men within it; and there came a great king against it and besieged it; now there was found in it a poor wise man, and he by his wisdom saved the city; yet no man remembered that same poor man. Then said I, wisdom is better than *Gevurah*, nevertheless the poor man's wisdom is despised and his words are not heard." (Ecclesiastes 9:16)

Samson was called a *gibor*.

GEVURAH (SEVERITY OR JUDGMENT) IN CONTEMPORARY KABBALAH

"Real strength [*Gevurah*] comes from being able to control ourselves. This kind of power results from much practice and concentration. It is common to react instinctively to problems with anger, fear, or inaction. Biologists call this the 'fight or flight' response to danger. If we have true strength, though, we can control that instinctive reaction and thoughtfully respond to new challenges." (Schwartz and Haas, p. 169)

"*Gevurah* is the quality of contraction and restraint. It stands in opposition to generosity. Restraint is the ability to say no even when social pressure is brought to bear. *Gevurah* represents universal justice as well; it understands that everything impacts and has repercussions. The tendency of *Gevurah* is to be excessively conservative, preferring things just as they are. Uncontrolled, *Gevurah* is stifling. It does not allow for any movement. It is strictly conformist, unspontaneous, rigid, and hypercritical." (Cooper, p. 90)

CHESED (KINDNESS) IN THE BIBLE

Eliezer, Abraham's servant, prays to God to find a wife for Isaac: " . . . send me good speed this day, and do *Chesed* with my master Abraham." (Genesis 24:12)

Eliezer, after telling Rebecca's brother Laban about his travels, says: "And now, if you will do *Chesed* and *Emet* (truth) with my master, tell me, if not, tell me, so that I may turn to the right hand or to the left." (Genesis 24:49)

Jacob, about to die, says to Joseph: "If now I have found favor in your sight, put, I pray, your hand under my thigh, and do with me *Chesed* and *Emet* [truth], do not bury me in Egypt." (Genesis 47:29)

God in the Ten Commandments: "For I the Lord Your God am a passionate God, punishing the iniquity of the fathers upon the children unto the third and fourth generation of those that hate Me, but doing *Chesed* to thousands of generations of those that love Me, and keep My commandments." (Exodus 20:6)

God to Moses from a cloud: "*Adonai, Adonai*, mighty, merciful, and gracious, long suffering and abundant in *Chesed* and *Emet* . . . " (Exodus 34:6)

"Thus says the Lord: Let not the wise man glory in his wisdom, neither let the mighty man glory in his might, let not the rich man glory in his riches, but let him that glories glory in this, that he understands and knows Me, that I am *Adonai* who does *Chesed*, *mishpat* [law], and *tzedakah* [justice] in the earth, for in these things I delight, says *Adonai*." (Jeremiah 9:23)

" . . . because I desired *Chesed* and not sacrifice, and knowledge of God more than burnt offerings." (Hosea 6:6)

"Sow for yourselves by righteousness, reap according to *Chesed*; break up your fallow ground, for now it is time to seek God until God comes and rains righteousness upon you." (Hosea 10:12)

"God has told you, humanity, what is good and what God demands of you, but to do justice, to love *Chesed*, and to walk humbly with your God." (Micah 6:8)

CHESED (KINDNESS) IN CONTEMPORARY KABBALAH

"Grace creates opportunities to do good things. Consciously finding the right way and the kindest way to handle situations and people produces an atmosphere of gentleness." (Schwartz and Haas, p. 169)

"*Chesed* is the quality of expansiveness and generosity, the part of us that yields even though another part says no. It operates best when there is no self-consciousness holding it back. The tendency of *Chesed* is to be extremely liberal, willing to try anything. Uncontrolled, however, it has the potential to smother the recipient. It has no self-limitation; it knows only how to bestow things. Pure generosity will keep piling the food high on the plate; it will spin cotton candy until it fills the circus tent; it will give away the family jewels." (Cooper, pp. 89-90)

APPENDIX C

Diagram of the Sephirot

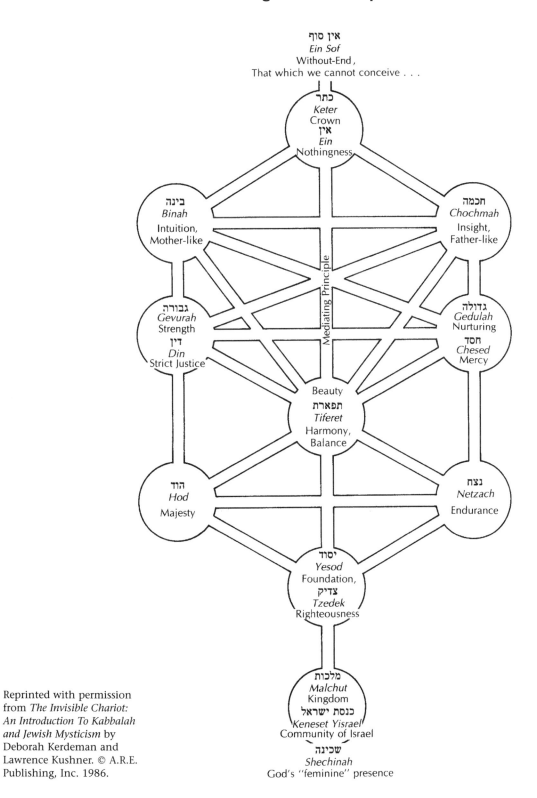

אין סוף
Ein Sof
Without-End,
That which we cannot conceive . . .

כתר
Keter
Crown
אין
Ein
Nothingness

בינה
Binah
Intuition,
Mother-like

חכמה
Chochmah
Insight,
Father-like

Mediating Principle

גבורה
Gevurah
Strength
דין
Din
Strict Justice

גדולה
Gedulah
Nurturing
חסד
Chesed
Mercy

Beauty
תפארת
Tiferet
Harmony,
Balance

הוד
Hod
Majesty

נצח
Netzach
Endurance

יסוד
Yesod
Foundation,
צדיק
Tzedek
Righteousness

מלכות
Malchut
Kingdom
כנסת ישראל
Keneset Yisrael
Community of Israel
שכינה
Shechinah
God's "feminine" presence

Reprinted with permission from *The Invisible Chariot: An Introduction To Kabbalah and Jewish Mysticism* by Deborah Kerdeman and Lawrence Kushner. © A.R.E. Publishing, Inc. 1986.

BIBLIOGRAPHY

Cooper, David. *God Is a Verb: Kabbalah and the Practice of Mystical Judaism.* New York: Riverhead Books, 1997.

The book features insights as to how to bring mystical Judaism into one's life.

Labowitz, Shoni. *Miraculous Living: A Guided Journey through the Ten Gates of the Tree of Life.* New York: Simon & Schuster, 1998.

The author presents his understanding of how to follow a spiritual path in one's everyday life.

Scholem, Gershom. *On the Kabbalah and Its Symbolism.* New York: Schocken Books, 1965.

———. *Major Trends in Jewish Mysticism.* New York: Schocken Books, 1941.

Both of these books are major resources on Jewish mysticism and *Kabbalah*. Scholem was the most famous scholar to popularize these topics long before the search for spirituality became widespread in the late twentieth century.

Schwartz, Dannel I., and Mark Haas. *Finding Joy: A Practical Guide To Happiness.* Woodstock, VT: Jewish Lights Publishing, 1998.

This book explores and explains how to find joy through the teachings of Jewish mysticism and *Kabbalah*.

CHAPTER 50

BA'BAYIT:
PARENT AND CHILD EXPLORING GOD, PRAYER, AND SPIRITUALITY TOGETHER

Michelle Shapiro Abraham

TOPIC:

God, Prayer, and Spirituality

TARGET AUDIENCE:

Children in Kindergarten through Grade 2 and their parents or grandparents. The Family Books are intended to be used at home as a follow-up to a classroom unit on prayer, God, and spirituality. They can also be introduced at a family education program or used as part of such a program.

TIME FRAME:

20 minutes to complete each Family Book

STAFF:

The Family Books are designed to be used by parents with their children. However, if used or introduced at a family education program, then a facilitator is needed to give directions to parents and children.

OVERVIEW:

Many parents wish to help their children grow spiritually. Yet, for many reasons, this is a difficult undertaking. The Family Books included in this chapter (see Appendixes) frame difficult spiritual issues in a child-friendly manner, thus providing a vehicle for parents to encourage and facilitate their children's spiritual development in an open and inviting way.

PURPOSE:

The purpose is to bring spirituality into the home in an explicit, but normative way that fits with the lifestyle of most families today. The Family Books provide another way for parents to interact with their children.

OBJECTIVES:

- Children will explore different ideas about God, prayer, and spirituality that are age appropriate.

- Parents and children will interact in their homes, sharing feelings and thoughts on the topics of God, prayer, and spirituality.

- Parents and children will create a home in which *kedushah* (holiness) is experienced, discussed, and explored.

CONTENT:

Exploring God: ideas about God; relationship to God; God as Creator; reasons for thanking God

Prayers and praying: thanking God; reciting blessings; praising God; making promises to God

Spirituality: *Kabbalistic* creation story; *tikkun olam* (repairing the world).

LEARNING MATERIALS:

- one copy per person of Family Books (Appendix A, p. 406 and Appendix B, p. 413)

- crayons, markers, or colored pencils

- glitter, glue, fabric pieces, scissors, and assorted other decorating materials

(Another approach is to make a collage using magazines, family photos, scissors and glue, or camera and film.)

LEARNING ACTIVITIES:

Suggestions to parents of ways to use the Family Books follow:

Instructions To Parents

In your home, find or create a comfortable space where you can sit, talk, read, write, and draw. Always do what feels comfortable for you and your child. Remember, there are no right or wrong answers to the issues/questions you will be discussing. First, spend whatever time is needed to complete the artistic side of the Family Books based on your child's interest in this type of activity. The child should be proud and satisfied with what he/she created.

The Family Books can be used in several ways. Here are some options:

Option #1: At Home

At bedtime, read through an entire Family Book at one time. Make notes of what your child says. On a day soon after, work together with your child on the art aspect of one of the Family Books. Read the instructions to your child, and let the child draw or make the collages. In the evening, read through the book again. Keep returning to the book at bedtime, on Shabbat, or during family discussion times to review and discuss what the child said, to add any new thoughts, and to give other family members a chance to share their ideas.

Option #2: At Home

Do a page or two at a time of a Family Book. Read what is on the page, then talk about it. Have the child draw or make a collage. When the Family Book is completed, read it through at bedtime. Keep returning to the book at bedtime, on Shabbat, or during family discussion times to review and discuss what the child said, to add any new thoughts, and give other family members a chance to share their ideas.

Option #3: At Home

Parent and child each complete a Family Book. Older children can make a Family Book, too, if this works in your family. This would allow an opportunity for all family members to share their ideas and feelings. Devoting significant time to these books also shows the level of importance that the parent attributes to the topic. Further, this is a wonderful way for all family members to share thoughts and feelings about God and to create a basis for sharing and discussing spiritual topics in the home.

Option #4: At Home

Use a camera and film to take pictures of the child's responses to the various questions. These photographs can send a powerful message about finding God and spirituality in everyday times, places, and activities. Be sure not to get carried away with the photography instead of focusing on what the child has to say.

Other Programming Options

Option #5: Family Education Program

Introduce the Family Books at a family education program on God, prayer, or spirituality. Spend a few minutes explaining their purpose and how to use them at home. Provide each family with a sheet of the different options for home use (options #1-4 above). The Family Books are also a good follow-up to family education programs on God, prayer, or spirituality. They may be distributed all at once or one at a time.

(Note: Family Books may be sent home after any family education program, regardless of the topic, to encourage more parent-child interaction around Jewish topics.)

Option #6: Family Education Program

Introduce the content of the Family Books and their purpose. Have the parents and children do the art part of the Family Book as part of the family education program. Share guidelines on how to read and discuss them in the home — at bedtime, on Shabbat, or during family discussion times.

Option #7: At Home

Use the Family Books as a follow-up to classroom lessons on the topics of God, prayer, and spirituality. Send home the books with the Instructions To Parents above.

EVALUATION:

Parents and children answer these questions: (1) What did you like about making and reading the Family Books?, (2) What did you learn about God?, and (3) What questions do you have about God?

WATCH OUT FOR:

Following are positive guidelines to give parents:

1. Let the children share their feelings and ideas before you share yours. Share your feelings and ideas first only if an ice breaker is needed.

2. Always do what you and the child feel comfortable doing.

3. Remember that there are no right or wrong answers. If the child asks a question you cannot answer, explain that it is a difficult question and that you will find an answer. Then consult with an educator, Rabbi, book, or other source. (Other chapters in *Teaching about God and Spirituality* may be helpful, too.) Be sure to report back to your child.

APPENDIX A

Family Book #1

A book by _____

Date _____

God created so many wonderful things in the world.
I can say "Thank you God" by saying a blessing over the things that I
can see, smell, hear, and taste in this wonderful world of ours.

Before I eat a meal I can say:

Blessed Are You, Adonai Our God, Ruler of the Universe,
Who creates bread from the earth.

My favorite meal is

---.

Here is a picture of me eating my favorite meal

When I go outside to play in the spring, everything is blooming and coming to life. The flowers come in every color of the rainbow - red and yellow and pink and blue and so many more! If I lean down and put my nose very close, I can smell how sweet they are!

When I smell the flowers I can say:

Blessed Are You, Adonai Our God, Ruler of the Universe, Who creates sweet smelling plants.

I think God created sweet smelling flowers because_____

This is a picture of me smelling the flowers.

Storms can sometimes be a little scary. But I know that storms can also be awesome! The lightening flashing and the huge bangs of thunder and the trees blowing in the wind all remind me of how powerful and amazing God can be.

When I hear the thunder I can say:

Blessed Are You, Adonai Our God, Ruler of the Universe, whose power and might fills the whole world.

My favorite thing that happens during a storm is:

This is a picture of the biggest storm I have ever seen!

There are so many beautiful things in the world that God created - animals, and flowers, and plants, and people.

When I see something that is especially beautiful, I can say:

Blessed Are You, Adonai Our God, Ruler of the Universe, Who has created such beauty in the world.

I think the most beautiful thing that God created is:

_____

This is a picture of the my most beautiful thing.

In the story of Noah in the Torah, God promises that God will never let it rain for so long that the earth is covered in water again. God puts a rainbow in the sky to remind everyone of this promise.

When I see a rainbow in the sky, I can remember God's promise by saying:

Blessed Are You, Adonai Our God, Ruler of the Universe, Who remembers the covenant and keeps promises.

Just like God, I can make promises too. One promise that I

have made is _____

I have kept this promise by _____

_____

The world that God created is really amazing! Saying a blessing is one way that I can say thank you to God.

One thing that I want to thank God for is:

_____

I can say a blessing thanking God for this by saying:

Blessed are You, Adonai Our God, Ruler of the Universe, who created

_____

(fill in what you want to thank God for)

This is a picture of what I thanked God for.

APPENDIX B

Family Book #2

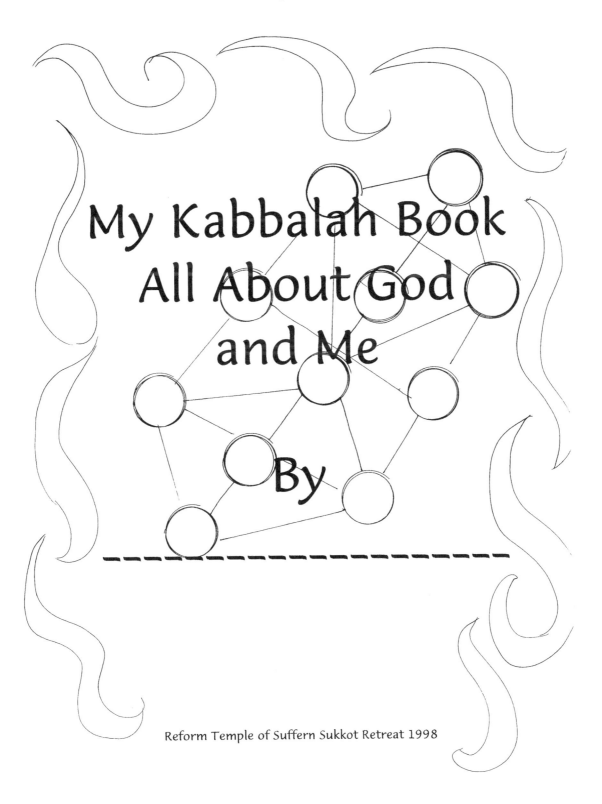

My Kabbalah Book
All About God
and Me

By

_____

Reform Temple of Suffern Sukkot Retreat 1998

In the very beginning, before there
was anything, there was God and God
was everywhere...

I used all of my crayon colors &
this is what I think the world
looked like before creation.

One day God decided that there should be
something else. So God decided it was time to
create the world. But first, God had to make room
for it. So, God had to make a giant empty space
with no God in it.

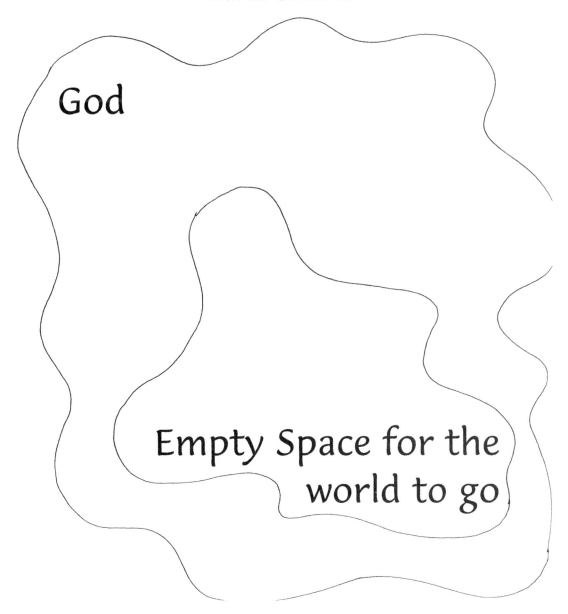

God

Empty Space for the
world to go

Once that empty space was there, God got worried. "I want to be part of creation," God thought. "I want to be there inside every blade of grass, and inside every person, and even inside every ant." So God came up with an idea. God put a whole bunch of Godliness inside big jars. God figured that God could put these big jars through out creation.

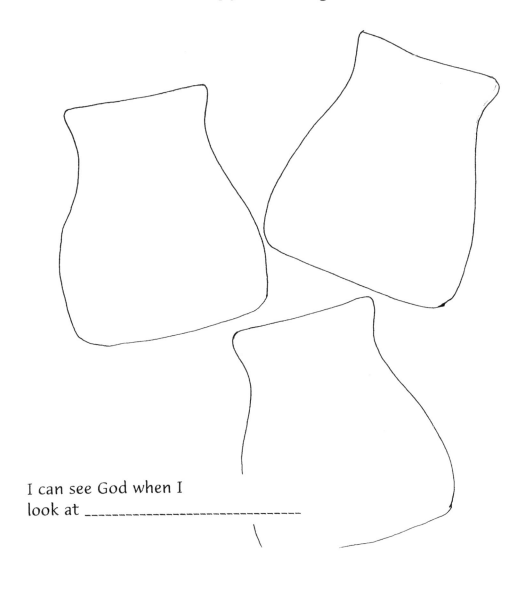

I can see God when I
look at _____

There was so much God and God made those jars
so full that something amazing happened.
Something scary and loud and amazing! All at once
all of those jars exploded!!

When the Jars exploded, I think it sounded like

_____

Just at that moment, when all of the jars exploded, something <u>really</u> amazing happened. The ENTIRE world was created!! Everything- from creepy red ants to the crashing oceans. People of all colors -- black, and white, and beige and brown -- and everything in between. Trees, and shrubs, and blades of grass. EVERYTHING was created!

This is my picture of EVERYTHING in the world!

And inside everything is a little bit of God. A little
bit of God that was splashed all over when the jars
exploded. If we look very carefully, we can find
God inside every one of us.

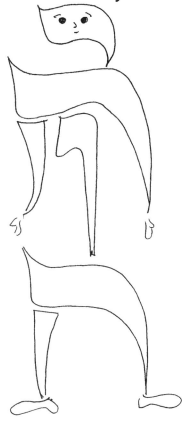

The Hebrew letters יהוה (yud-hey-vav-hey) stand
for the name of God.

Us people have a very important job in the world. You see, when those jars exploded sparks of God's light were spread all over the place. It is our special job to help God repair the world by finding those sparks. How do we do this? By being kind to others, and helping make the earth healthy and clean, and caring for those in need. Every time we do one of these mitzvot, we show some of God's light. If everyone helps, we can repair the world!

I can help repair the world by

_____

This is a picture of me making the world a better place.

CHAPTER 51

GOD AS A TOPIC FOR FAMILY CONVERSATION

Bev Fox

TOPIC:

Children and adults explaining, exploring, and sharing their views of God

TARGET AUDIENCE:

Grade 4 children and their families

TIME FRAME:

Weekend Retreat

STAFF:

At least one staff person was needed to explain what to do. Because of the group size, other staff members were used to set up, circulate, answer questions, and address concerns. Sometimes the group was divided into two sections, with one group doing one activity first, and then switching with the other half of the group to do a second activity. This splitting up of the group presents its own staffing needs.

OVERVIEW:

Nearly 200 hundred parents, fourth graders, and their siblings attended this weekend retreat on sharing views on and dialoguing about God. The retreat provided time for parents and children to sit together, talk about God, and learn more about Jewish views of God. Families received a source book of readings from children's texts and advice from experts on teaching about God. Stories and storytelling, text study, parent/child interview, drama, and visual arts were used to explore the topic.

PURPOSE:

The *kallah* provided a safe environment for parents and children to dialogue about their views of and feelings about God and expand their knowledge of Jewish views of God.

OBJECTIVES:

- The families will use biblical texts as a basis for exploring views of God.

- The parents and children will begin to identify the attributes of God that are meaningful to them.

- The parents will have the opportunity to be "spiritual seekers or role models" open to sharing what they feel about God with their fourth graders.

- The children will have the opportunity to dialogue with their parents about their feelings and views of God.

- The parents will have the opportunity to talk with other parents about how they talk to their children about God.

- All participants will become more aware and sensitive to their attitudes about God.

- All participants will think about the role of God in various Bible stories.

CONTENT:

Attributes of God; names of God; beliefs about God; perceptions of God; dialoguing and talking about God

LEARNING MATERIALS:
(for the God sessions)

- 1 God Source Book per family (see Appendix A, p. 424, for list of selections)

- 1 copy of the view of God interview for all fourth graders and their parents

- 1 *Siddur* for all fourth graders and their parents

- 1 copy per family of a Bible story (see Appendix A, p. 424, for Source Book and selected stories)

- 2 sheets black construction paper per family

- translucent paper in multiple colors

- gluesticks

- scissors

- pencils

LEARNING ACTIVITIES:

The sessions devoted specifically to exploring views about God were scattered throughout a weekend that conveyed a sense of *kedushah*, holiness, in the Shabbat atmosphere created through prayer, ritual, study, observance of *mitzvot*, and community. The specific sessions devoted to dialoguing and studying about God were:

- Thoughts on God: A Story and Discussion (Car Ride to the Camp Site)
  On the three-hour ride to the camp, students read the story *Old Turtle*. They talked about their perceptions of God, created a list of names of God, and jotted down questions about God.

- Views of God: Interviews and Text Study (Saturday Morning)
  Interview between parents and child; a discussion of views of God; study of the views of God presented in the *"Avot"* and *"Gevurot"* prayers that begin the *"Amidah"* (one hour). (See Appendix B, p. 426, for interview and text study questions.)

- Putting God into the Story: Bibliodrama (Saturday Afternoon)
  Participants create new versions of Bible stories by focusing on an unanswered question or issue that God helps address. God becomes an active participant, a major character in the telling of each story (for example, God discussing with Noah how to choose which animals to put on the ark, or Rachel talking with God about what she should do about Jacob's marriage to Leah). These versions are presented as skits to the whole community Saturday night. (See Appendix C, p. 427, for instructions.)

(Note: Use a basic children's text of the stories. Distribute a copy of a story to each group. A recommended source is *The Illustrated Hebrew Bible* by Ellen Frankel (Stewart, Tabori, & Chang). The biblical narrative episodes include: The Snake in the Garden of Eden, The Flood, The Tower of Babel, The Birth of Moses, The Golden Calf, Samson, Ruth and Naomi, David and Goliath.)

- Names of God: Stained Glass Windows (Sunday Morning)
  Create stained glass windows of the names of God based on the lists generated in the car and on a list of God's names found in the family resource book *Higher and Higher (L'ayla L'ayla): Making Jewish Prayer Part of Us* by Steven M. Brown (United Synagogue, 1996). (One hour)

EVALUATION:

Parents and children respond to the following questions:

- What was one important thing that you learned about your parent's or child's feelings or views about God?

- What was one important idea that you learned about Judaism's views of God from the texts or from other participants?

- In terms of God, what would you like to talk about when you return home?

- How can you make God more part of your family time and talk?

WATCH OUT FOR:

Some families are more comfortable than others talking about what is important to them as Jews. Some parents may be hesitant to speak about their views of God. Creating a safe space in which both parents and children feel comfortable sharing their views is important. Emphasize that there are no right or wrong answers, only honest ones. Furthermore, show both parents and children how texts such as the Bible, prayer book, and stories can be used to mediate a dialogue in which family members can explore different viewpoints and express their feelings about God.

APPENDIX A

God Source Book: Readings

The God Source Book distributed to each family includes the following readings:

Old Turtle, Douglas Wood. Duluth, MN: Pfeifer-Hamilton, 1992.

"How We Know about God: What God Looks Like?" In *Partners with God* by Gila Gevirtz. West Orange, NJ: Behrman House, 1995, pp. 9-11.

"Names of God," *Higher and Higher (L'ayla L'ayla): Making Jewish Prayer Part of Us* by Steven M. Brown. New York: United Synagogue of Conservative Judaism, 1996, pp. 62-64.

Coles, Robert. *The Spiritual Life of Children.* Boston, MA: Houghton Mifflin Company, 1990.

> Excerpt from Chapter 4, "The Voice of God," pp. 75-76, eight paragraphs, beginning with, "'Our God worries about us down here,' Avram told me a month or so after I'd returned from England . . . " through eighth paragraph beginning, "Yes. It wasn't much; but it was enough to give me plenty to think about." And eighth paragraph ending, "I'm glad I can turn to God and hear Him mention other kinds of days!"

> Excerpt from Chapter 11, "Jewish Righteousness," pp. 259-260, two paragraphs starting with, "Al, for instance said, 'My dad is easy-going most of the time, but sometimes he explodes . . . , '" and pp. 266-267, six paragraphs beginning, "His brother Aaron was contemplating another direction for himself: 'I'd like to be a teacher, like my favorite teacher, Mr. Benethon . . . . '" through sixth paragraph beginning, "Yes. It wasn't much; but it was enough to give me plenty to think about . . . " Sixth paragraph ending with, "I'm glad I can turn to God and hear Him mention other kinds of days!"

Kushner, Harold. *When Children Ask about God.* New York: Schocken Books, 1971.

Excerpts from Chapter II, "If God Isn't a Bearded Old Man in the Sky?" page 26, "What stirs or inspires one man leaves another cold. Two people go through the same experience; one finds his life transformed by it; the other remains indifferent. This can be equated with God treating us personally, each of us according to his own inner personality. Long ago, the Rabbis suggested that: 'God is like a mirror, which never changes, yet everyone who looks into it sees a different face' (*Pesikta d'Rav Kahana*, 109b, quoted in a *Rabbinic Anthology*, p. 6)." Plus, pp. 28-29, one paragraph, beginning, "Above all, never let us be afraid to say to our children: 'That is a very difficult question . . . . '"

Excerpts from Chapter III, "Children Ask about God," pp. 38-39, five paragraphs beginning, "We must realize the world is a frightening place to a young child . . . " Fifth paragraph starting with, "Probably the most important theological contribution we can make to our children at this point is to let them learn to trust *us* . . . " Fifth paragraph ending with, "your children will have difficulty believing in a God who is fair and loving." Plus, pp. 47-48, one paragraph beginning, "Whoever intended the fancy Greek-and-Latin word 'omniscient' (all-knowing) and attached it to God in an attempt to flatter or magnify Him . . . " Plus, p. 51, paragraph beginning, "Let us tell our children that there isn't a God-person in Heaven keeping track of what you do . . . " Plus, pp. 54-55, two paragraphs, beginning, "I might suggest that, instead of talking about 'where is God?' we rephrase the question and ask 'when is God?'"

Excerpts from Chapter IV, "Don't Blame God for 'Acts of God,'" pp. 102-104, five paragraphs beginning, "The problem of prayer in relation to God as we have come to understand Him is a difficult one and will be dealt with at length later . . . " Fifth paragraph starting with, "Yet we do utter such prayers at such times . . . " Fifth paragraph ending with, "they may be desirable as an outlet for our strong emotions and concerns."

Excerpt from Chapter V, "God and the Bible," p. 126, two paragraphs beginning, "For people who lived long ago and understood the world in the light of the best scientific knowledge of the time . . . "

Excerpts from Chapter VI, "The Vocabulary of Religion: Sin, Mitzvah, Repentance, Prayer," pp. 148, four paragraphs beginning, "The purpose of life is to grow to be the very best person you can be . . . ," fourth paragraph starting with, "We speak of commandments as being . . . ," fourth paragraph ending with, "We should do these things

because they help us become the sort of person we want to be."

Excerpts from Chapter VII, "Some Affirmative Ways of Meeting God," pp. 164-165, three paragraphs beginning, "God is the Power which makes it possible for us to become fully human." Plus, pp. 168-170, eight paragraphs beginning with, "Since a growing child spends more time thinking about himself than any other subject, it would be advisable to habituate him to finding God when he looks into his own heart and soul . . . " Eighth paragraph beginning with, "To understand God — not by talking about Him but by 'imitating' Him, . . . " eighth paragraph ending with, "we will make the 'little bit of God' within him a very real part of his world."

APPENDIX B

Views of God: Interview and Text Study Questions
(One hour)

Part One

In the first part of the interview, the fourth graders will ask their parents a series of questions. Please answer the questions as honestly as possible. There are no right or wrong answers to the questions.

- How do you imagine God?

- What are some of your doubts about God?

- Have you ever experienced a personal moment with God?

- If you were God, what would you do differently?

- Do you believe that God speaks to us through the Bible?

Part Two

In the second part of the interview, please indicate whether you agree or disagree with the following statements.

- I believe that God created the world.

- I believe that the Torah is the word of God.

- I believe that God listens to prayer.

- I believe that there is a divine force that directs all events for the good of humanity.

- I believe that God has no power to interfere in the affairs of the world.

- I believe that God exists inside of people.

- I think that it is important for all people to be moral and ethical.

- I try to serve God through my work.

- My important decisions are founded on my faith.

Part Three

The parents will now interview their children asking them questions about two prayers from the *"Amidah"* — the *"Avot,"* and *"Gevurot."*

Avot

- Why does the *"Avot"* say, "the God of Abraham, the God of Isaac, and the God of Jacob" and not "the God of Abraham, Isaac, and Jacob"?

- How do you think that Abraham thought about God? Remember, he was the first person to think about the concept of one God Who creates and commands?

- How do you think Isaac thought about God after the *Akedah*?

- How do you think Jacob thought about God after having lost Joseph and then finding him again by going down into Egypt?

Gevurot

The *"Gevurot"* talks about the wonderful things that God does in the world.

- The Hebrew word *gevurah* means mighty or hero. Make a list of the mighty acts of God. Are you surprised by the list? What would you have expected?

- Based on this prayer, how can we be like God?

- Who is a true hero?

APPENDIX C

Putting God Into the Story: Bibliodrama

Each small group consisting of a few families is to make up a skit to be performed Saturday night. The skit is based on the Bible story given to the group. The interesting nuance is that in each story you must add in the character of God as an active participant in addressing an unanswered question or issue that the text presents. God could have a conversation with one character in a dream, or on a side stage. God could appear to everyone. God could be represented as an angel. God can be a character in the skit, or your other characters can talk or pray to God. Be creative. The idea is to take what we have been talking about God and apply it to the traditional stories. In essence, we are creating our own *midrash*.

Begin by reading the story, preferably aloud. Understand who the characters are. Think about what roles each person in the group might play. Have some of your members take on the roles of some of the inanimate objects or normally silent participants in the story — the tree in the Garden of Eden, the ram in the sacrifice of Isaac. Determine what issue or question the text leaves unanswered that you want God to help address.

A few examples: If you were using the Adam and Eve story, you might have God in conversation with the snake about the snake's reason for tempting Eve. Perhaps God wanted to test human beings and asked the snake if he would tempt Eve. But the snake went too far, and that is why God still cursed it.

If you were doing the story of Moses and Yocheved, perhaps Yocheved has a conversation with God about what she should do with her baby. She could converse with God about how she could save her baby. Maybe God is the one to suggest she use a basket. Or perhaps it is only a prayer to God to watch over her son as she leaves him to his fate in the Nile.

If you are doing the Noah story, perhaps Noah has some conversations with God about why the world is being destroyed. Maybe there is even an argument. Or perhaps Noah turns to God to ask how to choose which animals should be paired to go on the ark.

Have fun, use your imaginations, and give each other insights into the story and God!

CHAPTER 52

GOD IS IN *THIS* PLACE: A FAMILY TREASURE HUNT

Ben Zion M. Kogen and Julie Jaslow Auerbach

TOPIC:

Identifying holy spaces where God is hiding; creating holy spaces

TARGET AUDIENCE:

Day School students in Kindergarten through Grade 8 and their parents. (This program can also be used in other settings.)

TIME FRAME:

2 hours

STAFF:

The family education coordinator at the day school planned the program with a committee of active laypeople. She worked with an Educator-in-Residence, an expert from outside of her community, in designing and implementing the program. The Educator-in-Residence was funded through a special grant. The Educator-in-Residence led the text study with the parents while other staff members led activities and crafts for the children. These additional staff members helped make certain that the family Treasure Hunt was running smoothly, some circulating around the building and others greeting families in a particular place. A music person, preferably someone who plays guitar, would enrich this program, although this is not essential.

OVERVIEW:

This program was part of a series of programs primarily for parents that focused on bringing God and spirituality into family life. The program featured both a family session (a Treasure Hunt) and a parent session (text study). The theme of the program focused on Jacob's realization, after his ladder dream, that God was in this place and he had not known of the place's holiness. While God often seems to be hiding or hidden, we can learn to recognize the places where God dwells, the holy places that we encounter in our daily lives.

PURPOSE:

This program helps students and their parents view their school as a holy place and what they do in it as potentially holy activities — ways of bringing God into their lives. By identifying the places where actions take place that reflect Jewish values, godliness can be brought to a place, making it holy and sanctifying lives.

OBJECTIVES:

1. The parents and children will view the school, a place in which they spend time, as a place where they can find God on a day-to-day basis.

2. The parents and children will identify the ways that they can find God, and bring God and holiness into their lives through different actions.

3. The parents will study texts about finding God in different places and spaces.

CONTENT:

Finding God in our lives, identifying the holiness of different actions

LEARNING MATERIALS:

- name tag, 1 per person and markers

- list of Jewish Values and Treasure Hunt Instructions, 1 copy per family (Appendix B, p. 433)

- text study materials, 1 copy per adult (Appendix C, p. 434)

- 1 copy of song sheets, 1 copy per each person

- pencils, 1 per family

- signs with Values written on them to identify Treasure Hunt places

- 12 baskets or containers for Treasure Hunt items

- Treasure Hunt items, 1 per family: notecard; sticker with the words "Reduce, Reuse, Recycle"; bird seed in plastic bag; Lost and Found sticker; name tag; sheet with kosher symbols; Band-aid

- toy bracelets or rings; bookmark; 1 per child

- candy; candy kisses; blue ribbons for missing soldiers; 1 per person

- certificate for completing the Treasure Hunt, 1 per family

- evaluation sheet, 1 per family

- microphone and extension cord

- blackboard, chalk, and eraser

LEARNING ACTIVITIES:

"God Is in *This* Place . . . " was the fifth theme in an ongoing series of learning opportunities, some for parents and others for families, on God and spirituality. Activities emanating from each program were layered into the classrooms through the classroom teacher or artists-in-residence, and into the home through take-home activities. The full series included the following sessions:

1. Exploring the "*Shema*" through the Life Cycle: Jewish Parenting in Action!

2. *Kiddush, Kaddish, Kodesh*: Connections in a Disconnect Time

3. *Brachot*: Navigating through the Life Cycle with Prayers and Blessings

4. To Bless and Be Blessed

5. God Is in *This* Place: A Family Treasure Hunt

Following is an overview of Session #5:

God Is in *This* Place: A Family Treasure Hunt

- Welcome Families and Introduction To Theme, through Songs – 20 Minutes

- Treasure Hunt: Finding God in the School Building – 30 Minutes

- Process Treasure Hunt – 10 Minutes

- Text Study for Parents with the Educator-in-Residence – 50 Minutes (See Appendix C for the texts. The authors recommend giving participants the texts in Hebrew, as well as in English, as some concepts may be more readily understood in the Hebrew.)

- Parallel activities for children by age grouping

- Closing – 5 Minutes

Each of these segments is described below.

Welcome Families and Introduction To Theme, through Songs

Welcome families to the program. Thank the people involved in planning the program. Introduce the Educator-in-Residence to the group.

Introduce the theme of the program, "God Is in *This* place," by singing songs. Two songs by Julie Silver are particularly appropriate: "I Am All Around" (on the album *Together*) and "Chazak, Chazak" (on the album *From Strength To Strength*). Words and music for both are in *The Julie Silver Songbook*.

Are there special places where God is hiding? Is

God all around us? Do we need to do anything to bring God in? As we read in *Parshat Terumah*, God said, "Let them build for me a sanctuary so that I may dwell among them." Is God living among us at this school? (Exodus 25:8)

Read the text: "Ya'akov awoke from his dream and said: 'Certainly God is in this place, and I did not know it.' Fearful, he said, 'How awesome is this place! This is none other than God's dwelling, and it is the gateway to heaven!'" (Genesis 28:16-17)

Our patriarch, Ya'akov, woke up from his dream with a new awareness. He learned from his dream that where he had been, God was present — it was a holy place. Today, we, like Ya'akov, will explore a familiar space and awaken — realizing that this familiar place, our school, is a place where we experience God all the time, but may not know it.

You will be going on a family Treasure Hunt. You will look for evidence of 12 values, each one marking another place where God is dwelling among us. Once you have located a Jewish value at a place where God dwells, you will take from the basket a reminder of the value. Please take the list of values and Treasure Hunt instructions (Appendix B), which contains an outline of the school in which to write where you found God. When you are finished, return to this room with your treasures, evidence of God's presence in this place!

Treasure Hunt Finding God in the School Building

Appendix A, p. 432, is an overview for staff that features the values; places in the school where the value was found; instructions for the families upon finding the place; and the name of the treasure item that is a reminder of the value, which families added to their bags.

Process Treasure Hunt

As the families return with their treasure bags filled, they receive a certificate of completion. As families complete the Treasure Hunt, ask them to take a few minutes to answer the following questions as a family:

* What were all the places in the school in which you found God?

* How does doing actions that fulfill these values — finding the hungry, guarding your tongue and what you say, etc. — bring God into your life? The school?

* What did you learn about where God dwells?

* If you were doing this same Treasure Hunt for the places where God dwells in your home, where would you find God? What values would you find in each room of your home?

Text Study for Parents with the Educator-in-Residence
(See Appendix C, p. 434, for the texts)

The Educator-in-Residence leads parents in study of texts about places where God dwells. (Children participate in parallel activities by age grouping.)

CLOSURE

Today we searched for God in our school. We have come to this place countless times. Sometimes in our studies, prayers, or activities, we acknowledge God's presence. These are times when we would expect to find God. Our Treasure Hunt reminded us that what we do in this place on a day-to-day basis brings God into our lives. We can find God in every nook and cranny of this school. The ground on which we walk is holy! God is near to us.

Sing "I Am All Around" by Julie Silver. (Families received a song sheet with the words.)

EVALUATION:

There was both written and oral evaluations of the program. The former was sent out accompanied by a thank-you note from the two lay chairpeople and the two educators. Sample questions included: (1) Please list two highlights of the program, (2) What were your goals for the program?, (3) Were the goals met? If not, what would have helped to enable you to meet your goals? (These last questions are critical; if the attendee's goals are not in sync with those of the programmer, the program may be perceived by the attendee as poorer than it was, and thus unsuccessful in the eyes of the educators. Similarly, the educator/programmer needs to know why he/she might have fallen short in their presentation.)

As this is an evolving workshop, the input of participants is always critical to the process. The evaluation form contained a place for comments on the format and the sharing of new ideas that were learned, as well as a request for other topics. Many follow-up programs have been created as a result of suggestions by a parent or a family.

WATCH OUT FOR:

In a program like this with a wide range of ages, it is important to make certain that the main concepts about God are presented explicitly. The connection between the activity and the concepts needs to be made clear at the beginning and the end.

Parents need to interact with their children in order for this program to reach its maximum success potential. Especially while on the Treasure Hunt, they need to ask their children questions, talk to them, explain things, and lead a family discussion. Parents should be ready to be students as well as teachers, for their children may have much to share.

Classroom teacher support before and after the program can be crucial in generating excitement about God and spirituality, recruiting participants, integrating the learning experience into their classrooms, and acknowledging the commitment to education of the participants.

(The authors would like to acknowledge the invaluable help of Cleveland's Solomon Schechter Day School parents, Sandy Laserson, and Debi Slater, whose creativity and energy helped make this program a success.)

APPENDIX A

Treasure Hunt Code Grid for Staff

Value	Place in School	Instructions	Treasure Item
Ahavat Shalom bayn Adam L'chavero — Bringing peace between people	Front office	Use this card to bring peace between you and someone else.	Notecard
Malbish Arumim — Clothing the naked	Coat closet	Take a moment to thank God for the clothing we are wearing.	Toy rings, bracelets, etc.
Bal Tashchit — Do not destroy needlessly or waste	Science room	Remember to Reduce, Reuse, Recycle!	Sticker with reduce, reuse, recycle
Ma'achil Re'ayvim — Feed the hungry	Kitchen	Have a piece of candy! Remember to recite the *brachah*	Candy
Shmirat HaLashon — Guard your tongue and what you say	Loud speaker in a classroom	May your words always be sweet!	Candy kisses
Tza'ar Ba'alay Chayim — Kindness to animals	Classroom with an animal in it	Here is some bird seed to feed the birds in your yard.	Bird seed
Hashavat Avaydah — Return of lost articles	Lost and Found	Is there something you have not returned? Write it down to remember to return it.	Lost and Found sticker
Talmud Torah — Studying Torah	Library	Here is a bookmark to mark your place of study.	Bookmark
Hachnasat Orchim — Welcoming Guests	Education Director's office	Welcome! We're glad you're here!	Name tag
Shmirat Kashrut — Keeping Kosher	Lunch Room	Here are some kosher symbols to look for the next time you are in the grocery store.	Kosher symbols
Refuah Shlaymah — Caring for the Sick	First Aid space	Take this Band-aid and save it for someone who needs it.	Band-aid
Ahavat Tzion — Love of Israel	Classroom with map of Israel	Put on this blue ribbon to remind you of your love of Israel.	Blue ribbon (reminder of Israeli soldiers captured, killed, wounded)

APPENDIX B

List of Jewish Values and Treasure Hunt Instructions

List of Jewish Values

Havaat shalom ben adam l'chavero Bringing peace between people — **1**

Malbish Arumim Clothing the naked — **2**

Bal Tashchit Do not destroy needlessly — **3**

Maakhil R'evim Feed the hungry — **4**

Shmirat HaLashon Guard your tongue and what you say — **5**

Tza'ar Baalei Chayim Kindness to animals — **6**

Hashavat Avedah Return of lost articles — **7**

Talmud Torah Studying Torah — **8**

Hachnasat Orchim Welcoming Guests — **9**

Shmirat Kashrut Keeping Kosher — **10**

Refuah Shlaymah Caring for the sick — **11**

Ahavat Zion Love of Israel — **12**

Treasure Hunt Instructions

Can you find the 12 Atomic Jewish Stars (see packet cover) in the rooms and halls of Solomon Schechter Day School? Can you match each to a Jewish Value on the list above?

When you do, write the name of the place and the number of the value in one of the "rooms" of your SSDS picture in the packet.

Once you have located a Jewish Value, you will see a basket with a treasure for you and instructions. Please read the instructions and take ONE of the items from the basket. Put it in your Treasure Hunt bag for use after the Hunt is completed.

When your "school" is filled with Jewish Values, return to the gym to be certified as having completed the Holy Spaces Treasure Hunt!

There are more than 12 Jewish Values at our school. See if you can find others. Note them, too! Each value you find marks another place where God is dwelling among us!!

APPENDIX C

Text Study: Creating Holy Spaces

Ya'akov awoke from his sleep and said: "Surely *Adonai* is present in this place, and I did not know it." Shaken, he said, "How awesome is this place! This is none other than God's dwelling, and it is the gateway to heaven!"

(Genesis 28:16-17)

And God said, "Do not come closer. Remove your shoes from your feet, because the place on which you stand is holy ground."

(Exodus 3:5)

God spoke to Moses, saying: "Speak to the entire community of Israel, and say to them: You shall be holy, because I, the Lord your God, am holy. You shall each revere [your parents], and keep my Sabbaths. I the Lord am your God."

(Leviticus 19:1-3)

APPENDIX

GOD: THE ETERNAL CHALLENGE

Sherry Bissell [Blumberg]

with

Audrey Friedman Marcus and
Raymond A. Zwerin

AN ⬤◖◉ MINI-COURSE • STUDENT MANUAL

Note: The following pages constitute the Appendix to *Teaching about God and Spirituality*, which consists of the entire text of the Student Manual for the inter-active mini-course entitled *God: The Eternal Challenge*. One of the first attempts at curriculum on the subject of God and currently a staple in Jewish schools, the mini-course is both a cognitive and affective learning experience for students in grades 7 and up. Beginning with an historical overview, it motivates students to explore God as Creator, Revealer, Redeemer, and Judge. Students confront such issues as God's unity, God's dwelling place, speaking with God, struggling with God, and the concept of Covenant. Readers are encouraged to make use of this course in their schools, at camps and retreats, and for family education.

Dedication
by Sherry Bissell [Blumberg]

This mini-course is dedicated to the memory of Rabbi Marcus Breger, who helped to make the leap of faith that has sustained and enriched my life, and to Audrey Friedman Marcus, whose faith in my work and ability has enabled me to continue.

Acknowledgment

Grateful appreciation to Shirley Barish for reading and commenting on the manuscript.

Graphic Design

Pam Levinson

Contents

Course: MC-112
Graded: 7th Grade and Up
Time: 10-14 hours

I NEED YOU GOD, WHY?

The Jewish People's search for God is not a new search. It has been our eternal challenge. As we search, we often have many questions about God. Take a moment and think quietly. Write some of your thoughts and questions about God here.

Thoughts about God:

Questions about God:

Nearly every religion is based on the existence of God or an Eternal Force. In Judaism, the God idea is central.

The Sh'ma
Hear O Israel, the Lord is our God,
the Lord is One.

Each time we recite the *Sh'ma*, we affirm our belief in one God.

Throughout our history, we Jews have wrestled with various concepts of God—wondering, confronting, seeking and finding God in many different ways. During this course, we will investigate these many concepts of God. Perhaps this study will help you to get in touch with the possibilities for experiencing God in your own life.

HOW DID THE IDEA OF YOU DEVELOP?

During biblical times, we Jews first encountered God as a tribal deity who told Abraham to leave the idol worshippers of his birthplace and to set out for a new land. As the new leader of a new people, Abraham came to know God as *shofeyt,* a judge who could not act unjustly.

A generation later, God appeared to Jacob in dreams, enabling him to become a better person and a stronger leader of his growing tribe of people. Then, God's working in history took clearer direction. Through Moses, God became the Redeemer who freed us from Egyptian slavery, the Lawgiver who gave us Torah on Mt. Sinai and the Source of our moral values. Through Joshua, God brought His people back into the land which He had promised to Abraham, Isaac and Jacob.

Prophets in the Bible enlarged our view of God. They taught that *Adonai* was more than just our God. Indeed, He was the Creator of the universe, the God of all peoples. His special relationship with Israel demands that we act according to His Torah; yet He also rewards and punishes all other nations on the basis of their moral behavior.

Since it is sometimes easier for people to relate to God in human terms, the Bible often personified Him. Thus we read about God as having an "outstretched arm and a mighty hand," or as "walking in the garden" or as being a "man of war."

To the Rabbis in the Talmud, God is all-powerful, all-knowing, awesome and removed. Yet He is also understood to be everywhere at once, all-spirit and without beginning or end. They addressed Him as *HaKadosh Baruch Hu* (the Holy One Blessed Be He) and understood that His *Schechinah* (indwelling spirit) lives within each and every one of us.

Through the past ten centuries, philosophers and teachers have added their ideas about God to those found in the Bible and Talmud. Some of these ideas are based on reason and logic. Some are mystical or secretive. Some have to do with emotionalism—a reaching out to God through song, dance and energetic prayer.

As you can see, Jewish understandings of God change and grow in every age. The idea of God is continuously evolving even today, because your ideas, too, are adding to that evolutionary process. The only things which do not change are God . . . and our people's need for Him. But in order to talk about God, we need to think of Him as more than just a pronoun. We need to know God's name.

Ways of relating to God ▼	God	Characteristics of God ▼
Direct Speech	Abraham	*Shofeyt* Judge Tribal Diety
Visions/Dreams	Jacob	Challenger
Burning Bush Mt. Sinai Tent of Meeting	Moses	Redeemer Lawgiver
Promise to Moses	Joshua	Restorer of People to the Promised Land
Visions/Dreams	Prophets of the Bible	Creator of All People Rewarder/Punisher
Bat Kol Study Prayer *Mitzot*	Rabbis of the Talmud	*Shechinah* *Hakadosh Baruch Hu* Spirit
Mysticism Emotionalism Logic	Philosophers	*Ein Sof* *Ribono Shel Olam*
?	Us	?
	God	

Hello, there, it's me
_____.

WHAT SHALL I CALL YOU?

What is important to a culture is often called by many different words or descriptions. For example, the Eskimo has many words for snow. The desert dweller has many words for camel. Americans have many words for vehicles. We Jews have more than 70 names for God.

What names for God do you know?

Did you mention *Elohim, Adonai, El Shaddai, Ehyeh Asher Ehyeh?*
God is called by each of these Hebrew names in the Bible.

Or did you write the names for God used in the Talmud and *midrashim* such as *Ribono Shel Olam, HaMakom, HaKadosh Baruch Hu?*

Names have power. The most significant Name of God has been especially powerful. It was revealed to Moses for the first time in the wilderness at the burning bush. This Name is unpronounceable. It is neither said in vain nor written on perishable material. So secret is it that only the High Priest of Israel in biblical days knew how to pronounce it, and he was allowed to say it only once a year on Yom Kippur. This name of God consists of four Hebrew letters—*yud, hay, vav* and *hay*. Whenever we see this ineffable Name, we read it as *Adonai.*

In order to avoid taking the name of God in vain accidentally, some Jews go one step further by intentionally changing all names for God. They say *Adoshem* instead of *Adonai* and *Elokaynu* instead of *Elohaynu.*

In writing the name for God in Hebrew, they substitute the letters *dalet yud, hay yud* or *yud hay* for the ineffable name. In carrying this principle over into English, they also write G-d instead of God and L-rd instead of Lord. While God's name is not written in Hebrew in this course, the word God is spelled out. The English word for God is only a reference word; it is not His name.

The names of God we have discussed so far describe His nature. Other names describe His work. These names include Creator, Redeemer, Giver of Torah and Judge. Let's see how these other names of God relate to you.

Find out the meaning of each of the following names for God by translating or defining them. Write your answers here:

ADONAI _____

ELOHIM _____

EL SHADDAI _____

HAKADOSH _____

BARUCH HU _____

EHYEH ASHER _____

EHYEH _____

HASHEM _____

HAMAKOM _____

TZUR YISRAEL _____

 בּוֹרֵא

Can I Call You The Creator?

Fill in the symbol representing the view which comes closest to your idea of creation:

☐ In six days, God created the heavens and the earth and everything therein.

△ The potential for life existed and, in time, it evolved naturally.

✴ Creation took place suddenly with a "big bang." It was an accident.

○ The earth and life have always existed.

After you have made your decision, join a small group of those who chose the same idea. Share your reasons for choosing this view. Then pick a representative from your group to share with the group as a whole.

The notion of God as creator need not pose a problem for modern people who are also open to scientific theories. The "big bang" theory suggests that this world was the result of the tremendous explosion of a black hole. But science can not explain where the material came from which made up the black hole. What is more, "In the beginning, God created the heavens and the earth" *(Genesis 1:1)*, implies a sudden act of creation—a divine big bang, if you will.

The famous Scopes monkey trial in Tennessee over fifty years ago pitted Darwin's theory of evolution against the biblical account of creation. These two accounts, however, are not necessarily contradictory. Evolution implies creation in time. The Bible also speaks of creation in time—six days. A "day" might well have been billions of years long.

Where did man and woman come from and how did they come to be? Even evolutionists and anthropologists today aren't certain. No matter how many remains they find, the missing link between ape and

human beings has not been found. Perhaps, as the Bible says, human beings are a unique creation. In any event, it is always possible to view Adam and Eve as man and woman in general and not just as two particular individuals.

Science is concerned with the *how* of creation—how the universe was formed, how *homo sapiens* developed. It neither accepts God nor denies Him as Creator. Judaism, which is mainly concerned with the *why* of creation, insists that without God, creation is meaningless. The world exists, that we know. If we only ask about how the world came into being, we might never be sensitive to the larger questions, such as what is our purpose here and who set our purpose for us.

The Greeks solved the whole problem of creation by insisting that the raw materials for the earth have always existed. Therefore, God, whom they called the First Cause, or the Divine Architect, merely took these materials and shaped them.

Judaism, on the other hand, asserts that only God existed eternally, before creation, and that He created the raw materials from which he shaped and formed the universe. The Hebrew word which means to create from nothing is בורא *boray*. Therefore, when we speak about God as creator, we call Him *boray*.

Can you think of any blessings or prayers in which the word *boray* refers to God?

What place does God have in your view of creation?

Now ask yourself, Can I call God בורא, the Creator?

Can I Call You The Giver Of The Torah?

IN BIBLICAL TIMES
The Jewish concept of God as *Notayn HaTorah* is called Revelation. Traditionally, Jews believe that the entire Torah, or written law, was given to Moses at Mt. Sinai. The Oral Law was also given to Moses and then passed on by word of mouth from sage to sage until it was finally written down as the Talmud.

Some say that Moses himself wrote the Torah, while others assert that Moses did so with God's inspiration. Some Jews argue that only the Ten Commandments were given at Sinai. Still others view the Torah as a collection of writings written by different groups of leaders, prophets and/or priests and edited through time.

Shavuot Window, by Victor Ries, Temple Beth Abraham, Oakland, California.

5

> "For this commandment which I command you this day is not too hard for you, neither is it far off. It is not in heaven that you should say: 'Who shall go up to heaven, and bring it to us, that we may do it?' . . . But the word is very close to you, in your mouth and in your heart, that you may do it."
>
> *Deuteronomy 30:11, 12, 14*

True Or False

What is your view of revelation? Below, mark the statements which you believe to be true or false.

1. _____ The Written and the Oral Laws were both given in completed form by God to Moses at Mt. Sinai.

_____ Only the Five Books of Moses were given by God to Moses at Mt. Sinai.

_____ Only the Ten Commandments were given by God to Moses at Mt. Sinai.

2. _____ The Torah is the work of Moses alone.

_____ The Torah is the work of Moses with God's inspiration.

_____ The Ten Commandments alone are the work of Moses.

3. _____ The Torah is the work of human beings alone.

_____ The Torah is the work of human beings inspired by God.

Whatever your view of what happened at Sinai or the nature of revelation, it is important to keep in mind that the idea of revelation has remained central in Judaism for over 3000 years. According to the Torah, God's covenant with the Jewish People was made not only with those who were with Moses at Sinai, but with all Jews in every generation—past, present and future.

The prophet Jeremiah said that Torah is not just an object to look at or hold in our hands. He preached that God would put His Torah within the people and write it upon our hearts. This means we must make it a vital part of our being. You see, Torah is more than just the first five books of the

Bible. "Torah" can also mean a commitment to living by Jewish values, by Jewish customs, traditions and ceremonies. To do "Torah" can also mean to commit oneself to a lifetime of Jewish study and learning. "Torah" can also mean a commitment to preserve, defend and support both life in general and Judaism as a way of life in particular. To make any or all of these commitments is to make Torah a vital part of our being.

In what ways do you make Torah a vital part of your being?

IN RABBINIC TIMES

In Rabbinic times the idea of revelation changed. The Rabbis taught that while the Bible was a record of God speaking to individuals such as Moses, Samuel and the prophets, such conversations ceased after Malachi, the last of the prophets. Did that

6

mean that communication between God and His earthly creatures ceased in the 5th century B.C.E.? The Talmud records that God's will continued to be received through a *bat kol*—a heavenly voice—which appeared to certain individuals aloud or in dreams. Through a *bat kol*, interpretations of Jewish law *(halachah)* and decisions of authority were said to be communicated. But the words spoken by the *bat kol* were not always followed because Torah, the Rabbis decreed, was no longer God's business, but was up to sages and students to interpret.

With a partner, consider this question: How does God continue to reveal things to human beings?

TODAY

Torah is not for any one generation alone. We have already learned that. It is for every generation to live by and to study and, in so doing, to find new insights in its teachings. As a Rabbi in *Ethics of the Fathers* said, "Turn it and turn it, for all is in it."

Before and after we read from the Torah we bless God as *Notayn HaTorah*. We speak of it as תורתו (His Torah), just as Mark, in his letter to God, calls it "Your book."

Dear God:
I read Your book and I like it. Did You write any others? I would like to write a book someday, with the same kind of stories. Where did You get Your ideas?
Best wishes, Mark

From *More Children's Letters to God*, compiled by Eric Marshall and Stuart Hample (N.Y.: Simon and Shuster, 1969). Reprinted by permission of the Sterling Lord Agency, copyright ©1967 by Eric Marshall and Stuart Hample.

Now ask yourself, can I call God נותן התורה, Giver of Torah, the Revealer?

?

". . . I am the Lord and I will bring you out from under the burdens of the Egyptians . . . and I will *redeem* you with an outstretched arm and with great judgments."
Exodus 6:6

גּוֹאֵל

Can I Call You The Redeemer?

Diaspora *(galut)* is what we call any place outside the land of Israel. At times various difficulties befell the Jewish People in the Diaspora. Such was the case when we were slaves in Egypt, captives in Babylonia, objects of persecution during the Spanish Inquisition and the victims of pogroms in Poland and Russia. Such was also the case during the nightmare years of the *Shoah.* At such times we raised our voice to God as גּוֹאֵל , and called upon Him to redeem us.

Egyptian Haggadah,
illustrated by hand using gold leaf,
published in 1928.

Redemption, therefore, means being rescued from a desperate situation and taken to safety. Redemption can apply to an entire people; it can also apply to an individual. When in trouble or despair, when fear or anxiety overwhelms, when in danger, during sickness or when life is threatened, it is then that God as Redeemer is called upon.

In a dictionary, look up the words *redeem* and *redemption*. Write your definitions here:

Redeem:

Redemption:

Did you list all the different meanings?

Read the *bracha* below:

Blessed are You, O Lord, who redeems Israel.

Siddur

Now repeat the *bracha*, substituting each of the various definitions you found for the word redeems.

Blessed are You, O Lord,

who _____ Israel.

Which definition seems best to you and why?

Inside the land of Israel Jews also faced serious difficulties from time to time. When the Babylonians laid seige to the First Temple, or the Maccabees had to fight the army of Antiochus IV, when the Romans forbid us to study Torah and even today, as hostile Arab nations surround Israel, we ask God for salvation יְשׁוּעָה . In Judaism, salvation is physical, not spiritual. We are asking to be saved from the cruel hands of enemies who stand ready to crush us.

Whether in Israel or in the Diaspora *(Galut),* Jews have dreamed of a time when all troubles will cease, when God will "stop the world," put an end to pain and suffering and bring about the *Olam HaBa*—the world to come. Some Jews believe that all this will be brought about by one man—*Mashiach*—whose identity will be revealed by the prophet Elijah. Other Jews choose to hope for the coming of a messianic age when all people will learn to care for and be considerate of one another. Both views reflect optimism about the future. This optimism stems from a belief that people can improve themselves and earn redemption from God.

"Oh Israel, wait for the Lord
For with the Lord is steadfast love
And great power to redeem.
It is He who will redeem Israel
From all their iniquities."

Psalm 130

"Redemption, like a livelihood, must be
earned each day."

Genesis Rabbah 20:9

Place your initials where you stand on the continuum below:

Explain your position on the continuum.

Place a P where you think the author of the above left *Psalm* would be on the continuum. Explain your answer.

Place an M where you think the author of the *midrash* from *Genesis Rabbah*, above left, would be on the continuum. Explain your answer.

God will
redeem us if
we deserve
redemption.

God will never
redeem us. We
must redeem
ourselves.

According to what you know of the Jewish tradition, what part do people play in redemption?

List all the ways that you can help to bring about redemption:

Now ask yourself, Can I call God גּוֹאֵל, Redeemer?

?

9

"... A king had an empty glass. He said, 'If I put hot water into it, it will crack; if I put icy cold water into it, it will contract.' What did the king do? He mixed the hot with the cold water, poured the mixture into the glass and it did not break. Similarly, said the Holy One, blessed be He, 'If I create a world which knows only my mercy, sins will multiply beyond all bounds; if I create a world which knows only my justice, how can such a world survive? Behold, I will mix my justice with my mercy and the world will endure.'"

Genesis Rabbah 12:15

Can I Call You The Judge?

It is only natural that when we do something wrong, we hope that it will be overlooked and forgotten. When we do something right, we would like praise and reward. For bad deeds we hope for mercy. For good deeds we want justice.

In our tradition we are taught that no person is totally good or totally evil. We are all a mixture of the two, and on Yom Kippur each year, our good deeds (*mitzvot*) are placed in a balance against our misdeeds (*avayrot*). It is up to us to lesson our misdeeds and increase our *mitzvot* each year. This is the process called *teshuvah* (repentance).

Sometimes as we see the world, especially in the newspaper headlines, it seems that evil triumphs and good is defeated. We are frustrated and angered by this. "Why is it so?" we ask. "Where is God's justice?" The prophet Ezekiel also saw such happenings. He explained that "God does not want the death of the wicked but that they should change their ways and live."

The Rabbis taught that God delights when the wicked repent. That's why He was so anxious to have Jonah go to Nineveh. On the other hand, God takes no delight in the death of the wicked who do not repent. When the Israelites had crossed the Reed Sea to safety while Pharaoh's army was drowning, the angels wished to offer a triumphal song of praise to God. But He refused them saying, "The work of my hands is drowned in the sea, and you would offer Me song?" (*Sanhedrin 39b*)

Out of the whirlwind God told Job that because human beings were created last and are really such a small part of the universe, we cannot hope to understand all things completely. We can only trust that all is as it should be. As in the parable of the king, God mixes mercy and justice in right measure when He judges this fragile world.

10

בָּרוּךְ אַתָּה יְיָ אֱלֹהֵינוּ מֶלֶךְ הָעוֹלָם דַּיַּן הָאֱמֶת

Blessed are You, Eternal our God, King of the universe, who is the Righteous Judge.

In the Jewish tradition, we recite the above blessing upon hearing of a person's death:

How is it possible to call God a Righteous Judge at such a sad moment?

A universal symbol for justice is a blindfolded woman holding a set of balancing scales. In what way does this symbolize justice?

Would this be an appropriate symbol for the justice of God? What other symbol might you use? Be prepared to defend your symbol in a debate.

If you knew that God judged each of your words and actions, how would this affect what you would say or do?

If everyone in the whole world thought they were being judged by God for everything he or she said and did, in what ways would the world change?

Now ask yourself, Can I call God דַּיַּן Judge? **?**

SUMMARY

We have considered a number of names for God and their meanings. Some names describe His nature, others His work in the world. But we have only scratched the surface. A quick look at the *siddur* gives us many more names for God. See how many you can find in the *siddur* in Hebrew or in English.

From among all the names for God which we have studied, which name gives you the most comfort?

To which names do you relate best?

HOW CAN YOU BE ONE?

שְׁמַע יִשְׂרָאֵל
THE LORD IS GOD THE LORD
IS אֶחָד

The Sh'ma

Hear
O Israel,
the Lord is
our God,
the Lord is
One.

Whenever we recite the *Sh'ma*, we are saying that God is One. This idea which forms the basis of our religion seems so simple and so obvious to us. Yet this idea is not as widely held as we might think. Let's see what we mean when we say God is One.

God is One and not none. Almost half the world, including Buddhists and Hindus, believe that there is no God as Jews define Him. Life and rebirth are punishment for desires and wrongdoings of a previous existence. Thus, there is no God, only life and the need either to escape it or to merge with it.

God is One and not two. When we Jews lived in Babylonia, we came into contact with the Zoroastrian religion which taught the principle of dualism. There are two gods—one the god of light and good, the other the god of darkness and evil. When evil seemed to triumph, it was because the god of evil triumphed over the god of goodness and vice versa. Dualism pits gods against each other and can lead to a confusion of values.

God is One and not three. One fourth of the world is Christian. The main belief of that faith is that God is essentially three: the Father, Jesus the son and the creative spark or Holy Ghost. In Judaism, the oneness of God's nature makes impossible the idea of the trinity.

God is One and not many. The Greeks, Romans, Norse, Egyptians, Babylonians and indeed, most early peoples, believed that gods created and ruled the world and that human beings were their playthings. There was a god for every function of nature, as well as chief gods and goddesses. Some scholars have said that this is the origin of the idea of angels or cherubim or seraphim in Jewish literature. Others believed that this was how the idea of calling God the Lord of Hosts began. Whether or not the scholars are correct, Judaism could never accept the idea of human beings as toys of the Divine. Although we seem to be alone in our idea, still we affirm *Adonai Echad*—God is One.

Think about the meaning of "God is One." With your eyes closed, say the *Sh'ma* over and over quietly, concentrating on *Adonai Echad.* Repeat the words slowly in English and Hebrew. What images or feelings did you have?

What is the importance to you or to our world of the Jewish belief in one God?

WHERE DO YOU LIVE, GOD?

According to tradition, God has had specific places to dwell. When we wandered in the desert for forty years, Moses built the Tabernacle as a place of worship. Inside this special tent were two rooms separated with a *parochet,* or curtain. One was open to the priests. There they lit the eternal light and the *menorah.* There they placed twelve fresh loaves of bread as a weekly offering. In the other room was the Holy Ark upon which stood two golden seraphim—angel figures. God, it was thought, sat upon their wings and used the Holy Ark as His footstool.

When Solomon built the First Temple in Jerusalem, he continued to use the idea of the two rooms. God, as King of the world *(Melech),* sat upon His seraphim throne. He was thought to be in residence there in Jerusalem. Only once a year, on Yom Kippur, the High Priest alone was allowed to part the curtain and enter this Holy of Holies.

In Rabbinic times, after the Second Temple was destroyed by the Romans, there was no Holy of Holies in which to imagine God dwelling. How could God who created the universe be contained in any one place, the Rabbis asked? After all, He is *HaMakom,* the place of the whole universe. He is the Holy One, Blessed Be He. He needs no specific holy place in which to rest His "feet." But if God is so large and wonderful, is He also too far from us who live on earth? No, the Rabbis answered. God as *Shechinah*—indwelling spirit—lives in the very heart and soul of every person.

A Chasidic story, like the one above, often makes what is difficult seem so simple.

In what places do you feel that God is especially close to you?

We read in another Chasidic story:

Think a moment about the story. In what ways do you let God into your life? When you do *mitzvot?* When you love, sing, pray? Complete the following:

I let God in when I

My family lets God in when

God dwells in the world when

Western Wall, Jerusalem.

"Whither can I go from your spirit?
Or whither shall I flee from Your presence?
If I ascend up into heaven, You are there;
If I make my bed in the netherworld, behold
You are there.
If I take the wings of the morning,
And dwell in the uttermost parts of the sea;
Even there would Your hand lead me . . ."

Psalm 139:7-10

Jewish tradition teaches that God lives everywhere—in our synagogues, in nature and our world, in our homes, in people and in the universe.

Have you ever sensed God's dwelling in nature? With a partner, share the memory of a beautiful moment (a sunrise, sunset, at the beach or the mountains). On the right, describe the scene. What made it beautiful? In what ways was God present in the moment you shared?

If you wish, write a poem together or draw your scenes below:

15

HOW SHALL I SPEAK WITH YOU?

"May the words of my mouth and the meditations of my heart be acceptable to You, Lord, my Rock and my Redeemer."

Siddur

Jews have always talked with God. We talk to Him in private and when we worship together. Sometimes our conversation has been one of love and mellow feelings. Yet there have also been times when we have struggled with God. We have prayed and we have doubted, we have praised and we have argued. But we have never ceased talking to God. This 4000 year old conversation has kept Judaism alive—growing, adapting, changing.

Now we will examine *how* we speak with God. As you search for your own ways to speak with God, what follows may be helpful.

עֲבוֹדָה I Speak To You With Others: Public Worship

Worshiping together, Jews speak with God. We have a set of prayers; we have traditions and rituals. Tradition invites Jews to pray three times a day. Praying together provides a sense of community and the opportunity to share the experience of worship with others.

Why do you think community worship is so important in Jewish life?

Worshiping together has always connected Jews to our history and helped us to be aware of each other and our mutual needs. Today, just as in the past, this link with the community is a vital and necessary one. When a person feels alone, when there is a death in the family, when someone is very happy and wants to express his or her joy or thankfulness, the community provides a framework in which those feelings can be valued and shared.

A Chasidic Rabbi spoke of joining himself to all Israel in worship so that he could help those who could not pray as well as He, and so that others who prayed with greater devotion could help him. In a public worship service, we can often raise our thoughts to God more easily because others are involved with us in prayer. That is why the prayers in a worship service rarely include the words "I" or "me," but usually "us" or "we".

Look through a *siddur*, the anthology which contains the words for our public worship. Notice the many times it says "we," "our" and "us." Read through the prayers *Ahavah Rabbah*, *Avot*, *Sim Shalom* and *Aleynu*. List the plural words that reflect community.

Temple Beth Israel, San Diego, California.

16

Make a survey of your friends and family. Ask them when and why they go to services and how they feel when worshiping together as a group of Jews. Compile their responses on a separate piece of paper and code them as follows:

X Put an X next to responses that involve a tie with the past.

S Put an S next to responses that involve being sociable.

F Put an F next to responses that relate to food.

R Put an R next to responses that relate to relaxing.

A Put an A next to the responses with which you agree.

Then answer the following question:
How has congregational worship (publicly speaking with God) helped ensure Jewish survival throughout history?

I Speak To You Alone: Private Prayer

"To pray is to take notice of wonder, to regain a sense of the mystery that animates all beings, the divine margin in all attainments. Prayer is our humble answer to the inconceivable surprise of living."

The Wisdom of Heschel by Abraham Joshua Heschel (N.Y.: Farrar, Straus and Giroux, 1975) p. 205.

Private prayer takes place at many different times—when we are afraid, when we seek comfort or at night when we think about our day. Sometimes we pray out of doors surrounded by nature; sometimes we pray inside, wrapped in our own thoughts. Even during public worship services, there are moments of silent meditation to allow for individual concerns.

Private prayer is an expression of our deepest emotions. It is a way of talking with God that enables us to confront honestly all of our feelings. While it is possible for these feelings to surface during public worship, we can best explore and express them in private, personal prayer.

The following passages express the emotional aspects of private prayer:

What emotions were expressed in each of the above readings?

1. "O Lord, my heart is not proud nor my look haughty;
I do not aspire to great things or to what is beyond me;
But I have taught myself to be contented
like a weaned child with its mother;
like a weaned child am I in my mind.
O Israel, wait for the Lord
Now and forever."

Psalm 131

2. "Holy, Holy, Holy is the Lord of Hosts, the whole
earth is full of his glory."

Isaiah 6:3

3. "Let everyone cry out to God and lift his heart up to Him, as if he were hanging by a hair and a tempest were raging at the very heart of heaven . . ."

Martin Buber, Ten Rungs

4. "I'm filled with love of God;
I know, my heart's desire,
My innermost love,
Isn't called by any name.
How can a name call forth,
What's more than even All,
More than the Good,
More than the Substance,
More than the being.
And I so love,
I say, I do, do love
The Lord of all."

Abraham Isaac Kuk

5. "Sing a new song unto God . . . Serve Him with joy—come before His presence with singing."

Psalm 100

6. *"Modeh Ani Lefanehcha.* I render thanks to Thee, Everlasting King, who has mercifully restored my soul to me; Thy faithfulness is great."

Siddur

With another person, try to describe the emotions expressed in #1 above. Without using words, act out, draw or touch each other's hands to express the emotion. Then move to another person and describe the emotions in the second passage. Continue until you have responded to all the passages.

Job, by Robert Cook.
Courtesy of the Sculpture Center,
New York.

Now write your reactions to the activity.

I Speak To You With Faith

How often do you say the word Amen?

What do you think Amen means?

By yourself, write your own personal prayer here:

Amen, as a Hebrew word, means faith.
When we say it, it is as if we said, "I believe that."

When are we most likely to say Amen?

Faith is a difficult idea to understand.
Sometimes it means to believe that things
will get better even when hope seems
impossible—to say yes, even when the
world says no.

"It really seems a wonder that I haven't dropped all my ideals
because they seem so absurd and impossible to carry out. Yet
I keep them, because in spite of everything I still believe that
people are really good at heart. I simply can't build up my
hopes on a foundation consisting of confusion, misery and
death. I see the world gradually being turned into a
wilderness, I hear the ever approaching thunder, which will
destroy us too, I can feel the sufferings of millions and yet, if
I look up into the heavens, I think that it will all come right,
that this cruelty too will end, and that peace and tranquility
will return again."

Excerpt from *Anne Frank: The Diary of a Young Girl*,
by Anne Frank. Copyright ©1952 by Otto H. Frank.
Reprinted by permission of Doubleday & Company,
Inc.

AMEN

19

Sometimes it means to look at life with a sense of optimism even though it is reasonable to be pessimistic.

**"I believe in the sun even when it is not shining.
I believe in love even when feeling it not.
I believe in God even when He is silent.**
Written on a cell wall in Cologne, Germany

Sometimes it means to believe that God will take care of all things in His world.

"I believe with perfect faith in the coming of the Messiah even though he tarries."
Maimonides

The Jewish People has time and again held beliefs such as these. Our faith in God has seen us through many crises.

Complete as many of the following sentences as you can.

In spite of _____,

I believe _____.

Because of _____,

I believe _____.

When _____,

I believe _____.

How is faith like love?

How is faith like awe or reverence?

Which of the following involve faith?

◯ When we say the *Sh'ma*

◯ When we help a friend

◯ When someone helps us

◯ When we see a rainbow

◯ When we say a prayer or blessing

◯ When Mordecai refused to bow down to Haman

◯ When a Russian Jew applies for an exit visa

◯ When a congregation begins to build its synagogue

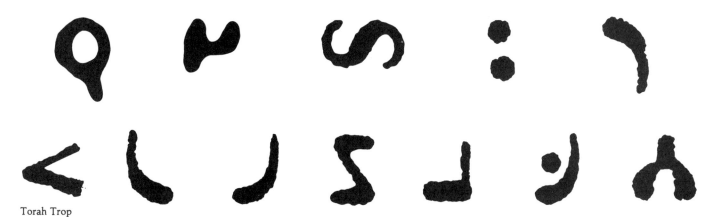

Torah Trop

I Speak To You With Song

A poet once said, "When words leave off, music begins." A word when sung seems to lift the spirit. In song we rise above ourselves. The heart soars. Perhaps that is why words of praise to God seem to demand a melody.

What book of the Bible means "songs?"

When do these songs appear in the worship service?

Why do they appear there? What function do they serve?

Read *Psalms 149* and *150*. What mood do they suggest?

Jewish worship services are traditionally sung. The *Shaliach Tzibor*, the rabbi or the *Chazzan* lead and the congregation follows.

What prayers can you sing?

There is a musical phrase for every word of the Bible. These melodies are noted in a system called *trop*. Look at the top of this page to see what some of the *trop* marks look like.

What are some reasons for wanting to sing words of Torah?

Which of these melodies seems especially meaningful to you and why?

In your synagogue, is Torah read or chanted?

Blessings are also sung. Do you know a melody for the

Blessing over bread

Kiddush

Blessing over Shabbat candles

Blessing over Chanukah candles

Torah reading

Shehechiyanu

Birkat HaMazon

?

What other blessings can you sing?

What parts of the Pesach *Haggadah* can you sing?

When Talmud is being studied, it is read in a sing-song manner. When *Kaddish* is recited, the leader and congregation become an informal choir as they take definite parts in reciting this special song of praise to God.

At a wedding or a funeral, parts of the services are sung. At the Shabbat table we sing *zemirot* to praise God for so wonderful a gift as this last day of the week.

Words are important, but the Chasidim taught us that the melody alone can lift us. They called a melody without words a *niggun*. A *niggun* is sung to such phrases as *Bim Bam, Hai Did De Dye, Ya Ba Ba*, etc. Make up your own *niggun*, song or piece of music and share it with the group.

I Argue And Struggle With You

Jewish literature is filled with accounts of Jews who have argued and struggled with God. Can you recall any of these?

Read *Genesis 18:23-33, Genesis 32:25-31* and *Deuteronomy 3:23-28.*

Not only Bible people argued and struggled with God.

"Good morning to You, Lord of the world.

I, Levi Yitzhak, son of Sarah of Berditchev, approach you with a legal matter concerning your people Israel.

What do you want of Israel?

You always say, 'Command the children of Israel . . .'

You always say, 'Speak unto the children of Israel . . .'

Merciful Father: There are so many other peoples in the world . . . Persians, Babylonians, Edomites, Russians, Germans, English . . .

What do they say? Our kingdom is the kingdom, our emperor is the emperor . . .

But I Levi Yitzhak, son of Sarah of Berditchev say

I shall not go hence nor budge from my place until there is a finish,

Until there is an end of our suffering . . .

Glorified and sanctified be His name . . ."

Rabbi Levi Yitzhak of Berditchev, 1740-1810

"'Do you hear?' Pinhas shouted defiantly. 'I will not fast.'

'I understand. You are right. One must not fast. Not at Auschwitz. Here we live outside time, outside sin. Yom Kippur does not apply to Auschwitz . . .'

'It is simple, I have decided not to comply with the law anymore and not to fast because in the eyes of man and of God I am already dead . . . Until now, I've accepted everything . . . I have told myself: "God knows what he is doing." I have submitted to his will. Now I have had enough, I have reached my limit. If he knows what he is doing, then it is serious; and it is not any less serious if he does not. Therefore, I have decided to tell him: "It is enough."'

(Pinhas, somewhat later)

'I have a confession to make . . . You know, I fasted . . . Yes, I fasted. Like the others. But not for the same reasons. Not out of obedience, but out of defiance. Before the war, you see, some Jews rebelled against the divine will by going to restaurants on the Day of Atonement; here, it is by observing the fast that we can make our indignation heard. Yes, my disciple and teacher, know that I fasted. Not for love of God, but against God . . . the only way to accuse him is by praising him.'"

From *Legends of Our Time*, by Elie Wiesel. Copyright ©1968 by Elie Wiesel. Reprinted by permission of Holt, Rinehart and Winston, Publishers.

Act out one of the biblical or post-biblical struggles or arguments with a partner. One of you argues; the other responds as God. Switch roles after a few minutes.

Which situation did you find most moving?

Which situation did you find most meaningful?

Jacob wrestling with an angel of the Lord

When we are in pain, when we can't get a handle on what the world is all about, when we are frustrated by the conditions of life, then it is appropriate to challenge God. Sometimes we plead with God as Moses did, and do not get our wish. At other times the argument enables us to see that what we wanted at first isn't really what we want at all, as in the case of Pinhas. And perhaps . . . an argument, such as Abraham's or Levi Yitzhak's even helps God. Through such confrontations, understanding begins and we can grow in the process.

Sometimes I Cannot Speak: Doubting You

Doubting God is *very* different from arguing with God. To *argue* with God is to confirm absolutely His being. We would never argue with someone who doesn't exist! On the other hand, to *doubt* God brings into question God's very existence.

Have you ever doubted God's existence?

Someone who doubts God all the time is an atheist. Is atheism a belief?

Which is easier, believing in God or not believing in God? Explain your answer.

Some people take an agnostic position. They say that since God is unknown and probably unknowable, they will neither believe that God exists nor believe that He doesn't exist. An agnostic position often keeps one from thinking at all about God and, therefore, prevents one from establishing, or attempting to establish, a relationship with Him.

Another position is called deism. A deist would say that there is a God and that perhaps He even created the universe. But once the universe was set in motion, God removed Himself from His creation and is no longer involved in it, nor is He reachable.

How does the deist position differ from the Chasidic statement on page 14 that God dwells wherever people let Him in?

It is obvious that many people have doubted, some for a lifetime and others from time to time during their life. Look at the following examples, and circle the position they represent—atheist, agnostic or deist.

0	atheist
?	agnostic
1+	deist

"'I walked today through the slums of life, down the dark streets of wretchedness and of pain . . . and as I walked I challenged God.

I walked today down the lanes of hate, hearing the jeers of bitter people, hearing the names as they cursed and spat: "Dago," Nigger," "Kike," "Jap." I saw the dejected people they stoned.

Why, God Why?

I walked today through war's grim dregs—over fields of blood, over graveless men. I saw the dead, the limbless, the pleading, the crying. I saw the pain, the waste. I smelled the odor of rotted flesh.

I saw the children gathered round—watching, naked, hungry, weeping, diseased, dirty . . .

Blinded with tears, I fled down these streets. I stumbled, then stopped. I shouted:

Why, God, Why? Why do you let human beings sin, hate, suffer?'"

Anonymous

"Suddenly I stopped. Near a stand of pines among the hillocks of clay I recognized the fraternal grave . . . A little further was another mass grave, that of the fourteen recently murdered Jews . . . I stood there, agonized. Here were four Jewish communities that yesterday had been bustling with life . . . Why? Why?

Suddenly my body shook. Above the howling of the wind I heard the voice of the old cobbler of Trok. It rolled over the frozen lake and whistled through the pines with a roar.

Layt din v'layt dayan! **There is no Law and no Judge!"**

"The Fraternal Grave of Four Jewish Settlements" by Abraham Eisen, translated from the Yiddish by Moshe Spiegel, from *Foroys* (Vilna, 1947).

0 ? 1+

0 ? 1+

KELLY & DUKE — BY JACK MOORE

0 ? 1+

Have there ever been times when you asked, "Why God, why?" as the author did in the first quotation?

What might cause someone to doubt God's existence some of the time?

What have you ever seen or read that caused you to feel as did the character in the Abraham Eisen story?

What might cause someone to doubt God's existence all of the time?

Draw your own cartoon about doubting or
not doubting God.

SUMMARY

Review the previous section on speaking
with God. Then, complete the following:

Where do you choose to speak to God?

In public worship

In private prayer

How do you choose to speak with God?

○ With humility

○ With awe

○ With love

○ With adoration

○ With gratitude

○ With joy

○ Through song

○ Through argument and struggle

○ Through doubt

○ Through faith

WHY DO YOU NEED ME, GOD?

We Are Partners With You: Covenant

In legal terms, a covenant is an agreement between two parties. In religious terms, it is an agreement between God and a person and/or God and a people. Look up the following covenants which God made with Noah, Abraham and Moses: *Genesis 9:1-15, Genesis 12:1-3, 17:1-27* and *Deuteronomy 30:15-16*.

For each of the three covenants, what are the people's responsibilities and what is God's promise?

There are those who say that as we keep our covenants, we not only *affirm* God's existence, we *allow* God's existence. This is demonstrated by the following quotations.

"Our rabbis daringly declare that only through the awareness of the children of Israel does the Lord exist in and for the world. It is written: 'You are my witnesses, said the Lord, and I am God' *(Isaiah 43:10).* **That means that if the people of Israel testify to God's existence, He exists; if they do not, He does not exist."**

Sifre Deuteronomy 34:6

	People's Responsibilities	God's Promise
Noah		
Abraham		
Moses		

In what way do you think God has kept His part of the covenant with Moses?

"Without Jews there is no Jewish God. If we leave this world The light will go out in your tent. Since Abraham knew you in a cloud, You have burned in every Jewish face, And we made you in our image . . ."

From "Without Jews" by Jacob Glatstein. Translated by Nathan Halper. From *A Treasury of Yiddish Poetry*, edited by Irving Howe and Eliezer Greenberg. Copyright © 1969 by Irving Howe and Eliezer Greenberg. Reprinted by permission of Holt, Rinehart and Winston, Publishers.

Is there a time limit on the covenant?

"There is a relationship between God and man that involves both God and man— there is a reciprocity. God is in need of man—and man depends on God."

"A Conversation with Abraham Joshua Heschel," Eternal Light script (N.Y.: Jewish Theological Seminary, 1973).

In the covenants between God and Abraham and God and Moses, how has the Jewish People kept its part?

28

Without you and your brothers and sisters, your parents could not be called Mother and Father. Without His people, God could not be called the God of Israel.

For what other reasons might God need us?

But Why *Me?*

Each of us is unique and has special gifts to give the world. Each gift provides an opportunity to serve God as shown in the following story:

Rabbi Yaakov Yitzhak, the Seer of Lublin, gave the following response to a disciple who asked to be shown one general way in which to serve God. "One way is through the teachings, another through prayer, another through fasting and another through eating. Everyone should carefully observe which way his heart draws him and then choose this way with all his strength."

Rabbi Jacob Isaac, Seer of Lublin,
1745-1815.

Does our relationship with God mean that we have special responsibilities in the world? If so, what are they?

What special gifts do you have that God needs?

Taking into consideration the idea of covenant in all the sources in this section, what is the relationship between God, Torah and Israel?

CONCLUSION

Look back through this booklet and think about the course. What have you learned about God?

Compare these thoughts and questions with those you wrote on page 1. What did you discover from the comparison?

Complete the following sentences:

What did you learn that has special meaning for you? Explain.

I believe in God when

I need God when

I pray to God when

I love God when

Write down the thoughts and questions that come to your mind now when you think about God.

I thank God when

I argue and struggle with God when

I doubt God when

I feel close to God when

God needs me when

Make a road map of your search for God.

What "baggage" did you take with you?

What obstacles did you face along the way?

Who helped you in your search for God?

Are you pleased with your journey so far?

In a unique way, you have begun the study of a subject which can occupy you for a lifetime. The course represents only one approach to the subject of God. Learning (Talmud Torah), worship/prayer, mitzvot (religious observances) and social action (gemilut chasadim) are other paths that lead to God. These paths are for you to pursue by yourself and with others.

Searching for God does indeed pose an eternal challenge! And often, it is in the search itself that God can be experienced.

31

GLOSSARY:
A VOCABULARY FOR THEOLOGY

Sherry H. Blumberg

The following is a list of words that are used in theological discussion and reflection. Teachers and parents who are speaking about theology and God should try as often as possible to use language appropriate to the age of the student. Knowing these terms and deciding when to use them is part of the teacher's skill and responsibility.

GENERAL TERMS

Antinomianism	A belief that faith alone is necessary for salvation.
Atheism	A belief that there is no God.
Agnosticism	Uncertainty about the existence or non-existence of God.
Constructivist Theology	Theology based on personal interpretation.
Creation	Usually refers to the account in Genesis. In Jewish tradition creation is believed to be *ex nihilo* (from nothing).
Creationism	The doctrine that all life is ascribed to a Creator God; a doctrine that each soul is unique, a distinct creation of God.
Creator	The belief that God is the One who creates *(Boray)* the world.
Covenant	The mutually binding agreement *(Brit)* between God and the Jewish people.
Deism	The Belief that there is a God, but God does not intervene in the affairs of humanity.
Epistemology	A theory of knowledge; the branch of philosophy that investigates how we come to know.
Eschatology	In theology, a concern with death and final things, such as heaven, hell, and judgment.

Existentialism	A chiefly twentieth century philosophical movement that embraces diverse doctrines. It centers on analysis of individual existence in an unfathomable universe, and the plight of the individual who must assume ultimate responsibility for his/her acts of free will without any certain knowledge of what is right or wrong or good or bad.
Explicit Religiosity	Outward signs of being religious, following traditions, ritual, norms.
Feminist Theology	Theological reflections based on the feminist critique or understanding of society and religion.
Free Will	Freedom of human beings to make choices that arc not determined by prior causes or divine intervention.
Grace	In Jewish tradition, God's mercy and forgiveness (*Rachamim*).
Hermeneutics	The theory and practice of text interpretation.
Immanent	Religious feeling that God is innate, within oneself, present in one's daily life.
Implicit Religiosity	Inward connection to religion in belief and faith.
Monotheism	Belief in One God.
Mysticism	The spiritual practice and belief that union with God is possible and desirable. A belief in a reality that is beyond normal perception.
Narrative Theology	Theological school concerned with the telling of story, the connection of the individual to the oral or written narration of a religious tradition.
Naturalism	A belief that God is part of nature and found in nature.
Omnipresent	A belief that God is everywhere.
Omnipotent	A belief that God is all powerful and can do anything.
Omniscient	A belief that God knows everything.

Ontology	In philosophy and theology, the study of being.
Particularism	Relating to one group or religion.
Piety	The state of holiness, an attempt to be very religious and close to God in one's feelings and actions.
Polytheism	A belief in multiple gods.
Predestination	The belief that everything is predetermined; there is no free will.
Prophets	Individuals called by God to speak for justice, righteousness, observance of God's ways, or to comfort and give hope.
Redemption	The saving or freeing of people and the soul (in Hebrew, *Geulah*). God is called Redeemer (*Goayl*).
Revelation	Disclosure of God's purpose for Jews in the Written and Oral Torah.
Ritual	Symbolic and often prescribed acts.
Salvation	In Jewish thought, deliverance from a difficulty; in other religions, preservation of the soul.
Soul	*Neshamah*, the breath, life source, or immortal part of human beings that is connected to God in some way.
Spirituality	A sensitivity to the non-material and intangible aspects of existence, usually connected to God and the transcendent.
Supernatural	Beyond the natural; a transcendent God.
Theism	A belief that there is a God or gods — usually a personal God concept that differs from deism.
Transcendent	A God image or religious experience that surpasses common or everyday experience, something that is outside and beyond.
Universal	Unlimited and boundless, common to many different religious traditions.

HEBREW TERMS

Adonai	Name of God, the surrogate pronunciation of *yud hey vav hey.*
Chasidut	Hasidic philosophy and writings.
D'vaykut	Cleaving and clinging to God (a major Hasidic principle).
Ehyeh Asher Ehyeh	Literally, I will be what I will be, a name of God revealed to Moses from the burning bush.
El	Singular noun meaning God.
El Shaddai	God Almighty, or God of the Mountains.
Elohim	Another name of God in the Torah; refers to the judging quality of God.
Kabbalah	The Jewish mystical tradition and mystical texts.
Kadosh	Holy, separate.
Kavanah	Intention, preparation; the inner approach to prayer.
Kedushah	Holiness.
Keva	The set standard order of prayer; the regular practice of praying.
Nefesh	Soul or breath.
Shechinah	The feminine quality of God; the spirit of God that travels with the Jewish people into exile.

RESOURCES FOR LEARNERS, TEACHERS, AND PARENTS

Roberta Louis Goodman

The popularity of God and spirituality in today's culture is reflected in the wide selection of materials available. This annotated resource section is not a complete listing of all materials and resources on teaching and learning about God and spirituality; that would require a book in itself. Rather, this is a selected listing of those that are the most useful and most appropriate for Jewish educational settings. (Many additional materials and resources are found in the annotated bibliographies of the chapters in this book.)

The selections include fiction and nonfiction, textbooks, videos, and web sites. Most of the materials were written for Jewish audiences, although some are geared to a more diverse audience. The entries are presented by categories: Early Childhood, Elementary School Age, Teens, Family Education and Parent Resources, Adults, and Teacher and Jewish Professionals.

An attempt was made to include materials that are readily available through Jewish publishers or major book vendors. The entries date predominantly from 1990 through 2001. In a few cases, earlier publications are listed. Complete citations of the materials and resources are provided to aid in finding them. In addition, a brief description of the contents or focus of each item is provided.

Early Childhood

Borosom, Martin. *Becoming Me.* Woodstock, VT: Jewish Lights Publishing, 2000.

Written in the personal voice of the Creator, this book presents the creation story with a focus on the relationship between the Creator and human beings. It conveys the closeness of human beings to the Creator. This version of the account of creation emphasizes the concepts of love, friendship, and our own existence in relationship to God.

Cone, Molly. *Hello, Hello, Are You There, God?* New York: UAHC Press, 1999.

This collection incorporates the stories about God found in the series *Hear, O Israel: The Shema Story Books.* Cone created these original stories about God to convey concepts such as learning, belonging, and love of God. A Teacher's Guide with background materials, activities for the classroom and family, objectives, and questions for discussion is available.

Kushner, Lawrence and Karen. *Because Nothing Looks Like God.* Woodstock, VT: Jewish Lights Publishing, 2001.

The authors present questions people have about God. Then they use real life examples to help children and their parents explore possible responses. Stories revolve around fear and hope, happiness and sadness, and other spiritual matters.

———. *How Does God Make Things Happen?* Woodstock, VT: Jewish Lights Publishing, 2001.

Here the authors offer concrete examples of how God gives us each day ways to change the world for the better.

———. *What Does God Look Like?* Woodstock, VT: Jewish Lights Publishing, 2001.

Filled with illustrated pictures and real life examples from a child's everyday world, this book compares what is all around us in our daily lives to God being omnipresent, everywhere. This awareness of God in our daily activities creates a sensitivity to that which makes our lives holy and special.

Sasso, Sandy Eisenberg.[1] *God's Paintbrush.* Woodstock, VT: Jewish Lights Publishing, 1992.

This beautifully illustrated book presents different ideas that provoke thinking about God and experiencing God in everyday life and the world around us. For example, thinking about rain as God's tears becomes a way of getting children to think about what makes God cry. Every two pages has a reflection and questions for children to discuss. A separate activity kit with teacher and student activities is available.

Elementary School Age

Brichto, Mira Pollak. *The God around Us: A Child's Garden of Prayer.* New York: UAHC Press, 1999.

———. *The God Around Us: Volume II.* New York: UAHC Press, 2001.

In these two volumes, beautiful, full color artwork and poetry are used to stimulate thoughts about God and prayer. The books impart knowledge that God is around us in the everyday.

Cone, Molly. *Who Knows Ten? Children's Tales of the Ten Commandments.* rev. ed. New York: UAHC Press, 1998.

These original tales use stories to convey the core ideas of each of the Ten Commandments.

Ganz, Yaffa. *Where Are You, HaShem?* New York: Mesorah Publications, 1989.

In this story, a young boy looks for God in many places. Finally, he realizes that God is everywhere.

Gellman, Marc, and Thomas Hartman. *How Do You Spell God? Answers To the Big Questions from around the World.* New York: William Morrow & Co., 1995.

Each chapter begins with a universal question, such as theodicy (why do bad things happen to good people?). Then answers are provided from different religious traditions. A Teacher Guide is available.

Gevirtz, Gila. *Living As Partners with God.* West Orange, NJ: Behrman House, 1997.

Building on *Partners with God* (see immediately below), this book focuses on helping students formulate an understanding of community and the Jewish people's Covenantal relationship with God. These concepts are presented through role models, important Jewish figures from ancient to modern times, who have fulfilled the Covenant by living as partners with God. Their insights and actions give glimpses into ways that we can live as partners with God in today's world. A Teacher's Edition is available.

———. *Partners with God.* West Orange, NJ: Behrman House, 1996.

Gevirtz turns difficult life questions into a textbook format. She addresses the profound questions about God by introducing a Jewish vocabulary for thinking and talking about God. The book fosters a personal search for God. The Teacher's Edition includes commentary on the concepts presented in the textbook and strategies that accommodate different learning styles.

Goodman, Roberta Louis. *God's Top Ten.* Los Angeles, CA: Torah Aura Productions, 1992.

This work, which is based on narrative theology, uses stories to convey an understanding of God. The stories, which are from classical and modern sources, help students explore and explain the meaning of each of the Ten Commandments. Questions that raise significant issues about life are interspersed. A Teacher's Guide is available, too.

I Have Some Questions about God. Los Angeles, CA: Torah Aura Productions, 2002.

---

[1]For a complete listing of all of Rabbi Sasso's books on God and spirituality for early childhood, see the bibliography for Chapter 16, "Tell Me a Story about God," p. 187-188.

These classroom materials are organized around 12 big questions that children in Grades 3 and 4 ask about God. Examples include: Does God punish people? Can praying make someone well? Rabbis, along with children, wrote answers to these questions. Exercises are designed to encourage students to reflect on and share their experiences of God in the world. Finally, stories about God stimulate thinking.

In God's Image. Los Angeles, CA: Torah Aura Productions, 1983. (Game)

This game, which is appropriate for Grades 4 through adult, is filled with examples of times when God has helped people. As participants roll the dice, they must either explain how people can help other people in the same way or name an organization that does the particular act of *gemilut chasadim*.

Kushner, Lawrence. *The Book of Miracles: A Young Person's Guide To Jewish Spirituality.* New York: UAHC Press, 1987.

The author uses *midrashic*, Talmudic, and biblical stories as a basis to present his own comments on the importance of maintaining one's awareness of the world around. Many beautiful and mysterious events occur every day.

Lester, Julius. *When the Beginning Began: Stories about God, the Creatures, and Us.* San Diego, CA: Silver Whistle, 1999.

Kirkus Reviews calls this book "an unusual and inventive, beautifully illustrated collection of Jewish tales interpreting the creation story in the Old Testament." Lester puts a *midrashic* spin on the 17 stories as he attempts to make the sacred come alive.

Pasachoff, Naomi. *Basic Judaism: Volume 3 God.* West Orange, NJ: Behrman House, 1987.

The third book in the series, this volume focuses on concepts related to understanding God and holiness, such as *emunah, brit, olam hazeh, olam haba, teshuvah.* A Teacher's Guide, Duplicating Masters, and Student Activity Book are also available.

Rosenthal, Yaffa. *Thank You, HaShem.* New York: Mesorah, ArtScroll Youth Series, 1983.

In this *alef-bet* book, each letter depicts something God created.

Sweetland, Nancy. *God's Quiet Things.* New York: William B. Erdmans Publishing, 1994.

This storybook shows how children can find God in nature.

Thompson, Marlene. *Let's Discover God.* West Orange, NJ: Behrman House, 1998.

This set of eight booklets for Grades K through 2 presents basic concepts about God (e.g., our Covenant with God, why we perform *mitzvot*, how we can act in God's image). The booklets are filled with poems, photographs, activities, discussion questions, and prayers and blessings. A Teacher's Edition is available.

Wise, Ira. *Missing the Mark.* Los Angeles, CA: Torah Aura Productions, 1990.

The *"Al Chayt"* prayer is central to the High Holy Day experience. This lesson presents the Jewish understanding that everyone "misses the mark" sometimes and needs to start again, addressing the concepts of *teshuvah* (repentance) and *cheshbon hanefesh* (personal assessment or review).

———. *T'shuvah, She Wrote.* Los Angeles, CA: Torah Aura Productions, 1990.

Teshuvah is more than saying one is sorry. It involves turning toward another person, turning toward God. This lesson uses both case studies and classical texts to convey the concept of *teshuvah*.

Wood, Douglas. *Grandad's Prayers of the Earth.* Cambridge, MA: Candlewick Press, 1999.

This book is filled with deep wisdom and insight about the spiritual life, and is presented in a way compatible with all religious traditions. One day, on one of many walks with his grandad, a school age boy asks about prayers. His grandfather shows him how the gift of each living thing is its prayer.

He explains that human beings pray in a variety of ways, sometimes with the words of their ancestors and sometimes with their own words. When the grandfather dies, a period of doubt sets in. In the end, it is his ability to pray that comforts the boy and makes him whole again.

———. *Old Turtle*. Duluth, MN: Pfeifer-Hamilton, 1992.

A classic, this non-denominational story begins with the animals arguing about the nature of God, each one tending to view God as similar to him or her. Old turtle, the wise one, tells the animals that all of their views of God point to what God is. He announces the arrival of human beings, who are reminders of what God is. When human beings forget this role, argue about God, and cannot find God, then they are destructive to the world. Joyfully, the people hear and learn from nature, returning to find God in one another and becoming God's representatives on earth.

Videos for Elementary School Age

god@heaven. 20 min., color. Ergo Media Inc.

Seven-year-old Adam sends an e-mail to the Western Wall in Jerusalem — "an e-mail direct to God." The audience shares Adam's frustration as days go by without a reply. Then, suddenly, this contemporary video's mix of theology and technology addresses an age-old question in a new and innovative way. An excellent way to begin a discussion of communication with God.

How Do You Spell God? 32 minutes, color. HBO.

Based on the book of the same name by Rabbi Marc Gellman and Monseignor Thomas Hartman, this thought provoking video embraces great questions and stimulates discussion. Children pose and answer many of the same questions presented in the book, sharing their insights, feelings, fears, doubts, and expectations. Comes with a study guide and student activities.

Teens

Bayer, Steve. *What Does God Do?* Los Angeles, CA: Torah Aura Productions, 1993.

This lesson introduces teens and adults to a Rabbinic concept of God and what it means to "imitate" God.

Bissell, Sherry [Sherry H. Blumberg], with Audrey Friedman Marcus and Raymond A. Zwerin. *God: The Eternal Challenge*. Student Manual and Leader Guide. Denver, CO: A.R.E. Publishing, Inc., 1980.

This mini-course presents frequently asked questions about God. These include: Where do you live, God? How shall I speak with you? Why do you need me, God? Each question is followed by a combination of activities, Jewish sources, and responses. The mini-course addresses the relationship between God and each individual, and presents different ways that God can be part of our lives. (For a reprint of the Student Manual, see the Appendix on p. 435 of this book.)

Goldstein, Niles E., and Steven S. Mason. *Judaism and Spiritual Ethics*. New York: UAHC Press, 1996.

In an attempt to identify spiritual ethics of Jewish conduct, behaviors that reflect our devotion to God, the authors present an exploration of the thirteenth century text, *Sefer Ma'alot Hamidot* (Book of Virtues and Values).

Goodman, Roberta Louis. *Test of Faith: An Instant Lesson on Faith Development*. Los Angeles, CA: Torah Aura Productions, 1985.

This Instant Lesson, perhaps the first published work to use faith development theory in a Jewish setting, challenges students to think about how they make meaning out of their lives. Activities include: trying to figure out at what stage the learner is and interpreting a story by answering significant meaning making questions.

Grishaver, Joel Lurie, et al. *When I Stood at Sinai*. Los Angeles, CA: Torah Aura Productions, 1992.

Written by a class of sixth graders, this volume invites students to tell their own stories about revelation, what it means to receive the Torah at Mount Sinai. The material can be used with Grade 6 through adults.

Kerdeman, Deborah, and Lawrence Kushner. *The Invisible Chariot: An Introduction To Kabbalah and Jewish Spirituality*. Denver, CO: A.R.E. Publishing, Inc., 1986.

Major ideas and concepts about *Kabbalah* are presented in an accessible and content rich way. Learners explore and reflect on their place in the universe, the roles they can play in repairing the world, and how their lives can be connected to God. A Leader Guide is available.

Levitin, Sonia. *The Singing Mountain*. New York: Simon & Schuster, 1998.

In this novel, contemporary Jewish identity and the search for spirituality are intertwined. Set in California and Israel, these themes are portrayed through the lives of two teenagers and their families.

Salkin, Jeffrey K. *For Kids — Putting God on Your Guest List*. Woodstock, VT: Jewish Lights Publishing, 1998.

B'nai Mitzvah are able to grasp the spiritual meaning of this life cycle event through a combination of advice and inquiry. Written as a guide for B'nai Mitzvah, the book presents core spiritual values of Judaism in an accessible way.

Sonsino, Rifat, and Daniel B. Syme. *Finding God: Ten Jewish Responses*. New York: UAHC Press, 1986.

While there is only one God, views about God have not been monolithic. Sonsino and Syme present ten different views of God from biblical through modern times in an accessible but sophisticated way. Some of the views are collective views of the Bible and the Rabbis; others are individual views of such Jewish philosophers as Philo, Maimonides, Luria, Spinoza, Buber, Steinberg, Kaplan, and

Fromm. The book helps people connect to Jewish sources and perspectives on God that are more well developed than their childhood images.

When Will the Messiah Come? Los Angeles, CA: Torah Aura Productions, 1986.

Using the form of a Talmudic argument, this lesson centers on questions of faith, including a discussion of the Messiah.

Videos for Teens

Oh, God!. 98 minutes, color, rated PG. Available from most video stores.

In this comedy, God calls on a supermarket manager to spread simple messages about life and the world. God appears in a golf cap and sneakers and laments having put pits in avocados. The movie raises questions about what God expects of us and how God works in the world. A teacher guide is available.

Oh, God! Book II. 94 minutes, color, rated PG. Available from most video stores.

God makes a trip to earth and teams up with an eleven-year-old girl to spread God's influence. She designs an advertising campaign for her school, but is expelled and sent to a psychiatrist for her ideas. This comedy raises questions regarding God's involvement in our day-to-day activities and our world.

Teens on Faith: A Spiritual Journey. 30 minutes, color. CBS.

Twelve high school students of diverse backgrounds talk about their search for meaning in a complex world and how their religious communities and commitments enter into this search. Two Jewish teens are featured. Issues triggered by the film are: practice based on parents' religious patterns, religious stereotypes, being attacked for what one believes, marrying out of one's religion, drugs and spirituality, and the importance of religious role models.

Family Education and Parent Resources

Bria, Gina. *The Art of Family Rituals, Imagination, and Everyday Spirituality*. New York: Dell, 1998.

Bria offers suggestions on how to assign special meaning to everyday tasks that make up home life.

Chopra, Deepak. *The Seven Spiritual Laws of Success for Parents: Daily Lessons for Children to Live By*. New York: Harmony Books, 1997.

Chopra reinterprets the seven successes of spiritual laws for adult growth for parents. Spirituality, he asserts, is a skill that involves living each day, one law at a time.

———. *The Way of the Wizard: Twenty Spiritual Lessons in Creating the Life You Want*. New York: Harmony Books, 1995.

Chopra suggests ways for parents to teach children spiritual values by incorporating spiritual goals into family life.

Gellman, Marc, and Thomas Hartman. *Where Does God Live? Questions and Answers for Parents and Children*. New York: Triumph Books, 1995.

The authors posit that it is important for parents and children to talk to one another about God and not just rely on clergy. Authored by a Rabbi and a Priest, the book supports such conversations by presenting an important theological question, answering it, and then giving parents and children a chance to respond. The theological questions are ones that parents and children are likely to have considered such as: What does God look like? Does God make miracles? When my pet hamster Elmo died, did he go to heaven?

Gordis, Daniel. *Becoming a Jewish Parent: How to Explore Spirituality and Tradition with Your Children*. New York: Harmony Books, 2000.

Even as he addresses customs and traditions of the holidays and life cycles, Gordis orients these rituals and symbols to larger questions about God and spirituality. He recommends that parents be worldview builders, helping develop their children's outlook on life, rather than thinking of themselves as information providers responding to questions about God. Gordis provides stories and suggestions for following this approach.

Heller, David. *Talking To Your Child about God: A Book for Families of All Faiths*. New York: Bantam Books, 1988.

Heller provides practical advice to parents about how to teach their children about God. Drawing on his professional training as a psychologist, he describes children's curiosity about God, provides suggestions on creating a healthy spiritual atmosphere at home, and helps parents examine their own place spiritually. He moves from laying the groundwork to offering ways of introducing the child to God, and helping the child find God.

Jenkins, Peggy. *Nurturing Spirituality in Children: Simple Hands-On Activities*. Hillsboro, OR: Beyond Works Publisher, 1995.

Simple lesson plans are presented for nurturing spirituality. Parents can use these with their children ten minutes at a time. Topics include teaching about compassion, and a sense of God.

Kushner, Harold S. *When Children Ask about God*. New York: Reconstructionist Press, 1971.

In this early book on teaching about God, Kushner presents his insights for parents and others.

Raff, Tamar. *Family Talk about God*. Tamar & Bruce Raff, 1993. c/o Irv Horn, 5077 Corinthia Way, Ocean Hills, CA 92056, tandbraff@aol.com.

This discussion guide presents ideas about God and questions for families to discuss. It provides ways of discussing a topic that is often difficult for parents to broach. This guidebook can be used as a family-centered supplement to any of the books on God or as an independent source book.

Wolpe, David. *Teaching Your Children about God: A Modern Jewish Approach*. New York: Henry Holt and Company, 1993.

Wolpe provides practical advice to parents about how to bring God into family life. He encourages parents to rediscover their spiritual roots. He describes how children view the world and God. He presents questions about life that lead us to God. Each chapter includes spiritual exercises or activities for family members and discussion questions that heighten awareness of God in our lives.

Adults

Ariel, David. *The Mystical Quest: An Introduction To Jewish Mysticism*. New York: Schocken Books, 1992.

This readable and comprehensive overview provides background on the history, nature, character, and principles of Jewish mysticism. The *Sephirot* are described. Ariel discusses the *Shechinah*, Torah, and soul from the perspective of mysticism, as well as the life of a mystic, modern mysticism, and the mystic quest.

————. *Spiritual Judaism: Restoring Heart and Soul To Jewish Life*. New York: Hyperion, 1998.

Ariel applies Jewish spiritual principles to daily life, focusing on such realms as prayer, essence, genius, and nature.

——-. *What Do Jews Believe? The Spiritual Foundations of Judaism*. New York: Schocken Books, 1995.

Chapters in this book address key theological concepts and questions about God, human destiny, good and evil, chosen people, meaning of Torah, *mitzvot*, prayer, Messiah, and why be Jewish.

Bernstein, Ellen, ed. *Ecology and the Jewish Spirit: Where Nature and the Sacred Meet*. Woodstock, VT: Jewish Lights Publishing, 1998.

The essays in this book present nature and the environment as integrated parts of people's existence. The book includes both first person accounts as well as traditional texts and commentary on finding holiness in nature. The author conveys strongly the

responsibility of human beings as partners with God to tend and care for the earth.

Biers-Ariel, Matt; Deborah Newbrun; and Michael Smart. *Spirit in Nature: Teaching Judaism and Ecology on the Trail*. West Orange, NJ: Behrman House, 2000.

This books blends nature, Judaism, and spirituality. The activities in the book stress the miracle and wonder of God's creations, the divine spark found in the natural world around us. The authors present Jewish sources and traditions that show how to sanctify God's creation.

Bookman, Terry. *The Busy Soul: Ten-Minute Spiritual Workouts Drawn from Jewish Tradition*. Woodstock, VT: Jewish Lights Publishing, 1999.

This guide presents easy to do spiritual exercises around the cycle of the year, with particular emphasis on holiday themes. For example, Purim includes themes of risk taking, *mazal* (luck), self-esteem, and self-reliance.

Borowitz, Eugene B. *Renewing the Covenant: A Theology for the Postmodern Jew*. Philadelphia, PA: Jewish Publication Society, 1991.

Borowitz presents his liberal theology centering around Covenant for the modern Jew. He presents his approach to thinking about one's relationship to God and how that translates into living as a Jew today.

Chopra, Deepak. *The Seven Spiritual Laws of Success: A Practical Guide To the Fulfillment of Your Dreams*. San Rafael, CA: Amber-Allen Publishing, 1994.

In the seven successes, personal understanding and harmony promote fulfilling relationships.

Cooper, David. *God Is a Verb: Kabbalah and the Practice of Mystical Judaism*. New York: Riverhead Books, 1997.

Cooper divides his presentation of *Kabbalah* and Jewish mysticism into four parts: (1) The Past (The Work of Creation), (2) The Present

(This World), (3) Higher Awareness (The Work of the Chariot), and (4) Beyond This Life (The World To Come). A highlight is his presentation of the path of the *tzaddik*, Jewish enlightenment, in which he describes numerous paths, including those of learning, respect, generosity, awe, purity, and moderation.

———. *The Handbook of Jewish Meditation Practices: A Guide for Enriching the Sabbath and Other Days of Your Life*. Woodstock, VT: Jewish Lights Publishing, 2000.

Cooper emphasizes taking time to revitalize and renew one's soul on Shabbat or throughout the week. He presents numerous mediation exercises and self-reflection techniques that help quiet and focus the mind and soul.

Dosick, Wayne D. *Soul Judaism: Dancing with God into a New Era*. Woodstock, VT: Jewish Lights Publishing, 1999.

In this do-it-yourself approach to spiritual living, Dosick provides exercises and suggestions for enriching daily life. He draws upon Jewish meditation, mysticism, and *Kabbalah*. Several practical approaches for deepening personal relationships with God are suggested, including praying and meditating, performing rituals and following observances, and utilizing the arts — song, stories, and dance.

Edwards, Lloyd. *Discerning Your Spiritual Gifts*. Cambridge, MA: Cowley Publications, 1998.

Edwards discusses spiritual gifts from different biblical perspectives. He presents a guide to discovering spiritual gifts through step-by-step exercises and self-evaluation.

Frankiel, Tamar. *The Gift of Kabbalah: Discovering the Secrets of Heaven, Renewing Your Life on Earth*. Woodstock, VT: Jewish Lights Publishing, 2001.

Frankiel combines scholarship and spiritual insight in tracing the evolution of *Kabbalah* in Judaism. She presents the connection that exists between the everyday life and the spiritual oneness of the universe. Practical suggestions and techniques for spiritual growth are included, such as mapping divine energies, the personal Tree of Life, and clearing the path of remembering.

Gillman, Neil. *Sacred Fragments: Recovering Theology for the Modern Jew*. Philadelphia, PA: Jewish Publication Society, 1990.

Each chapter of Gillman's book addresses a critical issue in Jewish theology today. Some examples are Revelation and suffering. In regard to Revelation: What really happened? Knowing God: how and what? Proving God's existence. In regard to suffering: Why does God allow it? Gillman weaves classic and modern texts with his own views in responding to these essential theological questions.

———. *The Way into Encountering God in Judaism*. Woodstock, VT: Jewish Lights Publishing, 2001.

Throughout history, Jews have expressed countless images of God. Arguing that metaphors of God change over time, Gillman presents this imaginative tradition.

Grishaver, Joel Lurie. *And You Shall Be a Blessing*. Northvale, NJ: Jason Aronson, 1993.

This book delves into how the *brachah* formula creates a process of prayer and infuses the act of saying a blessing with meaning.

———. *The Bonding of Isaac: Stories and Essays about Gender and Jewish Spirituality*. Los Angeles, CA: Torah Aura Productions, 1997.

This book examines issues of gender and spirituality through a weaving together of traditional texts with movies, books, and other elements of popular culture. Grishaver explores the ways that men and women approach their own spiritual and relationship needs.

Hoffman, Lawrence A. *The Art of Public Prayer: Not for Clergy Only*. Woodstock, VT: Jewish Lights Publishing, 1999.

Hoffman aims to remove obstacles to prayer and prayer services that stand in the way of everyday spirituality. He provides practical suggestions on how the worshiper and the leaders of services can make prayer a more meaningful experience.

Jewish Education News 16:1 (Winter 1995). Special Focus: God and Spirituality.

An extremely worthwhile issue of this CAJE publication that contains helpful and informative articles by outstanding educators, including, among others, Neil Gillman, Betsy Dolgin Katz, Roberta Louis Goodman, Sherry H. Blumberg, Michael J. Shire, Judith Z. Abrams, Arthur Kurzweil, Joel Lurie Grishaver, Yosi Gordon, Gila Givertz, and Saul Wachs. Carolyn Starman Hessel contributes "A Resource Guide for Teaching about God and Spirituality."

Kaplan, Aryeh. *Innerspace: Introduction To Kabbalah, Meditation and Prophecy.* Jerusalem, Israel: Moznaim, 1990.

This source provides a thorough and accessible description of the soul and *Sephirot* in mysticism.

Kedar, Karyn D. *The Dance of the Dolphin: Finding Prayer, Perspective and Meaning in the Stories of Our Lives.* Woodstock, VT: Jewish Lights Publishing, 2001.

This book focuses on learning to live in both the rational/material and the spiritual worlds. Kedar shares her views through stories, examples, and insights that suggest how to navigate this tension in one's own life.

———. *God Whispers: Stories of the Soul, Lessons of the Heart.* Woodstock, VT: Jewish Lights Publishing, 1999.

Through stories about ordinary people and her own life experiences, Kedar shows that the joy and pain in our lives have purpose and meaning. Some of the themes she deals with include: the Divine in each of us, hope, patience, acts of loving-kindness, forgiveness, learning from death, surrender, and balance.

Kushner, Harold. *When Bad Things Happen To Good People.* New York: Avon Books, 1981.

This classic deals with the question of theod-

icy, why bad things happen to good people. Kushner resolves the question by providing a theology that does not require viewing the bad things in our lives as God's punishment. Rather, he asserts, God plays a role in providing support and compassion to the sufferer.

Kushner, Lawrence. *GOD was in THIS PLACE & I, i did not Know: Finding Self, Spirituality, and Ultimate Meaning.* Woodstock, VT: Jewish Lights Publishing, 1991.

This is just one of the author's many books related to spirituality. Here he looks at the lives of Jews who provide insights into Jewish spirituality. Other worthwhile books by Lawrence Kushner are *The Book of Letters, The Book of Words, Eyes Remade for Wonder, Honey from the Rock, Invisible Lines of Connection,* and *The River of Light.*

Lamm, Norman. *The Shema: Spirituality and Law in Judaism.* Philadelphia, PA: Jewish Publication Society, 2000.

Lamm uses the *"Shema"* as his focus in exploring the relationship between spirituality and law in Judaism. He incorporates commentary from throughout the ages, as well as his own perspective.

Leder, Steven Z. *The Extraordinary Nature of Ordinary Things.* West Orange, NJ: Behrman House, 1999.

In a poetic, fluid style, the author presents the important messages behind ordinary events of our lives from birth to illness, from crunching on *matzah* to pulling weeds in the heat of the summer. He shows us how God is present in our everyday lives.

Levoy, Gregg Michael. *Callings: Finding and Following an Authentic Life.* New York: Harmony Books, 1997.

How does one follow one's true calling? Levoy offers strategies for sharpening the senses to cut through the distractions of everyday life. He identifies the many calls that we receive and the various channels through which they come.

Levy, Benjamin. *A Faithful Heart: Preparing for the High Holidays: A Study Text Based on the Midrash Ma'aseh Avraham Avinu.* New York: UAHC Press, 2001.

> Modeling the use of texts to examine spiritual issues, Levy presents texts from the Medieval work, *Ma'aseh Avraham*, a compilation of *midrashic* sources on Abraham. He translates and interprets the texts as a way of preparing individuals for the High Holy Days. Themes covered include *teshuvah*, belief in God, the efficacy of prayer, and making ethical choices.

Matlins, Stuart M., ed. *The Jewish Lights Spirituality Handbook: A Guide to Understanding, Exploring & Living a Spiritual Life.* Woodstock, VT: Jewish Lights Publishing, 2001.

> This anthology of Jewish scholars and writers is geared toward stimulating thought and providing tools for continuing on one's spiritual journey. It is organized around these five questions: What is Jewish spirituality? Where is spirituality found? When does spirituality enter? How do you forge the tools to make it happen? Why should spirituality be part of my life?

Moffatt, Betty Clare. *Soulwork: Clearing the Mind, Opening the Heart, and Replenishing the Soul.* Berkeley, CA: Wildcat Canyon Press, 1994.

> Moffatt encourages readers to explore their spiritual paths and connect with the richness of their inner lives. She stresses the importance of centering and balancing to achieve inner peace.

Moody, Harry R., and David Carroll. *The Five Stages of the Soul.* New York: Anchor Books, 1997.

> The authors identify the five stages of the soul as call, search, struggle, breakthrough, and return. They examine the relationship between these five stages and legends and myths from religious traditions.

Ochs, Carol; Kerry M. Olitzky; and Joshua Saltzman, eds. *Paths of Faithfulness: Personal Essays on Jewish Spirituality.* New York: KTAV Publishing House, 1997.

These essays by faculty members of Hebrew Union College-Jewish Institute of Religion in New York City present the spiritual journey of each of them.

Olitzky, Kerry M. *Jewish Paths toward Healing and Wholeness: A Personal Guide to Dealing with Suffering.* Woodstock, VT: Jewish Lights Publishing, 2000.

> Olitzky provides a Jewish framework for understanding healing and suffering. He offers healing rituals, Psalms, and prayers that can be used to precipitate or enrich the dialogue with God.

Olitzky, Kerry M., and Lori Forman. *Restful Reflections: Nighttime Inspiration to Calm the Soul, Based on Jewish Wisdom.* Woodstock, VT: Jewish Lights Publishing. 2001.

> Similar in format to its companion volume, *Sacred Intentions* (see immediately below), this book presents quotations followed by a reflection from a spiritual thinker aimed at enriching one's daily life and spiritual path.

———. *Sacred Intentions: Daily Inspiration to Strengthen the Spirit, Based on Jewish Wisdom.* Woodstock, VT: Jewish Lights Publishing, 1999.

> For each day in the secular calendar, an inspirational quote from a Jewish source followed by a reflection on the text is provided.

Plaskow, Judith, and Carol P. Christ. *Weaving the Visions: New Patterns in Feminist Spirituality.* San Francisco, CA: HarperCollins Publishers, 1989.

> Co-edited by a distinguished Jewish scholar, this anthology of essays puts Jewish women's spirituality into the larger context of feminist theology. Several of the essays focus exclusively on Jewish women's spirituality. Others help frame the issues with which women struggle as they find their spiritual place and voice in today's world.

Solomon, Lewis D. *Jewish Spirituality: Revitalizing Judaism for the Twenty-First Century.* Northvale, NJ: Jason Aronson, 2000.

> Solomon argues for a new approach to

Judaism, and suggests introducing Jews to spiritual practices. He draws on classical texts including Bible, Talmud, and *Midrash*, and deals with themes of love and compassion, humility, joyfulness, peace of mind.

Sonsino, Rifat. *Six Jewish Spiritual Paths: A Rationalist Looks at Spirituality*. Woodstock, VT: Jewish Lights Publishing, 2001.

Judaism offers many different paths to spirituality. Sonsino presents six different paths to God through acts of transcendence, study, prayer, meditation, ritual, and relationship and good deeds.

Spitz, Elie Kaplan. *Does the Soul Survive? A Jewish Journey To Belief in the Afterlife, Past Lives & Living with Purpose*. Woodstock, VT: Jewish Lights Publishing, 2001.

Spitz combines personal accounts of the afterlife and Jewish scholarship. Topics include reincarnation, past life memory, the work of mediums, and more.

Umansky, Ellen M., and Diane Ashton, eds. *Four Centuries of Jewish Women's Spirituality: A Sourcebook*. Boston, MA: Beacon Press, 1992.

This volume is a collection of writings by women that reflect their Jewish, religious self-identity. The material draws on a wide range of sources, including letters, sermons, essays, Responsa, *midrash*, diaries, poetry, ethical wills, and speeches from over 100 women. These sources and authors help capture and reclaim Jewish spirituality from a women's perspective.

Waskow, Arthur, and Phyllis Ocean. *A Time for Every Purpose under Heaven: The Jewish Life-Spiral as a Spiritual Path*. New York: Farrar, Straus and Giroux, forthcoming.

This book is a celebration of the great spiral of Jewish life and ceremony, incorporating the wisdom of the Bible and the Rabbis and exploring new rituals for the twenty-first and the fifty-ninth centuries. The authors show how the flow of a Jewish life fits together from one celebration to the next, and how

each moment can become a connection to a sacred community.

Wineman, Aryeh. *The Hasidic Parable*. Philadelphia, PA: Jewish Publication Society, 2001.

The author presents key parables reflecting the values and norms of the spiritual life for the Hasidic movement.

———. *Mystic Tales from the Zohar*. Philadelphia, PA: Jewish Publication Society, 1997.

Wineman translates and comments on eight of the most complete narratives from the *Zohar* and explores our relationship to God based on this classic text.

Wolpe, David J. *The Healer of Shattered Hearts: A Modern Jewish Approach*. New York: Henry Holt, 1990.

Through texts and traditions, Wolpe examines the role of God in our daily struggles, fears, and questions.

Organizations

Aleph — Alliance for Jewish Renewal.

The Aleph web site (www.aleph.org) defines Jewish renewal, describes programs and projects, offers a community network of Jewish renewal efforts, and provides access to a bookstore of materials on Jewish renewal.

Metivta.

Metivta, a Center for Contemplative Judaism, is a learning institution for Jewish wisdom that unites contemplative spirituality with study, introspection, and practice rooted in Jewish mystical tradition. Access to their web site is at www.metivta.org. In addition to courses and retreats, online offerings include a discussion forum, the opportunity to ask a question of a Rabbi, and inspirational writings. A new writing appears daily in addition to archived articles available for downloading or reading online. Scholars associated with Metivta include Rabbis Jonathan Omer-Man, Rami Shapiro, and Abraham J. Twerski.

Shalom Center.

The Shalom Center brings Jewish spirituality and community to the task of healing the world. At their web site, www.shalomctr.org, you will find worlds of action, worlds of spirit (Torah, prayer, seasons of our joy, life cycle events), go and study, go and act (teachers, books and tapes, and links), as well as many provocative articles.

Videos for Adults

I Ask for Wonder: Experiencing God. 60 Minutes, color. Available from the Board of Jewish Education of Greater New York.

In this inspiring video, Jews who have emerged from personal tragedy who are still filled with a spirit of faith discuss the different ways they encounter God. Among others, the program features a "running Rabbi" who is faced with cancer, a family with a disabled child that takes joy in the child's life, and Rabbi Harold Kushner who lost a son.

The Power of Prayer. 10 minutes, color. Dateline NBC.

A news short that appeared on television, this video focuses on people given a second chance at life who attribute their recovery to prayer. Featured is Dr. Larry Dossey, a Dallas surgeon, who has conducted research and written books on how one's physical well-being can be affected by prayer. This video can be used as a trigger for discussion of the importance of prayer as part of medicine.

Teachers and Jewish Professionals

Brown, Steven M. *Higher and Higher (L'ayla L'ayla): Making Jewish Prayer Part of Us.* New York: United Synagogue of Conservative Judaism, 1996.

One of the most frequently used pages from this popular looseleaf book is the list of approximately 100 names for God. Brown devotes a section of this book on prayer to

the language of faith, God talk. This resource provides both background material on the prayers and activities for use with teens and adults.

Coles, Robert. *The Spiritual Life of Children.* Boston, MA: Houghton Mifflin Company, 1990.

This classic by a Harvard professor and therapist presents insights into the spiritual and inner life of children. Cole has spent much of his career trying to understand life from the perspective of children. In this book, he shares stories from children of different religious backgrounds, including Jewish children, about their spiritual questions, experiences, and quests.

Chopra, Deepak. *How to Know God.* Philadelphia, PA: Miniature Editions, 2001.

Using brain research, Chopra outlines stages based on the brain's response. The stages are: flight or fight, reactive, restful awareness, intuitive, creative, visionary, and sacred.

Fowler, James W. *Stages of Faith: The Psychology of Human Development and the Quest for Meaning.* San Francisco, CA: Harper & Row Publishers, 1981.

This is Fowler's seminal work in which he describes in detail faith development theory and the stages.

Fowler, James W.; Karl Ernst Nipkow; and Friedrich Schweitzer. *Stages of Faith and Religious Development.* New York: Crossroad, 1991.

This volume contains a collection of articles about faith and religious development by prominent theologians and thinkers. A variety of theories, both stage theories and other approaches, are included in this volume.

Goodman, Roberta Louis. "Faith Development: A Jewish View." In *The New Jewish Teachers Handbook*, Audrey Friedman Marcus and Raymond A. Zwerin, eds. Denver, CO: A.R.E. Publishing, Inc., 1994.

This chapter provides an overview of faith development theory, which is about how people make meaning out of their lives. The theory's implications for and application to Jewish education are presented. Activities are described for each of Fowler's six stages of faith.

Handelman, Maxine Segal, and Roberta Louis Goodman. "God, Prayer, and Spirituality." In *Jewish Every Day* by Maxine Segal Handelman. Denver, CO: A.R.E. Publishing, Inc., 2000.

This chapter presents practical advice to early childhood educators about how to present God and prayer while nurturing the spirituality of young children.

Heller, David. *We Gave the World Moses and Bagels: Art and Wisdom of Jewish Children*. Philadelphia, PA: Jewish Publication Society, 2000.

This book is filled with short quotations and pictures by children, and in part it focuses on how Jewish children portray their spiritual beliefs. The author raises a question and then shares the answers of children, ages 5 to 12, from around the U.S. The book provides a glimpse into how children understand what it means to be Jewish.

Kohn, Shoshana. *We Gave the World Moses and Bagels: Lesson Plans for Jewish Students*. Philadelphia, PA: Jewish Publication Society, 2001.

This is a six-page insert of lessons for the classroom or home on the book *We Gave the World Moses and Bagels: Art and Wisdom of Jewish Children* by David Heller (see immediately above).

Pitzele, Peter. *Scripture Windows: Toward a Practice of Bibliodrama*. Los Angeles, CA: Torah Aura Productions, 1998.

Bibliodrama is a process of entering into the biblical text and creating *midrash* through improvisation. Created by Pitzele, bibliodrama provides a way of exploring the relationship between God and the Jewish people in biblical and modern times. This how-to manual presents practical ways of applying Pitzele's approach to Jewish educational settings.

Schein, Jeffrey, ed. *Connecting Prayer and Spirituality: Kol Haneshamah As a Creative Teaching and Learning Text*. Wyncote, PA: The Reconstructionist Press, 1996.

This source book makes the new Reconstructionist *Siddur, Kol Haneshamah*, into a study text. Sections address the teaching of prayer and spirituality in general, as well as provide approaches and lesson plans specifically geared toward *Kol Haneshamah*.

Walsh, Froma. *Spiritual Resources in Family Therapy*. New York: Guilford Press, 1999.

This collection of writings attempts to provide counselors with approaches to tapping into spirituality in therapeutic situations. The author's underlying assumption is that spirituality as an important aspect of the human condition can help lead to healing and wholeness. Yet, she asserts, many therapists are uncomfortable, unskilled, or unknowing in how to apply this to their practice. The editor is a professor of social work at the University of Chicago whose own religiosity and Jewishness have influenced her worldview and professional practice.

CONTRIBUTORS

MICHELLE SHAPIRO ABRAHAM is a graduate of the Rhea Hirsch School of Education at Hebrew Union College-Jewish Institute of Religion in Los Angeles. She is currently the Director of Education at Temple Shalom in Plainfield, New Jersey. Previously, she was the consultant on the Moral Education Initiative for the UAHC Department of Education. Ms. Abraham is the author of the UAHC Chai Family Education curriculum, and has developed and implemented many Family Education programs, several of which focus on God and spirituality.

RABBI HANAN A. ALEXANDER, Ph.D., is the former Editor-in-Chief of *Religious Education: An Interfaith Journal of Spirituality, Growth and Transformation.* He currently teaches in the Faculty of Education at the University of Haifa, and previously served as Vice President for Academic Affairs at the University of Judaism in Los Angeles.

JANICE P. ALPER is Executive Director of Jewish Educational Services in Atlanta, Georgia. A graduate of the Rhea Hirsch School of Education of Hebrew Union College-Jewish Institute of Religion, she has extensive experience in directing Jewish schools, writing curriculum, and developing family programs. She is the editor of *Learning Together: A Sourcebook on Jewish Family Education* (A.R.E. Publishing, Inc.) and co-author with Joel Lurie Grishaver of *Mah La'Asot, What Shall I Do?* (Torah Aura Productions).

DAVID S. ARIEL, Ph.D., is President of the Laura and Alvin Siegal College of Judaic Studies (formerly the Cleveland College of Judaic Studies). He is the author of *Spiritual Judaism: Restoring Heart and Soul To Jewish Life* (Hyperion), *The Mystic Quest: An Introduction To Jewish Mysticism* (Jason Aronson), and *What Do Jews Believe? The Spiritual Foundations of Judaism* (Schocken Books). He received his Bachelor's

degree at Hebrew University of Jerusalem and his Master's degree and Doctorate from Brandeis University in Jewish thought.

JULIE JASLOW AUERBACH received her M.A. from the Cleveland College of Judaic Studies. She is the Director of Jewish Family & Adult Education at the Gross Schechter Day School in Cleveland, Ohio. She was formerly a Curriculum Associate at the Jewish Education Center of Cleveland and a Senior Educator for Melitz, coordinating Project Numbers 2000 for North America, as well as a congregational education director. Ms. Auerbach made the musical contributions to *Jewish Every Day* and was a contributor to *Growing Together,* (both published by A.R.E. Publishing, Inc.). Her original children's songs are recorded on the cassette *Seasoned with Song.*

RABBI ALAN BREGMAN *(z"l)* was ordained at the Hebrew Union College-Jewish Institute of Religion. He was the UAHC Great Lakes Region Director for 25 years.

CATHLEEN COHEN, Ph.D., is a painter and poet, who teaches poetry writing in a variety of schools in the Philadelphia area. During the past several years, she has developed and taught a prayer curriculum at many supplemental Hebrew schools through the Aaron A. Gold Scholarship Program, coordinated by the Auerbach Center for Jewish Education and the Penn Literacy Network. She has published poetry in journals, such as *Harrisburg Review, Moment, Piedmont Literary Review,* and *Response,* and will have work included in an upcoming anthology, *The Paradoxes of Miriam,* to be published by Jason Aronson.

NADINE COHEN has a background in regular and special education and a Master's degree in Art Therapy. She has taught diverse cultures, abilities, and interests. She currently works as an art educator and art therapist with deaf and hard of hearing children in St. Louis, Missouri, while continuing to facilitate ongoing workshops in the Jewish community. Her work and studies allow her to explore further the interconnectedness of language and symbol in our lives.

RABBI WILLIAM DRESKIN is the Rabbi at Woodlands Community Temple in White Plains, New York. Along with co-author Kyla Epstein Schneider, he is a founding member of Beget Kefet, a musical *tzedakah* collective that educates and raises funds on behalf of Myriam's Dream.

RABBI MORLEY T. FEINSTEIN is the Senior Rabbi of University Synagogue in Los Angeles, California. A Phi Beta Kappa graduate of the University of California at Berkeley, Rabbi Feinstein received his M.A.H.E. and M.A.H.L. from Hebrew Union College-Jewish Institute of Religion. He previously served Temple Beth El in South Bend, Indiana and San Antonio's Temple Beth-El, and is a past Treasurer of the Central Conference of American Rabbis. One of the co-editors of the forthcoming Rabbis and Cantors manual, Rabbi Feinstein is the author of *The Jewish Law Review* (Torah Aura Productions) and *The Jewish Values Game* (A.R.E. Publishing, Inc.), as well as numerous articles.

BEV FOX is the Assistant to the Principal at Solomon Schechter Day School in Northbrook, Illinois. She holds a B.A. in Jewish Studies from UCLA and a Master's in Social Work from the University of Chicago. Jewish Family Education is one of her loves. The program included in this book was an outcome of her work at the Summer Whizin Institute 2000 at the University of Judaism.

LYNN LUTZ FRIEND has been a Jewish Educator for over 25 years. She holds a Bachelor's degree in Education and a Master's Degree in Social Work. She currently teaches art and Hebrew at North Shore Congregation Israel in Glencoe, Illinois. Most recently, she founded J.E.T.A., Jewish Experience Through Art, a company that

provides art based workshops and consultation to individuals and synagogues.

RABBI NEIL GILLMAN, Ph.D., is the Aaron Rabinowitz and Simon H. Rifkind Associate Professor of Jewish Philosophy at The Jewish Theological Seminary of America. In addition to ordination from JTS, he holds a Ph.D. in Philosophy from Columbia University. A former dean of the JTS Rabbinical School, Dr. Gillman is the author of *Sacred Fragments: Recovering Theology for the Modern Jew* (Jewish Publication Society), *The Death of Death: Resurrection and Immortality in Jewish Thought*, and most recently, *The Way into Encountering God in Judaism* (both published by Jewish Lights Publishing). Dr. Gillman is known for his unique talent of engaging adults in theological exploration that stimulates their religious growth.

RABBI JULIE GREENBERG is the founder and Director of the Jewish Renewal Life Center, a yearlong training program in Jewish spirituality, located in Mt. Airy, Philadelphia. She was ordained by the Reconstructionist Rabbinical College, and is currently completing a degree in relationship and family counseling. Rabbi Greenberg also has a private Rabbinic practice in which she teaches, counsels, and guides individuals and families moving through various life passages.

BARBARA R. GROSSMAN, Ph.D., received her doctorate in Theology and Pastoral Counseling from the School of Theology at Claremont. She completed her Master's in Religion and Psychology at Columbia University. Since 1990, her private practice in Lake Forest, California has focused on marriage, family, and child counseling. Dr. Grossman's interest in structural development as it applies to the quality of personal excellence, marriage, and family relationships, and participation in a community of faith is integrated in her practice, workshops, and writing.

MAXINE SEGAL HANDELMAN is the Director of Early Childhood Jewish Education for Jewish Community Centers in the Chicago area. She holds a Master's degree in Jewish Education from Hebrew Union College-Jewish Institute of Religion and Master's Degree in Early Childhood Education from Pacific Oaks College. The author of *Jewish Every Day: The Complete Handbook for Early Childhood Teachers* (A.R.E. Publishing, Inc.), Ms. Handelman has been a member of Rosh Chodesh groups in Jerusalem, Los Angeles, and Chicago.

RABBI BRUCE KADDEN was ordained at Hebrew Union College-Jewish Institute of Religion, and has served as Rabbi of Temple Beth El in Salinas California since 1984. He and his wife Barbara are the authors of *Teaching Mitzvot: Concepts, Values, and Activities*; *Teaching Tefilah: Insights and Activities on Prayer*; and *Teaching Jewish Life Cycle: Traditions and Activities* (all published by A.R.E. Publishing, Inc.).

BETSY DOLGIN KATZ, ED.D., is the North American Director of the Florence Melton Adult Mini-School, a two-year adult school located in 41 cities in North America. A former Chairperson of the Coalition for the Advancement of Jewish Education (CAJE), she is a member of the Board of Directors of the Covenant Foundation. Dr. Katz has published articles and curriculum on varied subjects in Jewish education, including teacher development, adult learning, teacher centers, and the Florence Melton Adult Mini-School. Her most recent publication is *Or Hadash, Let a New Light Shine* (UAHC Press), an adult curriculum on Jerusalem.

LINDA KAUFMAN is Music Specialist at Temple Beth-El in San Antonio, Texas, and Co-Director of the Beth-El Players, a resident theater production company in San Antonio that presents original plays based on Jewish folktales and *midrash*. Ms. Kaufman composes the music and serves as musical director for the troupe's productions. She also composed sacred pieces used in Temple Beth-El's Yom Kippur services, as well as new Passover and holiday songs that can be used in Religious School classes. She is a two-time Globe Award winner for music written for the Beth-El Players.

BEN ZION M. KOGEN is a Doctoral Candidate at the Jewish Theological Seminary of America. He has devoted his entire career to Jewish education, serving posts in congregational schools, community Hebrew schools, and a Solomon Schechter Day School. Mr. Kogen has served as a member of the Board of the Jewish Educators Assembly and CAJE.

HARRIET M. LEVINE is the Director of Education at Woodlands Community Temple, White Plains, New York. Prior to this, she served as Family Educator of Congregation B'nai Israel in Bridgeport, Connecticut. Ms. Levine received her M.A.R.E. degree from Hebrew Union College-Jewish Institute of Religion.

KATE MANN holds a Master's in Jewish Education earned through the interactive video-conferencing degree program at the Laura and Alvin Siegal College of Judaic Studies. Prior to becoming a Jewish educator, she was a dancer and dance educator in the Milwaukee Public Schools. She still works as a freelance choreographer. Currently, Ms. Mann serves as the Dance/Movement Specialist at Temple Sinai in Milwaukee, where she has spent 16 years developing kinesthetic teaching methods for religious education, Grades K-6. She has been a presenter at CAJE conferences and on the staff at Olin-Sang-Ruby Union Institute Camp.

RABBI CRAIG MARANTZ is the Associate Rabbi at Temple Israel in Omaha, Nebraska. Previously, he was Rabbi and Educator at The Temple in Atlanta, Georgia. He received a Master's degree in Jewish Education from the Rhea Hirsch School of Education of Hebrew Union College-Jewish Institute of Religion where he was also ordained, as well as a Master's degree from Stanford University.

RACHEL MEISELS received a B.A. at Towson University and another B.A. at Baltimore Hebrew University. She is a teacher at Goldsmith Early Childhood Education Center of the Chizuk Amuno Congregation in Baltimore, Maryland, where she has developed parent and family programs. She is the author of many songs and poems which are used in early childhood programs in Baltimore.

RABBI JORDAN MILLSTEIN was ordained by the Hebrew Union College-Jewish Institute of Religion. A Wexner Fellow, he currently serves as the senior Rabbi at Temple Emanuel in Worcester, Massachusetts.

CAROL OCHS is Coordinator of Graduate Programs and Visiting Professor of Philosophy at Hebrew Union College-Jewish Institute of Religion in New York. She recently co-authored *Jewish Spiritual Guidance: Finding Our Way To God* (Jossey-Bass) and completed an expanded edition of her book *Women and Spirituality* (Rowman & Littlefield Publishing). She is also the author of *Behind the Sex of God: Toward a New Consciousness — Transcending Matriarchy and Patriarchy; An Ascent To Joy: Transforming Deadness of Spirit; The Noah Paradox: Time As Burden, Time As Blessing* (University of Notre Dame Press); and *Song of the Self: Biblical Spirituality and Human Holiness* (Trinity Press International), as well as numerous essays and scholarly articles.

RABBI KERRY M. OLITZKY, D.H.L., is the Executive Director of the Jewish Outreach Institute in New York City. He is a fellow at the Center for Jewish Studies, Graduate and University Center, CUNY, and a fellow and consultant for Synagogue 2000, a transdenominational project to renew the synagogue. He is the author of numerous books and articles, including *Restful Reflections: Nighttime Inspiration to Calm the Soul Based on Jewish Wisdom;* and *Sacred Intentions: Daily Inspiration from Jewish Wisdom,* both with Lori Forman (Jewish Lights Publishing).

RABBI MARCIA R. PLUMB was ordained at Hebrew Union College-Jewish Institute of Religion in New York. She is the Director of the Spirituality Programme at Leo Baeck College-Centre for Jewish Education in London, and specializes in liturgy, ritual, and spirituality. She is

the founder of The Half-Empty Bookcase, an international Progressive Jewish Women's Organization, and The Jewish Women's Network, a European organization for Orthodox and Progressive women.

DR. DAWN ROBINSON ROSE is the former Director of the Center for Jewish Ethics and Assistant Professor at the Reconstructionist Rabbinical College in Philadelphia. Having received her doctorate from the Jewish Theological Seminary where she has taught Jewish Feminist Theology, she is currently concluding Rabbinical studies at the Academy for Jewish Religion.

RABBI STEVEN M. ROSMAN, Ph.D., M.S., M.A.H.L., M.S.C., D.A.P.A., is the Director of the Division of Complementary Medicine for ProHEALTH Care Associates, where he practices acupuncture, nutrition, and botanical therapies, stress management, and various forms of counseling. He is an internationally known stress management consultant, advocate for complementary medicine, and motivational speaker who has written ten books, including *Jewish Healing Wisdom* and *Jewish Parenting Wisdom* (both published by Jason Aronson), *The Bird of Paradise and Other Sabbath Stories,* and *Sidrah Stories* (both published by UAHC Press) and has authored numerous articles on Jewish education, storytelling, sports nutrition, stress management, and more. Most recently, he has contributed chapters to books on neurology and pregnancy and breast cancer.

RENA ROTENBERG received a B.A. from Brooklyn College of the City University of New York and an M.A. from Baltimore Hebrew University. She has been the Coordinator of Early Childhood Education at the Center for Jewish Education, Baltimore, Maryland since its inception in 1973. She has authored or co-authored many publications, including Curriculum Guides for Shabbat and Holidays (Center for Jewish Education, Baltimore), *Torah Talk: An Early Childhood Teaching Guide* and

Lively Legends — Jewish Values: An Early Childhood Teaching Guide (both published by A.R.E. Publishing, Inc.). She is a founding member of the National Jewish Early Childhood Network and the National Association of Jewish Early Childhood Specialists, as well as a member of the Early Childhood Education Committee of the United Synagogue of Traditional Judaism.

NANCY RUBIN holds a B.A. from Towson University. She was the Director of the Baltimore Hebrew Congregation Preschool in Maryland. She was a teacher at the school before becoming the Director. Actively involved in the building of a state of the art free standing preschool building at the congregation, Ms. Rubin consults with regard to building and equipping quality Jewish early childhood facilities.

RABBI JEFFREY K. SALKIN is the Senior Rabbi of The Community Synagogue in Port Washington, New York. A prolific writer and teacher, he is the author of many books on spirituality, including *Putting God on the Guest List: How to Reclaim the Spiritual Meaning of Your Child's Bar or Bat Mitzvah* (Jewish Lights Publishing) and *Searching for My Brothers: Jewish Men in a Gentile World* (Putnam).

RABBI SANDY EISENBERG SASSO has served as Rabbi of Congregation Beth-El Zedeck, Indianapolis since 1977. She was the first woman ordained by the Reconstructionist Rabbinical College in 1974, and received her Doctor of Divinity after 25 years in the Rabbinate. Rabbi Sasso also holds a Doctor of Divinity degree from Christian Theological Seminary. She is the author of many nationally acclaimed children's books, including *God's Paintbrush*; *In God's Name*; and *Cain and Abel: Finding the Fruits of Peace* (all published by Jewish Lights Publishing).

DANIEL S. SCHECHTER, a past president of a congregation, is the author of *Synagogue Boards: A Sacred Trust* (UAHC Press). He has served as editor and publisher of *Trustee* magazine. Mr.

Schechter has also been co-director of the liturgy development project of the Central Conference of American Rabbis, and chair of the Park Ridge Center for the Study of Health, Faith, and Ethics. He holds a Bachelor's degree from Brown University and Master's degrees in Education and Journalism from Columbia University.

RABBI JEFFREY SCHEIN, ED.D., is a graduate of the Reconstructionist Rabbinical College. He holds a doctorate in education in curriculum development from Temple University. Presently, he is a Professor at the Laura and Alvin Siegal College of Judaic Studies and the National Education Director for the Reconstructionist Movement. His books include *Growing Together: Resources, Programs, and Experiences in Jewish Family Education* (A.R.E. Publishing, Inc.), *Creative Jewish Education* (Rossel Books), *Targilon: A Workbook Charting the Course of Jewish Family Education* (JESNA and Jewish Reconstructionist Press), and *Connecting Prayer and Spirituality* (Reconstructionist Press).

KYLA EPSTEIN SCHNEIDER is learning and teaching in Cleveland. She received her Joint Master's Degrees in Jewish Education and Jewish Communal Service from Hebrew Union College-Jewish Institute of Religion in Los Angeles, and her B.A. from the University of Illinois. She served for 12 years as Synagogue Educator at both a large Reform congregation and a large Conservative congregation, and most recently was the Judaic Coordinator for Pardes, the New Jewish High School in Cleveland. An active board member of her synagogue, she has also held numerous board positions with CAJE.

RABBI ISAAC SEROTTA, ordained by the Hebrew Union College-Jewish Institute of Religion, holds a Master's degree in Jewish Education from the Rhea Hirsch School of Education. He is the spiritual leader of Lakeside Congregation for Reform Judaism in Highland Park, Illinois.

RABBI MICHAEL J. SHIRE, Ph.D., is Vice-Principal of the Leo Baeck College-Centre for

Jewish Education in London. He holds a doctorate from Hebrew Union College-Jewish Institute of Religion. His dissertation investigated curricular implications of the enhancement of religiosity in Jewish Education, the topic of his chapter in this publication. He is the author of the *Illuminated Haggadah* (Stuart Tabori, and Chang), *L'Chaim* (Chronicle) and *The Jewish Prophet* (Jewish Lights Publishing).

CARLA SILEN, a former English and Religious School teacher, is co-director of the Beth-El Players in San Antonio, Texas. Ms. Silen writes the scripts and the lyrics, as well as directs the company's productions, which range from musicals to more serious productions for the High Holy Days. She has joined with Ms. Kaufman in an ongoing project to turn Psalms into songs for children and to create new songs for the Jewish holiday cycle. She recently won a Globe Award for Best Original Script, "The Pirate Princess."

RABBI RIFAT SONSINO, Ph.D., is the spiritual leader of Temple Beth Shalom in Needham, Massachusetts. From 1996 to 2001, he was the editor of the *CCAR Journal*. Rabbi Sonsino is a graduate of the Law School in Istanbul, Turkey, and received his ordination from the Hebrew Union College-Jewish Institute of Religion in Cincinnati. He also has a Ph.D. from the University of Pennsylvania in Bible and Oriental Studies. He is the co-author of *Finding God: Ten Jewish Responses* and *What Happens after I Die?* (both published by UAHC Press) and the author of *Motive Clauses in Hebrew Law* (Scholars Press) and *Six Jewish Spiritual Paths* (Jewish Lights Publishing).

DR. JOANNE TUCKER, Ph.D., is the founder and artistic director of the Avodah Dance Ensemble. She received her modern dance training at the Juilliard School and the Martha Graham Studio and earned a Ph.D. in theater from the University of Wisconsin. Dr. Tucker is the co-author of *Torah in Motion: Creating Dance Midrash* and *Creative Movement for a Song: Activities for Young Children* (both published by

A.R.E. Publishing, Inc.). She leads workshops and is artist-in-residence at congregations, schools, and retreats throughout the United States, and teaches a seminar in liturgy as part of the Doctor of Ministry program at Hebrew Union College-Jewish Institute of Religion.

THE UAHC JOSEPH EISNER CAMP INSTITUTE FOR LIVING JUDAISM was founded in 1958 in Great Barrington, Massachusetts. Groomed sports fields, modern bunks, historic buildings, the finest ropes course in the northeast, two heated pools, and a renowned program of Jewish involvement and identity building make Eisner a remarkable and unique camp community. The current camp director is Louis Bordman. For more information, contact Eisner at 212-650-4130, Eisnerguy@aol.com, or access their web site, www.eisnercamp.org. Others who were involved in the program "Where in the World Is Adonai Echad?" were: **David Friedman** was the Director of Eisner Camp at the time the program was written up for inclusion in this book; **Aaron Katersky** served as one of Eisner Camp's Assistants Directors. He has been involved with authoring the camp's education program for the past five summers; **Jonah Pesner** is a Rabbi at Temple Israel in Boston, and a member of the Eisner Camp Program Advisory Committee. Rabbi Pesner was Eisner Camp's Education Director during the creation of the curriculum; **Zach Shapiro**, Assistant Rabbi of University Synagogue in Los Angeles, California, was Assistant Director of the UAHC Joseph Eisner Camp Institute during the creation of the curriculum; and **Jeffrey Sirkman**, Senior Rabbi of Larchmont Temple in Larchmont, New York, was Chairperson of the UAHC Joseph Eisner Camp Institute Program Advisory Committee for nearly a decade.

RABBI DAVID WECHSLER-AZEN is a graduate of Princeton University and was ordained at Hebrew Union College-Jewish Institute of Religion. After a Temple University Fellowship in Film, he produced the award-winning *Video Guide To Jewish Teaching* (UAHC Press), and has served in a variety of congregations. He currently serves as Associate Rabbi at Temple B'nai Or, Morristown, New Jersey, and works with elders at the Jewish Home and Hospital in Manhattan. Along with the program described in this volume, he teaches *Kabbalah* through baseball: kaBASEballah reveals some amazing correspondences between the *Sefirot* and the positions on the field.

RABBI SHAWN ISRAEL ZEVIT was ordained by the Reconstructionist Rabbinical College in 1998, and serves as the Director of Outreach & Community Development for the Jewish Reconstructionist Federation. He has over 20 years experience in spiritual leadership, human relations training, educational arts, teaching, and performing. Rabbi Zevit is a founding member of Shabbat Unplugged, Playback Philadelphia, the Bibliodrama Training Institute, the Institute for Contemporary Midrash, and Theatre Shalom Canada. He performs traditional and new music from his CD *Heart and Soul*.

INDEX